Families, Schools, and Communities

Together for Young Children

Third Edition

We dedicate this book to our families:

Clifford and Delores Stokum Couchenour
Bryan Maughan
Jay, Stacey, Chelsea, and Christopher Couchenour

James and Martha Douglas Chrisman
Cindy and Kate Chrisman

and to the many families, schools, and communities
that added to our nurturing.

D.C.

K.C.

Join us on the web at
EarlyChildEd.delmar.com

Families, Schools, and Communities

Together for Young Children

Third Edition

Donna Couchenour, Ph.D., C.F.L.E.
Kent Chrisman, Ed.D.

Shippensburg University

THOMSON
™
DELMAR LEARNING

Australia • Canada • Mexico • Singapore • Spain • United Kingdom • United States

THOMSON
DELMAR LEARNING

Families, Schools, and Communities: Together for Young Children, 3rd Edition
Donna Couchenour and Kent Chrisman

Vice President, Career Education Strategic Business Unit:
Dawn Gerrain

Director of Learning Solutions:
John Fedor

Managing Editor:
Robert L. Serenka, Jr.

Senior Acquisitions Editor:
Erin O'Connor

Product Manager:
Philip Mandl

Editorial Assistant:
Alison Archambault

Director of Production:
Wendy A. Troeger

Production Manager:
Mark Bernard

Content Project Manager:
Karin Hillen Jaquays

Technology Project Manager:
Sandy Charette

Director of Marketing:
Wendy E. Mapstone

Channel Manager:
Kristin McNary

Channel Manager:
Scott A. Chrysler

Marketing Specialist:
Erica S. Conley

Art Director:
Joy Kocsis

Cover Design:
Rose Design

Compositor:
ICC Macmillan Inc.

Library of Congress Cataloging-in-Publication Data

Couchenour, Donna L. (Donna Lee), 1950-
  Families, schools, and communities together for young children / Donna Couchenour, Kent Chrisman. — 3rd ed.
    p. cm.
  ISBN 1-4180-6719-9
  1. Early childhood education—Social aspects—United States. 2. Home and school—United States. 3. Community and school—United States. I. Chrisman, Kent. II. Title.
  LB1139.25.C67 2007
  371.19—dc22

                                        2007005160

NOTICE TO THE READER

CONTENTS

FOREWORD   x

PREFACE   xiii

PART I: Understanding Families

CHAPTER 1: A Theory-based Approach to Family Involvement in Early Childhood Education   3

Objectives   3

Key Terms   3

The Importance of Families and Communities in Children's Lives   3

Contextualist Theories   5

Bronfenbrenner's Bioecological Theory   7

Vygotsky's Sociocultural Theory   8

Family Systems Theory   11

Implications for Practice in Early Childhood Education   16

Guidelines for Developmentally Appropriate Practice   16

Key Characteristics of Early Childhood Programs Practicing Inclusion   18

National Association for the Education of Young Children Accreditation Performance Criteria   19

Division for Early Childhood (DEC) of the Council on Exceptional Children (CEC) Recommended Practices in Family-Based Practices   23

Family Support Movement   24

Summary and Conclusions   25

Chapter 1 Applications   26

Questions for Reflection and Discussion   26

Field Assignments   26

References   27

CHAPTER 2: Understanding Family Diversity   29

Objectives   29

Key Terms   29

Contextualist Theories and Family Differences   29

Ways in Which Families Are Different   31

Ethnicity, Race, and Culture   31

Economic Differences among Families   34

Gender Role Identity   39

Families and Religiosity   46

Geographic Region   48

Application to Early Childhood Education Programs   50

Celebrating Diversity   50

Inclusiveness   50

Ethical Considerations   52

Relating Diversity to Developmentally Appropriate Practice   52

Relating Diversity to Programs for Children with Special Needs   53

NAEYC Accreditation Guidelines   53

Professional Code of Ethical Conduct   54

Family Support Principles   54

Summary and Conclusions   55

Chapter 2 Applications   55

Questions for Reflection and Discussion   55

Field Assignments   55

References   56

CHAPTER 3: Developmental Issues in Families with Young Children   59

Objectives   59

Key Terms   59

Theoretical Foundation   59

Bioecological Theory   59

Family Systems Theory   60

Developmental Issues in Families   61

Transition to Parenthood 61

Sibling Relationships 64

Work and Family 70

Child Care 74

Extended Family Relationships 77

**Practical and Ethical
Considerations** 81

Family Support Principles 81

Code of Ethical Conduct 81

Summary and Conclusions 82

Chapter 3 Applications 82

Questions for Reflection and Discussion 82

Field Assignments 83

References 83

**CHAPTER 4: Family Strengths, Family
Functions, and Family Structure** 87

Objectives 87

Key Terms 87

Introduction 87

Defining Family Strengths, Functions,
and Structure 87

Family Strengths 90

What Makes a Family Strong? 90

What Factors Support Family Strengths? 92

Resilient Children 93

Family Functions 94

Historical and Contemporary
Purposes of Families 94

Causes of Change in Family Functions 96

Family Law 97

Family Structure 98

Variations in Family Form 98

The Meaning of Birth Order 101

Application of Chapter Information 102

Family Support 102

Early Childhood Programs 103

Summary and Conclusions 103

Chapter 4 Applications 103

Questions for Reflection and Discussion 104

Field Assignments 104

References 104

CHAPTER 5: Parenting 107

Objectives 107

Key Terms 107

Theoretical Perspectives 107

Bioecological Theory 107

Developmental Contextualism 108

Ways to Parenthood 109

Biological and Fertility Alternatives 109

Blended Families 111

Adoption 111

Foster Parents 113

Grandparents as Parents 114

Teen Parents 116

Responsibilities of Parents 117

Economic 117

Nurturance and Child Care 118

Attachment and Socialization 119

Building and Maintaining
Relationships 119

Character Education and Spirituality 120

Collaborating with Societal Institutions 120

Parenting Styles and Beliefs 120

Trends in Beliefs about Discipline
Strategies 122

Motherhood and Fatherhood 122

Mothering 123

Fathering 124

Parenting Beliefs 127

Child Development and the Role
of Children in Families 127

Interactions with Early Childhood
Educators 127

Summary and Conclusions 128

Chapter 5 Applications 129

Questions for Reflection
and Discussion 129

Field Assignments 129

References 129

CHAPTER 6: Family Stress 133

Objectives 133

Key Terms 133

Family Systems Theory 133

   Horizontal Stressors 134

Families and Unpredictable Stressors 135

   Family Violence 135

   A Particular Form of Family Violence:
Child Abuse 137

   Substance Abuse in Families 141

   Marital Transitions and Single
Parenting 143

   Homeless Families 145

   Families and Children with
Disabilities 147

   Families and Children with Serious
Illness 151

   Immigrant Families 151

   Migrant Families 153

   Military Families 155

   Children of Incarcerated Parents 156

The Role of Early Childhood
Educators 160

Summary and Conclusions 160

Chapter 6 Applications 160

Questions for Reflection
and Discussion 161

Field Assignments 161

References 161

PART II: Practice

**CHAPTER 7: A Family-Based Philosophy in
Early Childhood Education** 167

   Objectives 167

Key Terms 167

Rationale for a Family-based Philosophy
in Early Childhood Education 167

   The Example Set by Head Start 168

   Families in a Democracy 170

   Continuity 170

Family Support 176

   Responsibilities of Families and Schools 176

   Empowering Parents 177

Linking Parents and Teachers 177

   Parents as Consumers
of Children's Education 177

   Supporting School Policy and Families 177

Epstein's Framework for School, Family,
and Community Partnerships 179

National Standards from the PTA 180

   Additional Frameworks for
Understanding Family Involvement 181

Professionalism in Family-based Early
Education 182

   Confidentiality 182

   Advocacy 183

   Collaboration 183

   Understanding Roles and Boundaries 183

   Record-Keeping 184

Embracing Diversity 184

   Observing and Appreciating
Differences 184

   Understanding that Many Ways
of Interacting with Children Can
Serve Them Well 186

Evaluating the Family Involvement
Component in Early Education 188

Summary and Conclusions 189

Chapter 7 Applications 190

Questions for Reflection
and Discussion 190

Field Assignments 190

References 190

CHAPTER 8: Family-Staff Relationships 193

  Objectives 193

  Key Terms 193

  Building Relationships 193

    Communication 193

  Ongoing Communication 195

    One-Way Communication 195

    Two-Way Communication 199

    Effective Interpersonal
Communication 211

    Guidelines for Giving and Receiving
Criticism 216

    Assertiveness versus Aggression 217

  Conflict Resolution 217

    Some Ineffective and Inappropriate
Practices to Avoid in Interpersonal
Communication 219

    Helpful Attitudes for Effective
Interpersonal Communication 219

  Summary and Conclusions 220

  Chapter 8 Applications 220

  **Questions for Reflection
and Discussion** 220

  Field Assignments 221

  References 221

**CHAPTER 9: Supporting Young Children's
Learning at Home** 223

  Objectives 223

  Key Terms 223

  Theoretical Foundations 223

  Overview 223

  Families and Literacy 225

  Families and Science 226

  Families and Mathematics 230

  Families and Social Studies 232

  Summary and Conclusions 233

  Chapter 9 Applications 233

  Questions for Reflection and Discussion 233

  Field Assignments 234

  References 234

**CHAPTER 10: Parent Education and Family
Life Education** 237

  Objectives 237

  Key Terms 237

  Bioecological Theory 237

  **Philosophy about Programs
of Parent Education** 238

    Assessing Needs and Effects 238

    Format of Programs 240

  Methods of Parent Education 241

    Parent Education Packages 241

    Parent Education Books 241

    Parents as Teachers 243

    Home Instruction Program
for Preschool Youngsters 245

  Family Life Education 248

  **The Role of Early Childhood Educators in
Parent Education and Family Life
Education** 250

    Topics for Parent Education 250

  Summary and Conclusions 258

  Chapter 10 Applications 258

  **Questions for Discussion
and Reflection** 258

  Field Assignments 258

  References 259

**CHAPTER 11: Early Childhood Educators in
the Community** 261

  Objectives 261

  Key Terms 261

  Bioecological Theory 261

  **Community Involvement in Early
Childhood Education** 262

    Local School Boards 262

    Boards of Trustees and Advisory
Boards 263

Caring Communities   263

Referring Children for Additional
or Varying Services   264

Program Models   266

    Head Start   266

    Comer Schools   266

    Early Intervention   267

    Preschool Inclusion   270

    Other Models   271

Interdisciplinary Collaboration   273

    Benefits   273

    Challenges   273

Family-Centered Interprofessional
Collaboration   273

The Business Community   274

Professionalism in Early
Childhood Education   274

    Knowledge Base   274

    Continuing Professional Development   281

    The Movement to Leave No
    Child Behind   282

Summary and Conclusions   282

Chapter 11 Applications   282

Questions for Reflection
and Discussion   282

Field Assignments   283

References   283

CASE STUDIES   285

    Case 1:   Supporting Families in Infant
              Care Programs   287

    Case 2:   Challenges of Increasing Family
              Involvement   289

    Case 3:   Helping Family Members and
              Staff to Understand
              Developmentally
              Appropriate Practice   292

    Case 4:   Developmentally Appropriate
              Practices in Head Start   296

    Case 5:   Early Childhood Inclusive
              Practices   299

    Case 6:   Standardized Assessment   302

    Case 7:   English Language Learners   303

APPENDIX A: Websites for Professional
Development   305

APPENDIX B: The NAEYC Code of Ethical
Conduct and Statement of Commitment   310

APPENDIX C: NAEYC Academy for Early
Childhood Program Accreditation Standards
and Topic Areas   321

APPENDIX D: Responding to Linguistic and
Cultural Diversity Recommendations for Effective
Early Childhood Education: A Position Statement
of the National Association for the Education of
Young Children (1995)   325

APPENDIX E: Professional Preparation Excerpts
from NAEYC Initial Licensing Standards
for Early Childhood Teacher Certification   336

APPENDIX F: NAEYC Position Statement on the
Prevention of Child Abuse in Early Childhood
Programs and the Responsibilities of Early
Childhood Professionals to Prevent Child
Abuse   361

GLOSSARY   369

INDEX   375

FOREWORD

Since Bronfenbrenner's seminal work, *The Ecology of Human Development and Learning* (1979), the early childhood education profession has been "reconstructing" itself in relation to creating environments and strategies that empower children, families, communities, and the profession itself. This process of renewal and transformation has been stimulated by the most rapid and dramatic social, economic, and technological changes ever to occur in human history. Our conceptions of what families, schools, and communities are like or should be like are experiencing revolutionary paradigm shifts. Several changes are powerful in their impact on how children and families learn and function: New work and family structures require more parent time, but society has actually reduced its support and resources; new technology and related educational advancements require more education for people to function effectively, but society has not responded with increased educational quality for all people; our knowledge of parenting and child/family development has improved, but too many early childhood professionals and too many parents and citizens lack this new knowledge and skills; and a self-centered and individualistic society requires more parent/family skills and bonding time, yet our society has busied parents and families with mostly isolated activities that contribute to continued economic and environmental abuses. Certainly there are exceptions to the above stressors that are so real in all families, but one need only read the pages of Couchenour and Chrisman's book, *Families, Schools, and Communities: Together for Young Children*, to realize that the battle in the new millennium will be for a human competence that creates social decency and fosters spiritual and psychological relationships that empower everyone to be carers of each other.

Perhaps the most critical facet of Couchenour and Chrisman's work is their articulation of a theoretical construct that early childhood education professionals and concerned parents and citizens can use to develop strategies for having optimal conditions for everyone's learning and development. Their synthesis of the bioecological, contextualist, and family systems theory into a conceptual structure to use in addressing the many issues parents, children, families, schools, and communities experience is invaluable. The synthesis provides five important starting points for early childhood education professionals to use in crafting their "map" for being truly high-quality family helpers.

1. The human development and learning process is the result of everyone's effort; that is, it is an interactive and renewing process that is influenced by all parts of the human community.

2. An empowering approach to working with the diverse and ever-changing needs and contexts of children and families must replace a deficit-oriented way of relating to children and families.

3. The power of parents and families to nurture healthy and proactive ways of living in children can occur within various forms and structures. The key is for families to have strong and nurturing relationships with each other and their supportive helpers.

4. Early childhood educators must create diverse and adaptive ways to support families in a world of constant change and stress.

5. Early childhood educators must lead the way for "community transformation" to create family-embracing ways of functioning. Each of these "starting points" for crafting a new vision and new paradigm for helping create powerful families is addressed by Couchenour and Chrisman.

Children's school and life success is indeed embedded within the multiple bioecological systems of person and environment relationships. Couchenour and Chrisman point to several examples within the multiple life systems that impact families: individual bioecological dynamics, social interactions, economic involvement, and cultural and societal events and experiences.

Throughout history, families have needed nurturing and supportive relationships with the environment to thrive and contribute to the community. The need for a "systems" perspective of families is very critical in the complex and highly technological society in which parents and children now function. The prevailing belief that the individual can manage all of the factors that happen in life is myopic and distorted. As Couchenour and Chrisman so aptly describe, the challenges parents face in nurturing healthy and happy children are indeed great and require a total community structure to empower this critical child-nurturing function. Thus, the recognition that the human development and learning process is systemic requires us to approach parent, child, and family growth from an empowerment perspective. Engaging total families in the process of building on their strengths, identifying and addressing needs, and taking leadership in building strong communities are key strategies noted by Couchenour and Chrisman. This empowerment approach calls for the following:

- understanding that families are the caring people who commit themselves to the child's life-long well-being
- nurturing children and adults in the family to reach their full potential and engaging them in activities in which they become the leaders in their communities
- creating a sense of "mutuality" in families and in our professional and community relationships with families
- validating parents and children—and their helpers—as the most important people in our communities
- advocating and structuring schools and communities to be places in which parents, children, and families can renew and enrich their lives, thus empowering them to be the tremendously capable people they can be

Diversity in family and parenting forms and styles must be used as means to enrich and further develop family, child, and school-community strengths. If early childhood educators approach cultural and familial differences as sources of strength, so will parents, children, and other people in the community. As Couchenour and Chrisman suggest, the prevailing theme should be that of nurturing, caring relationships in all families by validating and valuing human differences as essential. This validating process can be achieved by early childhood professionals in several ways:

- highlighting parent achievements across the diversity of family and cultural groups in and beyond the community
- utilizing the diversity of parent and family talents as teaching resources for all children and teachers in the school
- helping parents see the strengths present in themselves and their children, and then engaging parents and children in developing their strengths and talents
- empowering everyone in the community to value and validate cultural diversity through needed social and economic changes

The only viable paradigm for developing successful family involvement in schools and communities is the partnership approach. This means crafting all facets of the family-school-community partnership together:

- learning about each other in relation to strengths, skills, and talents that can be used to empower everyone
- establishing equality in roles and relationships in family, school, and community, and in the transactions that occur between these groups
- seeing, treating, and affirming parents as the key leaders in families, and as powerful leaders in the family-school-community triad
- developing family-friendly strategies that invite parents and families to be actively engaged in school and community decisions
- using diverse strategies that account for the varying work and family schedules, and situations that today's parents and families experience
- valuing parents and family members as caring and capable people who are full members of the community team.

Early childhood professionals can provide the needed "leadership" in stimulating community transformation toward becoming a family-centered place to live and grow.

As the authors note, several important starting points provide the foundation for this transformational process:

- provide a "model" of family-centered functioning in the school and in relations with families and community members

- engage members of the community in the total school program in ways that empower them to take ownership of creating the very best schools for children and families

- educate the community on the key educational, social, and family needs that exist, and on strategies for addressing these needs

- advocate for policy changes that will strengthen families in the community

- participate in actions that help reshape the community toward being a positive force in the lives of families.

Couchenour and Chrisman offer a wealth of ideas and information for building a new and stronger commitment to children and families. Most important, they provide a conceptual structure for crafting new strategies and approaches to engage families, schools, and communities in building healthy and positive places for children. Further, they connect this structure to the profession's standards of quality, to the urgent needs of families, and to our desire for a better future for all of our children. We owe the authors a big thanks for developing this powerful tool for reshaping our approach to supporting children and families. We can best thank them, however, by becoming active partners in our schools and communities in creating strong and nurturing environments and relationships for children and their families.

Kevin J. Swick
Professor of Education
University of South Carolina—Columbia

PREFACE

This book was written to meet a need for a textbook that included a theoretical and research foundation for early childhood educators' work with families, schools, and communities. As societal changes are mirrored in schools, the use of a contextualist model as a basis for family, school, and community partnerships makes sense. For early childhood educators, the current findings by neuroscientists about the importance of early stimulation for optimal brain development point to the importance of supporting families. Further, early childhood educators are in a position of having knowledge that should be used by communities to enhance the lives of children and families.

New scientific information and current societal concerns about children's safety have led to a change in the charge of early childhood professionals. Teachers of young children must effectively involve families and communities in educating all of our children. Neglecting to do this at this critical time in history demonstrates both a lack of knowledge and a lack of caring about providing the best possible education for all children.

The *Instructor's Guide* to Accompany *Families, Schools, and Communities: Together for Young Children* provides philosophy, a research base, and resources for early childhood teacher educators. Using the Harvard Family Research Project as a foundation, the authors provide a framework for both family involvement content and effective teaching strategies. This textbook addresses the Harvard framework for content in at least the following ways:

General family involvement: Chapters 1, 7, 8, 10, 11
General family knowledge: Chapters 2, 3, 4, 5, 6
Home–school communication: Chapters 7, 8, 9, 10
Family involvement in learning activities:
   Chapters 7, 9, 10
Families supporting schools: Chapter 1, 7, 9
Schools supporting families: All chapters
Families as change agents: Chapter 1, 7, 9, 10

Use of this textbook along with assigned, focused field experiences will provide both breadth and depth of knowledge for early childhood educators, future and present. Further, for each chapter of the textbook, the *Instructor's Guide* delineates knowledge, attitudes, and skills; a variety of instructional strategies; and reading lists for additional information. Resources include an updated list of suggested readings for further information about the content of each chapter. Videos related to each chapter are included with instructional strategies.

We are especially pleased with and proud of an important addition to our *Instructor's Manual*. Dr. Rose Casement from the University of Michigan-Flint has compiled an annotated bibliography of children's literature to accompany many of the topics in this textbook. Rose's knowledge of high-quality children's literature and the significance of families in children's lives make this addition especially relevant.

We believe that early childhood educators will find this resource to be beneficial in their work to support families and children.

It is our hope that this book will serve as one important tool in early childhood teacher education. In addition to the information in this book, teacher education must provide a variety of strategies for teaching both novice and experienced early educators about working effectively with families and communities. Both undergraduate and graduate students who study about working with families must have field experiences and field assignments so that they can practice skills and adopt attitudes such as compassion, empathy, and tolerance.

New to the Third Edition

While maintaining the previous strengths of a strong theoretical foundation and emphasis on creating strong partnerships with families, the third edition of

Families, Schools, and Communities: Together for Young Children has been expanded to include the following:

- completely updated references, for both the research base and current practices

- deeper theoretical explanations

- greater emphasis on inclusive environments and early intervention

- an entirely new chapter on encouraging families to support young children's learning at home. Information is provided specific to family involvement with literacy, math, science, and social studies.

- new information regarding working with and supporting military families

- understanding and supporting foster parents and teen parents

- myths and facts about gay, lesbian, bisexual, and transgendered parents

- substantive information about child development content that is essential for implementation of strong advocacy efforts for young children and families

- increased information and advocacy approaches for children who have an incarcerated parent

- explanations of multiple frameworks for involving families in the education of their young children

- ways to professionalize newsletter formatting

- methods for assessing a parent or family conference

- two new timely topics for parent education and family support: Childhood Obesity and Teaching Financial Responsibility

- a new case study related to English Language Learners (ELL)

- the revised version of the NAEYC Code of Ethical Conduct and Statement of Commitment

- updated Web sites and Web resources have been incorporated throughout each chapter. The Web links can be retrieved directly through the

Thomson Delmar Learning Online Companion Website located at http://www.earlychilded. delmar.com.

Acknowledgments

We wish to acknowledge those who so ably assisted with this writing project. For the first edition, Rebecca Pettit provided a thoughtful review and many excellent suggestions for relating current theoretical perspectives to practice in early childhood education. Patty Keer Weibley's comments from her perspective as a parent with a young child, as well as a professional teacher, added clarity and authenticity. Anne Nickles, director of Shippensburg Head Start, provided us with many sources of invaluable information related to the family involvement component of Head Start. And she allowed us to keep the materials longer than we should have. We are grateful for the photographs submitted by Barbara Bartels and Gay Jones, and by the Szeles and McDaniel families. We are also grateful to Nancy Dymond, Teri Hilbinger, Beth Wachter, and Dr. David Lovett for providing parent voices beginning with the second edition, and to Louanne Burt for additional family stories. Shippensburg University supported a semester-long sabbatical leave for Donna in fall 2005, providing necessary time for the completion of this third edition. Tamara Smith served as an invaluable graduate assistant and provided extensive new resources through searches of current literature. Deb Schultz's work as a graduate assistant also was very helpful.

Our families demonstrated patience with our work on this book as we missed visits and events over the past several years. We are grateful to many extended family members for their interest in this project. The staff at Thomson Delmar Learning who have worked with us include Erin O'Connor and Philip Mandl. Their continuing support for new editions of this textbook have increased the quality of the final product. We are grateful for their varied ways of facilitating our work on this project.

The authors of this textbook began collaborating on professional projects in 1983. We worked together as friends and colleagues through 1994. Since then, we continue to collaborate in our work for children, families, and schools as spouses. Living together through the challenges and blessings of family life has influenced our understanding of the importance of family and community involvement in early education.

Donna Couchenour
Kent Chrisman

Reviewers

The authors are especially grateful to the following reviewers, enlisted by Thomson Delmar Learning, for their helpful suggestions, affirmation, and constructive criticism.

Sylvia J. Brooks
University of Delaware
Newark, Delaware

Judith A. Lindman
Rochester Community & Technical College
Rochester, Minnesota

Kellie Jo Sullivan
Brazosport College
Lake Jackson, Texas

Irene Cook
California State University, Bakersfield
Bakersfield, California

Gail Goldstein
Albuquerque Technical Vocational Institute
Albuquerque, New Mexico

Marie Brand
SUNY Empire State College
Saratoga Springs, New York

PART 1

UNDERSTANDING FAMILIES

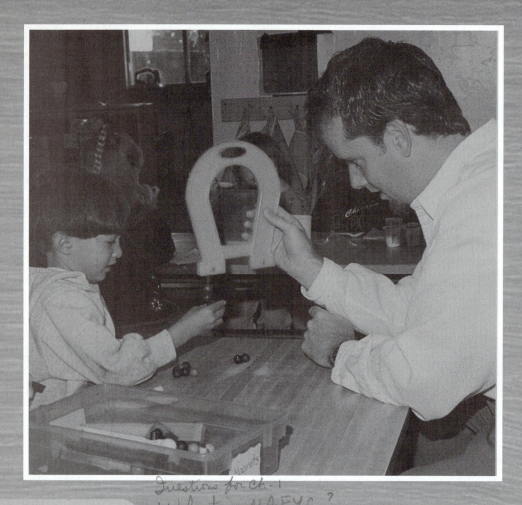

Questions for ch. 1
What is NAEYC?
What is DEC?

OUTLINE

Objectives

Key Terms

The Importance of Families in Children's Lives

Contextualist Theories
✓ Bronfenbrenner's Bioecological Theory
✓ Vygotsky's Sociocultural Theory
✓ Family Systems Theory

Implications for Practice in Early Childhood Education
✓ Guidelines for Developmentally Appropriate Practice (DAP)

Key Characteristics of Early Childhood Programs Practicing Inclusion
✓ NAEYC Accreditation Performance Criteria
✓ Division for Early Childhood of the Council on Exceptional Children Recommended Practices in Family-Based Practices
Family Support Movement

Summary and Conclusions

Chapter 1 Applications

Questions for Reflection and Discussion

Field Assignments

References

A Theory-based Approach to Family Involvement in Early Childhood Education

OBJECTIVES

After reading this chapter, you should be able to:

- relate the importance of families to young children's development according to three theoretical perspectives.

- understand the scientific basis for including family involvement in early childhood education.

- consider the categories of internal and external developmental assets necessary for optimal child development.

- apply principles of developmentally appropriate practice (DAP) and the family support movement in meaningful ways.

Key Terms

accreditation
✓bioecological theory
chronosystem
circumplex model
cohesion
✓contextualist theories
✓developmental assets
developmental
   contextualism

✓developmentally appropriate
   practices (DAP)
exosystem
family life cycle
family support movement
✓family systems theory
flexibility
horizontal stressors
inclusion

✓irreducible needs of children
macrosystem
mesosystem
microsystem
✓sociocultural theory
vertical stressors
zone of proximal development (ZPD)

continuity

The Importance of Families and Communities in Children's Lives

During the summer of 2005, divergent political philosophies echoed comments made nearly a decade earlier during the course of the 1996 U.S. presidential campaign. The debate centered on whether it takes a village or a family to raise a child. Political philosophies differ in this regard, but the argument is found to be faulty when the evidence from child development research is considered. Researchers and practitioners are well aware that in order to reach their optimal levels of development, children need both families and communities. For this reason, schools must strive to support and partner with both families and communities.

Partnership is a key to the establishment of successful relationships among families, schools, and communities. Partnership refers to equal rights for and responsibilities of all three entities. Further, partnerships imply that power bases are equal. Hierarchical models of family, school, and community collaborations will not lead to desired outcomes. That is to say, education professionals must work *with* families and communities through such mechanisms as two-way communication and shared decision-making.

Margaret Mead noted that children, of course, *have* needs, but that they also are *needed by* families and communities: "Of course we need children. Children are our vehicles for survival—for in them there is hope, and through them what has been, and what will be will not only be perpetuated, but also united." Thus, as Figure 1–1 demonstrates, children, families, and communities are entities that are interdependent with one another. In order for early childhood teachers to achieve the best results in their work with young children, this understanding must be practiced in every venue of a child's education. It is the goal of this book to provide details of both the scientific evidence and the best educational practice regarding forming partnerships among families, schools, and communities.

Two recent sources of evidence that inform early childhood educators about the essential need for such partnerships include the **developmental assets** work of the Search Institute (http://www.search-institute.org) and the work on the **irreducible needs** of children by Drs. T. Berry Brazelton and Stanley I. Greenspan.

The Search Institute has established a framework of developmental assets, or critical factors, necessary for children's healthy development. Recent research by associates of the Search Institute (http://www.search-institute.org) has led to the establishment of a framework of developmental assets, or critical factors, necessary for children's healthy development. Scholars continue to test and refine this framework,

but current child development understanding supports the assets as listed. The list of assets includes forty items for each period of development (infancy, toddlerhood, preschool, elementary school age, and adolescence) and demonstrates the importance that families, schools, and various community groups play in the lives of children. The assets for each developmental level are divided into twenty external assets and twenty internal assets. These external and internal assets, in turn, are divided into four subcategories, as seen in Figure 1–2.

"It takes a village to raise a child."

—**African proverb**

An examination of the four external asset categories (those that come from outside the child) shows

Figure 1–2	Categories for Developmental Assets

FOUR EXTERNAL ASSETS

Support—Children need care and love from families, neighbors, and community groups.

Empowerment—Children are empowered when communities value them and keep them safe and secure.

Boundaries and Expectations—Children need to know what is expected of them. Limits should be clear, realistic, and responsive.

Constructive Use of Time—Children need to have opportunities to play safely. Choices should be provided with many varied activities. Both developmental level and individual differences should be considered.

FOUR INTERNAL ASSETS

Commitment to Learning—Families and communities encourage children to be lifelong learners.

Positive Values—Children are exposed to examples of caring, fairness, social justice, integrity, honesty, responsibility, and healthy life choices.

Social Competencies—Children have opportunities to learn how to get along with others, to celebrate similarities and differences, and to peacefully resolve conflicts.

Positive Identity—Children have positive role models and responsive nurturing so that they can develop a sense of self-worth and caring for others.

Source: http://www.search-institute.org

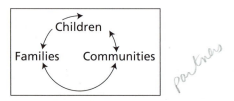

Figure 1–1   Children, families, and communities rely on each other.

that families and communities provide children with necessary care and love, with safety, with limits on expected behaviors, and with a variety of healthy activities. As you consider these categories, list examples that you have experienced either from your own childhood or from a child you have known.

Similarly, an examination of the four internal assets (those that come from within the child) shows that children need the ongoing support from families and communities to build strong positive identities. When children have such support, they are able to commit to being lifelong learners, exhibit positive values such as honesty and responsibility, learn social competence, and gain a positive sense of self. In order to develop these internal assets, young children are dependent on strong role models from both their families and communities.

Brazelton and Greenspan (2000), both pediatric medical professionals, note that over the course of the twentieth century and into the twenty-first, families with young children have faced more and different kinds of stress than in the past. They emphasize young families' need for support from sources outside the immediate family in order to best nurture their children. Our society, they believe, is in grave danger of failing our children. And when children do not get what they need for optimal development, society often pays the price. This cost includes the continuing presence of street gangs, drug and alcohol dependence, and ever-increasing prison populations.

The premise that all children have a right to sensitive nurturance and that no citizen has a right to ignore children's needs is a common thread throughout much of the work accentuating children's irreducible needs. This current and critical endeavor splendidly echoes the old African proverb, "It takes a village to raise a child".

Consider the developmental assets listed in Figure 1–2 and the irreducible needs of children noted in Figure 1–3. Note the areas of overlap.

> Examine overlaps between the "Developmental Assets" and "Irreducible Needs." Discuss how these two sources provide evidence for the necessity of partnerships among families, schools, and communities.

Contextualist Theories

Three **contextualist theories**—bioecological, sociocultural, and family systems—demonstrate relationships among children, families, and communities that are crucial to effective family involvement in early childhood education. When early childhood teachers apply these theories, their family involvement practices will be more authentic and supportive.

In this book, early childhood education is defined comprehensively as any program of care and education for children from birth through eight years of age. Early childhood educators, whether child care staff, preschool teachers, kindergarten teachers, or primary teachers, are a critical part of a healthy community for young children and their families. Healthy communities rely on families to perform a variety of functions for their children. (Readers have noted that even though this textbook is geared toward educational programs for children through age 8, many of the principles and applications are relevant for programs having children through age 12 years.)

When families cannot or do not perform these functions, communities may sometimes "pick up the slack" for the good of the children. As society changes, the expected functions of families and communities shift.

The roles that children serve and the expectations families hold for their children have evolved dramatically in the past 150 years. Moving from an agrarian society through the industrial revolution and into the information age has caused flux in all societal institutions. We have moved from seeing children as property of the father to perceiving them as individuals who have responsibility for themselves, from seeing them as miniature adults who have no rights to perceiving them as developing human beings who possess legal rights and need societal safeguards (deMause, 1974). For many, these changes in the family, so much easier to observe and critique compared to changes in larger societal institutions, signal doom. Thus, some people deny the need for families to rely on the larger community for support.

In this latter perspective, the "village" becomes an enemy. This is faulty logic, however, and can harm

Maslow's hierarchy

Early childhood education teachers are a critical component of a community for both young children and their families.

young children as well as their families by denying children and their families needed sources of support.

> *"Many things can wait. Children cannot. Today their bones are being formed, their blood is being made, and their senses are being developed. To them we cannot say tomorrow. Their name is today."*
>
> **—Gabriela Mistral, Chilean poet**

Good early childhood teachers have always known that frequent, effective communication with families is imperative in the provision of quality care and education for the youngest children. "The emphasis on parents in the settlement house movement of the 1880s, the nursery school movement of the 1920s, and the early intervention movement of the 1960s is exemplary of the parent participation tradition in early childhood education" (Powell, 1989, p. 1). Teachers have used traditional forms of communication, such as newsletters and conferences, when they are effective, but teachers also have created new and different strategies, such as interactive journals and portfolio parties, to adapt to individual circumstances.

Since the 1970s, when society saw an increase in the number of very young children in out-of-home care, a preponderance of early childhood literature supporting the need for family involvement has been

---

Figure 1–3   The Irreducible Needs of Children

All children must have the following needs met in order to grow and thrive:

- ongoing nurturing relationships
- physical protection, safety, and regulation
- experiences that consider the individual differences of children
- experiences that are developmentally appropriate
- appropriate limits, predictable structure, and reasonable expectations
- a stable, supportive community
- cultural continuity

Source: Brazelton and Greenspan, (2000)

---

written. Presently, we are seeing that the need is even greater than it was three decades ago. The latest research on early brain development reinforces our somewhat intuitive notion about the importance of teacher-family partnerships, emphasizing again that parents are not only children's first teachers, but probably also their most important teachers.

The concern about providing continuity in children's experiences is widely held as a rationale for positive and sustained relationships between early childhood teachers and family members (Powell, 1989). Early childhood literature and practice have assumed that continuity is necessary and good for children. Though little research exists to document this as an absolute, some theories offer substantial support for the importance of continuity in young children's lives. In early childhood education, the best way to provide continuity is to develop strong family-school/child care–community bonds.

> *"The reality is that learning does not begin when kids are age five. Learning begins well before they enter the schoolhouse. And what happens to children in their early years has profound impacts on the kind of entering students they will be."*
>
> **—Sharon Lynn Kagan, Professor at Teachers College, Columbia University, and past President of NAEYC**

Bronfenbrenner's Bioecological Theory

Urie Bronfenbrenner's (1979) **bioecological theory** provides substantial support for upholding practices of involving families in early care and education. This theory emphasizes the developmental notion that biological predispositions and environmental influences interactively affect human growth.

A great deal of current information supports the understanding of the interaction of the forces of nature (biology) and nurture (environment). This view is in opposition to the age-old argument in psychology about nature *versus* nurture. "It is time to reconceptualize nature and nurture in a way that emphasizes their inseparability and complementarity, not their distinctiveness . . . [I]t is . . . nature *through* nurture . . . [T]he coactivity of nature and nurture accounts for both stability and malleability in growth" (National Research Council and Institute of Medicine, 2000, p. 41). This and other similar evidence has led Bronfenbrenner to expand his earlier "ecological theory" to one that acknowledges such a shift in thinking about the influences of nature and nurture to "bioecological theory." A major impetus for Bronfenbrenner's development of this model was earlier research methods that produced narrow and inauthentic findings about human development from laboratory studies. He advocated for research methodologies that would make use of observational techniques in natural settings. That is, the importance of studying children in their homes, schools, and communities undergirds this developmental theory.

Bronfenbrenner's model consists of five systems (which are graphically represented by concentric circles). Current understanding of the model, however, perhaps is best described as the Process-Person-Context-Time design (Bronfenbrenner, 2001). Central to the model are the four concepts mentioned in this title:

Process—the changing or dynamic relationship between the person and the context(s).

Person—the individual, including his or her biological makeup and cognitive, emotional, and behavioral qualities. In the model, this concept is placed in the center of the nested circles.

Context—environmental systems, each of which is identified in the concentric circle model in Figure 1–4.

Time—viewed as multidimensional and including the historical period, the time in a family's life cycle, and the time in an individual's development. This concept is represented by the outermost circle of the model and labeled the **chronosystem.**

Possibly the most celebrated of these concepts is context, often shown as concentric circles. Each of the levels of the environment is believed to actively interact with the individual. Understanding these systems can help early childhood teachers to also understand, in turn, that influences on children include the immediate environment (microsystem) as well as other environmental levels (mesosystem, exosystem, macrosystem, and chronosystem). The five environmental systems, including the dimension of time, are described below.

Urie Bronfenbrenner's Bioecological Theory

http://www.psy.pdx.edu/
Click "Key Theorists and Theories" and then click "Urie Bronfenbrenner" (*Note:* Site under construction as of publishing date.)

Bronfenbrenner poses five environmental systems:

1. **Microsystem** is the setting in which the individual lives, or the near environment. This includes the home, school, and community. Often, in a study of home-program relationships, only this system is considered.

2. **Mesosystem** is the relationships between contexts in the microsystem. The relationship or the connection between two forms of microsystems influences children's behavior and development. For example, a telephone call from the teacher regarding a child's difficulties at school may affect parental treatment of the child at home.

3. **Exosystem** is a system removed from direct access of the individual, and has an indirect rather than direct effect on her. Examples of exosystems include parental work sites, extended family, and mass media.

What specific things in each context affect you?

4. **Macrosystem** is the culture in which an individual lives. Values and beliefs of a culture or subculture affect children and families. Western culture is more individualistic, whereas many non-Western cultures are collectivistic.

5. Chronosystem is the time or the sociohistorical context. The era in which one lives her life affects behavior and development.

Taking each of these systems into account in the process of development indicates the complex nature of ecological effects on children. Many experts believe that when professionals understand the nature of such effects, more appropriate and effective strategies for optimizing children's development can be incorporated into early education practices, such as creating strong connections between children's families and early education programs.

These systems are most frequently understood as a series of concentric circles, with the individual at the innermost circle (Figure 1–4). Based on his theory, Bronfenbrenner has written frequently about what children need from their families and what families need from the larger society.

Although many early childhood teachers are capable of and committed to providing excellent educational climates for young children, they do not have responsibility for each child throughout the child's life. Thus, even when teachers' functions are similar to parents' functions, a major difference exists between the two. This suggests that even though high-quality early education is extremely important for children's development, the family is even more important. For Bronfenbrenner, the importance of families for children goes beyond caregiving. He states unequivocally that parents are more capable of providing for the physical and psychological needs of a child when they have a third party who admires and loves them for their caregiving. So, a parent who has a loving relationship with another adult can more easily provide for children's needs. Bronfenbrenner summarizes human development as occurring "in the context of an escalating psychological ping pong game between two people who are crazy about each other" (1990, p. 31).

The converse is that some single or unattached parents may not always get the fuel they need from other adults to provide optimally for their children. Multiple sources exist for single parents to feel loved and admired; any of these sources that is healthy can support that parent's caregiving. Such resources may include grandparents or other extended family, faith communities, or friendships.

Further, workplace policies affect family relationships. As the adults in more families than ever are all working outside the home, the effects of the workplace conditions are felt by children. Flexible hours, part-time positions *with* benefits, and availability of quality child care offer tremendous support for families with children. Such jobs, however, are not readily available for many workers in the current economy. Many jobs are part time, without benefits, and the hours change at the whim of the employer or manager rather than to meet family needs.

As a theorist, Bronfenbrenner is unusual in his advocacy for changing social policy in ways that will positively influence children's development. His recognition that the culture makes a difference in children's lives, as expressed in his definition of the macrosystem, has led him to call for national action in both public and private sectors to demonstrate our care for children and our support for their families.

Vygotsky's Sociocultural Theory

Early childhood educators have increasingly looked to the work of Lev Vygotsky in their attempt to better understand the determinants of children's development. Certain aspects of this **sociocultural theory** are parallel to Bronfenbrenner's explanation of the importance of the external social world for a child's development (Tharp & Gallimore, 1988).

Vygotsky postulated that human knowledge is derived from culture. This means that much of what we "know" comes from our families and larger society. The holidays we celebrate and the ways we celebrate them exemplify knowledge based on culture. The food we eat, the way we prepare and serve it, and even our table manners result from experiences within our culture.

Much of the behavior of young children is rooted in family expectations. Some four-year-olds, for instance, have learned at home that "hitting back"

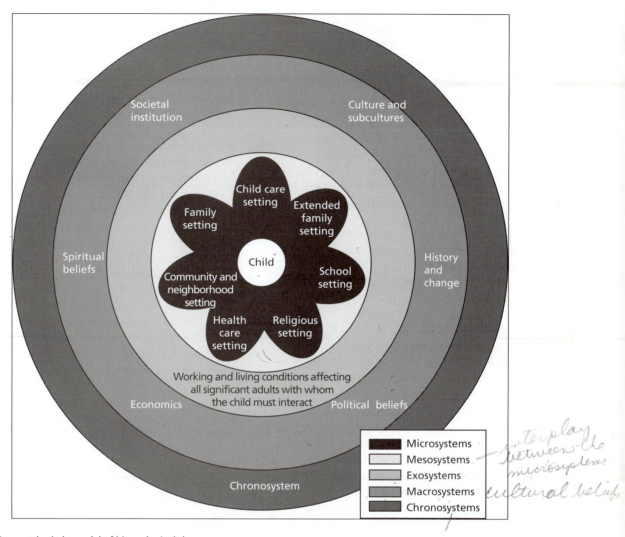

Figure 1–4   Concentric circle model of bioecological theory.
Source: Adapted with permission from Kostelnik, M. J., Whiren, A. P., Soderman, A. K., Stein, L. C., & Gregory, K. (2006). *Guiding children's social development* (5th ed.). Clifton Park, NY: Thomson Delmar Learning

is an acceptable solution to problem situations with peers or siblings. It is important for early childhood teachers who are dealing with children who have learned that hitting is permitted to realize that not only must they teach the child a new set of rules for getting along with others at school, but also that they must communicate with parents and solicit their support for acceptable school behavior.

On the other hand, early childhood teachers sometimes must accept differences of behavior in

children and accommodate these differences in the classroom. For example, teachers should support children's development of their home language. This practice demonstrates respect for a family's primary language and communicates that the early childhood staff values the family's culture. Further, children who speak more than one language have an asset that will serve them well in future endeavors.

Best practice in early childhood education points to viewing bilingual capabilities as an advantage for

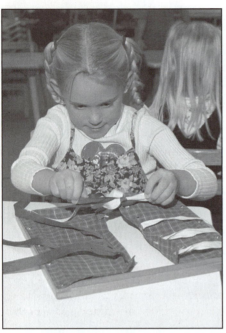

A child's development is dependent on both high-quality early education and the quality of family life.

young children. In fact, the National Association for the Education of Young Children (NAEYC) (1996, p. 1) recommends that teachers of young children "encourage and assist all parents in becoming knowledgeable about the cognitive value for children of knowing more than one language, and provide them with strategies to support, maintain, and preserve home-language learning." Early childhood teachers must "honor and support" families in order to recognize the value of each of their cultural values and traditions.

Position Statement on Responding to Linguistic and Cultural Diversity

http://www.naeyc.org/
Click "Publications"; click "Position Statements"

Lev Vygotsky's Theory

http://www.psy.pdx.edu/
Click "Key Theorists and Theories";
    click "Lev Vygotsky"

Another premise from Vygotsky is that thinking is determined by social and historical assumptions. For example, social assumptions related to limited gender roles influence thinking, even when one claims to be logical or unbiased. Many couples find that before they had children, it was easier to maintain an egalitarian relationship. However, after having children, the added responsibilities seem to affect the degree of egalitarianism, and many fathers take traditional roles as breadwinners, whereas many mothers take traditional roles as homemakers.

Inaccurate historical assumptions also may cloud our thinking. An excellent example of this is the one so many practicing teachers were taught as students: Columbus discovered America. But, this assumption raises a logical question: Could Columbus have discovered America when there were already people living here? We know now that there are more accurate ways of describing Columbus's explorations.

Of course, it is possible that our assumptions may also reflect greater accuracy than the above examples illustrate. Accurate social and historical assumptions affect our thinking in useful and productive ways.

For Vygotsky, the **zone of proximal development (ZPD)** is the mechanism by which development occurs. This ZPD is technically the difference between what a learner can do independently and what she or he can do with the help of a more experienced or knowledgeable "teacher." Note that for the purpose of cognitive development, a "teacher" might be a family member, classroom teacher, peer, or community member. This approach to understanding cognitive development emphasizes the collaboration between the learner and the "teacher." The ZPD has four stages (Vygotsky, 1962):

Stage 1: Performance is assisted by others who are more capable in the particular task.

Stage 2: Performance is assisted by the child herself as she moves toward self-regulation.

Stage 3: The child has internalized the task to a point that assistance would interrupt development. Performance is beyond both social and self-control; it is automatic and without self-consciousness.

Stage 4: Lifelong learning requires that the learner make recursive loops back to Stage 2 in order to improve or maintain skills.

An example of the first three stages of the ZPD is noted in the following anecdote.

> *Chelsea, age three, loves to sing and learns words to songs with ease. With this knowledge, her aunt sang a popular nonsense song to her one day: "Willaby, Wallaby, Wee, an elephant sat on me, Willaby, Wallaby, Woo, an elephant sat on you, Willaby, Wallaby, Welsea, an elephant sat on Chelsea." (stage 1)*
>
> *The child responded at first by staring and smiling. Her aunt continued singing, using the names of other family members: Christopher, mommy, daddy, and Bryan. Soon, Chelsea started to sing the words that were familiar to her such as "an elephant sat on Christopher" (stage 2 begins), and later that day she was singing "Willaby, Wallaby, an elephant sat on mommy" (more stage 2). She did not use the unfamiliar words that rhyme with a name and begin with a "w," such as "wommy" or "waddy," but listened carefully when her aunt did.*
>
> *Five days later, Chelsea visited her aunt again. At that point, she was singing the entire phrase and filling in names of her family (more stage 2). Several days later, Chelsea was singing the "Willaby, Wallaby" song without much effort or conscious thought as she played with blocks (stage 3).*
>
> *It is too soon to tell whether Chelsea might engage in the recursive loop if she forgets the words at a later date.*

When early childhood teachers apply concepts from sociocultural theory, they demonstrate respect for all families' values and traditions. The understanding that knowledge is rooted in one's culture—or, as Vygotsky put it, that thinking is determined by social and historical assumptions—may help teachers to analyze their own belief systems. For instance, some classroom or school-wide celebrations may be based on assumptions that come from the experiences or knowledge of the majority. Such events may cause some children and/or families to feel excluded or devalued by them. When this occurs, early childhood professionals must concern themselves with the ethical underpinnings of such celebrations.

Family Systems Theory

[handwritten: assumes that families have their own ways of approaching events in life, communication among + between each other, determine rules for structure + change + interacting c external organizat + individuals]

In addition to the developmental contextualist theory that has grown out of studies of human development across the life span, family sciences also has emphasized a *systems* approach: "In the **family systems theory,** everything that happens to any family member is seen as having an impact on everyone else in the family. This is because family members are interconnected and operate as a group, or system" (Olson & DeFrain, 1994, p. 16).

The following explanations of family systems theory include three models: developmental contextualism, circumplex, and family life cycle. All three of these models take a systems approach in that they view families as interactive systems in which children develop.

Developmental Contextualism Supporting Bronfenbrenner's notion that children develop in context, Lerner notes, "the family is not a context within which a child's ontogeny merely unfolds. Instead, the family is a dynamic context, one wherein a child is both transformer and is transformed. In addition, the child-family relation is reciprocally related to interactions with other key contexts of life, for example, the school and the peer group" (1989, p. 18). This point of view, **developmental contextualism,** evolved from an effort to connect human developmental theories that espouse a strong biological foundation and family sociology theories that emphasize the family as the central social institution.

[handwritten: Both biology + environment influence development]

Similar to the bioecological model, in which individuals are actively interacting with their contexts, development is viewed as bi-directional and dynamic. Lerner emphasizes the need for researchers to include variables from biology, psychology, sociology, and history so that a pattern of variables might be more comprehensively understood. He believes that it is only through such comprehensive studies that human development will best be dependably described. Further, he posits the centrality of dynamic interactionism to explaining human development. This concept emphasizes the synthesis of variables influencing each other as well as the individual. Essentially, the developmental contextualist view does not emphasize either nature or nurture as more essential, but rather supports the interaction of nature with nurture (or biology with context) as central to understanding influences on human development.

This view of human development is an optimistic one. The suggestion that people can acquire resources through various contexts in order to make the most of their own development can provide direction for many levels of education. In terms of early childhood education, it behooves us to work with children in their families and communities as well as at school or child care. Consideration for multiple levels of influence provides early education with information that can effectively support children's development and educational progress on such a variety of levels.

In addition to the developmental contextualist theory that has grown out of studies of human development across the life span, family sciences has also emphasized a *systems* approach. "In the **family systems theory,** everything that happens to any family member is seen as having an impact on everyone else in the family. This is because family members are interconnected and operate as a group, or system" (Olson & DeFrain, 1994, p. 16).

Circumplex Model   Several family systems models have been developed. The **circumplex model,** created by Olson and others, is intended to demonstrate how all family members are interconnected. Following are three concepts that are critical to this model.

1. **Cohesion or Togetherness. Cohesion** refers to the feelings family members have for one another, as well as the amount and kind of time they spend together. A recent revision of this theory added another level of cohesiveness, making a total of five levels:

   - disengaged/disconnected
   - somewhat connected
   - connected
   - very connected
   - enmeshed/overly connected (Olson & Gorall, 2003)

The three middle levels are viewed as balanced, whereas the extremes (disengaged and enmeshed) are termed unbalanced.

2. **Flexibility. Flexibility** refers to the ability of family members to change roles and amounts of power they hold over time. This category looks at how families balance stability with change. The five levels of flexibility are:

   - rigid/inflexible
   - somewhat flexible
   - flexible
   - very flexible
   - chaotic/overly flexible (Olson & Gorall, 2003)

Just as with cohesion, the three middle levels are viewed as balanced and the two extremes (rigid and chaotic) are seen as unbalanced. Figure 1–5 demonstrates the relationships among various levels of cohesion and flexibility.

3. **Communication.** Family communication is a mechanism for establishing and maintaining cohesiveness, and for supporting families to be flexible over time in order to best meet family functions. Thus, this dimension is considered to be essential in order for families to change in relation to their levels of togetherness or flexibility. The following abilities are included in this domain: listening, speaking, clarity, respectfulness, concern for others, and self-disclosure.

In order to explain the processes involved in family communication, the circumplex model has recently been updated to include another graphic, a couple and family map, that features all five levels of cohesiveness and flexibility. Further, this updated version allows variations in characteristics of the family to be mapped over time.

Measures of these three dimensions can lead family scientists or therapists to classify a family in one of three ways:

1. balanced families who have balance on both the cohesion and flexibility dimensions
2. midrange families who are extreme on one dimension but balanced on the other

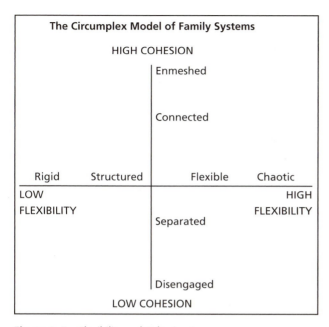

Figure 1–5   Flexibility and Cohesion Axes.

3. extreme families who are extreme in both cohesion (either too close, enmeshed; or too far apart, disengaged) and flexibility (either too loose, chaotic; or not flexible enough, rigid) (Olson & DeFrain, 1994)

Research with the Circumplex Model

http://www.prepare-enrich.com
Click "Research"; click "Circumplex Model Materials"

From these concepts, a total of twenty-five family variations can occur. Nine types of balanced families are:

somewhat connected and somewhat flexible
somewhat connected and flexible
somewhat connected and very flexible
connected and somewhat flexible
connected and flexible
connected and very flexible

very connected and somewhat flexible
very connected and flexible
very connected and very flexible

Twelve types of midrange families are:

disconnected with somewhat flexible
disconnected with flexible
disconnected with very flexible
overly connected with somewhat flexible
overly connected with flexible
overly connected with very flexible
inflexible with somewhat connected
inflexible with connected
inflexible with very connected
overly flexible with somewhat connected
overly flexible with connected
overly flexible with very connected

And, four types of extreme families are:

overly connected overly flexible
overly connected inflexible
disconnected inflexible
disconnected overly flexible (Olson & Gorall, 2003)

Because families are dynamic, this family systems theory points to the importance of the family's ability to change over time. For example, family cohesion is often higher in young couples and in families with young children than in families with adolescents. Teens' need to separate from their parents and find their own identities often leads to less cohesiveness during this stage of family life. Not surprisingly, families with young children often find that they become less flexible than they were before the first child was born and then become more flexible when the children become adolescents (Olson & DeFrain, 1994). Families with young children often have such tight daily schedules that flexibility lessens out of necessity.

Family Life Cycle   Using a model similar to Bronfenbrenner's, the expanded **family life cycle approach** espoused by Carter and McGoldrick (1999) employs a concentric circle representation with the addition of arrows for challenges that occur over time, **horizontal stressors,** and challenges that are embedded in particular families' patterns of relating, **vertical stressors.** Examples of horizontal stressors include developmental transitions, such as marriage, transition to parenthood, and "empty nest"; unpredictable events, such as chronic illness or sudden disability and unemployment; and historic events, such as hurricane disasters, war, and economic influences. Examples of vertical stressors include poverty, oppression, addictions, domestic violence, family myths and secrets, loss of leisure time, and genetic influences. The circles in this model represent from the innermost to the outermost: individual, immediate family, extended family, community, and larger society.

> The life cycle approach emphasizes that "families comprise people who have a shared history and a shared future. They encompass the entire emotional system of at least three, and frequently now four or even five, generations. . . . Relationships with parents, siblings, and other family members go through transitions as they move along the life cycle" (Carter & McGoldrick, 1999, p. 1).

Carter and McGoldrick also emphasize the importance of the family life cycle in order to best understand families. A family life cycle approach considers how families typically change over time. Relationships among family members take priority over family functions in this theory. Intergenerational relationships account for a great deal in how families move from one stage to another of the family life cycle process.

Most of the research and theory building done in this area is applicable to middle-class families in the United States. Families that differ culturally and economically from this group likely will not follow the same developmental cycle. This also may be true for families with various structures, such as single parent or blended family. It is important to understand that there is not a fixed sequence of life cycle stages for every family and that a flexible notion of predictable stages is helpful in understanding influences on individual development. For early childhood educators, the primary implication of this theory is that child development occurs within the context of the family life cycle.

Although there are several models of the family life cycle, some having as many as twenty-four phases, Carter and McGoldrick's work includes the following stages:

1. leaving home: single young adults
2. marriage: the new couple
3. families with young children
4. families with adolescents
5. launching children
6. families in later life

Because the emphasis in this text is on families with young children, this stage will be discussed further. Interestingly, Carter and McGoldrick refer to this stage as the "pressure cooker" phase of the family life cycle (p. 12), which may help early childhood educators understand and work more effectively with families of the young children they teach.

The "families with young children" period often requires immense adjustment by both parents. Each is moving, in terms of the family life cycle, from concern for the two of them as a couple to trying to balance child care, household responsibilities, and increasingly, a full-time job. Caring for children is a primary effort during this stage, so when any part of this tenuous balancing act goes awry, it may cause the children's caregivers or teachers to feel the effects of the couple's apprehension.

Achieving a successful balance depends on many factors: well children, job security, quality and affordable child care, housing, working conditions of home appliances, and reliable transportation. When any one of the factors is out of the ordinary or unexpected, the balance is threatened. Thus, when an early childhood teacher requests a conference or a parent meeting, parents of young children often are immediately aware of how scheduling such an event may complicate their "pressure cooker" schedule.

Further, when parents attend a conference or group family meeting, it is important that the time is planned carefully, that the starting time and ending time are communicated in advance, and that the time is well organized and used to benefit all concerned. In other words, educators must realize that a meeting might increase the pressure on families

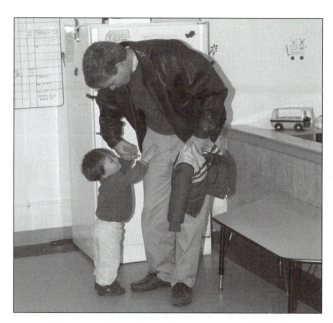

Parents may have concerns about balancing a full-time job and caring for their child.

and, therefore, must be as useful and efficient as possible.

Because moving to the young children phase of the family life cycle requires so much adjusting for new parents and other family members, engaging in rituals is often seen as a way of supporting the family. Both extended family and community are often involved in such celebrations. Common secular rituals marking this phase include baby showers, handing out cigars, posting lawn signs announcing the baby's gender, sending birth announcements, and newspaper announcements of births, while other rituals, such as baptism, christening, and bris, are based on religious tradition.

A number of social changes over the past generation have affected tasks and responsibilities across the family life cycle in the United States. Important examples of such changes include a lower birth rate, longer life expectancy, the changing role of women, the relocation of young families for jobs or education, and the increasing divorce and remarriage rate. Divorce is now so common that many social scientists see it as a normative event.

To demonstrate recent changes in families, please do the following:

1. Write down the number of children your parents have, the number of children that were in each of your parents' families as they grew up, and the number of children in your grandparents' families as they grew up. Add the total for each of the three generations. What did you find? *about # of children over generat*

2. Ask a relative about the ages at which your deceased relatives died. Note that current life expectancy for middle-class people in the United States is about 74 years. What did you find about earlier generations in your family? *regarding life expectancy*

3. What was your mother's role in the family in terms of working outside or inside the home? What were your grandmothers' roles? What roles do women in your own generation play? How have these changed over time? What are the reasons the roles have changed? *Have the men's + women's roles changed & why*

4. What was your father's role in the family in terms of working outside or inside the home? What were your grandfathers' roles? What roles do men in your own generation play? How have these changed over time? What are the reasons the roles have changed?

5. Has divorce and/or remarriage been an aspect of your immediate family? Your extended family? How has divorce or remarriage affected your family's life cycle process?

6. Do you live near your extended family? Have you ever moved with your immediate family? How does living near or far away from other family members affect relationships with grandparents, aunts, uncles, and cousins? *How does distance matter w/ extended family*

7. What is your family's philosophy regarding children? Speculate on how this philosophy might have changed over the generations.

Specific implications for early childhood educators that can be culled from family systems theory, include the following:

1. Teachers and caregivers need to remember the influence of all family members on children's behaviors. Influence may affect family members regardless of geographic distance or even after the death of some members. For example, one

family member may insist to the parent that the child should have a structured reading program emphasizing phonics. This causes the parent or other primary caregiver to question the school's whole language reading program.

2. Each family member may play a role in a child's life that may remain consistent or may vary, depending on the family's situation. For example, a grandparent may become more actively involved if a parent dies, divorces, or changes jobs.

3. Stress in the family may change the child's role and his relationships with other family members. The death of a parent or divorce may result in a child's greater role in providing emotional support for the remaining parent.

4. The function of myth may affect the child's behavior while she is at school. An example of one family myth, "We don't let anyone push us around," may influence the child so that she hits in response to conflict.

Implications for Practice in Early Childhood Education

Multiple sources, including both professional literature and professional associations, point to the importance of early childhood educators understanding and practicing family and community involvement. Early childhood professionals not only must demonstrate an understanding or knowledge base relating to families and communities, but also must apply their knowledge through allied attitudes and skills.

In terms of implications for practice, the following principles relating to family and community involvement are offered: Guidelines for Developmentally Appropriate Practice (DAP); Key Characteristics of Early Childhood Programs Practicing Inclusion; National Program Accreditation Guidelines; Division for Early Childhood (DEC) of the Council on Exceptional Children (CEC) Recommended Practices in Family-Based Practices; and the Family Support Movement.

> As you examine principles in each of the categories of this section, note specific knowledge, skills, and attitudes that are implied in each of the items.

Guidelines for Developmentally Appropriate Practice

"It is widely recognized that children vary on every measurable characteristic. Youngsters demonstrate individuality related to genetic, cultural, and contextual factors. Despite the rhetorical acceptance of such variability, conventional definitions of early development and learning have been more attentive to genetic and/or developmental variation than to cultural or contextual variation. Such a focus on genetic and developmental variability has had important and often negative consequences.

"In some cases, access to differing educational opportunities has been determined by assessments that ignore cultural competence and that use majority-culture norms to determine competence on a single dimension . . . .

"Developmental equivalencies are often not understood, and variation within cultures is often neglected. Individual, cultural, and contextual variables influence how children present themselves, understand the world, process information, and interpret experiences . . . ."

—**Kagan, Moore, and Bredekamp, 1995**

Bredekamp and Copple, in their book *Developmentally Appropriate Practice in Early Childhood Programs*, state that "developmentally appropriate practices derive from deep knowledge of individual children, and the context within which they develop and learn. The younger the child, the more necessary it is for professionals to acquire this knowledge through relationships with children's families" (1997, p. 22). They list eight guidelines to help professionals obtain this knowledge and establish reciprocal relationships with families of children in early education programs. These guidelines are as follows:

- Mutual respect, cooperation, shared responsibility, and negotiation of conflicts toward achievement of shared goals are requirements for effective family and school partnerships. All communication must be respectful of individual family members as well as of cultural values. Co-operation and shared responsibility point to the critical attitude of forming partnerships to reach shared goals. This attitude is in opposition to school and staff holding all of the power for resolution of conflicts. The professional's willingness and ability to negotiate will work to build strong and lasting partnerships with families and communities.

- Collaborative partnerships require regular, frequent, two-way communication with the child's family. Communication must begin early in the partnership and happen often. Understand that unilateral communication does not ensure that partnerships will be formed and thus, that optimal outcomes will ensue.

- Roles for parents include decision-making about children's care and education, as well as observation, participation, and decision-making regarding the program. Early childhood teachers must build in opportunities for family members to be active in the decision-making processes. Often, family experiences hold keys to improved decisions in early childhood programs. High-quality early childhood programs typically have open-door policies that invite family members to observe their children's educational program in action. Not only do teachers invite family participation, but they also encourage family members to initiate novel ways of being engaged in their children's education.

- The teachers' role includes sensitivity to families' wishes and respect for their preferences while maintaining professional responsibility to children. This guideline emphasizes the importance of the professional's responsibility to

children. Forming partnerships does not lead to the teacher capitulating to family members, but rather, indicates the importance of sharing professional knowledge in a manner that is sensitive to the family's concerns.

- Teachers and family members share their knowledge of the child through day-to-day communication and planned conferences. Teachers provide support to families to promote strengths and competence of family members. Working together, families and teachers are able to create methods of two-way, frequent communication that will be effective in supporting children's learning. It is likely that the form of communication will vary for different families, but the outcome of empowering families to participate in meaningful ways in their children's education should remain the same.

- Family members are involved in assessing and planning the program for individual children. Early childhood teachers provide necessary scaffolding to support families' full participation in regularly scheduled conferences, team meetings, and individualized family service plan (IFSP) and individualized education plan (IEP) meetings prior to, during, and following such meetings.

- The program links families with services and resources based on the concerns and priorities of program staff and families. Early childhood professionals can create resource files or handbooks with information about local agencies, helping professionals, and/or community events that are made readily available to families. Such resource compilations must be accurate and current. In the event that families need varying or additional services, early childhood teachers will work to seek such information from professional ties.

- All professionals who have information about the child will share that information with the family as children pass from one level or program to another. Early childhood teachers play a significant role in children's educational transitions. Sharing information with professionals in a new setting to support each child's learning may take the form of sharing files, conferencing, or responding to specific questions. Parents (or family members who are primary caregivers) should be given detailed, objective information about the child so that they can advocate as necessary as the child transitions from one environment to another.

The DAP guidelines form the basis for excellence as early educators design programs for family involvement. Each program's formulators will, of course, develop unique ways of implementing the guidelines. Generally, however, using these guidelines can help ensure that program staff, when faced with the inevitable questions and decisions that arise when a new program is implemented, acknowledge the importance of, and make decisions that reinforce, reciprocal relationships with families.

Position Statement on Developmentally Appropriate Practice

http://www.naeyc.org/
Click Information about NAEYC"; click "Position Statements"

See new position statement on inclusion

Key Characteristics of Early Childhood Programs Practicing Inclusion

Nearly all early childhood education programs practice some form of inclusion, whether in a way that has been planned or unplanned. In this context, *inclusion* refers to programs that enroll both typically developing children and children with identified disabilities. It is not uncommon for young children to arrive at their early educational setting, whether it is child care, preschool, kindergarten, or the primary grades, without having been identified as having a particular disability. Further, legislation regarding special education requires that children with identified disabilities be included in "regular" educational experiences. The following guidelines (Schwartz, Sandall, Odom, Horn, & Beckman, 2002) are provided as minimal

requirements for providing all children with a high-quality inclusive educational experience.

- *Inclusive early childhood programs enroll typically developing children and children with identified disabilities.* In addition, early childhood programs commonly enroll children with disabilities that have not yet been identified.

- *Staff members are well trained and competent in providing a high-quality early childhood program.* Teachers who are highly qualified in early childhood or special education must be prepared to extend their expertise as necessary to provide the most effective program for all children in it. Thus, early childhood educators must understand the individual needs of atypically developing children, and special educators must understand typical developmental milestones and behaviors.

- *The same daily schedule is available to all children.* Children must not be excluded from any activity. Early childhood educators must work with families and other professionals to accommodate any special needs.

- *The curriculum is developmentally appropriate and meets the needs of individual children.* The very term *developmentally appropriate* indicates that early childhood teachers are required to plan and implement educational experiences for the entire group of children that take fully into account children's individual differences and needs. Accommodating special needs must be practiced routinely.

- *All children have the support they need to participate actively in the program.* This support may take the form of technological adaptations, physical adaptations, or an extra set of adult hands to help as needed.

- *Adaptations and modifications are provided for individual needs. Specialized services are provided as needed.* Early childhood and special education teachers must have current knowledge regarding child development as well as mechanisms for accessing available services and accommodations.

- *All children are supported to engage in successful peer interactions.* All children need the support of their early childhood teachers to learn to get along with others. Teachers should be prepared to provide various levels of support as well as to accommodate individual needs as necessary, so that all children have sufficient opportunities to interact with peers.

- *Family members are active participants in various ways.* Application of all of the previously mentioned family and community partnership guidelines from Developmentally Appropriate Practices will be important for teachers to consider in inclusive early childhood programs. Teachers must interact with all families with respect and sensitivity.

- *Staff members and families collaborate to provide the best educational program for each young child.* The early childhood teacher's collaboration with families of children with special needs is necessary to ensure that each child's learning outcomes might be optimal.

National Association for the Education of Young Children Accreditation Performance Criteria

The National Association for the Education of Young Children (NAEYC) has devised a system of early childhood program standards and performance criteria that is administered by the NAEYC Academy for Early Childhood Program Accreditation. Programs serving infants through kindergarten, under any auspices, are eligible to apply for this national, voluntary accreditation. This program began in 1985 and has recently been "reinvented" in order to increase the accountability of all systems serving young children and their families. The primary purpose of this accreditation system is to encourage early childhood programs to participate in a structured approach to program improvement that considers all of the evidence-based components of high-quality early education. Those components are organized by focus areas and performance categories. See Figure 1–6 for more information.

More than 10,000 programs serving more than 850,000 children and their families are now accredited.

| Figure 1–6 | NAEYC Early Childhood Program Standards |

Focus Area: Children
Performance Categories: Relationships; Curriculum; Teaching; Assessment of Child Progress; Health

Focus Area: Teaching Staff
Performance Category: Teachers

Focus Area: Partnerships
Performance Categories: Families; Community Relationships

Focus Area: Leadership and Administration
Performance Categories: Physical Environment; Leadership and Management

See KDE website for self-study info

Four steps are involved in the process of accreditation. First, early childhood programs enroll in the extensive self-study in order to assess their strengths and areas needing work. After completing the self-study and undergoing a check to ensure that they meet eligibility requirements, programs submit their self-assessment report and officially apply for accreditation. The program then receives "Candidate" status, and NAEYC begins the process of scheduling a site visit. During the site visit, the program must demonstrate that it meets all ten program standards. More information is available at www.naeyc.org/accreditation/academy.asp.

Most of the ten program standards relate, in various ways, to family and community involvement, but we focus on the two standards specific to these topics: program standard 7, "Families," and program standard 8, "Community Involvement." The Families standard contains three categories:

- Knowing and Understanding the Program's Families
- Sharing Information Between Staff and Families
- Nurturing Families as Advocates for Their Children

See Figure 1–7 for a list of the performance criteria for each of the categories in standard 7.

tube deo on www.naeyc.org/academy/interested/whyaccreditation

Figure 1–7   Categories and Accreditation Performance Criteria for Program Standard 7—Families

KNOWING AND UNDERSTANDING THE PROGRAM'S FAMILIES

New and existing program staff develop skills and knowledge to work effectively with diverse families as a part of orientation and on-going staff development.

Program staff use a variety of formal and informal strategies (including conversations) to become acquainted with and learn from families about their family structure; their preferred child-rearing practices; and their socioeconomic, linguistic, racial, religious, and cultural backgrounds.

Program staff actively use information about families to adapt the environment, curriculum, and teaching methods to the families they serve.

To better understand the cultural backgrounds of children, families, and the community, program staff (as a part of program activities or as individuals) participate in community cultural events, concerts, storytelling activities, or other events and performances geared to children and their families.

Program staff provide support and information to family members legally responsible for the care and well-being of a child.

Program staff establish intentional practices from the first contact with families designed to foster strong reciprocal relationships and maintain them over time.

Program staff ensure that all families, regardless of family structure; socioeconomic, racial, religious, and cultural backgrounds; gender; abilities; or preferred language, are included in all aspects of the program, including volunteer opportunities. These opportunities consider families' interests and skills and the needs of program staff.

Program staff engage with families to learn from their knowledge of their child's interests, approaches to learning, and the child's developmental needs, and to learn about their concerns and goals for their children. This information is incorporated into ongoing classroom planning.

Program staff use a variety of formal and informal methods to communicate with families about the program philosophy and curriculum objectives, including educational goals and effective strategies that can be used by families to promote their children's learning. They implement a variety of methods, such as new family orientations, small group meetings, individual conversations, and written questionnaires, for getting input from families about curriculum activities throughout the year.

The program works with families on shared child-caregiving issues, including routine separations, special needs, the food being served and consumed, and daily care matters.

Families may visit any area of the facility at any time during the program's regular hours of operation as specified by the procedures of the facility.

The program facilitates opportunities for families to meet with each other on a formal and informal basis, work together on projects to support the program, and learn from and provide support for each other.

The program's governing or advisory groups include families as members and active participants. Family members are mentored into leadership roles by staff or other families in the program.

Program staff and families work together to plan events. Families' schedules and availability are considered as part of this planning.

SHARING INFORMATION BETWEEN STAFF AND FAMILIES

Program staff use a variety of mechanisms, such as family conferences or home visits, to promote dialogue with families. Program staff ask adults to translate or interpret communications as needed.

Program staff communicate with families on at least a weekly basis regarding children's activities and developmental milestones, shared caregiving issues, and other information that affects the well-being and development of their children. Where in-person communication is not possible, alternative communication practices are in place.

Program staff communicate with families on a daily basis regarding infants' and toddlers'/twos' activities and developmental milestones, shared caregiving issues, and other information that affects the well-being and development of their children. Where in-person communication is not possible, alternative communication practices are in place.

Continues

Figure 1–7 *(Continued)*

The program compiles and provides information about the program to families in a language the family can understand. This information includes program policies and operating procedures.

Program staff inform families about its systems for formally and/or informally assessing children's progress. This includes the purposes of the assessment, the procedures used for assessment, procedures for gaining family input and information, the timing of assessments, the way assessment results or information will be shared with families, and ways the program will use the information.

When program staff suspect that a child has a developmental delay or other special need, this possibility is communicated to families in a sensitive, supportive, and confidential manner, with documentation and explanation for the concern, suggested next steps, and information about resources for assessment.

NURTURING FAMILIES AS ADVOCATES FOR THEIR CHILDREN

Program staff encourage families to regularly contribute to decisions about goals for their child and plans for activities and services.

Program staff encourage families to raise concerns and work collaboratively with them to find mutually satisfying solutions that staff then incorporate into classroom practice.

Program staff encourage and support families to make the primary decisions about services that their children need, and they encourage families to advocate to obtain needed services.

Program staff use a variety of techniques to negotiate difficulties that arise in their interactions with family members. Program staff make arrangements to use these techniques in a language the family can understand.

Program staff provide families with information about programs and services from other organizations. Staff support and encourage families' efforts to negotiate health, mental health, assessment, and educational services for their children.

Program staff use established linkages with other early education programs and local elementary schools to help families prepare for and manage their children's transitions between programs, including special education programs. Staff provide information to families that can assist them in communicating with other programs.

To help families with their transitions to other programs or schools, staff provide basic general information on enrollment procedures and practices, visiting opportunities, and/or program options. Prior to sharing information with other relevant providers, agencies, or other programs, staff obtain written consent from the family.

The Community Involvement standard incorporates the following categories:

- Linking with the Community
- Accessing Community Resources
- Acting as a Citizen in the Neighborhood and the Early Childhood Community

Position Statement on Accreditation Criteria

http://www.naeyc.org.
Click "Information about NAEYC";
    click "Position Statements"

See Figure 1–8 for listing of performance criteria for each of the categories in standard 8.

"The purpose of the National Academy of Early Childhood Programs is to improve the quality of care and education provided for young children in group programs in the United States. The Academy achieves its purpose by developing training resources, disseminating public information about high quality programs, and administering a national, voluntary accreditation system for early childhood programs."

—Accreditation Criteria and Procedures

LINKING WITH THE COMMUNITY

Program staff maintain a current list of child and family support services available in the community based on the pattern of needs they observe among families and based on what families request (e.g., health, mental health, oral health, nutrition, child welfare, parenting programs, early intervention/special education screening and assessment services, and basic needs, such as housing and child care subsidies). They share the list with families and assist them in locating, contacting, and using community resources that support children's and families' well-being and development.

Program staff develop partnerships and professional relationships with agencies, consultants, and organizations in the community that further the program's capacity to meet the needs and interests of the children and families that they serve.

Program staff are familiar with family support services and specialized consultants who are able to provide culturally and linguistically appropriate services. They use this knowledge to suggest and guide families to these services as appropriate.

Program staff encourage continuity of services for children by communicating with other agencies and programs to achieve mutually desired outcomes for children and guide collaborative work.

Program staff identify and establish relationships with specialized consultants who can assist all children's and families' full participation in the program. This includes support for children with disabilities, behavioral challenges, or other special needs.

Program staff advocate for the program and its families by creating awareness of the program's needs among community councils, service agencies, and local governmental entities.

Program staff include information gathered from stakeholders in planning for continuous improvement, building stakeholder involvement in the program, and broadening community support for the program.

ACCESSING COMMUNITY RESOURCES

Program staff use their knowledge of the community and the families they serve as an integral part of the curriculum and children's learning experiences.

Program staff connect with and use their community's urban, suburban, rural, and/or tribal cultural resources.

Program staff inform families about community events sponsored by local organizations, such as museum exhibits, concerts, storytelling, and theater geared to children.

Program staff invite members of the performing and visual arts community, such as musical performers, traveling museum exhibits, local artists, and community residents, to share their interests and talents with the children.

The program engages with other community organizations and groups to cosponsor or participate in cultural events to enrich the experience of children and families in the program.

ACTING AS A CITIZEN IN THE NEIGHBORHOOD AND THE EARLY CHILDHOOD COMMUNITY

Program staff are encouraged to participate in local, state, or national early childhood education organizations by joining and attending meetings and conferences. Program staff are also encouraged to participate regularly in local, state, or regional public-awareness activities related to early care and education.

The program encourages staff to participate in joint and collaborative training activities or events with neighboring early childhood programs and other community service agencies.

The program encourages staff and families to work together to support and participate in community improvement or advocacy projects.

Program leadership builds mutual relationships and communicates regularly with close neighbors, informing them about the program, seeking out their perspectives, involving them in the program as appropriate, and cooperating with them on neighborhood interests and needs.

Program staff are encouraged and given the opportunity to participate in community or statewide interagency councils or service integration efforts.

Program leadership is knowledgeable about how policy changes at local, state, tribal, or national levels affect the services and resources available for children and their families.

Division for Early Childhood (DEC) of the Council on Exceptional Children (CEC) Recommended Practices in Family-Based Practices

In the *DEC Recommended Practices* book, Trivette and Dunst (2000) discuss two key features for early intervention (children with disabilities and children under age three) and early childhood special education (children with disabilities and children ages three through five) that family-based practices must include. The first feature is based on "resources and supports" (p. 40) and indicates that professionals must ensure that families have the necessary resources to engage in optimal child-rearing activities. The second feature relates to "family-centered helpgiving" (p. 41) and states that it is not only what is done with families that matters, but also how it is done. Ultimately, the goal is that "professionals must strengthen families' abilities to support the development of their children, in a manner that increases families' sense of parenting competence and not families' sense of dependency on professionals or professional systems" (p. 41).

> *"Respect for all children and families is a fundamental value supported by DEC. All children and families means all—including children with disabilities, children at-risk for school failure, children who live in poverty, children who are non-English speaking, children with gifts and talents, and all of their families."*
>
> **—Sandall, McLean, and Smith, p. 7**

Seventeen recommended family-based practices, organized into four categories, as follows:

1. Families and professionals share responsibility and work collaboratively.
   - *Family members and professionals jointly develop appropriate family-identified outcomes.*
   - *Family members and professionals work together and share information routinely and collaboratively to achieve family-identified outcomes.*
   - *Professionals fully and appropriately provide relevant information so parents can make informed choices and decisions.*
   - *Professionals use helping styles that promote shared family/professional responsibility in achieving family-identified outcomes.*
   - *Family/professionals' relationship building is accomplished in ways that are responsive to cultural, language, and other family characteristics.*

2. Practices strengthen family functioning.
   - *Practices, supports, and resources provide families with participatory experiences and opportunities promoting choice and decision making.*
   - *Practices, supports, and resources support family participation in obtaining desired resources and supports to strengthen parenting competence and confidence.*
   - *Intrafamily, informal, community, and formal supports and resources (e.g., respite care) are used to achieve desired outcomes.*
   - *Supports and resources provide families with information, competency-enhancing experiences, and participatory opportunities to strengthen family functioning and promote parenting knowledge and skills.*
   - *Supports and resources are mobilized in ways that are supportive and do not disrupt family and community life.*

3. Practices are individualized and flexible.
   - *Resources and supports are provided in ways that are flexible, individualized, and tailored to the child's and family's preferences and styles, and promote well-being.*
   - *Resources and supports match each family member's identified priorities and preferences (e.g., mother's and father's may be different).*
   - *Practices, supports, and resources are responsive to the cultural, ethnic, racial, language, and socioeconomic characteristics and preferences of families and their communities.*
   - *Practices, supports, and resources incorporate family beliefs and values into decisions, intervention plans, and resources and support mobilization.*

4. Practices are strengths- and assets-based.
   - *Family and child strengths and assets are used as a basis for engaging families in participatory experiences supporting parenting competence and confidence.*

- *Practices, supports, and resources build on existing parenting competence and confidence.*
- *Practices, supports, and resources promote the family's and professional's acquisition of new knowledge and skills to strengthen competence and confidence.*

The Division for Early Childhood of the Council on Exceptional Children
http://www.dec-sped.org/

Family Support Movement

Since the mid-1970s, the interdisciplinary **family support movement** has evolved from emphasizing program development to providing principles for national efforts in work with families. The essence of this movement constitutes "a fundamental change in the traditional belief systems, reflecting a change from assuming that the role of government is to be a resource for families in crisis to recognizing the responsibility of our society to promote the well-being of all families" (Weissbourd, 1994, p. 37). This movement clearly is an application of Bronfenbrenner's theory, emphasizing the importance of various systems as they relate to children and families.

At the heart of family support is community building. The best way to improve the lives of children and families is through caring communities. This movement sees such community support for all families as an "inherent responsibility of a democracy" (Weissbourd, 1994, p. 41).

> *"Family support is about investing in the promotion of the positive things that families want for their children. In the long term, family support is a societal investment in the creation of happy, healthy, productive citizens. This investment not only has an impact on the families who participate in services, it has a secondary impact on us all."*
>
> **—Family Support America (http://www. familysupportamerica.org/, retrieved October 7, 2005)**

Family Support America has outlined seven evidence-based premises (http://www.familysupport-america. org/, retrieved October 7, 2005*) on which programs of family support must be based:

- *Primary responsibility for the development and well-being of children lies within the family, and all segments of society must support families as they rear their children.* Teachers of early childhood education have a unique role in that they have been specially trained to understand and teach young children. Forming partnerships with families of these young children is the best way that early childhood professionals can support families in rearing of their children.

- *Assuring the well-being of all families is the cornerstone of a healthy society, and requires universal access to support programs and services.* Early childhood teachers must advocate for such universal access to all programs of early education, including child care, Head Start and other quality preschool systems, early intervention, early childhood special education, full-day kindergarten and developmentally appropriate primary grade education.

- *Children and families exist as part of an ecological system.* An understanding of Bronfenbrenner's bio-ecological theory leads early childhood teachers to view the complexity of influences on children and families. This knowledge provides for individualized responses to children and families.

- *Childrearing patterns are influenced by parents' understandings of child development and of their child's unique characteristics, personal sense of competence, and cultural and community traditions and mores.* Early childhood teachers have a responsibility to share accurate information about child development as a way to support childrearing competence and confidence. In doing this, teachers must respect and honor individual and cultural differences.

- *Enabling families to build on their own strengths and capacities promotes the healthy development of children.* Affirming the strengths of each family is an effective way to advance healthy development of children.

*This organization is no longer active.

- *The developmental processes that make up parenthood and family life create needs that are unique at each stage in the life span.* An understanding of contemporary issues facing families with young children will provide a strong basis for supporting those families. Further, providing specific resources and supports to those who need them, can aid successful navigation through such challenges and joys.

- *Families are empowered when they have access to information and other resources and take action to improve the well-being of children, families, and communities.* Early childhood teachers and programs can provide ongoing information about community events, helping agencies and current issues.

This perspective recognizes "that families are responsible for their children's development, and that no family can function alone" (Kagan & Weissbourd, 1994, p. xxi). Family support points to children and families' absolutely critical need for continuity between home and school. The family support movement believes that early childhood educators must become advocates not only for young children but also for the families and communities from which those children come.

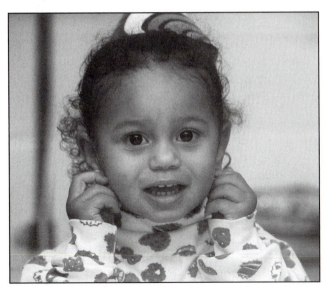

A child gains her identity and sense of self from her family.

A child gains her identity and sense of self from her family. When families' strengths are recognized and their needs are met through the community, they do better and children do better. Bowman (1994) explains how the family support movement changes our paradigm "from a prevention to a promotion model" (p. 41). This means we have evolved from defining families primarily as having deficits and thus defining our task as intervening to prevent problems, to seeing families essentially as having strengths and thus perceiving our task as providing resources to support and augment those strengths and thus promote families' well-being.

Family Focus
http://www.collaboratory.nunet.net

Institute for Responsive Education
http://www.resp-ed.org/

Summary and Conclusions

The information about theory and best practices in this chapter indicates that children do not arrive at early childhood programs having had the same experiences or coming from families who value the same experiences. This contextualist framework permits early childhood professionals to understand concepts related to building supportive partnerships with families, and then to apply those ideas to their work with young children and their families.

Young children do not enter educational programs on a level playing field. As members of families, they come to us with all of the positive, negative, and neutral experiences of their families' lives. Children have learned much about what to expect in their own social world before we see them in early childhood education programs. It is an increasingly important responsibility of early childhood educators to understand the importance of families in children's lives and to include various components from all families' lives in early education.

meredith Walls

Chapter 1 Applications

1. Using information from at least one theory discussed in this chapter, respond to the following comments from early childhood teachers or administrators:

    a. "My job is to teach the children, not to provide a shoulder for parents to cry on."

    b. "There are not enough hours in the day to plan, implement, and evaluate a family involvement program for my classroom."

    c. "I enjoy working with children, but not adults. That's why I wanted to teach."

    d. "How can I include a child with special needs in my center?"

2. Using information from at least one theory discussed in this chapter, respond to the following comments from family members who have children enrolled in early childhood programs:

    a. "I send my child to preschool so that she can learn. The teacher's job is to make sure she does. I resent being asked to volunteer in the classroom."

    b. "I did not like school when I was a student. I am not comfortable being in the classroom."

    c. "I don't want those teachers at my daughter's child care center telling me how to raise my children. I won't go to any of the parent meetings as long as they're telling me what to do."

3. Using information from at least one theory discussed in this chapter, respond to the following comments from community members who do not have young children:

    a. "I don't want my tax money going to support preschool programs in the schools. Parents should take care of their own children."

    b. "Good parents don't put their kids in child care. I will never do that to my children."

    c. "Families don't care about children like they used to. They want the community to build parks and to provide recreation so they can send their kids out of the house and ignore them."

Questions for Reflection and Discussion

1. When you think about teaching young children, how do you envision your role with families? How have your expectations changed since reading and reflecting on this chapter?

2. When you think about teaching young children, what do you think about the community's involvement or influences on children? How have your ideas changed since reading and reflecting on this chapter?

3. What is your understanding of the role of each of the following theories in developing exemplary family involvement programs in early childhood education?

    a. bioecological

    b. contextualist   *sociocultural*

    c. family systems

4. Using each of the three theories explained in this chapter, critique the guidelines for developmentally appropriate practice, national accreditation, and family support.

Field Assignments

1. Interview several early childhood teachers or administrators about the role families and community members have in their programs. Consider interviewing early childhood professionals in the following types of programs: Head Start, child care, public school, family center, and early intervention. Compare and contrast family involvement in each kind of program.

2. Interview some parents or other family members about their involvement in their young children's educational program. Consider interviewing family members who have children enrolled in various types of programs as mentioned in Assignment 1. What similarities and differences did you find?

References

Bowman, B. (1994). Home and school: The unresolved relationship. In S. L. Kagan & B. Weissbourd (Eds.), *Putting families first: America's family support movement and the challenge of change.* San Francisco: Jossey-Bass.

Brazelton, T. B., & Greenspan, S. I. (2000). *The irreducible needs of children: What every child must have to grow, learn and flourish.* Cambridge, MA: Perseus.

Bredekamp, S., & Copple, C. (1997). *Developmentally appropriate practice in early childhood programs* (rev. ed.). Washington, DC: National Association for the Education of Young Children.

Bronfenbrenner, U. (1979). *The ecology of human development: Experiments by nature and design.* Cambridge, MA: Harvard University Press.

Bronfenbrenner, U. (1990). Discovering what families do. In D. Blankenhorn, S. Bayme, & J. B. Elshtain (Eds.), *Rebuilding the nest: A new commitment to the American family.* Milwaukee, WI: Family Service America.

Bronfenbrenner, U. (2001). The bioecological theory of human development. In N. J. Smelser & P. B. Baltes (Eds.), *International encyclopedia of the social and behavioral sciences* (Vol. 10, pp. 6963–6970). New York: Elsevier.

Carter, B., & McGoldrick, M. (Eds.). (1999). *The expanded family life cycle: Individual, family, and social perspectives* (3rd ed.). Boston: Allyn and Bacon.

deMause, L. (Ed.) (1974). *The history of childhood.* New York: Psychohistory Press.

Family Support America. 2005. http://www.familysupport-america.org, retrieved October 7, 2005.

Kagan, S. L., Moore, E., & Bredekamp, S. (Eds.). (1995). *Reconsidering children's early development and learning: Toward common views and vocabulary.* Washington, DC: National Education Goals Panel.

Kagan, S. L., & Weissbourd, B. (1994). *Putting families first: America's family support movement and the challenge of change.* San Francisco: Jossey-Bass.

Lerner, R. M. (1989). Individual development and the family system: A life-span perspective. In K. Kreppner & R. M. Lerner (Eds.), *Family systems and life-span development.* Hillsdale, NJ: Lawrence Erlbaum Associates.

Lerner, R. M. (n.d.). A developmental contextual view of human development. http://gator.uhd.edu/~williams/child/Lerner.htm, retrieved January 5, 2005.

National Academy of Early Childhood Programs. (1991). *Accreditation criteria & procedures.* Washington, DC: National Association for the Education of Young Children.

National Association for the Education of Young Children. (1996). *Linguistic and cultural diversity—building on America's strengths.* http://www.naeyc.org/ece/1996/03.asp.

National Research Council & Institute of Medicine. (2000). *From neurons to neighborhoods: The science of early childhood development.* Committee on Integrating the Science of Early Childhood Development. Jack P. Shonkoff and Deborah A. Phillips, eds. Board on Children, Youth, and Families, Commission on Behavior and Social Sciences and Education. Washington, DC: National Academy Press.

Olson, D. H., & DeFrain, J. (1994). *Marriage and the family: Diversity and strengths.* Mountain View, CA: Mayfield.

Olson, D. H., & Gorall, D. M. (2003). Circumplex model of marital and family systems. In F. Walsh (Ed.), *Normal family processes* (3rd ed., pp. 514–547). New York: Guilford.

Powell, D. (1989). *Families and early childhood education.* Washington, DC: National Association for the Education of Young Children.

Sandall, S., McLean, M. E., & Smith, B. J. (2000). *DEC recommended practices in early intervention/early childhood special education.* Longmont, CO: Sopris West.

Schwartz, I. S., Sandall, S. R., Odom, S. L., Horn, E., & Beckman, P. J. (2002). "I know it when I see it": In search of a common definition of inclusion. In S. L. Odom (Ed.), *Widening the circle: Including children with disabilities in preschool programs.* New York: Teachers College Press.

Tharp, R. G., & Gallimore, R. (1988). *Rousing minds to life.* New York: Cambridge University Press.

Trivette, C., & Dunst, C. (2000). Recommended practices in family-based practices. In S. Sandall, M. E. McLean, & B. J. Smith, *DEC recommended practices in early intervention/early childhood special education* (pp. 39–46). Longmont, CO: Sopris West.

Vygotsky, L. (1962). *Thought and language.* Cambridge, MA: MIT Press.

Weissbourd, B. (1994). The evolution of the family resource movement. In S. L. Kagan & B. Weissbourd (Eds.), *Putting families first: America's family support movement and the challenge of change.* San Francisco: Jossey-Bass.

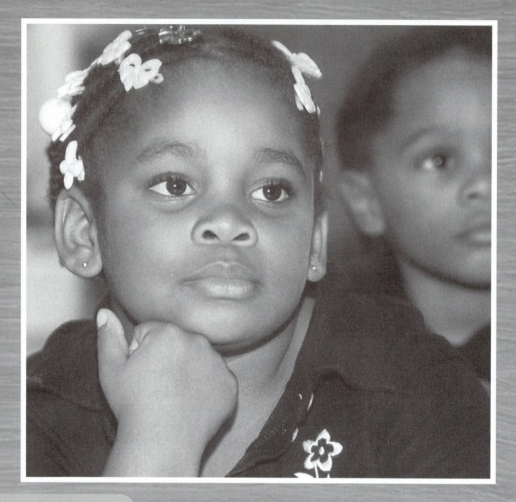

OUTLINE

Objectives

Key Terms

Contextualist Theories and Family Differences

Ways in Which Families Are Different

Ethnicity, Race, and Culture

Economic Differences in Families

Gender Role Identity

Families and Religiosity

Geographic Region

Application to Early Childhood Education Programs

Celebrating Diversity

Inclusiveness

Ethical Considerations

Relating Diversity to Developmentally Appropriate Practice

Relating Diversity to Programs for Children with Special Needs

Accreditation Guidelines

Family Support Principles

Summary and Conclusions

Chapter 2 Applications

Questions for Reflection and Discussion

Field Assignments

References

Understanding Family Diversity

OBJECTIVES

After reading this chapter, you should be able to:

- discuss ways in which the three guiding theories view family differences.

- relate ways in which families differ in terms of ethnicity, race, and culture;

all these listed influence the family, in turn the child!

- economics; gender roles; religiosity; and geographic region.

- reflect on implications related to family differences for early childhood educators.

Key Terms

culture	inclusiveness	Temporary Assistance for
ethnicity	race	Needy Families (TANF)
gender role	religiosity	

Them + Us Video   *Case Study on Toilet Training from "Giving It Some Thought"*

Contextualist Theories and Family Differences

Includes the broader social influence on family

Bioecological theory (Bronfenbrenner, 1979) informs teachers that differences in children's microsystems will account for differences in children's behaviors and development. The social environment provided to children by their families is directly driven by the family's identification with their race, culture, and ethnicity. Other factors that influence the microsystem include economics, gender, religion, and geographical region of residence.

In terms of financial influences, it is clear that the macrosystem, or the societal philosophy and practices of economics, affect microsystems (Garbarino & Ganzel, 2000). For example, families who are impoverished for reasons related to inability to compete for

employment in a capitalist society (e.g., disabilities, addictions, prejudice), often live in impoverished microsystems. These families live in situations that are often associated with early risk factors in children. Such risk factors include unsafe communities, malnutrition, lack of appropriate medical care, low-quality child care, and poor schools.

Vygotsky's sociocultural theory emphasizes the notion that knowledge derives from culture. Teachers observe differences in behaviors of children and their family members based on their culture's view of what is appropriate. Such knowledge cannot be disputed in favor of a teacher's or other dominant view. Children's very definition, and thus knowledge, of family is rooted in their particular culture.

Cultural differences, thus, lead to differences in understanding, in knowing, and in behaving. Children acquire their knowledge by interacting with

Children learn social expectation from family.

others who are important in their lives, especially parents and/or other primary caregivers. These daily, often ordinary interactions with one another provide children with the shared knowledge of the family's culture. Examples of this knowledge include selections of clothing, expected behaviors, choices of foods and how food is prepared, celebrations and rituals, and gender and other social roles. For example, the concept of "respect" is embodied through cultural differences in behavior: In some cultures, it is respectful to make eye contact, and in others, it is not; in some

African American Web Resources

University of California CLNet
http://clnet.ucr.edu/
Type in "Afro"; click "African American Internet Links"

Asian American Web Resources

Center for Educational Telecommunications
http://www.cetel.org/ Click "Resources"

Native American Web Resources

http://www.hanksville.org/
Click "Index of Native American Resources on the Internet"

Latino Web Resources

Latino Web
http://www.latinoweb.com
http://latino.sscnet.ucla.edu

Multicultural Web Resources

The Curry School of Education at the University of Virginia, Multicultural Pavilion
http://curry.edschool.virginia.edu/
Click "Centers"; click "Multicultural Pavilion"

New American Studies Web Resources

Georgetown University, Center for New Designs in Learning & Scholarship
http://lumen.georgetown.edu/
Click "cndls"; click "Projects; click "American Studies"

A child's knowledge of family is rooted in her culture.

cultures, it is respectful to refer to elders as "ma'am" or "sir," and in others, it is not. Similarly, in some cultures, it is expected that pork will not be served, and in others, it might be; in some cultures, women have specifically defined roles, and in others, they do not.

Family systems theory (McGoldrick, 1989) places great importance on ethnicity and culture as a factor in a family's beliefs, practices, and values. A family's income level is likely to influence many aspects of family decisions and behaviors. For example, many professional women who become parents celebrate the arrival of their first child at about the same age (31 to 35) that some lower-income women celebrate their first grandchild. Females and males are likely to experience family quite differently, from everyday behaviors to rituals and celebrations. "Religion also modifies or reinforces certain cultural values. Families . . . whose religion reinforces ethnic values, are likely to maintain their ethnicity longer" (p. 70). Families who live in close proximity to others of the same ethnic, racial, and cultural background are more likely to maintain the same norms; those who move away may become more homogenized into or more influenced by a dominant culture.

Recent research with same sex couples leads to new questions about the usefulness of a family life cycle model that might apply to all families (Johnson & Colucci, 1999). Findings indicate that lesbian and gay definitions of family often include close friends and other "families of choice." It is still unusual for families of lesbian and gay couples to have typical family rituals—e.g., weddings and wedding or baby showers—thus ignoring or denying such marker events with typical family rituals. Further, family titles do not exist for in-laws of the life partners of gay men or lesbians (Johnson & Colucci, 1999).

Ways in Which Families Are Different

We each have a picture of family in our head from our own experiences.

Families define themselves as a family. Membership in a family can be decided only by each member of that family. Thus, it is the role of early childhood educators to be aware of who constitutes each child's family. It is never the role of an early childhood educator to define the child's family for him or her. *Teachers should not attempt to alter a particular family's view about membership in that family.* Factors that make families different from one another include ethnicity, race, culture, economics, gender roles, religiosity, and geographic regionalism.

We must consider these differences if we are to best serve *all* children and *all* families in early childhood programs. It is commonly said that we should honor the humanity in everyone by celebrating our similarities, but it is also important to understand the multiple differences that exist among individuals and families. It is often just such a lack of understanding that leads to stereotypes, prejudices, and exclusion. As we address family differences, we cannot ignore the effects of poverty and discrimination on those differences.

Since when we hear or read the word *family* each of us tends to reflect on our own familial experiences, ignoring differences, it is important to give thoughtful attention to the topics of family diversity addressed in this chapter.

Look @ families from each of these perspectives

Ethnicity, Race, and Culture

Ethnicity "**Ethnicity** refers to a concept of a group's 'people-hood' based on a combination of race, reli-

Social groups w/ a shared history, sense of identity, geography & cultural roots.

gion, and cultural history, whether or not members realize their commonalities with each other. It describes a commonality transmitted by the family over generations . . . it is more than race, religion, or national and geographic origin . . . It involves conscious and unconscious processes that fulfill a deep psychological need for identity and historical continuity" (McGoldrick, 1989, p. 69).

Family ethnicity is sustained through "unique family customs, proverbs and stories, celebrations, foods, and religious ceremonies" (p. 110). Differences have been noted between the notions of self-concept and ethnic identity. Families often find it difficult to instill ethnic pride in their children in our pluralistic society (Stauss, 1995, citing Harriett McAdoo). Further, the effects of racism affect beliefs and practices in non-majority ethnic groups (McDade, 1995). *What is your ethnic background?*

It is this deep psychological need for identity that must be taken into account by early childhood professionals. The degree to which ethnicity is important to a given family, and thus to a given child, varies. Understanding these varying degrees will help early childhood teachers view each family's individuality as a strength and support children's sense of connection to their ethnic group. For instance, consider the following descriptions of three different families.

Chelsea is a three-year-old daughter of European-American parents. Her family portrait includes a picture of her mother, Stacey; her father, Jay; herself; and her five-month-old brother, Christopher. These family members live together in the same home in a small town in eastern Ohio. Living nearby, her paternal grandmother has almost daily contact with Chelsea's family. Her maternal grandparents live about fifteen miles away, and enjoy weekly visits with Chelsea's family.

Jamal is the five-year-old son of Janice. They live in St. Louis with Janice's mother, Dianne, and her long-time partner, Samuel. Jamal's family portrait includes his mother; his grandmother; Samuel; and Samuel's teenage daughter, Jalisa. Jamal calls his grandmother "Mamma" and his mother "Janice." Frequent family visitors include Dianne's mother and father who live in the same city, and Samuel's mother who travels from Chicago twice a year for a month-long stay.

by pursuing about past generations of your people

Understanding who you are

[handwritten margin note: Ethnicity is about the beliefs, values, attitudes that are past down. Race is physical features + others born]

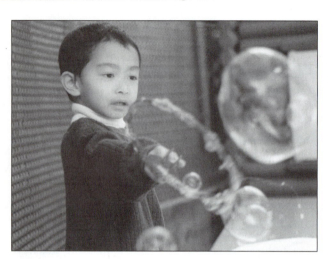

Understanding ethnic differences will help early childhood teachers support children's sense of connection to their ethnic group.

Robin, seven years old, is the youngest child in her Japanese-American family. She lives in Seattle with her parents, her maternal grandfather, and two older brothers. Her family portrait includes her mother, Marcia; her father, Paul; her grandfather, Ito; and 13-year-old twin brothers, Rodger and Raymond. Last year, Robin's family traveled to Kyoto, Japan, to visit her paternal grandparents.

> Consider your own ethnicity. What are some of your family's practices, attitudes, or beliefs that may have originated and been passed on from earlier generations? Also, consider how your personal views are similar to and different from your family's views.

"The first thing to remember about the American family is that it doesn't exist. Families exist. All kinds of families in all kinds of economic and marital situations, as all of us can see . . . . The American family? Just which American family did you have in mind? Black or white, large or small, wealthy or poor, or somewhere in between? Did you mean a father-headed, mother-headed, or childless family? First or second time around? Happy or miserable? Your family or mine?"

—Louise Kapp Howe, 1972

For family events in early childhood programs, teachers and other staff should plan for and be prepared to include a variety of family members, not just parents and siblings. Early childhood educators must go beyond traditional parent-involvement work to a more timely approach that emphasizes whole-family involvement. Welcoming grandparents, aunts and uncles, and family members who have no official title based on bloodline can be a critical factor in building successful family-school relationships.

Teachers too often talk of children who come from good homes and those who have troublesome families. Often, "good home" means one whose family structure is synonymous with the teacher's own, and a less than good home is defined as one whose structure differs from that of the teacher's. Thus, knowledge about cultural differences is a key to changing teachers' perspectives about diverse families.

> 1. Draw a picture of your family at the time you were born.
> 2. Next, draw a picture of your family when you were a preschooler.
> 3. Draw your family when you were in elementary school.
> 4. Draw your family during your middle school or junior high years.
> 5. Draw your family as it was when you graduated from high school.
> 6. Draw your family as it is today.
> 7. Draw your family as you expect it to be five years from now.
>
> Reflect on the following: How did your family change over time? How do you define family? On what did you base your expectations of your family in the future? Compare and contrast your drawings and reflections with others in your class.

Is the idea of family values one that is reasonable? Mellman, Lazarus, and Rivlin (1990) found in their research a high degree of consensus on love and emotional support, respect for others, and taking responsibility for actions. Perhaps these are the characteristics we should look for when we want to label a family as having a "good home."

Race   Ethnic differences go beyond race. The term **race,** based on physical differences, is often noted to be scientific in nature, as opposed to the sociocultural nature of ethnicity. In this regard, most sources tell us that three races of humans exist in the world: Negroid, Mongoloid, and Caucasoid. Each of these is defined by specific characteristics, such as skin tone, facial structure, and geographic origin. However, in authentic work with children and families, early childhood educators often realize that emphasizing race alone is not very helpful. This is seen most clearly in children of interracial families. The question "What race are you?" often is both confusing and irrelevant in the United States today. It is more helpful for early childhood educators to understand individuals within the diversity of families.

Wardle (1987) notes that we know little about interracial families. However, one point made strongly is that children from interracial families cannot choose to identify with the race of one parent over that of the other. This misconception is an oversimplified, misguided attempt to understand the unique difficulty that interracial children have with their need for identity. Wardle suggests that teachers work closely with parents (or other family members) to "feature cultural customs of both (or all) races represented in each interracial child, as well as create ongoing experiences for all children in which multicultural diversity is celebrated" (p. 58).

What Is Culture?
http://www.wsu.edu
Type in "culture"; click "learning commons—
    what is culture?"

Culture   **Culture** refers to the unique experiences and history of various ethnic groups. Cultural differences often indicate differences in views on the family and the community, differences in expectations of children, differences in child-rearing, and differences in the value placed on education.

Carol Brunson Phillips (1995) notes that early educators need to have an understanding about both

cultural beliefs include expectations of chi, child-rearing belifs, value of education

how culture is transmitted and how it is not transmitted. She has formulated six concepts to help with this understanding.

1. *Culture is learned.* Culture is not biological; teachers cannot identify a family's culture by how the family members look. Instead, each individual learns his culture's rules through daily living. Examples include table manners, interpersonal interactions, and ways of demonstrating respect.

2. *Culture is characteristic of groups.* An individual's characteristics are both cultural and individual. Unique personality traits are not culturally based. Cultural behaviors are rooted in groups. Some cultures may place greater emphasis on individuality or conformity than others.   *Ind. w/in the gr. may differ.*

3. *Culture is a set of rules for behavior.* "The essence of culture is in the rules that produce the behaviors, not the behaviors themselves" (Phillips, 1995, p. 5). So, culture is an influence on behavior, often a sweeping influence, but the behaviors alone are not culture. Behaviors commonly influenced by culture include types of clothing and flavors in foods.

4. *Individuals are embedded to different degrees within a culture.* Some families and individuals place more emphasis on cultural traditions than do others. Some Irish families may "act" more Irish than others; some Vietnamese families may "act" more Vietnamese than others; some African families may "act" more African than others. These are individual variations within cultures. Teachers should not expect all people of one culture to be equally involved with their cultural rules. Understanding of both cultural rules and individual differences in people of the same or similar culture is important.

5. *Cultures borrow and share rules.* Over time, cultures have influenced one another. Culture is not stagnant. As people from two or more cultures interact, cultures are affected and may undergo transformations.

6. *Members of a cultural group may be proficient in cultural behavior but unable to describe the rules.*

as teachers, we should strive to identify our cultural rules to better be able to underst other cultures rule

Because young children begin to learn their culture in their own home environments, behaviors seem natural to them. Not only can they not tell you why they engage in these behaviors, it is also likely they are not conscious of all of the behaviors they have learned from their culture. When one northerner spent her first Thanksgiving in the Deep South, she asked the cook, "Why do you put boiled eggs in the gravy?" Certain that there must be some interesting story or superstition related to this practice, she was surprised at the cook's response: "I don't know. That's the way my mother did it."

In their work to include families, teachers of young children may find it more profitable to consider not only a child's race but also her or his ethnicity and culture. It is more likely that knowledge of sociocultural factors would provide greater understanding to teachers than information about physical differences noted in definitions of race. Thus, including understanding of racial differences is most useful in the context of cultural and ethnic differences as well.

Consider each of the six concepts for understanding culture. Share an example of a behavior or expectation in your culture that relates to each concept. Reflect about how your actions or thoughts may be culturally based.

According to contextualist theories, nuclear families, extended families, and communities play varied roles in children's lives. One important factor in these variations is related to culture and ethnicity. It is frequently noted that in the United States, ethnic groups that are not dominant in the culture are more strongly influenced by extended families (McDade, 1995). Further, the macrosystem and chronosystem for cultural groups differ. Figure 2–1 illustrates differences in parenting characteristics and in the value placed on education among a variety of cultural groups.

Teachers sometimes unintentionally emphasize differences among groups of people, and the effect of this emphasis is assaultive rather than respectful toward diversity. One way to avoid making this emphasis

with preschool-age children is to "focus on the people in the child's world of today, not a historical world. *The goal with preschoolers is not to teach history, but to inoculate them against racism*" (Clark, DeWolf, & Clark, 1992, p. 8).

James A. Banks (1997) also reminds us that "an individual's identity with his or her ethnic group varies significantly with the times in his or her life, with economic and social status, and with the situations and/or setting." This statement should guide us as we work with families to focus on who they are right now; and that, in turn, will help us focus on children's needs and interests. Trawick-Smith (1997) states, "Only through a full understanding of parental beliefs, socialization practices, and family relationships can teachers meet the unique needs of individual children."

Economic Differences among Families

In the contemporary United States, children and families have vastly different experiences related to income and other resources. The following statistics on poverty among American children are provided by the Children's Defense Fund and taken from the U.S. Department of Commerce, Bureau of the Census. The poverty rates for children six years and under peaked at 25.6 percent (more than one of every four children) in 1993 and gradually declined to 17.8 percent (still very close to one of every five children) in 2000, but had risen by 2004 to 19.9 percent (nearly one of every five children). These rates are not uniform nationwide: They are lowest in New Hampshire (9.7 percent), Connecticut (10.5 percent), Alaska (11.2 percent), and Maryland (11.4 percent); child poverty rates are highest in the District of Columbia (33.9 percent), Mississippi (31 percent), Louisiana (30 percent), and Arkansas (25.9 percent).

Differences in rates of poverty are also obvious among ethnic groups. Figure 2–2 shows increases in child poverty from 2000 to 2004. "Extreme poverty" indicates that the families are living below one-half of the poverty level, or on about $7,610 a year or less (Children's Defense Fund, *State of America's Children*, 2005). (Note that the large increase in numbers of

Figure 2–1	Variations in Parenting and Educational Values

African-Americans

Parenting: Discipline often appears to be severe and punitive. Many parents emphasize high achievement and a strong work ethic. Boys and girls are socialized similarly, with emphasis on adaptive coping ability and emotional strength necessary for dealing with hostile environments (McDade, 1995).

Education: Traditional educational strategies may not meet the needs of some children in this culture. Research suggests that some males are particularly not well-served through the feminine orientation of most elementary classrooms (Hale, 1986). Many African-American parents emphasize education as the way to greater economic success.

Asian-Americans/Pacific Islander Americans

Parenting: Typically, children are encouraged to be independent and to respect authority. It is expected that they will be unquestionably obedient to their parents and often, they are expected to put the needs of their parents before their own. Parents desire children to be emotionally controlled, self-disciplined, and logical thinkers (McDade, 1995).

Education: These families typically emphasize education and high levels of achievement in their children (Hamner & Turner, 1996). The emphasis on the value of conformity may help children to adapt to expectations in U.S. schools.

Hispanic/Latino

Parenting: The family may take precedence over individuals and the expectation is for the family to be self-reliant. Individual achievement or responsibility is not valued in some families, but social skills are given a high priority.

Education: Hispanics as a group are increasing their educational achievement. Mexican-Americans are less likely to complete high school, however, than other Hispanic populations, with 56 percent of Mexican-Americans having less than a high school education (Hamner & Turner, 1996).

Native Americans

Parenting: Although there are differences by tribe, some common values are found related to parenting. Children are generally valued by adults, and this is shown in their inclusion in all social events as well as in parents' gentle styles of discipline. Important characteristics to foster in children include loyalty, humility, respect for elders, reticence, and diminished emphasis on personal gain and private ownership (McDade, 1995).

Education: Few Anglo teachers seem to understand tribal culture, while Native American children and families often feel a lack of cultural relevance in schools. Because silence is valued in tribes, children are comfortable with not answering questions in class, especially avoiding the risk of an incorrect answer and taunting by classmates. There is some movement toward having education under tribal control (Hamner & Turner, 1996).

Source: These descriptions are based on evidence from research and are not necessarily indicative of individual families. For further reading and understanding, see: *Early Childhood Development: A Multicultural Perspective* by Jeffrey Trawick-Smith and *Teaching Strategies for Ethnic Studies* by James A. Banks.

poor and extremely poor Latino children is related to an increase in the number of Latinos in the U.S.). For various ethnic groups, this proportion is even higher (see Figure 2–2).

In 1996, federal legislation was passed that included time limits for which adults could receive governmental financial aid. Under this policy, the Temporary Assistance for Needy Families (TANF), parents must go to work after receiving welfare for a maximum of two years, and families are limited to a lifetime total of five years' cash assistance. States may exempt up to 20 percent of their cases from the five-year limit. Because this legislation gave states the responsibility of implementing the mandates, a variety of designs has been put into place. Marian Wright Edelman, president and founder of the Children's

Figure 2–2	Comparison of Children in Poverty from 2000–2004		
	2000	**2004**	**% Increase**
Children in Poverty			
White, Non-Hispanic	4,018,000	4,507,000	12.2
Black	3,581,000	3,780,000	5.6
Latino	3,522,000	4,102,000	16.5
ALL	11,587,000	13,027,000	12.4
Children in Extreme Poverty			
White, Non-Hispanic	1,650,000	1,923,000	16.5
Black	1,581,000	1,908,000	20.7
Latino	1,168,000	1,459,000	24.9
ALL	4,634,000	5,561,000	20.0

Source: Children's Defense Fund

Defense Fund, notes that Minnesota stands out as a state that has "made it a goal to move families with children not just off welfare but out of poverty" (CDF Reports, 1997, p. 3). Further, Edelman writes, "There is no mystery about how to help families off welfare and out of poverty. States must provide the education, training, and work experience that parents need to compete for jobs with decent wages. States also need to remove the obstacles that often prevent parents from leaving welfare for work: lack of health care, transportation and child care" (p. 3).

Nearly a decade after the passing of TANF legislation, research continues to show that jobs alone are not enough to keep families out of poverty. Education and specialized training continue to be critical to the path out of poverty (Children's Defense Fund, *State of America's Children 2005*). Regrettably, it continues to be difficult for low-wage workers to participate in any kind of training or education that might help to lift them from poverty. The resources needed for child care, transportation, and tuition or fees are often serious barriers.

Early childhood teachers often take on the role of advocating for children and families with young children. Early childhood professional standards note that early childhood teachers must be "informed advocates for sound educational practices and policies" (Hyson,

2003, p. 60). Such practices and policies are related not only to children's immediate environments or microsystems, but also to the societal level or macrosystem. Early childhood teachers play an important role in being knowledgeable about and taking action for all levels of children's needs. Advocates understand that families must be able to earn a living wage; have access to health care; have reliable transportation; and have access to affordable, quality care for their children during the hours that they are required to work. At the macrosystem level, this involves contacting state and federal policymakers to provide information about the needs of young children and their families.

Frequently, educators' understanding of diversity does not include differences by family income or, to use the traditional term, social class. Yet financial resources have a tremendous impact on families, their practices, and their values. All parents are aware that poverty is a threat to children. Families living with scarce resources have had to learn the importance of meeting children's most basic needs.

> The U.S. Census Bureau (2000) reported that the poverty line for a family of three was below $13,290 per year in 1999, or less than $1,108 per month. Investigate costs in your locality for housing, food, health care, transportation, and other necessities. Comment on your findings.

Cheal (1996) notes that as a society, we have several reasons for concern about families and their risk for poverty. He highlights three reasons:

1. The risk of poverty is highest in early childhood.
2. Families with children do not reap enough benefits from government redistribution of income.
3. Current political views about the role of government do not allow for assisting poor families in meaningful ways.

Even after President Johnson's "War on Poverty" during the 1960s, and into the 1980s and 1990s, young children continued to have the highest risk of living in poverty. This has been especially true for those children living in families headed by women. The economic picture for these families remains bleak. Even when women are employed, they typically do not make enough money to provide reliable transportation to their jobs, pay for high-quality child care for their children, and maintain a safe and healthy home environment. "The risk of poverty among women has often depended heavily on the nature of their relationships with men" (Cheal, 1996, p. 55). Further, traditional gender roles have been discarded for these single mothers. Often, mothers have not been expected to be employed, but rather it has been socially desirable for them to stay home and raise their children. This belief is no longer held in regard to women on welfare (Cheal, 1996).

> Consider your opinion about maternal employment and child rearing. What do you believe is the prevailing attitude about this in contemporary society? Is there a double standard for poor and affluent mothers? Should there be?

The American dream for modern times included the notion that children should not have to rely on "the luck of the draw," that is, children's happiness and productivity should not rely simply on being born into a family at one economic level versus a family at another. With this view came the political notion that government would make an attempt to redistribute societal resources so that all children might benefit from them. (However, from 1978 to 1987, government expenditures on children decreased by 4 percent while those for the elderly increased by 52 percent [Danziger & Weinberg, as cited in Cheal, 1996].) Public school was one way of attempting to even out children's lives. The notion that all children would have equal access to good, effective education was one way of equalizing the chances for poor children (Cheal, 1996). One issue that faces education today involves seeking strategies for parity to those school districts having fewer resources.

> Research school funding for your state of residence. Are all schools/districts/counties funded equally, that is, are all children provided with equitable education resources? How are schools funded? What are the policy issues related to school funding for which early childhood professionals might advocate?

Unlike the perspective of past decades, however, the predominant contemporary political view of poor families is that they must be moved from welfare to work, and for the most part, they must achieve this on their own. Individual responsibility is now valued and expected. However, in the 1930s, at the time of the Great Depression, it was understood that poverty was not the result of individual failings, but rather that the economic structure of society played a very large part in family financial losses. Few policy makers today are willing to include societal explanations or responsibilities in their views on assisting the poor (Cheal, 1996). Some child and family advocates believe that these political views contain racist and sexist elements. Because many poor families are composed of women and children, and because the huge majority of policy makers are white and male, this is a very real possibility. In his extensive analysis about systemic causes of poverty, David Cheal (1996) notes that "the poverty of children is not accidental. It is the fixed position of children in a carefully graded system, in which the youngest children have the highest risk of poverty" (p. 182). He accurately refers to this planned system as "perverse."

> Consider the political views explained by Cheal (1996). Using bioecological theory, discuss how the views are related to the various systems. Create an action plan for child and family advocates that could address these perspectives from each of the systems.

Children's Defense Fund
http://wwwchildrensdefense.org

National Center for Children in Poverty
http://www.nccp.org

National Center for Policy Analysis: Welfare
http://www.ncpa.org/
Click "policy issues"; click "welfare"
    University Research on Families
http://www.childwelfare.com/

U.S. Census Bureau—Poverty
http://www.census.gov/
Click "poverty"

A review of research on low-income family involvement in children's education notes that while such families "strive to support their children's education, their overall levels of involvement are lower than those of families who do not live in poverty" (Boethel, 2003, p. 33). In addition to obvious barriers such as language differences and the lack of time, transportation, and child care, other barriers include cultural beliefs in which some families view the institution of school as the only source of education, a lack of understanding about the roles of family members at school, a lack of knowledge about subject matter that children are learning, and experiences of exclusion and discrimination (Boethel, 2003).

Early childhood professionals often criticize families for not being interested in their children's education or for their reluctance to volunteer in the education programs. A complete understanding or appreciation of the minute-to-minute stresses of families living in poverty may not be possible. However, an effort by the teacher to accept each family must be visible. Further, early childhood educators must support all families at the place they are. Wishing away family stress caused by a lack of resources does not work. Helping to meet their pressing needs is the first step to forming partnerships with some families. Sometimes, teachers of young children feel frustration when families do not send money or notes back to school as the teacher requested. Rather than assuming that the parents or responsible family members are apathetic or hostile, it is helpful to keep in mind that the family may be dealing with other needs that were more pressing, such as keeping the heat turned on or a medical appointment. In such instances, teachers must call on their own compassion and understanding. Use of gentle reminders and a call of concern will be much more fruitful than accusations.

A multitude of studies show that economic hardship puts many children at very high risk in the United States. Negative outcomes for children include difficult peer relationships, school problems, and low self-esteem (Bolger, Patterson, & Thompson, 1995; Brooks-Gunn, Klebanov, & Duncan, 1996). The stress of poverty makes parenting more difficult. The threat of violence in immediate neighborhoods is increasing in some communities. Involvement in their children's lives seems an impossible goal for some parents living in such desperate circumstances.

Families who live in poverty are often called on to pool their resources throughout their extended families and neighborhoods. Their very survival may depend on sharing child care arrangements and meals, as well as lending money. The addresses of poor families may change frequently as families move out of one home to live temporarily with others, and then, when finances get a little better, attempt to move back into a place of their own. In this need for mutual support seen in poor communities, some people rely on friendship networks for help as much as they do on extended family (Zinn & Eitzen, 1987).

Prejudice against families who receive "welfare" abounds. "For most Americans, the words *welfare recipient* evoke the image of a good-for-nothing freeloader who drives a Cadillac, uses food stamps to buy sirloin steak, or watches soap operas all day. It is a classic icon of American culture, routinely projected upon all who are receiving public assistance" (Rank, 1994, p. 2). In an effort to describe the lives of welfare recipients, including their strengths and their problems, Rank's research includes information from interviews with people about their lives. What he found is that, like most families, the parents in his sample want what is best for their children. "Their frustration," he notes, "comes from not being able to provide it (p. 70).

Planning for the future is not something that poor families can easily do, whether the reference is to the immediate future or to a time months or years from now. Unplanned or unexpected events such as illness, unreliable transportation, or requests from children's school for field trip money often have serious consequences on a family's financial plans. Working-class families often rely heavily on extended family for help. Siblings, parents, aunts, uncles, and cousins make up the primary social network in working-class families (Zinn & Eitzen, 1987). When adults in these families have economic stability, their lifestyles may appear much more like those of the middle class; however, when jobs are not stable, these families teeter on the brink of poverty. Many of these families are one or two paychecks away from the welfare rolls. A married mother of two children relates her feelings about applying for welfare.

We felt like it was a shameful thing to be doing, basically. And I remember when the in-take worker was going over our form and wanted to know what our income had been for the previous month, and we said, it was something like two hundred and fifty dollars. And she looked at us and she said, "Uhh, this can't be right, you couldn't live on this." And we said, "That's right, that's why we're here!" (Laughter.) I think we felt grateful that it was there. But it was a real blow to our pride. We had all kinds of . . . I mean . . . the way the public generally views welfare people, we had a lot of those same views. And it was really a hard thing for our pride to put ourselves in that position, and join that category of people. (Rank, 1994, p. 40)

People in the working class who are most likely to be affected by poverty are adults of childbearing age (25 to 44 years), the elderly (65 years and over), and children, especially under 1 year of age. The following percentages relate the likelihood that various age groups in the working class are living in poverty (Cheal, 1996):

Children, under 1 year	**53%**
Children, 1–4 years	50%
Elderly, 65+ years	48%
Adults, 25–44 years	29%
Young adults, 15–24 years	24%
Middle-aged adults, 45–64 years	21%

At the other end of the spectrum, affluent, professional, or middle-class families with young children may have little or no problem meeting their children's basic needs and amenities. But these families, too, may fall prey to situations that may be harmful to their young children. Concern for their progeny's success entangles some parents in the "superkid syndrome." David Elkind (1987) has written about "the hurried child" and those who are "miseducated." "Parents today believe that they can make a difference in their children's lives, that they can give them an edge that will make them brighter and abler than the competition" (p. xiii). Families with this goal for children pose another kind of challenge to early

childhood teachers, who try to plan developmentally appropriate educational experiences for children but are often confronted with parental requests to move their child up a grade or place them in accelerated groups.

It is critical to note that the risks children in poverty face are unmatched by any other single variable. Still, children from affluent families often contend with undue pressure related to expectations that are not consistent with early development. All children must live in environments that provide the developmental assets (www.search-institute.org) described in Chapter 1. In review, these assets include:

- support from families and communities
- empowerment through families and communities valuing them as children
- responsive boundaries and expectations
- opportunities to play constructively
- encouragement to be lifelong learners
- exposure to positive values that include fairness, caring, honesty, and responsibility
- opportunities to learn how to get along well with others
- experiences that help to develop a positive sense of self-worth and caring for others

Effective early childhood teachers can best help all families and communities by helping them understand that all of these assets are needed for healthy child development. When only two or three are emphasized, the necessary balance is overlooked and children may be stressed, neglected, or overcome with a sense of failure.

Gender Role Identity

"Women have always played a central role in families, but the idea that they have a life cycle apart from their roles as wife and mother is a relatively recent one, and still is not widely accepted in our culture. The expectation for women has been that they would take care of the needs of others: first men, then children, then the elderly. Until very recently, 'human development' referred

to male development and women's develop-ment was defined by the men in their lives." "They went from being daughter, to wife, to mother, with their status defined by the male in the relationship . . . ."

—Monica McGoldrick, 1989

An individual's gender role is "a set of expectations that prescribe how females or males should think, act, and feel" (Santrock, 1994). People's understanding of themselves as male or female, and what that means in their particular environment, is influenced by biological, social, and cognitive factors. Within any given family, the roles specified for males and females may be rigid or fluid. Families with rigid stereotypes are likely to view males as independent, aggressive, and power-oriented, whereas females are seen as dependent, nurturant, and uninterested in power. Research regarding the interaction of ethnicity and gender on traditional gender roles has shown that expectations for males and females vary according to ethnicity (McGoldrick, 1989).

The pluralistic culture of the United States contains many variations on gender roles. A feminist perspective on gender indicates that women and girls are competent in their own right. This conflicts with the traditional view of female existence as important only in relation to males.

Because early childhood teachers work with both female and male family members, it is important that teachers are aware of their own views about gender roles. Teachers may find it challenging to accept and support the role, whether traditional or feminist, that a particular parent has taken. For example, how would you react to the following situations, noting your own biases and preferences?

- In Suzanne's (age four years) family, Mr. Jaworski stays home with Suzanne and her younger brother, Tucker. Suzanne's mother, Dr. Stoner, who kept her maiden name, has built a successful career and travels on business at least six times a year.

- In Peter's (age seven years) family, Mrs. Jordan is a full-time homemaker. Peter and his two older brothers are enrolled in the elementary school in which you teach. Mr. Jordan has been in danger of losing his job because of cutbacks at his corporation.

- Debra's (age two-and-a-half years) mother, Ms. Meyer, is employed as an administrative staff member on a local university campus. She has insisted that you call her "Ms. Meyer," not "Mrs. Meyer." Debra and her mother live with Ms. Kennedy, who works on the grounds crew at the same campus.

Mother-headed families often have very different needs than father-headed, single-parent families do. First of all, there are many more of them in existence. It is estimated that as many as one-half of all children will spend some of their childhood years in a family headed by a single woman (Garfinkel & McLanahan, 1989). Single-parent families headed by women are much more likely to be poor than are those headed by men. Reasons for this include little or no support from fathers, the limited earning capacity of mothers, and the difficulties that come with trying to juggle the roles of sole breadwinner and sole caregiver (Burns & Scott, 1994).

Gender Development
http://www.psy.pdx.edu/PsiCafe/
Click "Areas"; click "Developmental Psychology";
    click "gender development"

Sexual Orientation and Gender Identity
http://www.aclu.org/
Click "Lesbian and Gay Rights"

As the social and economic climates have changed during the latter half of the twentieth century, women have been increasingly able to obtain employment that pays a reasonable wage. But comparisons with a number of other countries, most notably Sweden, show that in addition to access to employment that pays a living wage, mothers must also have access to affordable, high-quality child care and other family support services, and must be able to collect child support from the noncustodial parent (Burns & Scott, 1994). One mother who attempted to leave public assistance noted how crucial good child care is:

Well, I had two little bitty babies. And I was working at the time I got pregnant. So I tried going back to work when Stacy was about, say, two months old. And the lady that I got to baby-sit for me just didn't come up to par for me. And with me having the two babies, one was just walking and one was an arm baby, I made the decision that it's best for me to try to be here with them. And I know they were taken care of like I would have wanted them to be taken care of. So that's when I applied for aid. (Rank, 1994, p. 42)

Another topic related to gender identity centers on same-sex unions. Many educators have concerns about children of lesbian families. However, existing literature does not support the prejudice that children in lesbian families are worse off than other children (Burns & Scott, 1994). Figure 2–3 delineates myths and facts about gay, lesbian, bisexual and transgendered parents. The common view that children suffer from the lack of a father's presence, for instance, is not substantiated when children have relationships with multiple adults who have somewhat of a parenting role: friends, grandparents, and/or the biological father. When lesbian mothers have social, economic, and personal resources, "chosen, father-free parenthood" can meet children's needs (McGuire & Alexander, 1985). Further, comparisons of characteristics of lesbian mothers with women in general show the following for lesbian mothers:

- higher levels of education and professional training
- scored as more normal on psychological tests
- had more support and practical help from cohabiting partners than wives receive from husbands
- mother-child relationships were closer
- cognitive and social competence was normal or high
- sex role behavior was normal
- daughters chose more prestigious/traditionally masculine careers
- daughters reported higher popularity (McGuire and Alexander, 1985)

Figure 2–4 provides additional commentary.

Some beliefs about lesbian mothers that are shown to be empirically unfounded include that lesbian mothers have higher incidences of mental illness, are less maternal than heterosexual women, leave little time for parent-child interactions, and are generally unfit to be parents. Further, there is no research evidence to support the notion that children will be hindered in sexual identity development, that they are less psychologically healthy, or that they experience greater difficulties in social relationships than peers from heterosexual families. Actually, "children of lesbian mothers develop patterns of gender-role behavior that are much like those of other children" (Patterson, 1995).

It is important to realize that just as heterosexual-parent families differ from one another, great diversity also exists among gay and lesbian parent families (Patterson, 1995). Some gay and lesbian parents have biological children; others have adopted or foster children. Some have custody of their children; some have limited visitation with their children. Some are single-parent families; some are two-parent families. Some live in communities where their gay or lesbian identity is accepted; others live in communities that are not so accepting.

Concern about lack of father involvement in families or specifically with their very young children does not exist only when fathers are living out of the home. A British study by Jane Ribbens (1994) shows that contemporary child-rearing remains in the domain of women:

Issues of childcare, presumptions about the needs of children, and decision-making about how to deal with and relate to children are major preoccupations in women's everyday lives. Furthermore, a consideration of how women perceive, understand and resolve some of these issues around childrearing is essential to any analysis of gender relationships, divisions of labour and distributions of resources within households. (p. 29)

Further, Ribbens notes that it is generally the responsibility of the mother to create "the family." In this task, two processes are involved: (1) work on internal cohesion, making certain that the family members form a meaningful unit; and (2) work on

Figure 2–3	Myths and Facts about Gay, Lesbian, Bisexual, and Transgendered Parents

MYTH

Lesbians and gay men do not have children.

FACT

Lesbian, gay, and bisexual parents have biological children. They also have children through domestic and international adoption, artificial and donor insemination, foster care, and surrogacy.

MYTH

Gay men and lesbians have unstable relationships.

FACT

Gay men and lesbians often have committed, loving relationships. Sometimes these relationships are not open or obvious to others because of societal discrimination.

MYTH

Gay men and lesbians prey on children to recruit them to their "lifestyle."

FACT

Research indicates that children reared by gay or lesbian parents are no more likely to become gay or lesbian than children who grow up with heterosexual parents.

MYTH

Children who are in contact with gay men or lesbians face increased risk of being sexually abused.

FACT

Sexual abuse is caused by pedophilia, not sexual orientation. Ninety percent of sexual abuse cases involve a heterosexual male.

MYTH

Children raised by gay men and lesbians will be exposed to an "immoral" environment.

FACT

Morality is subjective. If all people were eliminated from the possibility of parenthood because of what someone believed to be immoral, there would be no parents left. In the United States, parents have primacy in decisions about providing a moral environment for their children.

MYTH

Families with gay or lesbian parents are not "real" families.

FACT

Lesbian and gay parents "cook dinners, change diapers, and take time off of work to care for children, help with homework, negotiate TV time, drive children to soccer practice, worry about child care, clean house, and read bedtime stories." Families define themselves.

MYTH

Gay men cannot be nurturing parents.

FACT

Research has shown gay fathers to be responsive to and supportive of their children.

MYTH

Discussing a gay or lesbian family member means you must talk about sex.

FACT

"As responsible parents, we are charged with speaking about sexuality to our children in accurate, appropriate and age sensitive ways. We want our children to have correct information and an understanding about how to interpret information that is congruent with our beliefs. However, to think that in order to discuss a lesbian, gay, bisexual, or transgendered (LGBT or GLBT) family member means one must automatically speak about sex, is wrong. When speaking of an LGBT relative, a responsible and caring parent can and should discuss such important issues as love, understanding, acceptance, diversity, and discrimination. To speak with young children about LGBT family members is to speak about what they understand most, family. For a child not to be able to talk about his or her family is not only discrimination, it is wrong."

MYTH

It is safer for children of lesbians and gay men not to talk about their families.

FACT

Strong schools will include information about all children's families in education programs. Strong schools must also provide an emotionally safe climate for all children through support for *all* families.

MYTH

Children raised by a gay or lesbian couple will not have proper male and female role models.

FACT

"Research suggests that our children are exposed to more people of the opposite sex than many kids of straight parents and even when our kids are not, there is no evidence to suggest that they are harmed."

Source: Family Pride Coalition, http://www.familypride.org, retrieved November 18, 2005.

Figure 2–4 Commentary on Lesbian and Gay Parenting

Mother's Day Guest Commentary
by C. Ray Drew and Kate Kendell

Until just recently, the existence of lesbian and gay parents went almost unrecognized in our culture. Much of our society simply believed that being a gay or lesbian parent was a contradiction in terms, and numerous negative myths promulgated that position. Heterosexist laws denied the possibility of parenting for openly gay/lesbian people, and penalized anyone with children from a prior heterosexual relationship with loss of visitation or custody.

The last ten years have changed this landscape dramatically. We now find ourselves in the middle of a "gayby boom" as countless thousands of lesbians and gay men choose to become parents. We have countered the Radical Right's argument that a family consists only of a heterosexual father, mother and children, with our community's family values of love, diversity, respect, caring and pride. We have proudly stated to the world that "love makes a family."

But is love enough? What happens when the "love" between a lesbian couple fades or sours? In recent years we have experienced a threat to our community's families as alarming as the Radical Right's hate campaign. In surging numbers, we have seen an insidious increase in the number of custody battles within the community involving lesbian couples, as biological mothers deny visitation to their former partners.

No one is at their best when a couple splits up. It is a time of serious emotional crisis. It is a time when it is easy to rationalize that a former partner's behavior is a reflection of a poor parenting bond with the child. Friends and family may feel protective and support the biological mom in her dismissal of her former partner. In the absence of laws to the contrary, it is tempting to redraw the family construction around heterosexist laws, take the child and cut the partner out of the family picture forever.

But can we use the heterosexist, anti-gay laws to assure that a former partner is denied the right to see her child and simultaneously demand that others recognize our family commitments? While together, a couple may have lamented the fact that their family was discriminated against by IRS laws, insurance regulations, social security policies and numerous laws that denied the legal recognition of their family. Sadly, after dissolution of the relationship, the biological mother can use those very laws to deny that the other parent was EVER a "real" parent.

In the legal world of non-gay married couples, an elaborate court system is ready to decide custody and visitation issues when the parents cannot do so. Even if one parent was only marginally involved the court nevertheless recognizes their status as parent. In the absence of identified harm to the child, even the less involved or marginal parent is granted some visitation.

The community and court standards reflect the parental rights and obligations of both parents.

When a lesbian couple breaks up, without a legally sanctioned relationship or legal recognition of their family, who decides what is in a child's best interests? Couples, who had a clear, unambiguous agreement that they would be equal parents to this child, suddenly become very unequal in the face of divorce. The biological mother has absolute power in these cases to determine the fate of the child and the privileges of the non-biological mother. In case after case, the biological mother has denied that her former partner is even a parent. Some courts have agreed, denying the non-biological mother's right to her day in court to seek any legal redress, much less be granted visitation with her child.

Are legal protections important? Of course they are. We need the protection for our families that legally sanctioned marriage provides. We need the protection of second-parent adoptions in the absence of marriage.

But more important than these legal protections we need to honor our agreements and our intentions with one another. Family is a social construction as much as a legal entity. If we are to truly have permanent parental and family relationships, we need a social ethic that says they are permanent. We need a consistent community value, which says that a commitment to parenting is lifelong. If we want our children to grow up secure in who they are and who their family is, they need to see a community with a strong sense of family, a community that maintains that standard even when couples break up.

Does love make a family? You bet. And when love doesn't last forever, the "family" still does. It is our commitment that will signal to society and our children just how seriously we take our own families.

Kate Kendell is the Executive Director of the National Center for Lesbian Rights, a legal resource and advocacy public interest law firm. C. Ray Drew is the Executive Director of the Family Pride Coalition International, an international LGBT family advocacy organization. Kendell can be contacted at NCLRsf@aol.com, and Drew can be contacted at GLPCI@GLPCI.org.

Source: With permission from C. Ray Drew and Kate Kendell. Mother's Day Guest Commentary (Online).

external boundaries, making certain that there are clear separations of the family from other social units.

> *Within the apparently "conventional" families in my own study, images of family togetherness did not always correspond to how things worked out in everyday interactions. While the women living with their husbands were quick to tell me their good qualities as fathers, in the details of their accounts strains could also become apparent in constructing "the family" with an involved father. Much of the care of preschool children occurs in women's worlds, either within or outside the home, and men are marginal to these worlds. (Ribbens, 1994, p. 64)*

After analyzing the information provided by the mothers in her study, Ribbens goes on to say that much of the mother-child time together did not occur within families at all, but rather in variations of networks of other women and their children. This finding brought Ribbens to the conclusion that observational studies are needed of mothers and their young children as they participate in "semipublic" settings such as play groups.

Fathers play very different roles within families than those of mothers. Only since the mid-1970s has much research been done on fathering. Contemporary society sees fathers essentially in one of two ways: either as increasing their involvement with their children, or as absent and having little emotional or financial responsibility for their children. Furstenberg (1988) refers to this as the "two faces of fatherhood." Early childhood teachers may observe these vast differences in the fathers of children in their care. Sometimes, fathers are so removed from the family that children have not met them or barely know them. Adults are often under the mistaken assumption, then, that the children's closeness to another adult male, grandfather, or uncle simply replaces their relationship with fathers.

Erna Furman (1992) writes about young children who have been "deeply affected by the loss of their father through death or family breakup" (p. 36). She notes that the loss of a father may cause long-term hardship for a child, but that those children who never had relationships with their fathers should also be of concern to educators. She tells of two such children. Felicity, at three-and-a-half years, had never met

her father. Her mother never talked about him and was certain that Felicity at this young age did not even think about her father. Felicity exhibited behaviors such as thumb-sucking and unceasing demands, however, that were determined by a therapist to be related to her desire to know her father. With this information, Felicity's mother tried to prepare her for possible disappointment and contacted her father to let him know of their daughter's wishes. In this case, the father responded and began to spend some time with his daughter. Even though contact between Felicity and her father was sporadic, the trust that the process generated between mother and daughter was a positive outcome to this situation.

In the second scenario, Ben also had not met his father. When Ben's toddler class planned visits by their fathers, his mother asked the teacher if Ben's beloved grandfather might come with him instead. When the teacher suggested that the mom ask Ben his opinion, the mom was surprised—and when she asked Ben, she was surprised again. Ben initially refused to have his grandfather go to school with him. Because he had never mentioned his absent father, Ben's mother assumed that meant he never thought about who his father might be. Once it was revealed that Ben did have questions about his own dad, his mother was able to explain that he lived far away and could not visit. Having this information and a new understanding, Ben was then willing to have grandfather accompany him to school.

So many teachers assume that because it is now common for children to live in homes without their fathers, that children simply accept or do not even notice the absence. Furman (1992) points out that when teachers observe carefully, however, they report situations with children that contradict this viewpoint. She says, "There are no easy answers to these human dilemmas, but respecting our children's thoughts and feelings has much to do with respecting ourselves and with building a community in which we all learn to respect one another. Respect, like charity, begins at home" (p. 37).

In his review of the research literature related to fathers and families, Parke (1995) notes that a great deal of research supports the fact that fathers spend less time with their children than do mothers. This is

Fathers can be competent caregivers of children.

true from infancy through adolescence. Other consistent findings from research are that fathers are competent caregivers of their children when they need to be, and fathers interact in qualitatively different ways with children than do mothers. Whereas mothers are more verbal and directed and use toys in their interactions, fathers are more physical and tactile with children. It seems reasonable to believe that both styles of interaction stimulate children and that children benefit from such differences.

Dads and Daughters
http://www.dadsanddaughers.org/
Click "Research agenda"

Family Support and Father Involvement
http://www.fcps.net/
Click "Research in Parent Involvement"; click "A
   Call to Commitment . . . "

What determines how involved fathers are in their children's lives? A variety of factors have been shown to contribute to any given father's interaction with his children. Parke (1995) uses empirical data to demonstrate that the following considerations are related to father involvement. It is evident that father involvement is based on a complex system of in-home and out-of-home variations.

- *Fathers' relationships with their own parents.* Those men who had positive interactions with their own fathers may model those with their children. However, there is also some evidence that men who view their relationships with their fathers as negative sometimes make an effort with their own children to increase positive feelings and interactions.

- *Fathers' belief systems about the roles of mothers and fathers.* Some men have more stereotypic ideas about what each parent should do with children. Others are more willing to be flexible in meeting their children's needs.

- *Attitudes of the mother.* Some mothers believe that they are the more important and competent parent, and restrict father involvement in various ways. As mothers are in the workforce full time, they may be increasingly willing to encourage a greater level of father involvement with their children.

- *Marital relationships.* When mothers provide support to fathers in their caregiving roles, fathers gain competence and confidence in relating to their children.

- *Timing of fatherhood.* Males who become fathers when they are adolescents tend not to be highly involved in their children's lives. Some of these fathers rarely even visit their children. Men who become fathers later in their lives often appreciate their children more and have greater self-confidence in their parenting. On the other hand, men who became fathers "on time" were more likely than older fathers to be physical with their children.

- *Family employment patterns.* Fathers typically spend a greater amount of time with their children when mothers are employed outside the home.

It also may be that the quality of father-child relationships changes when mothers are employed outside the home.

- *Work quality.* Difficult or stressful work conditions may cause fathers to be more disengaged with their children when they are at home. It is also believed that positive workplaces can enhance the quality of the father-child relationship.

Those who advocate for higher levels of father involvement do so in part because they believe it results in positive outcomes for children. Parke (1995) also discusses the research related to this area of interest. Following are some of the findings related to children whose fathers do not live with them:

- little effect of father contact on well-being of children 11 to 16 years
- no relation between father contact and children's social and cognitive development for children five to nine years

These findings are somewhat surprising in light of the emphasis on father involvement in children's lives. One explanation, however, is that father presence during the first three years may be the most important time. Several studies seem to support this point of view. Further, quality of interaction, versus just quantity of time spent together, seems to be important to father-child relationships.

Two aspects of the definition of *quality* are fathers' physical play and positive affect with their children. Young children whose fathers exhibit these two characteristics have been found to be more popular and have a higher degree of social acceptance from other children (Parke, 1995).

As with mothers, individuals in our society typically assume that all fathers are heterosexual. This is obviously not true. It is difficult to obtain an accurate count of the number of gay fathers in the United States today. The primary reason for this is that the prejudice and discrimination against these fathers threaten their relationships with their children. It is believed that the largest group of children of gay fathers today is composed of those who were born in heterosexual relationships of their biological parents before one or the other parent had identified themselves as lesbian or gay. Gay fathers commonly do not have custody of their children, nor do they often live in the same home as their children. This is partially a result of the legal system's bias against gay fathers. This bias is so pronounced that not only do courts rarely grant custody to gay fathers, they may even deny these fathers visitation rights based on the notion that gay fathers are negative influences on their children (Patterson, 1995).

Research on gay fathers is sparse. Patterson (1995), in her review of the literature on gay fathers, notes that they report differences in their parenting in comparison to heterosexual fathers. Gay fathers reported both greater warmth and responsiveness to their children, and more limit-setting. The few studies that have compared gay fathers and gay men who are not fathers have found that these fathers reported higher levels of self-esteem and fewer negative attitudes about homosexuality than did the non-fathers.

One of our culture's concerns about the effects of gay fathers on their children is whether having gay parents will affect the sexual identity of gay fathers' children. At this time, no research supports the notion that children of gay fathers will be homosexual in their orientation (Patterson, 1995).

As early childhood educators, our greatest concern for children from gay or lesbian families may be for their psychological and physical safety. However, this concern stems not from the dynamics within the family, but rather from the bigotry and hate that these families may receive from society.

Early childhood teachers may find themselves in situations where colleagues, students, parents, or people in the community are openly discriminatory toward *g*ay-, *l*esbian-, *b*isexual-, or *t*ransgendered-parent (GLBT or LGBT) families. It must be the early childhood professional's first responsibility to do no harm to children and families. Further, because it is known that families compose the most important relationship for all children, teachers must respect and support a child's parents and the relationships that children have with their parents.

Families and Religiosity

Due in part to the constitutional separation of church and state, education has been silenced about religion. This can make it difficult for early childhood educators to explore the role that it plays, if any, in children's families. Nonetheless, understanding the importance of **religiosity** in families is as critical as understanding a family's culture or economic status. Some teachers and schools, of course, do place religion within a family's culture, but, generally, because there has been so little attention given to family and individual differences related to religion in education, we have chosen to discuss it here.

The term *religiosity* refers to the degree of emphasis families place on religion in their lives. This may not be immediately evident to early childhood professionals, both because of the variety of religious practices and because of the tremendous differences in degree of practice from family to family. Some families may discuss their religion with teachers in the context of specific classroom practices such as holiday celebrations. Others may have unexpressed concerns, and still others may have no need to be open with their child's teacher about their religious views.

Black churches have historically provided a great deal of family support. Because members of these churches were often denied access to other forms of family support in the United States, church members intervened to assist with survival. Caldwell, Greene, and Billingsley (1994) note that black churches have had a social service role since their inception in the late 1700s. During the civil rights movement of the 1960s, black churches took on a political activist role. In the 1980s, when drastic cuts were made in public funding for social programs, these churches once again reached out to their communities to provide support to families. It is believed that family and church are "strong interactive institutions that are mutually enhancing in their influence on African American communities" (p. 142). Further, "Black churches are mediators that buffer and enhance the relationship between the family's informal social network and the larger formal societal network" (p. 143). One aspect of this "larger formal societal network" is the educational institution.

Religiosity
http://www.wikipedia.com
Type in "Religion"

Whether or not families discuss their religion with teachers, teachers must be aware that religious belief or practice may affect a child's behavior. For instance, Janice Hale (1986), a scholar in the area of African-American child development, speaks about the differences in black churches and Anglo churches. She notes that from very early ages, African-American children are active during church services. The expectation is *not* that they should sit still and be quiet, as so often is the case in Anglo churches. Imagine the shock, then, when these children come to school where they are expected to be still and quiet!

Variations in religious beliefs and practices must be respected by early childhood teachers, just as teachers respect differences in culture, ethnicity, gender, and abilities. One source that helps to explain the differences is *How to Be a Perfect Stranger: A Guide to Etiquette in Other People's Religious Ceremonies* (Magida, 1996). Knowledge about these differences is often the first step in helping teachers understand families' beliefs and, thus, is part of the foundation for building family-school partnerships. (Figure 2–5 provides additional commentary.)

> *"A nation that does not stand up for its children does not stand for anything and will not stand strong in the twenty-first century . . . . We must believe we can save all of our children and then do it!"*
>
> —**Marian Wright Edelman**

There are several additional sources that early childhood teachers can turn to for help with this subject. One is *How to Be a Perfect Stranger: A Guide to Etiquette in Other People's Religious Ceremonies* (Magida, 1996). Two others are accessible through the Children's Defense Fund (CDF), which organized a rally at the Lincoln Memorial in Washington, D.C., on June 1, 1996, that was attended by more than 250,000 child and family advocates. The rally was a call to *all* communities of faith to come together to "Stand for Children." Continuing the rally's momentum, CDF created a religious-action branch, including the Interfaith Child Advocacy Network and Congregations to Leave No Child Behind. The mission statement for the Interfaith Child Advocacy Network indicates that the network will "provide opportunities for educating congregations

| Figure 2–5 | All Faiths should be Fairly Treated in Schools |

Forget the home-run race. Litigation has now surpassed baseball as America's favorite national pastime.

The latest example of how quick we are to "call a lawyer" comes from Ohio, where a school district may face a lawsuit for closing school on Rosh Hashana and Yom Kippur (Sept. 21 and Sept. 30, respectively).

School officials argue that absenteeism is too high on those days to hold classes in any meaningful way. Some 15% of the students in the district are Jewish and most of them stay home or attend synagogue for two of Judaism's most significant holy days. In some schools, absences ran as high as 21%.

A group of parents—with the ironic name of Parents for Fairness—objects, claiming that closing the schools these two days would favor the Jewish faith over other faiths in violation of the First Amendment.

Who's right?

It's true that the First Amendment's establishment clause requires that public school officials be neutral among religions and between religion and nonreligion. The school board can't close the schools on Jewish holy days because it wants to favor Judaism.

But school officials have a good civic (or secular) purpose for their action: Too many students would be absent those days to conduct a normal school day. The closings are meant to serve the educational needs of all the students, not to advance a particular religion. Just because the policy also benefits Jewish kids doesn't make it unconstitutional.

It would be different if the district had a much smaller Jewish population. In that case, the best approach would be to allow Jewish students to be excused for services and require them to make up the missed work.

Beyond the legal issues, Parents for Fairness might want to think more about what they mean by "fairness." After all, the school calendar already favors the majority faith since no classes are held on Sunday and Christmas is a national holiday. Most Christians don't need to worry about the school schedule.

By contrast, minority faiths have to work around the existing calendar. Jews who observe the Sabbath have a problem participating in Friday night ball games and Saturday activities. Muslim students who wish to attend community prayer mid-day on Fridays sometimes have a hard time getting released from school.

This built-in advantage should be all the more reason for school officials to be sensitive to the religious needs of students from minority faiths. Of course, that rarely means closing school. But it does mean finding ways to accommodate requests where possible.

Rosh Hashana, by the way, is the Jewish New Year, a time of celebration but also of judgment. According to Jewish tradition, during the 10 days following Rosh Hashana, God examines the deeds of the people. For Jews, this is a time of profound self-examination and repentance.

At the end of this period, on Yom Kippur—the Day of Atonement—God makes a final judgment and forgives those who have truly repented. Many Jews fast for 25 hours and spend much of the day in the synagogue, praying for forgiveness.

Repentance, judgment, forgiveness. Nowadays a little time off for these things seems like a very good idea.

Source: With permission from Charles C. Haynes, Senior Scholar, Freedom Forum First Amendment Center. *Public Opinion*, Chambersburg, PA, September 1998

and the public about the needs of children, the solutions, and our common responsibility for addressing those needs" (http://www.childrensdefense.org/religiousaction/). Congregations to Leave No Child Behind pledge to educate about the needs and concerns of children, to provide outreach for children, to practice spiritual disciplines, and to advocate for children and families. With these movements, CDF has made a clear connection between advocating for children and families and religiosity.

Geographic Region

Geographic location affects what it means to be an American family just as other factors do. Perhaps those who have relocated to other geographic regions

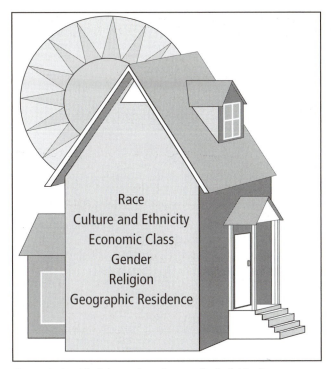

Figure 2–6 All of these pieces interact for individuality.

Race
Culture and Ethnicity
Economic Class
Gender
Religion
Geographic Residence

can understand best the differences among families that geographic placement creates, even among families of otherwise similar ethnicity, culture, economic class, and religiosity. Regional differences even affect gender role expectations.

Geographic differences are the result of the confluence of many factors, including climate, terrain, proximity to waterways, economy, industry, and history. Figure 2–6 demonstrates that all of the components discussed in this chapter interact to impact individual families.

As Figure 2–6 indicates, one of the elements affected by geography is poverty levels. Poverty rates for the nine census geographic divisions for 1994 demonstrate regional differences (Triest, 1997). The highest rate, 15.8 percent, existed in the west south-central region. Other areas whose rates were higher than the national average of 11.6 percent include east south-central, California, and New York. The lowest family poverty rate was in New England—8.2 percent—while the rates for the north central, middle Atlantic, south

Atlantic, mountain, and Pacific regions fall below the national average.

> Consider some of the notions you have about the people from one or two of the following regions: the Northeast, Southeast, Midwest, Southwest, Northwest, and Pacific. On what are your ideas based? What experiences have you had with people from regions other than your own?

Various stereotypes exist about people from different regions of the United States. Terms such as "salty New Englander," "Southern belle" and "Southern gentleman," "hillbilly," "farmer's daughter," and so on reflect images held by many living in other parts of the country. As with all stereotypes, a small part of these may be based in reality, but the ensuing pictures are far too narrow to be accurate or useful, and they limit our understanding of differences among people.

Sometimes, differences in dialect, slang, or variations in manners will lead to degrading others. Understanding expectations from various regional groups can help in having positive interactions with them. For example, a child whose family moved from the northeastern part of the country to the South soon learned that his teachers expected him not to reply to them with "Yes" or "No," but with "Yes, ma'am" or "No, sir." The child explained that this was difficult for him to learn because typically, when "ma'am" or "sir" was added to his speech in the past, it was not considered a sign of good manners, but, quite differently, a sign of sarcasm. Certainly, teachers should respectfully engage with students and expect respectful interaction in return, but it is important for teachers to understand how regional differences affect a child's understanding of what *respectful* means.

Another regional difference that teachers must be aware of is that priorities—the emphasis within a family of things that are of greater or lesser importance—may shift tremendously from region to region. In examining characteristics of Appalachian mountain families, for instance, Klein (1995) noted that connections between generations are critical for these families. Furthermore, most Appalachians emphasize the importance of spirituality over that of financial success. The consequent emphasis on humility among people of the Appalachians is often viewed by outsiders as making them "dull" and lacking self-esteem. After studying a number of characteristics that set this group apart from others, the author notes that educators must consider not only racial and ethnic differences but also those related to community and cultural heritage.

Alliance for Full Acceptance
http://www.affa-sc.org

Erase the Hate
http://www.ethonline.org/

Facing History and Ourselves
http://www.facinghistory.org

Museum of Tolerance
http://www.wiesenthal.com/
Select "Museum of Tolerance" from the
    drop-down menu

Teaching Tolerance
http://www.Tolerance.org

Tufts University Child and Family Web Guide
http://www.cfw.tufts.edu

50 Multicultural Books Every Child Should Know
http://www.soemadison.wisc.edu/
Type in "50 Multicultural Books"

Application to Early Childhood Education Programs

Celebrating Diversity

Celebrations and rituals are an important part of the human experience, but people celebrate for many different reasons and in many different ways. For instance, families may celebrate the same holiday but do it quite differently from one another. Other families may celebrate completely different holidays. One way to share information about the differences in the ways we celebrate is to have families come to early childhood programs to share their particular ways of celebrating.

Figure 2–7	Various Religious Celebrations and Traditions—Selected Web Sites

Kwanzaa

Kwanzaa is celebrated by many African Americans between December 26 and January 1. For African-American people who keep this African harvest holiday, it is a time of reaffirming themselves by focusing on their ancestors and culture. Traditions include the following:

Nguzo Saba: The seven principles
Kinara: Candleholder for seven candles
Mkeka: Straw or cloth place mat
Vibunzi: Ears of corn, one for each child in the family

One of Kwanzaa's guiding principles is applied to each of the seven days of celebration:

Umoja (oo-MO-jah): Unity of family and community
Kujichagulia (KOO-gee-cha-GOO-lee-yah):
    Self-determination
Ujima (oo-GEE-mah): Collective work and responsibility
Ujamaa (oo-JAH-mah): Cooperative economics
Nia (NEE-yah): Purpose (to set personal goals to benefit
    community)
Kuumba (koo-OOM-bah): Creativity
Imani (ee-MAH-nee): Faith

Source: Kwanzaa Information Center at http://www.melanet.com/, click "Kwanzaa Info Center"

In an effort to move to anti-bias approaches, some early childhood educators and institutions have done away with all celebrations. This is not necessary and may not even be desirable. Instead, it may be preferable to be sensitive to all ways of celebrating and to create celebrations unique to your classroom for special events such as new siblings, lost teeth, and other common developmental occurrences in families with young children. (See the information provided in the box "Selected Web Sites about Various Religious Celebrations and Traditions" and Figure 2–7.)

Inclusiveness

The ultimate goal for understanding diversity in early childhood education is to provide an *inclusive* environment. **Inclusiveness** means that each child and family can feel a sense of belonging, regardless of the commonalities or differences that exist between them and others in the group. This is a lofty goal, and because of many societal factors, may not be easily achieved.

As teachers plan class lessons and activities, and as they set classroom rules and policies, they must examine each lesson, activity, rule, and policy to ensure that it is inclusive. Even the most sensitive and knowledgeable teacher may err in this process. What is important, however, is not that we err, but rather what we do to correct the error when we realize that our classrooms are not inclusive. Compassionate, effective early childhood teachers collect information, ask for guidance, and change their classrooms so that inclusiveness prevails.

A review of research has led to the following recommendations of sources that can help early childhood teachers understand specific ways to support diverse families' involvement in their children's education. As stated in Chapter 1, inclusiveness is the key to strong family-school relationships, and "relationships are the foundation of parent involvement in schools" (Johnstone & Hiatt, as cited in Boethel, 2003, p. 71). Considering the importance of relationships as well as the existing empirical evidence, Boethel recommends the following practices for fostering an inclusive environment so that all families can participate:

- Be sure that all family involvement policies focus on including all areas of diversity. Such policies will relate to (1) frequent two-way communication with families; (2) adapting all family involvement components to meet diverse backgrounds, languages and circumstances; (3) involving representative families in planning and decision-making efforts; (4) providing effective professional development opportunities for teachers to work sensitively with all families; and (5) suggest and support possibilities for families to build their own capacities in order to effectively be involved in their children's education.

- The school principal plays a critical role in meaningful family involvement. Active support from a principal includes (1) frequent communication, with translation or in-home language; (2) informal meetings to check in with families about their interests, concerns, and questions as well as to update families on broad school concerns; (3) having a strong presence and active involvement at all school events; (4) prioritizing policies relating to family involvement; and (5) emphasizing the priority of family involvement with staff and families.

- Actively support and respect that all families have high aspirations for their children. Demonstrate appreciation for the efforts of parents and other family members.

- In order to best honor diversity, both similarities and differences must be acknowledged. "It is important for schools and community organizations not to simply ignore issues related to diversity or to act as if differences don't exist" (Boethel, 2003, p. 73). Acknowledgement of differences must include not only festive, lighthearted celebrations of food and customs, but also making a place for everyone at the decision-making table. In order for diversity to be truly honored, all voices must be heard.

- Teacher preparation programs and ongoing professional development must include in-depth content in the area of working with families, including those families who may be different from the teachers' own.

- Schools must help immigrant families understand the system. Inform all families through ways that they can understand what is expected of them and of their children in their student roles.

- Go the extra mile to support families in their involvement with children's education both at home and at school. Some recognized ways to do this include: (1) Making communication substantive by using families' home languages. (2) Making it do-able for immigrant families to participate in various ways. Be sure that someone from the parent organization is carrying out the charge to welcome all new families. Some of the ways to involve families is to increase their comfort level by requesting that they provide something from their culture, e.g., fundraisers that involve selling or auctioning food or other cultural products. (3) Getting into the community through home visits and/or involvement of school personnel in civic events.

- Trust is crucial, but it does not happen overnight. Keep in mind that each person has had past experiences and for some past experiences with schools have not always been positive. In addition to all of the previous points in this list, it may take time for teachers, principals and school communities to demonstrate that they can be trusted by families.

"Understanding that 'family involvement' may mean different things to different people can help both teachers and family members avoid misunderstandings and negative or stereotyped assumptions."

—Boethel, 2003, p. 35

"When we make choices about what to celebrate, let us be very conscious of who we are doing it for . . . . If we are doing it for the children, let us be conscious of all the subtle messages inherent in what we do and choose things to celebrate that are meaningful, developmentally appropriate, and healthy for them."

—Bonnie Neugebauer, 1990

Selected Web Sites about Various Religious Celebrations and Traditions

Various Faiths and Practices
Information about atheism, Buddhism, Christianity, Hinduism, Humanism, Islam, Native American religions, New Age, Shinto, Taoism, Wicca, and more
http://dir.yahoo.com/Society_and_Culture/
    Religion_and_Spirituality/Faiths_and_
    Practices
Click "Society and Culture"; click "Religion and Spirituality"; click "Faiths and Practices"

Jewish Holidays
http://www.aish.com Click "Holidays"

Jehovah's Witness
http://www.watchtower.org

Latter Day Saints (Mormon)
http://www.lds.org

Orthodox Church in America
http://www.oca.org

Scientology
http://www.scientology.org

Ethical Considerations

Relating Diversity to Developmentally Appropriate Practice

Bredekamp & Copple (1997) handbook on the Developmentally Appropriate Practice (DAP) includes the two primary components for appropriate practices in forming reciprocal relationships with families:

- *Caregivers form partnerships with parents through*: daily communication; building mutual trust; working to understand parents' preferences; and respecting cultural and family differences

    It must be noted that practices and attitudes work together to form such partnerships. Daily communications can build trust only when they are respectful, two-way, and objective. It is possible for teachers to communicate frequently and to be ineffective or assaultive if they are not sensitive to families' preferences or differences.

- *Members of each child's family are encouraged to be involved in ways in which they feel comfortable.* It is important for teachers to consider comfort level when they encourage families to be involved in their children's education. It is possible that a grandparent or cousin may be more comfortable volunteering in the classroom than a parent. In these cases, such family members often share relevant information with the parents. Early childhood teachers can look to various members of children's families for various kinds of involvement and then find ways to support those activities.

Relating Diversity to Programs for Children with Special Needs

The mission statement of the Division for Early Childhood (DEC) of the Council on Exceptional Children (CEC) includes "promoting policies and practices that support families" (http://www.dec-sped.org).

The DEC goals include:

- *Respecting families' diverse values, culture, and linguistic background.* When early childhood professionals are working with young children with disabilities, it is crucial to be sensitive to families' feelings and ways of working through the information that their child has a disability or multiple disabilities. In order to be sensitive to all families, diversity in values systems, cultural expectations and beliefs must be considered. Using the families' home language is absolutely necessary so that the family can best understand the child's needs and care.

- *Promoting parent professional collaboration.* The first consideration in building partnerships is the relationship between or among parents or other appropriate family members and professionals. Professionals must demonstrate respect for families as well as knowledge about their children's education. Creating positive relationships among families and professionals is one of the best ways to ensure that children can get all of their special needs met. Families and professionals communicate information about a child's disabilities that may be unique to their particular environment.

NAEYC Accreditation Guidelines

Guidelines from the National Association for the Education of Young Children (NAEYC) for early childhood program accreditation provide specific ideas for application that are based on the research evidence. Criteria from the accreditation guidelines compiled by the National Academy of Early Childhood Programs that relate to the "Families" Program standard (http://www.naeyc.org/accreditation/academy.asp) and to diversity are:

- New and existing program staff develop skills and knowledge to work effectively with diverse families as a part of orientation and ongoing staff development.

- Program staff use a variety of formal and informal strategies (including conversations) to become acquainted with and learn from families about their family structure, their preferred child-rearing practices, and their socioeconomic, linguistic, racial, religious, and cultural backgrounds.

- To better understand the cultural backgrounds of children, families, and the community, program staff (as a part of program activities or as individuals) participate in community cultural events, concerts, storytelling activities, or other events and performances geared to children and their families.

- Program staff ensure that all families—regardless of family structure, socioeconomic, racial, religious, and cultural backgrounds, gender, abilities, or preferred language—are included in all aspects of the program, including volunteer opportunities. These opportunities consider families' interests and skills and the needs of program staff.

- Program staff use a variety of mechanisms, such as family conferences or home visits, to promote dialogue with families. Program staff ask adults to translate or interpret communications as needed.

- The program compiles and provides information about the program to families in a language the family can understand. This information includes program policies and operating procedures.

Accreditation guidelines that relate to Community Relationships and diversity program standard are:

- Program staff are familiar with family support services and specialized consultants who are able to provide culturally and linguistically appropriate services. They use this knowledge to suggest and guide families to these services as appropriate.

- Program staff connect with and use their community's urban, suburban, rural, and/or tribal cultural resources.

Professional Code of Ethical Conduct

The early childhood profession "recognizes that those who work with young children face many daily decisions that have moral and ethical implications. The NAEYC Code of Ethical Conduct offers guidelines for responsible behavior and sets forth a common basis for resolving the principal ethical dilemmas encountered in early childhood care and education" (NAEYC, *Code of Ethical Conduct and Statement of Commitment*, http://www.naeyc.org/about/positions/PSETHOS.asp, p. 1 [(see Appendix B for complete document.)] Three of the seven core values of this code relate specifically to family diversity:

- Recognize that children are best understood and supported in the context of family, culture, community and society.

- Respect the dignity, worth, and uniqueness of each individual (child, family member, and colleague).

- Respect diversity in children, families, and colleagues.

In addition to the seven broad categories defined as core values, the Code of Ethical Conduct also includes *ideals* and *principles*. It is intended that the ideals reflect the aspirations or desired outcomes of ethical practice, whereas principles are statements to guide ethical conduct.

The following ethical *ideals* are particularly related to working with diverse families:

- To develop relationships of mutual trust and create partnerships with the families we serve.

- To welcome all family members and encourage them to participate in the program.

- To respect the dignity and preferences of each family and to make an effort to learn about its structure, culture, language, customs, and beliefs.

Ethical *principles* that are especially relevant to working with diverse families include:

- We shall not participate in practices that discriminate against children by denying benefits, giving special advantages, or excluding them from pro-

Early childhood education staff should respect, encourage, and foster cultural diversity in the classroom.

grams or activities on the basis of their sex, race, national origin, religious beliefs, medical condition, disability, or the marital status/family structure, sexual orientation, or religious beliefs or other affiliations of their families. (Aspects of this principle do not apply in programs that have a lawful mandate to provide services to a particular population of children.)

- We shall make every effort to communicate effectively with all families in a language that they understand.

- We shall use community resources for translation and interpretation when we do not have sufficient resources in our own programs.

Family Support Principles

Seven premises of the family support movement are described in Chapter 1. When reviewing these premises, it is evident that each one is stated in a way that is inclusive of all families. Basic understanding of these premises must lead to a respect for diversity and to the implication that early childhood educators must consider all families in decision-making regarding instruction, assessment, policies, and other aspects of educational programs.

Return to Chapter 1 and review the seven evidence-based premises from Family Support America. Choose two of these premises and reflect on how they relate specifically to work with diverse families and their children.

To listen to a father speak about the need for diversity education, go to the online resource at http://www.earlychilded.delmar.com.

This father of four discusses the need for diversity education to support his children's understandings of themselves and of others. He discusses some of the reasons that diversity is important and gives examples of what that might look like in school in this online voice.

Summary and Conclusions

Families differ in many ways. It is crucial that early childhood teachers work to increase their understanding of the differences among families and to interact sensitively with all families, bearing these differences in mind. Lifelong learning is a requirement for teachers in this regard, for as society changes, so families change.

Celebration of diversity leads to inclusive practices in early childhood education. Teachers' acceptance of differences among families is essential for each child to feel a sense of belonging in early education programs. Welcoming all families is a prerequisite for effective family involvement. Family members who view themselves as very different from teachers and other school personnel are less likely than other families to be involved in their children's education. It is the responsibility of early childhood teachers to foster a climate that encourages various types of family involvement so that all children may reap the benefits known to occur from home and school partnerships.

Chapter 2 Applications

1. A colleague, a primary grade teacher, tells you that because she has only one child in her classroom who does not celebrate Christmas and

twenty-three who do, she goes with the majority. So, for most of December, the class is involved in projects related to Christmas. How do you respond?

2. A mother of one of your kindergarten children tells you that you must not celebrate her son's birthday, nor may he attend any birthday celebrations for others because of the family's religious beliefs. What do you do about your tradition of celebrating each child's birthday?

3. When you request photos of each of your preschoolers' families for your bulletin board project, one child brings a picture of herself and two men. The child tells you that this is her with Daddy and Daddy's roommate, Ron, when they were on vacation at the beach. What do you do with the picture?

Questions for Reflection and Discussion

1. Consider the various forms of diversity discussed in this chapter. Discuss your experiences with each type of diversity.

2. Give an example of an experience from your past when you did not feel a sense of belonging or included in the situation. What do you think were the factors related to your feeling excluded?

3. Recall some common celebrations that you have observed in early childhood settings, either when you were a child or more recently. Identify some situations that were not inclusive. What are some ideas that you have for making the celebrations more inclusive?

Field Assignments

1. Interview a Head Start director or family coordinator about the benefits that quality early education has for low-income families.

2. Observe in a child care center, preschool program, kindergarten, or primary grade classroom. Note situations that you feel were

examples of a good understanding of diversity in families, as well as situations that excluded some children or families.

3. Interview a staff member of a religious community. Ask about programs that are offered that support families.

Ashley

References

Banks, J. A. (1997). *Teaching strategies for ethnic studies* (6th ed.). Needham Heights, MA: Allyn & Bacon.

Boethel, M. (2003). *Diversity: School, family, & community connections.* Austin, TX: National Center for Family & Community Connections with Schools, Southwest Educational Development Laboratory.

Bolger, K. E., Patterson, C. J., & Thompson, W. W. (1995). Psychosocial adjustment among children experiencing persistent and intermittent family economic hardship. *Child Development, 66,* 1107–1129.

Bredekamp, S., & Copple, C. (1997). *Developmentally appropriate practice in early childhood programs* (rev. ed.). Washington, DC: National Association for the Education of Young Children.

Bronfenbrenner, U. (1979). *The ecology of human development: Experiments by nature and design.* Cambridge, MA: Harvard University Press.

Brooks-Gunn, J., Klebanov, P. K., & Duncan, G. J. (1996). Ethnic differences in children's intelligence test scores: Role of economic deprivation, home environment, and maternal characteristics. *Child Development, 67,* 396–408.

Burns, A., & Scott, C. (1994). *Mother-headed families and why they have increased.* Hillsdale, NJ: Lawrence Erlbaum Associates.

Caldwell, C. H., Greene, A. D., & Billingsley, A. (1994). Family support programs in black churches: A new look at old functions. In S. L. Kagan & B. Weissbourd (Eds.), *Putting families first: America's family support movement and the challenge of change.* San Francisco: Jossey-Bass.

Cheal, D. (1996). *New poverty: Families in postmodern society.* Westport, CT: Greenwood.

Children's Defense Fund. (2005). *Children in the Nation.* http://www.childrensdefense.org. Retrieved November 16, 2005.

Children's Defense Fund. (2005). *The State of America's Children 2005.* http://www.childrensdefense.org. Retrieved November 16, 2005.

Children's Defense Fund. (2002). Every child deserves a fair start. http://www.childrensdefense.org/fairstart-faqs.htm.

Clark, L., DeWolf, S., & Clark, C. (1992). Teaching teachers to avoid having culturally assaultive classrooms. *Young Children, 47*(5), 4–9.

Division for Early Childhood. Mission of DEC. http://www.dec-sped.org.

Elkind, D. (1987). *Miseducation: Preschoolers at risk.* New York: Knopf.

Family Pride Coalition. (2004). Myths and facts. http://www.familypride.org/site/. Retrieved November 18, 2005.

Furman, E. (May 1992). Thinking about fathers. *Young Children, 47* (4), 36–37.

Furstenberg, F. F., Jr. (1988). Good dads—bad dads: Two faces of fatherhood. In A. J. Cherlin (Ed.), *The changing American family and public policy* (pp. 193–218). Washington, DC: Urban Institute Press.

Garbarino, J., & Ganzel, B. (2000). The human ecology of early risk. In J. P. Shonkoff & S. J. Meisels (Eds.), *Handbook of early childhood intervention* (2nd ed.). New York: Cambridge University Press.

Garfinkel, I., & McLanahan, S. (1989). *Single mothers and their children: A new American dilemma.* Washington, DC: Urban Institute Press.

Hale, J. (1986). *Black children: Their roots, culture, and learning styles* (rev. ed.). Baltimore: Johns Hopkins University Press.

Hamner, T. J., & Turner, P. H. (1996). *Parenting in contemporary society.* Needham Heights, MA: Allyn & Bacon.

Howe, L. K. (1972). *The future of the family.* New York: Simon & Schuster.

Hyson, M. (Ed.) (2003). *Preparing early childhood professionals: NAEYC's standards for programs.* Washington, DC: National Association for the Education of Young Children.

Johnson, T. W., & Colucci, P. (1999). Lesbians, gay men, and the family life cycle. In B. Carter & McGoldrick (Eds.), *The expanded family life cycle: Individual, family, and social perspectives* (3rd ed.). Boston: Allyn & Bacon.

Klein, H. A. (1995). Urban Appalachian children in northern schools: A study in diversity. *Young Children, 50* (3), 10–16.

Magida, A. (Ed.). (1996). *How to be a perfect stranger: A guide to etiquette in other people's religious ceremonies.* Woodstock, VT: Jewish Lights.

McDade, K. (1995). How we parent: Race and ethnic differences. In C. K. Jacobson (Ed.), *American families: Issues in race and ethnicity.* New York: Garland.

McGoldrick, M. (1989). Ethnicity and the family life cycle. In B. Carter & M. McGoldrick (Eds.), *The changing family life cycle* (2nd ed.). Needham Heights, MA: Allyn & Bacon.

McGuire, M., & Alexander, N. J. (1985). Artificial insemination of single women. *Fertility and Sterility, 43,* 182–184.

Mellman, M., Lazarus, E., & Rivlin, A. (1990). Family time, family values. In D. Blankenhorn, S. Bayme, & B. Elshtain (Eds.), *Rebuilding the nest: A new commitment to the American family.* Milwaukee, WI: Family Service America.

National Academy of Early Childhood Programs. (1991). *Accreditation criteria and procedures.* Washington, DC: National Association for the Education of Young Children.

National Association for the Education of Young Children. (April 2005). Code of ethical conduct. http://www.naeyc.org/about/positions/PSETHOS.asp. Retrieved November 19, 2005.

National Association for the Education of Young Children. Program accreditation. http://www.naeyc.org/accreditation/academy.asp. Retrieved November 18, 2005.

Neugebauer, B. (1990). Going one step further—no traditional holidays. Child Care *Information Exchange, 74.*

Parke, R. (1995). Fathers and families. In M. H. Bornstein (Ed.), *Handbook of parenting (Vol. 3): Status and social conditions of parenting* (pp. 27–63). Mahwah, NJ: Erlbaum.

Patterson, C. J. (1995). Lesbian and gay parenthood. In M. H. Bornstein (Ed.), *Handbook of parenting, volume 3: Status and social conditions of parenting* (pp. 255–274). Mahwah, NJ: Erlbaum.

Patterson, C. (1995). Lesbian and gay parenting. APA Online Public Interest. http://www.apa.org/pi/parent.html. Retrieved November 18, 2005.

Phillips, C. B. (1995). Culture: A process that empowers. In P. L. Mangione (Ed.), *Infant/toddler caregiving: A guide to culturally sensitive care* (pp. 2–9). Sacramento, CA: California Department of Education.

Rank, M. R. (1994). *Living on the edge: The realities of welfare in America.* New York: Columbia University Press.

Ribbens, J. (1994). *Mothers and their children: A feminist sociology of childrearing.* Thousand Oaks, CA: Sage.

Santrock, J. W. (1994). *Child development.* Madison, WI: Brown & Benchmark.

Search Institute. (n.d.) Developmental Assets. http://www.search-institute.org. Retrieved November 18, 2005.

Stauss, J. H. (1995). Reframing and refocusing American Indian family strengths. In C. K. Jacobson (Ed.), *American families: Issues in race and ethnicity.* New York: Garland.

Trawick-Smith, J. (1997). *Early childhood development.* Upper Saddle River, NJ: Merill-Prentice Hall.

Triest, R. K. (January–February 1997). Regional differences in family poverty. New England *Economic Review,* 3–18.

Wardle, F. (1987). Are you sensitive to interracial children's special identity needs? *Young Children, 42* (2), 53–59.

Zinn, M. B., & Eitzen, D. S. (1987). *Diversity in American families.* New York: Harper & Row.

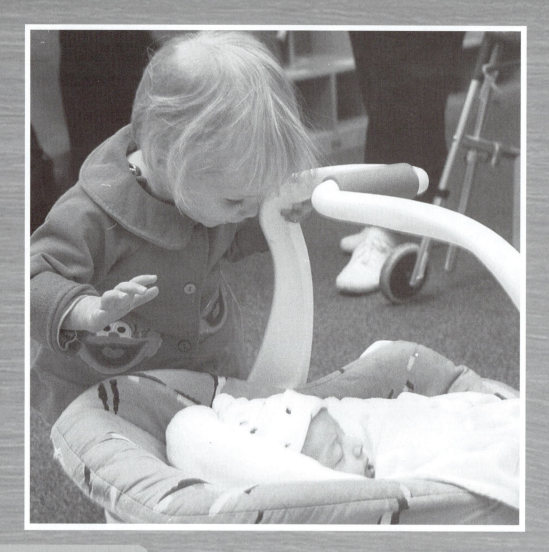

OUTLINE

Objectives

Key Terms

Theoretical Foundation
Bioecological Theory
Family Systems Theory

Developmental Issues in Families
Transition to Parenthood
Sibling Relationships
Work and Family
Child Care

Extended Family Relationships

Practical and Ethical Considerations
Family Support Principles
Code of Ethical Conduct

Summary and Conclusions

Chapter 3 Applications

Questions for Reflection and Discussion

Field Assignments

References

How might these issues affect family involvement in education?

Developmental Issues in Families with Young Children

After reading this chapter, you should be able to:

- understand developmental issues and transitions facing families with young children.

- relate the importance and effects of various social groups to young families.

- apply principles of family support and information from the code of ethical conduct to your work as an early childhood educator when working with families with young children.

Key Terms

child care "trilemma"
downsizing
extended family
 relationships

family-friendly work policies
family size
high-quality, affordable child
 care

maternal employment
sibling relationships
transition to parenthood

Theoretical Foundation

Bioecological Theory

Bronfenbrenner (2001) defines development "as the phenomenon of continuity and change in the biopsychological characteristics of human beings both as individuals and as groups" (p. 3). This chapter emphasizes changes that typically occur in families as they have children. Examining the particular issues that face families with young children in our society can help early childhood teachers increase their awareness of and sensitivity to these developmental transitions.

Keeping in mind the concentric circle model posed by Bronfenbrenner (explained in Chapter 1),

some additional information from this theory provides greater detail through ten propositions (Bronfenbrenner, 2001). Seven of the propositions most relevant to the content of this chapter are presented here. These propositions offer insights into the application of the theory, enabling teachers to better understand multiple influences on development.

Proposition I—A critical element of this theory is *experience*. Experience is both objective and subjective. This means that objective aspects of one's experience can be observed or assessed by another person. However, this theory posits a comparable influence on subjective aspects of experience, including an individual's feelings, beliefs, and values.

Proposition II—An individual develops in relation to reciprocal interactions with other people and objects

[handwritten margin note: Experience changes the way a person thinks as well as what a person does]

in their environments. Over time, these interactions must be more complex in order to support children's developmental progress. " . . . the informal education that takes place in the family is . . . a powerful prerequisite for success in formal education from the primary grades onward" (Bronfenbrenner, 1990, p. 33).

Proposition III—All of development is influenced by the characteristics of the individual and by all the systems (microsystem, mesosystem, exosystem, macrosystem, and chronosystem). Any of these determinants, whether biological or environmental, may be interacting with one or more other determinants at any given time.

Considering mesosystem effects, children are influenced by ongoing patterns of open, effective communication that build trust between and among the systems where children spend most of their time: home and early education settings. Parental workplace stress is a major factor in what happens at home, demonstrating an aspect of exosystem influences. The premise of an extensive study conducted by Parcel and Menaghan (1994) is that conditions in parents' workplaces affect the home environments that adults create for their young children. And, home environments affect children's cognitive and social development. (Findings that support this premise are discussed further in the "Work and Family" section of this chapter.) Macrosystem effects include public policies that influence child rearing, including availability of high-quality early education opportunities for all children.

Proposition IV—For all areas of a child's development (physical, cognitive, social, and emotional), it is necessary for children to interact with one or more individuals (especially adults who are in the parenting role) with whom the child develops a strong emotional attachment. Over time, these interactions not only build strong emotional ties, but they also must involve more complex interests for those involved in the relationship.

Proposition V—Strong feelings of attachment between children and those who are parenting them lead to children's motivation and curiosity. When children have this strong emotional foundation, they then express their interest in the world around them.

Proposition VI—In addition to strong, positive emotional bonds, children proceed to their optimal levels of development when their attachment figure has the involvement of another adult "who assists, encourages, spells off, gives status to, and expresses admiration and affection for the person caring for . . . the child. . . . Where there is an attachment to two or more parent figures, each can serve as a third party to the other" (Bronfenbrenner, 2001, p. 10). This level of support seems to be essential to adults in parenting roles in order for child outcomes to be most favorable. Families that have support, outlets for frustration, and caring others can provide more positive experiences for their children.

Proposition VII—Children influence their parents. Both child behavior and development affect the well-being of parents. Children with "easier" temperaments and a variety of interests and abilities may sway parental psychological development in a positive direction. Parents who are rearing children who display more challenges to the parents may exhibit a lower feeling of well-being.

Family Systems Theory

" . . . [B]ecoming a parent is one of the most definitive stages of life, a crossing of the Rubicon."

—B. Carter, 1999, p. 249

Family systems theory notes that " . . . becoming a parent shares the common characteristic of a change of membership and a change of function of its members" (Bradt, 1989, p. 235). The changes necessary in the family system with the birth of a first child are immense. For both new mothers and new fathers, balance between work and home undergoes an immediate and dramatic shift, as have their expectations regarding their responsibilities in these environments. Also, new parents feel continuously challenged about whether they have the capacity to live up to the responsibility for nurturing this new generation (Bradt, 1989). New parents may meet these challenges in very different ways, along a continuum of responses. Some parents insist that

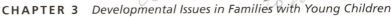
What can make Transition to parenthood diff & stressful (handwritten)

Developmental Issues in Families

Transition to Parenthood

The theoretical perspectives discussed above confirm that huge changes occur in families when individuals become parents. Thus, this transition is characterized by the changes that occur between parenting partners. Many of a couple's established patterns of behavior that have become routine for the couple will be changed with the arrival of a child. These changes in a couple's routine typically change the relationships with each other, as well as with other family members, friends, and coworkers. Some research exists to inform our understanding of what happens in the **transition to parenthood.**

A study in 1957 (LeMasters) revealed that 83 percent of new parents had experienced a serious amount of family distress following the birth of their first baby. The ideal of American family life is that a baby celebrates a couple's love, but this idealism quickly turns to exhaustion as parents expend the effort required to meet the nonnegotiable needs of a baby (La Rossa & La Rossa, 1981). Few new parents feel well prepared to meet the constant needs of newborns. Further, most new parents are surprised by the stress that is added to their lives. This indicates that little support is available for couples as they become parents.

Men and women report some differences in their transition to parenthood. Although both clearly feel the loss of nearly all free time, women are more likely to value their relationships with their babies. Fathers are more likely to act as if their babies are things to show to others, and they see babies as being less competent than do mothers. Even egalitarian couples begin to split family responsibilities in the direction of more traditional gender roles (LaRossa & LaRossa, 1981).

Children are influenced by ongoing patterns of open communication and trust at their school.

there is "nothing to" rearing children, and others become increasingly focused on their children. Most likely, there is middle ground between these perspectives that provides for a healthy response to meeting the new and demanding challenges for parents.

Challenges abound in families with young children. Changes in roles for parenting adults, changes in relationships with the other parent and extended family members, and changes in expectations regarding work and home responsibilities all work together to increase the difficulty of adjusting to even a joyous occasion. And yet, forming families and having children, remains a popular option. Ninety percent of all couples who can have children do have children. About 3,000 couples each year become parents (Belsky & Kelly, as cited in Carter & McGoldrick, 1999). *4 million babies yearly in U.S.* (handwritten)

"Being a parent, whether father or mother, is the most difficult task humans have to perform. For people, unlike other animals, are not born knowing how to be parents. Most of us struggle through."

—**Karl Menninger**

"The context of family relationships is continually in flux in the early months of parenthood."

—**Laurie Van Egeren, 2004**

Van Egeren (2004) found differences in co-parenting relationships between mothers and fathers as they made the transition to parenthood. Co-parenting is defined as "that part of the relationship between caregivers specifically directed toward parenting concerns . . ." (Van Egeren, 2004, p. 455). For example, this study (which examined only heterosexual married couples) found that in the first six months of parenting, fathers were more satisfied than mothers. Also, this study found that a major transition exists when new mothers who have taken on most of the child care and a significant amount of home and family responsibilities, return to employment outside the home. New roles for both parents commonly require negotiating the definition and assignment of existing tasks, as well as ways to share the added child care responsibilities. Further, fathers, but not mothers, reported more positive co-parenting when their babies had easy temperaments. This study also supports Bronfenbrenner's Proposition VI, the presence of a supportive third party. When husbands were warm and caring, both parents experienced co-parenting more positively.

New mothers report that they see it as their responsibility to create a family, "to produce a different sort of social unit" (Ribbens, 1994, p. 59) when the first child is born. Having a family, to most people, means having and caring for children. Even at this point in history, with so much emphasis on gender equality, it seems that both society and individual mothers perceive the mother's role as being that of ensuring the formation and integration of the family unit.

One reason for this move toward "traditionalization" is that larger systems in society—that is, the exosystem and macrosystem—do not support gender equity in parenting (LaRossa & LaRossa, 1981). So, even when couples attempt to fully share parenting, the workplace, extended families, and other social institutions often do not provide the necessary support for co-parenting. With so many parenting tasks to complete, tired new parents often do not see gender equity as a battle that they have the energy to fight or even can afford to fight. Thus, they give in to the system.

Fathers' and mothers' self-reports on their success with infant care also differ (Hudson, Elek, &

Fleck, 2001). For the couples in this study, fathers scored lower than did mothers at all three points of the study: when babies were two months, three months, and four months of age. However, mothers and fathers both scored increasingly higher on a measure of parental satisfaction over the same three time periods. One difference in the satisfaction results, though, was that fathers demonstrated higher scores in their parenting satisfaction with male infants.

It is believed that the differences found between fathers and mothers is a least partly a function of what it means to be a mother and what it means to be a father. As noted above, even in this era of less stereotypical gender roles, strongly held traditional views of mothering seem to endure. It is only recently that fathers have attended the births of their babies and have been expected to be engaged in infant and child care.

Woollett and Parr (1997) analyzed psychological tasks for women and men in their transitions to parenthood. Some interesting results from this research indicate that the men both looked forward to the birth more than the women and enjoyed childbirth more than the women. These researchers explain women's sometimes ambivalent feelings about parenthood as a reaction to the major transition inherent in becoming a parent. On the other hand, even though males are now expected to become parents who are enthusiastically engaged with their children, their role continues to be less defined by society and their transition to parenthood is less "abrupt."

The women in Woollett and Parr's (1997) study also commonly expressed depressive feelings as a postpartum reality. More information about postpartum depression is needed, but existing evidence that suggests that 8–15 percent of new mothers are affected by it and an even greater percentage (25–50 percent) experience depressive symptoms that are milder or of shorter duration (O'Hara, 1997, as cited in Feeney, Alexander, Noller, & Hohaus, 2003). The news media are now giving greater attention to postpartum depression, due in part to celebrity moms who have shared their stories. Depression has been connected to relationship anxiety coupled with the major life change of transition to parenthood (Feeney, et al., 2003). Other factors that were related to depressive symptoms included mothers' negative reactions to the news that they were pregnant and mothers' perceptions of their infants as difficult. Thus, couple adjustment in the transition to parenthood is seen as crucial for infant nurturance and positive developmental outcomes.

Another study found that common changes in emotional functioning during the transition to parenthood included depressive symptoms and stress (Perren, von Wyl, Burgin, Simoni, & von Klitzing, 2005). In this research, both mothers and fathers reported depressive symptoms during pregnancy as well as postpartum. For parents with prior mental health challenges, stress increased continuously to one year after birth. On the other hand, mentally healthy mothers had a decrease in depressive symptoms from pregnancy until infants were three months old, but then the symptoms increased again.

This longitudinal study explained that additional stress for both parents occurred when mothers returned to employment outside the home. For many of the parents in this study, that shift happened when the baby reached one year of age. Although stress around employment existed for all families, those with psychological dysfunction were believed to be at greater risk.

One point of concern related to research on the transition to parenthood is that most studies have used middle-class or upper-middle-class families. If these families are noting this much stress, what happens in families with fewer resources, human or material? Based on ecological theory, we can only hypothesize that a single mother with a low income will face even greater crises in this transition.

"The transition to parenthood is a major life event that effects all aspects of psychosocial functioning."
—Condon, Boyce, and Corkindale, 2004

The Cowans (1995) make an important point: It is clear that families need interventions to assist them during this critical transition. When parents adjust more easily, their relationships with their children are of higher quality. This relationship is a critical factor in the child's development and central to the child's success as a preschooler and an elementary student.

It is primarily for this reason that early childhood educators must be aware of the importance of various forms of support for all new parents in their transition to parenthood. Parents face a tremendous challenge especially with their first babies, but each new birth changes the family system and requires added support. As we celebrate births, we must be prepared to offer families the support, help, and care they need to reduce the negative outcomes associated with the transitions of becoming a family.

The trend of looking specifically at fathers' adjustment in the transition to parenthood is relatively recent. There is some evidence that pregnancy, rather than birth or infancy, is the most stressful time for new fathers (Condon, Boyce, & Corkindale, 2004; Woollett & Parr, 1997). A study that examined the adjustment of first-time fathers found that the men were "ill-prepared for the impact of fatherhood on their lives" (Condon, Boyce, & Corkindale, 2004, p. 56). Some of the explanations for this lack of preparedness include having few or no social support networks for fathering, feeling increased financial responsibilities and thus increased stress about work, having a lack of good role models for fathering, being confronted with idealized media and cultural images of childbirth and parenting, and feeling a reluctance to seek help for emotional problems.

Some efforts are being made to address the need to increase fathers' effectiveness and satisfaction during the transition to parenthood. One such effort is the New Fathers Network, an Internet-based program that offers a library of relevant information, a discussion forum, and e-mail access to advanced practice nurses (Hudson, Campbell-Grossman, Fleck, Elek, & Shipman, 2003). The response from program participants was generally positive. The researchers believe that this program or similar Internet interventions provide social support in a form that made fathers willing to use it. However, it is not known whether such a program would be effective with fathers in high-risk, adolescent, or diverse ethnic or socioeconomic populations.

Another Web-based program for first-time fathers is Boot Camp for New Dads (http://www.NewDads.com). This program bills itself as "a guy thing." In addition to the Web site, this intervention program includes parenting classes, at medical or other community centers, on topics such as diapering, when and how to feed your baby, soothing a crying baby, becoming your baby's burping buddy, introducing baby to pets, and helping mom cope. The program also includes a system for connecting with other dads. As with the New Fathers Network, this program seems to take seriously the task of increasing the social network about parenting for new fathers.

All of the research discussed above can be useful in helping early childhood educators understand the difficulties and stressors affecting women's and men's transitions to parenthood. This research, however, is limited in some important ways, because much of it has sampled only middle-class or upper-middle-class, white, married or partnered adults. Recently, however, some attention has been given to the transition as experienced by single, low-income mothers; adolescent fathers; and psychologically depressed mothers and fathers.

The members of nearly half of all female-headed households in the United States, or approximately 6.5 million such households, live below the poverty level. Many low-income women endure both mental health challenges and parenting difficulties. Another correlate to the high risk for this group of women is low social support. With this number of risks, it is clear that low-income, single mothers face greater difficulties with the transition to parenthood than more affluent, healthy, partnered mothers. One study (Keating-Lefler, Hudson, Campbell-Grossman, Fleck, & Westfall, 2004) found that many low-income, single mothers had "an array of emotions and mixed feelings" (p. 390), feeling both excited and overwhelmed. Further, the primary source of stress for these women seemed to stem from the loss of their earlier dreams for themselves as well as the loss of relationships with the babies' fathers and sometimes with their own families of origin. In addition, the women reported that having sole responsibility for an infant and few resources to meet those responsibilities caused great stress. Many of the women lacked transportation, did not have enough money to make ends meet, and were uncertain about how they were going to continue to provide for their children. A sense of isolation and sometimes hopelessness about

the ability to succeed in the future led to growing negative feelings in these women.

Given all of these concerns and their overall lack of support, low-income, single women have great difficulty in making a smooth transition to parenthood. This places both the mother and the child in the high-risk category. Thus, it is in the best interest of families, schools, and communities to ensure that alternative sources of support and resources are available for these families.

Information also is lacking about the transition to parenthood for adolescent mothers and fathers. Regarding adolescent mothers, it seems safe to assume, however, that when they are low-income and single, their youth and lack of employment skills add still more risk factors to the outcomes discussed above. An examination of the transition among adolescent fathers and their partners has shed some light on the details of the challenges that adapting to parenthood poses for these young men. Florsheim, Moore, Zollinger, MacDonald, and Sumida (1999) found that the same risk factors associated with the likelihood of becoming an adolescent father are also related to difficulties in adjusting to fatherhood. One of the most prevalent of these factors is antisocial-hostile behavior. Further findings, leading to concern for infant development, show that when the antisocial-hostile father is living with the infant's mother, her nurturing skills are negatively affected. This result did not occur when the parents were not living together, that is, the mothers' parenting did not seem to be as adversely affected by the father's behavior when he was not living with the mother.

An ongoing concern in these difficult adolescent relationships is that when fathers do not transition to their role as parents during the infancy period, they are more likely to become absent fathers and that " . . . risk begets risk, laying the groundwork for the intergenerational transmission of psychological dysfunction" (Florsheim, Moore, Zollinger, MacDonald, & Sumida, 1999, p. 13).

Sibling Relationships

As families grow, new relationships must be negotiated. As the first child becomes the big brother or big sister, parental roles also change. Attention to

Siblings w/ disabilities —
some children deeply care for
others resent

sibling relationships becomes a new challenge for parents who are often just beginning to feel more confident of their abilities. Young children typically react to the announcement about the coming of a new baby in a variety of ways that are influenced by individual differences in development and temperament. Chelsea, at age two and a half, responded to her parents' announcement about a new baby by stating, "No baby. Doggie." For young preschoolers, this may seem like a reasonable, desirable, and logical variation to the family composition.

Young children have a great deal to understand when a new sibling is added to the family constellation. Early childhood teachers frequently experience changes in children's behaviors at school when a new baby is expected or has arrived at home. In the above example, Chelsea seemed resistant to having a new baby in the family. By the time baby Christopher was born, however, she was three years old and seemed to have adapted to the notion: She commented frequently, "He's so nice." One day, however, Chelsea heard her mother refer to herself as "Christopher's mommy, too." The mother was surprised to realize that although Chelsea had gotten used to the idea of the baby living in their house, she had not necessarily understood that the baby also was her mother's child—and she was not prepared to share her mother! Adele Faber and Elaine Mazlish (1987), in their book, *Siblings without Rivalry*, provide a useful analogy to help parents understand some of the feelings of rivalry children may experience with the introduction of new siblings: The researchers suggest that parents try to imagine how they would feel if their spouse added a new spouse into the family!

Child developmentalists believe that sibling rivalry is common. However, when siblings do not get along well and engage in frequent conflict, the negative relationship affects family accord as well as individual children's development. Research indicates that siblings contribute both directly and indirectly to a child's development (Brody, 2004). Further, siblings can affect one another in positive ways as well as in negative ways. From a family systems perspective, the behavior of any one member of a family affects all the members of the family and their relationships with one another (Brody, 2004).

Direct ways in which siblings influence one another include those listed below.

- Older siblings teach new concepts and language skills to younger sibs.
- Older sibs become better teachers, gain confidence, increase their school achievement, and learn to balance their own needs with others.
- A balance of conflict and nurturance between or among siblings helps children to understand others' emotions and viewpoints as well as how to resolve conflict.
- Younger siblings who have aggressive older siblings are at risk for problems with conduct, academics, and peers.
- Older siblings can serve as a buffer for younger siblings in times of family upheaval (Brody, 2004).

Some of the indirect ways in which siblings influence one another include the following.

- Older siblings influence their parents' expectations for younger children. *How*
- Older children also influence teachers' perceptions about younger siblings in relation to academic ability and behavioral expectations. *How*
- Older children who have difficult temperaments or special needs may influence parental ability to provide appropriate nurturance to younger siblings.
- When older siblings do well in school and with peers, parents use more positive parenting strategies with younger children (Brody, 2004).

Sibling influences are also noted when parents or parenting figures treat siblings differently. In order to be a responsive parent, children's differences must be noted and cared for. However, when the differential treatment is seen as unfair by siblings, issues may arise.

- Poor emotional and behavioral functioning may occur when children perceive that siblings receive more warmth from parents than they do.
- Low self-esteem in children is related to perceptions of unfair treatment from parents.

Parents can mitigate these negative effects, however, by explaining to children the basis for differential treatment so that children understand the need to individualize parenting for developmental differences or special needs.

Family size, of course, influences family systems, especially the dynamics of sibling relationships. Hernandez (1993) discusses details related to growing up in larger families versus smaller families. The median family size had decreased from 6.6 in the 1890s to 2.9 in the 1940s. During the baby boom (1946–1964), the median family size rose to 3.4. Most recently, during the "baby bust," median family size has decreased to 2.1 Figure 3–1 demonstrates changes in average family size over time. Fewer siblings in the house means a marked change in the typical family's microsystem. Generally, young children today have fewer relationships within the family and a greater number of people with whom they interact in additional microsystems.

Hernandez's analysis indicates that the reasons for declines in family size are related to social, economic, and political changes. The first issue Hernandez (1993) addresses is that having many siblings is a mixed blessing: It creates the opportunity for caring sibling relationships, but less attention is available for each child from parents. Hernandez indicates that children from larger families receive less education,

and thus enter lower-status occupations and earn less income. Further, a great deal of research has pointed to the fact that increased interactions with parents leads to gains in children's verbal ability and school success. Smaller families provide greater possibility for parents to interact with children. This is likely one reason that young children currently have higher levels of language development when they enter preschool or kindergarten than was true of children in the past.

Children with Disabilities: Understanding Sibling Issues
http://nichcy.org

Helping Children Adapt to a New Sibling
http://www.nncc.org
Click "Articles and Resources"

How Foster Children Impact Sibling Relationships
http://www.fostercare.net/

Siblings in Adoption—Expanded Families
http://www.pactadopt.org/
Click "Articles of Interest"; click "siblings"

Many studies regarding the characteristics of only children have demonstrated that they are very similar to those of other children or that only children are even somewhat advantaged (Falbo, 1992). Conventional wisdom in U.S society points to a desire for two or three children, down from a generation or two ago. And conventional wisdom opposes planning for having only one child. Even adults who were reared as only children note that they wish they had grown up with brothers and sisters. Falbo notes that it is rare for an only child to have "strong positive feelings about his or her status because it is and continues to be nonnormative" (p. 77).

In her review of literature regarding only children, Falbo (1992) notes that only children scored higher than others on achievement motivation and self-esteem. They were not unique from other children in many personality traits, including dominance, generosity, autonomy, anxiety, and popularity.

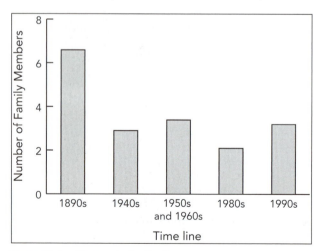

Figure 3–1   Changes in family size.

In childhood, the home lives of only children have been more likely to encourage intellectual activities such as reading, music, dance, and travel outside the country. In school, only children were not more likely than others to cause trouble or have special needs, but they were less inclined than others to demonstrate antisocial behavior, hyperactivity, dependency, or social withdrawal.

> *"Sensitive parenting . . . often requires that children in the same family be treated differently."*
>
> —Brody, 1998, p. 8

The primary reason for the decline in **family size** is a desire of individuals and couples to increase their social and economic standing or to keep from falling behind in their economic standing (Hernandez, 1993). The cost of having children has increased, and the economic benefit of having children has all but disappeared. As society has shifted from an agrarian emphasis to an industrial and technological one, each child's needs for housing, food, and clothing was no longer provided directly by the family, but, rather, families had to pay for goods and services. Not only was child labor restricted, but also school attendance became mandatory. During the twentieth century, quality of living has become tied to the increased consumption of goods and services that are produced outside of the home. In addition, parents' expectations about their own lives changed, and they perceive a need for more time for their own careers and recreation. Thus, many parents feel that their resources are too stretched to for them to consider having more than one or two children. Essentially, changes in the exosystem, macrosystem, and chronosystem have affected decisions about the size of the family in the microsystem. Childhood within the family context has experienced a "revolutionary shift" (Hernandez, 1993) from large to small families within the past 100 years. The downside of this shift from larger to smaller families is that children have fewer siblings who are potential companions throughout childhood and adulthood; the benefit is that children today receive more attention and resources from their parents.

Sibling relationships often challenge parents. Faber and Mazlish (1987) provide many examples from parents of such challenges. It seems that some degree of sibling rivalry may be inescapable within the family context. Parents claim not only that it is hard for them to understand why their children express such dislike for one another, but also that it is difficult to live with the sibling conflicts. Parents believe in the same paradigm used by researchers: that siblings are companions, friends for life. But children's actions rarely support this view.

Researchers interested in studying sibling relationships note that these interactions and emotions cannot be meaningfully studied outside the context of family and peer relationships. Further, research into sibling relationships may dispel the notion that parent-child relationships are the only significant ones in the processes of socialization (Buhrmester, 1992).

The causes of sibling rivalry or unity are not completely clear. Some of the factors influencing the quality of sibling relationships that researchers have examined include child temperament, parental depression, parent relationship with a spouse or partner, parenting strategies, and the interaction among any or all of these variables (Brody, 1998).

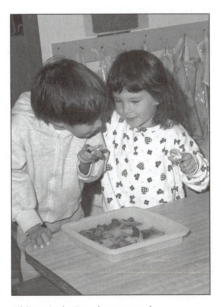

Sibling rivalry is to be expected.

Children with more difficult temperaments, particularly those who were less adaptable, more likely to withdraw from new situations, or emotionally intense, have displayed more troubled attitudes and behaviors with the birth of a new sibling. Further, highly active and siblings with different temperamental qualities have been found to engage in more conflict. Outside influences, including parenting style and family harmony, can assist siblings with these qualities to have more positive relationships with one another. For example, when parents have positive relationships with their children, the sibling relationship typically is more positive as well. However, when parents are negative and over-controlling, sibling relationships may be affected in a negative manner (Brody, 1998).

Evidence indicates that it is important for parenting adults to guide children's behavior and to set positive behavioral expectations. This might best be accomplished in the context of everyday problem-solving discussions with children rather than in the heat of disagreement. Conversely, when parents are aloof from sibling disputes, older siblings may take over, leaving younger siblings to be victims or, at least, to be negatively influenced both socially and emotionally. "Parental intervention in escalating conflict can reassure children that their parents are available to help and protect them when they are upset or in danger" (Brody, 1998, p. 13).

In any analysis of sibling relationships, it is important to keep in mind that there is a complex mix of influential factors. Considering only one or two possibilities will most likely lead to oversimplification of the relationship. Still, continuous positive family interactions that emphasize problem solving and conflict resolution seem to provide a strong basis for more positive sibling relationships.

Children with siblings who have developmental disabilities may face unique challenges in their relationships. It is not unusual for children to be taunted or teased about a sibling with a disability. Gath (1992) notes that a useful strategy for parents of children with disabilities is to provide an understandable explanation to children regarding their sibling's disability. There is some evidence that "life may be easier for a brother or sister when there is another normal *sic*

child in the family" (p. 103). Also, "the presence of other normal [*sic*] children in the family is a great comfort to the majority of parents, but conversely, the arrival of a second handicapped child in the same family increases the grief many times over and the presence of two children with mental retardation or other long standing disability in one family adds up to very much more than twice the burden of one" (p. 102). Other challenges to families who are rearing siblings with and without disabilities include issues of fairness in terms of expectations about behavior and opportunities, as well as overcoming sadness and distress about a child's disability.

"Generally, researchers have hypothesized that when one child has a disability, the sibling relationship would be less warm and positive. Surprisingly, the majority of studies have found the opposite pattern" (Stoneman, 2001, p. 135). Variability in these relationships exists in that when a child's disability is more severe, the interaction between siblings is reduced. Physical or cognitive impairment may hinder children from playing together in ways that are mutually enjoyable. Stoneman's (2001) analysis of differences in sibling relationships of typically developing siblings and of those where one sibling has a disability makes a critical point. Just because the two types of sibling relationships differ, does not mean that one trend is the best for all. "Relationship differences can be adaptive and can allow love and friendship to develop in the face of the obstacles imposed by disability" (Stoneman, 2001, p. 140).

Some concerns about sibling relationships would lead one to consider how differences in family structure might influence those relationships. For instance, how do marital transitions affect sibling relationships? Are biological siblings emotionally closer to one another than half- or step-siblings? What is the impact of sibling relationships in a single-parent family?

Anderson and Rice (1992), in their study of sibling relationships in non-divorced, divorced, and remarried families, found that some personality traits of siblings differed by gender. Girls demonstrated more positive behavior, such as empathy and support, toward brothers and sisters than did boys, but they also showed equal amounts of aggression and hostility as boys. Generally, the findings in this study supported the family systems notion that increased family transitions contributed to conflict or ambivalence in sibling relationships. Negative sibling relationships were more common in stepfamilies and divorced families than in non-divorced families. These researchers emphasize that despite the conflicts among siblings, children in all types of families demonstrated a great deal of positive behavior toward their siblings.

Although earlier studies have shown differences in the quality of sibling relationships between "intact" and re-partnered families, the work of Deater-Deckard, Dunn, and Lussier (2002) found greater similarities with siblings of both types of families in England. In addition to intact and re-partnered families, these researchers also included siblings from single mothers. The results demonstrated that siblings in the single mother families were more negative than those in the other families, but that they engaged in just as much positivity as siblings in the other types of families. Interestingly, in terms of understanding family context, the single mothers in this study also were found to engage in more negativity than the parents in intact or re-partnered families. Although most of the research on families in transition has emphasized parent-child interaction, it is important to gain additional information about sibling relationships, since it is well documented that these relationships do have a strong influence on child development.

Even though it is advantageous to be aware of the positive relationships and influences that exist among siblings, parents continue to be frustrated and sometimes overwhelmed by sibling rivalries. In a laboratory study of young siblings, Ram and Ross (2001) found that even very young children are capable of using positive negotiating strategies in order to settle conflicts. Some of the strategies that children used included turn-taking, sharing information about their own points of view, and asking questions of each other. As might be expected, when siblings had ongoing positive relationships with one another and seemed to like and care for one another, contention was reduced. It is possible that the family context (even though not studied in this research) provided siblings with ways to engage one another positively.

Another finding in this study was that the children seemed to be concerned about issues of equality as they played together. As they negotiated situations with one another, they seemed to emphasize that certain toys or playthings were equally desirable and thus, would take turns with that toy. Further, the researchers noted that a good selection of playthings probably works to reduce contentious interactions (Ram & Ross, 2001).

Parents who have shared their stories in workshops with Faber and Mazlish make it clear that sibling rivalry is difficult to live with. Hetherington (1992) notes that "sibling relationships are unique because they combine the affective intensity and reciprocity of peer relationships with many of the complementary processes associated with parent-child relationships . . ." (p. 11). She goes on to say that sibling relationships have both an intense emotional component and high levels of supportive and antagonistic behavior.

Faber and Mazlish, basing their suggestions on the work of Haim Ginott (1965), offer strategies for the following:

- communicating feelings in acceptable ways
- knowing when and how to stop children's hurtful actions toward each other
- avoiding negative and positive comparisons of children
- understanding the differences between equal treatment and meeting each child's legitimate needs
- intervening in rivalries when one sibling has a disability
- setting limits on fighting
- managing tattling
- viewing sibling relationships as important across the life span

The last chapter of Faber and Mazlish's book contains stories from parents who are trying to impact their children's relationships in a positive way. Some of the stories that are particularly moving are ones in which parents discuss contacting their own siblings and using the strategies they apply to their children to repair or rebuild their adult sibling relationships.

In what ways does the world of work impact families + in turn teachers of yc children?

Work and Family

Work and family patterns for families with young children have undergone seismic shifts since the 1960s. In 2002, more than half of all new mothers with a child under 12 months of age were in the labor force (Overturf-Johnson & Downs, 2005). Between 1961 and 1965, this figure was a little less than 17 percent. The increase in new mothers who are employed by the time their babies are a year old has been steady. See Figure 3–2 for details.

As might be expected, the percentages increased for mothers employed outside the home as their children got older. Figure 3–3 provides information about percentages of mothers in the labor force when their children were two and five years of age.

Families and Work Institute
http://www.familiesandwork.org
Institute for Child and Family Policy
http://www.childpolicy.org/

Today, early in the twenty-first century, the state of the economy is such that many families perceive a need for two full-time incomes. When both parents in two-parent families are working full-time, the result is a dramatic change in the functions that families can and do perform. Many who are concerned about children and families have called on employers to incorporate **family-friendly work policies** for their employees.

Along with other members of contemporary society, many early childhood professionals have strong opinions about when and whether mothers of young children should be in the workforce. Each family, however, must decide this issue for itself—and only each family can. For some families, this decision is a matter of simple arithmetic (earning the amount of income necessary to keep them solvent); for others, it is a matter of career building. Today, we are more accepting of "Mr. Moms" but still tend to think that women should be willing to consider various work options. Many see this issue as being more political than economic, however.

Although no expert expects a rapid turnaround regarding maternal employment, there has been some recent movement toward the notion of women having "flex-careers" as well as being more "family-centric"/less "work-centric" (Galinsky, 2004). Women with flex careers plan to take time out of the labor force while their children are young. Recently, a survey showed that 28 percent of women who do not yet have children plan to do precisely this in order to spend time with their children.

Contemporary new moms may be making this decision for many reasons, but one has to do with the phenomenon that many Americans are feeling

Figure 3–2	Percentages of Employed Mothers 12 Months after First Baby
1961–65	16.8
1966–70	23.9
1971–75	27.9
1976–80	38.8
1981–85	56.3
1986–90	60.8
1991–95	62.0
1996–99	64.6

Figure 3–3	Percentages of Employed Mothers 24 and 60 Months after First Baby	
Time Period	24 Months	60 Months
1961–65	22.5	33.5
1966–70	29.8	41.1
1971–75	37.0	50.0
1976–80	48.0	64.3
1981–85	63.0	69.9
1986–90	66.6	72.7
1991–95	70.2	78.6
1996–99	Not available	Not available

overworked (Galinsky, Bond, Kim, Backon, Brownfield, & Sakai, 2004): About 44 percent of respondents indicated that they feel overworked on a regular basis. There are indications that this chronic sense of being overwhelmed in the workplace will lead to greater amounts of depressive disorders. Clinical depression related to work stress is predicted to take over from cancer as the number one cause of death and disability worldwide by 2020 (World Health Organization, as cited in Galinsky, et al., 2004). In this context, the movement toward flex careers by women with young children can be seen as an act of self-preservation.

Despite the enormous changes in work-family patterns experienced by married-couple families in the United States over the past generation, dual-career couples are still the most common type, while couples consisting of the wife as breadwinner and the husband as homemaker remain the least common type, as the list below indicates (Cheal, 1996).

Dual-career couples 30%

Husband provider, wife co-provider 24%

Husband breadwinner, wife homemaker 19%

One partially employed 8%

Both partially employed 6%

Wife provider, husband co-provider 5%

Nonworking 5%

Wife breadwinner, husband homemaker 2%

Stress in the workplace is on the rise. **Downsizing** often means that each employee is required to do all the work previously done by at least two people. Both men and women report working longer hours than they would like. Emotionally, they are torn: They are grateful to have a job, but stressed by the workload and expectations. Workers who have children report even greater levels of stress and are coping less effectively than those without children. Fifteen percent of employed parents say they rarely or never do anything for fun with their children (Galinsky, 1994).

Many people believe that **maternal employment,** that is, mothers working outside the home, is always negative for both the women and their families. These people believe that if women would return to caring for their young children, both families and the economy would be better off. Ellen Galinsky points out that this is not always the case. In many dual-earner families, women bring home 40 percent of the total income. This is a significant proportion of household income, and it can be assumed that families would suffer a much lower quality of life without this income. Further, researchers since the early 1970s have examined the effects of maternal employment, and the conclusions are that other variables are more important for children's welfare than whether or not the mother is working outside the home. Some of these variables include variations in home life, effects from the specific work environment, and the availability of quality child care. So, employed moms who have a satisfying family life, a supportive work environment, and access to quality care for their children provide positive outcomes for children. Segments from both the exosystem and macrosystem can affect families in either positive or negative ways.

In a study of the relation of maternal employment to mothers' and teachers' ratings of children's temperament and social behavior, Farver, Couchenour, and Chrisman (1998) found that young children's mothers who were dissatisfied with their work status, whether they worked outside the home or stayed at home, rated their children as more problematic in terms of difficult temperament. Also, mothers who were younger and had less education and lower incomes were more likely to rate their children as difficult than did older, more educated, higher-income mothers. Further, teacher ratings of the children's behavior yielded some important results.

Teacher ratings of preschool children's behaviors by the categories in Figure 3–4 were examined in relation to mothers working full-time, part-time, or not working outside the home. Each of the high-end scores is marked with an asterisk. Keep in mind that high scores indicate difficulty relating to the characteristics of the preschool children. For mothers not working outside the home, only the "Hesitant" category was noted as significantly troublesome by preschool teachers. It is possible that children whose mothers are not employed outside the home have had fewer external social experiences, and thus, demonstrated hesitancy in social encounters in

Figure 3–4	Mothers' Work Status by Teachers' Ratings of Children's Behavior		

Not Working	Working Part Time	Working Full Time
Sociable	*	
Difficult		*
Hesitant	*	
Aggressive		*
Prosocial		*
Asocial		*
Hyperactive/Distracted		*
Anxious/Fearful	(No significant findings)	
Excluded	(No significant findings)	

preschool. For mothers who worked part-time, only "Sociable" was noted as a troublesome factor. This may be because some children experience inconsistency in their caregiving arrangements and other aspects of the daily schedule when mothers work part-time, thus leading to the possibility of difficulties in getting along with others. Teachers noted more areas of difficulty in children whose mothers worked fulltime: difficult temperament, including slower to accept new experiences and a greater frequency of negative emotional responses to others; higher levels of aggression; fewer pro-social interactions and more asocial behaviors; and greater levels of hyperactive/distracted behaviors.

One of the important concepts demonstrated in this study is the complexity of children's behavior and the outcomes of maternal employment. It is important to use information such as this in ways that positively affect all children and families in children's school experiences. For example, early childhood teachers can plan ways to support children who are socially hesitant in preschool. Another example is to redirect aggressive behaviors so that these children can have more successful social experiences.

It is important to note that this study does not show causal relationships between children's social characteristics and maternal employment. That is, one cannot stipulate from this study that maternal employment causes preschoolers to be aggressive or

asocial. It is possible that families sometimes choose for children to attend various types of preschools (including full-day child care) because they have assessed that their children would benefit from more social experiences with other children. This view might lead parents to make the choice for mothers to be employed outside the home. Additionally, there are other external factors that were not examined in this study, such as presence or lack of family-friendly characteristics in the workplace, extended family or other social supports for the family, special needs of children or siblings, marital satisfaction, and many others. More research needs to be conducted using a variety of factors before one can conclude that maternal employment causes particular social characteristics, positive or negative, in children. This is an important caveat, because the media often publicizes studies such as this one and suggests causal results that are not, in fact, supported by the research.

A primary stressor for working parents is a breakdown in their child care arrangements. Often, this happens when children are ill or their caregiver has an emergency. Further, a lack of empathy and negativism from the child's caregiver has a negative effect on both the mother's and the child's well-being. One of the most severe causes of distress for employed mothers and their children is inconsistency of caregivers.

In addition to child care worries, a variety of other workplace characteristics take a toll on employed moms. Those most notably affecting both marriage and children's development are overly demanding jobs, heavy workloads, job insecurity, long hours with no flexibility, lack of autonomy and lack of control over work schedules, unsupportive supervisors and coworkers, an unsupportive social atmosphere, and the perception of discriminatory practices. While long hours and demanding jobs are typically problematic, many fathers and mothers with complex, challenging jobs that they like have been found to be warmer, more responsive, and firmer with their children (Galinsky, 1994).

Parcel and Menaghan (1994) note the importance of examining information regarding both parents' employment rather than studying maternal employment alone. The title of their book, *Parents'*

Jobs and Children's Lives, represents their primary research question: How does parental employment affect children's cognitive and social development? Results of this study show complex ways in which children are affected by employment of their parents. Some of the more remarkable conclusions follow.

At ages three to six years, children's verbal facility, including vocabulary development, was related to both maternal and paternal characteristics, as well as to the home environment. Verbal facility was higher when the mother's work was complex and she received a good salary; verbal skill was also higher when the father had higher hourly wages. When either or both parents clocked overtime work, children's verbal ability was likely to be hindered. Married mothers with fewer children were likely to have preschoolers who had greater verbal skills.

Later reading and math achievement of children ages six to eight years was also related to some parental characteristics and the home environment. Parents' levels of education, as well as their hourly wages, were positively related to children's reading ability. Children who had higher reading achievement scores were likely to have mothers who were employed in more complex work. One exception to this, however, was when mothers had complex jobs and family size was increasing. In these cases, reading skills of young children were negatively affected. Children whose fathers worked less than full-time were negatively affected in their reading ability. Math skills were positively related to mothers' age and education but had no relation to fathers' age or education.

As with reading skill, math achievement was higher for children whose parents had higher hourly wages and when mothers' work had greater complexity. Some additional characteristics were noted for families of children who had higher math skill: One level of maternal part-time employment (21 to 34 hours per week) showed a positive association, while another level of part-time employment (35 to 40 hours per week) showed a negative association. The researchers speculate that when mothers work 21 to 34 hours per week, they may actually have less spousal support for home and family responsibilities, and/or inconsistent childcare arrangements. Both of these circumstances may increase stress and cause a

less positive home environment for children. (It is not clear why these employment patterns did not affect reading achievement in the same way.) Finally, math achievement was also higher in stable marriages and lower when a marriage ended or the family head was stably single. It seems that young children's math skill is more dependent on various home and family characteristics than is reading achievement.

Behavior problems were also examined in relation to parental characteristics, employment, and the home environment (Parcel & Menaghan, 1994). Mothers with positive self-concepts and higher levels of education were less likely to have children who manifested behavioral problems. Further, higher maternal wages, stable marriages, and stronger home environments were negatively associated with children's behavior problems.

Over and over again, this research points to the fact that maternal employment alone is not responsible for children's academic achievement or social development. Rather, complex interactions help to explain the child outcomes. In summary, when parents' time and energy are stretched too far, often due to both work and family situations, then children's development is likely to be hindered. However, when employment provides satisfaction and an increase in resources for the family without stretching parents too far, children are likely to benefit.

Companies are increasingly providing more work-family assistance to help families balance job and home responsibilities. Even though more work site programs, such as child care assistance, flexible time, and part-time and leave policies, are offered, it is typically those with higher job status who have more choices and greater access to these programs. Thus, white, upper-middle-class employees are receiving the bulk of these forms of support from employers. Although families that receive such supports from employers find them to be extremely helpful, this is yet another example of ways in which the gap between the haves and have-nots is increasing in today's society (Galinsky, 1994).

Much of Galinsky's research at the Families and Work Institute confirms the increasing incidence of family support programs in the workplace. It seems that corporations go through stages in their understanding of what types of family support programs are good for families and good for companies. Two areas of current interest are greater training for supervisors about how to support employees' family needs and creation of a family-friendly culture in the workplace.

Galinsky (1994) notes that our societal beliefs about work need to change if we are going to support families to a greater degree. Some of the traditional "deep-seated beliefs" that she says must change include the following:

- Time equals commitment.
- Presence equals productivity.
- People have to sink or swim.
- People issues and work issues are different.
- If it isn't unpleasant, it isn't work.
- If you give employees an inch, they'll take a mile.
- Employees must sacrifice their personal needs to get ahead.
- There is no connection between the work-family problems of employees and the company's productivity (p. 132).

Some beliefs that should replace these are the following:

- It is better to focus on work tasks than work time.
- People perform better when they are not hampered by personal pressures.
- Flexibility is a competitive issue and a management tool.
- Manage by empowering, rather than controlling (p. 132).

When workplaces provide more support to families, children reap the benefits. When children have greater opportunities for optimal development, all of society benefits.

Galinsky (1999) has more recently turned her research endeavors to asking children what they think about parental employment. One aspect of this research was concerned with children's views of the parenting they were receiving and measured this factor by using descriptor phrases such as "good values," "someone I can talk with," "appreciates me," and "is involved with my school." No differences were found in responses from children whose mothers were or were not employed outside the home. Other areas that this study examined included amount of time spent with parents, child care, and the effects of parents' jobs on children and child development. Results included the finding that children who spend more time with their parents when their parents were relaxed and calm saw them in a more positive way. Both quantity and quality of time matter to children. More children reported too little time with their fathers than reported too little time with their mothers.

Only half of the children in the study believed that their child care experiences were positive. Those children generally also felt that child care was good for their development. The problem here, however, is that too little high-quality child care exists to meet the needs of all children (Galinsky, 1999).

When children see that their parents are tired and stressed from their jobs, they often worry about their parents. Even though parents in this study seemed to be out of sync with their children's feelings, the children reported that the one thing they would change if they could is that their parents would be less stressed and less tired. Further, it was found that parents often do not share much information about their jobs with their children; they seem to see work as competing with children. This observation led some children to believe that parents did not like their jobs, when in fact, those parents reported liking their jobs (Galinsky, 1999).

This study broke new ground regarding the assumptions that adults make about work and children. Understanding the views of children can lead adults to behaviors that will yield more positive outcomes for children. These behaviors include spending a good amount of high-quality time with children, finding ways to reduce job stress, getting enough rest, understanding how to choose high-quality child care, and talking with children about some about the joys and challenges in their work.

Child Care

High-quality, affordable child care is not readily accessible to many families. The most common form of out-of-home child care used by families that need it is provided by friends or relatives in their home. In 1982, this was true for 63 percent of families needing out-of-home care (Hofferth, as cited in Greenman, 1984). But the number of child care centers and family day homes has increased dramatically in the past three decades. By 2002, of the 63 percent of children who were reported to have a regular arrangement for child care, 40 percent were in relative care and 14 percent were in non-relative care either in the home of the child's family or of the provider. About 35 percent of children under five who had a child care arrangement in 2002 were enrolled in some type of center or preschool facility. Approximately 6 percent of children in care were placed in licensed family home care. Also, 37 percent of children under five had no regular child care arrangement (Johnson, 2005).

> *"We have to ask whether this nurturance is possible in settings where caregivers are caring for four or more babies (and later six or more toddlers), are paid minimal wage, and given little training and little incentive to avoid staff turnover (among those who can get better jobs)."*

—Brazelton and Greenspan, 2000, pp. xiii–xiv

A variety of forms of nonparental or out-of-home care are possible. For many families, coming up with the best child care arrangement is a huge challenge. Families often decide from among the following choices: care by another family member, employing someone to come into the home (a nanny or au pair), family home child care, center care, or many combinations of these. States require child care centers to be licensed and many require family home caregivers to be registered or licensed. To best advocate for children, parents must understand the importance of licensed care. Essentially, state licenses demand only minimum requirements for conditions that maintain the health and safety of children. All children deserve at least this amount of protection.

A lot of attention has been given to the **child care "trilemma."** How can we balance quality of care, compensate child caregivers fairly, and keep quality care affordable for families?

Let's begin with the first point of the "trilemma." The importance of good quality care for children was mentioned previously in the section on families and work. Parents are more productive when they feel good about their children's care. A great deal of research on the outcomes of child care for children shows that when the care is of high quality, children flourish; but when the care is not good, it may be harmful to children's development. For example, children in high-quality care have been found to have higher mathematical ability, better thinking and attention skills, fewer behavioral problems, better work habits, and better relationships with peers than children in lower-quality child care situations. On the other hand, children in low-quality care have been found to have language and reading delays and to display more problematic aggression toward other children (Children's Defense Fund, 2005).

What is high-quality child care? Evidence from numerous studies of high-quality child care suggests that multiple components are necessary for positive outcomes in children's development. These components include:

- responsive adult-child interaction, including positive strategies for guiding children's behavior

- developmentally appropriate and effective curriculum that includes considerations for the academic integrity of curriculum selected

- authentic assessment that provides information to caregivers for planning curriculum as well as to share children's development, progress, and concerns with children's families

- family involvement in children's learning and development, both in and out of child care

- early education professionals who are well-prepared in child development and early childhood education

- small group sizes and good ratios of adults to children in the classroom

Some states have considered some or all of these components in their licensing requirements for child care homes and centers. However, given the still large number of centers that provide minimal or poor-quality care for young children, concerns in regard to increasing quality of child care continue. Since 1987, the National Association for the Education of Young Children (NAEYC) has administered a voluntary national early childhood program accreditation system. This accreditation requires that programs meet all of the criteria for providing high-quality care and education for young children and their families. Accreditation is one way for families to judge whether or not a child care center will provide good care for their child or children. (See Appendix C for NAEYC Accreditation Criteria.)

> *"High quality child care and early education are critical to the success of two national priorities: helping families work and ensuring that every child enters school ready to succeed."*
>
> **—Children's Defense Fund, April 2005**

The second point in the child care "trilemma" is that quality care is not cheap. In our society, parents are generally required to pay tuition. To make child care affordable for families, quality is too often compromised. One of the most serious problems with maintaining quality care is the high staff turnover. Turnover is high primarily because wages are low. It is not uncommon for child caregivers to earn minimum wage and to be employed part-time without benefits. It is not an exaggeration to state that parking lot attendants are usually paid better than child caregivers.

The Children's Defense Fund recently surveyed child care centers in cities and rural areas across the country (Schulman, 2000). This survey found a typical tuition range per year for child care for a four-year-old was $4,000 to $6,000, or more than $300 to $500 per month. Some child care costs as much as $10,000 per year for a four-year-old. Infant care is much more expensive than care for a preschooler, due in part to the smaller ratios of caregiver to child. Infant care was found to generally cost about $1,100 more per year than care for a four-year-old, or more than $400 to nearly $600 per month. Cost for child care was slightly lower in rural areas, ranging from $3,000 to $6,000 per year for a four-year-old. The average cost for infant care in rural areas was more than $4,500 per year. In many cities around the country, four years of child care cost more than four years of public college tuition. Consider the cost of child care in relation to the fact that many families with young children earn less than $25,000 per year. Further, a family with two parents working full-time at minimum wage jobs earns a little more than $21,000 per year. Clearly, the reality of child care costs hits working families' budgets quite hard—many families who live above the poverty level spend about 7 percent of their income for child care for one child.

Center for the Child Care Workforce
http://www.ccw.org/home/

Child Care Aware
http://www.childcareaware.org/

National Association for Family Child Care (NAFCC)
http://www.nafcc.org

National Association for the Education of Young Children—Accreditation
http://www.naeyc.org/
Click on "Accreditation"

National Child Care Information Center
http://nccic.org/

National Network for Child Care
http://www.nncc.org/

Wheelock College Institute for Leadership and Career Initiatives
http://institute.wheelock.edu

> Survey several centers in your region to calculate costs of child care for one year for a 4-year-old child and a 12-month-old child.

Several sources exist for helping families with low incomes to fund child care. The federal government provides such funding for families through the Child Care and Development Block Grant (CCDBG). These funds are limited, however, and it has been estimated that only one in seven of children who are eligible for funding actually receives it. Further, most states' funding guidelines are such that families making $25,000 per year are not eligible for these funds. A small amount of child care funding also is available through various state programs, the Temporary Assistance to Needy Families (TANF) program, and the Social Services Block Grant (SSBG) (Children's Defense Fund, 2005). Even with these sources, however, "the current funding level for child care assistance does not come close to meeting the needs of low-income working families" (Children's Defense Fund, 2005, p. 1).

As noted earlier, a critical component of high-quality child care is well-prepared early childhood education professionals. At this time, child care staff are not compensated in a manner that keeps them in the field. Low wages and the lack of benefits are related to the high turnover of child care staff, leading to another obstacle in maintaining quality programs for young children. Due to lack of rigorous requirements for these positions, coupled with low pay and absence of benefits, many caregivers of young children have little or no preparation for understanding children's development. Yet, they are entrusted to care for our youngest children.

In 2002, median hourly earnings for child care workers was less than $8.00, with the lowest 10 percent earning less than $6.00 per hour and the highest 10 percent earning more than $11.00 per hour. While benefits vary by place of employment, they are typically negligible (Bureau of Labor Statistics, 2004–05).

> *"There's a strong link between staff pay and the quality of the care children receive. Centers that are able to retain highly-trained staff are more likely to sustain high-quality care over time."*
>
> **—Wages and Quality, 2001**

Extended Family Relationships

With the prevalence of the nuclear family image as the ideal for today's society, **extended family relationships,** especially those with grandparents, are frequently overlooked in early education programs. "The separation of families into generational subsystems, referred to as the 'nuclear' and the 'extended' family, creates artificial separation of parts of a family" (Carter & McGoldrick, 1999, p. 11). However, it is true that unlike the common family configuration of

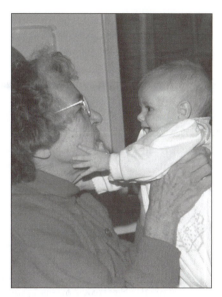

Extended family relationships, especially those of grandparents, are frequently overlooked.

two generations ago in the United States, most children do not live in homes with both their parents and grandparents. During the postwar, mid-twentieth century, the quality of living rose quickly for young families, and so it was expected that they would form their own households. This trend, however, has resulted in "vital connections" (Kornhaber & Woodward, 1981) between grandparents and grandchildren going unrealized. These researchers note that the missed connections are a detriment to both the children and the aging members of families. It should be noted, however, that many children have close emotional connections with their grandparents even if they do not share a residence with them. And, some grandparents intentionally forge these relationships even when geographic distance separates them from their grandchildren.

In their study of about 300 grandchildren ages 5 to 18 years, Kornhaber and Woodward (1981) noted that only about 5 percent of them had an intimate connection with at least one grandparent. This emotional closeness was fostered mostly by spending time together; no other factor was as critical to forming vital connections. Grandchildren who are given the gift of grandparents form emotional bonds second only to those they have with their parents. Because the parent-child relationship can be overcome by conflict at various times in the family life cycle, the grandchild-grandparent bond can serve a stabilizing purpose in the emotional life of children. With grandparents, children often feel unconditional acceptance and warmth. This study noted that when children do not have a grandparent-like relationship, they may suffer an emotional loss: ". . . grandparents and grandchildren are naturally at ease with each other while both have intense emotional relationships with the middle generation . . . grandparents and grand-children do not have to do anything to make each other happy. Their happiness comes from being together" (p. xiii).

The emphasis on the nuclear family often generates a perception of grandparents as "meddlers" or "child spoilers" rather than as people who can help to support the family (Kornhaber & Woodward, 1981). Given this view and the accompanying feeling of being unneeded, many grandparents move away from their grandchildren when the grandparents retire. Approximately 90 percent of grandchildren in this study had only sporadic contact with their grandparents, and the children and grandparents did not really know much about each other. Divorce also threatens grandparent-grandchild relationships. The divorce of children's parents often means that the children do not have intimate contact with at least some of their grandparents. Grandparents, parents, and grandchildren all seem to believe that a lack of grandparenting relationships in children's lives is not a tremendous loss. But today's families are overlooking history: "For the 40,000 years that humankind has been known to exist, children have typically been raised in tribes, clans, and variously extended networks of kin" (p. xix).

Foundation for Grandparenting
http://www.grandparenting.org

Grandparents Rights Center
http://www.grandparentsrights.org

If grandparents have lost their social significance in the United States, the research by Kornhaber and Woodward demonstrates that they remain an important emotional attachment for grandchildren. "Society . . . cannot change what a grandparent means to a grandchild" (p. 167).

. . . the real experts on the aged are children. Only children understand what elders are for, and only they can meet the real need of the aged: the need to be needed. Children need grandparents and grandparents need children, whether they are their own flesh and blood kin or surrogate grandchildren. And until these mutual needs are acknowledged and supported, the aged will never achieve more than begrudging respect, much less outright affection, as elders in American society. (p. 167)

Kornhaber (1996) has continued to collect data for the Grandparent Study that he and his associates began in the 1970s. Current results confirm prior findings of the "existence of a unique emotional relationship between grandparent and grandchild" (p. 36). An important positive characteristic of effective grandparent-grandchild relationships is a feeling of joy and fun. The following anecdote is one example of those feelings between a grandmother and her granddaughter.

Four-year-old Chelsea, who lives next door to her grandmother, frequently calls ahead to schedule play time with her. They play games together as well as engage in some messy play such as fingerpainting. Chelsea's grandmother, Dee, admits to trying to avoid the mess of fingerpainting one evening by reminding Chelsea that the plastic clothing protector that came with the fingerpaints had torn. Knowing the resourcefulness of her grandmother, Chelsea countered with, "You can find something to cover my clothes, Mumma." Sure enough, they found an old towel and the fingerpainting activity was on! Both parties reported having fun.

The Grandparent Study shows, of course, that roles are changing for women and men. Many contemporary women, having experienced the world of work outside the home, are now striving for a better balance between their work lives and home lives. One way many of them are attempting to do this is to reduce the number of hours they work outside of the home and to increase the amount of time they spend with family members. This seems to be good news for grandchildren. Grandfathers who may have had little time to spend with children earlier in their lives also seem to be setting priorities that involve their grand-children. One grandfather who worked two full-time jobs for many years found a great deal of pleasure in the time he spent with his preschool-aged grandson. As the grandson grew to adulthood, this relationship changed from playful interaction to one of genuine friendship. Other family members noted through the years how this pair seemed to really enjoy being together.

While role changes in contemporary society seem to contribute positively to grandparenting, some changes in contemporary families complicate the grandparenting role. In instances of divorce and remarriage, for example, the complexity of relation-ships or the sheer number of children and parents in-volved may interfere with children spending time with grandparents. The increased variations in family structure also contributes to confusion among family members about roles and identities. Some of these variations include:

- an increase in single-parent families
- single grandparents
- blended families
- grandparents serving as parents
- gay and lesbian partnerships (Kornhaber, 1996)

The research discussed above and a study by Kivnick (1982) examined the effects that grandchil-dren have on grandparents. Grandparents noted the following:

- recall of their own parenthood experiences as they anticipate birth of their first grandchild
- feelings of joy about arrival of grandchild, even when the timing of that birth was wrong for so-cial reasons
- wandering thoughts of immortality, connec-tions, spirituality
- impulse to see, hold, hear, care for, and indulge baby
- grandparent role central to their lives

- enjoying role as valued and esteemed elder in family

Kivnick (1982) found that grandparents at-tached a great deal of meaning to their roles with grandchildren and that the strength of this value was connected to the mental health of grandparents. The role of grandparent seemed to enhance the quality of life for the aging, thus contributing to positive mental health.

Research makes clear the importance of grand-children and grandparents in each other's lives. Some attention must be given to the middle genera-tion, the parents, so that they, too, might see the benefits of grandparents' presence in their children's lives. The need that young parents have to be

Figure 3–5	Guidelines and Ideas for Long-Distance Grandparents

- Find ways to continuously maintain communication
- Schedule family conferences to plan for continuous communication
- Discuss the difficulties of long-distance grandpar-enting with children's parents
- Pledge to spend as much time together as possible
- Create an action plan for ways and times to spend together
- Determine ways to use financial and material re-sources in ways that increase time to be together
- Plan for time for grandparent(s)/grandchild(ren) to spend together without presence of parents
- Make frequent use of technology. Give grandchil-dren disposable cameras to take pictures to send to you. Consider giving them a fax machine or a long distance phone card to stay in touch with you.
  - E-mail
  - Videoconference
  - Fax
  - Telephone
  - All forms of mail, including "snail" mail
  - Videotapes
  - Audiotapes

Source: Long-Distance Grandparenting
(www.grandparenting.org/Long-Distance.htm)

independent in this society detracts from the real support that grandparents can give, especially to their grandchildren. Although much of the research emphasizes the biological connection between grandparents and grandchildren, especially from the view of the grandparent enough information exists to support the value of the grandparent role in children's lives, and of the grandchild role in the lives of the aging, to give credence to programs for surrogate grandparents and grandchildren.

The following factors mentioned by Kornhaber and Woodward (1981) apply to surrogate situations as well as biological ones:

- young children are in awe of the elderly and can delight them
- the young and old have more time "to be"; parents are at an age where they must produce
- grandparents and grandchildren are relatively free of emotional conflict with each other
- grandparents are voices out of other times
- grandfathers are especially important as male figures for today's children who are so frequently missing those in their lives

In order to understand the value that grandparents have for children: observe interactions between young children and their grandparents, reflect on your own experiences with grandparents, and ask people of all ages about their relationships with their grandparents.

At age three, Chelsea was given an assignment in her preschool class to draw a picture of something for which she was thankful. She drew someone: her grandmother. Several months after Thanksgiving and that assignment, the drawing still has a special place on the grandmother's refrigerator. (Figure 3–6)

Neugarten and Weinstein devised five styles of grandparenting in 1964, a classification that continues to be useful to researchers and practitioners (Smith, 1995):

- formal—using prescribed roles for differentiating grandparents from parents
- fun seeker—viewing grandchildren as satisfying, and a primary role is to have fun with them

- surrogate parent—providing care for grandchildren
- reservoir of family wisdom—dispensing guidance, skills, or points of view to grandchildren
- distant—little contact with grandchildren, usually only for ritual occasions

It is likely that the style of grandparenting influences the grandparent-grandchild relationship. In addition to grandparents' style, other factors may affect these relationships. For example, grandparents' ages and health status affect their activity levels with grandchildren.

The most common source of child care for single-parent families is grandparents (Kennedy & Keeney, as cited in Smith, 1995). While this is true for all families, African-American grandmothers have long served as surrogate parents, often being more active in the parenting role than fathers who were present in the home (Pearson, Hunter, Ensminger, & Kellam, as cited in Smith, 1995). Grandparents who assisted teen mothers with children younger than two years of age were studied by Oyserman, Radin, and Benn (as cited in Smith, 1995). Although

Figure 3–6   "I am thankful for Mumma." Preschooler's drawing.

grandmothers in this study had little measured effect on children, the role of grandfathers as male role models for "nurturance and cooperation" was noted. It is generally seen as a positive for young children to have grandparents assist with parental roles.

Smith (1995) discusses two areas of practical concern related to grandparenting in contemporary society.

1. Workshops for effective grandparenting, with the purpose of helping to strengthen family relationships and communication.

2. Legislation in all fifty states providing grandparents with visitation rights when parents of their grandchildren divorce.

The existence of these two phenomena suggests that grandparents see their roles as relevant to the lives of their grandchildren. And as the research shows, grandchildren and grandparents often benefit.

Practical and Ethical Considerations

Family Support Principles

Considering the seven evidence-based principles of family support that can be found near the end of Chapter 1 in this book, the following five principles are most relevant to the developmental issues in families with young children. Of particular note is that the last four principles point to the need for society to support families in meeting their responsibilities to their children. In a complex, technological society such as that found in the United States, families cannot meet all of the needs of their children without support from other institutions. At the same time, such support to families helps them to meet their responsibilities to their children, forming the foundation of strong families for society.

- The developmental processes that make up parenthood and family life create needs that are unique at each stage in the life span. This chapter points out some of the salient and common concerns of families who have young children.

Based on current evidence, these issues include: the transition to parenthood, sibling relationships, work and family matters, child care, and relating to extended family members.

- Primary responsibility for the development and well-being of children lies within the family, and all segments of society must support families as they rear their children.

- Ensuring the well-being of all families is the cornerstone of a healthy society, and requires universal access to support programs and services.

- Enabling families to build on their own strengths and capacities promotes the healthy development of children.

- Families are empowered when they have access to information and other resources and take action to improve the well-being of children, families, and communities.

Code of Ethical Conduct

The National Association for the Education of Young Children (NAEYC) has developed a Code of Ethical Conduct for early childhood professionals. (See Appendix B for this Code in its entirety.) Noted here are the ideals for early childhood professionals in their work with families. Ethical responsibilities to families:

- To be familiar with the knowledge base related to working effectively with families and to stay informed through continuing education and training.

- To develop relationships of mutual trust and create partnerships with the families we serve.

- To welcome all family members and encourage them to participate in the program.

- To listen to families, acknowledge and build upon their strengths and competencies, and learn from families as we support them in their task of nurturing children.

- To respect the dignity and preferences of each family and to make an effort to learn about its structure, culture, language, customs, and beliefs.

- To acknowledge families' childrearing values and their right to make decisions for their children.

- To share information about each child's education and development with families and to help them understand and appreciate the current knowledge base of the early childhood profession.

- To help family members enhance their understanding of their children and support the continuing development of their skills as parents.

- To participate in building support networks for families by providing them with opportunities to interact with program staff, other families, community resources, and professional services (http://www.naeyc.org/about/positions/PSETH05.asp).

> **Consider the nine ideals for early childhood professionals' responsibilities to families in relation to each of the developmental issues for families with young children as discussed in this chapter. Discuss the strengths that you possess and challenges you face in regard to these ethical ideals.**

Summary and Conclusions

Although families differ in many ways, families rearing young children are likely to face similar situations and transitions. Family systems theorists point to this period in the family life cycle as a "pressure cooker," because parents with young children often are also in the early stages of their career or work life. Jobs may be less stable and incomes may be inadequate to support the family. Balancing family and work is a complicated, and ongoing task. Concerns related to caring for children, both in and out of the home, abound. New parents must establish new identities,

seeing themselves as mothers and fathers for the first time. Relating to extended families and in-laws may be challenging.

All families with young children need support. This support may come from other family members, friends, neighbors, and/or community groups. Families with too little support may require more from their children's early childhood programs. Teachers must be aware of all the demands and pressures made on families as they rear their young children. This knowledge serves as a foundation for incorporating practices into early childhood education that support families at this stage of the life cycle.

Chapter 3 Applications

1. The societal concern about the negative effects of maternal employment on young children was not echoed in the welfare reform legislation (as discussed in Chapter 2). Comment on why you believe the concerns were ignored in this legislation.

2. Plan and implement a way to disseminate information to parents of young children about the components of quality child care as provided in the National Accreditation Criteria.

3. Review and discuss the Faber and Mazlish model for parents to use in limiting sibling rivalry.

Questions for Reflection and Discussion

1. How would you explain the notion of family transitions to someone who has not read this chapter? What do family transitions mean for children in your care?

2. Can you provide examples from your own life of ways in which the macrosystem and exosystem have affected you?

3. What does the term "trilemma" mean in the child care discussion? Give an example from a real-life or hypothetical family situation.

4. Of what importance to your career in early childhood education is the discussion about grandparents?

Field Assignments *Jessica*

1. Interview some grandparents of young children (birth to eight years) about the role they have in their grandchildren's lives. Ask about their satisfaction with their role; would they change anything about it if they could?

2. Interview parents of young children about changes they made in their work and family life after the birth of their first child. What factors have facilitated their transition to parenthood? What factors have served as barriers? What work and family situations do these parents suggest would have been helpful?

3. Interview an early childhood educator about the effects she believes that maternal employment might have on the lives of young children.

4. Observe an early childhood program that has been accredited by the National Academy of Early Childhood Programs. Using the accreditation criteria highlighted in this chapter, note evidence of the criteria during the time of your observation.

References

Anderson, E. R., & Rice, A. M. (1992). Sibling relationships during remarriage. In E. M. Hetherington & W. G. Clingempeel (Eds.), *Coping with marital transitions: A family systems perspective.* Monographs of the Society for Research in Child Development, 57 (2–3, Serial No. 227, pp. 149–177).

Bradt, J. O. (1989). Becoming parents: Families with young children. In B. Carter & M. McGoldrick (Eds.), *The changing family life cycle.* Boston: Allyn & Bacon.

Brazelton, T. B., & Greenspan, S. I. (2000). *The irreducible needs of children: What every child must have to grow, learn and flourish.* Cambridge, MA: Perseus.

Brody, G. H. (June 2004). Siblings' direct and indirect contributions to child development. *Current Directions in Psychological Science, 13* (3), 124–126.

Brody, G. H. (1998). Sibling relationship quality: Its causes and consequences. *Annual Review of Psychology, 49* (1), 1–24.

Bronfenbrenner, U. (1990). Discovering what families do. In D. Blankenhorn, S. Bayme, & J. B. Elshtain (Eds.), *Rebuilding the nest: A new commitment to the American family.* Milwaukee, WI: Family Service America.

Bronfenbrenner, U. (2001). The bioecological theory of human development. In U. Bronfenbrenner (Ed.), *Making human beings human: Bioecological perspectives on human development* (pp. 3–15). Thousand Oaks, CA: Sage.

Buhrmester, D. (1992). The developmental courses of sibling and peer relationships. In F. Boer & J. Dunn (Eds.), *Children's sibling relationships: Developmental and clinical issues* (pp. 19–40). Hillsdale, NJ: Lawrence Erlbaum Associates.

Bureau of Labor Statistics. (2004–05). *Occupational outlook handbook, 2004–05 Edition, Childcare workers.* Washington, DC: U.S. Department of Labor. http://www.bls.gov/oco/ocos170.htm. Retrieved December 14, 2005.

Carter, B. (1999). Becoming parents: The family with young children. In B. Carter & M. McGoldrick (Eds.), *The expanded family life cycle: Individual, family, and social perspectives* (3rd ed.). Boston: Allyn & Bacon.

Carter, B., & McGoldrick, M. (1999). Overview: The expanded family life cycle: Individual, family and social perspectives. In B. Carter & M. McGoldrick (Eds.), *The expanded family life cycle: Individual, family, and social perspectives* (3rd ed.). Boston: Allyn & Bacon.

Cheal, D. (1996). *New poverty: Families in postmodern society.* Westport, CT: Greenwood.

Children's Defense Fund. (April 2005). *Child care basics.* Washington, DC: Children's Defense Fund.

Condon, J. T., Boyce, P., & Corkindale, C. J. (2004). The first-time fathers study: A prospective study of the mental health and wellbeing of men during the transition to parenthood. *Australian and New Zealand Journal of Psychiatry, 38,* 56–64.

Cowan, C. P., & Cowan, P. A. (1995). Interventions to ease the transition to parenthood: Why they are needed and what they can do. *Family Relations, 44,* 412–423.

Deater-Deckard, K., Dunn, J., & Lussier, G. (2002). Sibling relationships and social-emotional adjustment in different family contexts. *Social Development, 11* (4), 571–590.

Employment characteristics of families in 2001. Bureau of Labor Statistics. http://www.bls.gov/cps. Retrieved October 19, 2002.

Faber, A., & Mazlish, E. (1987). *Siblings without rivalry: How to help your children live together so you can live too.* New York: Avon.

Falbo, T. (1992). Social norms and the one-child family. In F. Boer & J. Dunn (Eds.), *Children's sibling relationships: Developmental and clinical issues* (pp. 71–82). Hillsdale, NJ: Lawrence Erlbaum Associates.

Farver, J., Couchenour, D., & Chrisman, K. (1998, July). The relation of maternal employment to mothers' and teachers' ratings of children's temperament and social behavior. Research poster presented at the Biennial Meeting of the International Society for the Study of Behavioural Development. Bern, Switzerland.

Feeney, J., Alexander, R., Noller, P., & Hohaus, L. (2003). Attachment insecurity, depression, and the transition to parenthood. *Personal Relationships, 10,* 475–493.

Florsheim, P., Moore, D., Zollinger, L., MacDonald, J., & Sumida, E. (1999). The transition to parenthood among adolescent fathers and their partners: Does antisocial behavior predict problems in parenting? *Applied Developmental Science, 3* (3), 178–192.

Galinsky, E. (1994). Families and work: The importance of the quality of the work environment. In S. L. Kagan & B. Weissbourd (Eds.), *Putting families first: America's family support movement and the challenge of change.* San Francisco: Jossey-Bass.

Galinsky, E. (1999). *Ask the children: What America's children really think about working parents.* New York: Morrow.

Galinsky, E. (2004). Moms in transition—going back to work. Families and Work Institute. http://www.familiesandwork.org/tips102004.html. Retrieved November 30, 2005.

Galinsky, E., Bond, J. T., Kim, S. S., Backon, L., Brownfield, E., & Sakai, K. (2004). *Overwork in America: When the way we work becomes too much: Executive summary.* Families and Work Institute. http://www.familiesandwork.org. Retrieved November 30, 2005.

Gath, A. (1992). The brothers and sisters of mentally retarded children. In F. Boer & J. Dunn (Eds.), *Children's sibling relationships: Developmental and clinical issues* (pp. 101–108). Hillsdale, NJ: Lawrence Erlbaum Associates.

Ginott, H. G. (1965). *Between parent and child: New solutions to old problems.* New York: Macmillan.

Greenman, J. (1984). Perspectives on quality day care. In J. T. Greenman & R. W. Fuqua (Eds.), *Making day care better: Training, evaluation, and the process of change.* New York: Teachers College Press.

Hernandez, D. J. (1993). *America's children: Resources from family government and the economy.* New York: Russell Sage Foundation.

Hetherington, E. M. (1992). Coping with marital transitions: A family systems perspective. In E. M. Hetherington & W. G. Clingempeel (Eds.), *Coping with marital transitions: A family systems perspective.* Monographs of the Society for Research in Child Development, 57 (2–3, Serial No. 227, pp. 1–14).

Hudson, D. B., Campbell-Grossman, C., Fleck, M. O., Elek, S. M., & Shipman, A. (2003). Effects of the new fathers network on first-time fathers' parenting self-efficacy and parenting satisfaction during the transition to parenthood. *Issues in Comprehensive Pediatric Nursing, 26,* 217–229.

Hudson, D. B., Elek, S. M., & Fleck, M. O. (2001). First-time mothers' and fathers' transition to parenthood: Infant care self-efficacy, parenting satisfaction, and infant sex. *Issues in Comprehensive Pediatric Nursing, 24,* 31–43.

Johnson, J. O. (October 2005). Who's minding the kids? Child care arrangements: Winter 2002. *Current Population Reports, P70-101.* Washington, DC: U.S. Census Bureau.

Keating-Lefler, R., Hudson, D. B., Campbell-Grossman, Fleck, M. O., & Westfall, J. (2004). Needs, concerns, and social support of single, low-income mothers. *Issues in Mental Health Nursing, 25,* 381–401.

Kivnick, H. Q. (1982). *The meaning of grandparenthood.* Ann Arbor, MI: UMI Research Press.

Kornhaber, A. (1996). *Contemporary grandparenting.* Thousand Oaks, CA: Sage.

Kornhaber, A., & Woodward, K. L. (1981). *Grandparents/grandchildren: The vital connection.* Garden City, NY: Anchor Press.

La Rossa, R., & La Rossa, M. M. (1981). *Transition to parenthood: How infants change families.* Beverly Hills, CA: Sage.

LeMasters, E. E. (1957). Parenthood as crisis. *Marriage and Family Living, 19,* 352–355.

Long-Distance Grandparenting. (n.d.). http://www.grand parenting.org/Long-Distance,htm.htm. Retrieved December 14, 2005.

National Association for the Education of Young Children. (April 2005). Code of ethical conduct and statement of commitment. A position statement of the National Association for the Education of Young Children. Washington, DC: NAEYC.

Overturf-Johnson, J., & Downs, B. (2005). Maternity leave and employment patterns: 1961–2000. *Current Population Report, P70-103.* Washington, DC: Census Bureau.

Parcel, T. L., & Menaghan, E. G. (1994). *Parents' jobs and children's lives.* New York: Aldine De Gruyter.

Perren, S., von Wyl, A., Burgin, D., Simoni, H., & von Klitzing, K. (2005). Depressive symptoms and psychosocial stress across the transition to parenthood: Associations with parental psychopathology and child difficulty. *Journal of Psychosomatic Obstetrics & Gynecology, 26* (3), 173–183.

Ram, A., & Ross, H. S. (November/December, 2001). Problem solving, contention, and struggle: How siblings resolve a conflict of interests. *Child Development, 72* (6), 1710–1722.

Ribbens, J. (1994). *Mothers and their children: A feminist sociology of childrearing.* Thousand Oaks, CA: Sage.

Schulman, K. (2000). The high cost of child care puts quality care out of reach for many families. Children's Defense Fund. http://www.childrensdefense.org/pdf/highcost.pdf.

Smith, P. K. (1995). Grandparenthood. In M. H. Bornstein (Ed.), *Handbook of parenting, volume 3: Status and social conditions of parenting* (pp. 89–112). Mahwah, NJ: Lawrence Erlbaum Associates.

Stoneman, Z. (2001). Supporting positive sibling relationships during childhood. *Mental Retardation and Developmental Disabilities Research Reviews, 7,* 134–142.

Van Egeren, L. A. (2004). The development of the coparenting relationship over the transition to parenthood. *Infant Mental Health Journal, 25* (5), 453–477.

Wages and quality in the child care industry. (September/October, 2001). *Jobs, Pay and the Economy.* http://www.uaw.org/publications/jobs_pay/01/0901/jpe04.html. Retrieved December 14, 2005.

Woollett, A., & Parr, M. (1997). Psychological tasks for women and men in the post-partum. *Journal of Reproductive & Infant Psychology, 15* (2), 159–184.

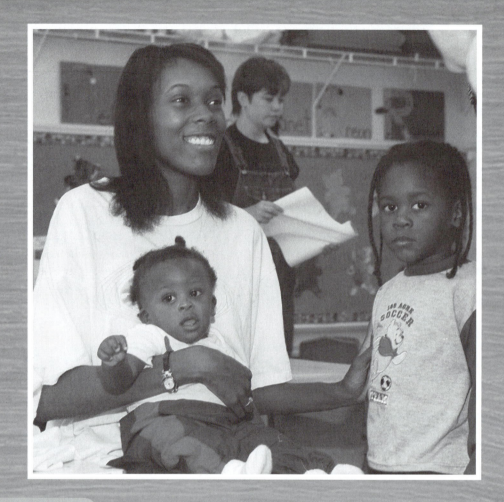

OUTLINE

Objectives

Key Terms

Introduction
Defining Family Strengths,
    Functions, and Structure

Family Strengths
What Makes a Family Strong?
What Factors Support Family
    Strengths?
Resilient Children

Family Functions
Historical and Contemporary
    Purposes of Families
Causes of Change in Family
    Functions
Family Law

Family Structure
Variations in Family Form
The Meaning of Birth Order

**Application of Chapter
    Information**
Family Support
Early Childhood Programs

Summary and Conclusions

Chapter 4 Applications

**Questions for Reflection and
    Discussion**

Field Assignments

References

CHAPTER 4

Family Strengths, Family Functions, and Family Structure

OBJECTIVES

After reading this chapter, you should be able to:

- discuss the meaning of the terms *family strengths*, *family functions*, and *family structure*.
- describe the factors that are related to changes in family strengths, family functions, and family structure.
- apply understanding about the strengths, functions, and structure of families to work in early childhood education.
- discuss factors associated with family resilience.

Key Terms

at-risk children
birth order
extended family
family accord
family functions

family pride
family strengths
family structure
family of orientation
family of procreation

nuclear family
resilient children
right of family integrity
primacy of parental rights

Introduction

Defining Family Strengths, Functions, and Structure

Scholars in family studies attach a great deal of importance to the concepts of **family strengths, family functions,** and **family structure.** It is critical that early childhood educators understand these terms. Thus, the meaning of each of these terms and the research supporting them are discussed in this chapter.

It is important for early childhood teachers to know what makes families strong. A great deal of study on this topic has occurred over the past two decades, and the research indicates that the factors that seem to be routinely related to strong families includeare **family pride** and **family accord.** Characteristics of family pride are mutual respect, trust and loyalty within the family, optimism, and shared values. The critical aspect of family accord is a family's competency in dealing with conflict (Olson, McCubbin, Barnes, Muxen, Larsen, & Wilson, 1989). For example, families that have ways of acknowledging and respecting differences among their members often demonstrate higher levels of accord. To create harmony, families may accept differences among members or use strategies for compromise.

Bioecological Theory   Bronfenbrenner's theory points to the importance of extended families as well as of larger social institutions acting in support of families. Individuals are affected, both positively and negatively, by their microsystems, or nuclear families. Larger social units, including the macrosystem, also affect nuclear families and the individuals within them. As society changes, the functions of the family also change. For example, consider the economic function of the family. As society's emphasis has changed from agrarian to industrial to technological, the family maintains an economic function, but the nature of that function has changed. Most families no longer produce all of their own food; instead, it becomes a function of contemporary families to purchase food from grocery stores, butcher shops, and specialty markets. Today, families are much more likely to pay for food with money rather than with labor.

As the nature of families continues to change, family functions continue to evolve. However, some of these functions change slowly enough that the typical family may not be consciously aware of the ways in which their members meet family responsibilities. Some young families often view such functional change as modern versus "old-fashioned." Others cling to family traditions that might provide positive support, such as grandparents participating in child care or negative responses to flexibility in gender roles. Nonetheless, families continue to remain at the heart of children's development. It is still the family that selects how each function or responsibility is managed.

Bronfenbrenner (1988) explains that families and the larger social contexts are clearly interdependent on one another. Strong families help to support society, and effective social systems are necessary to sustain families in meeting all of their obligations, particularly to young children. This proposition may be one of the best ways to understand the reason that "It takes a village to raise a child." And, certainly such villages must be composed of strong families!

> *"Other settings, such as school, church, or [child] care, are important to a child's development, but none can replace this basic unit of our social system: the family is the most humane, the most powerful, and by far the most economical system known for making and keeping human beings human."*
>
> **—Bronfenbrenner, 1988, p. 146**

Family Systems Theory   Early childhood teachers are most likely to be working with families who have young children, though, of course, not all families fit neatly into one stage at a time. As discussed in the previous chapter, the structure of families with young children changes dramatically with the birth of each new child. Loss of family members, either by death, divorce, or separation, may also occur during this stage. When early childhood educators understand how such losses affect family structure, as well as the common dynamics of families with young children, they can be better prepared to create positive partnerships with families.

Family systems theorists emphasize the stressors related to particular points in the family life cycle. Carter and McGoldrick (1989) note that three changes in family status are required of families as they transition to parenthood. These family status changes are written for two-parent families; however, new parents who are single and parents who are blending families may find that they must negotiate similar status changes in their families.

- *First Family Status Change.* In two-parent families, couples typically have to create space for children in the system that they have already established. How does baby fit in?

  Consider the five points in Figure 4–1 to increase your understanding about making space for children in a family. With these points in mind, what examples or issues have you experienced in your own families or observed in other families that illustrate this status change in families? How might this status change vary for single-parent families or for families with other structures?

- *Second Family Status Change.* Two-parent families must negotiate tasks related to nurturing children, consider new expenses and ways to manage finances, and balance house and family work with employment responsibilities. Figure 4–2

How will I/we take care of baby

Figure 4–1	First Family Status Change

1. Children may be born into a family that has:
   a. no space for them.
   b. space for them.
   c. a vacuum for children to fill.
2. Contemporary families have an emphasis on work outside the home, and devalue events and situations in the domestic sphere, including child-rearing.
3. Young parents often relocate and children then do not have strong ties to extended family members. Fewer available adults leads to less space for children in families.
4. At the other extreme is the child-focused family in which a child fills a vacuum left by a marital partner or the loss of parents' parents.
5. Changes in women's roles have affected family space for children. Women in the workforce are able to time children with more effective birth control methods than in the past. However, many families ignore the "greater complexity of tasks and relationships" (Carter & McGoldrick, p. 242) that the new baby brings (Bradt, 1989).

Source: Carter and McGoldrick, 1989

Figure 4–2	Second Family Status Change

Nurturing Children
- parents must make an emotional adjustment for others to care for their children
- couples arrange work schedules to provide for child care, and rarely see or interact with one another
- adjustment if one parent stays home to provide full-time care, leaving the workforce

Financial Management
- cost of child care
- changes in income related to caring for baby
- decision making related to new expenses for child

Housework
- balancing work and home responsibilities
- societal expectations and gender roles for mothers and fathers
- conflicts about who has each responsibility

Sources: Carter and McGoldrick, 1989; Bradt, 1989

Figure 4–3	Third Family Status Change

Parents
- What does it mean to be a mother? A father?
- How do past experiences influence these views?
- Taking roles and responsibilities of adults
- Must be available to nurture children

Grandparents
- Which set of grandparents is more involved and has more influence with their grandchild?
- How do grandparents affect the marital relationship?
- How much contact do new parents have with their child's grandparents? Has it changed since the birth of the baby?
- How do new grandparents see themselves providing for family continuity over the generations?

Sources: Bradt, 1989; Carter & McGoldrick, 1989

illustrates some of the details regarding the tasks that families need to regulate.

Given the three categories of the second family-status change noted in Figure 4–2, list some ways that families might address the challenges of regulating these tasks. How might single-parent families and two-parent families differ in the way they approach this status change?

- *Third Family Status Change.* Two-parent families find that they need to have new under-standing of themselves as parents and of their own parents as grandparents. As their roles are transformed, parents frequently deal with the issues listed in Figure 4–3. What factors come into play as mothers and fathers incorporate their new identities as parents into their previous identities? How might the relationship transformation differ for single-parent and two-parent families?

How do I now see myself in this new role + how do I now see my spouse + parents?

Consider the relationships that new parents form with their own parents, who are now in the grandparent role. Will these relationships differ according to family structure? Explain differences that might exist.

Olson's revised family map model is also useful for understanding family strengths, functions, and structure (Olson & Gorall, 2003). Through effective communication, families who are undergoing structural changes may find new ways of maintaining their balanced connectedness with one another. The realization that families are dynamic, continually changing in various ways, underscores why it is important that families learn to adjust their communication strategies. Those families who find that they can successfully balance change in ways that sustain their strengths, either with or without professional intervention, may have the greatest opportunity to fulfill all necessary family functions.

For example, one family with two young children, ages 6 years and 18 months, respectively, invited a newly widowed grandmother to reside with them. This change in family structure led to some changes in how functions were met. The grandmother volunteered to provide child care for the six-year-old when she returned from kindergarten each day, as well as provide full-time care for the 18-month-old. This functional change resulted in two additional changes: The parents' communication patterns with the grandmother increased tremendously and their travel time decreased, because they no longer needed to stop at the child care center before and after the commute to work. In addition, more time was available each evening for parents and children to increase their interactions. This family must continue to work to maintain flexibility as the kindergartner moves to first grade next school year and as both the toddler and the grandmother get older. Communication and adaptations will be needed on a regular basis.

Family Strengths

What Makes a Family Strong?

The first studies to examine family strengths occurred during the 1970s. Nick Stinnett (1979) and his associates found the following factors to be present in strong families:

Appreciation. Members of strong families make it a point to express appreciation to other family members. This expression might be through simple "thank-you" statements, performing acts of kindness in return, or giving a gift that recognizes the uniqueness of another family member. Demonstrations of appreciation help to maintain positive relationships in the family through feelings of warmth and caring.

Spending time together. Even though quality time is known to be an important factor for building healthy relationships, some quantity of time in shared activities is necessary as well. Many families have rituals or routines of time that they spend together such as eating dinner (or another meal) around a common table, holiday celebrations, game night, or even watching movies or sports events on television.

Open communication. Conversations at meal time, during leisure activities, or during a called family meeting all contribute to openness in communication. In our contemporary technological society, various forms of electronic communication must be considered, for example, e-mail, voice mail, and text messaging. However, face-to-face communication remains important in that it encompasses some of the other family strengths, such as spending time together and commitment to one another.

Commitment. The sense of commitment in strong families flows not only among individual family members, but also establishes a bond to the family unit. Thus, individual members might work together for the well-being of their family. Certainly, a commitment to supporting one another also adds to a family's strength.

Religious orientation or spirituality. For some families, this dimension relates specifically to religiosity and is practiced through church attendance, prayer, and consideration of scriptural lessons. For other families, spirituality is practiced more broadly in that they "see a larger purpose for their family than simply their own maintenance and self-satisfaction" (*Ages and Stages*, n.d., p. 6). Community or advocacy activities on a local, state, or national level are examples of ways that families might demonstrate this purpose larger than themselves.

Ability to deal with crises in a positive manner. All families *families* face crises, to a lesser or greater degree than others. *could* Part of dealing with a crisis lies in its very definition. *go for* Something that one family deems a crisis, another *assist* family may view as more routine. No matter how a family defines a crisis, strong families handle the stressors that they face in a positive way. This often means by coming together and supporting one another. For example, when a family member is diagnosed with a serious illness, others provide comfort and assistance with pressing responsibilities. Strong families deal with crises in ways that maintain their strengths in that they continue to spend time together, albeit the way they spend time might reduce leisure and increase the time spent working together.

The family strengths approach provides information about what makes a family healthy. Olson and DeFrain (1994) note that many of the strengths listed above can be placed in context with the three dimensions of the family circumplex model. Commitment and spending time together are related to family togetherness or cohesion; ability to deal with crises

Have available resources where

res. dysfunctional

and spirituality facilitate a family's flexibility; and appreciation for one another and effective interaction are aspects of the communication dimension. Early childhood teachers should note that research supports the presence of all of these characteristics in strong families. Teachers can best use this information by supporting families who engage in activities that exemplify these factors rather than criticizing families for a lack of any of these strengths. For example, in some communities, many families attend religious services on a particular night of the week. When teachers are aware of this, they may choose to assign homework on a schedule that supports this practice.

All research perspectives on family strengths indicate that understanding both family relationships and family interactions or behaviors are essential in understanding strong families. Olson (1989) delineated types of interactions that have been described for functional (versus dysfunctional) families. Figure 4–4 provides a list and explanation of eight kinds of interactions. As you read and reflect on these characteristics of functional families, consider how each factor leads to positive outcomes for families. On the other hand, take into account the opposite of each factor listed below (e.g., betrayal instead of pride, deceit rather than support) and the probable negative effects on families.

Figure 4–4	Characteristics of Functional Families

Healthy families

Family pride—Families are unified and loyal; they view their family positively and cooperate with one another.

Family support—Families spend time together and provide love and support to each member for a growth-producing environment.

Cohesion—In addition to cooperating with each other, members respect one another's individuality. Family members are interdependent without being too dependent or too independent.

Adaptability—In the face of change, families can adapt. Tasks may rotate or are completed by those who have time and skill. ✓ *Tasks all fall to one*

Communication—Both sharing of self and careful listening to others is important. *Vs. No listening*

Social support—Family members accept responsibility for supporting community endeavors. *No involvement in comm*

Values—Families who function well know their values and they work to practice and live by them. *Never thought of values*

Joy—Families know how to have fun together. *Don't spend time together*

"Among professionals and scholars who focus on the well-being of children, it is widely recognized that children do not do well unless families do well, and that families do not do well unless communities do well."

—Besaw, Kalt, Lee, Smith, Wilson, and Zemler, 2004, p. 1

Although some recent efforts have been made to include diverse families in research that examines family strengths and functionality, more information is needed about families of different cultures, ethnicities, and structures. One recent report (Besaw, Kalt, Lee, Smith, Wilson, & Zemler, 2004) provides some insight into "family strengthening in Indian America." Not surprisingly, given the importance of understanding any family in context, recent evidence points to the need to emphasize Native self-determination, that is, a plan for tribes to take control of policies and programs for supporting families. In this vein, one of the most important aspects for strengthening Native American families is attending to the sheer diversity among the hundreds of existing tribes.

Governmental efforts to create one-size-fits-all policies for Native Americans have failed for decades. For education professionals to understand why these programs have failed and what plans might work for effectively supporting strong Native families, it is vital that they become aware of two factors. First, educators must understand that the U.S. Constitution views each tribe as sovereign, just as each state and the nation is sovereign. Next, it is essential that educators become aware of the tremendous amount of oppression and discrimination faced by Native Americans, both historically and in the present. "Romanticizing tribal spirituality and culture or seeing it as solely historical is dehumanizing and a source of countless missteps in coming to a full understanding the nuances of the complicated ecological environment of Indian families and communities" (Besaw, et al., 2004, p. 20). Culminating conclusions in this report are:

1. Effective programs and policies for strengthening Native American families are self-determined.

2. Leadership can emerge from multiple levels of tribal society.

3. Family strengthening programs and policies must have "buy-in" from both the tribal community and the formal leadership of the tribe.

4. Effective family strengthening initiatives are institutionalized with the tribal government.

5. Effective family strengthening initiatives have a spiritual core based on the tribe's spiritual practices and beliefs.

6. Effective family strengthening initiatives are clearly based on cultural practices of the specific tribe.

7. Effective family strengthening initiatives focus on multiple systems including individuals, families and the tribe.

8. Effective family strengthening initiatives openly strengthen social networks for both children and families.

9. Effective family strengthening initiatives purposefully invest in the professional skills of trained tribal staff.

This report provides some greatly needed information about specific concerns relating to policies for strengthening Native American families. Clearly, however, more such information is needed to most effectively support all families. Viewing the needs of families through various ecological or systems approaches, such as the authors of this report have done, appears to be a constructive tool for both researchers and practitioners who are in positions to influence family strengths.

What Factors Support Family Strengths?

Because we know that young children are dependent on their families and that families have a tremendous impact on child development, it behooves early childhood professionals to foster ways in which the larger society might support specific factors related to strong families. Further, the family support movement (Kagan & Weissbourd, 1994) emphasizes that all families have strengths and all families need support. Looking for and supporting families' strengths, even in troubled families, is a useful strategy for early childhood teachers as they work to establish family-school partnerships. Figure 4–4 lists family strengths as defined by Kagan and Weissbourd (1994).

Building Family Strengths
http://www.clemson.edu/fyd/bfs.htm

Creating a Strong Family
http://www.extension.unl.edu
Click on "family"; click on "publications";
    click on "families"

Family Support and Children's Mental Health
http://www.rtc.pdx.edu/

From Family Stress to Family Strengths
http://www.cdc.gov
Type in "nasd"; type in "family strengths"

Resilient Children

Since the mid-1980s, researchers have concluded that some children, even in the face of great adversity, manage to overcome the odds against them to become relatively healthy, functioning adults. These **resilient children** exhibit "good developmental outcomes despite high-risk status, sustained competence under stress, and recovery from trauma" (Werner, 1995, p. 81). Most of the research in this area consists of studies of children from one or more of the following situations:

resilient families too.

- families of chronic poverty
- parent(s) suffering from serious psychopathology
- families that broke up in various ways
- children lacking nurturing (Werner, 1995)

Center on the Family
http://uhfamily.hawaii.edu

Family Resilience
http://outreach.missouri.edu/
Type "family resilience" into the Search field

Family Works, Inc.
http://www.familyworksinc.com/

Project Resilience
http://www.projectresilience.com/

By reviewing several longitudinal studies, Werner (1995) notes factors that seem to be consistent for **at-risk children** who proved to be resilient. An important element appears in the resilient child's temperamental makeup. They are easy children: active, affectionate, and good-natured. These children seem to bring forth positive responses from the adults who care for them, and they learn early to cope with adversity both by being self-sufficient and asking for help when they need it (Werner, 1995).

In addition to the child's temperament, family and community components also offer protection for at-risk children. A child who lives amid a great deal of family discord but still builds a relationship with at least one family member who is emotionally competent, stable, and willing to nurture that child, is more likely to become resilient. Further, community members, especially teachers, are often seen as a source of support when at-risk children are facing crises. Characteristics of these teachers are that they ". . . listened to the children, challenged them, and rooted for them . . ." (Werner, 1995, p. 83). Early childhood teachers often are in a prime position to assist and support children who live with so much adversity. Note that the teachers who help resilient children listen to them and demonstrate concern in their ongoing role as educators. Best educational practices in early childhood education call for such behaviors in teacher-child relationships.

Continuing interest in the study of resilience in children is providing access to more details about how families and schools can support children's inner strength to cope with challenges that they face (Brooks & Goldstein, 2001). Based on current research, Brooks and Goldstein explain ten ways that adults can help children to be more resilient or to be "can-do kids":

1. Respond to children empathically. Let them know that you understand their point of view, even when you are attempting to teach them another perspective.

2. Talk with children respectfully. Not only will children give you more attention when you are respectful with them, but they will also experience an excellent model for effectively communicating with others.

3. Be flexible, especially in order to find more effective ways of guiding children's behavior.

4. Provide some time for undivided attention for each child. If this is difficult, build it into your schedule.

5. Be accepting of each child's unique interests and personalities.

6. Create opportunities for children to contribute to the family or classroom. This teaches both helpfulness and responsibility.

7. Call mistakes "learning opportunities." Make it clear that avoiding mistakes also means fewer opportunities to learn something new.

Teachers have helped children by listening to them and demonstrating concern.

Figure 4–5   Family Functions

Economic—Families met their own economic needs; they produced what they needed to consume.

Prestige and Status—The family name was important.

Education—The family provided education, especially in the form of job training and household tasks.

Protection—Adults provided safety for children, and adult children took over this role as parents aged.

Religion—Religious practices in families included grace at meals and daily scripture reading.

Recreation—Home provided relaxation and physical activity for enjoyment.

Affection—Love was shared between spouses and through procreation of children.

8. Become aware of each child's strengths and help each child to see her or his own strengths as well as those of others.

9. Encourage children to solve problems and make decisions. Be present to support them in this process as well as afterwards.

10. Use discipline strategies that teach children self-control.

These ten suggestions might be implemented differently by parents or other family members than by early childhood professionals. Yet, the spirit of each idea can easily be practiced in both home and school settings.

Family Functions

The family is the essential unit for meeting several functions. It has been common for family sociologists to refer to seven traditional functions of the family: economic, prestige and status, education, protection, religion, recreation, and affection (Eshelman, 1988). Figure 4–5 provides a definition for each of these functions.

These functions have been viewed as important since at least the 1930s. As society changes, the precise view of each family function also changes. (For many, these changes evidence a diminished importance of family functions and, in turn, the demise of the family, and perhaps of all society.) Today, family science experts still view these seven functions as important for maintaining strong family units. However, the descriptions and examples for each of the functions have changed over time. These changes are delineated in Figure 4–6.

Families are able to meet the functions in a variety of ways, and a family's structure does not determine its ability to meet the functions. For example, specific demonstrations of affection vary from family to family. One family may express its love with words and another with actions. Some families show love through kisses and others through helping with chores. Further, families of a variety of structures can meet the functions as fully as any other family. It is possible for single parents to meet all of the functional needs for their families just as it is possible for a two-parent family or a blended family to do so. Essentially, the structure of the family does not indicate whether or not family functions are or will be met.

Historical and Contemporary Purposes of Families

Beliefs about family functions are often based on history or tradition, but as society changes, the ways in which families fulfill functions also change.

Figure 4–6	Family Functions, Past and Present

Economic ✓

Past—provided for all needs, goods, and services

Present—purchase many goods and services

Prestige and Status ✓

Past—family name

Present—profession, job responsibility, promotions, social opportunities in community

Education ✓

Past—taught children at home, especially for vocational and household responsibilities

Present—provide access to education, pay for it, advocate for and attain special services, form partnerships with educators

Protection ✓

Past—fathers especially were to keep the family physically safe

Present—choice of neighborhood, related to economic function

Religion

Past—practices in the home

Present—greater responsibility of religious institutions and society to instill spirituality and morality

Recreation

Past—activities and fun planned at home with families

Present—community-oriented sports, arts, nature, parks, and other activities

Affection ✓

Past—love shown through nurturance

Present—love shown by providing of "wants" and through various means of caring

---

Consider the function of education. In earlier times, the family was the primary educator, not only for infants and very young children but also frequently for adolescents, who were taught the family business or trade, as well as the tasks of caring for the home and family. Today, more than half of all families rely on out-of-home care for their babies during the first year of life. Many families seek some form of preschool education for children between the ages of three and five years, and nearly every child who is eligible attends kindergarten. Despite the home schooling movement in the United States, the vast majority of school-age children receive their elementary and secondary education at public or private schools. Further, many adolescents and young adults receive their career training outside the home. And, arguably, little attention or priority is given to youth regarding skills needed to care for homes and families.

Children, Youth & Family Consortium
http://www.cyfc.umn.edu

Forum on Child and Family Statistics
http://www.ChildStats.gov

So, even though the specific tasks of the education function have changed over several generations, families still have a function to seek and provide education for their children. When families need child care services for their infants and toddlers, they must choose from the available options those that best suit the needs of their family and their child. Some families choose to live in particular cities or neighborhoods because of the schools this enables their children to attend. And, frequently, parents and other family members pay for or assist and support students in their post-secondary education. Thus, many families continue to fulfill their function as their children's educators, but the ways in which they do so are very different from the ways of families in the past.

Galinsky and David (1988) quote Urie Bronfenbrenner regarding the connection among child care, families, and work: "One of the most important elements of good quality and one that is not usually discussed, is the importance of linkages between the family, the day care, and the world of work. If the child care enhances the power of family, there are excellent results for the child. If the family is undermined, then the outcome is not beneficial for the child" (p. 420). This comment makes it clear that systems of work, family, and child care affect one another, and that the outcomes for children are very predictable. When workplaces and educational settings hold families in high regard—and let them know it in a variety of ways—children benefit.

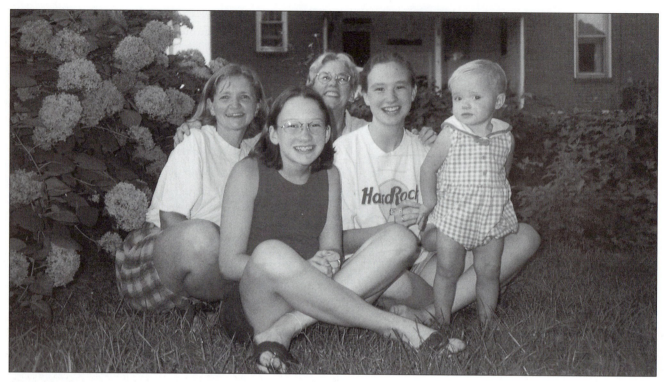

Strong families enjoy one another's company and express affection for one another.

Conversely, it is also important to note that children may be harmed when families are not honored.

Many early childhood programs include the idea of empowering parents as a goal in their family involvement plan. The Cornell Empowerment Group defines *empowerment* as "an intentional, ongoing process centered in the local community, involving mutual respect, critical reflection, caring, and group participation, through which people lacking an equal share of valued resources gain greater control over those resources" (Dean, 1991, p. 10). This group led a program for child caregivers and parents of children in child care that instructed participants in effective interpersonal communication, using skills such as active listening, assertiveness, and conflict resolution (Dean, 1991). The development of effective interpersonal skills is an important process for empowering parents. More information about interpersonal communication is discussed in Chapter 8.

- In addition to the economy, availability of credit, and the existence of child care, what other factors can you attribute to recent changes in family functions?

- How have functions changed just since you were a young child? Interview those in the previous two generations to gain firsthand information about how family functions have changed over that period of time.

- Speculate about some of the causes of these changes, especially those that occur beyond the microsystem.

Causes of Change in Family Functions

As changes occur in the systems beyond the microsystem, families need to accommodate to the larger society. For example, economic changes in the United States have affected many families by creating a need for two incomes. Along with the economic changes, a social change has occurred: young adults

Family pride is shown in portraits.

expect to have many of the luxuries with which they grew up and credit is readily available. At the same time, child care is more available than it was a generation ago. The complex interaction of these changes has affected the decisions that families make about work, as well as decisions relating to care and education of their children.

Family Law

In *The Rights of Families*, Guggenheim, Lowe, and Curtis (1996) provide current interpretations and details regarding family law. Included in this guidebook are the following topics: divorce and child custody, child support, property division, gay and lesbian families, adoption, and child abuse and neglect. In the introduction, the authors make an important point regarding the unique American viewpoint of those who advocate for public policies that support young children and families. They note that even more critical to the well-being of children and families, both historically and today, is the notion of being "free from

unjustified governmental interference" (p. xv). Guggenheim, Lowe, and Curtis go on to explain:

This is, in essence, a "hands off" view of family law, one that focuses heavily on a family's procedural rights. It is very different from other countries' conception of family rights, which reflect their society's commitment to the well-being of children and their families. Unlike the United States, many countries around the world believe that families need positive support in the form of paid childcare leave, national health insurance, subsidized day care, free universal preschool, child allowances, child support assurance, and free (or low-cost) higher education. The absence of such substantive rights for families in the United States is the subject of ongoing debate. (p. xv)

- **Consider both the U.S. "hands-off" perspective on family law and the view that families need positive support as noted by Guggenheim, Lowe, and Curtis (1996).**
- **Make a list of the pros and cons for each perspective.**
- **Share and discuss your list with a partner or in a small group.**

It is interesting to note that the U.S. Constitution makes no mention of children and families, yet courts have inherently upheld the rights of families. Two concepts that have been held in high esteem by the legal system include the **right of family integrity** and the **primacy of parental rights.** The right of family integrity includes the legal basis for parents to bear and rear children, and to guide those children according to their own beliefs. The primacy of parental rights upholds the strict limits of the Constitution to interfere with family life (Guggenheim, Lowe, & Curtis, 1996).

Some of the more common issues that are addressed in the family court system include:

- marriage, civil unions, domestic partnerships, prenuptial agreements

- family issues requiring legal intervention, such as domestic violence, paternity, adoption, child abduction, adultery, bigamy, polygamy, incest, orders of protection
- issues around terminating marriage, such as legal separation, divorce, annulment, child custody and visitation, child support, alimony, property settlements

Select one of the three categories of common issues addressed in family court and discuss related current topics that you have heard or read about, including areas of concern that might arise for early childhood professionals.

Family Support America
http://www.familysupportamerica.org

Family Structure

Another dimension of understanding families is structure. *Structure* refers to family membership. Some cultures define the family more in terms of the **nuclear family:** parents and their children. Others emphasize the **extended family,** including additional generations from both parents' families, their **families of orientation,** as well as siblings and their **families of procreation.** Figure 4–7 defines these terms.

Family structure refers to the makeup of a family: Who are the members of a particular family? Traditionally, in our culture, when families are depicted, it is common to see a mom, dad, son, daughter, and perhaps a pet or two.

Variations in Family Form

We tend to assume that Figure 4–8 realistically depicts a traditional family. Consider some other possibilities, however: that the adult male is the mother's brother; that the adult female is the father's sister; that the children are cousins being reared in the same home; that the family is blended. The possibilities are

Figure 4–7	Terms Related to Family Structure

Nuclear Family—Any two or more persons of the same or adjoining generation related by blood, marriage, or adoption sharing a common residence.

Extended Family—A family in which two or more generations of the same kin live together (extension beyond the nuclear family).

Family of Orientation—The nuclear family into which one was born and reared (consists of self, siblings, and parents).

Family of Procreation—The nuclear family formed by marriage (consists of self, spouse, and children).

Source: Definitions from Eshelman, 1988

Figure 4–8   People tend to assume that this is a realistic depiction of a traditional family.

endless. How many more possibilities can you produce? The same is true for the members of families depicted in Figure 4–9.

Figure 4–9   Structures of families take many forms.

As you prepare for your career in early childhood education:
- consider the list of services mentioned in the quote on page 97 (paid child care leave, national health insurance, and so on).
- note the advantages and disadvantages to families with young children if all services were available to families in the United States.
- interview a variety of citizens about their viewpoints related to one or more of these services.
- analyze the responses you receive from your interviews. Do your responses support the notion of individuals wanting to be free from governmental interference?

Family structure in the United States has changed considerably, as has been previously noted, and it continues to undergo many changes. The modern realities of diverse family structures, the dynamic nature of all families, and changes in societal trends and values have led scholars to categorize contemporary families as "postmodern" (Cole, Clark, & Gable, n.d.). Some of the many variations in structure that characterize U.S. families with young children include:

married nuclear families (spouses and child or children)

cohabiting families (unmarried partners and child or children)

single-parent families (unmarried parent and child or children)

joint-custody families (divorced or never married parents sharing custody of child or children)

blended or stepfamilies (spouses or unmarried partners with child or children from previous relationships)

same-sex partner families (lesbian or gay parents and their child or children)

multigeneration families (parent or parents reside with their parent(s) and their child or children)

grandparent-led families (grandparent(s) parenting their grandchildren)

Note that these variations are not mutually exclusive. For example, same-sex–parent families might also be blended; grandparent-led families might also be multigenerational, with children's aunts and uncles residing with them.

Despite the tremendous changes to family structure that occurred during the last half of the twentieth century and that continue to evolve into the twenty-first, the traditional family form often is still idealized in our society. The reality, however, is that this form is not, in fact, best for everyone. As early childhood educators, we sometimes forget this truth when making judgments about individual families. A case in point follows. One primary grade teacher had the responsibility to assign children in the first grade among four classrooms. In her own classroom, she placed only children who were living with both of their biological parents. One might say that she was aware of the research indicating that children who live in single-parent families are at greater risk for intellectual problems (National

Commission on Children, 1993) and that she held an idealized view of traditional families. The surprising point in this story is that this teacher herself had been a single parent and successfully reared a son. Discuss ethical concerns that you might have about this situation.

Although it is true that a strong marriage often provides a positive environment for rearing children, it is not the only family structure that accomplishes this goal. And while it is true that children in single-parent families are at greater risk, many of them have nurturant parents who are meeting their needs (National Commission on Children, 1993). Four important components of family structure have been identified by family researchers, regardless of the presence of a married couple (Ihinger-Tallman & Pasley, 1987).

1. **Division of labor.** Who is responsible for each family function?

2. **Rules of behavior.** What are the expectations for interacting with family members in everyday life?

3. **Family roles.** What behavior is expected for each position in the family? What does the mother do? The father? Each child?

4. **Power hierarchy.** Adult family members typically have more power than children. What happens when this is not so?

- For each of the four components listed, give examples from your family of origin.
- For each of the four components, give examples from your family of procreation or your expectations for your future family.
- Share your examples in a small group. Discuss commonalities and differences you find within your group.

Essential to understanding family structure is the realization that it is dynamic, that is, frequently changing. Whereas some families maintain the same structure for several years or even a decade or more at a time, all families undergo both loss and gain of members. Losses occur as a result of death, marital dissolution, or relocation. Families gain members through births, adoptions, marriages, and remarriages.

Sturgess, Dunn, and Davies (2001) examined young children's (ages four to seven years) perceptions of their relationships with family members and found that some children adjust more easily to changes in their family situations than do others. A key factor in this adjustment is related to children who have high levels of warmth in relationships with their mothers. Comparisons were made among children from non–step families, the biological children of the father from step families, and the stepchildren of the father from step families. A majority of children in non–step families (71 percent) and in biological children of father step families (62 percent) felt very close to their fathers. However, only 16 percent of stepchildren in stepfather families felt very close to their stepfathers. This study found further that those children who did not feel close to their resident fathers demonstrated more externalizing problems or "acting out" behaviors. Thus, even though educators can expect that the structures of postmodern families will continue to be dynamic, we must give attention to children who have difficulty with such transitions.

In addition to this research about the effect of parent-child relationships on children's adjustment during family transitions, some information about sibling relationships also has been related to children's adjustment (Deater-Deckard, Dunn, & Lussier, 2002). Negative sibling relationships in some families were found to be related to difficulties in adjustment, with biological siblings in single-mother families having the most negative relationships. More attention must be given to negative sibling relationships when children demonstrate difficulty with emotional adjustment.

The Meaning of Birth Order

One segment of family structure that has been of interest to researchers, families, and early childhood educators for many years is that of **birth order** of siblings. "When differences in birth order are found, they usually are explained by variations in interactions with parents and siblings associated with the unique experiences of being in a particular position in the family" (Santrock, 1994, p. 446).

Some behaviors have been found to apply more to firstborn children, regardless of the number of siblings that have followed that child's birth:

- more adult-oriented
- more helpful
- more conforming
- more anxious
- more self-controlled
- less aggressive

There is general consensus among child developmentalists that the presence of these characteristics is related to the demands and expectations placed on children by their parents. Being in the first position seems to be related to both higher levels of achievement and guilt, probably because the parents have some time to focus only on this firstborn. Research on only children has dispelled the popular myth that they are typically bratty and self-centered, and has found that, most often, only children have the positive characteristics of firstborns (Santrock, 1994).

Although popular notions exist about how middle children and youngest children are expected to behave, many researchers believe that birth order alone is an insufficient cause for variations in behavior. Following are some factors that are not considered in oversimplified beliefs about the birth-order explanation for behavior:

- number of siblings
- age of siblings
- spacing of siblings
- gender of siblings
- temperament of siblings
- individual characteristics of siblings such as talents, skills, interests
- health of siblings such as chronic conditions, disabilities, or life-threatening or terminal illness

Although one frequently hears that firstborns possess characteristics of perfectionism and reliability, that middle children avoid all conflict and are very loyal to friends, and that youngest children are irresponsible and charming, these complex character traits are influenced by much more than the factor of birth order.

Thus, although it is important to understand family dynamics, including that of birth order, it is best to not blame or credit a child's birth order for a set of behaviors. Sibling relationships, for instance, are an equally important factor in understanding children and their families.

On the other hand, some situations that we can be sure of are:

1. Living in a family is a unique experience that no two people perceive in exactly the same way.

2. A person is more strongly influenced by his or her family than any other group or system.

3. A person's birth order is one characteristic that typically has a lifelong effect on who that person becomes.

4. For those in any position of a family, there are many variables that influence a person—both positively and negatively (Graham, 2005).

Consider your own position in your family constellation. Now, reflect on how you might be both similar to and different from others who have the same place in their families. What factors do you believe might contribute to such similarities and differences?

Birth Order Affects Career Interests
http://www.osu.edu
Type "birthorder" into the Search field under
    Locate

Birth Order and Personality Differences
http://www.encouragingleadership.com/

The Effect of Birth Order on Intelligence
http://www.indiana.edu.
Type "intelligence and birth order" in the Search
    field

Application of Chapter Information

Family Support

It is important that we use research on family strengths, family functions, and family structure when planning family support policies and program-

ming. We also need to use information, however, to help us keep open minds about the widely diverse structures of families. Being aware of the risk at which divorce places children, for example, we might be tempted to judge parents who divorce as being self-centered and of not caring about their children. When we do not take all of the systems into consideration, it is easy to blame individual families for their inability to maintain a marriage or provide the best home for their children. But even if this assignment of blame were appropriate or accurate, early childhood teachers do nothing to help children by judging their families.

Thus, it is crucial that we understand the effect of larger systems on families and children. One of the most important of these larger systems is the economic one. Women with college degrees continue to earn less than men with high school diplomas. As a result, "children in one-parent families are six times more likely to be poor than children who live with two parents" (National Commission on Children, 1993, p. 20). After a divorce, women generally are worse off economically and men generally are significantly better off. Taking all of these facts into consideration, it is clear that divorce alone is not why so many young

When adults in the family provide loving care to children, it matters little whether they are parents, grandparents, aunts, uncles, or friends.

children are living in poverty. Inequality in the economic system must be factored into our understanding of this gloomy picture.

In the booklet *Strengthening and Supporting Families*, the National Commission on Children (1993) notes, "Decisions about marriage, divorce, childbearing, and parenting are intensely personal, but they are also influenced by cultural messages and by friends, family, and social institutions" (p. 20). Consider the bioecological systems in Bronfenbrenner's theory: They indicate, as does the preceding quote, that all segments of society have some responsibility for supporting families. As early childhood educators, we know that the most important reason for this societal support is that all children need and deserve homes filled with love and support.

Early Childhood Programs

When early childhood teachers understand that all families have strengths and all families need support, they realize that family structure is less critical than the accomplishment of family functions. Young children can be nurtured in many variations of family structures, and when adults in a family provide loving care to children, it matters little whether they are parents, grandparents, aunts, uncles, friends, or others.

> *"Building and maintaining positive relationships with families must resonate throughout programs—in the physical environment, in activities, in administrative and policy guidelines, and in programmatic features."*
>
> —**Barbara Bowman, 1994**

As specifics about how families fulfill the requisite functions evolve, so will the role of early childhood educators. In all early education settings, professionals must provide both care and education. As the saying goes, "We cannot educate young children without caring for them and we cannot care for young children without educating them." In support of this creed, both Bettye Caldwell and Magda Gerber have used the term "educare" for the primary function of early childhood education programs.

Summary and Conclusions

Early childhood practitioners must understand both family functions and family structure. Whereas many family functions have remained stable over time, the *nature* of those functions changes as society changes. It is because of societal changes that many families now seek to enroll their children in quality early childhood programs before their children are of traditional "school age." Family structure, the makeup of a family, influences how families manage their responsibilities. Single-parent families, by their nature, manage differently than most two-parent families. Blended families face challenges unfamiliar to original families of procreation.

Research points to certain characteristics that relate to strong families. When early childhood teachers apply their knowledge of these characteristics, the resulting program decisions and policies will then support families. It behooves professionals in early childhood education to provide support for the strengths in all families. Such support increases the likelihood of successful partnerships between home and school.

Chapter 4 Applications

1. Review the information about family strengths in this chapter. Thinking about a family that is familiar to you, comment on each of the strengths in relation to that family.

2. List ten families you know. Create a representation of each family's current structure or the structure when you had contact with them. Compare and contrast the families' structures. How do the variations among the structures of these families seem to affect specific functions of the family as discussed in this chapter?

3. How will you, as an early childhood educator, help ensure positive relationships with families (in the words of Barbara Bowman) through the physical environment, in activities, in administrative and policy guidelines, and in programmatic features?

Questions for Reflection and Discussion

1. How is knowledge about family strengths, functions, and structures useful to early childhood teachers?

2. How do you understand families differently after reading this chapter?

3. How will your teaching of children and working with families differ after reading about and reflecting on family strengths, functions, and structure?

Field Assignments

Technology

Before

1. Interview five people in your own generation. Ask them questions about how they view recent changes in the family. Note their comments. Critique the comments based on what you have learned about how changes occur in various levels of societal systems.

2. Create at least ten different representations of various family structures. Ask five adults to speculate about the relationships among the family members. Share your findings in class.

3. Interview an early childhood teacher about variations in family structure he has observed in the past three years. Ask the teacher to give you approximate percentages of the types of family structures currently in his or her classroom. Request comments from the teacher about any special or unusual circumstances. *Please note:* No names of families should be elicited for this assignment—respect confidentiality.

References

Ages and Stages Ejournal. (n.d.) Saskatchewan Psychology Portal. Strengths in families: Accentuating the positive. http://www.sesd.sk.ca/psychology/psych30/ejournalchildhood/agesandstages_families.htm. Retrieved January 5, 2006.

Besaw, A., Kalt, J. P., Lee, A., Smith, J., Wilson, J. B., & Zemler, M. (2004). The context and meaning of family strengthening in Indian America. A report to the Annie E. Casey Foundation by The Harvard Project on American Indian Economic Development.

Bowman, B. (1994). Home and school: The unresolved relationship. In S. L. Kagan & B. Weissbourd (Eds.), *Putting families first: America's family support movement and the challenge of change.* San Francisco: Jossey-Bass.

Bradt, J. O. (1989). Becoming parents: Families with young children. In B. Carter & M. McGoldrick (Eds.), *The changing family life cycle.* Needham Heights, MA: Allyn & Bacon.

Bronfenbrenner, U. (1988). Strengthening family systems. In U. Bronfenbrenner (Ed.), *Making human beings human: Bioecological perspectives on human development.* Thousand Oaks, CA: Sage.

Brooks, R., & Goldstein, S. (March 2001). Raising resilient children. *Parent's Magazine.*

Carter, B., & McGoldrick, M. (1989). Overview: The changing family life cycle: In B. Carter & M. McGoldrick (Eds.), *The changing family life cycle: A framework for family therapy.* Needham Heights, MA: Allyn & Bacon.

Cole, K. A., Clark, J. A., & Gable, S. (n.d.) Promoting family strengths. University of Missouri Extension, University of Missouri. http://muextension.missouri.edu/xplor/hesguide/humanrel/gh6640.htm. Retrieved January 5, 2006.

Dean, C. (1991, March). Bringing empowerment theory home: The Cornell parent-caregiver partnership program. *Networking Bulletin: Empowerment & Family Support, 2,* 10–13.

Deater-Deckard, K., Dunn, J., & Lussier, G. (2002). Sibling relationships and social-emotional adjustment in different family contexts. *Social Development, 11* (4), 571–590.

Eshleman, J. R. (1988). *The family: An introduction.* Needham Heights, MA: Simon & Schuster.

Galinsky, E., & David, J. (1988). *The preschool years: Family strategies that work from experts and parents.* New York: Times Books.

Graham, J. (2005). Birth order. Family issues facts: A fact sheet for families and people who work with families. University of Maine Cooperative Extension

Bulletin #4359. http://www.umext.maine.edu/onlinepubs/htmpubs/4359.htm. Retrieved January 5, 2006.

Guggenheim, M., Lowe, A. D., & Curtis, D. (1996). *The rights of families: The authoritative ACLU guide to the rights of family members today.* Carbondale: Southern Illinois University Press.

Ihinger-Tallman, M., & Pasley, K. (1987). *Remarriage.* Newbury Park, CA: Sage.

Kagan, S. L., & Weissbourd, B. (1994). *Putting families first: America's family support movement and the challenge of change.* San Francisco: Jossey-Bass.

National Commission on Children (1993). *Strengthening and supporting families.* Washington, DC: National Commission on Children.

Olson, D. H. L., & DeFrain, J. D. (1994). *Marriage and the family: Diversity and strengths.* Mountain View, CA: Mayfield.

Olson, D. H., McCubbin, H. I., Barnes, H. L., Muxen, M. J., Larsen, A. S., & Wilson, M. A. (1989). *Families: What makes them work.* Newbury Park, CA: Sage.

Santrock, J. (1994). *Child development.* Madison, WI: Brown & Benchmark.

Stinnett, N. (1979). In search of strong families. In N. Stinnett, B. Chesser, & J. DeFrain (Eds.), *Building family strengths: Blueprints for action.* Lincoln: University of Nebraska Press.

Sturgess, W., Dunn, J., & Davies, L. (2001). Young children's perceptions of their relationships with family members: Links with family setting, friendships, and adjustments. *International Journal of Behavioral Development, 25* (6), 521–529.

Werner, E. E. (1995, June). Resilience in development. *Current Directions in Psychological Science,* 81–85.

OUTLINE

Objectives

Key Terms

Theoretical Perspectives
    Bioecological Theory
    Developmental Contextualism

Ways to Parenthood
    Biological and Fertility
       Alternatives
    Blended Families
    Adoption
    Foster Parents
    Grandparents as Parents
    Teen Parents

Responsibilities of Parents
    Economic
    Nurturance and Child Care
    Attachment and Socialization
    Building and Maintaining
       Relationships
    Character Education and
       Spirituality
    Collaborating with Societal
       Institutions

Parenting Styles and Beliefs
    Trends in Beliefs about Discipline
       Strategies

Motherhood and Fatherhood
    Mothering
    Fathering

Parenting Beliefs
    Child Development and the Role
       of Children in Families
    Interactions with Early Childhood
       Educators

Summary and Conclusions

Chapter 5 Applications

**Questions for Reflection and
    Discussion**

Field Assignments

References

CHAPTER 5

Parenting

OBJECTIVES

After reading this chapter, you should be able to:

- discuss parenthood within the context of bioecological theory.

- understand the multiple roles of parents.

- explain differences in parenting beliefs.

- understand that a variety of adults may serve in a parenting role or parenting support role at some point in a child's life (grandparents, child care providers, and others).

Key Terms

adoption
attachment
authoritarian parenting
authoritative parenting
blended families
donor insemination

expressive (role)
indulgent parenting
instrumental (role)
nurturance
parenting
permissive parenting

public policies
spirituality
socialization
uninvolved parenting

Theoretical Perspectives

Bioecological Theory

What makes a parent? The most obvious answer is "biology." But beyond the biological connection that most parents have to their infants and children, what contributes to a mother or father's development as a parent? Bioecological theory explains this in terms of the systems surrounding the parent, both past systems and current systems.

A great deal of research on **parenting** style and skills shows that parents are very likely to parent the way they were parented. Thus, parents who were given supportive nurturance, care, and guidance have had positive models for parenting their own children in that manner. On the flip side, parents who were denied appropriate nurturance and care, as well as effective guidance, will have to work hard to overcome their experiences and learn to provide a more appropriate environment for their children.

Microsystem Effects Parental microsystems, both past and present, affect parents' behaviors with their children. Love and support from the other parent and significant others enable parents to do their best for their children. Recent research (Dunifon, 2005) has shown that when children of single parents also have a grandparent living in the home, the children's reading scores were higher than those of children living in single-parent homes without a grandparent present. This is in contrast to the many studies that have shown children from single parents doing worse academically than those who live with married parents.

Exosystem and Macrosystem Effects The exosystem and macrosystem also affect parenting. Extended families, workplace stresses and pleasures, neighborhoods, and faith communities can contribute to challenges and successes of parenting. The economy, the government, and the political climate certainly affect much of what parents are able to do for children. A recent report from the Children's Defense Fund (2001) lists the amounts spent on raising a child to age 18 for two-parent households at various income levels (see Figure 5–1).

   Public policies set by federal or state governments can affect parenting. Recent trends to cut welfare services for mothers who stay home to rear their children indicates a change in viewpoint about the role of parents. A generation ago, welfare policies were based on the premise that mothers *should* stay home to rear their young children. As societal expectations have changed about mothers in the workplace, the views about welfare have changed as well.

> "... [T]he United States also takes the lead, among developed nations ... with respect to poverty ... the data are consistent with the general trend among economically developed nations: children and families in the United States experience greater environmental stress. Further, many of the problems facing American families are not restricted to particular ethnic or economic subgroups. Rather, these conditions are pervasive, applying across the population spectrum."
>
> **—Urie Bronfenbrenner**

Chronosystem Effects Clearly, the chronosystem or era in which one is parenting affects parents and their children. In the 1950s and 1960s, most mothers with young children not only stayed home with their children but also were expected to do so by society. Currently, 79 percent of mothers with children under six years of age work outside the home (Children's Defense Fund, 2005). This change not only makes parenting very different, it also makes the kinds of support that families need very different. Many functions that once were accomplished in the home now require external support, most notably care for young children while any and all adults in the home spend most of their day in the workplace.

   Another aspect of the chronosystem's effect on parenting relates to the period of time in a child's development parenting is being assessed. For instance, effects of parental employment outside the home may be different for infants and for preschoolers. So, the chronosystem includes not only the historical era, but also the developmental period of a child's life.

Developmental Contextualism

The developmental contextualism perspective notes that both children and their parents are part of a larger world in which both generations have roles in addition to that of parent and offspring. For example, a parent may also be employee/employer, spouse/partner, sister/brother, friend, community volunteer, and daughter/son. Children may have roles as siblings, students, friends, grandchildren, and

Figure 5–1	Differing Costs to Raise a Child to Age 18

Income	Spent on Child
$38,000	$121,230
$38,000–$64,000	$165,630
$64,000	$241,770

nieces/nephews. This theoretical orientation is similar to the bioecological perspective in that multiple layers of systems affect and are affected by individuals. Thus, parenting provides a basis for child development "... *not* through their sole, main, or direct effects on children, but instead, through their embeddedness in a dynamic, multilevel system" (Lerner, Rothbaum, Boulos, & Castellino, 2002, p. 320).

Understanding parenting as a complex system related to variations in relational processes, individuals, contexts and time (both historical and developmental) will lead to new methods for data collection and analysis, but perhaps more importantly may also lead to more effective social policies. In other words, parenting is a process whereby "the parent shapes the child, but part of what determines the way in which parents do this is children themselves" (Lerner, et al., 2002, p. 321). When parents and their children have a good match of expectations and behaviors, parents are less challenged than when expectations and behaviors are disparate. And, yet, beyond this match or mismatch, other variables, such as cultural expectations and social supports, must all be factored into the larger picture in order to understand the complex process of parenting. One area of study that relates to this theory has to do with child temperament (or behavioral preferences and actions). Active, autonomous preschoolers seem to be a good fit for many U.S. parents. However, some Latino cultures

> **Consider both your thoughts and your feelings about parents and parenting. What do you believe to be the roles, responsibilities, and rights of parents in a family? How are mothering and fathering similar? How are they different? What are some common stereotypes about mothers and fathers? From where do these stereotypes come? How might the stereotypes be useful or damaging in your work with families of young children?**

Parents introduce their young children to community activities.

have expectations that children, no matter the age, should be compliant. In either case, multilayered systems influence parenting practices.

Ways to Parenthood

Biological and Fertility Alternatives

The most common way in which people become parents is through sexual intercourse that results in pregnancy. Sometimes, becoming a parent in this way is planned, and sometimes pregnancies are unplanned. Despite advances in the types and effectiveness of contraception, no method is 100 percent reliable. When sexual partners are married and conceive a child, most people assume that a child was planned. When partners are not married, many assume that the child was not planned. Of course, these assumptions may be correct or incorrect.

Advances in medical technology provide an array of options for people who want to become parents but who, for a variety of reasons, cannot or do not do so through traditional means. Current technological advances provide three alternative ways to reproduce: *in vitro* fertilization (IVF), **donor insemination**, and egg donation (Golombok, 2002).

Reproduction through *in vitro* fertilization continues to be widely referred to as the procedure that results in "test-tube babies." In the in vitro procedure, an egg is fertilized with sperm in a laboratory and the resulting embryo is placed in the mother's uterus. Most in vitro procedures at this time use an egg and sperm from the parents-to-be; however, donated eggs and/or sperm may also be used. About one in four births occurring from this technique are multiples, usually resulting in twins and sometimes in triplets (Golombok, 2002).

In the 1970s, the reality of test-tube babies was amazing. The first successful in vitro fertilization occurred in England in 1978. Since then, more than 500,000 births from this procedure have occurred around the world. The number of births from in vitro fertilization has increased greatly in the United States from 257 in 1985 to 11,342 in 1995. Even with a cost of more than $12,000 per trial, this alternative has become quite popular with couples who experience fertility problems (Miracle Babies, 1998).

The popularity of this alternative fertilization procedure has increased with its greater acceptance.

When Louise Brown was born at Oldham Hospital near Manchester, England, in July 1978, the world reacted as if she were a creature of science fiction. The first child conceived by in vitro fertilization—that is by uniting sperm and egg in a glass container—she was instantly known as the test-tube baby. Such was her notoriety that after leaving the hospital she had to be fed at midnight in a car on an empty street near the family's home in Bristol, since throngs of reporters made it impossible to reach the front door. For years neither she nor her working-class parents, Lesley and John Brown, could escape the global spotlight. The unrelenting scrutiny once prompted Brown, now a preschool nurse in Bristol, to admit, "Sometimes I wish it wasn't me." Despite the attention, she has emerged as a healthy, happy young woman. (Miracle Babies, 1998, p. 62)

Donor insemination, previously referred to as artificial insemination, is a procedure whereby sperm are transferred to the vagina with a syringe. Typically, this procedure is used when male partners are infertile. Lesbian partners also may utilize this procedure when they choose to become parents. Most often with sperm insemination, the birth mother has a genetic link to the child, but the father does not (Golombok, 2002).

The newest form of reproductive technology allows infertile women to conceive a child through the use of egg donation. Donated eggs are extracted from the donor through a complicated medical procedure and then fertilized in a laboratory, often with the prospective father's sperm. The fertilized egg is then placed in the birth mother's uterus. In the case of donated eggs, the father typically has a genetic connection to the child, but the mother may not (unless, of course, the egg donor is biologically related to the mother).

Early childhood educators probably are not aware of the conception or birth methods of the children who come to them. However, researchers have had some concern about the effects of various reproductive technologies on parenting capabilities (Golombok, 2002). Concerned about the stress that individuals or couples may have experienced due to infertility, as well as the stress caused by the possibility of coping with multiple births, researchers have hypothesized that those who use reproductive technology to become parents may exhibit some dysfunctional or ineffective parenting. However, after reviewing existing studies, Golombok (2002) concludes that "parents of children conceived by assisted reproduction appear to have good relationships with their children, even in families in which one parent lacks a genetic link with the child" (p. 355). Further, the research poses no evidence to indicate that children who have been conceived through these technologies are at any developmental risk. The most salient issue seems to center around parents telling their children about their methods of conception and if they do tell, when and how should they do so (Golombok, 2002).

Today, there are more alternative methods to becoming parents than thought possible even a few decades ago. While many ethical questions persist regarding these methods, those whose dreams of becoming a parent have been answered through medical technology remain appreciative. Technological advances often provide hope for those wishing to conceive or bear a child.

Blended Families

With greater frequency, both men and women are parenting both children that they conceived and those of their new spouse or partner. This is the case in **blended families.** Each partner in a blended family may bring her or his biological children to the new marriage. The parents in that household then attempt to provide care, nurturance, and guidance to children who may until very recently have been parented by someone else. Of course, parents do not always live in the same household with their children; many parents are carrying out their responsibilities with the added challenge of residing elsewhere.

Hanson, McLanahan, and Thomson (1996) note their puzzlement that the existing research regarding children in "stepfamily households" shows the absence of "a remarriage benefit." That is, that even though financial and other resources are greater than those in single-parent families, children are not better off. This concern led to the speculation that perhaps children in blended families experience higher levels of conflict than children in two-parent biological families. Their study examined eight variables related to the child's well-being: school performance, grade point average, school behavior problems, loss of temper or bullying others, sadness or withdrawing from others, sociability, initiative, and a global measure of quality of life. Children in their original two-parent families scored significantly higher on all areas of well-being except for grade point average. While these results are not surprising, it was unexpected that children in blended families would not be doing better than those in single-parent families, including in the areas of school performance and behavior problems. Children in single-parent families were significantly more sociable than those in reconstituted families. In an attempt to explain these results, the researchers studied parental conflict. Their results indicate that children in blended families experience higher levels of parental conflict than do other children. This is because they encounter more "intrahousehold" conflict than children in original families as well as "interhousehold" conflict, thus having two sources of possible family conflict. This is likely to increase their stress levels and lead to concern about the negative outcomes regarding child well-being noted by the researchers.

Private agencies 5000 – 40000

Adoption

International 7000 – 30000

Some individuals who want to be parents choose **adoption.** Adoption is a legal process that creates a non-birth family. Following the legal procedures, adoptive parents assume all of the rights and responsibilities held by birth parents (Guggenheim, Lowe, & Curtis, 1996). This path to parenthood was popular from 1950 to 1970 but has decreased in popularity since then, due, in part, to greater acceptance by society of single women keeping and raising their children. Available statistics show that from 2 percent to 4 percent of families include an adopted child (Guggenheim, Lowe, & Curtis, 1996; Rosenberg, 1992). In the United States, a little over half of all adopted children are parented by adults who are related to them (Stolley, 1993).

It has been commonly believed that adoption of children offered perfect solutions for both the relinquishing family and the adoptive family, as well as for the adopted child. Presumably, everyone's needs are met, and family life can proceed with ease, happily ever after. Elinor Rosenberg (1992) has, however, shown that differences exist between biological families and those in the adoption circle. Being aware of and paying attention to these differences can facilitate healthy adjustment by all of the members of the adoption circle: the birth parents, the adoptive parents, and the adopted child.

In an earlier time, a greater number of European-American infants were available for adoption. From the mid-1950s through the early 1970s, about 20 percent of infants of European-American single mothers were given up for adoption; in 1995, only 2 percent of this same category of mothers relinquished their infants (Chandra, Abma, Maza, & Bachrach, 1999, as cited in Brodzinsky & Pinderhughes, 2002). Several societal factors now exist that have reduced this number. Among the more obvious factors are less-negative responses to single

adeption.com

parenthood, the availability of contraception, and the legalization of abortion (Brodzinsky & Pinderhughes, 2002).

With this decrease in available European-American infants available for adoption, families wishing to adopt have moved increasingly to transracial (including children in foster care) and intercountry adoption, as well as to adopting children with identified special needs. Another fairly recent change in adoption practices is the trend to openness in all aspects of the process and policies. Although each of these practices is not without critics, many families and children are reaping the benefits of these changes.

It is important to note that birth parents do not typically see their decision to give up their child as an easy one. They often take advice from others or see adoption as their only viable alternative. Further, they have life-cycle issues related to this decision throughout their lives. Some of these issues include secrecy; anniversary dates, such as the child's birthday or the day on which the legal process was concluded; relationships to children born either before or after the adoption; intimate relationships; guilt; and lack of an official or social process for mourning the loss of a child given for adoption. It is certain that birth parents do not simply relinquish their child and then never look back. To the contrary, they may question the decision they made for the rest of their lives. Rosenberg notes that even into old age, such parents may wonder about the existence of unknown grandchildren. Today, we hear beautiful stories about reunions between birth parents and the children they relinquished. Not all of these stories have happy endings, however. Sometimes, lives become so complicated that families are unable to cope with such reunions.

Although early childhood teachers may not be aware if the parents they interact with are birth parents who have relinquished children, teachers are likely to be aware of families who have adopted a child. Although this may be a sensitive issue for families to share with teachers, due to the differences in biological family and adoptive family issues, it is helpful for teachers to have this information. One of the most common situations adoptive parents face is the realization that they were unable to have biological children. (Although this is not always the case, it is true for most adoptive parents.) Coming to terms with this loss can be challenging, and the pain it generates may continue to surface from time to time, especially if the parents' adoptive child is having some difficulty.

Rosenberg (1992) has created five phases for adoptive parenting, from the decision to adopt to the time that an adopted child reaches school age. Each phase has one or more developmental tasks associated with it. In the first phase, deciding to adopt, developmental tasks may include accepting the inability to reproduce, deciding to parent children outside of the bloodline, and deciding on the type of adoption that will be undertaken. The second phase is the adoption process. Tasks for this stage involve making both social arrangements (those relating to family and community) and legal arrangements. The third phase is the actual adoption. The primary developmental task for this phase is accepting a new member into an existing family. The fourth phase occurs during the child's preschool years, and parents' developmental tasks in this phase include acknowledging adoption as a fact in their family and deciding who, when, what, and how to tell about the adoption. The child's school-age years constitute the fifth phase, which requires adoptive parents to acknowledge adoption in the larger community.

Considering the family life cycle approach, adoptive families may engage in all of the usual tasks that are observed in the transition to parenthood and families with infants and young children. However, they have additional issues with which to cope. According to Brodzinsky and Pinderhuges (2002), these issues include:

- making the decision to adopt
- adjusting to adoptive parenthood
- discussing adoption with their child
- encouraging discussion about the child's birth family
- supporting the child in coping with adoption-related loss
- fostering a healthy, positive view about the child's birth and birth family

- cultivating positive self-esteem in the child
- assisting child in search for identity
- as child gets older, preparing for and providing appropriate assistance in contacting birth family

> **Review the typical life-cycle events and tasks for new families from earlier chapters in this text. Create a chart that demonstrates those charges along with additional challenges for adoptive families as noted above. Consider ways that early childhood professionals can provide support and sensitivity to adopted children and families.**

Adopted children also have issues that differ from those of birth children. Today, it is common to tell children the story of how they came to be a member of their family. These stories vary greatly for birth children, who hear about how they grew inside a special place in their mother's body, and for adopted children, who are told they were so special that their parents selected them. It can be safely said that all adopted children wonder about their birth parents; some adopted children are articulate and curious enough to engage their adoptive parents in discussion about this, while others are less inclined to be open about their questions, concerns, or desire for information.

These issues may vary for both parents and children in cases of racial or ethnic differences between adoptive parents and adopted children. In a newspaper editorial, Julie Higginbotham, a European-American mother of a Chinese-American daughter, commented on the insensitivity shown by strangers who ask questions and make comments about her daughter that are really none of their business. She has fielded questions such as: "Is she adopted?" "Where is she from?" "Was it really expensive?" The last paragraph of this editorial helps teachers and others to understand how adoptive parents feel about questions or comments that demonstrate such a lack of concern for parents' and children's feelings: "Alice was adopted, once upon a time. But now she is simply my child and our hearts are knit as tightly as any parent and child's can be. Alice is not a public exhibit. She deserves to be protected from adult questions that subtly invalidate her family's right to exist" (Higginbotham, 1998).

As teachers of young children, it is important to be sensitive to issues of adopted children and their families. Concern about terminology should be noted by teachers. Rosenberg (1992) tells about one preschooler who understood the common term "put up for adoption" to mean that all of the children who were available for adoption were placed on a shelf and waited for their adoptive families. Teachers of young children must understand that as adopted children and their families proceed through the life cycle, new issues are likely to arise that will require understanding on the part of professionals who work with them.

Foster Parents

"Foster parents provide care to children who cannot remain with their families by bringing these children into their homes" (Haugaard & Hazan, 2002, p. 313). From the beginning of the foster parent-child relationship, it is known that the relationship is expected to be temporary. *Temporary,* however, might mean a few days or a few years; the average stay of a child in a foster home is twenty-two months. The indefinite nature of the situation alone is a source of stress for children, foster families, and birth families.

Foster care in the United States has evolved over the centuries from colonial times to the present. At the beginning of the twenty-first century, the foster care system is beleaguered by too many challenges and not enough resources. The number of available foster families is decreasing as the number of children needing such placements is increasing.

A recent trend in some states is to have varying categories of foster families available for a range of children's needs. Examples of these categories include:

- emergency foster families who take children for very short periods of time on very short notice
- short-term foster families who take children who are expected to be able to return to their birth homes

- long-term foster families who care for children who will not return to their birth homes
- specialized care foster families who care for children with particular needs such as HIV positive
- treatment foster families who receive training to care for children with behavioral or emotional disorders
- kinship foster care that involves a family who is related to the child, typically grandparents or aunts or uncles (Haugaard & Hazan, 2002)

All categories of foster parents have in common some relationship issues that other parents do not typically have. In addition to their relationship with the child, foster parents also must work on creating productive relationships with both the birth family and the placement agency (Haugaard & Hazan, 2002). And, even as foster parents are working to build positive relationships with the child who is placed with them, they also must prepare for the eventual loss of that child. Foster parents must work with placement agencies so that the legal aspects of their relationship with the child for whom they care are handled appropriately. Further, foster parents frequently are in a role that requires them to help the child keep or build positive relationships with their birth families. All of these situations can be fraught with conflict that must be resolved for the good of the children and their relationships with their birth families.

These considerations point to the extraordinary challenges that face foster families on a recurring basis. Early childhood teachers may be aware when one of their students is living in a foster home. To support the child's academic progress and emotional well-being, teachers must have compassion and sensitivity for the challenges faced by everyone in this situation. Keep in mind that despite the difficulties faced by foster families, their efforts are based on the belief that they can help a child and his or her birth family in a time of dire need.

Grandparents as Parents

An increasing number of grandparents are providing all or most of the parental responsibilities for some children. In the recent past, it was common to have at least one grandparent living in the home with parents

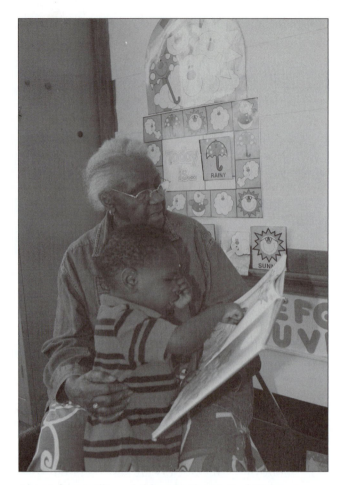

About four million children in the United States are living with grandparents or other relatives.

and children, in an extended-family living arrangement. Many children, though, now live with one or two grandparents, and the parents are not part of the child's daily life. Since 1980, this number has increased by 40 percent (Doucette-Dudman & LaCure, 1996). In 1997, available records indicate that about four million children in the United States are living with grandparents or other relatives (Bryson & Casper, 1998, as cited in Smith & Drew, 2002).

Parenting grandchildren complicates daily living. In addition to caring for the grandchild, or as often is the case, grandchildren, grandparents frequently work to create or maintain a relationship between the birth parent(s) and the child. Some experts believe that this is a crucial task for the children's healthy development. Legal issues related to grandparents and their grandchildren vary from state to state, and in many cases, are not clear. Some grandparents seek custody or adoption of their grandchildren, but many believe they are serving only as temporary caregivers and that the birth parent(s) will reassume the parenting responsibilities as soon as they can. The reality, however, is that even when the arrangement is perceived by all involved as temporary, it often stretches into years. When grandparents assume parenting roles, it is frequently because birth parents have been involved in alcohol or drug abuse and/or have physically, emotionally, or sexually abused the child(ren). The children may also be HIV positive or have other special needs. These desperate situations are often the catalyst for grandparents to attempt to save their grandchildren (Doucette-Dudman & LaCure, 1996).

In our society, some helping professionals and policy makers view it as odd that grandparents would want to parent or adopt their grandchildren. Some seem to be concerned that the relationships will confuse the children: For example, in these situations, the children's aunts and uncles, and maybe even their birth parents, take on sibling roles. As a grandmother raising her granddaughter, Doucette-Dudman makes an important point:

This is Sabra's life, she has known no other, she is not confused in any way. We have explained and will continue to elaborate on, her family connections. We (grandparents) are her parents because we parent. She also has birth parents, just like any other adopted child. Sabra loves them, too, but they do not parent. . . . Biological designations are practically irrelevant. (pp. 143–144)

Not only are grandparents discouraged from seeking full custody or adopting their grandchildren, but also few resources are available to them. In many situations, if grandparents did not assume the care of children, foster care would be necessary. The existing social service system allows for financial payments and medical insurance to those providing foster care, but grandparents are not eligible for these resources. Reverend Eduardo Yarde is quoted in *Raising Our Children's Children* (Doucette-Dudman & LaCure, p. 88):

With welfare reform, this is where the churches are going to play a crucial part. That's one sector that's been

neglected. My philosophy is that these grandparents have already raised their kids, they are under no obligation to raise more kids. And to me they are doing us, society, a favor. They are doing the State a favor. They should be rewarded for that. If we can't see that, we surely have lost sight of everything. The State really looks the other way, "Oh, that's grandparents." They don't even consider giving them some sort of support, nothing. And it's hard.

As grandparents raise their grandchildren, a number of difficulties have been documented (Kornhaber, 1993).

1. Without formal custody, grandparents have difficulty getting either preventive or emergency medical care for children.

2. Typically, insurance companies will not permit grandchildren to be included as dependents on policies.

3. Schools may not admit children who do not live with their parents and often deny authority of grandparents.

4. Social Security benefits for the children are available to grandparents only if they legally adopt.

5. Financial assistance from social service agencies is typically not available, not even resources available to foster families.

6. Housing regulations of grandparent residences may not allow children, or zoning laws may exclude grandchildren in the definition of single-family dwellings.

In their extensive review of grandparenthood, Smith and Drew (2002) conclude that "custodial grandparents are conducting a service to their communities as well as their families and need support at a national and community level to continue effectively" (p. 162). As one aspect of their advocacy for those over the age of 50 years, the American Association of Retired Persons (AARP), publishes a newsletter for "grandparents raising grandchildren," *The GIC Voice.* This free newsletter contains valuable information, including current medical, legal, and psychological facts. The Fall 2005 issue provides a clear description of federal legislation being proposed by both the House and Senate that would, if passed, provide various forms of support for grandparents and other family members involved in kinship care. That same issue of the newsletter also includes discussion of methods grandparents have used to help their grandchildren raise their test scores and ways that some schools are providing support for grandparents who are parenting their grandchildren. Early childhood professionals who wish to provide this valuable resource for their centers or schools can find more information at http://www.aarp.org/grandparents.

Having some knowledge about the stress that grandparents deal with in raising their grandchildren can help early childhood teachers to be sensitive to needs of the "parents" and children in these families. It is common for children being raised by grandparents to have special needs because of their biological parents' substance abuse or child abuse. Education systems are in a position to ease grandparents' stress; when educators and social service agency personnel work together, children and families benefit. Doucette-Dudman and LaCure issue a plea for teachers to have some understanding of and concern for grandparents who, out of "love and devotion," are nurturing their grandchildren.

Peggy Tuter Pearl (2000) suggests the following for teachers when grandparents are the primary caregivers:

- modify language in notes, letters, requests for signatures
- know who the primary caregivers of their students are
- allow extra time during conferences

Diannne Rothenberg (1996) includes a list of school strategies intended to help grandchildren in an article entitled "Grandparents as Parents: A Primer for Schools." Listed below are excerpts from this list. For a complete version and more information, go to http://www.ed.gov/databases/ERIC_Digests/ed401044.html.

- Anticipate transitional or adjustment difficulties, and act to minimize them.
- Look for children's strengths and build on them.
- Try not to single out children because of their family status.

To listen to a grandparent's voice, go to the online resource and listen to "Nancy." Nancy is a grandmother who is parenting her two grandsons (ages 9 and 14). She describes some of the issues in her role as both grandmother and parent in the personal online voice including legal, medical, and daily realities.

Teen Parents

When teens become parents, many family roles are altered in what family systems theorists refer to as "off time." In other words, adolescence is a time in U.S. society that is considered to have some freedom from major responsibility for others so that youth might seek their own identities. Further, in many families, grandparents may be quite young or in a family life cycle period when they are still rearing younger children. Thus, considering teen parenting from a family systems perspective, it can be noted that many family members are affected in ways for which they probably have not planned and are not prepared.

Although teenage pregnancy and childbearing rates are decreasing, the United States has the highest rate among most Western countries (Singh & Darroch, 2000, as cited in Moore & Brooks-Gunn, 2002). Most adolescents who give birth are not married; in 1998, 79 percent of teen mothers (15–19 years old) were single (Ventura, Mathews, & Curtin, 1999, as cited in Moore & Brooks-Gunn, 2002). Because, typically, neither teen parent is self-supporting, teen mothers often need help from their families, including their parents, grandparents, and siblings. Often, families of teen parents help with finances, child care, and transportation.

> *"Today, teenage parenthood is almost synonymous with single parenthood. Teenage mothers are disproportionately represented on welfare rolls and as high school dropouts. . . . The declining age of intercourse, the increasing rate of nonmarital births, and the disappearance of teenage marriage means that the young parent finds herself in a different situation today than previously."*
>
> **—Moore and Brooks-Gunn, 2002**

While it is clear that single teen mothers face many challenges that involve their own development as well as supporting their child's development, research shows that some buffers exist. Education is a particularly strong factor for successful results among teen mothers. Among the education-related factors that contribute to positive consequences for single teen mothers are being on expected grade level, having parents with more than a tenth-grade education, attending special schools for pregnant girls, and holding aspirations for continued education (Moore & Brooks-Gunn, 2002). Those teen parents who have opportunities to complete high school with special programs that include on-site child care are thus more likely to be able to support themselves and their child or children to a greater extent postgraduation.

How do adolescents parent? It is important to note that many individual differences exist in teen parenting styles and that these differences are related to variations in resources and experience, but some commonalities exist among teen parents based on the challenges these parents face. Many teen mothers are confronted by the common stressor of poverty. In addition to their own very low incomes, they may also come from families and live in communities that are negatively affected by circumstances of poverty. Research has shown that these harsh conditions can have negative effects on children of teen mothers through their adolescence and adulthood (Moore & Brooks-Gunn, 2002).

Reviews of existing research on adolescent mothers' parenting skills show that they appear to express warmth to their babies as much as older mothers do. However, teen mothers are neither as verbally responsive nor as emotionally available to their infants as would be beneficial for children (Moore & Brooks-Gunn, 2002). It is possible that children of teen mothers who live in multigenerational families may experience and benefit from greater verbal responsiveness and emotional availability from their grandparents. This is most likely to be true when the grandparents have higher levels of education and are not living in poverty.

Minimal information is available about young fathers, especially when they are not married to or living with their child's mother. Although the results from one national survey (Lerman, 1993, as cited in Moore & Brooks-Gunn, 2002) found that one-fourth of young fathers had daily contact with their children and one-half had weekly contact, the quality of the father-child relationship tends to decline over time. Some of the factors that are related to stronger father-child relationships include a close relationship between the teen parents, frequent visits and scheduled child care expectations, and involvement of the paternal grandmother (Coley & Chase-Lansdale, 1999, as cited in Moore & Brooks-Gunn, 2002).

Considering the challenges of teen parenthood, it behooves early childhood educators to be conscious of situations that are most supportive of families with young parents. Programs and policies that are geared to assisting teen parents with the challenges they face often lead to benefits for their children. On the other hand, negative influences emanating from teen parenthood can also stay with their offspring for a lifetime.

> This quote from A. A. Campbell (1968) is now viewed as classic: "When a 16-year-old girl has a child . . . 90 percent of her life's script is written for her." Based on available evidence, explain the meaning of this quote. Also, describe existing programs, policies and practices that might influence changes in the adolescent parent's life script.

Responsibilities of Parents

Economic

Parents have the ultimate responsibility for meeting all of their children's needs. Based on data from the Department of Agriculture Center for Nutrition Policy and Promotion, the Children's Defense Fund (2001) notes that a married-couple family earning less than $38,000 per year will spend $121,230 to raise a child to age 18. Those who make $38,000 to $64,000

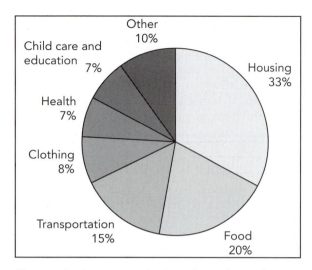

Figure 5–2   Percentages of estimated annual expenditures on a child by husband-wife couples with incomes of less than 38,000.
Source: Children's Defense Fund, Washington, DC. What it costs to raise a child. http://www.childrens-defense.org/factsfigures—costchild.htm

will spend $165,630, and those making more than $64,000 will spend $241,770.

In the United States, most people believe that parents bear the financial obligation for their children's expenses, which include health care, child care, shelter, food, and clothing (see Figure 5–2). This belief is so strong in our culture that we often ignore societal preferences and biases and assume all parents are capable of providing for their children's basic needs. This is not the case, however. For example, parents who have full-time jobs are more likely to have medical insurance for themselves and their children, and, thus, access to both preventive and emergency health care. Parents who work in entry-level, lower-paying jobs, even if they work full time, are less likely to have access to health insurance or to have their insurance paid for by employers.

Concern for the well-being of children who do not have health insurance has led the federal government to provide plans for young children. Specifically, in 1997, the federal government created the Children's Health Insurance Program (CHIP), so that uninsured children from low- and moderate-income families are eligible for regular checkups,

immunizations, doctor visits, eyeglasses, prescription drugs, hospital care, dental care, and other medical services (Children's Defense Fund, 2004). Although paying for medical expenses is still seen as a parental responsibility, some policy makers have noted that healthy children will cost society less in the future.

Nurturance and Child Care

Another responsibility of parents is to provide care and **nurturance** for their children. Traditionally, we have referred to this as "mothering" children. Even though many two-parent families currently find that two incomes are required, mothers are still seen as the parent who is responsible for and more capable of caring for children. "The research evidence clearly indicates that husbands share very little of the burden of raising their children and caring for their homes" (Hamburg, 1995, p. 11). Most single parents who are the primary caregivers for their children are mothers. In fact, only about 10 percent of all single-parent families are headed by fathers (U.S. Bureau of the Census as cited in Hamner & Turner, 1996).

Bioecological theory emphasizes the need for parents to have a system of social support in order to do their best at nurturing children.

*The establishment and maintenance of patterns of progressively more complex interaction and emotional **attachment** between caregiver and child depend in substantial degree on the availability and involvement of another adult or a third party—spouse, relative, neighbor, or formal service provider—who assists, encourages, spells, gives status to, and expresses admiration and affection for the person caring for and engaging in joint activity with the child. (Bronfenbrenner & Neville, 1994, p. 14)*

Note that early childhood teachers may serve as the "third party" to provide support to parents in their role as nurturers. Thus, it is critical that teachers understand this important role when planning the family involvement component in any program of early childhood education.

Child care outside the home continues to be viewed as a "women's" issue rather than a family or societal concern. Many policy makers continue to voice

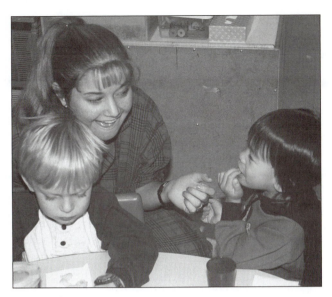

Early childhood education teachers may serve as the "third party" to provide support to parents in their role as nurturers.

Figure 5–3	Relationship of Attachment to the Child's Development: Physical, Cognitive, Social, and Emotional

Healthy attachments in infancy can lead to the following outcomes for preschool children:

Physical development—brain development, physical health

Cognitive development—skillful in problem solving, seeking maternal assistance when challenged, curious about new things

Social development—leaders with peers, self-confidence, sympathetic to others, competent in peer interactions, well-liked by others, considerate

Emotional development—ability to tolerate frustration, expression of positive emotions such as joy

the opinion that if mothers stayed home with their young children, there would be no need for child care centers. Oddly enough, these same people often call for "welfare mothers" to go to work.

It remains the parents' responsibility to choose child care for their young children. Many parents, in reality, have little choice. Accessibility and affordability are two areas of concern. Parents tend to rely on care that is close to home and that costs the least. Often, this means that parents sacrifice quality of care of their children for what they can afford. Current interest and concern for this issue at the federal level and initiated by Hillary Rodham Clinton is welcomed by many child and family advocates. High-quality child care costs more than most families can afford. Further, it is difficult to find.

Attachment and Socialization

The third area of parents' responsibility is related to their children's psychological well-being. Forming emotional attachments is crucial for children's healthy development in all domains. Attachment to parents is necessary for healthy physical, cognitive,

social, and emotional development. Figure 5–3 shows the relationship of attachment to all areas of child development.

Parents are the child's link to society. Early **socialization** experiences, including communication, play, and teaching behaviors, all happen within the context of the home. These early attachment and socialization experiences are thought to be a strong influence on children's development. Current research on brain development indicates that social interaction in the first three years of life creates important neuron connections for later learning. Parents are a child's first and foremost teachers, even if they employ other forms of care for their children at very young ages.

Building and Maintaining Relationships

Those in the parental role introduce others into the lives of their children. Extended family members, especially grandparents but also aunts, uncles, cousins, neighbors, friends, and siblings, become a part of the child's world. Parents sometimes rely on some people on this list to help with child care or just to socialize with their children. Families include others in varying ways, partly depending on their culture or ethnicity, and partly depending on their individual views. For some families, cousins are almost like siblings, while for others, cousins are almost strangers. These individual variations in family relationships are most often decided and implemented by parents.

Character Education and Spirituality

Spirituality, in its various forms, is seen as a parental responsibility, and most parents ensure that their spiritual beliefs are shared with their children. For many families, spirituality is defined as and dealt with in the context of organized religion. Many parents count on their church or temple to at least assist with this duty. Religion, along with other factors, influences "the kind of activities the family engages in, the limits set and the controls placed on children's behavior, and the set of expectations that parents hold for their children" (Hamner & Turner, 1996, p. 21).

For other families, morality is of higher value than religiosity. Moral behavior is often related in some way to spirituality or the meaning of life (Coles, 1990). Lickona, Schaps, and Lewis (1998) note that school programs of character education should state in the mission statement, "Parents are the first and most important moral educators of their children" (p. 55). In addition to this critical point, Lickona and his associates go on to say,

. . . [E]ach program should take pains at every stage to communicate with parents. To build trust between home and school, parents should be represented on the character leadership committee that does the planning. The program should actively reach out to "disconnected" subgroups of parents: All parents need to be informed about—and have a chance to contribute, react, and consent to—proposed core values and plans for implementing them. Finally, programs and families will enhance effectiveness of their partnership if they recruit the help of the wider community—business, religious institutions, youth organizations, the government, and the media—in promoting the core ethical values. (p. 55)

"Clearly we can all agree about the importance of teaching our children, both as individuals and as members of society, the importance of common values such as respect, responsibility, trustworthiness, and citizenship."

—**Richard Riley, Former U.S. Secretary of Education**

Collaborating with Societal Institutions

A newer responsibility of parents is that of relating to societal institutions and helping their children to do so, including early childhood settings. This is often a difficult responsibility for parents because they have had no models. This responsibility is related to the very topic of this textbook: How can early childhood education and families form partnerships that benefit not only children but also parents and teachers? For parents, working with their children's teachers often means finding effective means of resolving conflict, because parents and teachers may, at times, value different activities or behaviors for children. It is imperative that both parents and early childhood teachers address such conflict in ways that will best help children, while still respecting the family and maintaining the educational program.

Consider the Responsibilities of Parenthood that are discussed in this section of Chapter 5: economic, nurturance and child care, attachment and socialization, building and maintaining relationships, character education and spirituality, and collaborating with societal institutions. Critically assess the resources that parents need to meet each of these responsibilities. Finally, brainstorm ways that early childhood programs and communities might be able to offer various types of support to families in regard to each of the responsibilities.

Parenting Styles and Beliefs

Diana Baumrind has researched the topic of parenting styles for nearly four decades (1967, 1971, 1977, 1989). Early versions of Baumrind's typology of parenting styles included three variations: **authoritarian parenting, authoritative parenting,** and **permissive**

parenting. Further work in this area has led Baumrind to descriptions of four types of parenting:

- authoritarian
- authoritative
- indulgent
- uninvolved

These styles are based on two dimensions: amount of parental control and amount of parental warmth. Authoritative parents are high on both of these elements, whereas authoritarian parents are high on control and lower on warmth. Indulgent parents are lower on control and high on warmth, and uninvolved parents tend to the low end of both control and warmth. See Figure 5–4 for characteristics of parenting styles.

In addition to defining differences in parenting style, Baumrind has also shown that variation is parenting is predictive of children's behaviors and char-

acteristics. "Authoritative parenting, which balances clear, high parental demands with emotional responsiveness and recognition of child autonomy, is one of the most consistent family predictors of competence from early childhood through adolescence" (Darling, 1999). See Figure 5–5 for descriptions of child behaviors for each parenting style.

In the previous descriptions of parenting style, "control" refers to children's behavior. Thus, parents demonstrating those styles that emphasize greater control (e.g., authoritarian and authoritative) are

Figure 5–4 Characteristics of Parenting Styles

High Warmth

INDULGENT
- lenient
- allow self-regulation
- avoid confrontation
- do not value external
- exert few demands
- use personal messages & reflection

AUTHORITATIVE
- monitor behavior
- set clear expectations
- assertive, standards, supportive
- not restrictive or punitive

Low Control ——→ **High Control**

UNINVOLVED
- not pathologically neglectful
- little time/effort given
- expect compliance
- restrictive, directive
- punitive

AUTHORITARIAN
- obedience-oriented
- may be intrusive

Low Warmth

Figure 5–5 Child Behaviors Associated with Varying Parenting Styles

Authoritarian Parents—Firm control over children, punitive, little warmth or support provided to children

Associated Child Behaviors—Because children typically have fewer possibilities to interact with others, they have less social competence. Often, children are anxious and do not initiate activities. They have poorer communication skills and some are overly aggressive

Authoritative Parents—Consistent, loving, conscientious, secure in their ability to parent, set firm rules, communicate clearly, warm and unconditionally committed to their children

Associated Child Behaviors—More likely than other children to exhibit prosocial behavior such as sharing, sympathy toward others, and cooperation

Indulgent Parents—more responsive than demanding, lenient, do not require mature behavior, allow self-regulation, and avoid confrontation. Two types in this category: democratic—conscientious, engaged, committed to children; nondirective—especially lenient, without clear behavioral expectations

Associated Child Behaviors—may be involved in problem behaviors, mediocre academic performance, disrespectful to others, not popular with peers, higher self-esteem, good social skills, and less depression

Uninvolved Parents—low in both control and warmth, bordering on pathologically neglecting, but in normal range, little time or energy given to parenting, low commitment to children

Associated Child Behaviors—Perform most poorly in academic, social competence, self-esteem, self-regulation, do not handle independence productively concerned with employing strategies that lead to children doing what their parents expect of them. Another aspect of control that has been studied in regard to parenting is psychological control. This factor is what differentiates the notion of control for authoritarian versus authoritative parenting. Authoritarian parenting emphasizes high psychological control as well as behavioral control in that these parents expect their children to accept the parental values and goals without question. On the other hand, authoritative parents are likely to discuss children's views and to sometimes arrive at decisions based on input from the child (Darling, 1999).

Trends in Beliefs about Discipline Strategies

Even as existing research shows support for authoritative parenting, that is, for stating expectations and providing explanations to children about reasons for expected behavior, there is a current trend in parental beliefs and behaviors that ignores the importance of balance between "guiding limits and loving compassionate care" for young children (Brazelton & Greenspan, 2000, p. xviii). Families who are overwhelmed by responsibility are often attracted to simplistic discipline techniques that rely on punishments and rewards to control children's behavior. When used as a primary disciplinary method, these outdated approaches often lead children to either aggressive behavior or fearful, withdrawn behavior, neither of which supports children's optimal development. This "back-to-basics discipline ethic" does not consider children's need for sensitive nurturance and developmentally appropriate experiences (Brazelton & Greenspan, 2000).

Center for Effective Discipline
http://www.stophitting.com

Committee to Repeal Section 43 of the Criminal Code of Canada
http://www.repeal43.org

Parenting without Punishing
http://www.nopunish.net

Motherhood and Fatherhood

Even though we have come to accept the term "parenting," most families and teachers are aware that we have different expectations for mothers and fathers. One single mother reports an occasion when her mother commented on what a good job a particular single father who had custody of his son was doing. The conversation between the single mother and her mother went like this:

> **Mother:** *"John works so hard at his job and still is such a good father for Joshua."*
> **Daughter:** *"I work hard, too. And, I think I'm a good mother."*
> **Mother:** *"Of course you're a good mother. Women know how to take care of young children. It's natural for them."*
> **Daughter:** *"Working full time and being a mother is not easy."*
> **Mother:** *"Women have been having children and taking care of them for generations. It's not new for women your age."*

It is safe to say that many people in our society still believe that any woman who has a child knows automatically how to be a mother, but that not all men with children know how to be fathers. This belief sets quite a double standard for our expectations about parental responsibilities.

Generally, women experience greater fulfillment in their parental roles than men do, but they also see being a parent as more of a burden. Mothers feel restricted in other aspects of their lives due to their parenting duties (Goetting, 1986). Both of these feelings that are held by many mothers of young children, are easily traced to societal expectations. At very early ages, many girls play with dolls, and when asked what they want to be when they grow up, they say "a mommy." Boys, on the other hand, play with toys that are symbolic of the world beyond the home and, consequently, want to be pilots, police officers, or firefighters. They expect to be employed outside of the home, not to be restricted in their occupations by parenting duties.

In the 1950s, Parsons and Bales (1955) classified the role of mothers as **"expressive"** and the role of fathers as **"instrumental."** By this, these early scholars meant that mothers provided children with care and love, while fathers' direct role in caring for children was minimal. A father's position allowed him to be the tie the family had with the outside world. Although times have changed and more mothers of children under six work outside the home, we still observe tenacious vestiges of this perspective. When one parent does stay home to care for children, it is still most often the mother. And when parents divorce, mothers are still more likely to get custody of the children.

Current research has examined how mothers and fathers interact with their babies and young children. Many studies have found that mothers are more likely to provide the physical care such as feeding, bathing, and diapering, and fathers are more likely to play with their children. Also, mothers, whether they work outside the home or not, spend a great deal more time with their children than do fathers. Perhaps this accounts for why mothers find parenting more fulfilling *and* more restrictive.

It is interesting to ask children (if they are old enough to respond) who takes care of them in various ways such as who prepares their food, washes their clothes, makes doctor appointments, and plays with them. Children's perceptions are often quite accurate in terms of understanding which parent per-forms which duties. One school principal tells of waiting in the deli line at a grocery store when a four-year-old boy asked him, "Where is the 'girl' who lives with you? Why isn't she doing the shopping?"

> To check this information with families that you know, interview several families with young children and ask the following questions:
> 1. Who provides physical care of your children, including preparing meals, bathing, making certain of clean clothes, and so on?
> 2. If a child is ill, who stays home from work with the child? How is this decided?
> 3. Who makes medical appointments?
> 4. Who plays with the children?

Mothering

Preparation for the role of mothering includes the process that women go through to achieve a maternal identity as well as competency in this identity (Barnard & Solchany, 2002). This preparation continues throughout the pregnancy and into the postpartum period. Four maternal tasks have been distinguished as common in this preparation (Rubin, 1984, as cited in Barnard & Solchany, 2002). These tasks are:

Seeking safe passage. In preparation for her mothering role, a pregnant woman begins to take special care of their own health to keep her child safe through pregnancy, labor and delivery.

Ensuring acceptance of baby by important others. As an aspect of her maternal role, a pregnant woman begins to adjust her own life and relationships with others in ways that will accommodate the child's needs.

"Binding-in." This process relates to the pregnant woman's psychological attachment to the developing fetus and her future child. "The child begins to be real for the mother long before the child becomes real for family members and friends . . . " (p. 9).

Learning to give of oneself. Expectant mothers consider what they will be giving up to care for a dependent child as well as what they will gain from motherhood. Many mothers-to-be are concerned with their competency, especially when this is a new role for them.

Once women have become mothers, it is generally seen that they have three primary functions in this role (Winnicott, 1990, as cited in Barnard & Solchany, 2002):

1. *monitoring-surveillance*—Infants and young children must be constantly monitored and supervised in order to keep them safe. Beyond this, mothers also monitor their child's growth, development, health, and behavior. As children grow and develop, mothers accommodate their surveillance to the changing needs of children.

2. *expectant nurturing*—Mothers are typically children's primary caregivers. In this role, they expect to provide nutrition, a safe environment, health care, appropriate climate controls, and

meeting all of children's dependency needs. Again, as children grow and develop, mothers accommodate their nurturing to meet children's changing needs.

3. *responsive caregiving-social partner role*—In order to assist children in developing a sense of trust, mothers respond in a timely way to meet children's needs. This responsivity is crucial in teaching children that someone is always there to meet their dependency needs. "It is in the response of others that the child develops meaning of her or his behavior" (p. 16). Thus, responsiveness from mothers helps to support the social partner role with their infants and young children.

> *". . . [T]he goal of mothering is to develop an underlying, internal strength that fuels a healthy ego, supports a working conscience, and constructs strong internal working models consistent with individuality; and that the ultimate mothering goal is a child, who can enter adulthood as an autonomous, individuated, responsible person secure in her or his relationships."*
>
> —**Barnard and Solchany, 2002, p. 18**

Expectations of the mothering role change throughout infancy and early childhood. From a child's birth to three years of age, maternal responsibilities include providing food, safety, stimulation, and security; being emotionally available; and developing routines. From three to five years of age, mothers are responsible for setting consistent and reasonable limits and routines; modeling appropriate expression of feelings; and encouraging appropriate forms of autonomy. When children are five to eight years old, important tasks for mothers include providing discipline and limits; supporting emotional development; and creating awareness of values and beliefs of others (Barnard & Solchany, 2002).

Although many, perhaps most, mothers rise to the occasion and become warm, nurturing parents, it is known that for some women this capacity is reduced or difficult to attain. Such high-risk women seem to be too consumed with other issues to deal with the psychological tasks of preparing for motherhood. Some women are in abusive relationships, are addicted to various substances, are physically or mentally ill, or are in dire poverty. Some of the greatest risk factors for decreased competency in the maternal role include a childhood that lacked basic needs being met or that included abuse, past or current mental illness, ambivalence about the pregnancy and the birth of a child, and little ability to care for herself (Gabinet, 1986, as cited in Barnard & Solchany, 2002).

In their research of mothers of young children enrolled in Early Head Start, Barnard and Solchany (2002), found that when mothers had earlier trauma that had not been resolved, it was extremely difficult for them to make psychological space for their babies. These researchers propose that about 25 percent of new mothers have such unresolved trauma and for this reason they are not able to consider the needs of their babies. "When a baby is never taken into a mother's mind, the child becomes an emotional orphan whether or not a mother is physically present" (p. 20). This situation raises serious concerns about the development of a large number of young children in our society. These researchers recommend practices and policies that take into account the critical needs of children to be nurtured. One consideration is referred to as "allomothering." This view of nurturing children allows for the constant responsibility of child care to be spread out among several primary caregivers, for example, child care providers, extended family members, community agencies, and so on. They also point to the need for greater availability of high-quality child care services, as well as the importance of supporting parental involvement with child care providers. It is seen that high-quality early childhood education may be a good source for prevention of childhood difficulties based on a lack of ability to nurture that traumatized mothers evidence.

Fathering

Changes in either women's roles or men's roles in families lead naturally to changes in roles for the other. As mothers with young children are now more likely to spend more time in the workforce, one might expect that roles and responsibilities of fathers have also been adapted. Existing research points to the value of examining both quantity and quality of time that fathers spend with their young children. Typically, differences between mothers and fathers are noted in both of these ways.

Center for Successful Fathering
http://www.fathering.com

National Center for Fathering
http://www.fathers.com

National Fatherhood Initiative
http://www.fatherhood.com

Michael Lamb and his associates (as cited in Parke, 2002) have proposed three dimensions that are most relevant for studying father involvement:

1. *interaction*—This refers to fathers' direct contact with their children. Various types of activities, including playing and caregiving, are included in this dimension. Gradual increases in father interaction in two-parent families have been noted. One study (Yeung, Sandberg, Davis-Kean, & Hofferth, 2001, as cited in Parke, 2002) found that fathers interacted with their children 67 percent of the time of maternal involvement on weekdays and 87 percent on weekends. Most experts agree that mothers continue to spend more time with their children than do fathers. Generally speaking, qualitative differences in mother-child and father-child interaction exist as well. "Fathers are tactile and physical, and mothers tend to be verbal, didactic and toy mediated in their play" (Parke, 2002, p. 34). While these qualitative differences hold steadily in the United States, more recent cross-cultural evidence leads to the speculation that these differences most likely have cultural roots and so they are not purely based on biological gender differences of parents.

Some research provides support for the notion of "maternal gatekeeping." It has been noted that fathers engage in less interaction with their infants and young children when mothers are unwilling to yield responsibility of child care to fathers. Further, attitudes of mothers who engage in gatekeeping are more likely to be judgmental and lead to criticism of fathers' ways of interacting with their children (Allen & Hawkins, 1999, as cited in Parke, 2002). On the other hand, Bonney, Kelley, and Levant (1999, as cited in Parke, 2002) point out that when fathers are more highly involved with their children, maternal attitudes become more positive and this can lead to greater levels of father participation with their children.

2. *availability*—This dimension relates to fathers accessibility for their children. Availability, of course, may vary for those fathers who reside with their children when compared with those who do not live with their children. Also, as might be expected, when fathers work a greater number of hours, they are less available to and less involved with their children than those who work fewer hours. Fathers who hold high-stress jobs tend to be withdrawn from their children, whereas fathers who have positive work experiences demonstrate more supportive interactions with their children (Repetti, 1994, and Grossman, Pollack, & Golding, 1988, as cited in Parke, 2002).

In terms of father-child relationships, both father presence and quality of the relationship matters. However, even when fathers do not live with their children, it is possible for them to positively influence both the relationship and the child. Children have been found to do better both academically and psychologically when nonresident fathers use an authoritative parenting style. Another predictor of positive outcomes for children is related to the amount of child support paid by the nonresident father (Amato & Gilbreth, 1999, as cited in Parke, 2002).

3. *responsibility*—Fathers typically have different levels of responsibility than mothers in making sure that children are cared for as well as for

arranging that resources are available to meet children's needs. In fact, evidence indicates that even though both mothers and fathers are capable of obtaining child care, medical care, planning schedules, and supervising children, through the middle childhood years, mothers are much more likely to bear primary responsibility for their children (Parke, 2002). Those fathers who identified nurturance as an important part of their parenting not only had greater interaction time with their children, but also assumed more responsibility than did fathers who rated nurturance as less important to their roles (Rane & McBride, 2000, as cited in Parke, 2002).

"In most families, husbands notice less about what needs to be done, wait to be asked to do various chores and require explicit directions if they are to complete the tasks successfully . . . most couples continue to characterize husbands' contributions to housework or child care as 'helping' their wives."

—Coltrane, 1996, p. 175

As of 1996, it was estimated that there were approximately two million stay-at-home fathers in the United States. Frank and Livingston (2000) state that "Stay at home fathers recognize that caring for children and family is not emasculating; as their children become older they are likely to remain intimately involved with their children, aware of their friends, schoolwork, and activities, and active as the on-call parent who responds when the child is sick at school." If this description is accurate, then teachers need to become aware of the role(s) fathers play in the lives of their children and actively invite and welcome fathers at school. This awareness also helps teachers understand the family's caregiving arrangements.

An important point to be made when examining parenting behaviors is that fathers' roles are less "culturally scripted and determined" (Parke, 2002, p. 35) than are maternal roles. Whereas monitoring, nurturing, and caregiving are all universal expecta-

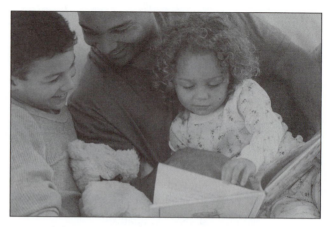
Stay-at-home fathers recognize that caring for children and family is not emasculating.

tions for mothers of infants and young children, social expectations for fathers seem to be more flexible and diverse. Some of the sources of these differences include fathers' experiences with their own fathers and families, early practice with caring for children, timing in the life cycle for becoming a father, attitudes about masculine roles, spouse or partner attitudes about paternal competence, and both positive and negative employment experiences.

Much of the research on child effects from paternal behaviors and attitudes has not been conducted so that clear cause can be related to fathering only. In reality, there is most likely a great deal of overlap on children's development from the effects of both mothers and fathers (and even other factors). "Although there is overlap between the effects of mothers and fathers on their children's academic, emotional and social development, evidence is emerging that fathers make a unique contribution to their children's development" (Parke, 2002, p. 56). At this time, several studies using different methodologies have concluded that high-quality relationships with fathers are correlated with higher amounts of empathy, both in childhood and adulthood.

In addition to research on fathering generally, more research is needed that looks at individual differences of fathers. One such study (Jain, Belsky, & Crnic, 1996, as cited in Parke, 2002) led to a typology of four kinds of fathers: (1) caretakers, (2) playmates-teachers, (3) disciplinarians, and (4) disengaged. Characteristics of the first two types of fathers included more highly educated, more prestigious employment, less neurotic and less consumed with daily hassles than the other two types. Clearly, more information about variations in fatherhood and effects on children will be helpful in understanding ways that professionals might intervene to foster more positive outcomes for all.

Parenting Beliefs

Parenting is one of the most important roles a person can perform. Yet, it is expected that parenting skills will come naturally. Because so many people do become parents in one way or another, this role is different from many others. Five differences have been noted (Bigner as cited in Hamner & Turner, 1996).

1. Women receive more pressure to become mothers than men do to become fathers.
2. Parenthood is not always voluntary.
3. Parenthood is irrevocable.
4. Parents receive very little preparation or guidance.
5. Parents develop and accommodate their parenting strategies as their children develop.

> **Consider the five parental roles. State your agreement or disagreement with each belief. Give real-life examples to support your view.**

Child Development and the Role of Children in Families

The ZERO TO THREE National Center for Infants, Toddlers and Families conducted a study that focused on the following questions: "How much do parents of babies and toddlers know about their children's intellectual, social, and emotional development at the earliest ages?" and "What are parents doing to encourage healthy development of their babies in these interrelated domains?" (Melmed, 1997, p. 46).

Results of this study are reported in nine points.

1. Parents know that early childhood is important but they do not understand the full significance of this period to human development.
2. Parents believe that they can impact emotional development more than intellectual or social development of their young children.
3. Parents see the first three years as not so important for the area of social development.
4. Parents emphasize nature over nurture when it comes to their children's intellectual development.
5. Parents play down the effect that outside child-care arrangements have on their children's development, especially if a stable home life is provided.
6. Parents are learning about children's needs as they parent rather than before they become parents.
7. Parents want information about early brain development, and specific information about what it means and what they should be doing for their children.
8. Parents emphasize their role in keeping their children safe, and seem not to know ways to match activities for and interactions with the development, interests, temperament, and moods of their children.
9. Parents desire to spend more time with their children.

Interactions with Early Childhood Educators

This study leads to many implications for early childhood teachers. One realization is that parents may

It is important that early education address all aspects of the child's development: physical, cognitive, social, and emotional.

deemphasize the importance of quality care outside the home, especially two-parent families who can provide well for their children. Those working in early care and education can feel devalued with this attitude. However, it will be important that early childhood professionals build on the importance of the family to children. Parents are vital to the young child's development, so finding areas of common ground and agreement between parents and educators is important. For this reason, it is essential that early education address all aspects of the child's development: physical, cognitive, social, and emotional.

Melmed (1997) suggests two parental needs that early childhood educators can help meet:

- information for understanding their particular children's feelings or needs, especially for difficult situations
- creative ways that they can spend more quality time with their children

What ideas do you have for each of these two ways to meet family needs?

While the ZERO TO THREE study emphasizes some similarities in parental beliefs about early development, Trawick-Smith (1997) outlines differences in beliefs about children related to culture, poverty, and oppression. Culture affects beliefs about

childhood through daily life and expectations; some see childhood as a carefree time to play and explore, others as a time to teach serious responsibility. Often, families and cultures who have endured great adversity in their lives have quite different belief systems than those who were fortunate to receive advantage and privilege.

As you review the nine points from the ZERO TO THREE study, consider how these statements might guide parent-teacher conferences and discussions. Understanding and appreciating parents' beliefs and knowledge of child development can help teachers and caregivers plan effective communications and interactions. Providing clearly worded statements about program goals and expectations can also help parents match their beliefs with the program's goals and expectations. Listening to parents can also help programs change and evolve to meet different expectations while still being grounded in developmentally appropriate practice.

Summary and Conclusions

Many parents have children through biological means. Others become parents in various ways. No matter how one becomes a parent, there are many responsibilities involved in this family role. All parents need support in providing the best for their children. Traditional mother and father roles continue to be common in today's society, but many children can and do thrive in alternative family forms, including single-parent families, gay and lesbian families, and families headed by grandparents. An authoritative parenting style is most effective in fostering children's optimal development.

Parents have legal rights as well as responsibilities for their children. It is very important that early childhood teachers understand the primacy of the family in the lives of young children. This understanding lends support for active family involvement in early childhood education. Teachers must initiate partnerships with family members, because whether the role of a child's parents is traditional or nontraditional, early childhood professionals increase children's opportunities for academic success by involving adults who parent the young children in their programs.

Chapter 5 Applications

1. Consider the results of the ZERO TO THREE study. Discuss the significance of each of the nine findings. How might early childhood teachers or administrators support families in each of these areas?

2. How might the way in which parents come to their parenting role affect their parenting philosophy and strategies? For example, how might adoptive parents differ from biological parents, and so on?

3. Discuss how specifics about each of the parenting roles have changed in the past generation or two. Also, discuss ways in which parents vary in carrying out each of the roles.

Questions for Reflection and Discussion

1. How will you involve all members of a family in your classroom? Will you differentiate requests for fathers and mothers?

2. How will you implement content from this chapter in your interactions with parents?

3. In what way is it helpful to understand variations in parenting styles and behaviors?

Field Assignments

1. Interview three mothers and three fathers about their interactions with their children. Compare the responses to research findings in this chapter.

Karen

2. Interview a parent from a blended family who is parenting both his or her biological child(ren) and a child or children of his or her spouse. Ask about both challenges and joys.

Carmen

3. Interview two early childhood professionals about ideas they have for creative ways parents can spend more quality time with their children. Share these ideas in class. Compose a class list of the best ideas to keep for a resource.

References

Barnard, K. E., & Solchany, J. E. (2002). Mothering. In M. H. Bornstein (Ed.), *Handbook of Parenting* (2nd ed., vol. 3), pp. 3–25. Mahwah, NJ: Lawrence Erlbaum Associates.

Baumrind, D. (1966). Effects of authoritative parental control on child behavior. *Child Development, 37*, 887–906.

Baumrind, D. (1967). Child care practices anteceding three patterns of preschool behavior. *Genetic Psychology Monographs, 75*, 43–88.

Baumrind, D. (1971). Current patterns of parental authority. *Developmental Psychology Monographs, 4* (1, Pt. 2), 1–103.

Baumrind, D. (1977). Some thoughts about childrearing. In S. Cohen & T. J. Comiskey (Eds.), *Child development: Contemporary perspectives.* Itasca, IL: F. E. Peacock.

Baumrind, D. (1989). Rearing competent children. In W. Damon (Ed.), *Child Development Today and Tomorrow* (pp. 349–378). San Francisco: Jossey-Bass.

Brazelton, T. B., & Greenspan, S. I. (2000). *The irreducible needs of children: What every child must have to grow, learn and flourish.* Cambridge, MA: Perseus.

Brodzinsky, D. M., & Pinderhughes, E. (2002). Parenting and child development in adoptive families. In M. H. Bornstein (Ed.), *Handbook of Parenting* (2nd ed., vol. 1, pp. 279–311). Mahwah, NJ: Lawrence Erlbaum Associates.

Bronfenbrenner, U., & Neville, P. R. (1994). America's children and families: An international perspective. In S. L. Kagan & B. Weissbourd (Eds.), *Putting families first: America's family support movement and the challenge of change.* San Francisco: Jossey-Bass.

Children's Defense Fund. (January 1998). What it costs to raise a child. *CDF Reports, 19* (1). http://www.childrensdefense.org/factsfigures—costchild.htm.

Children's Defense Fund. (May 2001). *What it costs to raise a child to age 18.* Washington, DC: Children's Defense Fund. http://www.childrensdefense.org/data/whatitcosts.aspx. Retrieved December 22, 2005.

Children's Defense Fund. (2004). Child Health, CHIP, Frequently Asked Questions. http://www.childrensdefense.org/childhealth/chip/faqs.aspx. Retrieved December 22, 2005.

Children's Defense Fund. (April 2005). *Child care basics.* Washington, DC: Children's Defense Fund.

Coles, R. (1990). *The spiritual life of children.* Boston: Houghton Mifflin.

Coltrane, S. (1996). *Family man.* New York: Oxford.

Darling, N. (1999). Parenting style and its correlates. Champaign, IL. ERIC Clearinghouse on Elementary and Early Childhood Education, Eric Digest. (ERIC Document Reproduction No. ED 427896.)

Doucette-Dudman, D., & LaCure, J. R. (1996). *Raising our children's children.* Minneapolis, MN: Fairview Press.

Dunifon, R., & Kowaleski-Jones, L. (2005). The influence of grandparents in single-mother families. Unpublished manuscript. http://www.cpr.maxwell.syr.edu/seminar/fall05/Dunifon_Kowaleski-Jones.pdf. Retrieved December 18, 2005.

Goetting, A. (1986). Parental satisfaction. *Journal of Family Issues, 7* (1), 83–109.

Golombok, S. (2002). Parenting and contemporary reproductive technologies. In M. H. Bornstein (Ed.), *Handbook of Parenting* (2nd ed., vol. 3, pp. 339–360). Mahwah, NJ: Lawrence Erlbaum Associates.

Guggenheim, M., Lowe, A. D., & Curtis, D. (1996). *The rights of families: The authoritative ACLU guide to the rights of family members today.* Carbondale: Southern Illinois University Press.

Hamburg, D. (1995). The challenge of parenthood. *The challenge of parenting in the '90's.* Queenstown, MD: The Aspen Institute.

Hamner, T. J., & Turner, P. H. (1996). *Parenting in contemporary society.* Boston: Allyn & Bacon.

Hanson, T. L., McLanahan, S. S., & Thomson, E. (1996). Double jeopardy: Parental conflict and stepfamily outcomes for children. *Journal of Marriage and the Family, 58*, 141–154.

Haugaard, J., & Hazan, C. (2002). Foster parenting. In M. H. Bornstein (Ed.), *Handbook of Parenting* (2nd ed., vol. 1, pp. 313–327). Mahwah, NJ: Lawrence Erlbaum Associates.

Higginbotham, J. S. (1998, November 12). *Adoption and privacy.* Harrisburg Patriot-News.

Kornhaber, A. (1993). Raising grandchildren. *Vital Connections, 14*, 1–4.

Kostelnik, M. J., Stein, L. L., Whiren, A. P., & Soderman, A. K. (1998). *Guiding children's social development.* Clifton Park, NY: Delmar Learning.

Lerner, R. M., Rothbaum, F., Boulos, S., Castellino, D. R. (2002). Developmental systems perspective on parenting. In M. H. Bornstein (Ed.), *Handbook of Parenting,* (2nd ed., vol. 2, pp. 315–344). Mahwah, NJ: Lawrence Erlbaum Associates.

Lickona, T., Schaps, E., & Lewis, C. (November/December 1998). Eleven principles of effective character education. *Scholastic Early Childhood Today*, 53–55.

Maccoby, E. E., & Martin, J. A. (1983). Socialization in the context of the family: Parent-child interaction. In P. H. Mussen (Ed.), *Handbook of child psychology* (4th ed., vol. 4). New York: Wiley.

Melmed, M. (1997). Parents speak: Zero to Three's findings from research on parents' views of early childhood development. *Young Children, 52* (5), 46–49.

Miracle babies. (October 12, 1998). *People.*

Moore, M. R., & Brooks-Gunn, J. (2002). Adolescent parenthood. In M. H. Bornstein (Ed.), *Handbook of Parenting* (2nd ed., vol. 3, pp. 173–213). Mahwah, NJ: Lawrence Erlbaum Associates.

Parke, R. D. (2002). Fathers and families. In M. H. Bornstein (Ed.), *Handbook of Parenting* (2nd ed., vol. 3, pp. 27–73). Mahwah, NJ: Lawrence Erlbaum Associates.

Parsons, T., & Bales, R. (1955). *Family, socialization, and interaction process.* Glencoe, IL: Free Press.

Pearl, P. T. (2000). Grandparenting. In L. Balter (Ed.), *Parenthood in America: An encyclopedia.* Denver: ABC–CLIO.

Rosenberg, E. B. (1992). *The adoption life cycle: The children and their families through the years.* New York: Free Press.

Rothenberg, D. (1999). Grandparents as parents: A primer for schools. (Report: EDO-PS-96-8). Urbana, IL. ERIC Clearinghouse on Elementary and Early Childhood Education, ERIC Digest (073). (ERIC Document Reproduction No. ED 401044.)

Smith, P. K., & Drew, L. M. (2002). Grandparenthood. In M. H. Bornstein (Ed.), *Handbook of Parenting* (2nd ed., vol. 3, pp 141–172). Mahwah, NJ: Lawrence Erlbaum Associates.

Stolley, K. (1993). Statistics on adoption in the United States. *The Future of Children: Adoption, 3* (1), 26–42.

Trawick-Smith, J. (1997). *Early childhood development: A multicultural perspective.* Upper Saddle River, NJ: Prentice Hall.

OUTLINE

Objectives

Key Terms

Family Systems Theory
Horizontal Stressors

Families and Unpredictable Stressors
Family Violence
A Particular Form of Family Violence: Child Abuse
Substance Abuse in Families
Marital Transitions and Single Parenting
Homeless Families
Families and Children with Disabilities

Families and Children with Serious Illness
Immigrant Families
Migrant Families
Military Families
Children of Incarcerated Parents

The Role of Early Childhood Educators

Summary and Conclusions

Chapter 6 Applications

Questions for Reflection and Discussion

Field Assignments

References

Family Stress

OBJECTIVES

After reading this chapter, you should be able to:

■ relate the effects of various unpredictable stressors in the lives of families with young children.

■ understand some of the societal beliefs that are at the root of various forms of family violence.

■ explain the grief process involved in a family's sense of loss.

Key Terms

adaptation	extreme families	immigrant families
adjustment	family coping	marital transitions
balanced families	family protective factors	midrange families
buoyancy	family recovery factors	migrant families
child abuse and neglect	family violence	resilience
crises	gender inequality	serious illness
disability	homeless	substance abuse
elasticity	incarcerated	vulnerability

Family Systems Theory

"Family stress can be defined as a real or imagined imbalance between the demands on the family and the family's ability to meet those demands."

—Clemson Extension, 2002

Some families are better able to cope with stress than others. Olson and his associates (Olson, Russell, & Sprenkle, 1989) found that of the three types of families categorized by the circumplex model (**balanced, midrange,** and **extreme**), balanced families have, and use, more resources for coping with stress. Some of these resources are good financial management skills, appreciation for the personalities of other family members, strong support from family and friends, and satisfaction with their quality of life. Further, balanced families are more likely to deal with stressors rather than deny them; they are more effective communicators and they have better problem-solving strategies.

Boss (1988) defines **family coping** as "the management of a stressful event or situation by the family as a unit with no detrimental effects on any individual in that family. Family coping is the cognitive, affective, and behavioral process by which individuals and their family system as a whole manage rather than eradicate stressful events or situations" (pp. 60–61). This definition implies that passively coping with traumatic situations may be detrimental to family functioning. Sometimes, however, giving up is required for a family to change. Boss (1988) notes that "even though it looks like failure when a family fails to cope, the failure itself can be positive" (p. 64). Thus, when families place too heavy an emphasis on coping, they may not adapt or change in ways that could increase their quality of life.

More recently, efforts have been made to study family stress and coping together in terms of family resiliency (McCubbin, McCubbin, Thompson, Han, & Allen, 1997). Family **resilience** is defined as "the property of the family system that enables it to maintain its established patterns of functioning after being challenged and confronted by risk factors **(elasticity)** . . . and the family's ability to recover quickly from a misfortune, trauma, or transitional event causing or calling for changes in the family's patterns of functioning **(buoyancy)**" (McCubbin, et al., 1997, p. 1). Research has led to the identification of family protective factors, that is, factors that protect against various risks, thus increasing a family's elasticity. Additionally, family recovery factors have been identified; these phenomena support a family's buoyancy.

Family protective factors (FPF) and **family recovery factors (FRF)** comprise the positive side of families' ability to cope with their **vulnerability** and **crises.** *Vulnerability* refers to the family's possibility of being faced with risk factors that have a negative impact on functions whereas the term, *crisis* refers to the possibility for a family's ongoing instability or dysfunction (McCubbin, et al., 1997).

The two family processes that have been found to be related to resilience are **adjustment** and **adaptation.** The process of adjustment engages a given family's protective factors in continuing to perform necessary functions even as they are faced with various risks. On the other hand, adaptation engages a family's recovery factors inasmuch as the family has the ability to "bounce back" or recover after dealing with crises. Although both protective and recovery factors are likely to be based on a given family's strengths, there is evidence that at various points in the family life cycle, particular forms of crises may be related to some common resources. For example, families of preschool children typically find community support and religious programs to be protective, while families of adolescents find family cohesiveness to be especially important (McCubbin, et al., 1997). Thus, it behooves early childhood teachers to attend to current evidence about protective and recovery factors for families of young children.

The previous paragraphs provide terminology in order to understand the evidence regarding family resilience. But they do not address the specific factors included in adjustment and adaptation, in recovery and protection. Figure 6–1 provides a list of general protective and recovery factors that are known to support family resilience.

> **Consider the ten factors that support family resiliency in Figure 6–1. Using your personal and professional experience, provide anecdotal evidence for at least three of these factors.**

Horizontal Stressors

Chapter 3 addressed the developmental issues typical for young families or families with young children. These horizontal stressors are specifically referred to in family systems theory as developmental stressors. Another type of horizontal stressor in this theory is the unpredictable stressor, affecting families regardless of the stage of the family life cycle (Carter & McGoldrick,

| Figure 6–1 | General Family Resiliency Factors |

1. *Family Problem-Solving Communication.* Families are challenged during times of risk or crises to use forms of communication that are affirming of one another. However, those families who are able to use such constructive means of communicating demonstrate an important component of family resilience.

2. *Equality.* Resilience is increased when all family members are empowered to be self-reliant and independent. Stereotypic gender roles that decrease women's authority or power can be a negative factor in terms of resilience. Of course, young children must be supported as they learn to become responsible members of the family.

3. *Spirituality.* Family spiritual beliefs and practices often provide comfort and support as families deal with unexpected, harsh realities.

4. *Flexibility.* Because crises often require families to change in at least some way, those families who are able to alter their roles, expectations, and even traditions have greater resiliency in the face of shifting circumstances.

5. *Truthfulness.* In order to move to helpful changes, families must operate in a realm of truth. Honesty within the family system as well as from external sources (e.g., medical, social services, legal) is necessary for healthy coping and recovery.

6. *Hope.* Families who can optimistically look forward to their future typically have greater resilience. This can be difficult in times of chronic disability or terminal illness. Yet, resilient families often find hope through a new generation as they lose members of older ones.

7. *Family Hardiness.* Hardy families pull together with strong resolve to get through crises. One factor in hardiness is commitment to working together, another is a family's belief that they can overcome difficulties.

8. *Family Time and Routine.* Family members build relationships with one another through time together, especially in common routines. When family members are dealing with crises, some semblance of normalcy tends to increase harmony and balance.

9. *Social Support.* Participation in existing networks of support including extended family, friends, and community all contribute to a family's resiliency. Sometimes, adding new social support systems, such as a single-parents network when coping with divorce, increases the ability to cope.

10. *Health.* Both physical and psychological health of family members increase protective and recovery factors for coping with crises. Because so many family crises relate to one or more members' ill health, an emphasis on healthy habits can support resiliency.

Source: McCubbin, McCubbin, Thompson, Han, and Allen, 1997

1989). The very nature of these stressors—their unpredictability—makes them difficult to cope with and to resolve.

Families and Unpredictable Stressors

Examples of unpredictable events include family violence, effects of substance abuse, homelessness, disabilities, various illnesses, and immigration.

Family Violence

Violence is prevalent in the lives of families in the United States. The very institution that should be providing love and nurturance is also the one in which violence is too often perpetrated. It is important that early childhood teachers have some understanding of the rate of violence, as well as ideas about why it is so common. Women and children are at greater risk of being victims of abuse than are men.

Straus (1991) discusses five social causes of **family violence:**

- high level of conflict inherent to family life
- gender inequality
- norms that allow violence in the family
- early training in violence within the family
- multiple risk factors, such as alcoholism, poverty, and societal violence

High Level of Conflict Inherent in Family Life

Some of the inherent conflicts in families arise from gender and age differences, involuntary membership in the family, family insulation or privacy, and the relationship of violence to conflict. These factors are considered to play at least some role in family violence. Any of these factors by itself is not viewed as the sole cause or reason for violence. Understanding the complexity of causes of family violence is important; one cannot predict that violence will exist in a given family based on the presence of one or more of these factors.

Gender and Age Differences. Most families are made up of both males and females, and have members of various ages. A great deal of research points to gender differences in values, priorities, interests, and notions about power. These differences lead to male-female differences in families. Some areas of difference include amount of income, activities and interests, and even television programming. In most families, these differences do not lead to violence, but when other factors are present, such differences seem to result in harm against females, younger children, or older family members. Although abuse can be committed against males, it occurs much less frequently, and they are less likely to be physically hurt by it. The generation gap also creates a number of areas of conflict. Different generations have different preferences for music, clothing styles, and how to spend their leisure time.

Involuntary Membership. Family members did not necessarily choose each other. Even though marriage partners in the United States are likely to have at one time chosen each other, many factors influence these choices, including the belief that they had many areas in common with one another. Marriage and parenthood often squelch some of those common interests. Responsibilities tend to take over each person, sometimes decreasing the sense of commitment to one another.

Children and parents do not typically choose each other. Rather, they get the "luck of the draw." Some children are fortunate to have parents who nurture and understand their needs without reverting to violent methods of child rearing. Others are less fortunate. The very fact that many family members

Family Preservation and Child Welfare Network
http://www.familypreservation.com

Family Violence Prevention Fund
http://endabuse.org/

— How home programs visitation can help

National Clearinghouse on Child Abuse and
Neglect Information
http://www.nccanch.acf.hhs.gov

National Coalition Against Domestic Violence
http://www.ncadv.org/

National Council on Child Abuse and Family
Violence
http://www.nccafv.org/

National Domestic Violence Hotline
http://www.ndvh.org/

are put together by circumstance rather than choice can cause tension among members. The old adage "You can choose your friends, but not your relatives" has more meaning than many people realize. This factor carries over to relationships with in-laws and stepchildren.

Family Privacy. Families are often insulated and have strong beliefs about being self-sufficient. The notion of privacy in the family can often be taken to an extreme. Spouses may speak to each other and their children in ways they would not want anyone else to hear. Behavior that is not observed by outsiders is less likely to be civil or humane, especially in the face of conflict. It is this factor—family privacy—that is overlooked by many when a pillar of the community is accused of spousal or child abuse. Family privacy, while of tremendous value, can also lead to harmful family secrets: "It's nobody's business."

Increasing Conflict Leads to Violence. As the amount of conflict increases in a variety of areas within a family, violence becomes more likely. Family privacy, sexism, and disparities in physical power increase the likelihood that a person believes that he is right—and has the right—to use his fists to settle conflict. This belief is accompanied by little chance of getting caught and the belief that "a good beating" will stop the behavior that is causing conflict.

Gender Inequality Many people believe that husbands are and should be the heads of households. This belief is supported in many informal ways throughout our society. Legal documents often list male names first, even in the case of co-ownership or joint income tax returns. Sometimes, this leads to a belief in male dominance and in the related belief that men have ultimate responsibility for all decisions and practices in their families. Research shows that "the greater the departure from gender equality, the greater the risk that physical force will be used to maintain the power of the dominant person" (Straus, 1991, p. 26). This is true even when females agree that males should be dominant. Even though male dominance is a factor in family violence, it is important to understand that most male-dominant marriages are not violent. Rather, **gender inequality** is one factor that makes violence more likely.

Society's Sanction of Violence Parents are permitted, and in some communities expected, to use physical punishment on their children. When child abuse laws were passed in the 1970s, most laws indicated that the intent was not to take away parental authority or the rights of parents to use physical punishment. A vast majority of parents use physical punishment, especially with young children. Fully 90 percent of parents support the use of such methods as necessary for child rearing.

Just as our cultural norms support spanking and other forms of physical punishment of children, they also frequently support hitting in marriage. Even though many say they oppose violence generally, large numbers of adults still note that there are some instances when spouses can and should be hit, especially those related to extramarital sexual affairs. It is never permissible to strike a colleague in the heat of disagreement, nor is it socially acceptable to use violence in any other social setting.

Early Training in Family Violence In families, violence is carried out by loving parents who are genuinely concerned about their children. The use of physical punishment for even small infractions teaches children that hitting within families is okay. "The problem is that these actions also teach the child the principle that those who love you are those who hit you" (Straus, 1991, p. 29). Research has shown that the more adults were physically punished as children, the greater the chance that they will hit their spouses as adults (Straus, 1983).

Multiple Causes In addition to the factors already mentioned, other factors that increase the probability of violence in families include alcoholism and other forms of substance abuse, poverty, and other types of stress on families. Again, however, none of these factors necessarily predicts family violence. Even though violence occurs in families at an alarmingly high rate, there are more nonviolent families than violent ones, even when several predictive factors for violence are in place. However, a family that possesses several of these factors is at a much higher risk for violence. One study showed that when factors were placed in a checklist format, as the scores on the checklist increased, so did violence increase (Straus, Gelles, & Steinmetz, 1980).

Research indicates that family violence is not committed by only a few very sick individuals. It is much more widespread than many people believe. Early childhood teachers must take seriously any indication that children in their care may have been abused. This is true even when the teacher tends to doubt the possibility of abuse because the child comes from a "good family."

A Particular Form of Family Violence: Child Abuse

The Child Abuse Prevention and Treatment Act of 1974, PL 93–247, defined **child abuse and neglect.** This law described abuse and neglect as "the physical or mental injury, sexual abuse, negligent treatment, or maltreatment of a child under the age of eighteen by a person who is responsible for the child's welfare under the circumstances which indicate that the child's health or welfare is harmed or threatened thereby" (U.S. Department of Health, Education, and Welfare, 1975, p. 3). Individual state statutes are based on this federal law and are available from county courthouses, state legislators, or state legislative libraries (Iverson & Segal, 1990).

Early childhood educators and child advocates often question the causes of child abuse. They wonder about the type of person who could hurt small children. Also, teachers are commonly concerned about safety and the best placement for children whose family members have abused them. Although many people believe that only someone with a severe mental disorder would harm a small child, reality does not bear this out. Historically, children have been viewed as the property of their parents, thus, they could be legally harmed or killed by parents. This perspective affected, and continues to affect, attitudes and behaviors toward children.

Until the 1974 law was passed, there were few safeguards for children whose parents maltreated them. In contrast, cruelty to animals was outlawed at least a century earlier. It was the Society for the Prevention of Cruelty to Animals (SPCA) that advocated for Mary Ellen in a widely publicized case of severe child abuse in 1874. This astonishing fact demonstrates that abuse of children has been an acceptable practice based in part on the low status of children in families and in society (Iverson & Segal, 1990).

Research over the past thirty years has demonstrated the ill effects of abuse and neglect on children. Early childhood educators are aware that these effects on children ultimately affect classroom dynamics. Based on ecological theory, Garbarino (as cited in Iverson and Segal, 1990) notes two primary causes of abuse as parental psychopathology and societal approval of physical punishment of children. It follows that preventive efforts must focus on both of these causes. Thus, family support services must include attention to families' mental health needs as well as to teaching parents alternative methods of discipline to physical punishment.

Some family characteristics have been shown to be related to abuse of children. In their review of literature, Iverson and Segal (1990) note the following factors:

- Parental experience includes models parents have for child rearing, especially from their own families and in their own cultures; skills for parenting; and understanding of child development.

- High levels of stress caused either by children or environment; poverty is especially stressful.

- Some characteristics of parents who abuse their children include physical or medical problems, intellectual deficits, lack of ability to form healthy parent-child relationship, marital problems, low self-esteem, immaturity, neuroses, dependency, and depression.

- Teen parents are more likely to possess the characteristics of parents who abuse because of their developmental levels. Because of their developmental stage, teens are consumed with themselves and often financially dependent.

These characteristics place them at higher risk for abusing their children.

Although the characteristics listed above place families at higher risk for child abuse, not all teen parents or those with intellectual deficits will harm their children. Understanding the risk factors should help professionals provide appropriate resources for preventing neglect and abuse of children. For example, parenting programs for those at risk might include not only information about what is best for their children but also child care for teen parents so that they are able to complete their education. Those living in poverty benefit from high-quality child care that provides sufficient time away from childcare responsibilities to enable them to finish school or take advantage of job training opportunities.

Effects of abuse and neglect on children are listed in Figures 6–2 and 6–3 (Iverson & Segal, 1990).

Early childhood teachers have a legal responsibility to report any suspected case of child abuse. For this reason, it is important that professionals be familiar with the indicators of physical, sexual, and emotional abuse and neglect of children, because this knowledge must be applied when teachers document the reasons they suspect abuse. Reporting an instance of possible child abuse is not intended to punish families, but rather to help them receive the interventions they need to help with managing their children and their lives.

Figure 6–2	Effects of Abuse and Neglect on Children

Infants and Toddlers

attachment disorders
aggressive toward peers and caregivers
not responsive to friendly overtures

Preschoolers

physically and/or verbally aggressive
destructive behavior
angry outbursts
less socially mature than non-maltreated children
play alone or watch others from a distance

School-agers

angry
aggressive
less impulsive than maltreated preschool children

KY Cabinet for Health + Family Services
KY 1-800-752-6200
Child or adult abuse

Many states have telephone hotlines for reports of child abuse. If you do not know your state's hotline or who to call, contact your State Department of Human Services. These departments have a variety of other names, including Public Welfare, Human Resources, Family Services, and Child and Youth Services. Check the social service agency listings in your local telephone directory for help. Please note that even though schools and child care centers often create procedures for teachers to report suspected cases of abuse or neglect through principals or directors, many states list teachers as those who are required to report to state officials.

When you call to report a case of suspected child abuse, it is likely that the individual taking your call will ask the following information:

• From where are you calling?

• What is your name? (You may choose to remain anonymous, depending on circumstances.)

• What have you observed that led to this call?

• What is the child's name?

• How old is the child?

• What are the child's parents' names?

• Where does the child go to school?

• Provide a description of the child.

• What is the child's address?

• Have you discussed your observations with the child or family members?

It is important for educators to understand that reports are made to child protective service workers, but that, ultimately, it is the legal system—the courts—that decides the outcome for abused children and their families. And, although agencies and courts have critical roles in attacking the problem of child abuse in our society, teachers of young children have an increasingly important role.

When the 1988 reauthorization of funding bill for the National Center on Child Abuse and Neglect was legislated, the importance of increased school involvement in the prevention, identification, and treatment of child abuse and neglect was noted (Cicchetti, Toth, & Hennessy, 1993). This recommendation arose from the research evidence that maltreated children's learning processes are interrupted or otherwise negatively affected. To optimize learning for children who have been abused and neglected, Cicchetti and his associates offer several suggestions for educators, details of which can be found in Figure 6–4.

Consider all eight of the recommendations for schools regarding maltreated children in Figure 6–4. Which items have you observed in practice? Which items do you believe are not commonly practiced? What are some barriers to putting these policies into practice? How might collaboration among schools and agencies increase positive outcomes for maltreated children?

| Figure 6–3 | Indicators of Abuse and Neglect |

PHYSICAL CHARACTERISTICS OF MALTREATED CHILDREN

Physical Abuse

Bruises, lacerations, welts, abrasions, fractures, or burns as follows:

unusual location:
- cheeks, lips, mouth, earlobes
- back, buttocks, back of legs
- external genitalia
- burns on soles of feet, palms of hands, back or buttocks

unusual appearance:
- clustered or patterned
- resembling the shape of an instrument
- on several different surface areas
- cigar or cigarette burns
- immersion (glove- or sock-like burns)
- rope burns (especially on neck)

suspicious circumstances:
- no explanation
- explanation does not fit injury
- patterns to the occurrence of injuries (e.g., after absences from school)
- repeated injuries or injuries in various stages of healing
- nonorganic failure to thrive

Neglect

Underweight, malnourished
Poor hygiene
Fatigue, constantly falling asleep

Bald spot on infant's head
Unattended physical problems or medical needs:
- chronic anemia
- severe diaper rash
- skin rashes
- tooth decay/gum disease
- head/body lice
- ringworm
- nonorganic failure to thrive

Sexual Abuse

Swelling, bruising or irritation around:
- genital areas
- anal areas
- mouth

Torn, stained, or bloody underclothing
Vaginal discharge
Pain/discomfort in walking or sitting
Anal ulcers
Genital pain or itching
Venereal diseases
Difficulty in urination
Pregnancy

Emotional Abuse

Physical symptoms of anxiety:
- psychogenic skin disorders
- pain with no physical basis
- ulcers
- unexplained vomiting

COMMON DESCRIPTIONS OF THE INTERPERSONAL BEHAVIOR OF MALTREATED CHILDREN

Physical Abuse	Neglect	Sexual Abuse	Emotional Abuse
Aggressive	Aggressive	Sexually aggressive or preoccupied with sex	Aggressive
Withdrawal	Withdrawal	Overly compliant	Suspicious
Avoidance	Suspicious/distrustful of others	Seductive	Avoids eye contact
Fearful of others	Unresponsive	Distrustful	Unable to make friends
Angry	Hostility	Fearful of opposite sex	Overly compliant
"Frozen watchfulness"		"Role reversal"	Overly non-compliant
Hostility		Withdrawn	Bizarre or inappropriate interpersonal behavior
		Isolated	

continues

Figure 6–3 *(Continued)*

BEHAVIOR SEQUELAE OF MALTREATMENT

Physical Abuse	Neglect	Sexual Abuse	Emotional Abuse
Self-abusive behavior	Irregular school attendance	Excessive daydreaming/ fantasizing	Self-abusive behavior
Lying	Begging, stealing, or hoarding food	Excessive sexual play/ masturbation	Hoarding food
Stealing	Lying	Self-abusive behavior	Referral to self in the third person
Truancy	Theft	Truancy	Thumb-sucking
Tics	Vandalism	Running away	Nail biting
Stuttering	Running away	Regressive/infantile behavior	Habit disorders—sucking, biting, rocking
Unpredictable	Daydreaming	Suicidal gestures	Obsessive or compulsive behaviors
	Bizarre eating habits	Insomnia	Insomnia
	Nail biting		Enuresis
	Tics		Truancy
	Stuttering		Running away
	Unpredictable		Destructive behavior

Source: With Permission from Iverson, T. J., & Segal, M. (1990). *Child Abuse and Neglect: An Information and Reference Guide.* Table 4–1, p. 72; Table 4–4, p. 95; and Table 4–6, p. 106

"Children have neither power nor property. Voices other than their own must speak for them. If those voices are silent, then children who have been abused may lean their heads against windowpanes and taste the bitter emptiness of violated childhoods. Badger every legislator from every county . . . let no editor or reporter sleep, until the remedy you want is granted. For you are the only voices of the violated child. If you do not speak, there is silence."

—Justice Francis T. Murphy. Cited in Doucette-Dudman and LaCure, 1996

Substance Abuse in Families

When family members use illegal drugs, or misuse alcohol or prescription drugs, children often suffer great difficulties. Parents who are addicted to drugs and/or alcohol typically cannot provide consistent nurturing for their children. Further, a family's economic

Resources for Information about Child Abuse and Neglect

National Center on Child Abuse and Neglect (NCCAN) 63 Inverness Drive East Englewood, Colorado 80112–5117
(303) 792–9900
http://www.nccanch.acf.hhs.gov

National Committee to Prevent Child Abuse
332 S. Michigan Avenue, Suite 1600
Chicago, Illinois 60604
(312) 663–3520
http://www.casanet.org/
Click "advocate's library"; click "abuse"

National Association of Counsel for Children 205 Oneida Street Denver, Colorado 80822
(303) 322–2260
http://naccchildlaw.org/

well-being is compromised when adults lose their jobs because of behavior related to **substance abuse.**

Mothers' prenatal use of alcohol and drugs may have dire consequences for newborns that last throughout life. Drinking alcohol during pregnancy may lead to babies having Fetal Alcohol Syndrome (FAS); the safe level of alcohol intake during pregnancy is not known. The characteristics of FAS include central nervous system disorders, growth lags, and facial deformity (Olson, 1994). Effects of maternal drug use on infants and young children include neurological immaturity, which is manifested in poor sleeping and eating patterns, poor self-control, inconsolability, hypersensitivity to the environment, and decreased ability to interact with others (Poulsen, 1994).

Figure 6–4	Policy Implications for Schools Educating Maltreated Children

The following recommendations are from the work of Cicchetti, Toth, and Hennessy (1993).

1. Assessments of maltreated children must include not only those for cognitive development and academic achievement but also those for the social and emotional domains. Because many abused children act out in school, too often the emphasis is on the behavior only and not on the emotional disturbance caused by abusive situations.

2. Intervention efforts must begin as soon as identification of maltreatment occurs. Schools may be the only setting in which such interventions can occur. Thus, courts and agencies must work with educators for positive outcomes. At this time, often interpretations of confidentiality procedures exclude educators and schools from appropriate levels of participation in intervention.

   Educators must increase their understanding of the importance of confidentiality in instances of abuse so that they can share appropriately in intervention efforts.

3. Early childhood teachers who are involved in intervention efforts should involve parents and other relevant family members. This creates the greatest possibility of continuity between environments.

4. The curriculum for maltreated children must be developmentally appropriate. Including all areas of child development in curriculum goals is essential so that these children have a greater chance for adjustment throughout their lives. Special planning and instructional support may be necessary for children to gain abilities and attitudes for cognitive, social, and emotional growth.

5. Specific training for teachers is necessary in regard to styles and strategies that are conducive to optimizing development of maltreated children. Teachers must recognize and avoid "any physically or emotionally abusive interchanges with children." The use of physical punishment must be forbidden. Too few teachers are trained in early childhood special education, especially in the area of emotional support.

   Research suggests that an extrinsic, behaviorally focused system for these children may interfere with their motivation. Thus, behavior modification programs should not be used with abused and neglected children. Instead, plans should include strategies for increasing the children's internal motivation while dealing with their emotional distress.

6. Teachers of young children are very important figures in children's lives. A positive relationship based on trust is important. Some current practices such as multiage grouping and looping are useful for abused children in that they may continue to build positive relationships with the same teacher or teachers for longer than one school term.

7. Because identification of abuse and neglect must come before any educational intervention can be offered, teachers and schools must improve their knowledge regarding recognizing and reporting instances of maltreatment. Having the attitude that reporting is required to help the child, not to punish the family, is also an important understanding.

8. Training must be provided so that child protective services workers and educators work together. Little progress has been made in this area and unfortunately, these groups of professionals often see the other group as problematic instead of working collegially toward more effective interventions. To be fair to individuals, the human services system and the educational system have not typically fostered these working relationships.

Source: Cicchetti, D., Toth, S. L., & Hennessy, K. (1993). Child Maltreatment and School Adaptation: Problems and Promises. In D. Cicchetti and S. L. Toth (Eds.), *Child Abuse, Child Development, and Social Policy* (pp. 301–330). Norwood, NJ: Ablex

Center for Interventions, Treatment and Addiction
   Research
http://www.med.wright.edu/
Type in "citar"

Center for Substance Abuse Treatment
http://www.samhsa.gov/centers/csat2002

Center on Addiction and Substance Abuse
http://www.casacolumbia.org/

Addiction to any substance (or condition) points to personality characteristics, disabilities, or impairments, each of which may have significant implications for an adult's ability to parent a child, and may predispose an adult to adopt an authoritarian, over-controlling, or under-involved style of parenting. Moreover, all abused substances alter to varying degrees an individual's state of consciousness, memory, affect regulation, and impulse control, and may become so addictive that the adult's primary goal is to supply his or her addiction to the exclusion of all else and all others in his or her life. These alterations likely have a marked influence, at any given moment, on the adult's capacity to sustain contingent, responsive interactions with an infant or young child (Mayes, 1995, p. 105).

Children who are growing up in homes in which one or more adults are addicted to drugs or alcohol are likely to be affected in one or more of the following ways:

- reverse roles with parent
- are fearful, angry, mistrusting, guilty, and sad
- are either over-responsible or under-responsible
- suffer chronic grief or depression
- are isolated from others
- have academic problems
- have learning disabilities (Krestan and Bepko, 1989)

Children living in families with alcoholism or drug abuse frequently need more support than classroom teachers can provide. Referring children to guidance counselors or other mental health professionals may be helpful.

"Numerous barriers stand between women, especially mothers, and drug treatment. For example, women often resist entering treatment programs because they must release their children to someone else's care and fear never seeing them again. Despite this reality, only a handful of residential drug-treatment programs accept women with their children. Treatment programs need to be developed that treat parents, especially mothers, in the context of their families."

—Zuckerman and Brazelton, 1994, p. 82

Marital Transitions and Single Parenting

Divorce and remarriage have become so common in our society today that some family experts believe that they may be developmental stressors rather than unexpected ones. However, because the consequences of divorce and remarriage for young children are often stressful, and because teachers and parents may disregard or discount the significance of these occurrences in the lives of children, we address these transitions here. Children may benefit from knowing other children and families in similar circumstances, but by and large, the changes in family structure are likely to generate concern for all family members.

In the United States, the divorce rate began to rise in the 1960s. Currently, almost 50 percent of marriages end in divorce. Most people who divorce eventually remarry. Remarriages in which children from previous relationships are present have a 50 percent higher rate of dissolution than those without children from previous relationships (Fields & Casper, 2001).

The number of single-parent families has also increased since 1970. In 2000, there were 10 million single-mother families, compared to 3 million in 1970. The number of single-father families also increased during that period, from 393,000 to 2 million. Compared to single-father families, single-mother families are more likely to have more than one child, to live below the poverty level, and to have never-married.

As the proportion of married couples has decreased, the proportion of U.S. families that are led by single mothers has increased. Single-parent families have increased both as a result of the divorce rate and a rise in the number of births among single women. Birth rates among single women continued to increase throughout the 1990s even as the divorce rate began to level off. Some experts predict that the divorce rate may soon fall to 40 percent (Emery, 1999; Fields & Casper, 2001).

Disagreement persists among scholars about the effects of divorce on children. Even though many studies have been completed in this area, families' experiences include so many variables that this has impeded researchers from declaring conclusive results. Robert Emery (1999), in his extensive review of research literature, has compiled "four global facts about consequences of divorce for children" (p. 35):

1. Divorce causes stress for children. Such stress is often related to the loss of frequent contact with one parent. Another common cause of stress has to do with the economic hardship families face as they divide one household into two.

2. Children whose parents divorce are at an increased risk for psychological difficulties, both internalized (depression, anxiety) and externalized (behavioral, conduct) problems.

3. Despite children's increased risk for psychological problems when their parents divorce, they are resilient in their coping.

4. Even with this ability to cope, children remain emotionally vulnerable when parents divorce. Even well-adjusted adults whose parents divorced when they were children report the existence of painful feelings, unhappy memories, and ongoing distress.

One of the many perplexing topics regarding divorce and children is cause and effect. It might be that children who display serious consequences seemingly from parental divorce may actually have suffered some distress or difficulties before the divorce, and that the source of those difficulties may be

troubled parents, relationship issues, parents who lack parenting skills, or parents who have mental health related issues. Of course, it is possible that parents in these situations are more likely to divorce and to have troubled children (Emery, 1999). In such cases, divorce may exacerbate children's behaviors, or it may cause family members or educators to notice these behaviors.

The resilience of children has been documented in research about divorce. Even though children from divorced families have more difficulties than children from married families, "time does appear to help divorced families to heal" (Emery, 1999, p. 61) Support and concern from caring adults is helpful to children experiencing divorce; however, the passing of time also is an important consideration. Researchers have found that most children show significant improvement in their adjustment two years after a divorce (Emery, 1999).

> *"Perhaps what is most insensitive and unjust is to arrive at the conclusions about divorce and its effects on children without carefully considering what we know, not just what we believe."*
>
> **—Robert Emery, 1999, p. 1**

A key question for early childhood teachers when examining the effects of divorce on young children is "What factors help children reach a healthy adjustment as their family structure changes?" First, parents can implement some strategies that will help to support children's increased adjustment to the new family structure. Galinsky and David (1988) share this advice for parents:

Explain the separation to the children and provide as much consistency as possible. Tell them where they will live, who will care for them, and when and how they will visit the noncustodial parent. Keep them updated on changes in advance of new situations.

Explain that the separation is not the child's fault and that it might take a while to feel better about it. Young children often believe that they caused the separation or divorce because of inappropriate behavior or a one-time wish. Parents most likely will need to frequently remind children that they were not the cause. Sharing feelings, both sad and optimistic, will be important for the healing process.

Encourage children to continue the discussion when they have concerns or questions. In addition to authentic conversations, children's books and media can provide a basis for discussion. Invite children to initiate conversation with you.

Provide support for children and yourself. Children and adults need various forms of social, emotional, and sometimes physical support as they adjust to new circumstances involved in divorce. Both personal (family and friends) and professional support is helpful.

Avoid promises, uncertain assurances, surprises, and extravagances led by guilt. Focus on what is real. Have fun together. Delight in the joys that exist in the relationship with your child.

Second, teachers and other community members can be excellent sources of support for children and parents as they adjust to their new living arrangements. Early childhood teachers can share the above advice for parents through newsletters or the establishment of special-interest parent groups. Further, school-wide groups for children have been found to be effective in supporting their adjustment to divorce. Such groups provide a place for children to share their feelings and experiences and to discuss their changing family relationships. Strategies to support children in these discussions through various **marital transitions** such as separation, divorce, remarriage, or other blended living arrangements are helpful. Effective programs teach children specific appropriate skills for problem solving, communication, and expression of emotions, including fear and anger (Emery, 1999).

To listen to a mother speak about single parenting go to the online resource located at http://www.earlychilded.delmar.com.

This single parent of two discusses the day-to-day responsibilities and relationships she has with her children. She also emphasizes the need for the school's support in helping her care for and educate her children in this insightful online voice.

Adjustment Tasks for Stepfamilies
http://www.stepfamilyinfo.org/

Divorce Education and Mediation Program
http://www.hamiltontn.gov/
Click "courts information"; click "circuit court clerk"; click "divorce education seminars"

Helping Children to Understand Divorce
http://www.muextension.missouri.edu/
Type in "Helping children understand divorce"

Primary Project
http://www.childrensinstitute.net
Click "programs for children"

Homeless Families

The number of **homeless** individuals in the United States today is increasing. Precise statistics are difficult to come by because of the elusive nature of homelessness; one estimate from 1990 indicates that 500,000 to 750,000 school-age children are homeless and that this number is growing (National Coalition for the Homeless, as cited in Kling, Dunn, & Oakley, 1996). Children's advocates agree that all young children have the right to a safe space to live. Much of our understanding about the optimal development of the whole child assumes physical and emotional safety. "The average homeless family includes two to three children under age five" (p. 3). It is believed that a common reason for homelessness is an inadequate supply of affordable housing combined with declining family incomes, even when the adults in the household are employed. In short, there is too little money to pay for available housing.

The effects on children of being homeless are vast. Among the difficulties are language and motor delays and unmet health needs. Behavioral problems and emotional disabilities are frequently found in children who live in shelters. In addition, many of the children's parents also are plagued with mental health problems (Hamner & Turner, 1996).

Living conditions among homeless families vary: some live in a shelter, some have lived in several shelters over a period of months, and others live with friends or extended families. When homeless families move in with another family, conditions are frequently overcrowded and offer no privacy. Stays may last for a few weeks or a few months, and the family may then move in with other friends or family members. For children in early childhood programs, these relocations often mean that they either drop out of the program (before mandatory school age) or change schools. These disruptions may be sudden and create difficult transitions for young children.

Education of Homeless Children and Youth
http://www.naehcy.org

Futures for Children
http://www.futuresforchildren.com/

Homeless Children's Network
http://www.hcnkids.org/

Homes for the Homeless
http://www.homesforthehomeless.com/

The Reading Connection
http://www.thereadingconnection.org/

Following are some characteristics of homeless children:

- sleep disturbances
- nighttime anxieties about possessions, even wearing their shoes to prevent theft
- lethargy and inattention at school
- may hoard food at school
- nutritional deficiencies
- delays in immunizations
- insecurity
- trouble playing with other children and making friends
- aggression
- anxiety
- language and other developmental delays (Kling, Dunn, & Oakley, 1996)

When parents are not able to provide shelter or security for their children, they often feel guilty and helpless: If they are not even competent enough to provide their children's basic needs, how can they possibly assist their children academically? Thus, the self-esteem of parents in homeless families is likely to be very low. Understanding these characteristics of homeless families and children can help early childhood teachers act sensitively toward them.

Early childhood educators must look for the strengths in homeless families, just as they look for strengths in other families. Research shows that although these families have almost no material possessions, they do have "the desire and the will to maintain the family unit regardless of continual changes in their life circumstances" (Kling, Dunn, & Oakley, 1996, p. 7). All children need consistency in classroom schedules and routines, but children without homes need this consistency even more. They are also likely to need some alone time at school because they often live in crowded situations.

Parents in homeless families may not be able to participate as active partners in their children's education. Often, for these parents, just getting their children to school is a huge accomplishment. So, extending special invitations to homeless parents, so that they can be included in school activities in ways they feel comfortable, may be a huge boost to their self-esteem. Following are some suggestions for early childhood educators who are working with homeless families:

- set up a parent lounge where support groups could form and meet regularly
- provide reading materials about child development, lists of and contacts for family services available in the community, and free activities for parents and children to do together
- set up a toy lending library
- formulate a plan for homeless children to borrow toys from school to take to the shelter
- provide banks for clothing, food, and first aid materials
- maintain appropriate confidentiality while helping families get available services

Reading materials about child development, family services available in the community, and free activities for parents and children to do together will assist early childhood educators who are working with homeless families.

Early childhood educators also should be aware of the Stewart B. McKinney Homeless Assistance Act of 1987, which provides some funding to states for serving homeless families. Teachers should contact their State Department of Education to find out what programs for homeless families are operating in their state (Kling, Dunn, & Oakley, 1996).

The following resources may be helpful in increasing teachers' understanding of working with children from homeless families:

National Alliance to End Homelessness 1518 K Street NW, Suite 206 Washington, DC 20005

(202) 638-1526

http://www.neh.org/

National Coalition for the Homeless

1439 Rhode Island Avenue, NW

Washington, DC 20005

(202) 659-3310

National Law Center on Homelessness and Poverty

918 F Street, NW, Suite 412

Washington, DC 20004

(202) 638-2535

http://www.nlchp.org/

Families and Children with Disabilities

"Children may be born with one or more disabilities, and they may acquire disabilities later in life because of accident or disease" (Hamner & Turner, 1996, p. 315). When a baby is identified with a **disability** at birth, parents often react with disbelief. Many parents perceive and experience this news as a loss, certainly the loss of a dream if not of a life (see Figure 6–5), and they must then proceed through the grief process. Although parents grieve in individual ways, some conditions of grieving seem to be common (Moses, 1983):

- denial
- anxiety
- guilt
- depression
- anger

"What's supposed to be the best day of your life turns out to be like a funeral."

—Robin Simons, 1987

Some factors are known to affect parental grief over the birth of a child with a disability. These include culture; religion; economic status; the nature of the disability; the family's ability to cope; the stability of the parents' relationship, the number, gender, and age of other children in the family; and the availability of support systems. Consider two or three of these factors and tell how you believe they might affect families who have a new baby that has been identified as having a disability.

Even when parents are coping well, families who have a child with disabilities face greater challenges than other families with young children. All infants and young children have many caregiving needs. Anyone who has cared for one healthy infant knows that it is a full-time job. But children with disabilities have even greater needs, which consume

| Figure 6–5 | Explanations for Each of the Conditions of Grief |

Denial—Parents who are informed that their child has a disability are so overwhelmed by shock and fear that denial is one way to cope. They are likely to look for complete cures for their child's condition, even when none exist.

Anxiety—Constant concern for the child, as well as for their entire family, often leads parents to feel extreme pressure and worry. Arrangements for the child's medical care and further testing often overwhelm already busy parents. Sleeplessness, irritability, and other symptoms associated with anxiety may become prevalent.

Guilt—"If only I had eaten better"; "If only I had had earlier prenatal care"; "If only I. . . ." Parents attempt to assess what they did wrong and how they are at fault for the child's condition.

Depression—Parents may feel overwhelming sadness about the loss of what their child might have been. Dreams have been shattered. Parents focus on the disability.

Anger—At whom should parents direct their anger? Not the child, not the medical staff, not each other, not families or friends. Sometimes parents blame others who have no responsibility for their situation because there is no logical place to direct the anger.

Acceptance—With warmth and support from professionals, family, and friends, many parents of children with disabilities come to accept not only their child, but also their situation. They begin to focus on the child's gains instead of their own loss at what might have been.

Children with Disabilities
http://www.childrenwithdisabilities.ncjrs.org/

ERIC Clearinghouse on Disabilities and Gifted Education
http://ericec.org

Exceptional Parent Magazine
http://www.eparent.com/

Federal Resource Center for Special Education
http://www.rrfcnetwork.org

Free Appropriate Public Education Site
http://www.fapeonline.org/

A Guide to Children's Literature and Disability
http://www.nichcy.org
Click "I"; click "literacy"

Individualizing Inclusion in Child Care
http://www.fpg.unc.edu/
On the Most Requested Pages' pull-down menu, click "Partnerships for Inclusion"

National Information Center for Children and Youth with Disabilities
http://www.nichcy.org/

Special Child
http://www.specialchild.com/

much more time than typically developing children. Further, it is often difficult to find substitute care so that parents can have a much-needed respite. Often, substitute caregivers do not feel that they have the additional knowledge or skills necessary to care for the child's special needs.

In addition to the challenge of caregiving demands, a second difference in families who have a child with disabilities is the level of stress. Hamner and Turner (1996) discuss the following causes of stress in these families:

- the need to feel "normal"
- lack of information about the child's condition
- concern about what the future holds for their child
- increased financial needs
- lack of sufficient support systems
- single parenthood

"I've heard this period called 'nothingness' and that's exactly how you feel. You can't move, can't think, can't do anything but feel—leaden, like a rock. There's nothing there—but that disability."

—Robin Simons, 1987

The one factor that seems to make a difference in helping families of children with disabilities to make a positive adjustment is the presence of informal support. Support from one's spouse is especially crucial. Families who share tasks within the family and have formal and informal support external to the family seem to cope best (Trivette & Dunst, 1992). Some planned programs for parents who have a child with a disability can include helping:

- all children to understand and relate to a child who is differently abled.
- parents to help their children to respond to teasing or comments about his or her disability.
- parents know what and how much to expect from their child's academic and social progress.
- parents with strategies to advocate for their children's optimal education.
- parents to know how and when to foster independence in their children with disabilities (Hendrick, 1998).

"I talk to other parents. There's no substitute for that. You find out you're not alone. You're not the only one with those concerns."

—Robin Simons, 1987

Since 1975, federal legislation—the Education for All Handicapped Children Act of 1975 (PL 94-142)—has mandated free public education for children with disabilities between the ages of 3 and 21 years. In 1986, additional legislation required that all states provide preschool programs to all children between three and five years who have been identified as having a disability. Thus, many early childhood teachers are working in education settings that include young children with disabilities (see Figure 6–6). Before the Education for All Handicapped Children Act was passed, most children with identified disabilities were not served by public schools or were served only in special classes. Some children were able to attend special schools for children with similar disabilities such as blindness or deafness, but many children did not receive appropriate education or related services.

One of the major pieces of the 1986 legislation is the emphasis placed on the importance of the whole family of children with disabilities. Instead of requiring an Individual Education Plan (IEP), this

---

Figure 6–6   PL 94–142 and PL 99–457

PL 94-142 (1975) The Education for All Handicapped Children Act renamed in 1990 to the Individual with Disabilities Education Act (IDEA)

To assure "that all handicapped children have available to them . . . a free appropriate public education which emphasizes special education and related services designed to meet their unique needs, to assure that the rights of handicapped children and their parents or guardians are protected, to assist states and localities to provide for the education of all handicapped children, and to assess and assure the effectiveness of efforts to educate handicapped children."

Also, this act required states to establish "procedures to assure that to the maximum extent appropriate, handicapped children, including children in public and private institutions or other care facilities, are educated with children who are not handicapped, and that special classes, separate schooling or other removal of handicapped children from the regular educational environment occurs only when the nature or severity of the handicap is such that education in regular classes with the use of supplementary aids and services can be achieved satisfactorily."

PL 99-457 (1986) The Infants and Toddlers with Disabilities Act (ITDA), now in IDEA

"ITDA requires provision of coordinated, multiagency, multidisciplinary services necessary to 'enhance' the development of infants and toddlers with disabilities. In addition to enhanced development, the law seeks to minimize the potential for developmental delay of children; eventually to reduce the need for special education and related services, and thereby reduce the cost of education for these children; to reduce the need for institutionalization and to 'maximize' their potential for independent living in a society; to work with families to assist them in meeting children's needs; and to assist the state and localities in meeting the needs of populations which are often underrepresented, for example, children living in poverty" (Guernsey & Klare, 1993, p. 250).

law requires an Individualized Family Service Plan (IFSP). Attention is given to the needs of the child's whole family. Given the research on the special challenges felt by families of children who have a disability, this approach is believed to be much more effective than planning only an educational program for the child (Figure 6–7).

In addition to the parent involvement requirements for typically developing children and their families, Head Start requires even more of the staff who are working with families who have children with disabilities. The following standards, included by Head Start, are excellent guidelines for all early childhood educators:

- support parents of children with disabilities
- provide information to parents on how to foster development of their child with disabilities
- provide observation opportunities for parents so that they can see activities described in child's IEP
- provide follow-up assistance to carry program activities over into the home
- refer parents to support groups or other parents whose children have similar disabilities
- inform parents of their legal rights
- inform parents of community resources available to them and help them to access the services
- identify needs related to the disability of siblings and other family members
- provide information regarding prevention of disabilities for younger siblings
- build parent confidence and skill in advocating for their children with special needs (Head Start program performance standards and other regulations, 1993, pp. 313–314)

"Sometimes I feel overwhelmed. How can I evaluate this program? How do I know this is best? Then I remember it's a team approach. I'm not in it alone. It's just my job to get the specialists I trust to talk to each other about it. I remind myself that they know programs, and I know my child."

—Robin Simons, 1987

Figure 6–7	Contents of IEPs and IFSPs

Each Individual Education Plan (IEP) and Individual Family Service Plan (IFSP) must contain:

1. Present levels of child's performance
   a. academic achievement
   b. social competence
   c. prevocational and vocational skills
   d. psychomotor skill
   e. self-help skills
2. Annual goals for child to achieve by end of school year
3. Measurable short-term instructional objectives that will assist the child in achieving the stated annual goals
4. Specific educational services needed by child including all special education related services, type of physical education program, and special instructional media and materials
5. Dates for services to begin and length of time to be provided
6. Description of how child will be included in regular education programs
7. Justification for type of educational programs prescribed
8. List of those responsible for various aspects of the IEP or IFSP
9. Objective assessment, at least annually, must be specified for measuring achievement of short-term goals
10. Teachers and parents must work together to decide on goals and how they should be achieved

Source: Federal Register, 41 [252], pp. 56966–56998

To listen to a mother of a child with a disability discuss her relationship with a school, go to the online resource located at http://www.earlychilded.delmar.com. Teri is the mother of a child with autism. She briefly describes the history of her son's development and her role as his advocate. Also, Teri discusses the school's role in his development and the need for a team effort in this personal online voice.

Families and Children with Serious Illness

Just as families with children who have disabilities face a major crisis at the time they are informed of their child's condition, so do families of children with a **serious illness.** Hilton Davis (1993) explains the intense feelings of families as they receive information concerning their child's illness. The diagnosis "brings with it irreversible change. The world is instantly transformed in a nightmarish way. The sudden need to adapt to dreadful circumstances is forced upon the parents, their child, and indeed the whole family. Potentially they have to change their whole way of life, amid the terrible pain or anguish implied by the words above. Their vision of the world, their values, their ambitions, their whole philosophy will be altered by this one event" (p. 1).

Medical advances have made it possible for more children to survive even with serious illnesses or disabilities. Not only are more children surviving, but health care professionals also are increasing efforts to enable these children to live as normal a life as possible. Thus, such children appear in greater numbers than ever before in early childhood educational programs. Each child's particular illness or disease will affect his special educational needs. Thus, it is important for early childhood teachers to have some knowledge of a child's illness, as well as general information about the child and family members (Figure 6–9).

Some serious illnesses cause greater concern than others in early education settings. Currently, children who are infected with HIV or have AIDS are among those who generate the greatest apprehension among teachers, other students, and the parents of other students. Often, children with these conditions are ostracized from society because of fears based on an inaccurate understanding of how the disease is transmitted. Additionally, families of infected children face incredible strains on their resources (Hamner & Turner, 1996) (see Figure 6–8).

Policies among early education programs vary widely on how they accept and deal with children with serious illness and their families. Generally, it is important that administrators and teachers understand the needs of all children and their families, and that they work with families to help them receive appropriate services. Although policies for dealing with seriously ill

Caring for Babies with AIDS
http://www.caring4babieswithAIDS.org/

Children's Memorial Hospital (Chicago)—
Neonatology
http://www.childrensmemorial.org/
Click "Specialties and services"; click "departments and programs"; click "Neonatology"

Chronically Ill Children: How Families Adjust
http://www.nurseweek.com/
Click "Education/CE"; type in "chronically ill children"

STARBRIGHT Foundation
http://www.starbright.org

children vary, confidentiality and the rights of children and their families must be the first priority of any policy. It will be necessary for teachers to comply with policy and to take precautions for their own safety such as wearing gloves when coming into contact with children's body fluids.

Davis (1993) offers four guidelines for those who are working with families of ill children:

1. Respect the parents.

2. Parents have the major role in dealing with their child's illness.

3. Professionals work *with* and *for* families, not *on* or *instead* of them.

4. The most important thing for professionals is to really listen to family members as they confer.

Immigrant Families

Immigrant families often feel divided between two sets of emotions. On one hand, they are sad about losing their country of origin and leaving behind family, friends, familiar ways of doing things, and the ease of communicating in their native language. On the other hand, they are hopeful about the new opportunities that living in the United States brings, and look forward to improving the quality of life for themselves and their children (Lieberman, 1995, p. 28).

As teachers welcome immigrant families into their programs, it is important for them to keep these

Figure 6–8 HIV/AIDS

"HIV is a retrovirus that infects white blood cells, the brain, the bowel, the skin, and other tissues.

Transmission of the virus occurs through sexual or parental blood contact, or from an infected mother to her fetus or infant. Infection results in a wide spectrum of illness and a high fatality rate.

The most severe manifestation of HIV infection is acquired immunodeficiency syndrome (AIDS)....

AIDS cases among children have increased rapidly since the first reports in 1982" (Simonds & Rogers, 1992).

Children contract the virus from their mother in three ways:

1. in utero as a fetus
2. during birth
3. by breastfeeding

Not all children born to HIV mothers contract the virus; estimates are that about 25 percent to 40 percent do.

Children with AIDS commonly have other illnesses and disorders including pneumonia, serious bacterial infections, skin disease, diarrhea, developmental delays, and neurological dysfunction. Most children with HIV develop AIDS in three to three-and-a-half years, and for most of these children, the disease is fatal.

Treatment is typically through drugs, and new treatments are evolving.

Early childhood education teachers should speak in short sentences and simple words to help immigrant children understand.

dual emotions in mind. It is usually easier for teachers to understand the joyfulness and excitement about coming to the United States, but the accompanying sense of loss is just as real for these families.

As immigrant families enter their new country, change is sudden and all-encompassing. One immediate and profound change may be that of language: If the family does not speak English, language barriers may be difficult to overcome. This causes great stress, which may lead to anxiety or depression (Lieberman, 1995). Also, as children are immersed in a new culture, families may be concerned about a loss of family values and traditions. Teachers can help reduce some of the stress that these families face by applying the following points:

- Consider the language difference. Speak and write in ways that the family can understand. Use short sentences and simple words to ensure that they understand.

- Explain the daily schedule and routine activities of the class. Take time to explain what happens in the program and to listen to parents' questions or comments.

- Acknowledge that there may be some tension between the family and the staff. It probably is not personal, but rather is based on cultural differences. Think about what you can do to communicate more effectively with the family and thus overcome as many of these tensions as possible.

- Ask questions about the family and their expectations for their children. Avoid getting too personal and do not give advice. Instead, listen carefully so that you can learn about the family.

Health Coverage for Legal Immigrant Children
http://www.cbpp.org
Type in "health coverage"

Identifying and Serving Immigrant Children Who Are Gifted
http://ericec.org

Immigrant Children Exceed Expectations
http://www.ilw.com/

Figure 6–9	Description of Some Chronic Illnesses of Children

Juvenile-Onset Diabetes—When too little insulin is secreted by the pancreas, juvenile-onset diabetes results. Needs: precise balance of diet, exercise, and insulin by injection; close monitoring of sugar levels is necessary two to three times daily. Snacks may be required during the school day.

Asthma—A chronic lung disease with bronchial sensitivity to many different stimuli. Wide variation in needs of children with mild cases to those with severe cases. Modifications in environment may be necessary to reduce allergens and irritants. Children with severe cases may have a lot of absences and need home-based educational services.

Spina Bifida—Improper closure of spinal column prenatally leads to spina bifida. Difficulties with movement in the lower body; child may not be able to move legs, and have little or no control of bowel and bladder. May need a wheelchair, braces, or crutches; retardation is possible. Schools must provide accessibility to all educational programs.

Cleft Palate and Other Craniofacial Anomalies—Degree of these problems varies from minimal to great. Disfigurement of child's face is difficult issue for child and family to deal with. Some anomalies easily corrected by surgery; others more complicated. Children have a high risk for ear infections and hearing loss.

Congenital Heart Diseases—There is a wide variety of structural anomalies in the development of the heart. Surgery often helpful; it is very expensive; may help problems, not typically a total cure. Child has restrictions on daily activities after surgery and must be carefully monitored. Uncertainty about survival.

Leukemia—Most common childhood cancer begins with anemia, weight loss, and sometimes bleeding. An excessive number of white cells in the blood. Child is frequently hospitalized, receives a large amount of medication, and radiation therapy with major side effects. Uncertainty regarding remission and survival.

Hemophilia—Genetic disease in which blood clotting factor is absent and leads to uncontrolled bleeding. Nearly all affected are male. Often, bleeding occurs without an injury present. Painful arthritis may accompany disease; may require surgery or strong medication. Some treatment with blood products may now be done at home or school; requires fewer hospitalizations.

End-Stage Renal Disease—Extremely severe complication of variety of conditions affecting kidneys. Treatments include dialysis and transplants. When disease begins in infancy, high rate of failure to grow. Survival rate for these children increasing.

Sickle Cell Anemia—Results from abnormality in structure of hemoglobin. This affects shape of cells, and these cells have trouble passing through veins and smaller blood vessels. Risks include lack of oxygen to any body organ and to certain kinds of bacteria which cause bone infections and meningitis. Symptoms include anemia, diminished growth, and late onset of puberty. Children are hospitalized frequently and need strong pain medication.

Cystic Fibrosis—Children with CF have major chronic lung disease and frequent lung infections. Great strides have been made in treating this disease. Diagnosis is usually made in the first two years of life based on poor weight gain and frequent lung infections. Children need equipment for respiratory care, medications, and special diets.

Muscular Dystrophy—More common in boys, this disease involves progressive weakness of large muscles in legs first, and then extends to other muscles of the body. Diagnosis does not usually happen until about age five or six years, even though cause is genetic. Treatment is very limited.

Source: Perrin, J. M. (1985). Introduction: Severe and chronic illness in childhood. In N. Hobbs, J. M. Perrin, & H. T. Ireys (Eds.), *Chronically ill children and their families.* San Francisco: Jossey-Bass PL 94–142 and PL 99–457.

- Establish a warm and trusting environment for all families and children. If you have concerns about the child or practices of the family, a trusting relationship will allow for ways to express the concern and for you to work in partnership with the family (Lieberman, 1995).

Migrant Families

Migrant families move from one location to another and from one job to another for financial reasons (Chavkin, 1991). And yet, migrant families are among the poorest in the United States (Lopez, Scribner, & Mahitivanichcha, 2001). It is difficult to estimate the number of migrant families in the United States, but there may be as many as 1.5 million migrant farmworkers (Shotland, 1989). Although little information is available about migrant families, it is known that there is diversity among their lifestyles (Chavkin, 1991). Some of this diversity might be related to the three primary geographic migration routes: East Coast, Mid-continent, and West Coast (Shotland, 1989).

Ethnicity and culture also contribute to the diversity of migrant families. Those farmworkers who migrate through the southern states and along the eastern seaboard are most often African Americans, Mexican Americans and Mexican nationals, Anglos, Jamaican and Haitian blacks, and Puerto Ricans. Those who migrate through south Texas and move through the Midwestern and western states are most often Mexican Americans and Mexican nationals, as well as some Native Americans. Migrant workers who travel the West Coast through California to Oregon and Washington are also most often Mexican Americans and Mexican nationals. Some of these farmworkers are also southeast Asians (Shotland, 1989).

Many factors may lead to poor health in adults and children in migrant families; these factors include continuous relocation, extremely low wages, hard physical work in the fields, unsafe farm equipment, poor nutrition, and lack of consistent medical care. Huang (1993) discusses health problems related to prenatal care, agriculture as a dangerous occupation, and poverty. Poverty contributes to ill health in numerous ways; among them are malnutrition and poor sanitation in substandard housing that lacks indoor plumbing for toilets or drinking water. These risk factors contribute to health-related problems in many segments of the population, of course, but migrant families are particularly susceptible to an extremely high number of them.

Many people who migrate for economic reasons speak only their native language or have limited use of English. Along with migrants' frequent relocations, language barriers obstruct their access to many human service programs available to others in the United States (Chavkin, 1991). These characteristics also impact the children's ability to succeed in school as well as families' involvement in their children's education (Menchaca & Ruiz-Escalante, 1995; Martinez & Velazquez, 2000).

Teachers of young children from migrant families must emphasize the strengths that the children bring from this lifestyle. Because they have lived and traveled in several states and often in at least two countries, children have information and perspectives to share that differ from those of other children (Gonzales as cited in Menchaca & Ruiz-Escalante, 1995). When teachers respect and celebrate all cultures and experiences among children in the classroom, including those of migrant children, all children have a greater chance for success. Further, teachers must make all children feel welcome as members of the classroom community of learners, regardless of the length of their stay (Huggins, as cited in Menchaca & Ruiz-Escalante, 1995). Moving from one school to another is a challenge for young migrant children, and early childhood teachers can support them by leading efforts to include them and making the classroom a safe place for all.

For all young children, family involvement in education contributes to academic success. It may be necessary for teachers to redefine their views about family involvement beyond a traditional view of participation in parent groups, attendance at school functions, and helping children with homework into a broader view that will encourage marginalized families "by building on each family's cultural values, beliefs, and economic positionality" (Lopez, Scribner, & Mahitivanichcha, 2001, p. 257). Some examples of ways that teachers can support migrant family involvement include:

- placing needs of families as the number one priority
- developing meaningful, authentic relationships with parents
- empowering parents by valuing their essential nature to children's success in school
- genuinely welcoming family members in a personal way to school function
- providing specific educational services to help migrant children and families
- collaborating with agencies in order to effect families' basic and health needs, as well as academic needs (Lopez, Scribner, and Mahitivanichcha, 2001)

Anchor School Project
http://www.anchorschool.org

Migrant Education Program
http://www.ed.gov/
Click "programs"; click "ED programs";
    click "Migrant Education Programs"

Migrant Head Start
http://www2.acf.dhhs.gov
Click "Head Start"; click "Head Start Bureau";
    click "Programs and Services"

Military Families

In 2000, the Department of Defense statistics showed that the total U.S. military force had 3,324,888 members with about 41 percent serving in active duty, that is, not reserve units. Of the active-duty members, nearly 55 percent were married. Fourteen percent of active duty service members were female and 64 percent were 30 years of age or younger (Mancini & Archambault, 2000). Recent increases in married military members and in the number of female members have led to changes in expectations for military life, heightening concerns about family issues (Drummet, Coleman, & Cable, 2003).

In addition to reviewing military force statistics, Mancini and Archambault (2000) also noted pressing concerns from service members and families as follows: availability of commissary and selection and cost of items; health care information and issues; poor status of base housing and lack of attention to solving housing problems; tuition assistance for military spouses; rates of pay and cost of living calculations; and the need for affordable child care. A major area of study has been the topic of financial stability of military families. About 47 percent of military families reported financial security, 30 percent reported occasional financial difficulty, and 22 percent reported tough financial circumstances where they were "in over their heads." Most junior enlisted officers reported having less than $1,000 in savings and 7 percent of active-duty members obtained loans for expenses to make a required relocation.

While some stressors are common to the majority of military families, other stressors may be less common and yet challenging to those families faced with such obstacles. One of these challenges is coping with the stress related to children with disabilities. Along with financial and child care concerns faced by a large majority of military families, it has been reported that supporting children with special needs can increase parents' stress. Evidence also exists, however, that families who have a child with disabilities rise to the occasion and make necessary adjustments when provided with helpful support and services. Researchers recommend that because these families often have unmet needs for community services and parent networks, active coordination of such services must be offered to families (Russo & Fallon, 2001).

In addition to financial concerns, three unique stressor events for military families have been documented: mandated relocations, separation from family members, and reuniting with family members (Drummet, et al., 2003). An increased sensitivity to these and other military family issues has arisen since the Gulf War during the early 1990s, when dual-career military couples and single parents were among those who were deployed suddenly, forcing them to find long-term care for their children in a matter of hours. These issues affect approximately 3.36 million children of military families (Ryan-Wenger, 2001).

The frequent and mandated moves required of military families also demand a great deal of adjustment and adaptation from them. Not only must the household reorganize for a new living space, but the relocation is likely to involve major geographic distance, sometimes internationally. New climates and cultural change also provide challenges for families. Both positive and negative effects have been documented for children in such relocations. The stress caused by each relocation has generally been found to be relatively short-lived for most children. However, some helping professionals continue to believe in a "military family syndrome" in which children exhibit high degrees of psychopathology. Although LaGrone (1978), as cited in Ryan-Wenger (2001), connected such psychopathology to authoritarian parenting styles, family conflicts, and a lack of permanence in families, no comparisons were done with nonmilitary families having similar characteristics. Presently, existence of this syndrome does not seem to be grounded in reality. In fact, some researchers have found quite the opposite: that relocations sometimes have a positive outcome on children's academic achievement (Drummet, et al., 2003).

Adult military family members also have stressors related to frequent and distant relocations. The sheer work and concern for children and other family members can easily lead to both physical and emotional exhaustion (Pollari & Bullock, 1988, as cited in Drummet, 2003). The loss of social networks—family, friends, coworkers, and community—as well as concern about finding new social networks in the next community is a source of stress for adults as well as children. Adult family members who relocate with the military member often face interruptions in their careers and new job searches after the move is made (Drummet, et al., 2003).

The second major stressor that has been documented for military families has to do with separation from family members. "Deployment is uniquely different from relocation, because deployment seldom includes the family unit. Therefore, a second unique facet of military life is the ever-present possibility of deployment of one or both adults from the family" (Drummet, et al., p. 281). "Since 1990, the number of United States military personnel deployed for war and operations other than war has been at an all-time high" (Ryan-Wenger, 2001, p. 236). The most common issues related to these family separations relate to care of the children, maintaining a positive couple relationship, negotiating roles and tasks in the family when one or both adult members are away on duty, reduced social support, and the effects of mass communication information that may provide inaccurate information.

Caring for children when a family member has been deployed is always challenging. However, this challenge might be exacerbated when the military family member is a single parent or when both parents are deployed to active duty. At these times, caregivers may not be aware of children's daily routines or special needs, yet step up to provide care for the children in the best way they can. Children whose parents have been deployed are likely to demonstrate behavioral issues that include anxiety, sleep disturbances, and phobias, as well as more frequent physical illness.

Of course, these symptoms may be greater for children whose family members are in combat situations (Drummet, et al., 2003). Very little research has been done to examine children's fears and concerns when a parent is serving in a war zone. It seems that many families prefer to protect their children by not asking them about their perspectives and feelings when one or both parents are at war (Ryan-Wenger, 2001). Sensitivity is important, but some evidence exists that whether or not a child is asked about her or his perspective, children are thinking about war. When asked "What would happen in your family if there was war?" one eight-year-old girl who had a parent serving in active duty replied, "My family would be killed, shot, stabbed, and they might be hurt" (Ryan-Wenger, 2001).

While it is clear to many people that military relocations and separations are stressful for families, the reuniting of such families is often viewed as a greatly anticipated, joyful event. Frequently, military family reunions are just that—happily anticipated. At the same time, however, reunions require an enormous amount of adaptation from all family members, and this typically creates stress around such reunions. Figure 6–10 provides a list and brief explanation of six factors that relate to family stress related to reunions (Drummet, et al., 2003).

Children of Incarcerated Parents

About two million children in any given year have at least one parent who is **incarcerated** in a state or federal prison, or in a local jail (Bilchik, Seymour, & Kreisher, 2001). Since the rate of incarceration has been growing throughout the 1990s and into the twenty-first century, greater numbers of children will be affected by this in the future. The number of children with incarcerated parents has grown by more than 50 percent since 1991 (Federal Resource Center for Children of Prisoners, n.d.). Fathers are most likely to be incarcerated, but there has been an

Figure 6–10	Factors Related to Military Family Stress at the Time of Reunion

Roles and Boundary Issues. When a military family member is deployed, other family members are required to pick up the functions that that person contributed to the family. Adjusting to the change and then adjusting again when the family member returns does not always occur without objections. Also, the returning individual might feel frozen out of family processes.

Household Management. Those who manage the household while the deployed member is away may find new success or may be frustrated by what they view as failure. In either case, management issues will most likely move to at least a more shared responsibility with the returning family member.

Honeymoon Effect. Upon the immediate return of the family member, a tremendous amount of joy and relief may overshadow any concerns about family issues. This period may last for various lengths of time, with some families moving gradually to dealing with such concerns, others avoiding concerns, and still others dealing suddenly with a concern, particularly if it seems like a looming crisis.

Social Support. In the excitement of reunion, families might overlook their existing sources of social support outside the family in order to re-establish familial ties. It seems that families who have a balance between outside social networks and family ties have an easier time adjusting through the reunion period.

Parent Rejection and Anxiety. Very young children may not remember or recognize a returning parent. Adult expectations for children to quickly assume relationships with the parent may cause additional anxiety in children.

Physical and Mental Condition of Military Family Member. When military family members return from deployment, they may not be in the same health status as when they left. Both physical injuries and emotional issues may change the expected nature of the reunion.

Source: Drummet, Coleman, and Cable, 2003

increase in female incarcerations. About 8 percent of the two million children who have an incarcerated parent have mothers who are incarcerated (Bilchik, et al., 2001).

Little information exists about the specific effects of parental imprisonment on children. However, because it is known that these families are more likely to be living in poverty and/or affected by substance abuse and violence, the effects are complicated by a number of negative environmental factors. When parents are taken into custody, children are confused, and their world immediately becomes chaotic. Many children believe that they might be responsible for their parents going to jail. The family separation created by parental imprisonment is traumatic for children, especially if the incarcerated parent is a primary caregiver.

Common responses from children with incarcerated parents include a variety of emotional and behavioral difficulties, such as withdrawal, aggression, anxiety, and depression. These children are likely to do poorly in school, and beyond early childhood they are at risk for abusing illegal substances and commit-

ting crimes (Bilchik et al., 2001). Because of the trauma associated with a sudden separation from a parent, children may suffer from post traumatic stress disorder (PTSD), which includes symptoms such as withdrawal, hyperalertness, sleep disturbances, guilt, and impaired memory and concentration (Jose-Kampfner, as cited in Young & Jefferson-Smith, 2000).

In addition to emotional and behavioral risk factors, children with incarcerated parents also are likely to feel embarrassed and isolated about having a parent in prison. They may attempt to keep others from knowing about the incarceration, by either remaining silent about the information or covering up the truth. Although the very nature of incarceration in our society is to punish the perpetrators of crime, care must be taken to ensure that children of incarcerated parents are not also punished because of their parents' illegal acts.

A common pattern of dealing with children whose parents are incarcerated has been to help support the children without dealing with their concerns about their parents or the issue of incarceration. Often, no one mentions the parent or the imprisonment in conversations with these children. Even incarcerated parents themselves, in reaction to their own guilt, may distance themselves physically and emotionally from their children. However, these responses only cause children to feel isolated and rejected. Children, not understanding that their parents may be acting out of guilt or embarrassment, see the parents' behavior as a lack of love for or interest in them, perhaps caused by something that they did (Young & Jefferson-Smith, 2000).

Programs for children whose parents are incarcerated are being created in many cities and states, and with input from organizations that have called attention to the needs of children in this situation. Families in Crisis provides a program for school-age children with both educational and therapeutic interventions. Services are provided to both children and parents in order to support strong family bonds that help children cope successfully (Bilchik et al., 2001). Girl Scouts Beyond Bars is a partnership program between correctional departments and Girl Scout councils, and was created to continue relationships between young girls and their incarcerated mothers (http://www.ncjrs.org/txtfiles/girlsct .txt).

Although fewer women than men are currently incarcerated, a greater number of programs seem to exist to support them in their parenting role both as they are imprisoned and on their release. This may be because women are often in the role of primary caregiver. However, Mendez (2000) makes the point, supported by his research, that incarcerated men also have an interest in their children and in increasing their parenting skills.

Fathers and Children Together (FACT) is another program supported by Families in Crisis. Young fathers between the ages of 18 and 21 who are about to be released from the Manson Youth Institute in Connecticut are provided with services to encourage them to be supportive fathers to their young children (Bilchik, et al., 2001).

A Bill of Rights for children of incarcerated parents has been created by the San Francisco Children of Incarcerated Parents Partnership (2005). Figure 6–11 illustrates the eight rights of children, as well as sample actions or areas for advocacy relating to incarcerated parents.

"I was nine when my mom got arrested. The police came and took her. I was trying to ask them what was going on and they wouldn't say, and then everything went so fast. I guess they thought someone else was in the house. I don't know. But nobody else was in the house. They arrested her and just left us there. For two or three weeks I took care of my one-year-old brother and myself. I knew how to change his diapers and feed him and stuff. I tried to make breakfast in the morning and I burnt my hand trying to make toast. I had a blister.
I wasn't really afraid. I was just trying to take care of my brother. That was my goal— to take care of him. Sometimes he would cry because he probably would want to see my mom."

—Dave, San Francisco Children of Incarcerated Parents Partnership, 2005

Caregivers and teachers of young children may find it difficult to know how to support children of incarcerated parents. The first step for those who are working with these young children is to understand the confusion and trauma they have faced. Further, early childhood teachers should be prepared to provide a sense of security at school by listening to children's concerns and by providing unconditional nurturance. Answer children's questions in the best and most honest way possible, respect the significance of family bonds, and seek assistance from the family and other professionals as necessary. Be sure to maintain confidentiality regarding sensitive information (Reilly & Martin, n.d.). Finally, early

Families in Crisis
http://www.Familiesincrisis.org
Child Welfare League of America Center for Children of Prisoners
http://www.cwla.org
Click "Programs"; click "Children with Incarcerated Parents"

| Figure 6–11 | Rights and Actions/Advocacy for Children of Incarcerated Parents |

RIGHT

I have the right to be kept safe and informed at the time of my parent's arrest.

ACTIONS

Develop arrest protocols that support and protect children. Examples: avoid sirens and lights in nonemergency situations; when possible, allow parent to say good-by and handcuff out of sight of children or have officers give age appropriate explanations.

RIGHT

I have the right to be heard when decisions are made about me.

ACTIONS

Train relevant staff to recognize and address children's needs and concerns; be truthful with children; listen to children so that their concerns are heard and understood.

RIGHT

I have the right to be considered when decisions are made about my parent.

ACTIONS

Review current sentencing laws in relation to its impact on children and families; include services and support to families and children during and after an arrest; include family impact statements in pre-sentencing investigation reports.

RIGHT

I have the right to be well cared for in my parent's absence.

ACTIONS

Offer support to new or ongoing caregivers; subsidize guardianship for children whose parents are incarcerated; when a parent is arrested, include agencies such as child welfare to help families deal with the crisis.

RIGHT

I have the right to speak with, see, and touch my parent.

Source: San Francisco Children of Incarcerated Parents Partnership, 2005

ACTIONS

Provide access to visiting rooms that are child-centered, non-intimidating and conducive to bonding; consider proximity to family when siting prisons and assigning prisoners; encourage child welfare departments to facilitate contact.

RIGHT

I have the right to support as I face my parent's incarceration.

ACTIONS

Provide training to relevant professionals to recognize the needs and concerns of children whose parents are incarcerated; provide access to helping professionals with specialized training in working with children whose parents are incarcerated; each state should include 5 percent of its corrections budget for family support during and after incarceration.

RIGHT

I have the right not to be judged, blamed, or labeled because my parent is incarcerated.

ACTIONS

Create opportunities for children of incarcerated parents to communicate with and support each other; create support for incarcerated parents so that they can work to become better parents and citizens—and then there would be a truth fit to tell their children.

RIGHT

I have the right to a lifelong relationship with my parent.

ACTIONS

Re-examine the 1997 Adoption and Safe Families Act that requires states to begin proceedings to terminate parental rights when child has been in foster care for fifteen of the past twenty-two months and for six months for children under three years; inform incarcerated parents of this law; designate a family services coordinator at prisons and jails; support incarcerated parents upon reentry into society by helping them to find employment and apply for benefits.

childhood educators should use the knowledge base from existing research and family support programs to advocate for greater numbers of appropriate interventions that will serve to keep family bonds strong, reduce the likelihood that parents will return to prison, or that their children will also go to prison, and decrease severe emotional challenges for children whose parents are or have been incarcerated.

The Role of Early Childhood Educators

As early childhood teachers prepare to work with an ever-increasing number of children with serious health concerns, several criteria must be included in their professional preparation:

- knowledge of legal requirements for each special need
- knowledge of health requirements for each special need
- understanding of family systems effects on children
- practicing effective strategies to support families as well as planning high-quality early education for the children
- advocating for needs of all children and families
- expansion of capacity to demonstrate compassion

Although it is true that a teacher preparation program for entry-level teachers cannot possibly anticipate every situation novice teachers might encounter, it seems evident that more emphasis should be placed on understanding the various needs and strengths of families in stress. Even under difficult circumstances, many families find ways to cope or to adapt. Furthermore, as teachers face a variety of

It is the teacher's ethical obligation to exercise the idea of lifelong learning.

challenging situations, it is their ethical obligation to exercise the idea of lifelong learning to ensure the best early education for each child and appropriate support for each family.

Summary and Conclusions

All families face stressful events. Some forms of stress can be predicted, such as the birth of a new baby or a planned relocation. Other stressors faced by families with young children, however, are unique and may be unexpected. Violence in families causes stress for all members, whether or not they are being abused. Stress also is caused by poverty and related economic factors; in extreme situations, families may lose their homes and all of their possessions. Serious illness or disabilities in young children lead to many chronically stressful situations. Some family stress may be the result of poor planning by or dysfunction in families. Much of this stress, however, is unpredictable and perhaps unavoidable.

Families cope in different ways. Those who have support and resources may find it easier to function at the time of a crisis. Others find it very difficult to adapt.

Early childhood teachers can offer support by listening and showing compassion when families need support. It may be necessary for teachers to refer children or families for additional or alternative services. Guidelines for ethical behavior require that early education practitioners form partnerships with all families based on trust and positive regard.

Chapter 6 Applications

1. Review the information on factors related to family violence in U.S. society. Give an example from your life experiences that helps to explain or support each of these factors.

2. Consider the information provided in this chapter about various serious illnesses experienced by families with young children. Which of these illnesses do you know something about from experience? pg.153

3. When a young child is born with or acquires a disability, it affects the entire family. Considering the information in this chapter along with your own life experiences, how will you view children with disabilities in your classroom? How will you view parents of children with disabilities as they voice their expectations to you? What challenges and joys do you predict when working with young children with disabilities and their families?

Questions for Reflection and Discussion

1. When you think about working with families of young children who have a major source of family stress, what do you see as your strengths? What areas of concern do you have about your reactions to the various stressors?

2. How will you decide on the extent and limits to which you will be involved in families experiencing stress?

3. How might you best prepare yourself as an early childhood educator to deal with the types of unpredictable family stress discussed in this chapter?

Field Assignments

1. Call the administrator of a homeless shelter or women's shelter in your area. Ask about what the needs are, and how you might be able to help young children and families at the shelter. Consider a toy drive, clothing drive, food drive, or collection of supplies such as paper, markers, glue, or other items; tutoring school-age children; or reading to children.

2. Observe in an early intervention program. Note the activities, participation, family involvement, and forms of assessment. If possible, ask the administrator about roles for early childhood educators in such programs.

3. Interview a children's protective services agent. Ask about experiences with family members who have been identified as child abusers. Discuss ways in which early childhood teachers and protective services workers might collaborate.

References

Bilchik, S., Seymour, C., & Kreisher, K. (2001). Parents in prison. *Corrections Today, 63* (7), 108–111.

Boss, P. (1988). *Family stress management.* Newbury Park, CA: Sage.

Carter, B., & McGoldrick, M. (1989). Overview: The changing family life cycle: A framework for family therapy. In B. Carter & M. McGoldrick (Eds.), *The changing family life cycle.* Needham Heights, MA: Allyn & Bacon.

Chavkin, N. F. (1991). Family lives and parental involvement in migrant students' education. (ERIC Document Reproduction No. ED 335174.)

Cicchetti, D., Toth, S. L., & Hennessy, K. (1993). Child maltreatment and school adaptation: Problems and promises. In D. Cicchetti and S. L. Toth (Eds.), *Child abuse, child development, and social policy* (pp. 301–330). Norwood, NJ: Ablex.

Clemson Extension. (2002). *From family stress to family strengths.* Clemson, SC: Clemson University.

Davis, H. (1993). *Counseling parents of children with chronic illness or disability.* Leicester, England: British Psychological Society.

Doucette-Dudman, D., & LaCure, J. R. (1996). *Raising our children's children.* Minneapolis, MN: Fairview Press.

Drummet, A. R., Coleman, M., & Cable, S. (2003). Military families under stress: Implications for family life education. *Family Relations, 52* (3), 279–287.

Emery, R. E. (1999). *Marriage, divorce, and children's adjustment* (2nd ed.). Thousand Oaks, CA: Sage.

Federal Resource Center for Children of Prisoners. (n.d.). Retrieved September 7, 2002, from http://www.cwla.org/programs/incarcerated/frccpabout.htm.

Fields, J., & Casper, L. M. (June 2001). America's families and living arrangements. *Current Population Reports.* Washington, DC: United States Department of Commerce, Economics and Statistics Administration, United States Census Bureau.

Galinsky, E., & David, J. (1988). *The preschool years: Family strategies that work from experts and parents.* New York: Ballantine.

Guernsey, T. F., & Klare, K. (1993). *Special education law.* Durham, NC: Carolina Academic Press.

Hamner, T. J., & Turner, P. H. (1996). *Parenting in contemporary society.* Needham Heights, MA: Allyn & Bacon.

Head Start program performance standards and other regulations. (1993). Washington, DC: U.S. Department of Health and Human Services.

Hendrick, J. (1998). *Total learning.* Columbus, OH: Merrill.

Huang, G. (1993). Health problems among migrant farmworkers' children in the U.S. (ERIC Document Reproduction No. ED 357907.)

Iverson, T. J., & Segal, M. (1990). *Child abuse and neglect: An information and reference guide.* New York: Garland.

Keeping incarcerated mothers and their daughters together: Girl Scouts beyond bars. (October 1995). Retrieved September 7, 2002, from http://www.ncjrs.org/txtfiles/girlsct.txt.

Kling, N., Dunn, L., & Oakley, J. (1996). Homeless families in early childhood programs: What to expect and what to do. *Dimensions of Early Childhood, 24* (1), 3–8.

Krestan, J., & Bepko, C. (1989). Alcohol problems and the family life cycle. In B. Carter & M. McGoldrick (Eds.), *The changing family life cycle.* Needham Heights, MA: Allyn & Bacon.

Lieberman, A. F. (1995). Concerns of immigrant families. In P. L. Mangione (Ed.), *Infant/toddler caregiving: A guide to culturally sensitive care* (pp. 28–37). Sacramento: California Department of Education.

Lopez, G. R., Scribner, J. D., & Mahitivanichcha, K. (2001, Summer). Redefining parental involvement: Lessons from high-performing migrant-impacted schools. *American Educational Research Journal, 38* (2), 253–288.

Mancini, D. L., & Archambault, C. (2000). What recent research tells us about military families and communities. DoD Family Readiness Conference, Phoenix, AZ.

Martinez, Y. G., & Velazquez, J. A. (2000). Involving migrant families in education. (ERIC Document Reproduction No. ED 448010.)

Mayes, L. C. (1995). Substance abuse and parenting. In M. H. Bornstein (Ed.), *Handbook of parenting, vol. 4: Applied and practical parenting* (pp. 101–125). Mahwah, NJ: Lawrence Erlbaum Associates.

McCubbin, H. I., McCubbin, M. A., Thompson, A. I., Han, S., & Allen, C. T. (1997). *Families under stress: What makes them resilient?* 1997 American Association of Family and Consumer Sciences Commemorative Lecture, Washington, DC.

Menchaca, V. D., & Ruiz-Escalante, J. A. (1995). Instructional strategies for migrant students. (ERIC Document Reproduction No. ED 388491.)

Mendez, Jr., G. A. (2000). Incarcerated African American men and their children: A case study. *Annals of the American Academy of Political and Social Science, 569,* 86–101.

Moses, K. (1983). The impact of initial diagnosis: Mobilizing family resources. In J. Mulick & S. Pueschel (Eds.), *Parent-professional partnerships in developmental disabilities services* (pp. 11–34). Cambridge, MA: Academic Guild.

Olson, D. H. L., Russell, C. S., & Sprenkle, D. H. (1989). *Circumplex model: Systematic assessment and treatment of families.* New York: Haworth Press.

Olson, H. (1994). The effects of prenatal alcohol exposure on child development. *Infants and Young Children, 6* (3), 10–25.

Perrin, J. M. (1985). Introduction: Severe and chronic illness in childhood. In N. Hobbs, J. M. Perrin, & H. T. Ireys (Eds.), *Chronically ill children and their families.* San Francisco: Jossey-Bass.

Poulsen, M. (1994). The development of policy recommendations to address individual and family needs of infants and young children affected by family substance use. *Topics in Early Childhood Special Education, 14* (2), 275–291.

Reilly, J., & Martin, S. (n.d.). Children of incarcerated parents: What is the caregiver's role? Retrieved September 7, 2002, from http://www.canr.uconn.edu/ces/child/newsarticles/CCC743.html.

Russo, T. J., & Fallon, M. A. (2001). Helping military families who have a child with a disability cope with stress. *Early Childhood Education Journal, 29* (1), 3–8.

Ryan-Wenger, N. A. (April 2001). Impact of the threat of war on children in military families. *American Journal of Orthopsychiatry, 71* (2), 236–244.

San Francisco Children of Incarcerated Parents Partnership. (2005). *Children of incarcerated parents: A bill of rights.* Stockton, CA: Friends Outside.

Shotland, J. (1989). Full fields, empty cupboard: The nutritional status of migrant farmworkers in America. Washington, DC. Public Voice for Food and Health Policy. (ERIC Document Reproduction No. ED 323076.)

Simonds, R. J., & Rogers, M. F. (1992). Epidemiology of HIV in children and other populations. In A. C. Crocker, H. J. Cohen, & T. A. Kastner (Eds.), *HIV infection and developmental disabilities: A resource for service providers*. Baltimore: Paul H. Brookes.

Simons, R. (1987). *After the tears: Parents talk about raising a child with a disability*. Orlando, FL: Harcourt Brace.

Straus, M. A. (1983). Ordinary violence, child abuse, and wife-beating: What do they have in common. In D. Finkelhor (Ed.), *The dark side of families*. Beverly Hills, CA: Sage.

Straus, M. A. (1991). Physical violence in American families: Incidence, rates, causes, and trends. In D. D. Knudsen & J. L. Miller (Eds.), *Abused and battered: Social and legal responses to family violence*. New York: Walter de Gruyter.

Straus, M. A., Gelles, R. J., & Steinmetz, S. K. (1980). *Behind closed doors: Violence in the American family*. Garden City, NY: Doubleday.

Trivette, C., & Dunst, C. (1992). Characteristics and influences of role division and social support among mothers of preschool children with disabilities. *Topics in Early Childhood Special Education, 12* (3), 367–385.

U.S. Department of Health, Education, and Welfare, Office of Human Development/Office of Child Development, Children's Bureau/National Center on Child Abuse and Neglect. (1975). Child abuse and neglect: The problem and its management. (DHEW Publication No. OHD 75–30073.)

Young, D. S., & Jefferson-Smith, C. J. (2000). When moms are incarcerated: The needs of children, mothers, and caregivers. *Families in Society, 81* (2), 130–141.

Zuckerman, B., & Brazelton, T. B. (1994). Strategies for a family supportive child health care system. In S. L. Kagan & B. Weissbourd (Eds.), *Putting families first: America's family support movement and the challenge of change*. San Francisco: Jossey-Bass.

PART 2

PRACTICE

OUTLINE

Objectives

Key Terms

Rationale for a Family-based Philosophy in Early Childhood Education
The Example Set by Head Start
Families in a Democracy
Continuity

Family Support
Responsibilities of Families and Schools
Empowering Parents

Linking Parents and Teachers
Parents as Consumers of Children's Education
Supporting School Policy and Families

Epstein's Framework for School, Family, and Community Partnerships

National Standards from the PTA
Additional Frameworks for Understanding Family Involvement

Professionalism in Family-based Early Education
Confidentiality
Advocacy
Collaboration
Understanding Roles and Boundaries
Record-Keeping

Embracing Diversity
Observing and Appreciating Differences

Understanding that Many Ways of Interacting with Children Can Serve Them Well

Evaluating the Family Involvement Component in Early Education

Summary and Conclusions

Chapter 7 Applications

Questions for Reflection and Discussion

Field Assignments

References

A Family-Based Philosophy in Early Childhood Education

Rationale for a Family-based Philosophy in Early Childhood Education

Families are children's first teachers. By the time children arrive in early childhood education settings, they have already had many experiences from which to learn. In optimal home settings, young children will have learned a great deal that prepares them for entry into early education. But, children from some home settings will experience a lot of discontinuity in their lives when they begin child care or school.

Even after children begin formal early education—child care, preschool, or kindergarten—families continue to be the primary force in their development. With this understanding, it is imperative that programs of early childhood education adopt a family-based philosophy.

In order to create effective, meaningful programs of family involvement in early education, teachers must have an understanding of family from both a research a theory perspective. Content from the first section of this textbook, "Understanding Families," was intended to provide information about families so that early educators might apply that information to their educational practice. Too little attention is currently given to early childhood teachers having deep knowledge of family systems theory (Christian, 2006). Establishing family involvement programs without a scientific understanding of families may lead to shallow or transitory efforts with families. Authentic partnerships are more likely to be developed when early childhood professionals have a categorically strong knowledge base in understanding families. "It is critical to use these explanations to better serve children and families rather than for the purpose of blaming or trying to 'fix' families" (Christian, 2006, p. 13).

As we understand more about families in general as well as the families with whom we work specifically, it is clear that family involvement must be varied and abundant. Opportunities for families to participate with their children in the support of their education should take into consideration the obligations and strengths of each family.

Even though multiple barriers exist for practicing family involvement in children's education, being aware of these obstacles can help teachers to overcome their negative impact on outcomes for early childhood programs. Even though early childhood education as a field has been more inclusive of families and communities than have other levels of education, there are still many ways that early educators can enhance their efforts in this realm. Common barriers that have been identified for all levels of education (Shartrand, Weiss, Kreider, & Lopez, 1997) include the following:

1. *School environments commonly discourage family involvement.* This is often so because lack of time and/or preparation of teachers as well as a traditional philosophy of schools having a narrow focus on children's educational needs alone.

2. *Families and schools have different preferences and different expectations for the nature of family involvement in children's education.* School staff members are frequently concerned with activities that encourage families to support school programs and participate in PTAs or PTOs. On the other hand, many families also are interested in advocacy and decision-making roles, often less popular variations with teachers. This "disconnect" between parents and teachers in the definition or values can lead to stalemates in actual levels of family or community involvement.

3. *It is common for teachers and families to view involvement in a negative light.* Teachers may complain about parental lack of concern, while parents may feel like unwelcome and uninvited participants in their children's education.

4. *Family diversity as it relates to culture, ethnicity, language, employment patterns, and family structure challenges schools and families working toward increased family involvement, even when both parties value and desire family and community engagement with schools.*

5. *Teacher preparation programs are generally lacking in providing pre-service teachers with knowledge, skills, and dispositions for working with families.* Increasing attention to knowledge about families, along with skills and dispositions for forming strong partnerships with families, is a key to appreciably increasing the emphasis on the reality of family involvement in their children's education.

> **Consider the five common barriers to family involvement in their children's education as outlined by Shartrand, et al. (1997). Using various contexts or systems (as in Bronfenbrenner's bioecological theory), create at least one solution for each of the five barriers.**

The Example Set by Head Start

Since its inception in 1965, family involvement has been a component of Head Start's comprehensive educational plan for working with children of low-income families. Many leaders in early childhood education believe that the success of Head Start would not be so remarkable without the emphasis on families.

Currently, The Head Start Vision for Parent Involvement includes three primary goals:

- support for parents in their role as primary educator, caregiver, nurturer, and advocate for their children
- support for parents in their own personal development
- support for parents as decision-makers for themselves, their children, and their Head Start program (*Head Start Handbook of the Parent Involvement Vision and Strategies*, 1996)

In supporting parents as the first educators of their children, Head Start teachers are aware that parents have enrolled their children in the program so that their children receive the educational benefits the program provides. Appreciating parents' efforts is important to this goal. Similarly, it is important for teachers to accept that whoever is doing the parenting (mothers, fathers, grandparents, or others) needs support from early childhood teachers in this role, because such acceptance increases the chances for successful partnerships. Like the descriptions of Head Start's three main goals, above, the following sample strategies to support parental nurturance have been taken from the *Head Start Handbook of the Parent Involvement Vision and Strategies* (1996):

- providing opportunities for parents to learn about child development
- sharing developmentally appropriate activities that parents and children can do together at home
- encouraging parents to visit and participate in the classroom to observe and later discuss how children learn and develop
- fostering participation in decisions about the classroom
- involving parents of children with disabilities in developing their child's individualized educational plan

Head Start programs encourage parents to visit and participate in their child's activities.

The premise of the second goal, supporting parents' personal development, is that parents' personal growth affects their children's development and learning. Thus, the purpose of the second goal is to help parents set goals for themselves so that their development ultimately benefits their children. The Head Start decision makers who defined this goal understood the importance of the family system to children's development. Some areas for parents' personal development for which Head Start programs may provide assistance or resources are:

- increasing skills for everyday life, such as planning and preparing nutritious meals
- planning for family life together
- identifying strengths and skills that they already possess that might help in managing family life or in finding a job
- working on skills they would like to learn or improve, such as effective and appropriate discipline of their children, or how to use a computer
- learning how to reduce stress and increase wellness
- creating opportunities to interact with other parents of young children and to build friendships

Figure 7–1 Roles of Families in U.S. Society that Provide an Emphasis on Family Involvement in Early Education

Doctrine of Parental Rights—Parents have legal rights and responsibilities in regard to their children. As educators, we often note parental responsibility, especially when we judge that it is not being fulfilled. However, family involvement in education principles must include the importance of parental rights as well.

Family Influences on Children—There is no doubt that parents are children's first teachers. Current brain development research points us to the fact that the child's first three years are critical as a time of learning. Early childhood educators and others in the community must help to support parent efforts even before children come to school.

Democratic Principles—Families living in a democracy have the privilege of choosing how to rear their children. At the same time, with all of these choices come huge responsibilities for meeting children's needs. Early childhood professionals can provide information to parents so that they can make knowledgeable choices as they fulfill their responsibilities.

- being involved in a community of others who value their language and culture
- working with teams of parents and Head Start staff to participate in community activities or to address community issues
- setting goals for themselves and making progress in the achievement of the goals

The preceding list of strategies offers many possibilities. Variations in programs and communities may restrict or increase these possibilities. Early childhood staff who are sensitive to and understand the strengths and needs of parents may be able to assist them in choosing one or two of these areas as priorities. It is also possible that parents who are veterans of Head Start may be willing to serve as mentors to new parents as they work to meet their goals.

Head Start has been successful in creating a sense of community among its staff and clients. This works to benefit children, teachers, and families. One of the keys to this community-building effort is that parents—as partners with Head Start staff—are included in decision making throughout all aspects of

the program, including the following:

- the children's curriculum
- choices of health services available to children
- planning for parent involvement activities
- activities to work on at home with their children
- ways to volunteer for Head Start
- choices about which committees or groups on which to serve

Families in a Democracy

Powell (1989) notes three premises about the role of families in U.S. society that provide a purpose for an emphasis on family involvement in early education (Figure 7–1).

- the doctrine of **parental rights**
- family influences on children
- democratic principles

Rights and Responsibilities of Parents   In a democracy, citizens have both rights and responsibilities. The rights and responsibilities related to parenting have legal and cultural roots. Professional educators must understand parental rights just as they understand and insist on parental responsibility. In this light, teachers must respect the primacy of the role that parents have with their children.

Continuity

From Home to School   In addition to the critical role families play in the lives of young children, early educators have long been concerned about children's adjustment as they enter a formal educational program. The very nature of moving from home to school causes a great deal of discontinuity in a child's world. Many experts believe that **continuity** of experience is beneficial to children and that some of the discontinuity caused by moving from home to school may be bridged when family members have opportunities to communicate frequently with their children's teachers (Powell, 1989).

Carlos entered a part-day preschool program when he was just a little over two-and-a-half years. Each day, his mother, Gina, walked into the school with him and stayed with him while he explored in the block center and sometimes the sand table. As children were invited to the group time rug, Carlos reached for his mother's hand and tears streamed down his face. Gina hugged Carlos and told him that she would be back to pick him up later. Carlos joined the others for group time, singing and moving, participating fully. Carlos continued to cry each day for almost two weeks when it was time for his mother to leave. The school staff encouraged Gina to stay as long as she wanted. Suddenly, one day, Carlos walked with Gina to the group time rug with a big smile on his face— the moment this parent had been waiting for! As Gina left the school that morning, teachers noticed tears streaming down her face. When Gina returned to pick up Carlos later that morning, she told one of the teachers that she did not realize that she was going to feel sad when Carlos happily left her to join the other children.

Transitions during the Day

Continuity refers to both **linkages** and amount of **congruence** between educational programs and families of the children they serve. Linkages are the types and frequency of communication between home and school; congruence is the amount of similarity that schools and homes have in terms of values and goals for children, use of language, and adult-child interaction patterns (Powell, 1989).

To increase the continuity that children realize between home and school, it is the professional responsibility of early childhood educators to plan, implement, and evaluate the linkages they have with families. To be considerate of all families, teachers may need to use more than one type of communication; that is, written and verbal. Increased frequency of communication between home and school also increases continuity for children. Many early childhood education programs state in their policy manuals that they require one parent-teacher conference each year. It is important that the planned or formal conference be combined with other forms of more frequent informal communication with families. Further, communication must include some method of two-way communication, not just one-way communication from school to home. Teachers must also consider variations in nonverbal communication. Suggestions for a variety of strategies are included in Chapter 8.

Congruence of expectations and values between home and school is an important aspect of continuity. It does not take much experience for an early childhood teacher to realize that her objectives will not always be viewed as equally important by children's families. Variations in families' educational and income levels and culture or ethnicity may lead to incongruence of expectations for children between home and school. The many other family factors discussed in the first six chapters of this text also are likely to contribute to differences between educators and parents in their goals for young children.

One school district superintendent, Dr. Clarke, tells about a conversation he had with a parent of a first grader. Dr. Clarke explained to the parent that by using strategies deemed to be developmentally appropriate for young children, the teacher was encouraging children to think for themselves. He went on to explain that children would grow to love learning. The parent interrupted him by saying, "I don't want my daughter to think for herself. I want her to do what I say." This incongruence between the school's philosophy of encouraging a child's autonomy in learning and the parent's value of compliance is one that educators frequently observe. What family, cultural, and societal factors do you believe might have influenced this mother's viewpoint?

"Schools have choices. There are two common approaches to involving families in schools and in their children's education. One approach emphasizes conflict and views the school as a battleground. The conditions and relationships in this kind of environment guarantee power struggles and disharmony. The other approach emphasizes partnership and views the school as a homeland. The conditions and relationships in this kind of environment invite power sharing and mutual respect, and allow energies to be directed toward activities that foster student learning and development. Even when conflicts rage, however, peace must be restored sooner or later, and the partners in children's education must work together."

—Joyce Epstein, 1995

Conflicts may arise

Communication with parents should be face-to-face, and the interaction should occur in a private place where confidentiality is maintained.

Although it has been assumed that young children benefit from greater continuity between home and school, there is little research support for this perspective. However, it is possible that when the discontinuity between the two settings is too great, children may fail at school (Powell, 1989). It is possible that there is an optimal level of discontinuity in which children will learn to adapt to a variety of settings and that such adaptation is beneficial to children. Powell discusses Lightfoot's (1978) distinction between creative conflict and negative dissonance. Viewing creative conflict as preferable to negative dissonance, the difference seems to lie in the balance of power or mutual respect between home and school. Some educators have been known to give up on the idea of family involvement when the sources and degree of conflict become too great. However, a balance of power and demonstrations of mutual respect are likely to lead to positive outcomes, even in conflict.

It is important for early childhood teachers to understand that family involvement is not just about families helping the school. This perspective assumes the school or the teacher is the base of power. Establishing a family-based philosophy in early childhood education does not do away with conflict with

What is it about?

families. However, it may generate creative conflict that leads to solutions that are beneficial to children, families, and teachers.

Leah was a five-year-old kindergartner reading on the fifth-grade level. In the beginning of the year, her mother was worried that Leah would learn nothing during the year in the developmentally appropriate kindergarten classroom. After two months of observing the teacher and the class, and having frequent heated discussions with the teacher and the principal, the mother finally confided to another parent that her child was very happy and was gaining many unexpected skills.

It is obvious from this example that creative conflict is not always resolved immediately, but may be a process that takes some time.

When there are discontinuities between settings, Bronfenbrenner (1979) noted some assumptions that early childhood teachers can work toward in order to enhance the development of children and their families as they function in various settings.

1. *First, attempt to agree on goals.* Schools can inform parents of goals for children in their early education program. This allows parents, as consumers, to consider the various educational options they have for their child.

2. *Second, supportive linkages are required between the two settings.* Teachers should radiate support for all children and families in their classrooms, because the lack of such support or perceived negative feelings about a child's family may lead to unfavorable outcomes for the child.

3. *Third, it is helpful to have a parent or other close family member from the home setting accompany the child to school.* This often means spending time with the child in the new setting rather than just dropping the child into it. Teachers will need to invite family members to do this because often it is not what families expect. Issue the invitation before the school year begins, so that for the first few days of school, family members can plan their day around this practice. Keep in mind that work or other demands may prohibit some families from spending time with their child as they enter school.

4. *Fourth, communication strategies should be two-way, especially when the topic of communication is personal to the child or family, rather than serving as an announcement for all children in the class.*

5. *Finally, Bronfenbrenner points out that communication should be face-to-face whenever possible.* This is especially true for sensitive topics, when teachers may be tempted to take the easy way out by sending a note home with the child. If timely face-to-face contact is not possible, a telephone conversation is better than a written message. Whether such contact takes the form of telephone calls or face-to-face discussions, it is imperative that the interaction occur in a private place and that confidentiality is maintained.

Transitioning to Preschool   Greater numbers of preschool programs now plan for extensive forms of supporting young children and their families with the transition from home to school. This situation holds true for preschools for typically developing children, for inclusion preschools, and for those that are designed specifically for children with identified disabilities. Since family involvement is essential in meeting the educational goals for all young children, early childhood educators and early childhood special educators note the importance of a parent or family component in any transition program design.

Preschool continues to be offered under a variety of auspices in the United States. Preschool programs might:

- be public or private.
- be part-day or full-day.
- meet five or fewer days a week.
- be church-related or secular.
- practice inclusion or enroll primarily typically developing children or those with identified disabilities.
- be taught by qualified early childhood specialists or by someone who has no or minimal qualifications in early education.
- be developmentally effective or use approaches that do not incorporate an understanding of child development.

When preschools plan for family involvement in children's transition from home to school, children adjust more readily and the stage is set for parents or other family members to become engaged in their children's early education. Methods that preschools use for transitioning include enrollment visits and observations, information sessions for families, handbooks with details about school policies and programs, and having only small groups of children in classes for the first few days of school so that children receive more individualized attention.

Transitioning from Preschool to Kindergarten
Some early education programs have created both formal and informal activities for supporting children and their families as children move to kindergarten or first grade. Typically, this transition involves a new location, many new people, and vastly different expectations. Often, the essence of this kind of transitioning program is a scheduled meeting for the parents, with one or more of the kindergarten teachers informing parents about what their children should know and be able to do in order to be ready to succeed in kindergarten. Such informational sessions can be somewhat helpful, but they typically do not provide children or families with support or resources for ensuring future success. It is more helpful to offer comprehensive programs that include opportunities for greater communication.

Many Head Start programs have developed and maintained "networks and collaborative relationships within their communities . . ." in order to assist children and families as they transition "to the next stage of their lives in their communities, carrying with them the supports and strengths they have developed in Head Start" (*Head Start Handbook*, 1996, p. 13). In the Head Start transitioning program, staff attempt to provide opportunities to experience the next steps, not only to hear from the kindergarten teacher but also perhaps to schedule visits to the classrooms, and to observe the teacher and children in action.

A transition activity booklet, *Connecting Head Start Parents to the Public School Setting*, is provided by some Head Start programs to parents as their children prepare to enter kindergarten. Figures 7–2, 7–3, and 7–4 contain excerpts from this very useful guide.

Figure 7–2	Why Parents Should get Involved in Their Child's Education

✓ **GUIDING PRINCIPLES IN HEAD START PROGRAMS**

1. Parents are the most important teachers their children will ever have.
2. Parents know their children better than anyone else.
3. Parents are responsible for their children.
4. Parents' attitudes affect their children's motivation to learn.
5. Parent involvement increases children's academic achievement and success in life.
6. Parents are in the best position to supervise children's leisure time. They should limit television watching and encourage homework, reading, and conversation.
7. Parents are the strongest advocates for their children.

Source: Epps, W. J. (n.d.). *Connecting Head Start parents to the public school setting.* Florissant, MO: Southern Research Associates

In Pennsylvania, the Capital Area Intermediate Unit provides the "Transition to School: A Planning Guide for Parents" for families of the preschoolers who are attending their programs and who will be moving to school district kindergartens. These preschool programs are especially for children with identified disabilities. Goals stated in the planning guide are:

- to explain the transition process
- to provide information to help parents plan for their child's programs
- to provide information about public school options for children with disabilities

Topics that are included in this guide are shown in Figure 7–5.

Home Visiting **Home visiting** is one way some early childhood programs have found to be effective in helping children transition from home to school. Listed below are reasons to conduct home visits, procedures to follow, cautions to consider, and some guidelines for the visit.

Reasons to Implement Home Visits

- helps the child feel comfortable with a new adult
- helps the teacher get to know the child (and family) in their own setting
- helps to build trust and communication between the teacher and the family
- lets the teacher see the child in her home environment

Procedures for Home Visits

- check your school's procedure regarding home visiting
- confirm the visit with the administrator
- contact the family in advance to set a time and date, and clarify directions (*Note:* Some families may prefer to meet in a public place, such as a library or fast-food restaurant.)

Figure 7–3	What Parents Can Do to Help at Home

TIPS FOR PARENTS

1. Read aloud to your child every day.
2. Select television and video programs that serve specific purposes.
3. Give your child meaningful tasks/chores around the house that s/he is responsible for carrying out.
4. Correct inappropriate behavior in a calm, meaningful way.
5. Take advantage of all family outings to teach your child something new or reinforce something already learned.
6. Practice identifying road and other safety signs with your child.
7. Make it an ongoing practice to engage your child in conversations about different topics.
8. Set aside a period of quiet time where everybody in the home is involved in silent reading or meditation.

Source: Epps, W. J. (1998). *Connecting Head Start parents to the public school setting.* Florissant, MO: Southern Research Associates

Figure 7–4	A Parent Guide for Parent/teacher Conferences and Conference Tips for Parents

1. Write down questions and comments you want to make a day or two before the conference.

2. Be sure you let the teacher know that you have come to the conference with some questions or concerns.

3. Share with the teacher your child's feelings about friends at school, school activities, transportation, meals, or other topics.

4. Listen carefully and take notes for the future.

5. Ask questions before accepting recommendations from the teacher about behavioral plans, special services, and other areas.

6. Be sure to let the teacher know if there are words, terms, or phrases that are not familiar to you, or if you are unsure of the meaning.

7. If more time is needed, request another conference.

8. Be sure to thank the teacher for her concern about your child.

CONFERENCE TIPS FOR PARENTS

1. be confident
2. be on time
3. be organized
4. be positive
5. be open and honest
6. be assertive, not aggressive
7. be on topic; discuss your child, not other children or parents

Source: Adapted from Epps, W. J. (1998). *Connecting Head Start parents to the public school setting.* Florissant, MO: Southern Research Associates

Figure 7–5	Content for Families in "Transition to School: A Planning Guide for Parents"

Introduction

- Goals for the Guide
- Statement about audience for Guide
- Quick checklist for transition that includes a calendar with dates for meetings from October through May and contact information

Part 1 Questions and Answers about Transition

- What does transition mean?
- Why parents need to be involved in transition
- What happens during the transition year?
- How does a multidisciplinary team complete an evaluation of each child?
- What is an Individualized Education Plan (IEP)?
- What is the parent's role in the evaluation report and IEP meeting?
- What do parents need to do to ensure child's eligibility for special education services through the school district?
- What services does the school district offer?
- Should I register my child for kindergarten?
- What is the role of my child's present Early Intervention team in the transition?
- Who should I call for information about services for my child in a private school?
- Who should I call about home school services for my child?

Directory of School District Contacts for Preschool Transition

Source: Pennsylvania Capital Area Intermediate Unit Preschool Programs

Part 2 Information to Help Me Discuss My Child's Skills

Section A: Typical developmental expectations for children

 The 3-year-old
 The 4-year-old
 The 5-year-old

Section B: Child Profile

Parent reads a short description for each of the following areas and then responds to "My child is able to . . . " and "My child has not yet learned to . . . "

Cognition	Self-Care
Communication	Social Interaction
Movement	

Ten sentence completions, such as "My child likes _____," "My child's favorite toys are _____," and "My biggest concerns about my child are _____."

Section C: Parent Classroom Observation Form

Instructions for scheduling observation visits are provided.

Guiding questions for parents to consider while observing in a Kindergarten Classroom as well as Kindergarten Level Programs for Special Needs Children are provided.

Part 3 Resources

Section A: Glossary of Special Education Terms

Section B: Definitions of Disabilities from Federal and State Regulations

Section C: List of Parent Advocacy and Support Groups and Agencies, with Contact Information

Safety Considerations for Home Visits

- make visits only with a coworker
- take a cell phone
- leave if the situation appears to be unsafe

What to Do during Home Visits

- introduce yourself
- ask about the family: How many children are in the family? How long have they lived at this residence?
- briefly explain the school day to the children and the family
- ask whether there are questions or concerns
- invite the family to visit you at school and provide them with ways to contact you

> **With the information that you have about transitioning programs for preschool and kindergarten programs, reflect on ways that transitions might be helpful to all entities: children, families, teachers, and communities at other levels of early education as well.**

Family Support

Responsibilities of Families and Schools

"In the family support movement, families are viewed as the dominant support for children's development. Partnerships between families and helping agencies—including schools—must acknowledge families' primacy" (Bowman, 1994, pp. 52–53). The importance of the child's family to her development and education cannot be overstated. Further, if family needs are met and support is available, children have a much greater chance at success. When families are overburdened with stress from poverty, illness, or violence, they cannot meet their own needs or those of their children.

Bowman discusses four themes that are often used to justify differences in academic achievement among those who have lower income or are not members of the dominant culture.

1. Certain characteristics of the child such as ethnicity or lack of self-esteem are barriers to learning.
2. Values from home conflict with school-valued learning and skill development.
3. Discriminatory practices and inequality in the distribution of resources cause disadvantages to poor children and those who are not from the dominant culture.
4. School practices affect individuals and groups differently.

These themes show that, in fact, there is little agreement about why children of color do not do well in school. Teachers need to consider that different children are likely to need different programs to help them succeed (Bowman, 1994).

Listed below are examples of how teachers can plan different programs to meet the needs of more children.

1. Plan activities and projects that are not costly. When the cost of an activity (for example, field trips) is high, seek external funding.
2. Include a variety of resource guests from different careers, income levels, and racial-ethnic groups.
3. Plan for active/passive times each day to meet differing needs. Include music, movement, quiet, individual, and small group choices for various activities throughout the day.

Suggested School Practice Changes

1. When planning school-wide events, include participants from various racial-ethnic and income level groups throughout the year.
2. Invite a variety of racial-ethnic leaders to speak and participate in school activities.
3. When purchasing books and other instructional materials, always consider the racial-ethnic and income level representations in the visual images.

4. Plan for differing time and space needs to meet unique needs such as before- or after-school care, unique transportation arrangements, and unique language accommodations.

Two excellent resources for ideas to meet unique needs are:

The Anti-Bias Curriculum, Louise Derman-Sparks, NAEYC, Washington, DC.

Starting Small (video and teacher's guide), Teaching Tolerance, Southern Poverty Law Center, Montgomery, Alabama.

Empowering Parents

Well-educated, affluent parents typically have very different interactions with their children's teachers than do their less-well-off counterparts. Schools are often criticized for having greater concern for the well-being of the school as an institution than for the individual children and families that are being served by them. It is possible that Head Start's successful family involvement model for **empowering** parents is not the model that would best serve other populations. Considering that parents who have higher levels of education and income may already feel empowered and assert themselves easily with teachers and administrators, goals for family involvement with such parents should differ from those of family involvement with low-income or less-well-educated parents. Regardless of the situation, however, authentic communication is necessary to foster growth-producing relationships between parents and teachers. Some family involvement activities that are traditional (such as open houses, conferences, fairs, and so on) may be effective, but it is necessary to assess these activities on an annual basis to make sure that they have not become meaningless rituals.

Empowerment is identified by Coleman and Churchill (1997) as only one theme for guiding a program's philosophy of parent involvement. Additional themes considered by these authors are parenting, identifying and developing family strengths, preparing children for future schooling, providing information about community resources, modeling appropriate learning opportunities for children at home, and

improving interpersonal relations between professionals and families. As they assess the needs together, families and teachers may choose one or more of these themes and develop goals together for specific family involvement. New themes are likely to evolve as partnerships are formed and nourished.

> **Add some other ideas for themes to the list generated by Coleman and Churchill. Discuss which family characteristics might be more suited to each theme.**

Linking Parents and Teachers

Parents as Consumers of Children's Education

In tuition-based early childhood education programs, it is obvious that families are consumers. In public education, the parent's role as consumer is less obvious but no less true (Kostelnik, Stein, Whiren, & Soderman, 1993). Parents have made tremendous investments in their children and expect teachers to have some idea of how important those children are (Figure 7–6). To practice a family-based philosophy, early childhood teachers must begin to understand that they are serving both children and their families. In a sense, the role of early childhood teachers and other staff members takes on several new perspectives when this idea is incorporated. This does not necessarily mean that teachers will agree with every request a family member makes, but it does mean that teachers will respect and understand that those requests are often made in the best interests of the child. Further, when conflict arises between a teacher and a parent, the teacher assumes a professional role in working to resolve the conflict.

Supporting School Policy and Families

It is not impossible to support both school policy and families. Careful listening to parent concerns and reflective responses will often lead to creative problem-solving. When school policies are based on what education professionals believe to be best practices, teachers can explain the purpose of the policy to families (Figure 7–7). More details about effective interpersonal communication are included in Chapter 8.

The Partnership for Family Involvement in Education, U.S. Department of Education, has produced posters outlining seven good practices for families.

Figure 7–6	A Parent Looks Back

As my daughter begins her last semester of college, I am amazed at how quickly the years have flown and how time for both of us seems to be measured by school years. It all seemed so short: preschool, kindergarten, high school graduation, and now I even have lodging reservations for her college graduation weekend!

Brief, almost fleeting, and yet, so many milestones have been accomplished. Overall, I am very pleased and even appreciative of the educational endeavors that she and I chose for her 16+ years of education.

In the beginning, I placed her in a private school.

She was almost four. Her years at the private school led to kindergarten and first and second grades. While there, she was exposed to lots of reading, typing, some Spanish, computers, and her two favorite pastimes to this day: drama and roller skating.

Next came a culture shock for her: public school.

This presented a larger class size, diversity, school spirit, and busing. She barely missed a beat in the adjustment. She was bused to an inner-city school.

She adjusted well and even ran for school president and won! I was pleased with her elementary school experience. I was especially pleased with two teachers who recognized that special creative streak in her and rewarded her for her individuality.

Looking back, there is very little that I would change. I have loved seeing her achieve, stretch, be challenged, and most of all grow into a lovely, well-read, very verbal individual. It was 90 percent education and encouragement and 10 percent community outlets, church, and her mom, grandmother, and beloved uncle.

—Cindy Chrisman

Figure 7–7	Examples of School Policies Based on Best Practices

Best Practice—Teachers work in partnership with parents.

School Policy—A variety of two-way communication strategies are used to meet needs of each family. Schools ask families about useful and preferred means of communication.

Best Practice—Teachers and parents work together to handle differences of opinion as they arise.

School Policy—A plan for conflict resolution is in place and shared with all parents. Family members work with staff to develop the plan.

Best Practice—Teachers solicit and incorporate parents' knowledge about their children.

School Policy—Assessment procedures require conferences with parents. Information is shared appropriately with parents before the time of the conference so that they are prepared to make meaningful use of the time with the teacher. Family members share information about their child that will be used by staff when assessing children.

Best Practice—Parents have opportunities to be involved in ways that are comfortable for them.

School Policy—Parents are informed about a variety of ways in which they can be involved with their children's education, both in and outside the classroom. And families share with staff their skills, interests, and preferences.

Using the motto "Education is everybody's business!" the Partnership poster includes these practices.

1. *Take the time.* Moments talking at evening meals and visiting the library, museum, or zoo make a difference.

2. *Read together.* It's the starting point of all learning. Read with your youngsters.

3. *Use TV wisely.* Limit viewing to no more than two hours a school day.

4. *Stay in regular contact with your child's teacher.* Check homework every day.

5. *Meet with your child's teacher and principal.* Compare your school program with standards of excellence so your children can reach their full potential.

6. *Know where your children are.* Support community efforts to start after-school and summer programs.

7. *Talk directly to your children.* Share the values you want them to have and about the dangers of drugs, alcohol, and tobacco. It could literally save their lives.

Early childhood teachers can share these practices with families in a variety of ways. Providing parents with information, such as the criteria for quality programs in early education based on guidelines for developmentally appropriate practice or national voluntary accreditation criteria, gives them knowledge so that they can appropriately evaluate their children's education. Many early education programs provide their goals for children and philosophy of teaching and learning in handbooks and orientation sessions for parents.

Epstein's Framework for School, Family, and Community Partnerships

In her theory-building work, Joyce Epstein (1995) notes the existence of **overlapping spheres of influence** in the lives of children. Her idea that home, school, and community are all important in each child's education has led her to discuss types of involvement as well as examples and practices.

> *The way schools care about children is reflected in the way schools care about the children's families. If educators view children simply as students, they are likely to see the family as separate from the school. That is, the family is expected to do its job and leave the education of children to the schools. If educators view students as children, they are likely to see both the family and the community as partners with the school in children's education and development. Partners recognize their shared interests in and responsibilities for children, and they work together to create better programs and opportunities for students. (Epstein, 1995)*

From the preceding quote, one notes that Epstein's framework places children as central. When

families, schools, and communities are truly partners, the possibility of a "caring community" exists. Epstein identifies the following terms as critical to understanding her framework for partnership:

- family-like schools — *accepting, caring atmosphere*
- school-like families — *emphasize imp of school, learning activities*
- community-minded families — *emphasize service to other*
- family-friendly schools and communities *Think of needs of modern families*

> **Before reading any further, note some characteristics that you believe to be important to each of the four terms above.**

According to Epstein (1995), family-like schools recognize individuality in children and welcome all families; school-like families recognize children as students and learners, and encourage their success; community-minded families (including students) help their neighbors in a variety of ways; and family-friendly schools and communities consider the needs and realities of contemporary families. See Figure 7–8 for a Checklist for Family Friendliness in Schools. What items would you place on a similar list regarding school friendliness for families?

Six types of involvement or caring have been recorded by Epstein: parenting, communicating, volunteering, learning at home, decision-making, and collaborating with the community. It is suggested that schools utilize all six types of involvement for balance in their partnerships with families and communities. Figure 7–9 provides a brief explanation of each of the six types.

Epstein and her associates make it clear that creating a comprehensive caring community takes a lot of time and a lot of hard work. Organization and planning are required. They suggest the appointment of an action team and at least a three-year plan. Thus, partnerships are a process, not events. Before beginning the work of the action team, it is important to gather information about the school's existing practices. One way to collect this information is through use of the standards listed in Figure 7–10.

Figure 7–8	Checklist for Family Friendliness in Schools

	Almost always	Most of the time	Sometimes	Rarely	Almost Never
Parent meetings are problem-focused.	5	4	3	2	1
Parents are informed about classroom activities.	5	4	3	2	1
Parents are viewed as a source of information.					
Parental input is valued.	5	4	3	2	1
Parents come to school for positive reasons.	5	4	3	2	1
Parent meetings are held at various times.	5	4	3	2	1
Teachers discuss parents in a positive manner.	5	4	3	2	1
Teachers avoid gossiping about families.	5	4	3	2	1
Parents are informed when their children are doing well.	5	4	3	2	1
Teachers make it a point to invite all parents to school functions.	5	4	3	2	1
Are relationships between parents and teachers generally seen as positive?	5	4	3	2	1
Did most parents of children in the school succeed in school themselves?	5	4	3	2	1

Source: Rosenthal, D. M., & Sawyers, J. Y. (1996, Summer). Building successful home/school partnerships: Strategies for parent support and involvement. *Childhood Education*, pp. 194–200.

Figure 7–9	The Keys to Successful School-Family-Community Partnerships. Six Types of Involvement

EPSTEIN'S KEYS TO SUCCESSFUL SCHOOL-FAMILY-COMMUNITY PARTNERSHIPS

1. **Parenting**—Assist families with parenting skills and setting home conditions to support children as students, and assist schools to understand families.
2. **Communicating**—Conduct effective communications from school to home and from home to school about school programs and children's progress.
3. **Volunteering**—Organize volunteers to support the school and students.
4. **Learning at home**—Involve families with their children in homework and other activities.
5. **Decision making**—Include families as participants in school decisions and develop parent leaders.
6. **Collaborating with the community**—Coordinate resources and services from the community for families, students, and the school, and provide services to the community.

Source: Epstein, J., Coates, L., Salinas, K. C., Sanders, M. G., & Simon, B. S.-(1997). *School, family, and community partnerships: Your handbook for action.* Thousand Oaks, CA: Corwin Press.

National Standards from the PTA

The National Parent Teacher Association (PTA) has had as its primary goal for more than 100 years, "affirming the significance of parent and family involvement . . . in support of children and their education. . . ." With this in mind, and the increasingly powerful evidence from research to support family involvement in education, the PTA, using Epstein's six types of involvement, has created national standards.

The purpose for the standards is threefold:

1. to promote meaningful parent and family participation
2. to raise awareness regarding the components of effective programs

---

Figure 7–10	Listing of Standards from the National PTA

NATIONAL PTA STANDARDS FOR FAMILY INVOLVEMENT

Standard I—Communicating
Communication between home and school is regular, two-way, and meaningful.

Standard II—Parenting
Parenting skills are promoted and supported.

Standard III—Student Learning
Parents play an integral role in assisting student learning.

Standard IV—Volunteering
Parents are welcome in the school, and their support and assistance are sought.

Standard V—School Decision-making and Advocacy
Parents are full partners in the decisions that affect children and families.

Standard VI—Collaborating with Community
Community resources are used to strengthen schools, families, and student learning.

Source: http://www.pta.org/programs

---

3. to provide guidelines for schools that wish to improve their programs (http://www.pta.org/programs/invstand.htm, retrieved February 20, 2003)

For each of the six standards for family involvement, the National PTA has provided quality checklist, including **quality indicators.** Figure 7–9 summarizes the standards. On the Web, go to http://www.pta.org/programs for the entire checklist, including quality indicators.

Additional Frameworks for Understanding Family Involvement

Although Joyce Epstein's framework for partnerships is, at this time, the most well-developed one with a strong organization, the National Network of Partnership Schools (NNPS), frameworks with alternative perspectives have also been examined. Staff at the Harvard Family Research Project (Shartrand, et al., 1997) have identified Epstein's approach as *functional*, referring to its emphasis on specific purposes and roles for family, school and community partnerships.

 National Network of Partnership Schools (NNPS) **www.coso.jhu.edu.** Click "programs"; click "National Network of Partnership Schools"

The Family Involvement Network of Educators (FINE) **www.gse.harvard.edu.** Click "faculty & research"; click "research projects"; click "Harvard family research project"; click "FINE network"

---

resources available throu membership in comm. networks

James Coleman's framework for partnerships is referred to as *social capital.* In his groundbreaking mid-1960s research, "Coleman concluded that a student's home environment had more impact on test scores than any other factor, even school curriculum or student body characteristics" (Lynn, 1997). The notion of social capital points to the importance of relationships among individuals and institutions, in our case, families, schools, and communities. Central to this approach is that families are invested in their children's learning, negotiating differences in values in order to best benefit children's education, and skills in communicating with families in ways that demonstrate authentic caring (Shartrand, et al., 1997).

Parent empowerment best describes Moncrieff Cochran's framework of family involvement in children's education. Because schools have such a central place in U.S. society, they are in a unique and constructive situation to encourage empowerment of parents, families and communities (Cochran & Dunn, 1991). "Empowerment is a process through which people and communities grow toward more equitable, respectful interrelationships with themselves, and their environment. . . . In order for . . . relationships to become more equitable, the balance of power usually must change" (Dean, 2004). Attitudes that are fundamental with this framework include believing that:

- all parents want what is best for their children
- all parents want to be good parents
- parents are not only children's first, but also their most important teachers (Shartrand, et al., 1997)

Further, a knowledge base that provides understanding about societal power structures, oppression, and discrimination is necessary to build partnerships with all families in the school community. Early childhood teachers must work to comprehend the effects of dominant groups and institutions on oppressed people. Thus, skills must be gained in order to communicate respect to all families and to help build confidence in those who need such support (Shartrand, et al., 1997).

Luis Moll has defined *cultural competence* as a necessary emphasis for family involvement. This emphasis on cultural competence requires teachers to look beyond what they observe in classrooms. Moll's research found that "many families had abundant knowledge that the schools did not know about—and therefore, did not use in order to teach academic skills" (North Central Regional Educational Laboratory, 1994). For example, many rural families knew a great deal about agriculture, farm or ranch management, carpentry, and electricity, and, further, these families shared their knowledge and skills through informal community networks. Moll believes that tapping into these strong networks can be very helpful for schools.

Relating the cultural competence model to language learning and literacy leads educators to understand the importance of bilingual students taking advantage of their home languages (North Central Regional Educational Laboratory, 1994). Knowledge and skills central to this framework include teachers':

- awareness of their own beliefs and prejudices that influence building partnerships with all families.
- knowledge about cultural variations in parenting and education.
- skills in gaining translators and creating ways to communicate with all families.
- knowledge of variations in communication styles of various groups of people.
- skills to incorporate family "funds of knowledge" into student learning at home and at school (Shartrand, et al., 1997).

It is vital that early childhood teachers consider all four of these frameworks as they prepare to work with all families. Many teacher preparation programs place little emphasis, generally, on understanding families and even less emphasis, specifically, on acquiring a deep understanding of and the skills to work with families who are culturally different, systems of power and oppression, and engaging in primary interactions with families to help build their confidence.

> What challenges do you face as you reflect on specifics of the four frameworks for building partnerships? What strengths do you already possess? Develop a plan for your professional progress based on at least one of the frameworks.

Professionalism in Family-based Early Education

Professionalism in early education is enhanced when all staff uphold their responsibilities to children and families. Due to their low pay, early childhood educators are often regarded as having low status in U.S. society. Still, it is imperative that these educators view themselves as professionals and see the need and their responsibility to apply the knowledge, skills, and values of the discipline. Although it is true that much is expected of early childhood teachers and that typically they are not compensated fairly for their work, professionalism must be evident.

Following are some of the components of professionalism for early childhood educators.

Confidentiality

Early childhood teachers must be able to maintain confidences shared by families. The nature of the job frequently makes early childhood teachers privy to information that may cause embarrassment or harm to a family. Information gleaned through observation, as well as information in formal records, must be kept in confidence. Teachers should make it clear to family members that it is their professional responsibility to maintain confidentiality and that they will not share information unless the family authorizes them to do so.

Requests to share information should be made only for the purpose of providing assistance to the family or child enrolled in the program. Responsibility for safeguarding confidentiality includes obtaining family consent when sharing information, obtaining family consent when inviting others to team meetings, keeping files secure, never gossiping or talking casually about a family, and respecting confidences coworkers share with you (*Family Partnerships,* 1998). See the **NAEYC Code of Ethical Conduct,** in Appendix B of this book, for statements on written and verbal confidentiality for both children's and families' rights to privacy.

The **Family Education Rights & Privacy Act (FERPA)** is a federal law designed to protect the privacy of a student's education records. Under this act, parents have the right to inspect and review all of the student's education records maintained by the school. Parents have the right to request that a school correct the records believed to be inaccurate or misleading. Generally, schools must have written permission from the parent or eligible student before releasing any information from a student's record. For more information about FERPA, visit http://www.ed.gov/offices/Om/ferpa.html.

Advocacy

Advocating for children and families is also a professional responsibility. **Advocacy** can happen within your school or center, in a town or city, in regional or state government, and at the national or international level. Advocacy may be done in person, through e-mail or letters, and by telephone.

Early childhood professionals may advocate within both private and public agencies, as well as with elected and nonelected public officials. For a detailed description of advocacy methods and strategies, read *Advocates in Action: Making a Difference for Young Children* (Robinson & Stark, 2002).

Collaboration

Professionalism with families also extends into the community through collaboration with other agencies and programs. Collaboration may be minimal (informing parent of opportunities), or more extensive (budgeting time and money for collaborative efforts). Collaboration may be necessary to improve or extend support for families, obtain services for children, or increase knowledge about certain conditions. For further information about family-community collaboration, read "New Directions for Parent Leadership in a Family-Support Context" (Langford & Weissbourd, 1997).

Understanding Roles and Boundaries

Early childhood teachers should be familiar with the roles and tasks included in their job descriptions. Work with families and children is frequently done on a deeply personal level. Sometimes, some personal disclosure on the part of the professional is effective, but it is critical that teachers are aware of professional boundaries in their relationships with children and families. Demonstration of caring must be balanced with limits in professional relationships. When friendships develop with either families in the program or with colleagues, it is important that professional boundaries be maintained in the interest of fairness to all. Some strategies that can be helpful in managing professional roles and boundaries include having accurate job descriptions, adhering to policies and procedures, not taking sides in family disputes, skill in assertive communication, knowing how to delegate when a boundary conflict may occur, and respecting

Professionalism in early education is enhanced when all staff members uphold their responsibilities to children and families.

professional boundaries with colleagues (*Family Partnerships*, 1998).

Record-Keeping

Having accurate and current records about children as well as relevant family information is useful for assessment of children. Further, such documentation can be invaluable if referrals for additional or alternative services are necessary. All records must be kept in a locked cabinet so that they are confidential. Keeping notes about informal and formal conferences with family members can serve as a reminder when planning for the group or for individual children. Observations of children in the classroom and in other settings provide meaningful information when compiling evaluations.

> *"Programs are only as good as the individuals who staff them."*
>
> **—Head Start Advisory Council on Services for Families with Infants and Toddlers**

Embracing Diversity

When early childhood educators attempt to form a family-based philosophy, a willingness to acknowledge and respect family differences is required. Cultural differences in families lead to very different approaches to parenting young children. Some families believe that children are fragile and that families are the protectors of children; other families believe that children are tough and independent, and that families are the trainers of children (Trawick-Smith, 1997). **Diversity** in families is part of the richness of our pluralistic culture.

Observing and Appreciating Differences

For any given teacher, one of the parenting approaches just mentioned may be the one they find to be most appropriate. It is important that early childhood professionals work to understand and respect various parenting approaches. Rather than judging the family, teachers can use the information about parenting approaches to better understand the child in their care. When necessary, differences in practices

and expectations between families and schools should be discussed. Open communication can lead to an understanding of the opposing point of view. Teachers can offer to share resources when parents ask questions or seek help with some area of difficulty. Teachers also should realize that a child's family can be the greatest resource for understanding the child.

> *"We live in an increasingly diverse world. As an early childhood educator you are almost certain to have close contact with people who have different racial, economic, cultural, and linguistic backgrounds and different lifestyles. This diversity offers challenges and opportunities. Although you may have moments of discomfort and self-doubt, you also have the possibility of gaining new appreciation and insights. Each bias and prejudice that you overcome brings you a step closer to helping all children to reach their potential."*
>
> **—Feeney, Christensen, and Moravcik, 1996, p. 12**

You will teach children who come from a variety of family structures. Encouraging members of a

It is important that early childhood educators acknowledge and respect cultural diversity.

child's family to participate in school functions is an important aspect of early childhood family involvement. Frequently, this might mean inviting a parent (or other family member) who does not live with the child to participate in ways that are comfortable for all family members. Sometimes, parents who do not live together, will both attend the same parent-teacher conference, or they may request separate conferences with their child's teacher. Keep in mind that each family defines itself. It is the role of the early childhood teacher to include all family members, not to judge who is a "real" mother or "real" parent.

Some barriers to implementing a multicultural framework in classrooms have been identified by Swick, Boutte, and Van Scoy (1996). The following factors become barriers when early childhood teachers do not engage in ongoing personal and professional development.

Barrier #1: Cultural stereotypes. People are stereotyped when others have minimal or inaccurate information about them. When those in the dominant culture have low self-esteem and are insecure, they tend to foster intergenerational prejudices.

Barrier #2: Social isolation. Having experiences with people from a variety of different cultures often helps to understand those cultures. However, those who have social contact only with others who are similar in culture and beliefs may lack information necessary for understanding differences.

Barrier #3: Tradition. By continuing the same activities in the name of tradition, schools can create exclusionary practices. When traditions are not inclusive, they must be reevaluated and modified, or dropped. All forms of bias must be considered including racism, sexism, ageism, as well as unfair limits placed on those with disabilities.

Barrier #4: Excessive conformity. Expectations that everyone conform to the majority are sometimes stated as being "democratic." This view, however, ignores a crucial aspect of democracy: that everyone has a voice and deserves to be represented. While in a vote, majority rules, this is not the case for everyday events in educational settings. Children can learn to celebrate their differences.

"Schools also need to recognize the effect they have on children's multicultural development. Some teachers have limited understanding of their student's cultural backgrounds. The resulting erroneous beliefs must be transcended through staff development, personal reading and enrichment, and through personal growth experiences. Institutional practices of tracking, ability grouping and rigidly defined graded systems need to be replaced with more inclusionary strategies such as multiage grouping, cross-cultural peer learning and more personalized instruction. Unquestioned rituals and policies imprison culturally different children within an inequitable and insensitive environment. . . . Inappropriate and inaccurate labeling has led many children to years of academic failure."

—**Kevin J. Swick, Gloria Boutte, and Irma Van Scoy, 1996**

Strategies for Overcoming Barriers

1. *Repeatedly invite guests, speakers, and representatives of a variety of cultures into the school program.* Plan education and recreational activities together.

2. *Use various media to show different cultures and promote the celebration of those differences.* For example, display posters depicting many cultures and change them throughout the year, use children's literature with different racial-ethnic and socioeconomic levels represented in positive ways and use videos depicting a variety of cultures in positive ways.

3. *Plan celebrations throughout the year that involve diverse communities and include food, music, dance, visual, and language traditions.*

Anti-Bias Curriculum   Louise Derman-Sparks and her associates (1989) have created a model approach for implementing curriculum goals related to understanding and respect for diversity in early childhood education. In the words of this group:

Anti-bias curriculum embraces an educational philosophy as well as specific techniques and content. It is value-based: differences are good; oppressive ideas and behaviors are not. It sets up a creative tension between respecting differences and not accepting unfair beliefs and acts. It asks teachers and children to confront troublesome issues rather than covering them up. An anti-bias perspective is integral to all aspects of daily classroom life. (Derman-Sparks and the A.B.C. Task Force, 1989, p. x)

Even though the emphasis of the anti-bias curriculum is on teaching and learning in early childhood classrooms, there are ways to consider this philosophy in work with families and communities. The authors of this curriculum dedicate an entire chapter to setting goals and working with parents. Including work with parents, they say, is "vital" to the effectiveness of this approach in early childhood education. The authors include the following goals:

- to establish genuine parent/teacher dialogue that opens up discussion of each other's points of view and seeks to gain clarity, understanding, and solutions agreeable to both teacher and parent

- to provide information that facilitates parent awareness of how young children develop racial-ethnic and gender identity, and the ways in which sexism, racism, and handicappism negatively affect healthy socioemotional and cognitive growth

- to create safe settings for parents to discuss with each other the issues raised by anti-bias work and to increase their ability to integrate anti-bias perspectives in their child-rearing.

- to facilitate development of children through joint parent/teacher problem solving and mutual support

- to involve parents in curriculum development, implementation and evaluation (Derman-Sparks *and* the A.B.C. Task Force, 1989, p. 97)

It is clear that carrying out these goals challenges most, if not all, early childhood professionals. The value systems held by some families are on a collision course with the values held by those who believe in an anti-bias approach to education. Various reasons exist for this. Some families have not given these ideas much thought, and although they may have some stereotyped ideas based on political or religious ideology, they may also begin to consider the importance of

understanding and respecting all people with whom they interact on a regular basis—for example, the people in their child's school. Other families agree with the importance of anti-bias curriculum but have not actively shared their beliefs with their children. Finally, still other families have already embraced, and practice, the philosophy of respect for all people.

For early childhood programs that are serious about implementing an anti-bias approach, the creators of this curriculum offer a nine-session plan for parent group meetings. Topics include the following:

1. Introducing Anti-Bias Curriculum
2. Gender Identity and Sexism
3. Creating Nonsexist Home Environments
4. How Children Develop Racial Identity and Awareness
5. Creating Antiracist Home and School Environments
6. Sexism and Racism in Children's Books
7. Talking with Children about Disabilities
8. Children's Books about Differently-Abled People
9. Advocating for the Rights of the Differently-Abled

Strategies and resources are suggested for each of the above topics. Although this outline is a useful beginning for informing parents about an anti-bias philosophy in educating young children, it is not exhaustive. Attention is not given to some specific groups that are oppressed, including low-income families, gay and lesbian people, overweight people, and older people. Clearly, it is the intent of this educational philosophy to eliminate all oppression and to advocate for fairness for all people.

Figure 7–11 contains suggestions for parents who seem to be reticent about involvement in their children's education (Lee, 1995).

Understanding that Many Ways of Interacting with Children Can Serve Them Well

Early childhood teachers work with both children and their families. We can best teach children by

Figure 7–11	Strategies for Involving Reticent Parents

Reaching Out to Reticent Parents

Suggestions offered by parents who participated in the study about how to reach out to reticent parents who seldom take part in school activities.

1. Encourage active parents to stress the importance of participating in school activities.

2. Urge children to encourage and remind their parents to attend school activities.

3. Invite parents to visit school and observe their children any time, and reassure them that they will be given a friendly welcome when they come to school.

4. Clearly indicate to parents that a language difference need not be a primary concern for parents who are interested in getting involved at school.

5. Invite interpreters to come with parents for open house and back-to-school-night activities, or encourage teachers to have interpreters present.

6. If two or more parents belong to the same Asian ethnic group, reassure them that they are free to speak in their own language to each other during parent meetings. This way, Asian parents who are able to communicate in English may help others to understand the discussions.

7. Reserve some time to communicate with Asian parents alone after the parent meeting (e.g., on back-to-school night) so that Asian parents do not feel that they have been ignored.

8. Visit reticent parents in their homes. In general, Asian parents respect teachers and feel honored when their children's teachers visit. Asian parents also view that teacher's willingness to come forward as a sign of sincerity (Shen & Mo, 1993). Parents are more willing to be educational partners when they learn that teachers make an effort to reach out to them.

9. Sometimes, children inhibit parents' participation because they feel embarrassed by their parents' inability to communicate well in English. They sometimes wish their parents would not appear at school. Convey that a language difference is not a negative trait.

10. Provide an opportunity for parents in the same Asian group, whose children attend the same school, to get acquainted with one another.

11. Schedule parent-teacher conferences to enable parents from the same Asian group, with children in the same class, to visit school at the same time. This way, reluctant parents may not feel as threatened by the unfamiliar school environment and may be encouraged to communicate with the teacher.

12. Asian parents who speak English and are familiar with school procedures can give introductions regarding the following matters to reticent parents from the same Asian group: school registration procedures, immunization, school volunteer programs, parent-teacher conferences, school educational goals, grading and evaluation systems, etc. Holding meetings about these issues in a parent's home might provide a less threatening environment for the reticent parent. Schools may also conduct seminars in parents' native tongues to help them become familiar with basic features of the school system such as educational services and programs, extracurricular activities, and procedures for assessment and evaluation of children (Yao, 1988).

13. Send notes to parents from time to time. The note could be a one- or two-sentence progress report, or it may be something that would make parents smile, such as, "Do you know what your child did today that gave us a good laugh?" or "Would you like to know what interesting thing your child did today?"

Source: Lee, F. Y. (March 1995). Asian parents as partners. *Young Children, 50,* 4–7. With permission from the National Association for the Education of Young Children.

---

including their families in a variety of ways. As we provide quality early childhood education programs for young children, we are also supporting and caring for families (Feeney, Christensen, & Moravcik, 1996). Adults in families have many ways of nurturing and providing for their children; they have values that may differ from the teacher's values. When early childhood teachers can assess family strengths and not see these differences only as deficits, then it is more likely they will enjoy successful partnerships with families of children in their programs.

| Figure 7–12 | Continuum of Parent Involvement |

HIGH
- Parents, trained by teacher, assist in classroom in such learning activities as reviewing writing samples, assisting at learning centers, or helping with computer use.
- Parents in classrooms reinforce processes and concepts introduced by teachers.
- Parents in classrooms practice with children on vocabulary words, number facts; help them enter answers on computer cards.
- Parents read to children in the classrooms.
- Parents make classroom presentations or present hands-on activities in areas of expertise.
- Parents participate in committees that directly influence school curricula and policies. Committees consist of parents, teachers, and administrator(s).
- PTA parents work on sponsorship and implementation of curriculum-related and family-oriented activities, e.g., cultural arts contests, displays, family fun night.
- Parents make instructional materials for classroom use, as directed by teachers.
- Parents assist in school library, checking out and shelving books.
- Parents participate as room mothers or room fathers.
- Parents supervise on class trips or chaperone at school functions.
- Parents visit classrooms during American Education Week or back-to-school night.
- Parents attend classroom plays, presentations.
- Parents attend school assembly programs.
- Parents attend competitive games, athletic events at school.
- Parents attend promotion ceremonies.
- Parents attend parent-teacher conferences.
- Parents are encouraged to help children with homework at home.
- Parents are involved in PTA fund-raising activities.
- Parents are asked to join PTA.
- Parents are encouraged to read school's handbook for parents.
- No parental involvement.

LOW

Source: Galen, H. (January 1991). Increasing parental involvement in elementary school: The nitty gritty of one successful program. *Young Children, 46,* 19. With permission from the National Association for the Education of Young Children.

Evaluating the Family Involvement Component in Early Education

As with any other component in quality early childhood education, it is important that early childhood teachers and administrators evaluate the success of family involvement. In planning for evaluation, it may be helpful to use the Continuum of Parent Involvement identified by Galen (1991). To evaluate this in a logical and consistent manner, a program must first identify its goals for family involvement. Both short-term and long-term goals may be identified. Examples of goals, strategies, and methods of evaluation are provided in this section. Please note that Figure 7–13 is a sample and not indicative of a comprehensive family involvement plan for early childhood education.

The results of evaluation of family involvement activities help program staff to be aware of their successes as well as of areas that need attention. Program assessment should lead to new goals that continue to build partnerships with families.

Figure 7–13	Sample Family Involvement Plan for Early Childhood Education

Goals	Strategies	Evaluation Methods
Providing program information regarding the philosophy of teaching and learning to all new families	Providing written brochures at the time of application, providing handbooks at the time of enrollment Personal explanations of program by director or other staff Teacher-led parent meeting that explains the program early in the year	Noting that the program philosophy has been added to the handbook or a brochure Having parents sign that they have read and understand the philosophy Asking parents to submit questions or comments that will be addressed in a parent meeting to increase their understanding of program philosophy
Creating an orientation to the program for both children and families	Classroom visits before school starts Making curriculum resources available to families Providing explanations or listings of all support services available	Filing the plan for orientation including how and when orientations are conducted Ask participants to complete a rating form about the usefulness of the orientation Ask family members who have been in the program for at least a year for suggestions for orientation topics and formats
Scheduling home-school conferences at least twice during the school term	Designing flexible schedules to meet family needs Including children when appropriate in conferences Involving other staff, other family members, or advocates when appropriate Giving parents a list of suggested questions they might ask during conferences	Recording dates and times of conferences Collecting evaluations from family members about the usefulness of conferences and suggestions for improvement
Making family members feel welcome as classroom volunteers	Matching family members' interests or skills with classroom needs Preparing materials and space in advance for parents Informing parents of daily schedule and exceptions to the schedule Consistently welcoming parents throughout the day Personally inviting each parent or family to participate in the classroom	Request feedback from volunteers who frequent the classroom Send questionnaires to those who do not volunteer to request information anonymously about what the program staff can do to increase their comfort level Self-evaluate which families you feel most comfortable having in the classroom and how you might increase comfort level of others

Summary and Conclusions

To practice a family-based philosophy in early childhood education, teachers must have knowledge of families and value the primacy of families in children's lives. In early childhood education, Head Start has provided a model program for partnerships between programs and families. Since 1965, Head Start has had a primary goal of empowering parents to take responsibility for their lives and for those of their children. High expectations have been coupled with various forms of support for families. Teachers in family-based early education programs see themselves as support for children and their families.

Policies in early childhood education programs must incorporate current understanding about parents as their children's first teachers. Family involvement must be a priority for early education professionals. As programs for children are planned and implemented, the central role of families must be incorporated in a variety of ways.

Chapter 7 Applications

1. The most important aspect of family involvement in education is that parents spend time with their children. Describe some ways you can help to foster this, even when parents are not volunteering in the classroom.
2. Explain the concept of continuity in children's lives. Give examples of ways early childhood professionals can increase continuity for children.
3. How might a perspective of parents as consumers of early education affect parent-teacher relationships?

Questions for Reflection and Discussion

1. Make a list of topics that should be included in a family-based philosophy of early childhood education.
2. Which areas of practicing a family-based philosophy will challenge you? In which areas do you possess experience or strengths?
3. How will particular early education settings (e.g., child care, public school, Head Start, and so on) affect your philosophy about family involvement?

Field Assignments

1. Ask several parents of young children about care and education arrangements they have made for their children each day. Note the number of transitions some very young children deal with daily.
2. Interview three early childhood teachers about the responsibilities they believe parents have for their children's early education. What suggestions would teachers give to parents of young children related to these responsibilities?
3. Interview three parents of young children about responsibilities they believe early childhood teachers have for their children's early education. What suggestions would parents give to teachers related to these responsibilities?

References

Bowman, B. (1994). Home and school. In S. L. Kagan & B. Weissbourd (Eds.), *Putting families first: America's family support movement and the challenge of change*. San Francisco: Jossey-Bass.

Bronfenbrenner, U. (1979). *The ecology of human development: Experiments by nature and design*. Cambridge, MA: Harvard University Press.

Capital Area Intermediate Unit (CAIU) Preschool Program. (2005–06). Transition to school: A planning guide for parents.

Christian, L. G. (January 2006). Understanding families: Applying family systems theory to early childhood practice. *Young Children, 61* (1), 12–20.

Cochran, M., & Dunn, C. (1991). Home-school relations and the empowerment process. *The Elementary School Journal, 91* (3), 261–269.

Coleman, M., & Churchill, S. (Spring 1997). Challenges to family involvement. *Childhood Education*, 144–148.

Dean, C. (2004). Empowering partnerships with families. *Innovations in community and Rural Development*. Cornell Community and Rural Development Institute. www.cardi.cornell.edu/community_capacity/community_action/000283.php. Retrieved January 24, 2006.

Derman-Sparks, L., & the A.B.C. Task Force. (1989). *Antibias curriculum: Tools for empowering young children*. Washington, DC: National Association for the Education of Young Children.

Epps, W. J. (1998). *Connecting Head Start parents to the public school setting: A transition activity booklet.* Florissant, MO: Southern Research Associates.

Epstein, J. (1995). School/family/community partnerships: Caring for the children we share. *Phi Delta Kappan, 76,* 701–712.

Epstein, J., Coates, L., Salinas, K. C., Sanders, M. G., & Simon, B. S. (1997). *School, family, and community partnerships: Your handbook for action.* Thousand Oaks, CA: Corwin Press.

Family partnerships: A continuous process. Training guides for the Head Start learning community. (1998). Washington, DC: U.S. Department of Health and Human Services.

Feeney, S., Christensen, D., & Moravcik, E. (1996). *Who am I in the lives of children?: An introduction to teaching young children.* Englewood Cliffs, NJ: Prentice Hall.

FERPA Web address: http://www.ed.gov/offices/Om/ferpa.html.

Galen, H. (January 1991). Increasing parental involvement in elementary school: The nitty gritty of one successful program. *Young Children, 46,* 19.

Head Start Handbook of the Parent Involvement Vision and Strategies. (1996). Washington, DC: U.S. Department of Health and Human Services.

Kostelnik, M. J., Stein, L. C., Whiren, A. P., & Soderman, A. K. (1993). *Guiding children's social development.* Clifton Park, NY: Delmar Learning.

Langford, J., & Weissbourd, B. (1997). New directions for parent leadership in a family-support context. In S. L. Kagan & B. T. Bowman (Eds.), *Leadership in early care and education.* Washington, DC: National Association for the Education of Young Children.

Lee, F. Y. (1995, March). Asian parents as partners. *Young Children, 50,* 4–7.

Lynn, L. (September/October 1997). Family involvement in schools: It makes a big difference, but remains rare. Harvard Education Letter. http://www.edletter.org/past/issues/1997-so/family.shtml. Retrieved January 24, 2006.

National PTA. http://www.pta.org/programs/invstand/htm. Retrieved March 9, 1999.

North Central Regional Educational Laboratory (1994). Funds of knowledge: A look at Luis Moll's research into hidden family resources. *CITYSCHOOLS, 1* (1), 19–21.

Powell, D. (1989). *Families and early childhood programs.* Washington, DC: National Association for the Education of Young Children.

Robinson, A., & Strk, D. R. (2002). *Advocates in action.* Washington, DC: National Association for the Education of Young Children.

Rosenthal, D. M., & Sawyers, J. Y. (1996, Summer). Building successful home/school partnerships: Strategies for parent support and involvement. *Childhood Education,* 194–200.

Shartrand, A. M., Weiss, H. B., Kreider, H. M., & Lopez, M. E. (1997). *New skills for new schools: Preparing teachers in family involvement.* Harvard Family Research Project. http://www.ges.harvard.edu/hfrp/pubs/onlinepubs/skills/chptr1.html. Retrieved January 22, 2006.

Starting Small. Teaching Tolerance Curriculum. Montgomery, AL: Southern Poverty Law Center.

Swick, K. J., Boutte, G., & Van Scoy, I. (Winter 1995–96). Families and schools: Building multicultural values together. *Childhood Education,* 75–79.

Trawick-Smith, J. (1997). *Early childhood development: A multicultural perspective.* Upper Saddle River, NJ: Prentice Hall.

OUTLINE

Objectives

Key Terms

Building Relationships
Communication

Ongoing Communication
One-Way Communication
Two-Way Communication
Effective Interpersonal Communication
Guidelines for Giving and Receiving Criticism
Assertiveness versus Aggression

Conflict Resolution
Some Ineffective and Inappropriate Practices
  to Avoid in Interpersonal Communication
Helpful Attitudes for Effective Interpersonal
  Communication

Summary and Conclusions

Chapter 8 Applications

Questions for Reflection and Discussion

Field Assignments

References

Family-Staff Relationships

OBJECTIVES

After reading this chapter, you should be able to:

- discuss attitudes and practices necessary for effective communication among families, child care, and/or schools.

- understand the most effective communication strategies for specific situations.

- apply effective conflict resolution practices in the family involvement component of early education.

- familiarize yourself with useful Web sites to build and support family-staff relationships.

- learn strategies for responding to a variety of interactions with families.

Key Terms

active listening
codependency
conflict resolution

empathy
interpersonal
  communication

self-disclosure
two-way communication

Building Relationships

Communication

Family systems theory emphasizes the importance of communication for establishing healthy, functional families. Effective communication also is vital to building relationships among professionals and families. When professionals implement strategies for effectively communicating with families, they serve a twofold purpose: (1) to establish strong partnerships, and (2) to model methods of communication that families might choose to use in order to strengthen their familial bonds. Clear communication is an essential professional tool for early childhood teachers and administrators who wish to develop productive partnerships. When we communicate effectively with others, each voice is empowered (Swick, 2003).

Attitudes   A perspective that views teachers and parents as partners in children's education is a very powerful one. The sense of common purpose and mutuality is a strength of the partnership notion (Swick, 1991).

Establishing a positive relationship with parents begins with their first phone call to the school or with their first visit, and it involves everyone in the school. For example, the person who answers the phone or greets the family on their arrival may set the tone for the entire visit. Incidental meetings with staff often provide families with useful information.

What makes a positive or healthy relationship? Clearly, any relationship depends on more than one person's attitudes and behaviors. However, it is also true that one person with certain understandings and skills can help positively direct a relationship. It is the duty of professionals to obtain these understandings and skills and to take the responsibility of directing the interactions with students' families and with community members. For example, it is teachers' responsibility to avoid using derogatory terms when describing a family, because using such negative language can degrade or disempower families. In addition, when teachers make such negative statements, it is difficult for them to overcome the negative attitudes and beliefs those statements express and thus, may make it impossible for that teacher to have an empowering relationship with a given family (Garbarino, 1992, as cited in Swick, 2003).

Some emotional and behavioral characteristics are known to be related to healthy relationships. The following are included by Hanna (1991) in her discussion of this topic:

High self-esteem—Teachers who love and accept themselves are more likely to demonstrate caring and acceptance of others.

Freedom from *codependency*—Teachers who are not extremely dependent on others, serving them and sacrificing their own needs, possess a trait that is important for positive relationships.

Genuineness—Honest, open, authentic teachers avoid game-playing in relationships with others.

Warmth—Caring for others, even with their faults, helps to maintain healthy relationships.

Empathy—Trying to understand the behavior of others and the underlying meaning of that behavior is an important characteristic of building relationships.

Self-disclosure—Balancing how much and what you disclose about yourself with family and community members can be a challenge. A certain kind and amount of **self-disclosure** is related to other characteristics of healthy relationships such as genuineness, warmth, and **empathy.**

Fairness and dependability—Over time, teachers have the opportunity to demonstrate that others can trust them to be fair-minded and to follow through as they have committed to do.

Energizing feelings—As teachers build relationships with families and their communities, they are likely to leave a situation feeling energized by the possibilities communicated. Experience with such situations is likely to positively influence teachers to work on relationships with parents and other community members.

Consider the characteristics of healthy relationships just mentioned. Think about a teacher that you had in the past who seemed to excel in one or two of those areas. Share some examples of teacher behaviors that you believe demonstrate these characteristics. Which of these areas do you see as your strengths? In which areas could you use some practice?

The U.S. Department of Education lists seven tips for building partnerships with families. These tips are:

- work together
- assess needs
- survey resources
- share information
- seek experienced collaborators
- set goals
- decide on measures of success

When these behaviors drive the work that educators and families are participating in together, the results will not only be stronger partnerships, but also greater progress for children's education. A complete description of these tips may be found at http://www.ed.gov/pubs/PFIE/families.html.

Practices

Written Communication   One of the initial contacts with parents is usually a letter welcoming their child to the school. Although this letter may be sent

Communication can happen in a variety of ways.

by the director or principal, it also should include information and perhaps a greeting from the classroom teacher. The content of all the written information sent home to parents needs to be clear and worded positively. Always proofread for correct spelling and grammar. The initial information should be covered in welcoming, supportive, and inviting ways.

Written communications can include brochures about the early childhood education program that contain a statement of the program's philosophy and goals for children, as well as information about school policies and the staff.

Communication in Person. When parents visit the school or center for the first time, it is important that both written and human resources are available. Personal communication should include pleasant greetings, a tour of the building and grounds, introductions to teachers and other staff, and an opportunity to ask questions. Figure 8–1 provides one format for interviewing parents or family members who are new to the early childhood program. Be sure to note that this form can be adapted to include additional topics. Currently, a focus of U.S. society is young children's health, nutrition, and fitness. So, item four in Figure 8–1 could include a "t. What are some healthy snack and meal ideas for young children?" Considering other current concerns, what would you choose to add (or delete) from this interview form?

Family involvement in early childhood education thrives in programs that practice an open-door policy. Written and personal communication should make clear to parents that they are welcome at the school any time, that they are partners in their child's education, and that their voice is important to the school. Examples of ways in which families are involved in the early childhood program could be shared at this initial visit.

Many early childhood professionals have found it useful to provide parents with a family handbook during orientation or initial enrollment. These handbooks commonly include a statement of the philosophy of the school's educational program and information about goals or expected outcomes for children, family involvement opportunities, daily schedules, operating policies and procedures, and individual classrooms.

Ongoing Communication

One-Way Communication

The following strategies are examples of one-way communication from school to home.

Newsletters Sending newsletters home from school is one way to help parents stay informed about and connected to school events. Including columns by teachers, children, administrators, and parents allows for a variety of voices and perspectives. This format makes it more likely that a larger number of parents will actually read the newsletter.

Suggestions for topics of interest and concern to families with young children include the following:

- the meaning of developmentally appropriate practice
- the importance of play for young children
- multiple intelligences
- the meaning of pretend play for young children
- early literacy
- nutrition
- understanding children's physical and motor development

Figure 8–1	Parent Interview Form

1. Would you like to work with the children in the classroom?
2. What would you prefer doing in the classroom if you were to come?
3. Name something special that you can do or make, or something you know about that you would be willing to share with the children.
4. I'm going to read a list of items to you. Tell me if you have ever felt a need to know more about any of these items by answering either yes or no. (Interviewer: Please check appropriate category.)

		Yes	No
a.	How to teach my preschool children		
b.	Whether my child is developing appropriately		
c.	Services provided by community agencies to which I have a right		
d.	How to communicate better with my children		
e.	How to help my children interact better with others		
f.	How to discipline my children		
g.	How to make toys and other things for my children		
h.	How to tell whether my child is progressing in school		
i.	What to do when my children do things that I do not consider proper (temper tantrums, thumb-sucking, bad manners)		
j.	How to play with my children		
k.	Where to take my children so they can have a nice time and learn		
l.	How to help my children retain their cultural heritage		
m.	How to use and develop the talents and skills that I know I have		
n.	How to refrain from hitting my child		
o.	How to guarantee that my child will succeed in school		
p.	How to talk to teachers		
q.	How to help my child learn a second language when I don't speak a second language		
r.	How to extend language learning		
s.	How to use my home environment as a learning experience for my children		

5. What is your opinion of preschool parents coming together at least once a month to talk and learn more about the areas to which you answered "yes?"
6. If you felt that this parent meeting is a good idea, how can we make sure that the meetings are worthwhile for parents?
7. Would you be willing to help organize the first parent meeting?
8. Are there other ways you might be willing to help with the parent meetings?
9. Name something special that you can do or make, or that you know about that you would be willing to share with other parents.

Source: Hohmann, M., Banet, B., & Weikart, D. P. (1979). *Young Children in Action,* High/Scope Press. Reprinted with permission from the High/Scope Educational Research Foundation

- understanding children's intellectual development understanding children's social and emotional development

- appropriate strategies for moving from diapers to potty

Columns about these topics and many others are provided for use by early childhood programs in *Family-Friendly Communication for Early Childhood Programs* (Diffily & Morrison, 1996).

> **Considering information about newsletters in this section of the textbook, design an outline or template that you might use as a basis for your newsletters to families. Be sure to demonstrate as many principles as possible from the "Newsletter" segment, as well as Figures 8–2 and 8–3, so that your newsletters are relevant to families.**

Especially important in a newsletter are dates of upcoming events and brief explanations or descriptions of school activities. Providing both a listing of current activities and those further into the future will remind parents and help them in planning busy schedules. A sample page from a newsletter is found in Figure 8–2. Figure 8–3 suggests content for newsletters to families.

The following ideas were selected from an article by Bob Krech titled "Improve Parent Communication with a Newsletter" (1995):

- The main goal of the newsletter is to answer parents' questions before they ask them.

- Try to keep the newsletter to one page.

- Always remember to thank parents, at least once, in your newsletter.

Electronic newsletters, or e-newsletters, are being used more frequently by early childhood professionals as a tool for connecting with families. The advantages to sending electronic newsletters include the instant delivery capability and low cost. Of course, because not all families have access to the technology

| **Figure 8–2** | What We Can Do to Help Our Children Learn |

What We Can Do to Help Our Children Learn:

Listen to them and pay attention to their problems.
Read with them.
Tell family stories.
Limit their television watching.
Have books and other reading materials in the house.
Look up words in the dictionary with them.
Encourage them to use an encyclopedia.
Share favorite poems and songs with them.
Take them to the library and get them their own library cards.
Take them to museums and historical sites, when possible.
Discuss the daily news with them.
Go exploring with them and learn about plants, animals, and geography.
Find a quiet place for them to study.
Review their homework.
Meet with their teachers.
Do you have other ideas?

For sale by the U.S. Government Printing Office
Superintendent of Documents, Mail Stop: SSOP
Washington, DC 20402-9328

Source: Reprinted with permission from the U.S. Department of Education

required to enable them to receive e-newsletters, it is important that e-newsletters not replace other forms of communication (Walker, 2005).

The following design tips are offered for either electronic or hard-copy newsletters:

- **Readers experience three stages of relevance**

  Stage 1: Within 3 to 7 seconds, readers decide whether they are interested by scanning headlines, titles, photos, and captions.

  Stage 2: Readers take from 1 to 90 seconds to decide whether they continue to be interested. Graphic organizers such as short paragraphs, bulleted lists, page borders, and column dividers are useful tools for this stage.

  Stage 3: When readers get to stage 3, they often continue reading the newsletter or put it aside to be sure to read at a later time.

| Figure 8–3 | Suggestions for Newsletter Topics |

What to Include in Newsletter Columns

Activities for home:
> those that children would do alone or with siblings or peers
> those that parents would do with children
> those best suited for family outings

Explanations of activities and routines at school:
> upcoming field trips and special events
> importance of play, music, outdoors, etc.

Announcements of child or family-related community activities:
> art, drama, music, films, sports, service

Information about school staff:
> introductions or bios
> recent professional development activities

School changes or announcements:
> those caused by weather conditions
> those due to construction/repairs/maintenance

Articles on parenting, guidance, health, and safety:
> ideas for different seasons
> travel guidelines and activities
> developmentally appropriate toys or gifts for children

Reminders:
> tuition due dates and other fees
> change of clothes, diapers, special dietary needs
> field trips
> closing times and related policies

Parent or family association activity announcements:
> meetings
> fundraising events
> volunteer opportunities

- **Layout of document**

  Readers view a document in a "Z"-shaped path, so that whatever is in the upper-left quarter of the page is seen first. Typically, readers then look across to the upper-right quarter of the page. Thus, the most important and relevant information should be in these two areas. Readers next move their eyes diagonally to the bottom-left portion of the page, which is considered the "dead zone." So, it's a good idea to add interest here with a photo, graphic, or picture. Finally, readers move to the page's lower-right quadrant. This is the best place to communicate desired actions from the reader.

- **Typeface/fonts**

  Most readable—Times New Roman and Courier. Use for text.

  Modern and fun—sans serif fonts such as Helvetica and Tahoma. Use for titles, headlines, and captions.

  Bolded—slows readers. Use only for five to seven consecutive words.

  Underlining—also slows readers.

- **Graphics and color placement**

  Readers (a) follow direction of movement in any picture, and (b) follow the direction of the way a picture is facing. Use directional pictures to move reader toward important content.

  Color is powerful and should be used to establish balance on any page.

- **Alignment**

  Align text to the left for informality, friendliness, and readability.

  Justified text is more formal and professional, but slightly harder to read.

  Use hyphens sparingly—no more than three in a single column (Walker, 2005).

Notes Notes to families can take a variety of forms and serve a variety of purposes. One form is the standard note sent to all parents in the school or class. This type of note is useful for informing parents about occasions such as field trips or picture days, or about activities for which parents need to either give permission or send items to school (Figure 8–5).

More personal notes include teacher-generated communications regarding a child's academic or behavioral progress. It is important to balance the types of notes and not use them for sending home only negative messages. Incorporating celebratory or

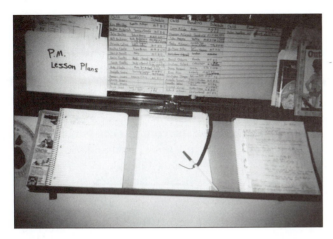

An available notebook for parents to jot messages allows teachers to keep up with individual family needs.

congratulatory notes when something has been done well helps parents keep a balanced perspective about their child, the teacher, and even their own parenting. What experiences have you had with personal notes from teachers? What points of consideration do you believe to be important when drafting such notes? Critique the notes sent by teachers to families in Figure 8–6.

Announcements Announcements should be made in a variety of formats over different lengths of time. Providing families with an annual calendar that contains important dates helps to keep everyone informed in a timely way about upcoming events. Sending school-wide announcements home with children is another strategy. Posting signs on doors and at pickup points helps remind families of upcoming events or activities.

Placing emergency announcements on the school's voice-mail system also helps to get information to parents. Some schools have an information line that is updated daily with a new recording that family members can call for information on upcoming events. Placing long-term announcements in newsletters and discussing them at parent meetings reinforces dates and other event information.

Daily Information Sheets Some centers and schools use preprinted forms that are completed each day by

---

Figure 8–4	Sample Daily Information Sheet

Harrisburg Child Development Center

Daily Information Sheet—Infants

DATE _____   CHILD'S NAME_____

Time of arrival _____   Brought by _____

Supplies brought   Staff signature _____
____ diapers   ____ soft toy for cuddling
____ change of clothing   ____ other _____
____ food/milk

....

Meals/feedings

Time_____   Description/amount _____
Time_____   Description/amount _____
Time_____   Description/amount _____
Time_____   Description/amount _____

....

Diapering times and notes

Time_____   Notes _____
Time_____   Notes _____
Time_____   Notes _____
Time_____   Notes _____

....

Sleep schedule and notes

....

Activities enjoyed

....

Developmental milestone(s)

....

Comments or concerns

---

classroom staff and sent home to families. These sheets contain information that can be useful to parents: what the child ate at each mealtime and snacks, the child's sleep schedule, activities that the child particularly enjoyed, accomplishments or developmental milestones observed, and special comments or concerns.

Two-Way Communication

Frequently, **two-way communication** between home and school is essential. Two-way communication between families and early childhood teachers offers

Figure 8–5   Sample Note Sent Home to All Families in the School or Class

November 13, 2006

Dear _____ ,
    School pictures will be taken on Friday, November 20. Both individual packets of photographs and group photos for each classroom will be available for purchase. We expect all prints to be available by December 11. Individual packets are priced at $12.50 and class pictures are $2.50. All picture money is due by December 16. Please call your child's teacher if you have questions or concerns.

Stacey Blades
School Director

---

distinct advantages to one-way communication strategies. These methods focus on developing ongoing communication "in which both parties are equals, contributing valuable information to the discussion" (Kagan & Cohen, 1997, p. 22). Useful two-way communication techniques are discussed below.

Planned Conferences   Planned teacher-family conferences must occur in a quiet place where information can be shared calmly and confidentially. Teachers should have all notes, portfolios, and other necessary materials ready at the time of the conference. It is recommended that the child's strengths be reviewed first, both to begin the meeting on a positive note before discussion of concerns or areas for improvement and to ensure that the conference gives a complete picture of the child's development and progress. Some professionals recommend the use of a "compliment sandwich," in which the early childhood teacher begins and ends the meeting with a positive comment, so that these comments "sandwich" the middle of the conference, during which the teacher and family members discuss their concerns. It may also be helpful for the teacher to begin the meeting by mentioning three positive areas before discussing areas of concern. It is important that positive comments be authentic and meaningful, not

empty statements whose purpose is only to make three hollow "positive" comments. When teachers need to conference with parents because of a particular concern, the preference for a balance between positive and negative information often is overlooked. The strategies mentioned above aid in achieving such equilibrium.

Keep a record of the conference, including brief documentation of the topics discussed. Some early

---

Figure 8–6   Sample Personal Notes to Parents or Families

Note #1

Dear Mr. Connors,
    I just wanted to let you know that the work you've done to help Chris with his spelling words has paid off! He got 100% on his test this week.
Congratulations to both of you!

Sincerely,
Kate Olijiwa

Note #2

Dear Ms. Lin,
    Sara has been having some problems on the playground for the past three days. Please call me during my phone hours, Monday through Thursday from 2:45–3:15 p.m., so that we can discuss this.

Steve Elliott

Note #3

Dear Jackie,
I wanted to let you know how much I appreciate your help in the classroom for the past three weeks. You are very good at supervising children during their learning centers time. I hope you will continue to come each week this school term. Thanks for your time and efforts in our classroom.

Martha Douglas

Figure 8–7   Sample Conference Form

Date _____

Time _____

Location _____

LIST OF TOPICS TO BE DISCUSSED:

_____

_____

_____

_____

Teacher comments

_____

_____

_____

_____

Parent comments

_____

_____

_____

_____

Action to be taken:

Type	By whom	Accomplished by (date)
_____	_____	_____
_____	_____	_____
_____	_____	_____
_____	_____	_____
_____	_____	_____
_____	_____	_____
_____	_____	_____

Signatures:

Teacher(s) _____   Parent(s) _____

_____   _____

_____   _____

childhood programs have duplicate forms that teachers use when preparing for and holding conferences; one copy of the form stays on file at the school, and the other is given to the parents. It is also useful for these forms to include a place for follow-up by the teacher and parents after the conference (Figure 8–7).

Conferences should be planned for times that are convenient for all family members who wish to attend. Many family members have some schedule flexibility if they know conference times and dates in advance. Others' schedules are less flexible, however, and such family members may need to schedule conference times that take place before or after the school day, for instance.

Routine conferences are frequently quite short, fifteen to twenty minutes, which is sufficient for a fairly quick overview of a child's progress. More time may be needed, however, if serious concerns are to be shared.

Children may be included and involved in conferences when it is deemed appropriate. Following are some examples of appropriate topics for children to be included during conferences:

- reviewing portfolios
- discussing problem situations
- outlining a new plan of action
- sharing relevant information

Naturally, the child's age, as well as any extenuating circumstances, would be considered when deciding whether to include him in the conference.

Involving other teachers and school staff is recommended when they are involved in the topic of discussion. Following are examples of other staff who might be involved:

- counselors
- nurse
- director or principal
- itinerant teachers or other staff
- social service coordinator
- cafeteria or playground supervisor

If parents have not met these people or do not see these staff members on a regular basis, it may be necessary to introduce parents to them. Also, it is a good idea to briefly explain to parents the reason for the additional staff members' attendance at the conference.

In turn, invite parents to bring others who are concerned about the child with them to the conference. It can be helpful for parents to have a support-ive other person present for several reasons. Sometimes, it is not possible for both parents in two-parent families to attend. In addition, single parents are likely to appreciate support from another concerned adult. Parents may want to invite the following:

- a friend
- grandparent of child
- child's caregiver
- significant other

Figure 8–8 provides a sample of a comprehensive self-assessment form that an early childhood teacher might use in order to increase awareness of the complexity of leading an effective conference.

Unplanned Conferences. Sometimes, a conference with parents or other family member needs to be arranged quickly. These conferences are likely to be held before or after school. Some guiding principles for unscheduled conferences are listed below.

1. Move to a quiet area away from other children and families.
2. Ask for someone else to supervise the children in your care, if necessary.

Telephone calls are a convenient and sometimes necessary way to remain in contact with parents.

Figure 8–8	Self-Assessment of a Parent/Family Conference

I. Setting

A. Appropriateness of Setting

Meeting setting has distractions and is in a public environment	Meeting setting has some distractions and is in a public environment	Meeting setting contains distraction and is private	Meeting setting is quiet and private
1	2	3	4

II. Level of Preparation

A. Preparation for Family Conference

No records/student work available for family member(s) viewing	Few records/student work available for family member(s) viewing	Some records/student work available for family member(s) viewing	Several records/student work is available for family member(s) viewing
1	2	3	4

III. Greeting

A. Greeting to Family Member(s)

Teacher is not welcoming	Teacher is somewhat welcoming	Teacher is welcoming	Teacher's welcome is warm and genuine
1	2	3	4

IV. Nonverbal Communication

A. Eye Contact

Teacher does not make eye contact	Teacher makes little eye contact	Teacher makes frequent eye contact	Teacher makes appropriate eye contact
1	2	3	4

B. Facial Expression

Teacher's facial expression is not warm or inviting	Teacher uses very little facial expression	Teacher's facial expression occasionally shows warmth	Teacher's facial expression is often warm and inviting
1	2	3	4

C. Head Movements

Teacher does not move head during conference	Teacher occasionally moves head during conference	Teacher frequently moves head during conference	Teacher uses head movements at appropriate times throughout conference
1	2	3	4

continues

Figure 8–8   (Continued)

V. Body Language

A. Respect for Others' Personal Space

Teacher frequently invades personal space of other(s) 1	Teacher occasionally invades personal space of other(s) 2	Teacher invades personal space a little 3	Teacher demonstrates respect for family members' personal space 4

B. Posture

Teacher's posture is very relaxed or very stiff 1	Teacher's posture is often very relaxed or very stiff 2	Teacher's posture is sometimes too relaxed or too stiff 3	Teacher's posture is appropriately relaxed and professional 4

VI. Verbal Communication

A. Amount of Time Speaking

Teacher speaks less than 10% or more than 90% of the time 1	Teacher speaks less than 20% or more than 80% of the time 2	Teacher speaks less than 40% or more than 60% of the time 3	Teacher speaks about 50% of the time 4

B. Use of Assertive Speech

Teacher uses aggressive or passive speech 1	Teacher uses occasional aggressive or passive speech 2	Teacher uses some assertive speech 3	Teacher uses mostly assertive speech 4

C. Voice Tone/Clarity

Teacher's speech is quiet, muffled or loud 1	Teacher's speech is low 2	Teacher's speech is frequently clear and appropriate in tone 3	Teacher's speech is consistently clear and appropriate in tone 4

VII. Verbal Responses

A. Length of Comments

Teacher's comments are long or terse 1	Teacher's comments are somewhat long or terse 2	Teacher's comments are sometimes appropriate in length 3	Teacher's comments are concise and with meaning 4

Figure 8–8   (Continued)

B. Use of Open-ended Comments/Questions

Teacher consistently uses closed (yes/no) comments/questions 1	Teacher frequently uses closed (yes/no) comments/questions 2	Teacher sometimes uses closed (yes/no) comments/questions 3	Teacher typically uses open-ended comments/ questions to encourage family participation 4

VIII. Language

A. Use of Professional Language

Teacher uses inappropriate language/ poor grammar 1	Teacher uses some inappropriate language/ poor grammar 2	Teacher mostly uses appropriate language/ good grammar 3	Teacher typically uses appropriate language/good grammar 4

B. Use of Positive Speech

Teacher phrases comments negatively 1	Teacher frequently uses negative comments 2	Teacher sometimes uses positive comments 3	Teacher typically phrases comments positively 4

IX. Attitude

A. Avoiding Codependency

Teacher is overly dependent on others 1	Teacher frequently is too dependent on others 2	Teacher is sometimes autonomous 3	Teacher is typically autonomous 4

B. Fairness and Dependability

Teacher does not demonstrate fairness or dependability 1	Teacher sometimes demonstrates fairness or dependability 2	Teacher frequently demonstrates fairness and dependability 3	Teacher consistently demonstrates fairness and dependability 4

C. Self-disclosure

Teacher frequently discloses personal information 1	Teacher occasionally discloses personal information 2	Teacher discloses a little personal information 3	Teacher does not disclose inappropriate personal information and sets up reasonable boundaries 4

continues

Figure 8–8   (Continued)

X. Warmth

A. Genuineness

Teacher is not genuine 1	Teacher is occasionally genuine 2	Teacher is frequently genuine 3	Teacher is consistently genuine in words and actions 4

B. Empathy

Teacher is not empathetic 1	Teacher is occasionally empathetic 2	Teacher is frequently empathetic 3	Teacher is empathetic in words and actions 4

XI. Acceptance

A. Willingness to Accept Others

Teacher demonstrates disapproval of family differences 1	Teacher does not demonstrate acceptance of family differences 2	Teacher shows some acceptance of family differences 3	Teacher is accepting of and accommodating to family differences 4

XII. Active Listening

A. Listening skills

Teacher interrupts family member 1	Teacher does not listen to family member 2	Teacher attends to but does not reflect family member's statements 3	Teacher actively listens and reflects family member's statements 4

B. Use of "I" messages

Teacher uses blaming words and attitude 1	Teacher does not use "I" messages 2	Teacher occasionally uses "I" messages 3	Teacher frequently uses "I" messages and explains her viewpoint as appropriate 4

XIII. Criticism

A. Receiving Feedback

Teacher reacts aggressively or passively 1	Teacher responds with obvious irritation or does not acknowledge feedback 2	Teacher acknowledges feedback 3	Teacher responds appropriately with words and actions 4

Figure 8–8 (Continued)

B. Giving Feedback

Teacher is aggressive with criticism	Teacher uses blame when criticizing	Teacher criticizes without offering help or support	Teacher sandwiches constructive criticism with compliments and offers support
1	2	3	4

XIV. Conflict Resolution

A. Identifying the Issue/Problem

Teacher does not define issue clearly or problem	Teacher is somewhat in defining issue unclear or problem	Teacher is a little in defining issue unclear or problem	Teacher clearly defines issue or problem and checks to see if family member has common understanding of issue or problem
1	2	3	4

B. Consideration of Family Member's Ideas

Teacher does not get information from families about their ideas	Teacher gets little information from families about their ideas	Teacher gets some information from families about their ideas	Teacher considers ideasof families in an active way
1	2	3	4

C. Consideration of Family Member's Concerns

Teacher does not get information from families about their concerns	Teacher gets little information from families about their concerns	Teacher gets some information from families about their concerns	Teacher considers concerns of families in an active way
1	2	3	4

XV. Goal Setting

A. Focusing on the Future

Teacher consistently dwells on past situations	Teacher frequently dwells on past situations	Teacher sometimes looks to the future	Teacher consistently looks to the future
1	2	3	4

B. Identifying goals

Teacher does not identify goals	Teacher unilaterally identifies goals	Teacher and family create common goals	Teacher and family create common goals and a plan for achieving them
1	2	3	4

continues

Figure 8–8   (Continued)

XVI. Use of Appropriate Content

A. Knowledge of Evidence of Developmentally Appropriate Practice

Teacher shows no evidence of knowledge of DAP	Teacher shows little evidence of knowledge of DAP	Teacher shows some evidence of knowledge of DAP	Teacher shows consistent evidence of knowledge of DAP
1	2	3	4

B. Use of Bias

Teacher consistently expresses bias	Teacher expresses some bias	Teacher does not express bias	Teacher consistently expresses respect
1	2	3	4

XVII. One-Way Communication

A. Newsletters, E-mail, Phone Calls

Teacher does not use any one-way communication	Teacher rarely uses one-way communication	Teacher frequently uses one-way communication	Teacher consistently uses forms of one-way communication in effective ways
1	2	3	4

XVIII. Two-Way Communication

A. Face-to-face Communication

Teacher avoids face-to-face communication	Teacher rarely engages in face-to-face communication with families	Teacher sometimes engages in face-to-face communication	Teacher consistently invites families to engage in forms of two-way communication
1	2	3	4

XIX. Resources

A. Appropriate Resources

Teacher does not provide family members with resources or suggests inappropriate resources	Teacher rarely provides or suggests resources	Teacher sometimes provides or suggests resources	Teacher consistently provides and suggests appropriate resources for families
1	2	3	4

Figure 8–8	(Continued)

XX. Closure

A. Summary

Teacher does not summarize meeting 1	Teacher summarizes only part of meeting 2	Teacher summarizes meeting 3	Teacher and family member together provide summary of meeting 4

B. Plan for Future Contact

Teacher does not plan future contact 1	Teacher mentions need for futurecontact, but no plan or action is addressed 2	Teacher suggests definite plan for the future 3	Teacher and family member agree on a future date and agenda for next conference 4

Source: Created by Tamara Smith, Early Childhood Education Graduate Student at Shippensburg University (2006)

3. If the family member has initiated the conference, listen carefully to the concern before commenting or responding.

4. If you need more time to gather information, tell the family member you will contact him as soon as possible, and then do it.

5. If you have initiated the conference, thank the family member for agreeing to meet with you on such short notice and determine how much time is available.

6. Plan a follow-up meeting to give direction or closure.

Phone Calls   Telephone calls are a convenient and sometimes necessary way to remain in contact with parents. Some teachers call families at a prearranged time each week that is convenient for the family. Other teachers set a weekly time to make short calls as follow-up related to concerns noted earlier in the week. As always when communicating with parents, be sure to share positive comments during calls with families as well as using calls to quickly check on any concerns you might have. When planning to call families, however, keep in mind that some families are not accessible by phone, and that there are situations for which phoning is not a reasonable communication alternative, such as when the teacher and family speak different languages or when too many distractions are in the environment. Listed below are suggestions and guidelines for contacting families by phone.

Before phoning a family:

- determine whether it is agreeable to call a work number for a conference.
- consider advance scheduling for a phone conference.
- send information home ahead of time so that parents can prepare for the conference.

During the call:

- maintain confidentiality when making the phone call and after the phone call is completed (central offices or teacher work areas are not the best place for privacy).
- be polite and calm.
- try to maintain the time limit agreed on in advance.
- conclude the call with a follow-up plan.

| Figure 8–9 | Excerpts from a Journaling Experience |

A Concern About Four-Year-Old Nicole's Withdrawn and Passive Approach to Activities at Preschool.

Journal for: Nicole Williams

From Teacher(s)

10/2 Nicole joined in play with other children a little more quickly than usual today. After scanning the room briefly, she walked to the art center and joined two others in their work on a mural for our farm theme.

10/4 I didn't realize Nicole had so much farm experience. She has been more enthusiastic than ever with this topic. What other interests or experiences has Nicole had that we might use to build on this positive experience?

From Parent(s)

10/2 I'm glad to hear about Nicole's artwork with the others. She actually seemed excited about the farm mural.

Her grandparents live on a farm, and she has always enjoyed the animals and the machinery.

10/5 She likes babies; a new cousin visits us often. She also likes to watch the construction crew working at the end of our street. This summer, she started to be interested in various insects. Thanks for using information from us to help Nicole at school.

After the call:

- make notes about the call.
- send a follow-up note to families. Include a positive or optimistic statement.

Journaling   Maintaining a journal that is sent back and forth between parents and teachers is an increasingly popular method of communication (Figure 8–9). Journaling with a parent is an excellent communication mechanism under the following conditions:

- both the teacher and the family agree to and are committed to this type of communication
- confidentiality is maintained
- the families are literate and comfortable writing their comments

- frequency of writing has been established and agreed upon by both parties; frequency should be assessed occasionally during the school term and modified as deemed necessary
- a reliable courier process has been established, such as use of children's backpacks or wire notebooks, and routine days have been planned for sending and returning journals

Electronic Mail   As computer networking becomes accessible to more people in our society, e-mail may become a very useful tool for maintaining communication with families of children in early childhood programs. A few guidelines and concerns about this type of communication are listed below.

- Be aware that e-mail communication may not be private. Avoid sharing highly sensitive information by this method.
- Employers may not want family members to receive personal e-mail at work. Be sure to check with parents about this before sending e-mail to their workplace.
- Many families still do not have access to e-mail. This communication method should not be used in a way that would exclude families without access.

Home Visits   Early childhood programs with very strong family involvement components often include home visiting as one aspect of their efforts to create strong partnerships between families and teachers. For example, the Head Start performance standards require that teachers make at least two visits to homes of all enrolled children, unless the parents decline the visits. Reasons given for requiring home visits are as follows:

- making connections between the home and program settings
- learning more about parent-child interactions
- developing positive relationships, which allow parents and staff to get to know one another
- identifying learning opportunities in home environments
- identifying techniques that can be generalized to other children in the family

- focusing individualized attention on family strengths, interests, and goals (Head Start Program Performance Standards and Other Regulations, 1993, p. 144)

Head Start regulations offer alternatives to families who prefer not to have a home visit. Visits may take place at the Head Start site or another place that is deemed to be both safe and private. When safety concerns arise for staff who are required to make home visits, Head Start regulations provide some precautions. Staff who make home visits are highly trained, well-supervised, and have access to support services such as monitoring systems or having another staff member make the home visit with the teacher.

These guidelines are useful for other early childhood programs implementing a home visit component. It is important that early childhood professionals be polite and respectful when arranging for and during the visit. Selecting a mutually acceptable time for the appointment, and arriving on time are important factors. It is often helpful to define the visit's ending time when making the appointment. During the visit, teachers must use effective interpersonal skills and keep in mind that their role changes when in the context of interactions in a family's home. In home settings, the teacher is the guest and must take the lead from the family. Typically, teachers are in the comfort of their own classroom when they meet with family members. Thus, during home visits, the balance of power is shifted somewhat. While it is true that home visits take a huge time and energy commitment from early childhood teachers, such visits often make the family feel valued and cared about, thus generating an increased level of partnership between families and schools.

Effective Interpersonal Communication

When any two people attempt to communicate, they may misunderstand one another: Clarity may be lacking. Emotions may be heated. Vocabulary may differ. Effective strategies for clear communication can be learned, and practicing these strategies leads to a more natural approach for both speaker and listener.

As you contemplate the following approaches to communication, be cognizant that "cultural learning needs to extend to our daily interactions and the way we see each other as learners" (Swick, et al., 1995/96, as cited in Swick, 2003). Some multicultural learning strategies that are known to be effective include (Comer, 1997; Powell, 1998; Swick, 1993, as cited in Swick, 2003):

- Early childhood teachers must acquire accurate information on children and families from cultures other than their own.

- Families and teachers/staff can work together to have relevant, constructive exchanges and joint activities to assist in understanding cultural differences.

- Families and teachers/staff can work together to plan interesting, enjoyable classroom activities that relate to authentic cultural learning.

- Partnership events should have multiple emphases, such as food, music, talents, ideas, and concerns shared in warm, sensitive ways.

- Education programs planned through partnerships to increase everyone's understanding of various cultures and groups in the community.

- Include representatives of families and communities to ensure that cultural content in the school curriculum is accurate, meaningful, and inclusive.

Active Listening **Active listening** is a process whereby the listener communicates to the speaker that she values what the speaker is saying. An important criterion for active listening is that the listener is not evaluating the content or the speaker but is genuinely open to the speaker's point of view (Gordon, 1970). It is important for teachers to listen to parents to understand their perspective and to be aware of the issues they believe are important. Some teachers find that truly listening to others poses a challenge because the role of a teacher is often to give instruction to others without entering into an extensive dialogue. Another challenge for teachers involves hearing parents' concerns—or complaints—without becoming defensive. Parents may be emotionally charged about an issue. When this occurs, try to listen for the emotion and understand that it is coming from real concern about their children.

Active listening is more easily accomplished when teachers believe in partnerships with parents and have the belief that parents have knowledge about their own family system that can be helpful information to teachers. This ability of a teacher to actively listen to family members is an extremely important application of the bioecological model of human development.

Following are some behaviors associated with active listening (Hanna, 1991):

- Attentive body position
  —comfortable distance between the communicators
  —being on the same level, e.g., both sitting or both standing
  —facing the other person as each of you speaks
  —relaxed body posture, slightly leaning toward the other
  —hands at sides or in lap

- Eye contact
  —maintain eye contact by looking at other's face
  —eye contact is recommended for 50%–75% of time in interaction

- Facial expression
  —facial reaction to what is being said include a smile, frown, or look of surprise at appropriate times
  —change of expression with content of conversation

- Head and body movements
  —nodding the head for feedback to speaker
  —other body movements used as feedback to speaker

- Touching
  —arm is a neutral area generally okay to touch
  —consider appropriateness of touch

- Verbal responses
  —short comments such as "oh" or "I see" offer encouragement
  —open-ended questions to support the speaker
  —paraphrasing to be sure you understand the point the speaker is making
  —expressing your interpretation of the speaker's feelings

These active listening behaviors should be modified to meet the needs of different families and settings.

As teachers attempt to incorporate these skills into their communication with families and other community members, they soon understand why Hanna states that "good listening is not for the lazy" (p. 186). Helping professionals in many fields find it helpful to practice behaviors related to listening. Working with a partner, practice the above list of listening skills. After you have practiced for about ten minutes, evaluate yourself on each of the skills. Which skills have you already mastered? With which listening behaviors will you need more practice?

Often, early childhood teachers have limited amounts of time for conferencing and other interpersonal communications with parents or other family members. Due to these time constraints, teachers may be tempted to bypass the importance of listening to parents and to move too quickly to offering solutions or telling parents that their concerns are unfounded. In these situations, it is often true that actively listening to parents' comments may be more satisfying to the parent and thus may provide for ongoing positive communication.

An example of this was shared by a child care center director. Parents of a three-year-old who was slightly injured on a balance beam requested a conference with the director. The classroom teacher had already "warned" the director that these parents were upset and wanted to have that piece of equipment removed from the classroom. Because this was the only recorded accident with the balance beam in more than ten years of that teacher's career, the teacher believed strongly that it should not be removed. The director met with the parents, listened to their concerns, and said he was sorry that their son had gotten hurt. After having a chance to be heard and to realize that school personnel were concerned about their child's injury, the parents withdrew their request to have the balance beam taken from the classroom. Further, they increased their involvement with the center's parent organization and advocated for the center with prospective parents (Figure 8–10).

Reflecting   Reflecting families' concerns, issues, feelings, suggestions, and complaints allows the teacher to repeat what he has heard. This method

Figure 8–10	Examples of Active Listening in Conversation

Parent: Emily's mother and I have separated. Emily and her brother are living with me. I just wanted you to know so that if something unusual happens at school, you may be better able to help Emily. She is sometimes very sad at home.

Teacher: You're concerned about how your separation is affecting Emily.

Parent: Yes. We hear so much about the effects of divorce on young children. She has been such a joyful child, and now it's hard to see her be so sad.

Teacher: I know that this has been a difficult time for both you and Emily.

Parent: Thank you for understanding my concerns.

Teacher: Let's stay in close communication about Emily during this difficult time. You can call me at school or at my home phone.

Figure 8–11	Teacher Phrases that Help in Reflective Dialogue

"Let me restate what I heard you say."

"To help me remember clearly, may I rephrase your concerns?"

"To help me work on these problems, may I write out some of your complaints?"

"Thank you for sharing your suggestions. I will summarize them to our director. This is the list I have made."

gives parents an opportunity to correct or modify the teacher's understanding of the conversation. Reflecting also gives the teacher an opportunity to fully comprehend the meaning of the message being communicated by the parent. Frequently, reflection becomes an excellent problem-solving tool because it increases clarity in **interpersonal communication** (Figure 8–11).

I-Messages and We-Messages Using *I-messages* permits teachers to speak from their own perspectives without offending parents. An I-message clearly places the responsibility and the viewpoint of the message on the speaker. Thus, it does not communicate guilt or accusation, as do statements that begin with "You should. . . ." Many professionals find that although I-messages are effective in practice, they have not learned to speak that way in their interpersonal conversations. Some find that it feels "unnatural." Because this strategy is so effective, however, especially when speakers are in the heat of emotion, it is advantageous for early childhood teachers, whether in training or in service, to practice or role-play using I-messages. Gordon (1970) describes three components of an I-message:

1. State concern about other's behavior from your perspective.
2. Pin down the concrete effect the behavior has on the teacher.
3. State feelings teacher has as a result of the effect.

I-messages are effective, not only in working with families but also in all interpersonal contexts, including work with children (Figure 8–12).

I-messages are useful because they reduce threat from a powerful figure, but there are times when *we-messages* are more effective than I-messages. We-messages identify a problem in a group or in a

Figure 8–12	Examples of Effective I-Messages

Situation—Parent stops teacher in hallway to discuss a concern about his child's progress.

Teacher—"I must be in the classroom now. I'll be glad to phone you after school to arrange for a time for us to talk. Where should I call you?"

Situation—Parents walk into director's office and begin to yell.

Director—"I can tell you're upset about something. Let me get some information from you so that I can figure out what I can do to help."

Situation—Grandmother complains to teacher about her daughter's lack of attention to her child.

Teacher—"I'm sorry you feel so bad about this. I believe that if someone were to read to Jess every day, it would help her a great deal. Is there any chance we could work on this together?"

relationship rather than focus on one individual's problem and another individual's behavior. Examples of we-statements include "We don't have enough affection" or "We ought to have more flexibility" (Burr, 1990).

We-messages are used to emphasize the closeness in relationships; thus, such communication should not be used for casual relationships between educators and family members (Burr, 1990). In early childhood education, however, some caregiver and family member relationships span several years with a great deal of close contact occurring. Often, the topics discussed in these relationships are personal: children's difficulties, parents' feelings, a variety of family transitions. In such cases, when teachers want to emphasize the teacher-family partnership in working for children, using we-messages may be helpful.

There may be times when it makes sense to combine we-messages with I-messages. This is especially true when the speaker wishes to emphasize the sense of connectedness between the parties, but also wants to add an element of uncertainty to the comment in an effort to establish more open communication. An early childhood teacher who has had an ongoing relationship with Calvin's parents stated, "I don't think we want Calvin to forget his work anymore." The parents readily agreed, and together they—teacher, parents, and Calvin—set out to solve the problem.

An Example of Building Communication between Teachers and Families

My first experience with realizing the importance of communication between myself and my teacher was when my daughter was in first grade. We were fortunate to be placed in the classroom of Mr. M. months after moving to one state from another. Mr. M. had a total open door policy and stressed the fact that his policy meant we were welcome any time and without notice.

Mr. M. had a monthly "Family Night" where the students invited the entire family, even grandparents, to come into the classroom and share their daily activities. Several times during the year he also had "Game Board Night" where the family brought and shared playing games with the class. Not only did "Family Night" and "Game Board Night" help my husband and

me support and encourage our daughter's education, but also pre-pared her younger brother for what it would be like when he started school. He did not have any of the typical first day jitters because he was so familiar with the school.

The class also witnessed the importance of socialization skills between families and friends. Throughout the year, we had parties and activities out of the school setting as well. We actually made some of our closest friends during this period of our lives and they are still involved in our lives today, five years later.

—**L. B., mother of two**

An Example of Ineffective Communication between a Teacher and a Parent

When my son was in Kindergarten, I was not prepared for what was to come. We had had a wonderful experience with our daughter from kindergarten all the way to the third grade, and did not realize how a bad situation could avalanche.

Our son was very prepared and excited to start school, and up to this point, we had felt he was very bright. After only two weeks of school, the teacher escorted my son out of the school at the end of the day to have a discussion with his mom about his behavior. This discussion took place in front of all the students and parents that were walking out of the building at the end of the day. Needless to say, my son was devastated, and I was shocked and appalled. I suggested that we go somewhere and discuss this in private, but the teacher did not have time for that so the conversation continued on the front lawn about how my son yells out answers to questions without raising his hand, can't stay in his seat, and wastes time doodling after assignments are done. I listened to what she had to say but did not make many comments because I felt I needed time to process the information.

After discussing the situation with my husband, I decided to ask her to cooperate with me and keep a behavior journal that I would read each day and, surprisingly, she agreed to do so. My son gave the journal to his teacher for two or three weeks, and she never made an entry so we assumed things were okay until conference time when we heard the same complaints as before. When asked about the journal, she simply said she did not think it would help. Needless to say, this was a long battle that totally turned my son against school and reading.

My son is now in the first grade with a wonderful teacher and is eager to learn. On the first day of school, we were getting dressed and he said, "Mommy, do you remember last year when I kept saying I was dumb and you said I was smart?" I said "Yes" and he said, "Well, I finally figured out what happened. I got yelled at so much last year until my brain just shut down."

As the saying goes, out of the mouths of babes!

> **Consider the differences between the two examples of teacher communication. Give some examples from each of the two situations that relate to how individuals have been empowered or degraded. How do these methods of communication affect the development of partnerships? Examine Swick's four communication behaviors for trust-building, below, and explain how they are present in or absent from these examples.**

If we are to develop authentic, essential partnerships with families, we must cultivate trust with them. Swick (1993, as cited in Swick, 2003) notes that there are four communication behaviors that are most likely to build trust among families, schools, and communities for strong partnerships:

Approachability—making others feel comfortable and secure

Sensitivity—understanding others in supportive ways

Flexibility—adapting to needs or concerns of others

Dependability—counting on one another to provide continuity

When early childhood teachers implement these four communication behaviors, they will provide strong leadership for creating necessary partnerships.

Nonverbal Communication As we have seen, the use of language is critical to effective interpersonal communication. It also is important, however, to examine nonverbal communication practices. Following are some behaviors that are components of nonverbal communication:

- personal space
- gestures and posture
- touching
- facial expression
- eye contact
- vocal cues (Knapp and Hall, 1992)

The concept of *personal space* includes physical distance between people who are engaged in conversation. Clearly, individual differences in personality lead to differences in comfort level of personal space. Cultural backgrounds and the nature of the relationship of those in conversation (Knapp & Hall, 1992) also are factors related to preferences in personal space. Early childhood teachers who are observant and sensitive to family member's preferences for physical space will be able to demonstrate respect in their interactions.

"Gestures are movements of the body . . . used to communicate an idea, intention or feeling" (Knapp & Hall, 1992, p. 187). Consider the many gestures that are used to communicate nonverbally throughout the course of a day. How do you gesture for "hello" and "good-bye?" When giving someone directions, gesturing is often as helpful as the words you use. How do teachers use gestures meaningfully in the classroom? Touching when communicating can have many meanings? Knapp and Hall (1992) list the following ways in which touch is used:

- positive affect
- negative affect
- play
- influence
- interaction management
- interpersonal responsiveness
- accidental
- task-related
- healing

> Observe at least two people who are conversing. Note the kinds of nonverbal communication strategies that they use. How did nonverbal communication contribute to the meaning and understanding among those you observed? Did you observe individual differences? How might you increase your sensitivity to nonverbal modes of communication in your work with young children and their families?

Individual differences have been observed in both gesturing and touch. Culture and gender play a role in these differences.

Facial expressions can communicate a lot of information or just a little. Because of individual differences and complexity involved in interpretation of facial expression, sensitivity is needed when interacting with others. Some people are very expressive, while others demonstrate little affect. There are times when facial expression alone does not reveal an individual's honest feelings. For example, nervousness can lead one to smile or even giggle at an inappropriate time. Variations are also observable in the nature and amount of eye contact. How do you use eye contact? What is your belief system about those who look others "right in the eye"?

Vocal cues such as hesitating and pausing may be used to emphasize a point or to demonstrate reflective listening. Practices such as saying one word more loudly or softly than others in the sentence and consistent or inconsistent rhythm in a person's speech contribute to the meaning of communication (Knapp & Hall, 1992).

". . . our actions speak louder than our words. Bronfenbrenner (1979) notes that children watch closely what we do with each other more than they listen to what we say to each other. Clearly, our modeling of behavior is more important than almost anything else we do. Yet, the nonverbal aspect of communication has been largely neglected in the education of human service professionals."

—**Swick, 2003**

Guidelines for Giving and Receiving Criticism

Teachers often find it difficult to deliver criticism to family members—at least, they often find it difficult to do so in an acceptable manner. Is it possible to give negative information in a positive manner? Yes, but the challenge is to do so clearly and honestly. It is often helpful to rehearse what you want to share and how you want to say it, as well as to choose a suitable time and place for the communication. The use of I-messages is recommended. Be sure to criticize the specific behavior or situation, not the whole person. As stated previously, offering a compliment before giving a criticism may make the situation less uncomfortable for the parent or other person with whom you are talking (Hanna, 1991). In other words, attempt to make the criticism as constructive as possible. This permits the other person to work toward a solution.

Consider the following examples of criticism. Using the preceding guidelines, note what is constructive and what may be destructive about each example. How would you change each one to make it more constructive?

1. During a scheduled conference with parents of a kindergartner, the teacher says, "I have some concern about the way you discipline Kate. She says that you hit her when she misbehaves. You should know better than that!"

2. In a note to the family of a preschooler, the teacher writes: "Nicole has been dropped off at school at 7:30 this week. School begins at 8:00. You may not bring her to school before 7:45. Thank you, Ms. Farver"

3. In a newsletter, a first-grade teacher includes the following in her letter to families: "Some parents have questioned our rule about not bringing special playthings from home. After some discussion, the school staff has decided to keep this rule. Please do not permit your child to bring toys to school."

Teachers must be prepared to receive criticism as well as to deliver it. Teachers may be prepared to hear criticism in some instances, while, at other times, the criticism may take them by surprise. To maintain positive communication with families, it is helpful for early childhood professionals to have skills in accepting and responding to criticism. If you agree with the criticism, admit your mistake—although this is not easy or comfortable, it is the responsible action and enables continued open communication with families. Let the person who voiced the criticism know that you agree with her and briefly state the reason for your behavior. Finally, indicate to her what you will do to change the situation or your behavior to prevent similar occurrences in the future (Hanna, 1991). Using these guidelines, write appropriate responses to the following criticisms from family members (assuming you agree with them).

1. "I thought you only served healthy snacks at this child care center. Jason told me that he had a chocolate cupcake for afternoon snack yesterday."

2. "I got a notice about the parent meeting tonight just two days ago. That's not enough time for me to make all the arrangements that are necessary to come to the meeting."

It may be even more difficult to respond to criticism with which you do not agree because there is greater likelihood of negative emotions arising. You may feel that a criticism is inaccurate or unfair. These feelings often lead to an emotional or out-of-control response. Taking a deep breath or silently counting to three is useful for some people when they are aware of such emotion. Responding in a calm manner gives a better chance of allowing communication to continue. When you disagree with a criticism, a comment such as "I guess I see this differently from you" or "I have another point of view about what may be the wisest course of action." Give some reasons for your perspective and suggest the possibility of another discussion in the future.

Assertiveness versus Aggression

In efforts to be polite and professional, early childhood teachers often overlook the importance of assertiveness in interpersonal communication. Assertiveness does not rule out flexibility or partnerships; instead, it allows teachers to have a voice about their preferences and feelings. Assertiveness is not the same as aggressiveness. A primary difference is that assertiveness enhances interpersonal communication, and aggressiveness discourages or inhibits communication. Assertiveness is self-focused, not other-focused (Lerner, 1989). Thus, an assertive response typically uses an I-message and does not blame or attack others. Blaming and attacking often are aggressive and counterproductive in forming partnerships. For example, "I have some concerns I would like to discuss with you about Kelly being sleepy at school" is more effective than "You need to make sure that Kelly gets enough sleep every night."

Boutte, Keepler, Tyler, and Terry (1992) discuss techniques for involving "difficult" parents (see Figure 8–13).

Conflict Resolution

When authentic relationships are developed with families, it is inevitable that some conflict will occur. Avoiding conflict is not the best solution to dealing with it. Instead, efforts at resolving conflict peacefully and effectively must be learned and implemented. One difficulty is that people bring their existing ideas and feelings about conflict with them: Some people believe it is impolite to share a difference of opinion, while others are shy, and still others may present a different point of view in a hostile, rather than an effective, manner.

Essentially, **conflict resolution** often takes the form of problem solving. Problem solving typically is a process that contains several steps, which are outlined below. Problems with, between, and about families are common in the life of a teacher. The following strategies are designed to reduce conflict and increase the chances for healthy resolution of a problem.

1. Clearly define the problem at hand. If there is more than one problem, define each one.
2. Let all participants share their viewpoints.
3. As the teacher, reflect each participant's concern.
4. Review any relevant school policy or procedure.

Figure 8–13	Selected Techniques for Involving Difficult Parents

	The parent who exhibits antagonistic behavior	The parent who frequently complains or is negative	The parent who exhibits shy/ unresponsive behavior	The parent who is illiterate or is not skilled in Reading or speaking English
Encourage attendance at all parent—teacher conferences	X	X	X	X
State and restate purpose(s) of the conference	X	X		
Show or tell concrete and specific examples of child's work or behavior	X	X	X	
Do not argue with a parent or become defensive	X	X		
Seek the assistance of other staff when needed	X			X
Elicit parents' ideas and incorporate them into a plan		X		
Frequently state positive strategies or work accomplished		X	X	
Ask open-ended questions and allow for plenty of discussion time	X			X

Source: Adapted from: Boutte, G. S., Keepler, D. L., Tyler, V. S., & Terry, B. Z. (1992). Effective techniques for involving "difficult" parents. Young Children 47 (3), 19–22

5. Assure the parents that they have been heard and that their issue will be addressed in one of the following ways:

   a. changes will be made (specify the changes)

   b. additional participants will be invited into the discussion, such as the principal, the director, a counselor, or a social worker

   c. another child or family will be contacted, if necessary, to resolve the problem

Many early childhood programs find it useful to specify guidelines for conflict resolution.

Including these procedures in a parent handbook or newsletter indicates to families that their opinions and views are respected and taken seriously. Such guidelines include the following:

1. First, take your concern to the person directly involved.

2. If the conflict cannot be resolved between the two parties, the guidelines specify who is the next person to be contacted. Typically, this is someone in an administrative or supervisory role.

3. The third person acts as mediator, listening to both perspectives and suggesting a resolution.

4. Some programs will have a process that continues with an appeal or taking the situation to an executive director or board.

Some Ineffective and Inappropriate Practices to Avoid in Interpersonal Communication

In addition to understanding the skills related to effective communication, it is also important to acknowledge that certain behaviors are often detrimental to building relationships. Teachers are advised to be aware of and avoid the following practices:

1. becoming defensive, argumentative, or combative closes communication

2. accusing the child or family is not productive

3. name-calling is never appropriate

4. gossiping about families is unprofessional

5. belittling or berating a child because of a conflict with his family is unethical

6. reacting so emotionally or irrationally that there is no opportunity for reconciliation is detrimental to all concerned

Helpful Attitudes for Effective Interpersonal Communication

Behaviors and practices are not the only things that affect positive communication. Attitudes are also

It is important for early childhood education teachers to develop mutually respectful working relationships with families.

important. For some teachers, the following attitudes may be more "natural," and some teachers may find that they need to work to develop these perspectives. Such work, though, will be well worth it when good communication with family members is achieved. Hanna (1991) lists the following attitudes as helpful:

- valuing mutual respect
- honesty
- open to lifelong learning and growing
- willing to share your experiences and ideas
- able to express feelings in appropriate ways
- knowing appropriate content for discussing in professional contexts
- flexibility
- a sense of humor
- ability to think critically and to problem-solve

Discuss the preceding list of attitudes with a partner. Think of a real-life example for each attitude. Think of one or two additional attributes to add to this list of helpful attitudes for effective communication.

Examples of successful programs in building family-staff relationships can be found on the Northwest Regional Educational Laboratory Web site, www.nwrel.org. Other ideas for supporting parents, including information about the No Child Left Behind Act (NCLB) and the Individuals with Disabilities Education Act (IDEA), can be found at the National Coalition for Parent Involvement in Education Web site, http://www.ncpie.org. These sites can help teachers and parents find ideas for building family-school partnerships.

Summary and Conclusions

While most teachers receive some preparation in classroom management of children, very few receive extensive instruction in communicating effectively with parents and other family members, especially in conflict situations. Conflicts or confrontations with parents are very difficult and may not be easily or quickly resolved. They often require great amounts of time, effort, energy, and knowledge. The importance of building and maintaining relationships with families cannot be overstated. Relationships built on trust and understanding go a long way in helping both parties in their efforts to resolve conflict.

Understanding the family is a great resource for teachers to use if a conflict arises. Having an established, mutually respectful working relationship with families prior to a conflict can be very helpful in proceeding to a resolution. Professional ethics and professional practice give school personnel the guidance to sustain their compassion and conduct as they work with families in sensitive and difficult situations, as well as in routine interactions.

Chapter 8 Applications

1. Plan a conference with parents about each of the following situations.

   a. A two-year-old has been biting other children. You meet with the parents of the child who is biting.

   b. A preschooler has become increasingly aggressive during outdoor time.

   c. A second-grader is not making expected progress in reading.

2. At the end of the school day, family members come to you with the following situations. What do you say or do?

   a. A father of a kindergarten child is angry and shouts at you that his daughter was not permitted to check out a library book yesterday at the regularly scheduled library time.

   b. The grandmother of a two-year-old tells you that her grandson has been bitten two days in a row and that she expects you to "throw the biter out of the program."

   c. A mother is late picking up her infant for the third day in a row. She is nearly in tears, saying that she is not able to leave work on time to pick up her baby by closing.

3. Create a newsletter article that explains to families the importance of each of the following early childhood education practices:

   a. free play

   b. developmentally appropriate practice

   c. authentic assessment

   d. family involvement

   e. celebrating diversity

Questions for Reflection and Discussion

1. List situations that might occur in the early childhood classroom for which two-way communication strategies between home and school would be preferred over one-way communication strategies.

2. Getting some parents to come to regularly scheduled conferences can be difficult. What are some strategies you could try for getting such hard-to-reach parents to have a conference with you about their child's progress?

3. What is your typical response to a conflictual situation? Do you avoid it, respond emotionally, or use effective strategies for resolving conflict? Which strategies will you work on for future use in the early childhood profession?

Field Assignments

1. Interview several parents who have their children enrolled in early childhood programs. Ask them about the kinds of communication they have with their child's teachers or the program's administrator. Ask whether they are satisfied or whether they would prefer more communication. If they would prefer more communication, ask about kinds of communication they would like.

2. Contact a number of early childhood education teachers. Inquire whether they have produced parent newsletters. If so, request copies of the newsletters to place in your file.

3. Contact an administrator of an early childhood program. Ask whether there are policies regarding conflict resolution between home and school. If so, are the policies printed in a parent handbook? If possible, get a copy of the policy.

References

Boutte, G. S., Keepler, D. L., Tyler, V. S., & Terry, B. Z. (1992). Effective techniques for involving "difficult" parents. *Young Children, 47* (3), 19–22.

Burr, W. R. (1990, July). Beyond I-statements in family communication. *Family Relations, 39* (3), 266–272.

Diffily, D., & Morrison, K. (Eds.). (1996). *Family-friendly communication for early childhood programs.* Washington, DC: National Association for the Education of Young Children.

Gordon, T. (1970). *P.E.T.: Parent effectiveness training.* New York: Peter H. Wyden.

Hanna, S. L. (1991). *Person to person: Positive relationships don't just happen.* Englewood Cliffs, NJ: Prentice Hall.

Head Start program performance standards and other regulations. (1993). Washington, DC: U.S. Department of Health and Human Services.

Hohmann, M., Banet, B., & Weikart, D. P. (1979). *Young children in action* (pp. 328–329). Ypsilanti, MI: High/Scope Press.

Kagan, S. L., & Cohen, N. E. (1997). Not by chance: *Creating an early care and education system for America's children.* New Haven, CT: The Quality 2000 Initiative.

Knapp, M. L., & Hall, J. A. (1992). *Nonverbal communication in human interaction.* New York: Holt Rinehart and Winston.

Krech, B. (1995). Improve parent communication with a newsletter. *Instructor, 105* (2), 67–73.

Lerner, H. G. (1989). *The dance of intimacy: A woman's guide to courageous acts of change in key relationships.* New York: Harper & Row.

Swick, K. (1991). *Teacher-parent partnerships to enhance school success in early childhood education.* Washington, DC: National Education Association.

Swick, K. J. (Summer 2003). Communication concepts for strengthening family-school-community partnerships. *Early Childhood Education Journal, 30* (4), 275–280.

Walker, T. (Summer 2005). *The director's link.* Chicago, IL: McCormick Tribune Center for Early Childhood Leadership at National Louis University.

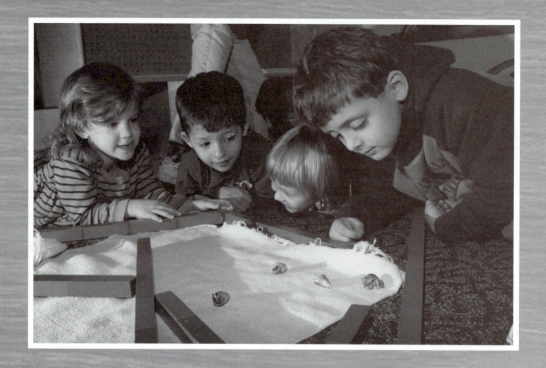

OUTLINE

Objectives

Key Terms

Theoretical Foundations

Overview

Families and Literacy

Families and Science

Families and Mathematics

Families and Social Studies

Summary and Conclusions

Chapter 9 Applications

Questions for Reflection and Discussion

Field Assignments

References

Supporting Young Children's Learning at Home

OBJECTIVES

After reading this chapter, you should be able to:

- understand how the subject areas of literacy, math, science, and social studies can be supported by families at home.

- understand how teachers form partnerships with families and encourage them to support children's learning at home.

- use some of the resources available in each subject area.

- create programs that support families' involvement in each subject area.

Key Terms

anti-bias
literacy

professional associations

tolerance

Theoretical Foundations

Bioecological theory points to specific effects on development that emanate from interactions between and among various microsystems. Bronfenbrenner emphasized this phenomenon with the concept of the mesosystem. Not only will home and school environments independently impact children's development, but the interactions or relationships of these environments with one another create additional influences (Bronfenbrenner, 1979). Thus, it is essential that teachers and other early education staff form partnerships with families and communities to support children's learning in all content areas.

One way to implement this concept is to consider Joyce Epstein's notion of not only creating family-friendly schools, but also creating ways to support school-friendly families. The National Network of Partnership Schools has identified "learning at home" as one of the six keys for family involvement in their children's education (Epstein, Coates, Salinas, Sanders, & Simon, 1997).

Overview

Young children understand the content of literacy, science, mathematics, and social studies differently than do older children and adults. Thus, family members may need help understanding how young children think about the concepts related to these subjects or content areas. The **professional associations** in **literacy** (International Reading Association), mathematics (National Council for Teachers of Mathematics), science (American Association for the Advancement of Science), and social studies (National Council for the Social Studies) include in their standards and publications statements about the importance of family involvement in helping children to understand content from each subject area. These associations do not suggest that families directly teach these subjects, but, rather, that family members' actions and activities at home can support and enhance learning at school. "Learning at home" refers specifically to "encouraging, listening, reacting, praising, guiding, monitoring, and discussing, not 'teaching' school subjects" (Epstein, 2001, p. 412). The professional associations listed above suggest that early childhood programs involve parents in such activities as family game nights, various activities in their homes, and strategies with their children throughout the day. Through these activities, families can explore these subjects with their children and expand their children's conceptual understandings without resorting to drilling or content memorization.

Epstein (2001) discusses relevant findings from recent research, including:

- Single parents, parents who work outside the home, parents who live far from school, and fathers are typically less involved *unless* the school organizes activities that meet the specific needs of these groups.

- Nearly all families want their children to succeed, so families appreciate information from schools that supports them in helping their children.

- Nearly all children want their families to be active partners in their school experiences.

- Caring communities can be intentionally built through strong partnerships.

- Effective programs are comprised of different components at different schools. Partnership practices must match the needs, interests, time

Caring communities can be intentionally built.

availability, talents, and developmental levels of children and families in specific schools and communities.

The next sections of this chapter delineate the need for partnerships between schools and families to support children's learning in each of the above-mentioned subject areas. Early childhood teachers play a vital role in supporting families in this work with their children.

National Network of Partnership Schools
http://www.csos.jhu.edu
Click "programs"; click "National Network of
   Partnership Schools"

International Reading Association
http://www.reading.org

National Council of Teachers of Mathematics
http://www.nctm.org

American Association for the Advancement
   of Science
http://www.aaas.org

National Council for the Social Studies
http://www.ncss.org

[handwritten margin notes: Language Dev. is imp to later reading; Env. print wordplay, board games, cooperative play; phonological awareness through adult directed activities; interacting as babies of lang.]

Families and Literacy

Families influence children's language and literacy learning in a variety of ways, both before the child's enrollment in an early education program and after formal education begins. A basic way that families affect literacy development begins in infancy, when families act, react, and interact with babies in conversation and other language exchanges during feeding, diapering, and play activities. When family members respond to a baby's needs, actions, and expressions with vocalizations of their own, children are provided with opportunities for hearing a wide variety sounds. As the child's language develops in later infancy, toddlerhood, and the preschool years, families continue to support literacy through a variety of means, including:

1. having conversations, that is, give-and-take interactions involving and responding to spoken language.
2. regular reading times (e.g., or bedtime stories).
3. the availability of books and writing materials.
4. daily opportunities to use and gain understandings about language and symbols in context (such as stop signs, cereal boxes, closed caption during TV shows). *Env. print*
5. regular trips to libraries and bookstores.
6. regular opportunities to hear and use positional words, such as on/off, up/down, above/below, near/far, etc.

Willam Teale (2000, as cited in King & McMaster, 2000) has stated that "Children from low income families may have been read aloud to as little as 25 hours total prior to entering first grade while children from middle income families typically have been read to 1,250 hours." Family literacy has been identified as such an important component of school success that over the last decade the federal government has defined it in various pieces of legislation. Current federal definitions of family literacy include the following aspects:

a. Interactive literacy activities between parents and their children

b. Training for parents that regards them as the primary teachers for their children and full partners in the education of their children

c. Parent literacy training that leads to economic self-sufficiency

d. An age-appropriate education to prepare children for success in school and life experiences (Based on the Reading Excellence Act, 1998; the Workforce Investment Act; Even Start; Head Start; and the Community Service Block Grant Act)

Families can encourage and support language development through the use of formal and informal word play, including peek-a-boo games and pat-a-cake with very young children, "I Spy" games with preschoolers and kindergarteners, and board games such as *Concentration* and *Monopoly* with elementary aged children. All of these types of play enrich children's vocabulary, help children develop language skills by using contextual clues, and give children valuable experience in practicing literacy in playful situations.

Owocki (1999) provides information about facilitating literacy learning through play. This book emphasizes, in addition, the importance of teachers collaborating with families as they implement developmentally appropriate methods for teaching literacy through play. Further, Leong, Bodrova, Hensen, and Henninger (1999) explain relationships between play and literacy in terms of four major literacy skills that are accomplished through play:

1. the ability to learn deliberately through planning, developing, and continuity of play
2. the development of symbolic representation as children imagine that objects can be many different things
3. the practice of oral language as children talk through the pretend scenario, creating a script of what will happen in play
4. the preparation for literacy through the introduction of content-related skills and concepts, including reading and writing, practice with encoding and decoding meaning, matching voice to print, and correspondence of sounds and symbols

As teachers implement play strategies to support children's literacy learning at school, they will also work with families to provide them with information about ways they can extend children's play at home so that families, too, encourage literacy through play activities.

Families can support language development while engaging in everyday activities, such as watching television or traveling in the car with children. As situations are presented in TV shows, family members can ask questions, expand understanding, listen to children's ideas about what is happening, and simply have conversations about program content. While in the car, family members can encourage children to look at traffic signs, billboards, and license plates; to say and spell town names; to read the numerals on speed limit signs; and to have conversations about landmarks. Car time is also an opportunity to sing songs, chant, and to play word and memory games.

Early childhood teachers can help families understand the language and literacy development of their children in a variety of effective ways. These can include, but certainly do not need to be limited to, sending home newsletters that contain nuggets of literacy information, thus informing families over time; hosting school programs for parents and other family members related to language development; and providing brochures, DVDs, and/or Web site addresses about language and literacy strategies. Discussion during family conferences is another forum for language and literacy information sharing.

Dickinson and Tabors (2002) have written that ". . . teachers must actively reach out to families, building on their strengths while guiding them toward the kinds of home language and literacy activities that will help their children achieve the educational success that families desire for their children." These researchers found three dimensions of children's experiences during preschool and kindergarten that are related to later literacy success:

- exposure to varied vocabulary
- opportunities to be part of conversations that use extended discourse
- home and classroom environments that are cognitively and linguistically stimulating

Families and Science

Understanding that young children view the world differently than adults means that adults' explanations about the world need to be based on children's current levels of understanding. Crowley and Galco (2006) found that the most important outcome of everyday parent-child scientific thinking "may not be the content children acquire, but the interests, habits, and identity they form as someone who is competent in scientific thinking." Listed below are some major points that are useful in working with families with young children to develop and support scientific thinking:

- Children learn science best when it is active (e.g., exploring magnets, cars on ramps, water play).
- Children learn science best when they have opportunities to talk and work with other people.
- Children learn science best when they are the scientist (not just a science word learner).
- Children learn science best when the topic of exploration is related to their own experiences (e.g., food, plants, wheels, care of animals).
- Children learn science best when adults listen to their ideas and questions and then respond to and expand on children's interests.

Sharing the above information with families may be done through newsletters, workshops, e-mail, or display areas of the school that are accessible to families. First, when early childhood educators help families learn how to support children's science learning at home, it is important to provide families with information about how science is addressed at school. When families have this information, early childhood programs can build on it by sharing specific information with families about how they can support scientific explorations at home. The American Association for the Advancement of Science (AAAS; 1991) lists as part of

---

RESOURCES FOR SUPPORTING LITERACY IN FAMILIES

The following resources are helpful in supporting these three dimensions of home language and literacy activities.

General Resources for Supporting Literacy in Families

Booklets

- *Helping Your Child Become a Reader*
  U.S. Department of Education
  Office of Intergovernmental and Interagency Affairs
  400 Maryland Ave. SW
  Washington, DC 20202

- *A Child Becomes a Reader (Birth through Preschool): Proven Ideas from Research for Parents* (Spring, 2003)
  The Partnership for Reading
  RMC Research Corporation
  Portsmouth, New Hampshire

Resources from the International Reading Association (IRA)

Videos

- *Read to Me*—introduces parents to the importance of reading aloud to their children (13 minutes).

- *Becoming a Family of Readers*—features parents and their children modeling book sharing (10 minutes)

Brochures for Parents

- *Making the Most of Television: Tips for Parents of Young Viewers*

- *Get Ready to Read! Tips for Parents of Young Children*

Resources from the National Association for the Education of Young Children (NAEYC)

Article

- *Hey! Somebody Read to Me!* By M. C. Ulmer (2005). *Young Children, 60,* (6). Washington, DC

Brochure

- *Raising a Reader, Raising a Writer*

Web Sites:

- The Partnership for Reading
  http://www.nifl.gov/
  Type in "partnership for reading"
- Even Start Family Literacy Program
  http://www.ed.gov/
  Click "Offices"; click "ED structure"; click "Office of Elementary and Secondary Education"; type in "Even Start"
- National Institute for Literacy (NIFL)
  http://www.nifl.gov/
- National Center for Family Literacy
  http://www.famlit.org
- Pennsylvania Center for the Book
  http://www.pabook.libraries.psu.edu
  Click "family literacy activities"

---

their standards for professional teacher preparation the following:

The importance of the family to the learning of the young child is emphasized by the National Education Goals that were established by Congress and the nation's governors in 1990. A parent's statements that "I was never good in math" or "I never had a scientific mind" are often communicated to young children and can stifle a child's desire to learn those subjects. Partnerships between school and family are essential to overcoming these and other obstacles in early childhood programs.

Figure 9–1 outlines several school-family science partnership scenarios.

Once families understand how science is taught at school, early childhood teachers can go on to explain to families that young children view the world differently than adults do, which means that adults' explanations about the world need to be based on children's current levels of understanding. Crowley and Galco (2006) found that the most important outcome of everyday parent-child scientific thinking "may not be the content children acquire, but the interests, habits, and identity they form as someone who is competent in scientific thinking." Listed below are

| Figure 9–1 | Science Activities for Families of Young Children |

Activity	Science Content
Pointing out basic characteristics of objects (e.g., colors, shape, number, size, weight)	Increases children's discrimination abilities to sort and name by categories
Naming objects, plants, body parts, events, weather, processes	Provides language for children's developing classification systems
Discussing and explaining how things around the house work: clocks, pipes, toys, television, CD player	Helps children understand the mechanics of commonly used machines with which they have experience
Investigating questions or interests together (i.e., looking up information in books or on the internet)	Gives children models for learning to investigate questions

useful ideas for working with families of young children to help them help their children develop and support scientific thinking. Children learn science best when

- it is active (e.g., exploring magnets, playing with cars on ramps, playing with/in water).

- they have opportunities to talk and work with other people.

- they are the scientist (not just a science word learner).

- the topic of exploration is related to their own experiences (e.g., food, plants, wheels, care of animals).

- adults listen to their ideas and questions and then respond to and expand on children's interests.

This information can be shared with families through newsletters, workshops, e-mail, or displays in family-accessible areas of the school.

Of course, for school-family science partnerships to be effective, early childhood professionals must be knowledgeable about and comfortable with both teaching science and interacting with families to create partnerships. Chrisman (2006) conducted a four-year project (2002–2006) investigating the effects on early childhood teachers' abilities to teach science and to create partnerships with families when they received professional development both through methods of teaching science to young children and with strategies for implementing family involvement. In the project, science content and activities were based on the Developmental Approaches to Science, Health and Technology (DASH) curriculum, and family strategies were based on the work of Epstein and the National Network of Partnership Schools (Epstein, Sanders, Simon, Salinas, Jansorn, & Van Voorhis, 2002). The preliminary results from this research (final results are expected in 2007) indicate that teacher attitudes about both science with young children (through third grade) and family involvement changed positively with focused professional development in both areas. Further, teachers reported an increase in planned activities for including families in supporting children's learning.

In 2003, the AAAS launched the Partnership for Science Literacy, an initiative to increase public awareness, particularly among parents, families, and caregivers of Latino/Hispanic, African-American, and other minority and underserved students regarding the value and importance of science literacy for their children's futures. This initiative provides information and resources to help families find out more about science and about the kind of science education that helps all children. The partnership, a joint project of AAAS (through its Project 2061 and Education and Human Resource directorates) and TryScience.org, was launched with funding from the National Science Foundation.

The initiative is built around the following key messages:

- Science education is for every child.
- Science is around you in your life every day.
- Parents and families can make a huge difference in their child's science education.
- Science is a lot of fun.

Additional useful information on this subject comes from Koralek and Colker (2003), who emphasize the importance of both families and communities in supporting science learning for young children. The following ideas were adapted from their book, *Reflecting, Discussing, Exploring: Questions and Follow-Up Activities.* This source views the importance of both families and communities in supporting science learning of young children.

1. What strategies can help to communicate to families what their children are doing and learning in the areas of science?
2. Most families are legitimately concerned with developing their children's literacy skills. How might you communicate with families about the important connections between science and literacy, or between mathematics and literacy, in a jargon-free and interesting way?

Houghton Mifflin Education Place
http://www.eduplace.com/
Click "science"

Science for Families Update
http://kidscience.blogspot.com

Try Science
http://www.TryScience.org
Click "parents"

National Science Education Standards
http://www.nap.edu/
Type in "nses"

3. Families love to see photographs of their own children: How can you use photos to help family members experience the wonder of their children's science learning?
4. Every community is different, yet each offers many opportunities for everyday scientific investigations. Identify those in your community and share ideas with families to explore together.

Ideas related to science and family involvement are regularly posted on the Early Years Science blog. Visit http://science.nsta.org/earlyyearsblog to read more about science and young children. The following selections are taken from the site.

We had a family science night with the theme of "Saving the Wetlands." All the stations had to do with wetlands in danger. We got a lot of information from our Coastal Bend Bays and Estuaries foundation and invited people from the community to bring activities. One person works at our waste water treatment plant and brought in an activity. We also have had a family literacy night that incorporated science and literacy with children's trade books about a certain topic. "NSTA Recommends"* has numerous resources.

Posted by Marilyn Cook on 1/22/2006 2:52: 38 PM (reprinted with permission):

A book of take-home science activities that I'm using suggested sending home little bottles of the primary colors of paint so that students could mix the secondary colors at home. 1) "Little bottles" were very expensive. 2) Red, yellow, and blue colored transparencies were not available at our office supply store for overlapping. 3) Colored tablets were available, but the shipping cost more than the tablets. After racking my brain for weeks, I finally "eureka-ed" that I could put drops of red, blue, and yellow food coloring in separate cups, let them dry, and then send them home for students to "reconstitute" by adding water to make cups of water of the primary colors. In three separate empty cups, students could mix the primary colors to make secondary colors at home in a cost-efficient manner.

* *"NSTA Recommends" is a regular column printed in* Science and Children. *National Science Teachers Association (http://www.nsta.org).*

Science nights provide families opportunities to see activities firsthand.

Families and Mathematics

Just as with science, young children understand math concepts differently than adults do. So, it is important to help family members understand both these differences and how young children gain mathematical skills and concepts. The National Council of Teachers of Mathematics (NCTM) and the National Association for the Education of young Children (NAEYC), in a joint position statement (2002), recommend the following for early childhood programs: "Build on children's varying experiences, including their family, linguistic, and cultural background; their individual approaches to learning; and their informal knowledge."

This position statement further indicates that resources are needed to support families as partners in developing their young children's mathematical proficiency. The NCTM and NAEYC recommend activities such as family math nights and take-home activities, including math games and manipulative materials tailored to children's ages and developmental levels. Teachers might consider creating a math corollary to the popular literacy packs used by children and families. Math packs could include graph paper; a variety of manipulatives, such as Legos, unit blocks, geometric shapes, and patterning activities;

| Figure 9–2 | Suggestions for Families to Support Young Children's Mathematical Understandings and Learning at Home |

Suggestions for families of ways that they can support young children's mathematical understandings and learning at home.

- In the morning:
    Discuss events of the day: what comes first, next and last
    Discuss patterns (in clothing, on toys, etc.)
    Encourage estimates (how many bites of cereal in a bowl, etc.)
- Sing songs in the car that have math content:
    "Five Little Monkeys"
    "One, Two, Three, Four, Five (Caught a Fish Alive)"
    "One, Two, Buckle My Shoe"
- Read books with mathematical content:
    The Doorbell Rang, Pat Hutchins
    Moja Means One: Swahili Counting Book, Muriel Feelings
    Read Aloud Rhymes for the Very Young, Jack Prelusky

Additional Family Math Resources and Ideas for Involvement

- *Family Math* by Grace Coates and Jean K. Stenmark
    Available from: Lawrence Hall of Science
    University of California
    Berkeley, CA 94720-5200
    http://www.lhs.berkeley.edu
    (510)642-1823
- Web Sites:
    Houghton Mifflin Education Place
    http://www.eduplace.com/.
    Click "math"
    National Council of Teachers of Mathematics
    http://www.nctm.org/.
    Click "resources for families"

and tools, such as compasses and measuring instruments. Math and literacy skills could be integrated by adding books with mathematical themes.

Copley (2000) has written, "Teachers, schools, and early childhood programs may want to use existing

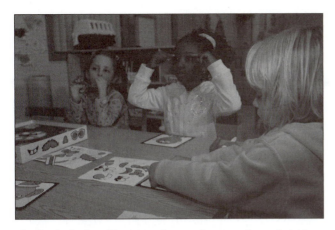

Photos help families experience the wonders of their children's mathematics learning.

resources to help get families on board with math learning. Among these are materials from NCTM, programs from Family Math (Coates & Thompson) and resources available on the Internet . . . "She further states that such approaches focus parents' attention on children's learning and understanding. Figure 9–2 lists excerpts from Activities for Families with Young Children (http://www.ed.gov/pubs/EarlyMath/activities1.html).

Smith (2006) includes the following ideas for involving parents in a school mathematics program:

- Explain your (math) program philosophy and methods through multiple means, including at open houses, in letters and notes and at parent-teacher conference

- Make videos about math activities in your classroom and be sure to show children's interest and enthusiasm

- Start a lending library of children's books with math-related themes

Koralek (2003) also lists several ideas for involving families and communities in math activities for young children. These include:

- developing a plan for "Family Mathematics Night" when families could learn about and

actively participate in their children's mathematics curriculum.

- taking photos to help family members experience the wonders of their children's mathematics learning. Some ideas might be adding captions or having children write "thought balloons" to the photos and creating displays or documentation panels.

" . . . [I]t takes a community and a family for real success . . . . We have long known that family members are a child's first teachers. Some of us were fortunate enough to learn counting on our grandfathers' knees and to learn to read similarly, using a daily newspaper . . . . [W]e might be more effective if we capitalized on the education that families and a student's community may have provided before the student came to school . . . . The real message here is that we may be missing opportunities when we do not use family and community members to help students learn."

—Johnny Lott, Past President, NCTM, 2003

Figure 9–3 recaps some of the guidelines for families that the National Council of Teachers of

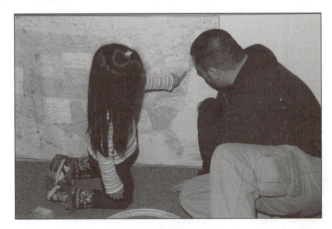

Using a wide variety of informational sources supports children's social studies understanding.

Figure 9–3 — National Council of Teachers of Mathematics (NCTM) Guidelines for Families

- Be positive! Have a "can do" attitude and relate math to other activities that require hard work and persistence, such as learning to play a sport or musical instrument.
- Link math with daily life. Use examples such as reading a map, creating and following a budget, understanding discounts of sale items, pointing out shapes and patterns.
- Make math fun. Play board games, solve puzzles, and participate in brain teasers with your child.
- Learn about math-related careers by researching careers along with qualifications and expectations in regard to mathematical understanding.
- Have high expectations. Math, like literacy, must be for all children. Be sure to advocate for good math opportunities.
- Support children in doing their homework, but do not do it for them. Serve as a guide or facilitator; ask your child to explain it to you as a review procedure or to check on where help might be needed.

Mathematics proposes. Consider ways that early childhood teachers might make meaning of these guidelines in their work with families.

Families and Social Studies

Social studies curricula for young children differ from the curricula for history, geography, economics, and government for older children. Activities and lessons are based on the cognitive and social understandings of young children in preschool, kindergarten, and primary grades, and thus look different from the lessons and teaching methods used in the upper elementary levels. Therefore, it is necessary to plan home- and community-based social studies activities that support early learning. Helping families understand these differences is an important first

step in planning family involvement. Figure 9–4 provides a list of guiding principles for interdisciplinary educational experiences in social studies for the early childhood years.

As discussed in Chapter 1, fundamental to creating effective family partnerships for any subject area is the early childhood teachers' understanding and appreciation of families' varied histories, cultures, and traditions. Building family social studies activities around this knowledge encourages family involvement in home-based social studies learning. Louise Derman-Sparks (1989) has written extensively about creating **anti-bias** activities. Her work features many examples of how to build inclusive strategies for families that support a social studies curriculum. Another resource for planning social studies activities with families is in the *Starting Small* (1997) series,

---

Figure 9–4 — Guiding Principles for Educational Experiences in Social Studies for Young Children

1. Integrity of content and authenticity of instruction must be maintained. Methods of inquiry should be used to gain knowledge.
2. A learning community that incorporates a balance of student-initiated and teacher-initiated experiences is optimal.
3. Use democratic methods that lead to children assuming appropriate levels of responsibility in order to gain confidence.
4. Provide many opportunities for children to interact with others who differ in ability, experiences, ethnicity, gender, and culture.
5. Respect diversity of thought, culture, and language.
6. Support children in the use of a wide variety of informational sources.
7. Use multiple symbol systems such as those used in language, math, music, art, graphs, charts, and tables.
8. Assess both process and outcomes of children's learning

Source: Consortium for Interdisciplinary Teaching and Learning (1994)
http://www.socialstudies.org/positions/interdisciplinary/

| Figure 9–5 | Sample Social Studies for Families of Young Children |

Activity	Age Level	Content
Draw a map of your house	Pre-K–K	Map-making (geography)
Draw a map of your neighborhood	K–Primary	Map-making (geography)
Make a chart with two columns indicating "Needs" in one and "Wants" in the other	K–Primary	Beginning understandings of economics
Make a collage of photos of either family members or friends	K–Primary	Family history (historical understandings)
Use a map to find all of the places your family members or family friends live	2nd–3rd grade	Map reading (geography)
Add the dollar amounts of each item of your favorite meal	Primary	Beginning understandings of costs (economics)

produced by the Southern Poverty Law Center, which is part of SPLC's *Teaching Tolerance* curriculum and available to teachers and schools at no cost. This curriculum is unique in its emphasis on developmentally appropriate explanations and examples relating to respect and **tolerance.** Both of these resources include activities and suggestions for involving members of the community in classroom activities.

Figure 9–5 lists family involvement activities with their corresponding social studies content.

Summary and Conclusions

Family and community members can be involved in activities that support understandings of young children in each of these content areas. Children's mathematical, literacy, scientific, and social studies thinking can be enriched and expanded without resorting to drilling or memorization. Families can learn about and understand the thought processes of young children, and this, in turn, can enable them to better relate to their children's ideas and conceptual frameworks. When teachers build partnerships with families and community members to support children's learning at home and at school, greater success is inevitable.

Chapter 9 Applications

1. Plan a program for families and/or the community to introduce one of the subject areas: literacy, math, science, or social studies.

2. Create a newsletter for families that explains one of the subject areas.

3. Collect some of the resources mentioned in the chapter resources and references and organize them as a file for current or future use.

4. Using photos of children at work, create a display or documentation board of math, literacy, science, or social studies activities and invite parents and other family members to review the activities.

Questions for Reflection and Discussion

1. What subject area would be the most challenging for you to share with families? Why?

2. What strategies would you prefer to use in involving families in each of the subject areas? Describe a plan for implementing the strategies that you prefer.

3. Discuss reasons that early childhood teachers are called on to build not only family-friendly schools, but also school-friendly families.

Field Assignments

1. Create materials that early childhood teachers could use to support families in engaging in children's learning at home. Ask an early childhood teacher to review the materials and to make recommendations about changes that would increase the effectiveness.

2. Interview several families of young children about how they support children's learning at home. Ask about what resources would be helpful to them in their efforts to do this.

3. Work with several other students and an early childhood education or community setting to plan, implement and evaluate one of the following events for professionals, families and children: family literacy, math, science or social studies.

References

Bronfenbrenner, U. (1979). *The ecology of human development: Experiments by nature and design*. Cambridge, MA: Harvard University Press.

Chrisman, K. (2006). *Preliminary results of the School Improvement Project: funded from the Dale Kann Endowment*. Shippensburg University Foundation.

Coates, G. D., & Thompson, V. (1999). Involving parents of 4 and 5 years olds in their children's mathematics education: The FAMILY MATH experience. In J. V. Copley (Ed.), *Mathematics in the early years* (pp. 205–14). Reston, VA: NCTM; Washington, DC: NAEYC.

Copley, J. V. (2000). *The young child and mathematics*. Reston, VA: NCTM; Washington, DC: NAEYC.

Copley, J. (Ed.). (2004). *Showcasing mathematics for the young child*. Reston, VA: NCTM.

Crowley, K., & Galco, J. (2001). *Everyday activity and the development of scientific thinking*. Museumlearning.com: University of Pittsburgh.

Derman-Sparks, L., & the A.B.C. Task Force. (1989). *Anti-Bias Curriculum: Tools for Empowering Young Children*. Washington, DC: NAEYC.

Dialogue on Early Childhood Science, Mathematics and Technology Education. (1991). *American Association for the Advancement of Science*. Washington, DC.

Developmental approaches to science, health and technology. University of Hawai'i: Curriculum Research & Development Group.

Dickinson, D. K., & Tabors, P.O. (2002). Fostering language and literacy in classrooms and homes. *Young Children*, 57 (2): 10–18. Washington, DC: NAEYC.

Early Childhood Mathematics Education: Promoting Good Beginnings. (April 2002.) A joint Position Statement of the National Association for the Education of Young Children and the National Council of Teachers of Mathematics. http://www.nctm.org/about/position_statements/earlychildhood_statement.htm. Retrieved July 5, 2006.

Early childhood: Where learning begins. *Mathematics*. (June 1999). http://www.ed.gov/pubs/EarlyMath. Retrieved July 5, 2006.

Epstein, J. (2001). *School, family, and community partnerships: Preparing educators and improving schools*. Boulder, CO: Westview Press.

Epstein, J., Coates, L., Salinas, K. C., Sanders, M. G., & Simon, B. S. (1997). *School, family, and community partnerships: Your handbook for action*. Thousand Oaks, CA: Corwin Press.

Epstein, J., Sanders, J. G., Simon, B. S., Salinas, K. C., Jansorn, N. R., & Van Voorhis, F. L. (2002). *School, family and community partnerships: Your handbook for action* (2nd ed.). Thousand Oaks, CA: Corwin Press.

Koralek, D. (2003). *Spotlight on young children and math*. Washington, DC: NAEYC.

Koralek, D. & Colker, L. J. (Eds.). (2003). *Young children and science*. Washington, DC: NAEYC.

Leong, D., Bodrova, E., Hensen, R., & Henninger, M. (1999). *Scaffolding early literacy through play*. Paper presented at the annual conference of the National Association for the Education of Young Children. New Orleans, LA.

Owocki, G. (1999). *Literacy through play.* Portsmouth, NH: Heinemann.

Project 2061. American Association for the Advancement of Science. http://www.project2061.org/publications. Retrieved July 5, 2006.

Smith, S. S. (2006). *Early childhood mathematics* (3rd ed.). Boston, MA: Allyn & Bacon.

Starting small: Teaching tolerance in preschool and early grades (Teaching Tolerance Project, 1997). Montgomery, AL: Southern Poverty Law Center.

King, R. & McMaster, J. (2000). *Pathways: A Primer for Family Literacy Program Design and Development.* Louisville, KY: National Center for Family Literacy.

Resources Mandy
Games
Book
Leappad
Online programs

Jeniesha
ABC fish during bath time

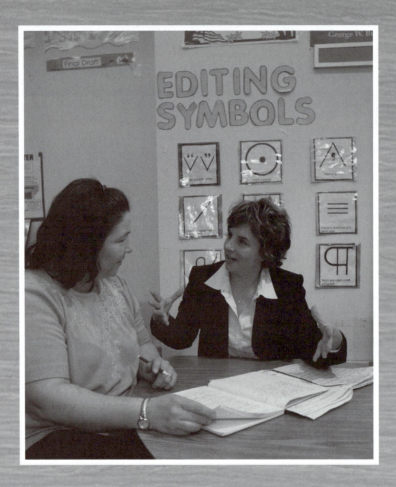

OUTLINE

Objectives

Key Terms

Bioecological Theory

**Philosophy about Programs
of Parent Education**
Assessing Needs and Effects
Format of Programs

Methods of Parent Education
Parent Education Packages
Parent Education Books
Parents as Teachers

Home Instruction Program for Preschool
Youngsters

Family Life Education

**The Role of Early Childhood Educators
in Parent Education and Family
Life Education**
Topics for Parent Education

Summary and Conclusions
Chapter 10 Applications
Questions for Discussion and Reflection
Field Assignments
References

Parent Education and Family Life Education

OBJECTIVES

After reading this chapter, you should be able to:

- understand the theoretical foundation for parent education and family life education.

- discuss and implement a number of strategies for parent and family life education.

- relate the role of early childhood teachers in providing parent and family life education.

Key Terms

family life education   parent education

Bioecological Theory

Social support important for parents to help them in their task of parenting.

Bronfenbrenner's bioecological model supports the premise of parent education in that there is a need for parents to have access to strategies that support all areas of their children's development—intellectual, social, and moral (Bronfenbrenner & Neville, 1994). As children develop, they require "progressively more complex activity," and it is especially important that these interactions exist between the child and parents or parental figures. Central to this model of human development is the special importance of appropriate interactions between children and adults who are committed to the child's well-being over their entire lifetime. This theory stresses the crucial concept of enduring emotional attachment for optimal child development.

Further, this model stipulates the importance of a third party who "assists, encourages, spells, gives status to, and expresses admiration and affection for the person caring for . . . the child" (Bronfenbrenner & Neville, 1994, p. 14). Parents should also be aware or educated about the importance of having someone support them as a parent. Bronfenbrenner notes that ideally this third person would be a spouse and that the context of marriage ideally supports this concept. However, if the marriage is not providing such support for each parent, other mechanisms will be needed to do so. Children's development is enhanced when their parents have support for their caregiving. Often, grandparents carry out this family responsibility.

Bronfenbrenner also notes the relevance of mutual respect and communication "between the principal settings in which children and their parents live their lives" (p. 17). So it is necessary for parents

Why do we have parent meetings or programs? To support parents in their task not judge or tell how.

and teachers or caregivers to communicate on a regular basis and to be able to believe in each other. When parents' workplaces provide flexible schedules, part-time jobs with benefits, and other programs that support families, a child's development is likely to be enhanced.

Programs of **parent education** and **family life education** should include application of the theoretical premises from bioecological theory. This means that such programs always respect the primacy of the family and are designed with the understanding that the basic purpose of parent education and family life education is to support parents in the important task of child rearing, not to undermine or judge their efforts.

Philosophy about Programs of Parent Education

An undergraduate student in an early childhood teacher preparation program reported to her instructor that she would not be permitted to hold a parent meeting at the center to which she was assigned for her practicum. The director at the center told the student that parents of children at the center told her that they "do not want to be told how to raise their children." Before one jumps to conclusions about the parents' lack of interest, let us hypothesize about what led to such comments. Consider the following list:

- experts on discipline being paid to speak to large audiences in school districts or other early childhood programs, indicating a one-method-fits-all approach
- family values (a need to customize information)
- lack of support given parents in our society
- lack of understanding about the need for communication between home and school for child's optimal development
- relative newness of very young children being in care outside the home
- few programs adopting a family support model

Reflect on each of these possibilities. Can you think of others? While the center director in the story might have concluded that parents in that center did not want or need parent meetings, other conclusions might better reflect best practices in early education. If it seems to be a widespread concern of parents that parent meetings are to indoctrinate them, then attention probably needs to be given to the source of that perspective.

It is also important for early childhood professionals to note differences in parenting that may be related to ethnicity. (Some of these differences are noted in Chapter 2.)

Parent education programs however, have been less successful among ethnic minority groups, possibly because they are based on and reflect Anglo-American middle-class values. Service providers have demonstrated that parents from ethnic minority groups and from low socioeconomic groups attend and complete parent education programs if the setting and the content are compatible with their values and their lifestyles (McDade, 1995, p. 286).

Thus, it becomes the responsibility of early childhood teachers to understand parenting differences and to find appropriate ways to share information with their particular clientele.

Assessing Needs and Effects

Programs of parent education should not be provided as a unilateral attempt to tell parents how to rear their children. Instead, the philosophy, the driving goals, behind such a program should be to offer support for families. One way to initiate such a program is to do a needs assessment with families. Figures 10–1 and 10–2 show two formats of needs assessments.

> *"It is usually assumed in our society that people have to be trained for difficult roles: most business firms would not consider turning a sales clerk loose on the customers without some formal training; the armed forces would scarcely send a raw recruit into combat without extensive and intensive training; most states now require a course in driver's education before high school students can acquire a driver's license. Even dog owners often go to school to learn how to treat their pets properly. This is not true of American parents"*
>
> **—LeMasters and DeFrain, 1983, pp. 75–76**

Figure 10–1 Needs Assessment A

At the Campus Early Learning Center, we offer monthly group meetings for parents and other interested family members. Each school term, we ask parents to rank their top three (3) choices of topics for which we might plan. Please rank your first choice as #1, second choice as #2, and third choice as #3. Also indicate days and times that you prefer and please return this form to the Director's Office by September 10. Thanks for your feedback.

_____ Appropriate and effective discipline

_____ How children learn

_____ New information from brain research

_____ Family involvement in children's education

_____ Preparing your child for kindergarten

_____ Healthy nutrition

_____ The importance of play for children's development

_____ Sibling rivalry

_____ Other: _____

_____ Other: _____

Day of the week that I prefer: (please circle all that apply)

Sunday   Monday   Tuesday   Wednesday
Thursday   Friday   Saturday

Time of day that I prefer (please circle all that apply):

Morning
Lunch time
Afternoon
Evening
Additional information about scheduling of meetings:

Figure 10–2 Needs Assessment B

As we plan for the parent/family involvement component of our program, your responses to the following questions will help us to determine some program content. We would appreciate your responses to the following questions by September 15. Please place your completed form in the box outside the Director's Office.

1. Age(s) of children in family _____

2. Who lives in your home? _____

3. What are your three biggest parenting challenges?
   a.
   b.
   c.

4. What questions do you have about how children learn and develop?
   a.
   b.
   c.

5. Do you have questions regarding our school curriculum?
   a.
   b.
   c.

6. What television programs does your child watch? About how much time each day does your child watch TV?

7. What kinds of play or activities does your child like?

Must assess after program ✳

It is typical that information sessions have been held for large groups of parents without any evaluation of what happened in homes after the session. Too often, even immediate feedback from parents regarding the program is not solicited. Professionals in early education cannot overlook the need to assess effects of their family involvement activities. Figures 10–3, 10–4, and 10–5 show examples of evaluation forms to be completed by family members after they have participated in planned school activities.

Figure 10–3 Sample Assessment for a Group Parent Meeting

Time and date of meeting: _____

Location: _____

Topic: _____

1. What was the best thing that happened at the meeting?

2. What changes should be made for future meetings?

3. Other comments?

| Figure 10–4 | Sample Assessment for a Group Parent Meeting |

Time and date of meeting: _____

Location: _____

Topic: _____

1. The information presented is useful to me.
   Very   Somewhat   A little   Not at all

2. The information was presented in an interesting manner.
   Very   Somewhat   A little   Not at all

3. The date and time were convenient for me.
   Very   Somewhat   A little   Not at all

4. Based on this meeting, how likely are you to attend another meeting?
   Very   Somewhat   A little   Not at all

5. I felt comfortable asking questions or responding to the presenter's questions/comments.
   Very   Somewhat   A little   Not at all

6. I believe that group parent meetings generally are important.
   Very   Somewhat   A little   Not at all

7. Comments:

| Figure 10–5 | Sample Assessment for a Group Parent Meeting |

Time and date of meeting: _____

Location: _____

Topic: _____

1. The thing I learned that will be most beneficial to me is
   _____.

2. I wish there had been more information shared about
   _____.

3. My time and day preferences for future meetings are
   _____.

4. At a future meeting, I would like to have information shared about _____.

5. Services the school could provide to ensure that I could attend more parent meetings are
   _____.

6. My suggestions for future parent meetings include
   _____.

Format of Programs

Powell (1989, 1994) discusses emerging directions for parent education that is sponsored by early childhood education programs. Following are some recent changes in both content and format for effective parent education.

1. Matching designs for parent education to the particular population being served is important. Matching is based on the "expressed need" of the parents rather than on the perceived needs by those planning the programs. Further, models that individualize programs based on parents' needs are believed to be more effective than planning group programs to meet each need.

2. Defining the role of the education professional in a way that encourages empowerment of parents is another recent change. The professional who acts as facilitator rather than all-knowing dispenser of knowledge is typically more effective. Understanding of adult learning supports the notion that when parents have a more active role in their education, they are more likely to change their behavior and use strategies that may be more beneficial to their children.

3. Finally, programs of parent education are responding to the notion in bioecological theory that parenting is enhanced when parents have social support and other buffers against stress in their lives. When parents have the support they need, their functioning as parents is strengthened. This idea broadens the notion of parent education for early childhood teachers. Consider not only information about child development, effective guidance strategies, healthy nutrition, and other content traditional in parent education programs but also services that support parents such as parent night out, support groups for single parents, or coordinating the sharing of services such as car pools or children's clothing exchanges.

There is little research to support specific types of parent involvement or parent education practices. Until recently, a belief existed that any kind of parent involvement in early childhood programs, or any content and format for parent education was certainly preferable to none. This view must be questioned in light of the theoretical basis for the family support movement. Concern about the effects of parent education on both children and families must be emphasized.

Current expectations for high-quality early childhood programs universally include the importance of family involvement, but often little detail is given about specific attitudes and strategies that are effective. Based on existing knowledge and theory, Powell (1989) delineates four dimensions that should be incorporated by early childhood teachers into their family involvement plan.

1. Be careful to respond to parents' needs in planning and implementing programs for them. A mismatch, even when the professional believes she is acting in the best interest of children, will not be effective and is likely to subvert the intention.

2. The programs must be managed collaboratively. Using a deficit model of the professional directly telling the clients how to change their parenting, is not an effective means of education. Conversations that are respectful and formats that are collaborative are far more effective strategies than one in which there is an "expert" and an "amateur."

3. The focus of parent education programs must be balanced on the needs of both children and parents. Using parent education as a way to directly affect child outcomes is risky. Concern for parent needs as well as child needs better serves the entire family. At the same time, sharing details about children's developmental needs should not be overlooked. This balance can be difficult to achieve, and for that reason, must be emphasized in planning, implementing, and evaluating the educational program.

4. One aspect of parent education that is frequently sacrificed to time limitations is that of open-ended discussion. Parents' experiences are most often shared and affirmed or disputed with this approach. Open-ended discussion is a strategy that is favored by many participating in adult education; child caregivers who attended training and then participated in focus groups for data collection by a researcher noted that they especially liked the focus groups, even though that strategy was only accidental to the training (Chrisman, 1996). The temptation to cut the open-ended discussion in parent meetings is one that leaders should not give into because participants frequently rate this time of the session as one of the most valuable.

Methods of Parent Education

When early childhood education staff decide to plan for parenting education for their particular population, they may consider several existing programs. Most of these programs have stated objectives so that staff and parent representatives might review several programs and then make decisions.

Parent Education Packages

Two popular parent education packages are based on the theoretical works of Adler (1923) and Dreikurs and Soltz (1964). Both the Systematic Training for Effective Parenting (STEP), created by Dinkmeyer, McKay, and Dinkmeyer (1980), and Active Parenting, created by Popkin (1983), focus on the goal of teaching children responsibility. Strategies for teaching responsibility include use of natural and logical consequences, reflective listening and I-messages, and democratic family meetings (see Figures 10–6, 10–7, and 10–8).

Parent Education Books

How to Talk So Kids Will Listen and Listen So Kids Will Talk, created by Faber and Mazlish (1980), is a program of parent education that is intended for parents to use individually. This plan for parents is based on the theoretical work of Haim Ginott (1969) (see Figures 10–9 and 10–10).

Raising Good Children from Birth through the Teenage Years is a parenting resource written by Thomas Lickona (1983). This plan is based on the

Teaching Respect *Communicating*

Figure 10–6 — Summary of STEP

Reasons parents need training are (1) rapid social change; and (2) increasing social equality for all people. The "democratic revolution" means adult-centered systems of rewards and punishments no longer fit the needs that humans have to be successful in society. The STEP system, a democratic child-rearing approach, is based on mutual respect between parent and child, and equality in terms of human worth and dignity. That is, children have as much right to be treated with respect as do adults. Two critical components of STEP are communication and encouragement. This system encourages parents to provide opportunities for children to make some decisions and to be responsible for their decisions. The use of natural and logical consequences replaces rewards and punishments.

There are topics for nine group sessions:

1. Understanding Child Behavior and Misbehavior
2. Understanding How Children Use Emotions to Involve Parents and the "Good" Parent
3. Encouragement
4. Communication—Listening
5. Communication—Exploring Alternatives and Expressing Your Ideas and Feelings to Children
6. Developing Responsibility
7. Decision-making for Parents
8. The Family Meeting
9. Developing Confidence and Using Your Potential

Materials in the package include a leader's manual; a parent handbook with problem situations, charts, points to remember, and a personal plan for improving relationships; two video cassettes; a script booklet for videos; a discussion guidelines poster; charts summarizing major concepts and principles; certificates for participants; and publicity aids.

Source: Dinkmeyer, McKay, & 1983

Figure 10–7 — Summary of Active Parenting

Goal—to develop innovative methods of presenting existing effective parenting practices to the millions of parents who can benefit from them.

Based on the work of—Alfred Adler, Rudolf Dreikurs, Carl Rogers, Robert Carkhuff, and Thomas Gordon.

Two beliefs about parenting—1. Parenting well is extremely important. 2. Parenting well is extremely difficult.

Three assumptions—1. Most parents have sufficient love and commitment to parent well. 2. Most parents have not been given sufficient information, skills, or support. 3. This can be disastrous in modern society in which children openly reject traditional parenting methods. "Courage is the greatest gift a parent can give a child." (Alfred Adler)

The following topics are included in six sessions:

1. The Active Parent: concept of equality, styles of parenting, fallacy of reward and punishment, courage, responsibility, cooperation, winning positive relationships
2. Understanding Your Child: how children develop, building blocks of personality, family constellation, understanding behavior, four goals of children's behavior, four mistaken goals of misbehavior, parenting and anger, and helping children use their anger
3. Instilling Courage: what is encouragement?, how parents discipline their own children, turning negatives into positives, how to show confidence, building on strengths, valuing the child as she is, stimulating independence
4. Developing Responsibility: responsibility, freedom and the limits to freedom, the problem-handling method for parents, who owns the problem?, I-messages, natural and logical consequences, mutual respect
5. Winning Cooperation: communication: road to cooperation, avoiding communication blocks, listen actively, listen for feelings, connect feelings to content, expressing love
6. Democratic Families in Action: family council meeting, six good reasons for regular meetings, how to get started, a word about the agenda, ground rules, emphasizing the family unit.

Materials in the package include a leader's manual, a parent handbook, two videocassettes, an action guide (parent workbook), and promotional materials.

Source: Popkin, 1983

theoretical work of Kohlberg (1964), emphasizing the importance of child development and how children come to understand the difference between right and wrong (Chrisman & Couchenour, 1997) (see Figure 10–11).

Two approaches that are currently being marketed for parents are Assertive Discipline (Canter & Canter, 1985) and 1–2–3 Magic (Phelan, 1995). Concern about the use of these programs with young

Figure 10–8	Critique of STEP and Active Parenting

These approaches are very similar and so have similar strengths and areas of concern. Based largely on the work of Alfred Adler, both methods provide excellent information about effectively communicating with children. Family meetings and democratic methods are very good ways to interact respectfully with children.

The notion that children learn responsibility through mutual respect holds up well in existing research. Active Parenting has a broader base and includes ideas from Carl Rogers and others.

A weakness in both packages is that not enough attention is paid to developmental or individual differences in children. Neither do they mention much about cultural differences in families. The strategies seem best for children six or older and are likely to be viewed more positively by middle class or affluent families. Even with these limitations, these packages may be useful to share with parents in your early childhood program. Be sure they understand that this is just one set of useful strategies and not the only method acceptable.

Figure 10–9	Highlights of *How to Talk So Kids Will Listen and Listen So Kids Will Talk*

Based largely on the work of Haim Ginott. Methods of communication affect relationships and children's behavior.

The goals of the authors include finding a way to live with each other so that we can feel good about ourselves and help the people we love feel good about themselves, finding a way to live without blame and recrimination, finding a way to be more sensitive to one another's feelings, finding a way to express our irritation or anger without doing damage, finding a way to be respectful of our children's needs and to be just as respectful of our own needs, finding a way that makes it possible for our children to be caring and responsible, and breaking the cycle of unhelpful talk that has been handed down from generations.

Topics in the book are:

1. **Helping Children Deal with Their Feelings**—connections between how kids feel and how they behave; when kids feel right, they behave right; adults often deny children's feelings; suggestions provided to help with acknowledging feelings

2. **Engaging Cooperation**—describe what you see, give information, say it with one word, talk about your feelings, write a note

3. **Alternatives to Punishment**—point out a way to be helpful, express strong disapproval of inappropriate behavior, state your expectations, show the child how to make amends, give a choice, take action, allow child to experience consequences of misbehavior, problem-solve by talking about child's feelings and needs, brainstorm together, write down all ideas, decide on one and follow through

4. **Encouraging Autonomy**—let child make choices, show respect for child's struggles, don't ask too many questions, don't rush to answer child's questions, encourage child to use sources outside the home, don't take away hope

5. **Praise**—praise and self-esteem, describe instead of evaluating, describe what you see and feel, sum up the child's praiseworthy behavior with one word

6. **Freeing Children from Playing Roles**—look for opportunities to show the child a new picture of herself, put child in situations where she can see herself differently, let child overhear you say something positive about her, model the behavior you want to see, be a storehouse for your child's special moments, state feelings and expectations about child's old behavior

Source: Faber and Mazlish, 1980

children is widespread. Research is not available concerning the effects of either approach; however, best practices in early education generally are in opposition to these plans (see Figures 10–12 and 10–13).

Parents as Teachers

Some parent education models for parenting young children are centered on home visitation. The Parents as Teachers (PAT) program, which originated in Missouri (Burkhart, 1991), is one such approach. Trained parent educators visit homes soon after the birth of a child. They provide practical details and support to parents concerning the child's needs for optimal development.

Parents as Teachers is built on two premises.

1. All families have strengths.
2. Parents are the experts on their child.

Home visitors are specially trained and certified through the Parents as Teachers National Center in St. Louis, Missouri. The original program included

Figure 10–10	Critique of *How to Talk So Kids Will Listen and Listen So Kids Will Talk*

This approach offers parents many useful strategies for keeping open communication with their children. These strategies ultimately are likely to help to build positive relationships. And positive relationships are an excellent basis for children's developing skill at self-control. The authors of this method are concerned for both parents and children and increasing the quality of family life for each member. Some parents find the strategies a little artificial sounding when they first begin, but that may be because in general, we lack effective interpersonal capabilities in our society. With practice, many adults feel that the strategies become more natural to them.

Adults place expectations on children, not just for blind compliance to their wishes but also for responsibility in the family. This approach is useful not specifically just for disciplining children, but for all interaction with them. Thus, parents are offered suggestions for their entire relationships with children, not only for disciplining them. This approach is generally viewed as a useful one and is highly recommended.

training for working with families of children from birth to three years. Additional training is now available for families with three- to five-year-old children. The program is comprised of four components.

1. *Home visits.* Visits by certified home visitors to homes of new parents are individualized. The task of home visitors is to provide child development knowledge and child-rearing information, and to support parents in using this material within their family.

2. *Group meetings.* Group meetings are scheduled for times that parents who work outside the home are available such as Saturdays or evenings. Often, the emphasis in a group meeting is on parent-child activities to emphasize the importance of family interaction on the child's development. At meetings, families have opportunities to share successes and concerns about their children and to receive feedback from staff members or outside experts.

3. *Developmental screening.* Parents and parent educators are encouraged to observe and monitor the child's development; these ongoing informal assessments often provide useful information about the child's progress or developmental delays. Formal screenings are conducted annually beginning at one year of age. When problems are identified in children's development, parents are helped with resources for appropriate forms of intervention.

4. *Connections with community resources.* Parent educators assist parents in making connections with resources in their particular communities. Examples of possible resources include libraries, health clinics, and programs for children with identified special needs (http://www.parentsasteachers.org, accessed July 4, 2006).

Evaluation research completed on Parents as Teachers over the past 15 years confirms the following:

- At age three, children enrolled in this program were significantly more advanced in language, problem solving, and social development than comparison children.

- Children who participated for at least one year scored higher on the Kindergarten Inventory of Developmental Skills than others.

- At the end of first grade, PAT children scored higher on standardized reading and math tests than others.

- In fourth grade, PAT "graduates" scored higher than the control group on the Stanford Achievement Test.

- By age three, more than half of PAT children with observed developmental delays were on target for expected typical development.

- Even when PAT children and families have many characteristics associated with high risk for educational failure, the children are placing above national norms (http://www.parentsasteachers.org, retrieved July 4, 2006)

Recently, the Parents as Teachers National Center has undertaken a new initiative in the form of a revised version of the curriculum with a neuroscience base. This use of new research available on brain development is an exemplary model of an existing

Figure 10–11 Summary and Critique of *Raising Good Children*

This approach uses developmental theory and research as a basis for parenting strategies. The underlying theme is noted in this quote, "A child is the only known substance from which a responsible adult can be made."

Lickona assumes that a primary goal for parenting is to foster moral development. He states ten big ideas from the moral development approach to parenting:

1. Morality is respect.
2. Kids develop morality slowly and in stages.
3. Respect kids and require respect in return.
4. Teach by example.
5. Teach by telling.
6. Help kids learn to think.
7. Help kids take on real responsibilities.
8. Balance independence and control.
9. Love kids and help them develop a positive self-concept.
10. Foster moral development and a happier family at the same time.

Lickona also offers specific parenting strategies that are supported by child development research for various age groups:

Infancy—love your baby; provide consistent care; smile and talk to baby often

Toddlerhood—set reasonable limits; provide space for safe exploration; give choices; only say no when you mean it; ignore undesirable behaviors; use distraction; use logical consequences if necessary

Source: Lickona, 1983

Threes—teach manners; provide habit of helping; read stories with labels such as "naughty" or "nice," but avoid saying "bad girl"

Fours—offer choices to give child decisions to make; take time to have fun together; reaffirm old limits and set new ones; require kids to give good reasons; assign chores that give a role in the family

Fives—be the authority figure children need; fives believe they should obey, so use opportunities to remind them of this belief; reinforce manners and other desirable behavior; begin to teach values about why some things are wrong

Sixes to eights—offer explanations and reminders, but be firm; appeal to reciprocity or equal exchange; negotiate and compromise in a spirit of fairness; talk about feelings; help them to know what your expectations are; nurture a loving relationship

Critique—This approach is concerned both with the parent and the outcome to the child. The goal is child-centered, in that the short-term and long-term effects of parenting strategies on children are geared toward fostering morality. These approaches are supported by a large body of research literature. Variations by ages of children are helpful to parents. Parents can read short segments of the book related to the particular age of their child. It may be helpful to have a professional who is knowledgeable in child development provide support for parents beginning this approach. This book is highly recommended as an approach to parenting.

---

program adding new scientific advances. The revised design has been named The Born to Learn Curriculum. Currently, assessments are being conducted to measure results of this approach to Parents as Teachers (http://www.parentsasteachers.org).

For more information:
Parents as Teachers National Center
St. Louis, Missouri
(314) 432-4330
http://www.parentsasteachers.org/

Home Instruction Program for Preschool Youngsters

Home Instruction Program for Preschool Youngsters (HIPPY) was developed by the National Council of Jewish Women in Jerusalem in 1969. HIPPY USA was started in 1984 in Tulsa, Oklahoma. This national network provides training and assists local communities with start-up materials. Funding for HIPPY USA comes mostly from three sources: training service fees, royalties from the sale of curriculum materials, and grants from foundations and corporations (http://www.hippyusa.org/, retrieved July 4, 2006).

Figure 10–12   Summary and Critique of *Assertive Discipline*

Goal—"to help parents take charge before the problems with their children get out of hand" (p. 6).

The authors state, "Assertive Discipline should be used when your everyday approaches to handling children's behavior haven't worked. If talking with your children, reasoning with them or understanding their feelings doesn't help improve their behavior, then it's time for Assertive Discipline" (p. 2). "Through Assertive Discipline, we will teach you how to take charge in problem situations and let your children know you must be the 'boss'" (p. 3).

The step-by-step plan for this approach is:

1. Communicate assertively. Avoid arguments and praise children when they behave. This approach attempts to teach parents how to speak assertively, how to use non-verbal messages, how to handle arguing, and how to catch children being good. The authors emphasize the use of praise and "super praise" for desired behavior.

2. Back up your words with actions. Plan how you will respond if they do or do not listen to you. The authors discuss how to use consequences for inappropriate behavior, how to handle "testing," and how to provide positive support.

3. Lay down the law. Set up a systematic Assertive Discipline plan. Use "parent-saver" techniques; conduct a "lay down the law" session with your children. Suggested disciplinary actions for minor behavioral problems:

Source: Canter & Canter, 1985

Separation
Taking away privileges
Physical action to remove child or object
"Do what I want" before you do anything else grounding
Suggested actions for serious behavior problems:
"I am watching you:" close monitoring of all behavior, even violating privacy
Tape recording child with sitter or at school
Unannounced visits
Room grounding: no TV, stereo, phone, games or toys; leaving only for school, bathroom, and eating
Out-of-home grounding with a neighbor or relative
Positive consequences for desirable behavior: choosing dessert, extra TV time, a jelly bean, choose a treat, stickers, later curfew, reading a story together, point system, fishing trip with dad

Critique—The field-testing aspect considers only the effects of the approach on parents and children's compliance with parents. No effects on children have been studied. The approach is authoritarian in nature.

Some strategies may be useful for parents, but the Assertive Discipline concept is not recommended by experts in child development. This punishment and reward system does not provide a foundation for children to develop responsibility or respect.

In this parent education program, paraprofessionals [× not necessarily parents] are trained to provide services to families in their homes. The emphasis is on helping parents prepare their three-, four-, and five-year-old children to succeed in school. Storybooks, creative games, and activity packets are shared by paraprofessionals in home visits and at group meetings. Parents practice the activities with paraprofessionals before using them with their children (http://www.hippyusa.org/, retrieved July 4, 2006).

Starting a HIPPY program in a local community involves the seven following steps:

1. review HIPPY program requirements

2. conduct need assessment in local community

3. hold a preliminary meeting with community leaders and other interested parties

4. secure funding from local and state sources

5. submit application to HIPPY USA

6. hire or assign a training coordinator

7. sign an agreement with HIPPY USA

HIPPY USA claims the following benefits for children, parents, and the paraprofessionals involved in the program.

For children:

• skill development

• confidence

Figure 10–13	Summary and Critique of 1–2–3 *Magic*

Goal—"When you finish with this book, you will know exactly what to do, what not to do, what to say, and what not to say in just about every one of the common everyday problem situations you will run into with your kids" (p. iii).

Phelan states his viewpoint about the role of parents early in the book, "When your kids are little, your house should be a dictatorship where you are the judge and jury" (p. 13). His view of children is stated with a quote from another writer, "'Childhood is a period of transitory psychosis.'" Phelan goes on to explain, "She meant that kids, when they are little, are sort of nuts! They are born unreasonable and selfish, and it is our job—and a teacher's job—to help them become the opposite" (p. 12).

Guidelines for this method:

1. Methods must be used exactly as described in the book.

2. Both parents should use the techniques.

3. Single parents can use the methods effectively by themselves.

4. Grandparents, baby-sitters, and other caregivers have found the methods helpful.

5. The kids should be in good physical health.

Premises of this approach:

1. To stop behavior, use the 1-2-3 "counting" procedure. "That's 1."

Source: Phelan, 1995

"That's 2."
"That's 3—take 5."

2. To start behavior, choose from six tactics:

Sloppy positive verbal feedback (PVF): Praise or reinforcement should be given often.

Kitchen timers: Set timer as deadline for starting desired behavior.

Docking system: If you don't do the work, money is docked each time.

Natural consequences.

Charting: Give stickers or marks for completing tasks.

Information about active listening, self-esteem, and reflecting feelings is added to chapters near the end of the book. In this section, the author warns parents about the dangers of overusing the 1-2-3 counting approach and suggests the importance of listening to their children. However, when the listening turns into an attack by the child, parents are urged to count.

Critique—In this approach to parenting, adults have all of the responsibility to control children, with children being given very little opportunity to develop self-control.

A great deal of research shows that children who are parented primarily through a punishment and reward system do not develop a sense of responsibility or conscience.

- better adapted to the classroom when they begin school

For parents:

- increased sense of their own abilities
- satisfaction of teaching their children
- excitement of seeing children's development
- a time for fun and learning with their children
- a positive relationship with another adult (paraprofessional) who cares about them and their children
- connect with other agencies in the community

For paraprofessionals, many who have been parents in the program previously:

- an opportunity to help others in a leadership capacity

- often a first job
- a step to a permanent job elsewhere

For more information:
HIPPY USA
220 East 23rd Street
New York, New York 10010
(212) 532-7730
http://www.hippyusa.org

Evaluation research on HIPPY programs in the United States confirms the following information:

- In second grade, children who had participated in HIPPY were higher on school performance and in teacher ratings of motivation and adaptation to the classroom.

- HIPPY children had fewer absences.

- HIPPY children were perceived by their teachers as better students.

- Through parent training in specific techniques for book reading, HIPPY children had higher involvement and interest in this activity.

HIPPY emphasizes growth for parents and paraprofessionals at least as much as it does for children. There seems to be even greater evidence for the success of the program with adults than with children. HIPPY USA suggests that future research focus on needed improvements in the program as well as details about variations required by local communities (http://www.hippyusa.org/, retrieved July 4, 2006).

Family Life Education   *Includes Developmental Issues of families*

Family life education incorporates a broader view of the needs of families. In addition to parenting, family life education includes topics such as marriage, family relationships, sex education, and work-family issues (Darling, 1987). Family life education is currently driven by ecological theory, emphasizing "wholeness and integration" (p. 819). The family life approach places skills and knowledge about parenting in the context of all of family life, thus making it a broad and diverse approach (see Figures 10–14 and 10–15).

Family life education, when incorporated into early childhood teacher education, would lead to discussions and the generation of knowledge about the following areas:

- challenges of families from varying socioeconomic backgrounds and how these situations affect involvement of families in their children's education

- concerns of families from differing ethnic, religious, racial, and sexual orientation backgrounds about their place in the culture of the school

- effects of stressors facing families such as divorce, remarriage, and death in establishing family-school relationships

Figure 10–14	Family Life Education Substance Areas for CFLE

1. Families in Society includes marital choice, minority families, gender roles, work, and family

2. Internal Dynamics of Families includes family stress and crises, conflict management, violence, special needs in families

3. Human Growth and Development over the Life Span includes prenatal and infancy through adulthood and aging

4. Human Sexuality includes biological determinants, sexual values and decision making, sexual response and dysfunction

5. Interpersonal Relationships including communication skills, romance, intimacy, and responsibility

6. Family Resource Management including goal-setting, allocation of resources, consumer issues, and decisions

7. Parent Education and Guidance includes parenting rights, practices, variations, and roles across the life cycle

8. Family Law and Public Policy includes social services, education, taxes, civil rights, and economic support laws

9. Ethics including social attitudes and values, our pluralistic society, social consequences of choices, and technological changes

10. Family Life Education Methodology including planning, implementing, and evaluating effective techniques

- strategies for sensitively including various family forms such as foster parents, grandparents, and other extended family members who serve as parents or guardians (Coleman and Churchill, 1997)

One example of a focus area for Certified Family Life Educators (CFLEs) is military family relocation, separation and deployment, and reunion (Drummet, Coleman, & Cable, 2003). Specific content areas for family life educators to address in their work with military families include the following:

A. Culture

1. Military culture requires total commitment from military members as well as from their family

Figure 10–15	Griggs' Criteria for Evaluating Family Life Education Material

Evaluation of a family life education program should consider the following:

- accuracy of content
- clear presentation
- nonjudgmental in tone
- logically organized
- interesting and challenging
- material leads to existing goals, objectives, or outcomes
- appealing format
- no sexism, racism, or cultural bias
- appropriate level for intended participants
- active learning required
- reflects various stages of family life cycle
- recognizes variations in family structure
- acknowledges changing roles of family members

Source: Griggs, M. B. (October 1981). Criteria for the evaluation of family life education materials. *Family Relations, 30* (4), 549–555

members. Confidentiality does not apply to doctor-patient or counselor-client relationships, making formal interventions questionable for those in the military. Family life educators could assist with formation of self-help or support group with proximity to military bases.

2. Military communities are ethnically diverse. Locations of bases and required relocations and deployments make it difficult to stay in close touch with family members. Also, racism, sexism, and other biases may be problematic depending on the region to which military members have been deployed. Family life educators can provide an essential educational service by sharing information about the local culture, long-distance measures of staying in touch with families, as well as ways to make the most of living in an unfamiliar culture.

B. Separation

1. Issues related to separation vary by and are influenced by family structure: single parents, dual-military families, one parent military and other civilian, and others. Family life educators must demonstrate sensitivity to these variations by assessing each family's needs and providing assistance to the military in developing surveys to get information that would assist retention efforts.

2. Separations affect finances of military families. Family life educators can assist families to plan ahead with separation plans so that legal (power of attorney), medical (for dependent children) and ongoing financial commitment (housing, food, utilities, credit debts) issues can be handled in their absence. Also, family life educators can assist parents who are separated from their young children maintain contact with the children and their caregivers.

C. Methods of Communication

1. Reliable communication is necessary for military families to maintain cohesiveness with their military family member. Family life educators sometimes hold workshops for family members about maintaining communication. They encourage methods such as having the deployed family member tape record a number of stories for children to listen to as they desire and creating family scrap books of pictures and stories that families can "read" and remember happy times together. Family life educators can also encourage children to keep scrap books of their activities so that when the military family member returns, they can share together in what might have been missed on a daily basis.

2. Gaining information about the safety and well-being of deployed military members is not always an easy process. Family life educators encourage family members to attend sessions held by the military for predeployment.

D. Employment Needs of Military Spouses

1. Because military members are deployed or relocated without much notice, spouses often are faced with career dilemmas that can lead the family to be dissatisfied with military life. Family life educators can provide various forms of assistance in this arena, such as helping military

spouses to link with related internet sources as well as jobs that are done primarily online. Also, collaboration with the military decision makers regarding the importance of programs to address issues related to spousal employment would help to support families.

E. Assistance with Relocation

1. First, military families need to know choices about housing for their upcoming relocations. Information about types of housing, community resources, and schools can help to soften the challenges of forced relocation. Family life educators might help to set up networks of families, communities, and military personnel to provide such information.

2. Financial aspects of relocating create challenges for many military families. Family life educators often provide workshops on budgeting and debt management as well as establish networks of trained peer financial counselors.

F. Programs for Relocated Children

1. As children relocate with their military families, they face frequent adjustments to new communities and especially to new schools. Family life educators might set up a system for supporting children's adjustment that would include family tours of schools and collaborating with school staff to create buddy systems for children new to the community. Buddies might be put into place even before the relocation so that a social connection is made prior to the move.

G. Assistance with Family Adjustment during Reunion Periods

1. Military families, often overcome with joy at the knowledge of an impending reunion, may be surprised at the challenges they will face with this transition. Family life educators can make families cognizant of the ups and downs often realized during times of reunion and they can also establish support groups on a base or in a nearby community to support families in this specific transition (Drummet, Coleman, & Cable, 2003).

This example of ways in which family life educators can support military families is only one of the many avenues served by highly qualified CFLEs. Their knowledge base and skills can be applied to many diverse family life circumstances in ways to help families navigate through difficulties to successful outcomes.

The National Council of Family Relations (NCFR) sponsors the only national program to certify family life educators (CFLE). Family life education provides skills and knowledge to enrich individual and family life. For more information about family life education, go to http://www. ncfr.org/ and click "CFLE Certification."

The Role of Early Childhood Educators in Parent Education and Family Life Education

Early childhood professionals must not presume to know the needs of their particular families in terms of parent and family life education. Instead, suggest possibilities for changes in parenting approaches by having families complete assessments. Families should always have a voice in the content and format of educational opportunities made available to them.

It is the responsibility of early childhood teachers to be aware of the pros and cons of any parent or family life education offered to families. If a packaged program is used, discuss the downside of the program as reviewed by experts in the field. Also, ask parents about what they like about and find useful in the program, as well as what is less appealing to them.

Topics for Parent Education

In this section, ten topics for parent education are discussed that are recommended for inclusion in most early childhood education settings. Nine topics deal with play, developmentally appropriate practice, positive guidance, limiting television, homework, early brain development, family literacy, childhood obesity, and financial responsibility. These seem to be frequently requested from parents and/or staff. The remaining topic, healthy sexuality development, is not one that is often discussed by either parents or staff. However, it is included in this book because recent research (Couchenour & Chrisman, 1996; Couchenour, Chrisman, & Gottshall, 1997; Chrisman, Gottshall, Koons, & Couchenour, 1998) into this topic found that early childhood teachers do not believe they have enough preparation in this area or that family involvement is required when this topic is addressed in early childhood education programs.

For each of the topics, a variety of formats may be used for dissemination. Some strategies for educating parents about these topics with the information provided herein include sections of parent handbooks, orientation sessions, workshops, newsletters, brochures, videotapes prepared so that parents can check them out at their convenience, mini-conferences with several speakers around the theme, or panel discussions. Use of several formats or strategies for any one topic is likely to increase the effectiveness of educating parents. Early education staff may also wish to divide any of the topics into smaller segments for any one session or strategy.

Topic One: The Value of Play for Young Children

Purpose: To explain to parents of children enrolled in an early childhood program the value of play to all areas of children's development, including physical, cognitive, social, and emotional. (Placing a list of outcomes for children at each learning center is helpful for parents as they volunteer in the classroom or simply learn about child development.)

Goals for Parents:

1. To explain how children learn through play and that play is a child's work.

2. To articulate a definition and list the characteristics of play.

3. To describe what children learn as they play in various learning centers around the classroom and outdoors. Examples are:

   dramatic play—vocabulary development, cooperation, role identification, and concept development

   blocks—spatial relationships, problem-solving, patterning, measurement, creativity, cooperation, and vocabulary development

4. To observe and facilitate play in home settings.

Concepts to Highlight:

1. Children learn very effectively through play.

2. Play has the following characteristics:

   a. it is intrinsically motivated

   b. it is the child's choice

   c. it is active

   d. it is child-directed

   e. it is fun

3. Teachers have the following responsibilities regarding play:

   a. it is planned

   b. it meets the needs of children

   c. space is organized for safety and best educational results

   d. ample time is allocated in the daily schedule for effective learning through play

   e. the teacher interacts with children during play in ways that support the child's choices

4. Play fosters physical development. Both large muscles and small muscles are used for increased gross motor and fine motor skills.

5. Play fosters cognitive development. Children, who from two to seven years are master players, are likely to become master workers soon after that, often during third grade.

6. Play fosters social development. Cooperation is required to play well with other children. Sometimes, children lead and sometimes, they follow when they play. Children take on a variety of different roles when they play.

7. Play fosters emotional development. Children gain ability to express themselves in a variety of appropriate ways. Self-esteem is enhanced through play.

8. Stages of play related to social development are solitary, parallel, associative, and cooperative.

9. Stages of play related to intellectual development are sensorimotor or practice, constructive, dramatic (or pretend), and games with rules.

10. Effective practice in early childhood education emphasizes play as a useful method for teaching and learning.

11. The teacher's role for fostering children's play includes setting up the environment and interacting in ways that enhance the play.

Resources:

Dimidjian, V. J. (Ed.). (1992). *Play's place in public education for young children.* Washington, DC: National Education Association.

IPAUSA.org. *The American Association for the child's right to play.* http://www.ipausa.org/. Retrieved January 26, 2006.

Jones, E., & Reynolds, G. (1992). *The play's the thing: Teachers' roles in children's play.* New York: Teachers College Press.

National Network for Child Care. (1994). *Play is the business of kids.* http://www.nncc.org/Curriculum/better. play.html. Retrieved January 26, 2006.

Rogers, C. S., & Sawyers, J. K. (1988). *Play in the lives of children.* Washington, DC: National Association for the Education of Young Children.

Sawyers, J. K., & Rogers, C. S. (1988). *Helping young children develop through play: A practical guide for parents, caregivers, and teachers.* Washington, DC: National Association for the Education of Young Children.

Wasserman, S. (1990). *Serious players in the primary classroom: Empowering children through active learning experiences.* New York: Teachers College Press.

Children learn effectively through play.

Topic Two: What Is Developmentally Appropriate Practice?

Purpose: To provide for parents of children enrolled in an early education program the meaning of the term "developmentally appropriate practice."

Goals for Parents:

1. To define and explain the term "developmentally appropriate practice."

2. To understand the role of professionals in planning, implementing, and assessing developmentally appropriate educational practice.

3. To discuss the importance of school, family, and community partnerships in fostering high-quality programs for young children.

Concepts to Highlight:

1. Definition of developmentally appropriate practice in early childhood education is three-pronged:

   a. understanding of child development and learning

   b. attention to individual differences in children's strengths, interests, and needs

   c. knowledge of each child's social and cultural contexts

The role of the early childhood professional is to enhance children's development and learning.

2. The role of early childhood professionals is expansive:

   a. to create a caring community of learners

   b. to enhance children's development and learning

   c. to construct appropriate curriculum for the group and for individual children

   d. to authentically assess each child's development and learning

   e. to establish reciprocal relationships with families

3. Developmentally appropriate practices consider all areas of children's development: physical, cognitive and language, social, and emotional.

4. It is necessary to understand the inaccuracy of common myths about the meaning of developmentally appropriate practice, including:

   a. there is only one way to implement developmentally appropriate programs

   b. developmentally appropriate classrooms are unstructured, chaotic

   c. teachers do not plan or teach anything in a developmentally appropriate classroom

   d. developmentally appropriate practice requires that existing curricula be "watered down" and that children fall behind academically

   e. academics have no place in developmentally appropriate programs

   f. developmental appropriateness is just a fad, soon to be replaced by another fad.

5. A variety of teaching and learning strategies are used in developmentally appropriate practices, including play, small groups, large groups, cooperative learning, and direct instruction. No one method is relied on exclusively; methods are based on how children learn.

Resources:

Bredekamp, S., & Copple, C. (1997). *Developmentally appropriate practice in early childhood programs* (rev. ed.). Washington, DC: National Association for the Education of Young Children.

Clemens, S. G. (1983). *The sun's not broken, a cloud's just in the way: On child-centered teaching.* Mt. Ranier, MD: Gryphon House.

Conant, B. *Answers to commonly asked questions concerning developmentally appropriate practices.* http://www.users.stargate.net/~cokids/dapQnA.html. Retrieved January 26, 2006.

Developmentally appropriate practice in early childhood programs. (1998). http://www.naeyc.org/about/positions/pdf/PSDAP98.PDF. Retrieved January 26, 2006.

Dodge, D. T., & Bickart, T. S. (1998). *Preschool for parents: What every parent needs to know about preschool.* Naperville, IL: Sourcebooks.

Kostelnik, M. J. (May 1992). Myths associated with developmentally appropriate programs. *Young Children, 47* (4), 17–23.

Mr. Rogers talks with parents. [videotape, 43 min.]. Washington, DC: National Association for the Education of Young Children.

National Association for the Education of Young Children. *Ten signs of a great preschool.* http://www.naeyc.org/ece/1996/01.asp. Retrieved January 26, 2006.

Whole language learning. [videotape, 20 min.]. Washington, DC: National Association for the Education of Young Children.

Topic Three: Positive Guidance

Purpose: To explain to parents that discipline is a tool for children's learning and not only about submitting to adult expectations.

Goals for Parents:

1. To understand that when they guide or discipline children, they affect the whole child.

2. To explain that children learn appropriate behaviors through adult modeling and teaching.

3. To describe the effects of various types of discipline on children's development.

4. To foster strategies of positive guidance in their own parenting.

Concepts to Highlight:

1. Positive guidance approaches teach children appropriate behaviors.

2. Positive guidance demonstrates respect to children and models respectful interactions.

3. Positive guidance teaches children to appreciate themselves and others as worthwhile individuals.

4. Positive guidance helps children to use conflict resolution strategies as they interact with other children.

5. Positive guidance considers reasons for children's misbehavior or mistaken behaviors.

6. Positive guidance uses a proactive approach, including creating an environment conducive to learning and less likely to cause children's misbehaviors.

7. Positive guidance creates positive relationships between children and adults as adults model respectful behaviors.

8. Strategies for positive guidance help to build partnerships between parents and teachers.

9. Positive guidance nurtures peacemaking and justice.

10. Positive guidance provides opportunities to resolve conflicts in nonviolent ways.

11. Punishment produces harmful consequences to young children.

12. Punishment does not teach children appropriate behaviors.

Resources:

Condon, C., & McGinnis, J. (1988). *Helping kids care.* Oak Park, IL: Meyer-Stone Books and the Institute for Peace and Justice.

Gartrell, D. (2007). *A guidance approach for the encouraging classroom* (4th ed.). Clifton Park, NY: Thomson Delmar Learning.

Gartrell, D. (2003). The power of guidance: *Teaching social-emotional skills in early childhood classrooms.* Clifton Heights, NY: Delmar.

Honig, A. S. (1996). *Behavior guidance for infants and toddlers.* Little Rock, AR: Southern Early Childhood Association.

Kaiser, B., & Rasminsky, J. S. (1999). *Meeting the challenge: Effective Strategies for challenging behaviours in early childhood environments.* Ontario, Canada: Canadian Child Care Federation.

McGinnis, K., & Oehlberg, B. (1988). *Starting out right: Nurturing young children as peacemakers.* Oak Park, IL: Meyer-Stone Books and the Institute for Peace and Justice.

Nunnelley, J. C. (2002). *Powerful, positive and practical practices: Behavior guidance strategies.* Little Rock, AR: Southern Early Childhood Association.

Topic Four: Limiting Television

Purpose: To help parents understand that young children are particularly vulnerable to potentially harmful effects of too much television viewing.

Goals for Parents:

1. To be aware of what the potentially harmful effects of watching too much television are.

2. To be sensitized to the effects of television violence on young children.

3. To identify high-quality children's programming and videos.

4. To create alternatives to television/video viewing.

5. To plan for family viewing time.

Concepts to Highlight:

1. Television has a lot of power to influence children's thinking and behavior.

2. Children may become less caring and more fearful when they view too much television violence.

3. Adults have responsibility to protect children from possible harmful effects of television. Set clear limits and rules about television watching.

4. Parents should monitor all of children's television viewing. It's okay to ban programs that are unacceptable.

5. There is more violence in programming now than when parents were children.

6. When children watch television, they are missing out on play and social experiences that are important to their development.

7. Schools and families can work together to decrease television viewing and to increase better alternative activities for children.

8. Letter-writing campaigns to stations and companies that advertise can be organized by school, family, and community partnerships.

Resources:

Healthy habits for TV, video games, and the Internet. KidsHealth for Parents. http://kidshealth.org/

parent/positive/family/tv_habits.html. Retrieved January 26, 2006.

Horton, J., & Zimmer, J. (1994). *Media violence and children: A guide for parents.* [brochure]. Washington, DC: National Association for the Education of Young Children.

Levin, D. E. (1998). *Remote control childhood? Combating the hazards of media culture.* Washington, DC: National Association for the Education of Young Children.

Television and children. Child Development Institute. http://www.childdevelopmentinfo.com/health_safety/television.shtml. Retrieved January 26, 2006.

Topic Five: Homework

Purpose: To help parents understand reasons and expectations for homework in the primary grades.

Goals for Parents:

1. To explain the purpose of homework for primary children.

2. To understand parents' role in helping with homework.

3. To implement effective strategies for assisting children with homework.

Concepts to Highlight:

1. Two common reasons for homework in primary grades:

   a. to practice skills

   b. to collect information, or observe something at home or out of the school setting

2. Homework teaches responsibility and good work habits.

3. Reasonable amount of homework time for first through third grades is fifteen to thirty minutes.

4. Strategies for helping children with homework include:

   a. reminders

   b. setting up a quiet place to work

   c. scheduling time to do homework before other activities

   d. communicating with teachers about expectations and how homework is used at school

Resources:

Bickart, T. S., Dodge, D. T., & Jablon, J. R. (1997). *What every parent needs to know about 1st, 2nd, & 3rd grades:*

An essential guide to your child's education. Naperville, IL: Sourcebooks.

Homework. Olney, MD: Association for Childhood Education International. http://www.acei.org/brochure. htm. Retrieved December 26, 2006.

National Education Association. Help your student get the most out of homework. http://www.nea.org/parents/homework.html?mode=print. Retrieved January 26, 2006.

National PTA National Standards for Parent/Family Involvement Programs. (1998). http://www.pta. org/programs/. Retrieved November 25, 1998.

PBS Parents. Supporting your learner: Helping with homework. http://www.pbs.org/parents/goingtoschool/helping_homework.html. Retrieved January 26, 2006.

Topic Six: Healthy Sexuality Development

Purpose: To help parents understand that early sexuality development is related to all areas of children's development: physical, cognitive, social, and emotional.

Goals for Parents:

1. To have an awareness of typical behaviors or questions young children have related to sexuality.

2. To relate their own discomfort with discussions of sexuality.

3. To use appropriate responses to foster healthy sexuality in their children.

Concepts to Highlight:

1. Sexuality is about who we are, not just a set of behaviors.

2. Children are curious about sexuality, just as they are about most everything else that they encounter.

3. Some aspects of sexuality relate to physical development:

   a. body functions

   b. male/female differences

   c. body parts

   d. pleasant sensations

4. Some aspects of sexuality relate to social development:

   a. gender roles

b. identification of gender

c. social relationships with those of same and opposite gender

5. Some aspects of sexuality relate to emotional development:

   a. high self-esteem is related to feeling good about who you are

   b. affection is learned in early family relationships

   c. empathy and respect are required for successful relationships

6. Some aspects of sexuality relate to cognitive development:

   a. understanding of facts about reproduction

   b. understanding of family and cultural values about sexuality

   c. understanding why one is labeled as a boy or a girl

7. Teachers and parents must work together to create appropriate responses for fostering healthy sexuality development in young children.

8. Fostering healthy sexuality can be a barrier to sexual abuse.

Resources:

Chrisman, K., & Couchenour, D. (2002). *Healthy sexuality development: A guide for early childhood educators and families.* Washington, DC: National Association for the Education of Young Children.

Couchenour, D., & Chrisman, K. (1996). Healthy sexuality development in young children. *Dimensions of Early Childhood, 24* (4), 30–36.

Lively, V., & Lively, E. (1991). *Sexual development of young children.* Clifton Park, NY: Delmar Learning.

Sexuality and U. The development of sexuality from infancy to puberty: Developmental outcomes, common behaviors, concerns, and learning objectives. http://www.sexualityandu.ca/eng/health/SCD/. Retrieved January 26, 2006.

Sexuality Information and Education Council of the United States (SIECUS). Families are talking: SIECUS resources for families. http://www.familiesaretalking.org/resources/rsrc0000.html. Retrieved January 26, 2006.

Wilson, P. M. (1991). *When sex is the subject: Attitudes and answers for young children.* Santa Cruz, CA: Network Publications.

Topic Seven: Early Brain Development

Purpose: To help parents understand the importance of brain development in the early years of a child's life.

Goals for Parents:

1. To have an awareness of typical brain development.

2. To know some implications of brain development theory for families.

Concepts to Highlight:

1. The importance of multisensory play in brain development.

2. The importance of conversation, singing, and language.

3. The negative effects of unmonitored television viewing.

4. The relationship between emotional development and healthy brain development.

Resources:

Good Beginnings Alliance. Early brain development. http://www.goodbeginnings.org/brain.htm. Retrieved January 26, 2006.

Healy, J. M. (1994). *Your child's growing mind: A practical guide to brain development and learning from birth to adolescence.* New York: Doubleday.

National Association for the Education of Young Children. Early years are learning years. http://www.naeyc.org/ece/eyly. Retrieved December 26, 2006.

Nebraska's Early Childhood Training Center. Early brain development. http://www.esu3.org/ectc/brain.html. Retrieved January 26, 2006.

Parents' Action for Children. Brain development. http://www.iamyourchild.org/learn/parenting/development/braindevelopment/. Retrieved January 26, 2006.

Topic Eight: Family Literacy

Purpose: To help parents understand ways to support literacy development at home.

Goals for Parents:

1. To have an awareness of the importance of reading to, with, and being a role model for children.

2. To understand the importance of providing books, writing materials, and other literacy supports during early childhood.

3. To be able to discern fads or gimmicks from age-appropriate literacy stories.

Concepts to Highlight:

1. Singing, playing, and reading to and with your children are important literacy strategies.

2. Making time to read together each day is important

3. Talking with your child and responding to their sounds, words, and questions is important for language development.

Resources:

Herb, S., & Willoughby-Herb, S. (2002). *Connecting fathers, children, and reading.* New York: Neal-Schuman.

National Association for Education of Young Children and the International Reading Association. (1998). *Raising a reader, raising a writer.* Washington, DC: National Association for the Education of Young Children.

National Center for Family Literacy. http://www.famlit.org/. Retrieved January 26, 2006. http://www.pabook.libraries.psu.edu/familylit/defaul.html. Retrieved January 25, 2006.

Topic Nine: Childhood Obesity

Purpose: To help parents understand the long-term health concerns associated with childhood obesity as well as provide strategies for families to increase children's health and wellness.

Goals for Parents:

1. To know the definition of obesity in children.

2. To gain an awareness of the long-term health risks associated with childhood obesity.

3. To be prepared to implement ways to increase children's activity levels.

4. To obtain a variety of healthy meal and snack suggestions.

Concepts to Highlight:

1. The ability to recognize characteristics of childhood obesity at different developmental stages in children.

2. An understanding of serious medical risks associated with childhood obesity.

3. How families can implement exercise and fitness regimens.

4. Healthy nutrition through the use of the new food pyramid, with emphasis on daily foods such as fruits and vegetables, protein and calcium sources, and fatty snacks as "occasional" food choices.

5. How schools/centers and families can work together to battle childhood obesity.

6. Recess and outdoor play during the school day is important for children's overall health and wellness.

7. The vital role of educators in teaching children about healthy food choices and physical activity.

Resources:

American Heart Association. Exercise (physical activity) and children. http://www.americanheart.org/presenter.jhtml?identifier=4596. Retrieved January 26, 2006.

KidsHealth. The food guide pyramid. http://kidshealth.org/kid/stay_healthy/food/pyramid.html. Retrieved January 26, 2006.

Kid Source. Childhood obesity. http://www.kidsource.com/kidsource/content2/obesity.html. Retrieved January 26, 2006.

Mayo Clinic. Childhood obesity: What parents can do. http://www.mayoclinic.com/health/childhood-obesity/FL00058. Retrieved January 26, 2006.

MyPyramid.gov. Steps to a healthier you. United States Department of Agriculture. http://www.mypyramid.gov/. Retrieved January 26, 2006.

Promoting physical activity and exercise among children. (1998). *ERIC Digest.* http://www.ericdigests.org/1998-2/exercise.htm. Retrieved January 26, 2006.

Topic Ten: Teaching Financial Responsibility

Purpose: To help parents understand ways that they can teach their children how to manage money and to make financial decisions.

Goals for Parents:

1. To increase understanding about how children learn financial responsibility.

2. To discuss spending, saving, making financial decisions and being a wise consumer.

Concepts to Highlight:

1. The difference between wants and needs

2. Setting good examples for being wise consumers and good financial managers

3. Discussion of family budgets to help children understand how money works

4. Deciding on children's allowances and how to help them spend, save and share

5. The relationship of work to earning money

6. Planning ahead by budgeting

7. Understanding the role of financial institutions with families

Resources:

Children and money. Institute of Consumer Financial Education. http://www.financial-education-icfe.org/children_and_money/index.asp. Retrieved July 4, 2006.

Managing money: Needs vs. wants. PBS Kids. http://pbskids.org/itsmylife/money/managing/article2.html. Retrieved July 4, 2006.

McKinnon, S. (2004). Allow an allowance. *Consumer Economics Update*. University of Missouri Extension. http://extension.missouri.edu/ceupdate. Retrieved July 4, 2006.

Social Studies for Kids. (n.d.) Want vs. need: Basic economics. http://www.socialstudiesforkids.com/articles/economics/wantsandneeds1.htm. Retrieved July 4, 2006.

Summary and Conclusions

Early childhood teachers can provide much needed support for parents and their caregiving responsibilities. However, it is important that professional personnel provide information that is perceived as being needed by family members. Further, information should be shared in sensitive ways. When parents feel as though they are being criticized or degraded, they are not likely to participate in parent education sessions. It is essential that teachers respect family strengths and cultural differences in parenting values.

In addition to being sensitive to families, early childhood educators must use their knowledge of child development and parenting styles to critically analyze appropriate topics and strategies for parent and family life education. Several popular parent education packages are analyzed in this chapter. New programs undoubtedly will be developed, however, and it is the responsibility of early childhood professionals to become aware of them as they are implemented and to promote those that will foster healthy practices for families. Programs that do not consider current understanding of child development and the importance of the early years should be screened and not recommended for use by parents or teaching staff.

Chapter 10 Applications

1. Assess one parent or family life education program using the concepts from bioecological theory as discussed in this chapter.

2. Discuss the concerns held by many early childhood educators about Assertive Discipline and 1–2–3 Magic. Why do you believe these programs have so much popularity?

3. What is the difference between parent education and family life education?

Questions for Discussion and Reflection

1. How would you design a parenting education or family life education program based on the guidelines from this chapter?

2. How would children benefit from use of the guidelines presented in this chapter? How would families benefit? How would early childhood teachers benefit?

3. Discuss the pros and cons of the following strategies for parent education: meetings, newsletters, the Internet, and the resource room.

Field Assignments

1. Attend a parent meeting held by an early childhood program. Discuss the content and format of the meeting you attended in relation to information from this chapter. What were the best points about the meeting? What suggestions do you have for change?

2. Interview three parents who have their children enrolled in an early childhood education program about their thoughts related to parent education. Ask questions about content they would be interested in and format they would prefer.

3. Interview an early childhood teacher about her perspective on parent or family life education. Does this teacher feel prepared to provide these kinds of programs? Are they needed? Do families want them?

References

Adler, A. (1923). *Practice and theory of individual psychology.* New York: Harcourt, Brace and Company.

Bronfenbrenner, U., & Neville, P. R. (1994.) America's children and families: An international perspective. In S. L. Kagan & B. Weissbourd (Eds.), *Putting families first: America's family support movement and the challenge of change.* San Francisco: Jossey-Bass.

Burkhart, A. D. (1991). *Parents are important teachers.* Kansas City, MO: Westport.

Canter, L., & Canter, M. (1985). *Assertive Discipline for parents: A proven, step-by-step approach to solving everyday behavior problems.* New York: Harper & Row.

Chrisman, J. K. (1996). *The effects of training on child care providers' attitudes and practices.* Unpublished doctoral dissertation, University of Louisville.

Chrisman, K., & Couchenour, D. (1997). Comparing faith-based parenting guides: An on-going task for the faith community. *Church and Society, 88* (1), 99–104.

Chrisman, K., Gottshall, A., Koons, T., & Couchenour, D. (1998, November). *Incorporating early sexuality development into early childhood teacher preparation programs: A qualitative study.* Paper presented at the meeting of the National Association for the Education of Young Children, Toronto, Ontario, Canada.

Coleman, M., & Churchill, S. (1997, Spring). Challenges to family involvement. *Childhood Education,* 144–148.

Couchenour, D., & Chrisman, K. (1996). Healthy sexuality development in young children. *Dimensions of Early Childhood, 24* (4), 30–36.

Couchenour, D., Chrisman, K., & Gottshall, A. (1997, November). *Teaching about healthy sexuality development in young children.* Paper presented at the meeting of the National Association for the Education of Young Children, Anaheim, CA.

Darling, C. (1987). Family life education. In M. B. Sussman & S. K. Steinmetz (Eds.), *Handbook of marriage and the family.* New York: Plenum Press.

Dinkmeyer, D., McKay, G., & Dinkmeyer, D. (1980). *STEP.* Circle Pines, MN: American Guidance Service.

Dreikurs, R., & Soltz, V. (1964). *Children: The challenge.* New York: Hawthorn Books.

Drummet, A. R., Coleman, M., & Cable, S. (July 2003). Military families under stress: Implications for Family Life Education. *Family Relations, 52* (3), 279–287.

Faber, A., & Mazlish, E. (1980). *How to talk so kids will listen and listen so kids will talk.* New York: Avon Books.

Ginott, H. G. (1969). *Between parent and child.* New York: Avon Books.

Griggs, M. B. (October, 1981). Criteria for the evaluation of family life education materials. *Family Relations, 30* (4), 549–555.

Kohlberg, L. (1964). Development of moral character and moral ideology. In M. L. Hoffman & L. W. Hoffman (Eds.), *Review of child development research* (vol. 1). New York: Russell Sage Foundation.

LeMasters, E., & DeFrain, J. (1983). *Parents in contemporary America.* Homewood, IL: Dorsey.

Lickona, T. (1983). *Raising good children from birth through the teenage years.* New York: Bantam Books.

McDade, K. (1995). How we parent: Race and ethnic differences. In C. K. Jacobson (Ed.), *American families: Issues in race and ethnicity.* New York: Garland.

Phelan, T. W. (1995). *1–2–3 Magic: Effective discipline for children 2–12.* Glen Ellyn, IL: Child Management.

Popkin, M. (1983). *Active parenting.* Atlanta, GA: Active Parenting.

Powell, D. (1989). *Families and early childhood programs.* Washington, DC: National Association for the Education of Young Children.

Powell, D. (1994). Evaluating family support programs: Are we making progress? In S. L. Kagan & B. Weissbourd (Eds.), *Putting families first: America's family support movement and the challenge of change.* San Francisco: Jossey-Bass.

OUTLINE

Objectives

Key Terms

Bioecological Theory

Community Involvement in Early Childhood Education
Local School Boards
Boards of Trustees and Advisory Boards

Caring Communities

Referring Children for Additional or Varying Services

Program Models
Head Start
Comer Schools

Early Intervention
Preschool Inclusion
Other Models

Interdisciplinary Collaboration
Benefits
Challenges

Family-Centered Interprofessional Collaboration

The Business Community

Professionalism in Early Childhood Education
Knowledge Base
Continuing Professional Development

The Movement to Leave No Child Behind

Summary and Conclusions

Chapter 11 Applications

Questions for Reflection and Discussion

Field Assignments

References

Early Childhood Educators in the Community

OBJECTIVES

After reading this chapter, you should be able to:

■ understand the reasons for and effectiveness of collaborative efforts for children and families.

■ acquire information about appropriate strategies for discussing referrals for special services with families.

■ understand the goals and outcomes of early intervention services.

■ appreciate the importance of community resources to best meet the needs of all children and families.

Key Terms

community resources
early intervention
interdisciplinary
    collaboration

preschool inclusion
professional ethics

professional standards
referral

Bioecological Theory

The community for the early childhood teacher is not just a theme for a unit, as in community helpers, but is an ongoing reality each day. Understanding how the community affects the children, families, school, and the early childhood teacher helps in planning, reflecting, and organizing the curriculum, as well as other aspects of a developmentally appropriate program.

Awareness of **community resources** and lack of resources provides teachers with important information. Knowing what is available and what is not immediately available helps teachers define appropriate action and alternatives for decision making. When

communities support families and young children, everyone benefits. As community members, early childhood professionals can find many incidental ways of advocating for young children and their families (see Figure 11–1).

Currently, the public education, health, and child welfare systems are working to combine their efforts "especially in addressing the needs of poor children and families. This is occurring in large part because program staffs recognize that the interactive effects of inadequate academic mastery, ill health, poverty, and family dysfunction are toxic for families and neighborhoods" (Massinga, 1994, p. 103). One strategy that will increase effectiveness and reduce stress for families is to provide services "all at once in one place" (p. 103).

Figure 11–1	Typical Community Resources

Many communities have these resources for families. Check your local telephone directory or chamber of commerce for contact information.

Hotlines for crisis intervention
Child care (may be listed as day care)
Preschool education programs
Head Start
Literacy Council
Early intervention services
Resource and referral agencies
Library
Individual and family counseling agencies
Employment counseling/training
Red Cross
Food banks
Women, Infants, & Children (WIC)
Human services or welfare offices
Health care services
Hospital
Mental health/mental retardation services
Planned parenthood
Parenting support groups
Parents without Partners
United Way

In the book *Grassroots Success!* (Washington, Johnson, & McCracken, 1995), the authors suggest asking the following questions to be sure that schools and families are prepared for and continue to support each other:

- How well does the primary curriculum reflect current research about developmentally appropriate practice?

- What information do parents of newborns seek?

- Are kindergarten entry requirements fair and appropriate?

- Can all young children receive their immunizations?

- How could neighborhood stability be increased?

- What instills a love of reading in young children?

- How could community awareness about the importance of children's early experiences be raised?

Community Involvement in Early Childhood Education

Public education in the United States has a history and tradition of local control through elected boards of education. Many private or nonprofit institutions also have voluntary boards, either as policy making or advisory bodies.

Local School Boards

Local elected boards of education have a wide variety of responsibilities for educational issues within communities. Following is a list of common responsibilities of school boards:

- ensuring efficient operation of all schools in jurisdiction

- establishing local tax rates

- ensuring that school policies and practices agree with state statutes

- reviewing and securing contracts for services

- approving the budget and all purchases

- appointing superintendent and other personnel

- reviewing the educational program and student progress

- approving instructional programs to meet needs of all students (http://www.jefferson.k12.ky.us/ Click "About Us"; click "Board of Education")

School board meetings are public events, and the times and dates of meetings are provided in newspapers and other community communications. Parts of school board meetings may be closed to the public, however, when members go into "executive session" for various items of business.

Because education is the business of the entire community, it is necessary for concerned citizens to become involved. Typically, local boards of education have specific procedures for citizens who wish to make public comments. Phoning the local school district office is a good way to find out these procedures. The following guidelines are recommended as a means of making an effective presentation:

- When called to speak, go to location specified, speak clearly, and state your name and any group you are representing.

- Make your statement, including supporting evidence or examples. Also, suggest a course of action you are requesting of the board.
- Consider making copies of your comments for board members and school district leaders.
- Limit your comments to one issue.
- Always be polite. (http://www.jefferson.k12.ky. us/ Click "About Us"; click "Board of Education")

> Have you ever attended a school board meeting? If so, what was your experience? If not, plan to attend to learn about how local communities affect educational practice.

One current trend that some school districts are following is site-based management and planning. In this approach, family members often play a crucial role in decision making. The degree of parental authority allowed by school boards varies across districts.

Reasons to Encourage Family Involvement in Local School Boards

- to learn about current local issues related to education such as curriculum topics, special education, plans for new or innovative facilities, transportation, and district-wide policies
- to demonstrate support for teachers and programs at school board meetings
- to voice parent and family perspectives during the open discussion segment of a school board meeting

> Contact an administrator of a private or nonprofit early childhood program in your community. Ask about the existence and responsibilities of board members. How has the program benefited from the existence of a board?

Boards of Trustees and Advisory Boards

Early childhood programs that have related policy-making or advisory bodies often find such boards to be useful in their planning and fund-raising efforts. Having a variety of community members serve on these boards from various professions including education, health, legal, and business, creates wide-ranging support for the program. Responsibilities allocated to these boards differ greatly depending on whether they have policy making or advisory capacities.

Some of the responsibilities that are performed by boards include:

- implementing tuition and fee changes
- creating programmatic changes, such as dates and times of operation; additional programs offered in summer such as school age summer camps; increases in enrolled children; and family involvement opportunities
- defining guidelines for new services that are being proposed, such as offering various classes at child care such as dance, gymnastics, and art
- implementing program and service evaluation by staff and families
- writing a mission statement and annual or long-term goals for the center
- making budget recommendations
- serving on hiring or personnel committees
- recruiting volunteers and services from community sources

Caring Communities

It is clear by now that not only should community resources be tapped as they are needed for intervention, but also that families need communities to be involved in nurturing all children. The 1991 Report of the National Task Force on School Readiness expounds on the need for comprehensive support for all young children and families in the United States. Included in this call for comprehensive support are the following:

- health care
- security in family life

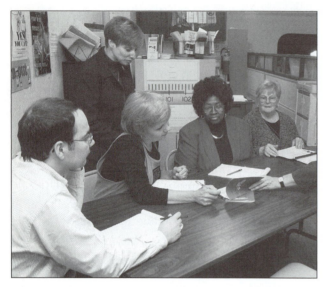

Policy making or advisory bodies are useful in supporting and planning for early childhood programs.

- high-quality early education
- linkages among services

According to this report, quality early education should not stand alone but, rather, should be integrated with other services in the community. Schools and programs should be visible in communities.

In *Ready Schools* (1998), the National Education Goals Panel lists important steps that can be taken by communities that care about preparing all children for kindergarten.

- Encourage parents to read to their children.
- Help parents connect with parent education programs such as Parents as Teachers and family literacy programs.
- Urge parents to take children for regular health examinations and immunizations.
- Urge pediatricians to share with parents the importance of reading to their children as well as effective parenting strategies.
- Help parents know how to find quality early education programs.
- Support national accreditation of local child care centers.

- Encourage parents to utilize early intervention services when necessary.
- Support programs that help teen parents to complete their education and learn effective, appropriate parenting skills.

"One of the first things we learned when we all went to education school twenty years ago—to work with the whole child. I don't know how we got away from that. But we have. Once we start meeting the needs of the whole child again, we'll begin to see real academic improvement . . . . We need to attach more social workers to the school who can go into the home and provide more services directly to children and families, taking care of bad teeth and nutrition and abuse. We've got to do this now, in the preschools and elementary schools—and in fact, before the child is born, with good prenatal care for mothers. We can't do it later. There's no way."

—Sheila Mae Bender, early childhood teacher, Louv, 1990, p. 343, as cited in The Report of the National Task Force on School Readiness

The Search Institute has identified a framework of forty developmental assets for children and adolescents based on research regarding healthy child development. Developmental assets for infants, toddlers, preschoolers, and elementary age children can be found at http://www.search-institute.org. These assets include the child, the family, and the community. More information is detailed in Chapter 1.

Referring Children for Additional or Varying Services

Sometimes, it becomes evident to an early childhood teacher that a child needs some additional support to succeed academically or socially. When teachers are aware of services available in the community, they are better equipped to refer children to the appropriate agencies, services, and programs to best meet the needs of each child. This becomes critical when the teacher is working in a program or school in which there are few support services (such as guidance counselors, social workers, or child psychologists). Without specialists in other disciplines, the early childhood teacher becomes the only qualified advocate for young children in the education system. When children have special needs, early childhood teachers and families alone cannot meet them. Additional professional advice and services are frequently necessary.

Referral is often required when children have difficulty in the classroom. Such difficulty may be academic, behavioral, or developmental. After efforts to individualize have been attempted and when the teacher believes that more information is needed to best help the child, with family agreement, other appropriate professionals are called in to assist the child. Many referrals are related to the child's physical health, including vision, hearing, or level of activity or inactivity. Other referrals may be related to immediate crises such as family financial difficulty or a death, an illness, or another family transition.

Referrals by the early childhood teacher most often need to be made in coordination with the program administrator. Effective administrators give support to teachers as they proceed through the referral

process. Examples of early childhood programs in which services are integrated include Head Start, Comer Schools, the Kentucky Educational Reform Act (KERA), and most early intervention designs.

To recommend special services for a child, it is important that early childhood teachers confer with parents beforehand, and that teachers follow appropriate procedures before, during, and after the conference. Abbott and Gold (1991) note the following procedures:

1. Collect a great deal of objective data about the child's behavior and development. Keeping a file of the child's work can be very useful.

2. Arrange for a conference with the appropriate family members. Be sure to indicate the purpose for the conference. It is likely that this will not be the first conference you will have had with this family.

3. Be well prepared for your conference. Collect all work and notes you want to share. Think through what you will say and how you will say it. Discuss the changes that have been made by school personnel to help the child in your classroom. Be prepared with information about possible referral sources. (See examples in Figure 11–2.)

Figure 11–2 Problems and Appropriate Referral Agency/Person

Problem	Appropriate Referral Agency/Person
Child behavior concerns	Child psychologist
Child nutrition concerns	Nutritionist, WIC, food stamp program
Child abuse	Human services agency, family therapist
Speech/language concerns	Speech therapist, speech clinic, health department hearing screening
Concern about vision	Health department vision screening, ophthalmologist
Chemical dependency	Health department, hospital
Domestic violence	Domestic violence shelter hot line, legal aid, family counseling, police
Creditor problems	Credit counselor
Utility payment difficulties	Community Action, United Way
Childhood illness	Health department, pediatrician, support group for specific illness
Developmental delays	Special education office, school district office, early intervention programs
Childhood poisonings	Health department lead screening clinic, poison control center
Family loss	Grief counselor

Source: Stephens, K. (September/October 1994). Aiding Families with Referrals. *First Teacher,* 34–35

4. During the conference:
   - be sure the space is comfortable and private.
   - check with family members about their perceptions of the child's behavior or development that is of concern to you.
   - note that you will assist in exploring sources when all information leads to a logical conclusion that additional help would benefit the child. Share resources available to your program or from your community.
   - avoid using the term "special education" (using it is premature at this point), and *do not, under any circumstances, guess at a diagnosis.*
   - strive for agreement to have a specialist assess the child based on the data collected by you and the family.
   - expect some emotion from the family. Keep your anxiety about this difficult topic in check. Use effective interpersonal communication skills.

5. Arrange for the assessment.

6. After the assessment, plan to meet with the family members to discuss the recommendations from the specialist and how you can best facilitate that implementation. In the case of a need for special education services, be sure to review and follow the procedures that have been mandated.

Program Models

Head Start

Started in 1965 with federal funding, Head Start was and remains a model comprehensive early childhood program. As its name indicates, this preschool program was originated because many children from economically distressed families were not doing well in school. The goal was to counter the effects of poverty for both young children and their families. Head Start emphasizes the whole child, including educational, medical, dental, nutritional, mental health, and family support services (Feeney, Christensen, & Moravcik, 1996) (see Figure 11–3).

Figure 11–3   Components of Head Start Programs

Education—Head Start provides early childhood education through high-quality classroom experiences and regularly scheduled home visits to families.

Health—Head Start programs ensure timely immunizations; health screenings including vision, hearing, dental, and speech and language development; nutritious meals; and nutrition education for families.

Parent Involvement—Head Start empowers parents to be their child's first teacher, achieve leadership skills, join committees, and volunteer in the classroom.

Employment possibilities with Head Start and training and financial support for continued education are additional options for family members.

Social Services—Head Start staff provides services and makes referrals to families that are undergoing crises that may be related to violence, substance abuse, physical or mental health needs, unemployment, and others.

Disabilities—Children with disabilities are included in the early education component. Therapies and services that are needed are coordinated through Head Start.

Family Literacy—Information is shared about general equivalency diplomas, adult basic education, and literacy programs. Parents are encouraged to read daily with their children.

Source: All About Head Start produced by National Head Start Association

---

Head Start hires staff to coordinate all aspects of the program. It is common to see all Head Start staff, including food-service workers and bus drivers, at professional development workshops that focus on child development. Head Start programs not only serve the children and families enrolled in the programs, but also are increasing local human resources in their broader communities by offering job training and by reducing the need for remedial programs and placement in correctional facilities (Lazar & Darlington, 1983; Schweinhart & Weikart, 1980).

Comer Schools

The Comer Schools were instituted in 1968 and led by James Comer in New Haven, Connecticut. Dr. Comer believes that children can learn and succeed only when all of their needs are addressed. Thus, emphasizing the whole child, he implemented successful public school reform in New Haven (Weissbourd, 1996).

Comer Schools attend to healthy child development by placing six "developmental pathways" at the center of the educational process: children's needs related to physical, cognitive, psychological, language, social, and ethical development. Also, rather than assessing children in the standard contemporary way—in relation to academic progress—Comer Schools assess children through the six pathways (Comer School Development Program, 2001).

The philosophical foundation of Comer Schools is based on key assumptions:

1. When families and communities cannot support children's development, children begin school with impairments to their learning ability.

2. All children will be supported and expected to meet high standards that will lead to preparation for modern employment and citizenship.

3. Tracking and lowered expectations for minority and ELL students are denied in the Comer model.

4. All students are entitled to the opportunity to reach their utmost potentials.

5. The six developmental pathways must be considered in order to provide education that leads to academic learning.

6. Educational experiences must be provided so that children can have developmental opportunities that have been lacking in their lives.

7. Schools need families and communities to work in partnership with them in order to achieve these goals (Comer School Development Program, 2001).

This model uses a structure of three teams:

school planning and management—made up of teachers, administrators, support staff, and family members who parent

student and staff support—made up of the principal and staff members with knowledge of child development and mental health (e.g., psychologist, social worker, counselor, and nurse)

parent team—made up of family members (Comer School Development Program, 2001)

The Yale Child Study Center has in place a School Development Program to assist districts that are interested in implementing the Comer model. Essentially, the Comer Schools operate as communities that have been created to support children and their families. Figure 11–6 demonstrates a model of the Comer School Development Program process.

Early Intervention

Programs of **early intervention** are those that are designated for children with special needs or are at risk for developmental disabilities from birth to three years of age (see Figure 11–4). Public law 99–457 requires that comprehensive services be provided for all eligible children. In addition to education for young children with disabilities, a variety of therapies and support services are included for them and their families. Public Law 105–17 (1997 amendments to the Individuals with Disabilities Act) contains information about the evolving nature of legal requirements for early intervention services (Ramey & Ramey, 1998).

> *"Times have changed. We have realized that our old views were too simple and our focus on the child needed to be expanded to include the family and its complex support network. The child-focused recipes have been supplemented or even supplanted by family-centered approaches to service."*
> **—McWilliam and Bailey, 1993**

Current recommended practice in early intervention typically concentrates on four areas.

1. *Family-centered practices*—recognizes the family as central to each child's development

2. *Practices with children*—considers each child's individual needs and strengths, engages children in developmentally appropriate experiences, and uses play as well as incidental experiences in teaching and learning

Figure 11–4   Early Intervention Series—Sample Program

Developmental Delays

Many children risk developmental delays due to premature births, abnormal muscle tone, seizure disorders, hydrocephalus, or other unidentified factors. Early intervention programs have proven to be highly effective with children who have virtually any type of developmental delays.

Benefits of Early Intervention

- enhances the development of infants and toddlers with special needs
- provides a support network for families of children with developmental disabilities
- reduces the effect of developmental disabilities among infants and preschoolers
- lowers cost to society through the reduced need for special education programs in schools

Space Coast Early Intervention Center (SCEIC) Program

The focus of this unique program is an interdisciplinary approach that includes normally developing children in the classroom learning alongside their peers. This interaction allows for role-modeling from peers and prepares the children for the eventual mainstream experience. The team spirit nurtured at SCEIC encourages teachers and therapists to cross boundaries in a cooperative manner using the newest and most developmentally appropriate techniques employed in the field.

Infant Program—Birth to approximately 18 months.

(Holmes Regional Medical Center provides this component of care.) The infant program concentrates on family involvement. The parents receive home programming suggestions from the therapists. These activities are designed to be implemented by the parents during the child's regular daily routine, such as feeding, diapering, or bathing. An occupational therapist and speech/language pathologist provide one to two hours of therapy per week for each child and parent on an individual basis. This training is designed to be continued on a daily basis by the family, striving to influence developmental gains through the home environment.

The families in the infant program receive an Individualized Family Support Plan (IFSP). This plan focuses on the needs and goals of the child and the family. The plan is reviewed and updated on a six-month cycle. Referrals for the infant program come from neonatologists and local area pediatricians.

Therapy is much more effective when parents and other caregivers follow through at home.

Transition Class—18 months to 2 years (provided by SCEIC).

The transition class meets five mornings a week. The class focuses on motor developments, self-feeding skills, and ways to cope with the physical environment.

The teachers, in conjunction with the therapists, aid the children in making choices, developing self-assurance and independence, and improving their language and cognitive skills.

Each family also receives an IFSP. Families, teachers, and therapists review and update each IFSP biannually and redevelop it every year.

Toddler Program—Two years to three years (provided by SCEIC).

The toddlers come to the Center three mornings a week. The program focuses on age-appropriate and developmentally appropriate activities for children to develop cognitive and social skills. This includes gross and fine motor, socialization, communication, cognitive, perceptual, and feeding skills.

An IFSP is also designed and updated for each child.

Preschool Program—Three years to six years (provided by SCEIC).

The preschoolers attend five days a week. The preschool program focuses on pre-reading, pre-writing, and pre-math skills. The staff provides a whole realm of real-life and hands-on experiences that offer the environment to develop pre-readiness skills.

Figure 11–4 *(Continued)*

To accurately assess each child's progress, an Individualized Education Plan (IEP) is designed. Here, too, families, teachers, and therapists review and update this plan biannually.

Mainstreaming—A major difference between SCEIC and other programs is the concentration on mainstreaming and/or inclusion. The Center believes that the more children with special needs are involved with their normally developing peers, the more it enhances their opportunities for learning the social skills necessary to help them be truly accepted.

SCEIC's children are fully integrated and share in activities such as story time, art projects, songs, finger play, snack time, and playground fun. All children are learning to share, take turns, and make friends in a cooperative environment. This approach helps children learn their own teaching skills and gain more self-confidence, which allows them to build a symbiotic relationship in the process. This is an important point, considering many of our children will be mainstreamed into the public schools. Our "typically developing" children learn that being different is acceptable and not something to be afraid of or shamed by.

Interacting with children with special needs and learning to accept them is a valuable experience for all children.

Socialization—Our Center gives the children opportunities for social interaction with members of the community. The children attend shows and concerts, and go to pet stores, restaurants, supermarkets, farms, and other real-life destinations. Regular field trips are essential to the growth and development of our children.

Our children have been invited to attend chamber of commerce events and other civic group meetings. Public awareness is crucial in order for all children to be accepted and valued. If the community has an awareness of what the Center does, and if children with special needs are able to participate in daily life activities, then people at large will be much more accepting.

Family Education & Support—Parent education and support is critical to the families involved at SCEIC.

Mothers, fathers, foster parents, grandparents, and other family support members are viewed as vital to their child's development, as are the teachers and therapists on staff. Parents work with the staff to evaluate their child, set goals and objectives, implement the program to reach these goals, and reassess their child's progress.

SCEIC provides the setting for parental involvement and education through class participation, consultations with staff members, and monthly support meetings where ideas can be shared. Support meetings offer a time for parents to interact with each other as well as with outside presenters and staff members. This networking provides an outlet for discussion of parental concerns specific to the family's needs.

Children deserve a chance to succeed in our society.

We Need Your Help

SCEIC's efforts are made possible through funds received from individuals, organizations, foundations and corporations, as well as tuition and annual fundraising.

More than 80 percent of our budget directly benefits the children and less than 10 percent of our budget comes from state funding. Investments from our community are what allow us to continue our programs.

For more information, call (407) 729-6858.

Space Coast Early Intervention Center

3661 S. Babcock Street, Suite D

Melbourne, FL 32901

(407) 729-6858

http://www.sceic.com

Source: With permission from Space Coast Early Intervention Center

3. *Inclusive practices*—provides opportunities for young children with disabilities to interact and learn with typically developing young children

4. *Collaboration in delivering services*—coordinates an appropriate team of professionals to meet the needs of children and families such as special educators; early childhood educators; pediatricians; social workers; physical, speech, and occupational therapists; psychologists; and others (McWilliam and Bailey, 1993)

In order to emphasize a family-centered approach to early intervention services, a family strengths model has been advocated. The family-strengths approach in early intervention is viewed as being a significantly different way of working with families than has been typical in the recent past. Using this approach, all professionals who provide services to children and families via early intervention programs acknowledge the existing strengths in individual families and attempt to build on those strengths. Professionals build trusting relationships with families so that families can be viewed as partners in the intervention process. In the family-strengths approach, the goal shifts from merely providing families with services to supporting and empowering families as they pursue solutions to whatever problems they are facing (Dunst, Trivette, & Mott, 1994).

When assessing children for early intervention services, it is important to attend to various aspects of functioning that might be related to cultural, ethnic, religious, or language diversity. The United States' diverse population makes it incumbent on professionals to consider the importance of cultural competence for both children and families. The role of families in early intervention may vary, based on diverse views and values of families. Professionals, as they work to build trusting relationships with families, will make note of differences. Respect must be given to both differences in families and the need that children and families have to be culturally competent (Guralnick, 2000).

For early childhood and early intervention practitioners, the issues of quality and efficacy of early intervention programs must be addressed. What are the characteristics of high-quality early intervention programs? And, what factors of early intervention programs make them effective for supporting development of young children with disabilities? Ramey and Ramey (1998) have extensively reviewed the existing research in this area and have subsequently put forth six principles "based on studies of children from economically impoverished families, children with biological risk factors, children with combined psychosocial and biological risks, and children with developmental disabilities diagnosed in infancy" (p. 111). See Figure 11–5 for a listing and descriptions of the six principles.

Preschool Inclusion

Revisions in the Individuals with Disabilities Education Act (PL 105–17, IDEA) mandate that inclusive programs have highest priority for placement of children with special needs. **Preschool inclusion** programs are those classroom settings that enroll children with and without disabilities. Individual programs may describe additional requirements for their philosophies of inclusion so not all inclusive programs look alike. Some of these programs are found in public school systems, but many districts still do not offer preschool classes for typically developing children. Thus, more common places to find instances of preschool inclusion are in Head Start and community-based programs (Odom, 2002).

Successful preschool inclusion programs consider needs of children and families at all levels of

Families are often eager to talk to each other.

Figure 11–5	Six Evidence-Based Principles for Effectiveness in Early Intervention Programs

#1 Developmental timing: When early intervention begins earlier in a child's life and continues for a longer period of time, benefits are generally greater than for those that begin later and are implemented for a shorter period of time.

#2 Program intensity: Those programs that operate the most hours per day, the most days per week, and the most home visits per week have greater positive outcomes than those that programs that provide less intensive services. Further, children and families who participate the most demonstrate the greatest developmental gains.

#3 Direct (vs. intermediary) provision of learning experiences: Direct educational services provided for children with disabilities provide more effective change towards developmental progress than do those programs that provide parent training or training for other intermediaries alone.

#4 Program breadth and flexibility: When early intervention programs provide a larger number of services with a broad focus, children's gains are greater than when programs are simplistic or narrowly focused. Further, programs that incorporate flexibility to meet various needs of children and families are also shown to be more effective than programs providing only a rigid structure.

#5 Individual differences in program benefits: Some children benefit more from early intervention programs than do others, based at least in part on the severity of their disability or risk situation.

#6 Ecological dominion and environmental maintenance of development: Continuing environmental supports are necessary for children to maintain gains achieved through early intervention. These supports are necessary so that children can maintain positive attitudes and behavioral gains.

Source: Ramey & Ramey, 1998

Bronfenbrenner's systems (Odom, 2002). Research with families of children in inclusive programs has shown that the most common concern is that individual children's educational needs are met. As with all high-quality early childhood programs, partnerships between teachers (and other staff) and families is of great importance. Families of young children with disabilities face many decisions in terms of provision of services for their children. When preschool staff share information through frequent clear communication, families are able to make the best decisions for their children (Beckman, Hanson, & Horn, 2002).

Other Models

Other models exist in which teams of professionals from a variety of disciplines collaborate to make joint decisions with families about young children's education and care. Such teams have the advantage of regular meetings to share information and plan incrementally, depending on the needs of the child and family.

Instructional Support Teams One example of an interdisciplinary model is the Pennsylvania model of team planning in public schools. In this model, the Instructional Support Team (IST) members are typically composed of the child's teacher, the building administrator, parents, counselor, and a certified teacher employed as an IST specialist from the school district. Usually, one of the team members expresses a concern about a child's development in some area and a meeting is called. At the meeting, all team members may express their concern or perspective. The team then arrives at a consensus or plan, which is implemented for a thirty-day period. At the end of this period, the team is reconvened to assess and consider further options as needed.

United Way's Focus on Our Future In York County, Pennsylvania, a successful child care initiative has been in place for several years. In 1995, three primary purposes were identified.

1. To focus attention on quality, affordable, available child care as integral to York County's human and economic infrastructure.

2. To assess community needs and develop an action agenda to improve early care and education for children and families.

3. To facilitate linkages among business, government, education, families, and others to move forward with a community action agenda.

After a great deal of study, the United Way's Focus on Our Future defined three goals based on the national "trilemma" regarding child care and strategies for achieving the goals.

Goal 1: Advance high-quality child care programs

- adopt and implement quality standards for York County child care services

- assist child care programs in achieving national accreditation

- provide training to providers for achieving necessary competencies for national accreditation

- develop a model to improve compensation for child care providers

- provide parent education about quality child care

- provide community education about the importance of quality child care

Goal 2: Address the needs of unserved and underserved families seeking child care

- increase the number of affordable quality child care spaces

- provide support for providers to increase the number of spaces for infants and children with developmental disabilities

- study the need for child care beyond traditional workdays

Goal 3: Develop and support public and private efforts to make quality child care affordable

- forge partnerships with public and private entities including churches and businesses

- promote employer participation in family-supportive benefits

- provide funding for tuition assistance for training child care providers

- assist child care providers with cost-effective strategies

- advocate for state and federal policies for expanding subsidized child care and support for early education

In its latest brochure, Focus on Our Future creatively used data from current brain research to compare Pennsylvania's spending on children at various stages. In an effort to get state policy makers to understand the importance of providing funding to early care and education programs, the brochure notes that 85 percent of brain development occurs by age three.

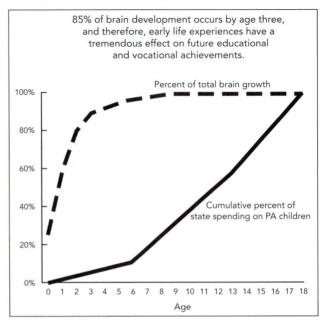

Figure 11–6 Graph Viewing Percent of Total Brain Growth With Cumulative Percent of Pennsylvania State Spending on Children. (Estimates Produced by Pennsylvania Partnerships for Children as Part of the National Association of Child Advocates Children's Budget Watch Project and Reprinted with Permission of the Pennsylvania Partnership for Children)

View the graph above (Figure 11–6) and note the percentage of state spending on young children compared to later years. What's wrong with this picture?

United Way Success By 6 Based on evidence relating to early brain development, the national United Way originated a community-based partnership model to deliver programs offering demonstrated solutions in early development in order to ensure that children from birth to age six years are "healthy, nurtured and ready to succeed" (United Way Success By 6, n.d.). Beginning in Minneapolis in 1988, Success By 6 programs now number more than 350 in the U.S. and Canada. The mission statement for Success By 6 states, "Success By 6 encourages and facilitates collaborations and partnerships to unite our community's businesses, government, service providers, advocates, educators, and families to ensure that our young children are born healthy, remain healthy, nurtured, and ready to successfully enter school by age 6" (United Way Success by 6, n.d.).

Project Even Start   Even Start is a federally funded program with the following components:

- adult literacy (adult basic education or instruction for English language learners)
- parenting education
- early childhood education
- interactive parent and child literacy activities

Even Start supports family literacy services for parents and children, primarily from birth through age seven, and has three related goals:

1. To help parents improve their literacy or basic educational skills
2. To help parents become full partners in educating their children
3. To assist children in reaching their full potential as learners

Interdisciplinary Collaboration

Benefits

The benefits of **interdisciplinary collaboration** as described in the previous sections of this chapter are as follows:

- utilization of specialists to best help children and families
- a consensus-building method in which the team recommends a course of action as well as ways to implement it
- resource availability, including funding, from a variety of sources

Challenges

While the benefits are extremely worthwhile, those who have worked at interdisciplinary collaboration have also met with challenges, some of which follow:

- coordination of a number of people for scheduling
- explanation of procedures and language pertinent to each discipline represented

- conflicting views about goals of education or understanding of how children learn
- a lack of or difficulty reaching a consensus about the best course of action to follow

Family-Centered Interprofessional Collaboration

A human services approach to create partnerships among families and professionals from diverse disciplines such as health, education, and social work is known as family-centered interprofessional collaboration. "Central to the family-centered interprofessional curriculum and practicum experience is the understanding that family empowerment and professional collaboration serve as building blocks to help families . . . beliefs will lead to effective, skilled, and caring family/professional interactions which will change the plight of children and families in the 21st century" (Davidson, Taba, Yamashita, & Ambrose, 1998, p. 3). Work in this interprofessional collaboration actually calls for a new paradigm for preparing human service workers, including early childhood teachers. "It is the teamwork and care that professionals and families offer to one another that enables all to identify, understand, and reach goals that ultimately benefit children and families" (p. 4). Collaborative efforts are quite complex, and it seems that when such a model is used in professional preparation, it is more likely that teachers, health providers, and social workers will implement interprofessional collaboration into their practice. It is likely that the wave of the future will be to include interprofessional collaboration models in early childhood teacher preparation programs.

The following principles are central to family-centered interdisciplinary collaboration (Davidson et al., 1998).

1. Family members and professionals work together to ensure interagency coordination to provide improved services for children and families.
2. Collaborators recognize and respect the knowledge, skills, and experiences that families and all professionals bring to the effort.

3. The development of trust is integral to the collaboration.

4. Open communication is expected so that all feel free to express themselves.

5. All cultural traditions, values, and family diversity are honored.

6. Negotiation is essential to collaboration.

7. The mutual commitment and shared vision of families, professionals, and communities serve children and families.

Collaboration is a drastically different way of providing services to families than existing methods and systems. It will take time before this revolutionary approach can vastly change ways of working with families. But the effort must begin. If early childhood professionals can, early in their teaching preparation, be provided with understanding of and respect for diversity and the realization that families are children's first teachers and primary nurturers, they will be better prepared for their future careers. Understanding families is necessary for early childhood professionals to succeed in the new millennium.

> *"We in business, along with all segments of society, are increasingly aware of the vital significance the earliest years have on childhood development. High quality child care is a key component of a positive experience in those formative years. By supporting high quality child care for children of our employees, York County businesses gain in employee loyalty and help ensure that their children will grow to be constructive members of society."*
>
> **—Louis J. Appell, Jr., President of Susquehanna Pfaltzgraff Co.**

The Business Community

Some businesses have made a commitment to supporting family involvement in children's education. "'Family-friendly' businesses have at least one of the following policies: allowing time for employees to get involved with schools; initiating, implementing, and funding specific programs that promote family involvement in education; and providing resources to employees on how to become more involved in their own children's education" (Strong Families, Strong Schools, 1994, p. 31).

Some employers contribute to family involvement in education by providing their employees with the option of working on *flextime*. Several models for flextime exist: Core hours may be required, usually in the middle of the day, such as between 10:00 a.m. and 2:00 p.m. Employees can then choose to arrive at work early or stay late. Some businesses allow for flextime at lunch, by allowing employees to either extend or shorten the lunch hour, then make up the difference in an agreed-upon manner. Following are other ways that employers support families:

- part-time positions
- job sharing
- alternative work schedules for full- or part-time employees
- flexible policies that allow for employee absences on the first day of school, school holidays, or to attend special events at school
- offering seminars and resources related to parenting and parent involvement in education
- child care options, such as on-site care or vouchers for discounts at the center parents choose (Strong Families, 1994)

Another way that businesses link to education is through direct contributions of money or equipment to schools. Some businesses organize volunteer programs and encourage employees to volunteer in various ways for the schools in their communities. When business, education, and families link their efforts in these and many other ways, communities become more caring and everyone benefits.

Professionalism in Early Childhood Education

Knowledge Base

The basis for professionalism stems from a variety of sources. A major source of professional information in early childhood education can be found in the study of child development. Early childhood educators rely on their understanding of children's development when planning educational programs, building or furnishing environments, and making recommendations to families.

In addition to this child development foundation, early childhood teachers also depend on pedagogical information from the field of early childhood education. Together, the National Association for the Education of Young Children (NAEYC) and the Division of Early Childhood (DEC) of the Council for Exceptional Children (CEC) have created a professional development document for their members (NAEYC, 1994). NAEYC has also developed a statement of professional ethics for those in the early childhood field (NAEYC, April 2005). These can be found in the appendices.

An Ethical Call to Advocacy One of the principles in the above-mentioned Code of Ethical Conduct is related to the early childhood professional's responsibility for participating in child and family advocacy efforts. Advocating for children and families requires both a professional knowledge base and professional commitment. Skills for advocacy work at the local, state, and federal levels have been widely addressed in a variety of sources. To be effective early childhood advocates must know how to contact decision makers and to draw from a knowledge base of child development.

The following ten "Big Ideas" are intended to provide advocates with evidence about children's development (see Figure 11–7).

Big Idea #1. Women's prenatal health is important to a child's optimal development.
Optimal health for babies and children is dependent on pregnant women receiving early and regular prenatal care. When such prenatal care is not available, not affordable, or not accessible, there are great risks for both short-term and long-term physical harm. Healthy maternal nutrition is critical for healthy prenatal development. Existing social programs, especially Women, Infants & Children (WIC) provide healthy foods for pregnant and nursing mothers and their children.

ADVOCACY FACT: Women who receive WIC services have better birth outcomes than their non-WIC peers. Babies are less likely to be born prematurely, mothers are more likely to receive adequate

Figure 11–7	Ten "Big Ideas" for Early Childhood Advocates

1. Women's prenatal health is important to a child's optimal development.
2. Biological and environmental factors influence the process of development.
3. Families are children's first and most important teachers.
4. Experiences in children's daily lives have profound effects on their development.
5. Individual differences in children must be understood.
6. Discrimination for or against any group of children must be avoided.
7. Infancy is a period of rapid growth and development.
8. Contrary to popular opinion, children ages 1–3 years are not "terrible twos", but rather "terrific toddlers".
9. Preschool children must have access to high quality, developmentally effective education.
10. Primary education must be designed to meet the unique development of children of this age.

prenatal care, and infant and fetal mortality rates decrease (Women, Infants & Children Program, Office of Nutrition Services, West Virginia Department of Health and Human Resources, http://www.wvdhhr.org/ons/wic.asp, retrieved January 4, 2004).

Advocacy issues surrounding prenatal care include costs for medical care and insurance, availability and affordability of transportation to medical centers or offices, prescription costs for vitamins or other necessary drugs, and employer leave policies. Obstetrician/gynecologists are medical doctors who provide comprehensive prenatal care that includes educational and social services, as well as medical and nutritional care. It is not uncommon for low-income women to have difficulty accessing the medical system and, thus, to have trouble obtaining good prenatal care. Advocacy for prenatal care must include informational components that help all citizens understand the necessity of good prenatal care, so that *all* children have the opportunity for optimal development.

Other issues include rehabilitation for intervention services related to drug or alcohol abuse. Infants and young children can pay dearly for the mistakes of their mothers. It is critical that rehabilitation for substance abuse be readily available to women who may conceive. Although some people believe that women who abuse drugs or alcohol should be punished rather than rehabilitated, children need their mothers. Opportunities for overcoming addiction is a benefit to both mothers and children. Rehabilitation services are needed in all areas of the country, urban and rural.

Big Idea #2. Biological and environmental factors influence the process of development.

A child's development is influenced by many factors, both biological and environmental. Most child development experts now believe that nature (biology) and nurture (environment) each have nearly equal bearing in developmental outcomes for children. However, it is not accurate to assume that a child is, in effect, "half nature and half nurture." A better understanding of this concept informs us that nature and nurture continually interact with each other in the process of development. For example, children who are born with disabilities identified at birth, such as Down syndrome or spina bifida, achieve greater developmental progress when early intervention programs and appropriate medical care are available and accessible. The interaction of nature and nurture is obvious when early educational programs and medical care contribute to the child's development and increasing abilities.

The most crucial area for advocacy efforts related to this principle of development is the availability and accessibility of early intervention services for infants who are born with identified disabilities. Some types of disabilities, such as ADHD and language delays, cannot be identified until children are a little older. Even then, early intervention is more effective than later intervention. Children who do not receive professional assistance with a language delay often are frustrated and act out, leading to behavioral difficulties. However, when children get therapeutic support as soon as possible, the environmental efforts

contribute to early successes and more optimal long-term outcomes.

"Well-designed, well-funded early interventions can have large and significant effects on school readiness and subsequent child outcomes."

—Janet Curie

Big Idea #3. Families are children's first and most important teachers.

When those who are parenting receive support from extended family or community sources, they are better able to provide for children, economically as well as socially. While it is true that "it takes a village to raise a child," it is children's families who most often connect them to the village.

The bond that exists between infants or young children and their primary caregivers (usually parents) is known as attachment. Many child development experts believe that this bond has both a biological and a social component. It is this powerful bond that leads to the critical relationship that exists between caregiver and child. Strong bonds between parents and their children lead to families being early and influential teachers. Thus, in order for children to develop physically, cognitively (intellectually), socially and emotionally (including morally), parents need to have experienced healthy relationships in their own families and communities. These relationships offer various forms of support to young parents, including child care, financial assistance, moral support, and social networks.

Head Start is based on the premise that families are children's first and most important teachers. This comprehensive early childhood education program founded in 1965 has family involvement at the heart of all of its components. In addition to providing high quality preschool education for children of low-income families, various programs are also provided to support family involvement in children's education.

One area of advocacy related to this principle of child development is that all families need support. When families have not been able to create these sources of support within their own families or communities, family support programs can be very helpful. Such programs often provide educational programs for parents and for children, as well as preventive medical care for all family members. Other programs may offer financial assistance with home heating bills or other necessities. Advocating for increased funding for Head Start programs is essential for continuing the work of this highly successful early intervention program.

> *"If we truly care for our children, we must cherish their parents."*
>
> **—John Bowlby**

Big Idea #4. Experiences in children's daily lives have profound effects on their development. Child care, whether within or outside of the family, must be of high quality in order to best support each child's optimal development. Many adults admit to a lack of awareness of the effects that high-quality or low-quality child care programs have on young children. Even when families are providing their children with all possible nurturing and socialization experiences, it is still critical that children's daily experiences outside the home also consider all of the children's needs. More than 80 percent of children four years of age and younger spend at least part of their day in nonparental care. When this care is not high quality, it negatively affects children's development. Research has shown that high-quality child care programs have good adult-child ratios, small group size, well-qualified teachers, developmentally effective curricula and assessment, as well as support for family involvement. Good care leads to increases in children's cognitive and language development, as well as more positive social interactions with peers and adults.

In poor-quality care, staff turnover is often high and this reduces caregiving consistency for children. Teachers are not well trained, children are expected to behave in ways that are not developmentally appropriate and family involvement is not encouraged. Such programs can lead to negative effects on children, including behavioral issues and less progress in cognition and language development.

Advocacy for high quality child care continues to be a high priority. In many cases, tuition or fees paid by parents must pay for all the costs of child care. This often means that four years of child care can cost as much as four years of college. Many families with young children do not have economic resources to afford the high quality care that all children deserve.

ADVOCACY FACT: The most important aspect of quality early childhood education is the nature of the interaction between teacher and child. Professional development for early childhood teachers must emphasize this.

Children who are victims of maltreatment, whether it is abuse, neglect, or both, suffer long-term negative consequences from such experiences. Even very young children may express anger through aggression towards other children and adults, angry outbursts, and engaging in destructive behaviors. Children who have been abused have great difficulty in relating to others. Advocates must work toward preventing child abuse and neglect. Parenting education and quality early education for children can help to reduce the rates of child abuse. But, when children have been abused or neglected, it is crucial that intervention strategies consider support for both children and parents. Any suspected case of child abuse can be reported to the State Department of Human Services. Most states have hotline numbers specifically for reporting suspected child abuse.

Big Idea #5. Individual differences in children must be understood. Even though children go through similar stages of development, they do so at different rates with individually different qualities. Biological factors in a child's individual makeup must be addressed in order to best meet every child's needs. Some of these factors are related to a child's personality and interests; some to body shape, size, and ability; and some to a child's thinking and learning capabilities. Although biological factors must be considered as we understand children's individual differences, supportive environments may decrease what are believed to be a child's limitations. On the other hand, negative environments may hinder even children possessing biological "gifts."

Parents, teachers, and other adults who work with young children must have information about individual differences so that all children feel accepted for who they are. This acceptance is necessary for development of healthy self-esteem. Children's accomplishments should be recognized, whether or not they are part of the adult's value system. For example, a family that holds athletics in high regard must acknowledge a child's musical talent as being as valuable as athletic ability. Teachers must openly value the strengths of all children and provide opportunities for all children to build on their existing strengths and to try new challenges.

Advocacy in this arena is related to understanding social and emotional development of children. At the same time that we value the importance of early literacy and numeracy initiatives, we must also know how to support children's sense of self-worth. Advocating for parenting education, teacher education, and staff development to include applications for social and emotional development will lead to a greater emphasis on the whole child.

> *"Thinking about children as individuals enables adults to adapt programs and strategies appropriately and to be responsive to the variations that exist among children."*
>
> **—Sue Bredekamp and Carol Copple**

Big Idea #6. Discrimination for or against any group of children must be avoided. All children deserve to have their needs met, regardless of ability, gender, family structure, socioeconomic status, religious affiliation, race, ethnicity, geographic location, or culture. Children who, in any way, are not in a majority group in the United States, risk discriminatory policies and oppressive conditions. Thus, advocates for children should be prepared to lobby against discrimination.

> *"If we are to reach real peace in the world, we have to begin with children."*
>
> **—Gandhi**

When people are oppressed by others in society, the negative effects are infinite. Although many people prefer to deny the negative effects of discrimination, this is not helpful to children and families who are members of ethnic minority groups in the United States and who suffer from these effects. If we are to celebrate any progress that has been made in the area of civil rights, we must also look to what remains to be accomplished in terms of creating fairness for all citizens. The very presence of discriminatory practices in our society often leads to a double disadvantage of being both oppressed and poor.

Babies born into poverty are prone to negative consequences in all areas of their development. They are less likely to receive good nutrition and medical care than other children, thus impeding their optimal physical development. They often live in areas where schools and community services have a lower tax base, thus are poorly funded. Often times, parents in low-socioeconomic families are overburdened by the number of hours they must work and have little time or energy to foster positive relationships with their young children.

Families living in poverty are often stereotyped as being lazy or shiftless. This often is not the case, however, and advocates must understand the ways that societal economics affects individuals and families. As the national economy has evolved, many "blue-collar" jobs that paid a sustainable wage have been lost. Further, as the number of households headed by women have increased, household income has decreased, because traditionally female jobs tend to pay less. And, for the past thirty years, a reduction of government benefits to poor families has increased the risk that these families will not have access to health care and other necessities for their children.

ADVOCACY FACT: The United States has the world's second highest rate of children living in poverty—22.4 percent (America's Babies: The ZERO TO THREE Policy Center Data Book Notable Facts).

The remaining four topics relate to specific time periods in children's development. At each period throughout childhood, children have specific needs that *must* be met. Drs. T. Berry Brazelton and Stanley Greenspan refer to these needs as *irreducible,* meaning absolute. Developmental time periods are: infancy, toddlerhood, preschool, and school-age. *Children can't wait.*

> *"Many things can wait. Children cannot. Today their bones are being formed, their blood is being made, and their senses are being developed. To them we cannot say tomorrow. Their name is today."*
>
> **—Gabriela Mistral, Chilean poet**

Big Idea #7. Infancy (birth–one year) is a period of rapid growth and development. Infants need nutritionally sound diets for their developing bodies. This involves both a financial issue with the costs of foods for the infant (and the family) but also education of the caregivers about what types of foods are most beneficial for the baby. Information detailing the positive effects from breastfeeding must be shared as well.

> *"There is no finer investment for any country than putting milk into babies."*
>
> **—Winston Churchill**

Babies' brains grow very rapidly. Current research about brain development during the first year of life points to the importance of early experiences: All infant experiences can impact brain growth, either positively or negatively. Nurturing environments with responsive caregivers increase a baby's neural connections and eventually lead to a child's more positive behavior. On the other hand, environmental deprivation can decrease brain activity and later lead to less appropriate behavior in children. Infants learn through all five senses and benefit from many things to look at, touch, smell, taste, and hear. Because so much learning and growth takes place in this first year of life, child advocates must work for parenting education and high-quality out-of-home care for infants.

In order to reach optimal levels of development, infants must form healthy attachments with their parents and other primary caregivers. In order to form such bonds, babies need responsive caregiving from consistent adults. Early attachment leads to an ability to trust caregivers and is the foundation for good mental health throughout life. Again, working for more opportunities for parenting education as well as good out of home child care will increase the likelihood that all infants will have opportunities to form attachments.

Big Idea #8. Contrary to popular opinion, children ages one to three years are not "terrible twos," but, rather, "terrific toddlers." Toddlers need many of the same things that infants do: good nutrition and medical care, responsive caregiving and an interesting, stimulating environment. However, this exciting period is frequently misunderstood by adults who may be challenged by the rapid development that occurs from one to three years of age. Children of this age have gone from being completely dependent on adults to wanting to be able to do things for themselves. And, oh, they can do so many things: walk, talk, feed themselves, take their own clothes off, sometimes put their clothes on, and play.

Brain development continues to be rapid during this stage. At birth, the brain is 25 percent of its adult weight and by the second birthday, it is 75 percent of its adult weight. Play is a critically important contributor to development during this time—as a matter of fact, toddlers learn best as they play. A little before the age of two, most children begin to pretend, so toddlers need many opportunities to play with a variety of toys and objects. Pretend play should be fostered by adults because it is now known to be an important marker for intellectual development.

Caregivers should allow plenty of time to play and also begin to set reasonable limits on the child's behavior. Toddlers need many reminders about what is correct and appropriate behavior; they are, after all, just learning about expected behaviors. It is important to foster competence at this age by supporting the child's developing skills. Even though some adults want to overprotect or pamper one- and two-year-old children, toddlers interpret such intent as doubt about their abilities and may begin to doubt themselves. All of this can lead to a negative sense of self-esteem. Limit setting may not be well received by toddlers, but it is important to teaching toddlers how to get along with others. Obviously, it is essential to set limits that prevent children from hurting themselves or others. Reminders and redirecting behaviors are generally more effective than punishment at this age. Because young children think differently than adults do, they are unable to connect the consequence that adults see as "logical" with the mistaken behavior.

Advocacy efforts for this stage of development should continue to emphasize health and nutrition, parenting education, and quality outside of home care. Child caregivers who work with children this age need to have specialized training to understand this unique period of development.

ADVOCACY FACT: 39 percent of children from birth through three years are in child care thirty-five or more hours per week (America's Babies: The ZERO TO THREE Policy Center Data Book; Notable Facts).

Big Idea #9. Preschool children (3–6 years) must have access to high-quality, developmentally effective education.

Preschoolers continue to need good medical care and nutrition. Even though brain growth and all types of development are a little less rapid during these years, children still flourish in positive, nurturing environments.

Play remains a crucial activity for children this age. This is actually the age when play is truly a child's work. Safe environments and nurturing adults are prerequisite for children's play. Encouragement and opportunity should be provided for pretend play with other children. High-quality educational programs for children in preschool and kindergarten have play at the center of the curriculum. Excellent early childhood teachers use play as an instructional strategy. Research evidence that links pretend play with early literacy development supports an emphasis on play.

Child care settings, whether in centers or family homes, must be high quality if children are to reach their full potentials. Because welfare reform now requires that low income mothers must work or be in a job training program it is important that all available child care be safe, affordable, and developmentally appropriate for all children. Unfortunately, the United States does not have federal consistent regulation that guarantees safe, affordable, and age-appropriate care for children in out-of-home settings nationwide. Instead, each state legislates its own regulations. The advocacy issues surrounding this issue include increased funding to support quality child care for low-income families and to increase family leave benefits for working parents.

ADVOCACY FACT: 30 percent of preschool children in the U.S. are cared for in child care centers (Casper, 1997).

Most states now partially support preschool programs through public education funding. Advocates must emphasize that an understanding of preschool child development must drive the curriculum in such programs. Teachers must be specially prepared in early childhood education. Family involvement must be a high priority in these programs. Only about one-half of all states include a requirement that family involvement topics be included in teacher preparation programs.

> *"Every facet of early learning programs and practices is interrelated with parent and family dynamics . . . . Above all else, families can validate and strengthen schools in ways that enhance the status and functioning of teachers, staff and children alike."*
> —Kevin Swick, 2003

Some children with special needs or disabilities are identified at birth. Many children, though, have needs that are not readily observable. As they begin to spend more time away from their homes in child care, preschool, or kindergarten, teachers or other professionals may observe and refer such children for assessment and additional educational support. According to federal law, all children with disabilities are eligible for early childhood special education. Advocates should lobby for all preschool children with special needs to have access to inclusive education programs. Teachers should be well versed in both early childhood and special education; some states offer specific state certification to early childhood special education teachers.

Federal legislation related to these topics that has been enacted includes: Temporary Assistance for Needy Families (TANF), the Child Care Development Block Grant (CCDBG), and the Individuals with Disabilities Education Act (IDEA). All of these laws require regular reauthorization and are often threatened with reductions.

Big Idea #10. Primary education (6–8 years) must be designed to meet the unique development of children of this age.

These young children also need continuous medical care and good nutrition. Currently, in the United States, childhood obesity has been declared an epidemic. Children who are obese at this age are at risk for diabetes and heart disease at increasingly younger ages. Obesity is being blamed on several factors: fast food that is high in fat calories, media and computer games that require little activity, and families who are so busy that they are serving their children greater amounts of fast food. Because this is a societal problem and because children this age cannot regulate their own healthy nutrition, the responsibility of solving this situation falls on all of us. Families must have access to adequate information about healthy nutrition, including healthy choices that can be made even at fast-food restaurants. Schools must examine their breakfast and lunch menus, and, maybe more importantly, consider eliminating soda and sweets from vending machines and celebrations and replacing them with juice, fruits, and vegetables. Further, schools can be very helpful in regard to increasing children's activity levels through physical education, recess, and active outdoor learning experiences.

Early childhood is a unique period in human development and, therefore, requires unique educational experiences. Young children think differently than older children, and this should be reflected in kindergarten and primary grade (first through third) classrooms. Those experiences include having teachers who are specially prepared in early childhood education; safe, active learning environments; language-rich curricula; and support for high levels of family involvement.

Many families use community services for before and/or after school care for their primary age children. Even though children may spend relatively little time in these settings, the quality of this care is important for healthy child development. Young children experience stress as they transition from one setting to another. When staff in before- and after-school programs collaborate with families and schools, children's needs can be met. Choices for children should include homework help, nutritious snacks, active play (inside and/or outside), and opportunities to interact with friends. It is important to have well-trained staff and a curriculum that is planned with individual children in mind.

Most children with disabilities are now being placed in inclusive classrooms in public schools. It is important that all professionals involved in programs of inclusion have training and support to best meet the needs of all children. Too often, school districts do not have adequate funding for all children with identified disabilities. Some teachers feel that they are not encouraged to make referrals for kindergarten children due to such lack of resources in local districts. Advocates can advance the need for greater funding from state and federal governments so that all mandates from these entities are financially supported.

ADVOCACY FACT: Recommended class size for first, second, and third grades is 15–18 children (National Association for the Education of Young Children).

Continuing Professional Development

Professional standards and **professional ethics** are necessary in early childhood education because of the potential for abuse, neglect, or mistreatment of the very young children who are given by their families into the care of others. Without such standards, programs and teachers would be left to their own authority as the source of appropriate behavior. Professional conduct must ultimately be embodied in the teacher, caregiver, or administrator, but that does not mean that each early childhood staff member is to create his own standards with each incident or situation.

By using professional standards and ethics, early childhood teachers are able to engage in the best known practices. It is through such a professional community that highest standards can be continuously defined and revised in the best interest of

Children reap the benefits when parents or other family members read to them each day.

children and their families. Such a professional community is a source of support and guidance for practicing early childhood teachers. According to the systems approach, teachers of young children benefit from such support. In turn, children and families benefit from the work of the early childhood professional community.

> *"It is everyone's responsibility to be committed to education. And it shouldn't be limited to parents—anyone in the community should be encouraged to think of the local school as 'their' school and should seek active participation in what goes on there."*
>
> —Lois Jean White, 1998 National PTA president

The Movement to Leave No Child Behind

Under the leadership of Marian Wright Edelman, the Children's Defense Fund has initiated a public awareness campaign. Leave No Child Behind attempts to create a climate that encourages action by policy makers on children's agenda. Included in the agenda are the following issues:

- child care and Head Start
- education
- family education
- nutrition
- housing
- child welfare
- gun safety

For more information about the status of this initiative, go to http://www.childrensdefense.org/.

Summary and Conclusions

Early childhood educators must form partnerships, not only with families, but also with members of the larger community. Connections among early childhood program professionals, agency personnel, and the business community serve to increase support and services to young children and their families. The support of the entire community for high-quality early childhood education encourages excellence.

Moving beyond home and school partnerships, relationships with the community are needed to provide a caring society for children and families. Knowledge about community resources is essential as early childhood educators attempt to meet the needs of all children and families in their care. Since its inception, early intervention for young children with identified disabilities has used a collaborative model.

Collaborative efforts between education and business have shown to be extremely beneficial to children, families, education, and the community. Although often seen as challenging work, collaboration often leads to positive results for all entities. Educational programs often become more effective with the deep knowledge that is gained when teachers work with other community members. Families, schools, and communities, working together for young children, can support and nurture each other.

Chapter 11 Applications

1. Role-play a conference with family members whose children have demonstrated the following behavior in the early childhood education program:

   a. nearly always choosing to play alone

   b. increasingly aggressive behaviors with peers

   c. frequent negative moods

2. List and describe all of the components of the comprehensive early childhood education program Head Start. What do you see as the benefits to children and families enrolled in this type of program?

3. Explain why early childhood teachers should not label children or guess at a diagnosis.

Questions for Reflection and Discussion

1. What concerns would you have about meeting with family members to discuss referring their child for special services? What are the benefits of such referrals?

2. What are the characteristics of a professional in early childhood education?

3. List and discuss benefits and potential conflicts in collaborative efforts.

Field Assignments

1. Visit a Head Start or early intervention program. If possible, ask about the role community members and community agencies play in the program. What agency sponsors the program? Are any volunteers involved?

2. Collect information about resources available in your community (or the one in which you plan to teach) that would be helpful to families of young children.

Layla 3. Interview an early childhood teacher about his involvement in any interdisciplinary collaboration. Ask about the challenges and the benefits of such work.

References

Abbott, C. F., & Gold, S. (1991). Conferring with parents when you're concerned that their child needs special services. *Young Children, 46* (4), 10–14.

Beckman, P. J., Hanson, M. J., & Horn, E. (2002). Family perceptions of inclusion. In S. L. Odom (Ed.), *Widening the circle: Including children with disabilities in preschool programs.* New York: Teachers College Press.

Casper, L. M. (1997). Who's minding our preschoolers? *Current Population Report*s (P70–62). Washington, DC: Bureau of the Census.

Comer School Development Program. (2001). About Comer SDP. http://info.med.yale.edu/comer/about/overview.html. Retrieved January 26, 2006.

Currie, J. What we know about early childhood interventions. Joint Center for Poverty Research, JCPR Policy Briefs, 2 (10). http://www.jcpr.org/policybriefs/vol2num10.html. Retrieved January 4, 2004.

Davidson, D., Taba, S., Yamashita, L., & Ambrose, A. (1998). *Bridging out: Lessons learned in family-centered interprofessional collaboration.* Honolulu: Health and Education Collaboration Project, Hawaii Medical Association.

Dunst, C. J., Trivette, C. M., & Mott, D. W. (1994). Strengths-based family-centered intervention practices. In C. J. Dunst, C. M. Trivette, & A. G. Deal (Eds.), *Supporting and strengthening families* (vol. 1): *Methods, strategies and practices.* Cambridge, MA: Brookline.

Feeney, S., Christensen, D., & Moravcik, E. (1996). *Who am I in the lives of children?* Englewood Cliffs, NJ: Prentice Hall.

Guidelines for preparation of early childhood professionals. (1996). Washington, DC: National Association for the Education of Young Children.

Guralnick, M. J. (2000). Interdisciplinary team assessment for young children: Purposes and processes. In M. J. Guralnick (Ed.), *Interdisciplinary clinical assessment of young children with developmental disabilities.* Baltimore: Paul H. Brookes Publishing Co.

Lazar, I., & Darlington, R. (1983). *As the twig is bent: Lasting effects of preschool programs.* Hillsdale, NJ: Lawrence Erlbaum Associates.

Massinga, R. (1994). Transforming social services: Family-supportive strategies. In S. L. Kagan & B. Weissbourd (Eds.), *Putting families first: America's family support movement and the challenge of change.* San Francisco: Jossey-Bass.

McWilliam, P. J., & Bailey, D. B., Jr. (1993). *Working together with children & families: Case studies in early intervention.* Baltimore: Paul H. Brookes Publishing Co.

National Association for the Education of Young Children. (April 2005). Code of ethical conduct and statement of commitment. http://www.naeyc.org/about/position/PSETH05.asp. Retrieved June 17, 2006.

National Association for the Education of Young Children. (April 2005). Code of ethical conduct and statement of commitment. http://www.naeyc.org/about/position/PSETH05.asp. Retrieved June 17, 2006.

National Association for the Education of Young Children (1994). *Personnel standards for early education and early intervention: A position statement of the Association of Teacher Educators, the Division for Early Childhood and the National Association of the Education of Young Children.* Washington, DC: Author.

Odom, S. L. (2002). Learning about the barriers to and facilitators of inclusion for young children with disabilities. In S. L. Odom (Ed.), *Widening the Circle: Including children with disabilities in preschool programs.* New York: Teachers College Press.

Ramey, C. T., & Ramey, S. L. (February 1998). Early inter-vention and early experience. *American Psychologist (53)* 2, 109–120.

Ready schools. (February 1998). Washington, DC: National Education Goals Panel.

Schweinhart, L. J., & Weikart, D. P. (1980). *Young children grow up: The effects of the Perry Preschool on youth through age 15.* Ypsilanti, MI: High/Scope Foundation.

Search Institute. (2000). http://www.search-institute.org.

Stephens, K. (September/October 1994). Aiding families with referrals. *First Teacher,* 34–35.

Strong Families, Strong Schools. (1994). Washington, DC: U.S. Department of Education.

Swick, K. (2003). Working with families of young children. In J. P. Isenberg and M. R. Jalongo (Eds.), *Major trends and issues in early childhood education* (pp. 69–79). New York: Teachers College Press.

United Way Success By 6. (n.d.). Success By 6. http://www.uwbg.org/initiatives/successbysix. Retrieved January 26, 2006.

Washington, V., Johnson, V., & McCracken, J. B. (1995). *Grassroots success! Preparing schools and families for each other.* Washington, DC: National Association for the Education of Young Children.

Weissbourd, R. (1996). *The vulnerable child.* New York: Addison-Wesley.

Women, Infants & Children Program, Office of Nutrition Services, West Virginia Department of Health and Human Resources. http://www.wvdhhr.org/ons/wic.asp. Retrieved January 4, 2004.

CASE STUDIES

The following seven case studies are intended to be used in a variety of ways by the instructor and students using this textbook. The authors believe that they provide some situational dilemmas commonly experienced by many early childhood teachers. They can be used for a one-time discussion or repeated as greater knowledge, skills, and experience lead to greater depth of understanding by students.

Supporting Families in Infant Care Programs

The Teacher

Tricia Clooney graduated two years ago with a bachelor's degree in elementary and early childhood education. She is certified in her state to teach prekindergarten through the eighth grade. In her senior year of college, Tricia was assigned to an infant center for her preprimary field experience. This practicum was a turning point for Tricia, in that now she knew just the age group with which she wanted to work. Being outgoing and independent, Tricia enjoyed the flexible child care environment with some routine and new challenges everyday. She not only enjoyed the infants but also found that she was very competent at working with families.

The Early Childhood Program and the Community

Soon after graduation, Tricia was hired as one of three infant teachers at Grasshopper Hill Child Care Center. She was thrilled. The director, who received her degree in elementary education eight years prior, oversees sixty children and twelve staff members, some of them part time. She has been directing this center for five years; before that, she worked for two years as a kindergarten teacher in another center. Although some of the other teachers in the center have professional preparation as early child-hood teachers, Tricia's two colleagues in the infant room, Lil and Roxie, have high school diplomas and regularly attend required training sessions. Roxie is the veteran teacher in this group, with five years' experience with infants at this center. Lil started working in this room just three months before Tricia was hired.

Grasshopper Hill Child Care Center is located in a rural area of southern Indiana. Most of the families who enroll their children at this center are employed in the nearby town of Summitsville. Major employers in Summitsville include a hospital, mall stores, public schools, a textile factory, and several restaurants.

Tricia's Dilemma

Tricia began her work at the center with very high hopes. She carefully studied about developmentally appropriate practices during her early childhood teacher preparation. Understanding the importance of an infant's environment and the necessity of interacting with babies as they are cared for, Tricia approached her work very seriously and enthusiastically. Some of the staff who had been there for a while expected that as Tricia "got her feet wet," her enthusiasm would decline and she would treat her work as a job, not as a calling. Two years later, Tricia is still enthusiastic and serious about caring for infants. At times, Lil has been known to roll her eyes as Tricia shares the latest information about brain development during a child's first three years. Roxie, though, listens and asks questions. Together, Tricia and Roxie work to implement best practices; Lil does her job caring for babies, completing necessary paperwork and interacting with parents as necessary. Having just completed a graduate course that included information about the family support movement, Tricia was eager to add to the center's existing family involvement plan. She had many ideas and lots of energy to work on them.

Tricia discussed with the director the possibility of creating a family resource room in a small storage area that was no longer used by staff. Additionally, she wanted to incorporate both family social events and programs for parent education at Grasshopper Hill. Lil finally spoke up: "How can we give the best care to babies and do all that work required for your family involvement ideas? I think that we'll begin to forget that the babies need us. Some of our babies' families don't even have time for them as it is. We need to pay attention to these babies, not to their parents. That's not our job." Even though Roxie found Tricia's ideas to be interesting, she had to admit that she wasn't sure when they would find the time in their very busy days to do even more. And she had to admit that she liked this job because of the babies; she wasn't sure that she enjoyed working with adult members of their families.

Tricia's Reaction

Although not completely surprised by Lil's and Roxie's concerns, Tricia was disappointed that they did not seem to want to try to provide more support for families at Grasshopper Hill. Tricia empathized with the moms, dads, and grandparents who sometimes seemed to feel guilty as they dropped off their infants, and most often seemed exhausted when they picked them up after the day's work. Tricia sometimes helped her sister, who is a young professional and the single parent of a toddler; she knew firsthand the challenges that working parents face because they want to provide the best care possible for their young children.

Tricia responded to Lil's comments from her own life experiences. She noted that life is difficult for parents as they try to balance their work and family obligations. Lil also responded from her life experiences: "Parents today want it all. They aren't willing to do without new homes, new cars, and vacations. They let us raise their children because they can't be bothered." These comments did surprise Tricia. She had not realized how different her viewpoint about families was from Lil's.

Tricia had permission from the director to set up a parent resource room and to begin to plan for family events at the center. She intended to conduct a needs assessment of families who had children enrolled in the infant and toddler rooms at Grasshopper Hill. Lil informed Tricia that she was not willing to work on her own time to help with any of these events. Roxie was torn; she did not feel as though she could use her personal time to work on family involvement, but she might be able to help during work hours. Lil warned both Tricia and Roxie that caring for the babies was what they were hired to do.

Questions for Reflection and Discussion

1. Explain the perspective of each of the three teachers: Tricia, Lil, and Roxie. With which do you most identify?

2. Discuss your life experiences that may affect the perspective you take in this situation.

3. Using information from this textbook, explain how incorporating family support programs with early childhood education may benefit families, schools, and communities.

Challenges of Increasing Family Involvement

The Teacher

Amy Gottleib completed her bachelor's degree in early childhood education. She was an honor student all through high school, and she received some criticism from the guidance counselor as well as some of her teachers when she shared her dream of teaching young children. "You're too smart for that," they commented. Her parents and siblings all had graduate degrees and worked as professionals in a variety of fields including engineering and business. However, they supported her desire to teach. During her student teaching experiences, Amy was all the more encouraged to teach in one of the primary grades. She loved being in the classroom with first and second graders. Her cooperating teachers and university supervisors were impressed with Amy's seemingly natural rapport with these young children.

In Amy's teacher preparation program, an emphasis was placed on the importance of family involvement. Many strategies were included for ways to involve families in their children's education. Research was shared that pointed to the importance of family involvement for children's academic success.

The Early Childhood Program and the Community

After graduation in December, Amy was a popular substitute teacher in her home school district. She was called nearly every day before the winter break. At the end of the month, a principal called to ask her to serve as a long-term substitute for a second-grade teacher. She immediately agreed to take this position, even though this school served mostly children from upper-middle-class families. Amy's preference had always been teaching children from less privileged backgrounds because she felt they needed her more than others did.

The South Shore School District is made up of a large area, some of it rural and some of it suburban. Since children attend neighborhood schools in this district, school populations tend to be economically homogeneous. The elementary schools have kindergarten through fifth grades. The school in which Amy is employed, Golden Oaks, has three classrooms of each grade and a fairly traditional approach to education. Many teachers have been employed at this school for twenty or more years. They have a reputation for high expectations and no nonsense. The principal, Mr. Brooks, is in his first year as principal after teaching seventh grade in a neighboring district for five years. Amy, now called Ms. Gottleib, is stepping into a second-grade class that had been taught by Ms. Nan Notting. Ms. Notting had taught for thirty years; she was known as an effective teacher who was firm with children and held high standards.

Family Involvement Traditions at Golden Oaks

Golden Oaks Elementary School has a history of a strong Parent Teacher Association group. The primary function of this group has been fund-raising. The money this group has raised has been used to purchase computers and other technology, as well as to provide for more field trips than the district can financially support. In addition to fund-raising, parents have assisted with holiday parties and other events when teachers felt a need for more adult supervision. Essentially, family involvement at Golden Oaks has centered on parents, especially mothers, supporting teachers and curriculum. Most often, parents initiated the carrying out of this function, not school personnel.

Ms. Gottlieb's Approach

Amy spent a great deal of time planning for and reflecting about her new position before her actual beginning day, January 4. Amy had carefully written lesson plans for the entire first week of school. She had spent time in the classroom arranging the environment and getting acquainted with curriculum materials that were available to her. Amy implemented a hands-on program with several learning centers. She interacted frequently with the large group, as well as small groups and individual children. She greeted the children in the morning and said good-bye to them at dismissal. Her rapport was excellent. The children liked her and were eager to do their work. Ms. Gottleib challenged her students with projects and supported their interests.

Additionally, Amy drafted a letter to family members, introducing herself and inviting them to participate in the classroom in several different ways. She enclosed an interest survey for parents to complete and sent the letter and survey home with the children on her first day.

By the end of the week, Amy had received only four of the twenty-two interest surveys she sent to parents. She was surprised and concerned about this, but she was also very busy with other teaching responsibilities. Over the weekend, she decided that she would send a reminder home to the parents on Monday.

Some Reactions to Amy's Ideas

On Tuesday morning, Amy received three completed family interest surveys and a note from an unhappy mother regarding the survey. The note read, "Ms. Gottleib, I don't understand the reason for this survey. You are the teacher. Ms. Notting did all of the teaching without parental assistance. I hope that you are capable of teaching our children at Golden Oaks. Sincerely, Gloria Noteworthy." At the end of the day, Mr. Brooks called Amy into his office. After some polite conversation, he asked her how things were going. Although she was feeling a little disconcerted about Gloria Noteworthy's comments, she shared her enthusiasm for teaching the second graders. Mr. Brooks gave some positive feedback he had heard from some other teachers about Ms. Gottleib's attitude. Then he shared with her that Ms. Noteworthy had complained to him about the parent interest survey. She also told him that she had phoned three mothers who had children in the same class and that they all resented receiving this survey from the "new teacher."

Amy's Reaction

Now, Amy was really stunned. It had not occurred to her that inviting parents to participate in their children's education could be seen in any negative way. She absolutely believed that children had more success when teachers formed partnerships with family members. She sent the interest survey for the sole purpose of being the best teacher she could be. It was a surprise to her that a parent would interpret this letter and survey as her inability to teach their children. She was hurt, confused, and a little less confident in herself after this situation.

Questions for Reflection and Discussion

1. Explain the perspectives of Ms. Gottleib, Ms. Notting, Ms. Noteworthy, and Mr. Brooks. With which do you most identify?

2. Discuss your life experiences that may have influenced the way you think about this scenario.

3. Using information from your textbook, discuss why inviting family involvement and collecting information about the interests of family members are often useful strategies for early childhood teachers.

Helping Family Members and Staff to Understand Developmentally Appropriate Practice

The Teacher

Rick Ramirez completed requirements for a state teaching certificate in early childhood education. He had returned to college after working for three years in accounting. Rick received a bachelor's degree in business, and after some experience, decided that he really wanted to teach. He had always appreciated the special characteristics of young children but never really considered a career in education. He and his wife have a four-year-old daughter and a six-month-old son. Spending time with his own children influenced his decision to become certified in early childhood education.

Rick excelled in and enjoyed his student teaching experiences. He was placed with a kindergarten teacher, Sally Aysse, who loved her job. Together, they planned and implemented a full-day program based on developmentally appropriate practices. The children learned as they played. The classroom had many print materials and appropriate software for use by the children. Children made choices regarding learning centers and projects. Rick was aware of how effective this active learning environment was for young children.

Ms. Aysse and Mr. Ramirez collected work samples and provided portfolios to share children's progress with their family members. Parents frequently volunteered in the classroom and the teachers had frequent interaction with nearly every family. Having this experience as well as other field experiences associated with his early childhood education coursework, Rick was confident and believed that he was well prepared to teach young children.

The Early Childhood Program and the Community

Rick interviewed for a kindergarten position with a private school, Harmony Academy, in the city of Harmony. The school was well established in this urban setting, providing education for children from kindergarten through twelfth grade for nearly fifty years. Rick felt that he had interviewed well with the principal. Members of the board, including parents and community professionals, also interviewed all prospective teachers for Harmony Academy. Although that proved to be a challenge, Rick thought that he had demonstrated what he knew about teaching young children as best he could.

Three weeks passed before the principal phoned Rick to offer him a job teaching kindergarten at Harmony. Although the salary was somewhat less than that of the suburban public schools in the area, Rick rationalized that the school was close to his urban home and he would save money by using public transportation. Besides, at this time, there were no other kindergarten positions in the area; Rick realized he especially wanted to teach children this age.

Rick's New Job

Two weeks before the start of school, Harmony Academy scheduled professional development for all teachers. In the morning, teachers met in interest groups, and in the afternoon, they worked to prepare their classrooms. Rick decided to join interest groups so that he could get to know the other early childhood teachers at Harmony. It turned out that neither the other kindergarten teacher nor the first- and second-grade teachers had early childhood certification. Both first-grade teachers were elementary certified, the kindergarten teacher had a degree in social work, one second grade teacher was certified to teach English at the secondary level, and the other second grade teacher had a business degree and was currently enrolled in a teacher intern program at a nearby college. Rick soon found that his early childhood education vocabulary did not mean much to his colleagues. He became more reticent and listened carefully to the words of his colleagues.

Rick began to really look forward to the afternoons and setting up his kindergarten room. He clustered desks and chairs to make some group arrangements, and he set up six learning centers around the room. On the third afternoon, Sandy Yates came by the classroom and introduced herself as a classroom aide for kindergarten and first grades. She had been assigned to work in Mr. Ramirez's kindergarten every Wednesday. After introducing herself, Sandy volunteered to place the desks and chairs in rows and to make name tags for the back of each child's chair, noting that that is what she typically did to help the kindergarten teachers. Rick was aghast that a classroom aide would suggest changing his room arrangement but

responded that he would like to have name tags for each child to wear on the first day of school. After Rick and Sandy decided how to construct the name tags, Sandy worked on them and Rick went back to his desk.

Education at Harmony Academy

By the first day of school for the children, Rick had come to realize that the philosophy of his teacher education preparation and his beliefs about how young children learn best were not common among the teachers at Harmony. The other primary teachers had not been exposed to current best practices in early childhood education; some of them used the same teaching methods their own elementary teachers had used many years ago. Harmony Academy had such a reputation for excellence that Rick could hardly believe these teachers' viewpoints. The principal of the school had experience at the secondary level and concerned herself much more with the curriculum and teachers for tenth, eleventh, and twelfth grades. She was not readily available to any of the primary teachers, so Rick had had little contact with her, even during the two weeks of professional development.

Kindergarten children came to school on buses with the older children. Because many families were dual-career, the board had decided several years ago to establish full-day kindergarten programs at Harmony. Because Rick realized that he would not have a ready opportunity to meet his children's parents, he phoned each family before the start of school. He had many short, pleasant conversations with parents, but he also left messages for four families that had not been returned.

The first day of kindergarten brought eighteen five-year-olds into Rick's classroom. He greeted them and met with them on the circle rug to inform them about the day's schedule.

Each child had a turn to tell about how he or she got ready and came to kindergarten that day. For most of the day, children were actively engaged in learning centers. They spent some time outdoors and had two large group story times. Rick had renewed confidence about his ability to teach by the time the children left for the day.

Rick's First Official Feedback

On Wednesday of the first week of school, Sandy Yates was in Mr. Ramirez's kindergarten to assist him. He had a plan for her to work with individual children at two different learning centers and then to be stationed near the large climbing apparatus during outdoor time. He also asked her to copy some letters he was sending home to parents and to place the letters in the children's cubbies.

Friday morning before the children arrived at school, the principal had left a message for Rick to come by her office at 3:45 p.m., the end of the school day. Surprised by the message, Rick got through the school day with a little anxiety. At 3:45, he met Mrs. Rivers in her office. She apologized for seeing so little of him his first days on the job and then asked how he was doing. Mrs. Rivers was surprised by Rick's enthusiasm for teaching the kindergartners. She was expecting him to state concerns about how best to teach these young children. After she recovered from her surprise, she informed him that Sandy Yates had come to her with some concerns that she and two of the children's parents had about too much playtime in Rick's kindergarten day. It seemed that several people had a lot of concern that children in this kindergarten class would not be learning what they were expected to know as students at Harmony Academy.

Rick's Reaction

Initially, Rick was confused. He had had almost no contact with Mrs. Rivers since he had been hired. Other than some workbooks in the classroom, few curriculum materials existed. Rick had expected that since he had specialized preparation in early childhood education that he might serve as a model for the other teachers, even though they had more experience than he did. Now, he was being criticized because he was applying a model in his classroom consistent with current best practices.

Sometime during the evening, it occurred to Rick that he had plenty of information to share with the principal, the classroom aide, his colleagues, and parents of the kindergarten children. He devised a plan for writing and sending a letter to parents each week that would explain the importance of play and active learning for children in this stage of development. Rick also shared similar information with the others who expressed concern about his methods.

Rick learned from the other kindergarten teacher that they each had a small allowance to purchase books and materials. He decided to purchase information for parents—books and brochures—to help them understand how children think and reasons for their behavior.

Reaction of Others

Principal Rivers' belief was that kindergarten was not really very important and she did not want to invest a lot of her time with the issue of play in kindergarten. She was rarely seen and remote regarding this issue. Sandy Yates remained skeptical about the value of play; however, she did as she was asked in Mr. Ramirez's classroom because she wanted to keep her job. Some parents found the information on play to be not only interesting, but relevant to what they observed in their children. Several of these parents began to actively support Mr. Ramirez's approach to teaching. Other parents continued to question him and state concerns throughout the year.

Slowly, a few more parents came to believe that just maybe, Mr. Ramirez knew what he was doing.

Questions for Reflection and Discussion

1. Explain the perspectives of Mrs. Rivers, Ms. Yates, Mr. Ramirez, and the kindergarten parents. With which view do you most easily identify?

2. Discuss your life experiences that may have influenced your perspective on this issue.

3. Using information from the textbook, discuss ways in which teachers might effectively share information regarding children's development and how they learn.

How did his way of comm help the situation?
How was he working to form partnerships?

Developmentally Appropriate Practices in Head Start

The Teacher

Jenny Kim was just completing an associate degree in early childhood education from her county community college. During her two years of teacher preparation, Jenny had many hours of experience at the campus child care center. She completed the required practicum there and had also been employed as a student assistant to help staff the center in late afternoons. Jenny often had opportunities to interact with parents and other family members when they came to pick up their children. She began to feel quite comfortable chatting with parents, informing them about how their child's day had gone, and taking messages for the morning child care staff.

Jenny had been required to visit other early childhood settings. She spent at least two hours in an early intervention program, a Montessori preschool, Head Start, and a United Way-funded child care center. With the information she gained from her coursework and from these visits, Jenny knew that her goal was to be a lead teacher in a Head Start program in the nearest city, New Rock.

After her graduation in May, she accepted a position with a YWCA summer camp program, leading the prekindergarten group. Later in the summer, she interviewed for a position with Head Start. Jenny was offered a position as assistant teacher. Even though she wanted a lead teacher position, she accepted the offer and began her Head Start work in the middle of August.

The Early Childhood Program and the Community

New Rock has a large Head Start program. Twenty preschool classrooms exist in various parts of the city. Home-based programs are also a part of the New Rock Head Start. With a population of about 100,000, New Rock has a variety of communities, some of them more economically prosperous than others. Also, some neighborhoods are more culturally diverse than others. All of the Head Start preschools are held in churches and agency buildings in the downtown area. Transportation is provided for all of the children enrolled in the program.

Jenny was assigned to be an assistant teacher in Alice Jones' room. Ms. Alice has been a lead teacher for four years. She accepted this position after she worked for two years as an assistant teacher and completed her bachelor's degree in child development. Ms. Alice greeted Jenny at the beginning of their week of professional development meetings before the start of school. Jenny was pleased to hear that the classroom she would be working in was based on developmentally appropriate practices. The campus child care center from which she gained most of her experience had been accredited by the National Academy of Early Childhood Programs, so Jenny had developed many skills that would be useful in her new job.

Jenny in Head Start

The night before the first day for children to come to school, Jenny could hardly sleep. She was thrilled to be working in Head Start. Alice and Jenny worked together to plan for all aspects of the first day. Jenny believed that Alice valued her contribution and that she could make a difference in the lives of the children.

The first week of school was everything that Jenny had hoped it would be. She loved the children, she felt capable, and Alice was an excellent role model. At the end of the week, when Jenny and Alice had their daily planning meeting, Alice mentioned that next week parents would be volunteering in the classroom. One of their tasks was to assign parents to specific days and times, as well as to think through in advance what the parents could do to contribute in the classroom. Alice had already collected information from them about their interests and available times.

Jenny remembered reading about the importance of family involvement to the Head Start program. There had even been a guest speaker from New Rock College during professional development week who had provided innovative strategies for involving families in their children's education. Although she had experience interacting with family members, it was rare at the campus child care center that parents came to the classroom to volunteer. There seemed little need for more adults when staff and students provided very good ratios of adults to children. The child care center did have some meetings and events for family members, but since they were often at the same time as Jenny had a class, she had not attended them.

During the second week of the Head Start year, many parents and other family members volunteered in the classrooms. Each day, there were at least three adult volunteers in the classroom. Alice had organized a chart in advance and directed each volunteer throughout the course of the day. Everything seemed to be well organized and to flow; Alice was as adept at working with the adults as she was with the children. At the beginning of the next week, Alice was ill; the director asked Jenny if she could take over as lead teacher for the few days Alice expected to be out and to have the volunteers as assistants. Jenny agreed to this plan; she was actually pleased to have the opportunity to "be in charge" for a few days.

As children and parents entered the classroom on Jenny's first day of lead teacher duty, she greeted them all. Most of the children and all of the adults seemed happy to be there. Jenny had carefully planned a group time that would have the children actively involved and then easily transition the children into learning center activities. The parents who were volunteering that day included one mother, Lois LeGrange; one father, Pete Stovall; and one grandmother, Felicia Sanchez. Lois was assigned to the blocks center, Pete to the art center, and Felicia to the dramatic play center. Lois and Pete sat on chairs at the periphery of each of their centers and next to each other. Soon after the children were busy at play, the two parents started talking with one another. This continued, even when children were asking them questions and in need of some direction or redirection. Although Jenny could not be sure, it seemed that they were talking about Felicia. They looked in her direction on occasion and then talked some more. Jenny did not think that she should intervene in this situation in front of the children, so she chose to ignore it. A few minutes later, Felicia raised her voice and threatened to "send you to time out if you don't stop that." Again, although Jenny was uncomfortable with this approach to disciplining children in the classroom, she did not want to correct the adult in the presence of children. She began to feel very nervous and stressed. By the end of the day, Jenny was questioning whether having family volunteers in the classroom was such a good idea. It seemed to work for Alice, but she'd rather have just the teachers in the classroom.

Questions for Reflection and Discussion

1. Explain the perspectives of Alice, Jenny, Lois, Pete, and Felicia. With which of these viewpoints do you most easily identify?

2. Discuss your life experiences that might relate to the perspective you have taken for this scenario.

3. Referring to the textbook, what knowledge and skills might help Jenny feel more prepared to work with family volunteers in the classroom?

Early Childhood Inclusive Practices

The Teacher

Olivia Ali married right out of high school. She and her husband had three children in eight years. When her youngest child entered first grade, Olivia enrolled in college. In a neighboring town, just twelve miles away, a state university offered a degree in early childhood special education. Olivia knew she wanted to teach; she researched the job market for education majors and found that teachers in this area were likely to be in demand for quite some time. In just six years, Olivia would complete her degree. This meant that she could be employed in a teaching position before their oldest child began college.

During her teacher preparation program, Olivia learned a great deal about children's development, various disabilities and their effects on children and families, and the importance of an interdisciplinary, family-focused philosophy for programs of early intervention. She had opportunities for observation and participatory field experiences in a variety of early childhood settings, some of them inclusive, and others that enrolled only typically developing children or children with identified disabilities. She observed a variety of teaching strategies and teachers with varied kinds of preparation and levels of experience.

Olivia's research paid off. As soon as she graduated, she interviewed for two positions and had offers to teach in both of them. She chose the position that was closest to her home. She would be a member of an interdisciplinary team for an inclusive early intervention program with primary responsibilities for the education component. Most of her work would be planning, implementing, and assessing an educational program for three small groups of children ages one to three years. She was very excited about teaching and evaluating the children's progress. Olivia also was responsible for a home-based program for infants identified as having a disability and their families. Many hours were also to be spent with an interdisciplinary team, planning and evaluating services for every child and every family.

The Early Childhood Program and the Community

The inclusive early intervention program that hired Olivia is supported by state and federal funds. The local school district is the contact point for the program, with the district's director of special education having a supervisory role over the early intervention coordinator. Twenty children are being served by the center-based program and twelve children are enrolled in the home-based program. Of the twenty center-based children, four are typically developing and sixteen have identified disabilities such as pervasive developmental disorder, Asperger's disorder, Down syndrome, and cerebral palsy. All of the home-based children have identified disabilities.

Briarville is a small town with a population of about 22,000 and sparsely populated rural areas nearby. Families do not often migrate from the area, so many families have lived there for several generations. Education is not always as high a priority as most of the local educators would like, but there has been a lot of support for the early intervention program. Concern about children with disabilities and their families is evident in Briarville. Fund-raisers have been successful, and the local newspapers and radio station have provided publicity.

Olivia's Doubt

Before long, Olivia's pleasure about getting the position she wanted turned to concern. She did not enjoy or feel confident in the team meetings. The physical therapist, occupational therapist, speech therapist, psychologist, and family services coordinator all seemed to know exactly what each child needed. Sometimes, one or more of them seemed to dominate the session. When she explained the play-based curriculum that she had been prepared to implement, the others passed it off as fluff. They questioned her about what she was teaching, both in her small group sessions and in her home-based plans. At times, one of the therapists would come to her classroom and pull a child out for therapy that was missed earlier in the week for some reason or other. This would occur without advance planning or notice.

Further, nearly all of the parents (or another family member) stayed with their children during the two-hour preschool sessions that were held twice each week. So, instead of Olivia teaching four or five children in her classroom, she was coordinating family members and providing assignments for them to complete with their children during the remainder of the week. Often, there would be five or six adults in the classroom and just four children. This role of teacher was very different from the one Olivia had envisioned for herself. She wanted to teach children, not be a family services coordinator. In her frustration, she began to question why families of

these young children could not just let them come to preschool for four hours a week. She would be glad to compose newsletters, call families as necessary, and have conferences with them. But she began to resent their presence. Just when she organized the children for a short group time, invariably one or more of the children would go to their parents or look at a parent and cry.

Even though she studied about the importance of interdisciplinary, family-focused models for early intervention, she questioned how this program was being operated. She wished that she had another educator in her workplace to talk with about her doubts and concerns. All she wanted to do was teach; how had she missed what early childhood special educators really do?

Viewpoints of the Others

Parents noted that Olivia was very warm when interacting with their children. She prepared a bright, cheery, appropriately stimulating environment for the children. Olivia planned interesting activities for the babies whose homes she visited. However, several family members commented to the coordinator that Olivia seemed remote to them. They often did not feel welcome during preschool groups.

Other professionals at Briarville's early intervention program either paid little attention to the new teacher or began to feel irritated that she did not seem to come to team meetings with a cooperative attitude. The coordinator overheard two of the others discussing their frustration regarding Olivia's presence at team meetings.

The coordinator decided to move up a meeting that had been planned with Olivia. The meeting was intended to be the regularly scheduled conference after thirty days of employment. However, it seemed that something needed to be done sooner. Olivia was worried when she received a message from the coordinator asking whether they could meet after her afternoon preschool group the next day.

Questions for Reflection and Discussion

1. Explain the perspectives of Olivia, family members, other early intervention professionals, and the coordinator. With which do you most identify?

2. Discuss your life experiences that may affect the perspective you take in this situation.

3. From the textbook, what information might help Olivia see the need for such a family-intensive approach to early intervention? Which skills might help to increase her confidence in this situation?

Standardized Assessment

The Teacher

Vera Wozniak was a second-grade teacher in a rural school district. She was asked to serve on a district-wide assessment committee. During the third meeting of the committee, the district psychologist recommended that a standardized test be administered to all second-grade students. Vera stated that the test was not age-appropriate and that reading level could be better assessed in other ways. After several discussions, the majority of the committee voted to approve the use of the test in the second grade.

The Early Childhood Program and the Community

As news of the decision was shared at faculty meetings in the district, Vera began to hear from kindergarten, first- and second-grade teachers. Many of them stated that they did not think it was appropriate to give a standardized test in a primary grade. Some parents of first-graders also began to ask questions about the test and asked Vera if they should send their child to a summer school or buy a reading program to "get ready" for the test.

Viewpoints of Others

After hearing these discussions, Vera decided to go to the principal, Mrs. Vellines. During their discussion, Mrs. Vellines revealed that the superintendent was very pleased that the committee had recommended the test since the district's reading scores were not at the state recommended levels.

Vera left the meeting feeling very frustrated. She knew that second graders were too young for a standardized test. She decided that she would make copies of articles she had read from NAEYC and International Reading Association (IRA) and share those with other teachers and parents. After sharing this information, a group of parents asked to be on the agenda for the next school board meeting. These parents spoke at the meeting and expressed their frustration that children were being pressured simply to get the test scores up. The superintendent agreed to review the plan.

The next day, Vera was asked to meet with the principal and the superintendent.

Questions for Reflection and Discussion

1. Explain the perspectives of Mrs. Vellines, the parents, Vera, and the superintendent.

2. Describe which resources Vera should take to the meeting.

3. How would Vera explain her reasoning in involving parent in this issue?

English Language Learners

The Teacher

Lance Scott was beginning his third year of teaching kindergarten when the suburban school district in which he teaches decided to create a full-day kindergarten program. Lance was informed by the school principal, Dr. Cassidy, that the decision makers believed it had become necessary to provide a full-day program to counteract the effects of families' spoken language on their young children. The emphasis on English as the required language in local and state political arenas was the impetus for this decision. Although Lance had taken several years of Spanish in both high school and college and had learned a little Bosnian from some friends, he was uncertain how to incorporate this knowledge into his teaching of young children. Besides, many teachers and community members were often heard to support immersing ELL into English-only classrooms. So, perhaps, his teaching would not need to change in any way, even with increasing numbers of ELL learners.

In the previous two years, Lance had had little contact with families who did not speak English. Even though some of the children in his kindergarten program were immigrants, their families were bilingual and communicated fairly clearly with him in English. One of his kindergarten colleagues, though, had a child whose family insisted on a translator for the annual conference as well as for newsletters and notes that the teacher sent home. This request was viewed as inappropriate by the teacher and most of the school staff. The result was that written communication essentially was kept to an absolute minimum to avoid any need to translate.

The Early Childhood Program and the Community

Due to an increase in available state funding, the superintendent and the local school board saw the necessity of increasing instructional time for five-year-olds, especially because there had been a recent change in attendance zone demographics. Just five years ago, the number of children classified as English language learners was less than 1 percent of all kindergartners. The next school year would see this rise to 6.5 percent and the prediction in the next ten years is that nearly 10 percent of all kindergartners were likely to be English-language learners. The general attitude about this change in demographics reflected at the school and in the community was that when people came to the United States, they should plan to acculturate and to speak English as quickly as possible. The state legislature had recently begun discussions about requiring schools and other institutions to use English only in all communications.

Viewpoints of Others

Lance was somewhat concerned that there was almost no concern being voiced about how children learn to speak and understand an additional language. Instead, the opinions that were most frequently stated all seemed to reflect political or personal statements about the importance of learning English for U.S. citizenship. Some comments focused on illegal immigration.

Lance approached some of his colleagues and the school principal to request information about professional development for staff that would relate to their responsibilities for English language learning. A common response from colleagues was that the school district should hire specialized personnel to "handle" these issues. The principal did not seem to think that the superintendent or school board would support funding for such a position.

Lance's Situation

As the new school year was fast approaching, no firm decisions were made or shared with teachers about their specific responsibilities for teaching children in their classrooms who were identified as ELL. However, when Lance received his class list of twenty kindergarten children, four of them were identified as ELL. He was facing the dilemma of moving forward as if full-day programming were his only new challenge, or attempting to find some appropriate information for his professional development related to teaching young ELLs and working with their families.

Questions for Reflection and Discussion

1. Explain the perspectives of Lance, the school principal, other teachers, and the community.
2. What are the professional issues related to best practices in early education that need to be emphasized in this case?
3. Using resources regarding the importance of incorporating children's home language into their learning, what points would you make to support Lance's hunch that seeking professional development related to ELL is valid?

Websites for Professional Development

Family Involvement in Early Childhood Education

(Please note that because Internet resources are time-sensitive and URL addresses may change or be deleted, searches should be conducted by association name and/or topic.)

A Guide to Children's Literature and Disability
http://www.kidsource.com/NICHCY/literature.html

Alliance for Full Acceptance
http://www.affa-sc.org/

Asian Nation: The Landscape of Asian America
http://www.asian-nation.org

Association for Childhood Education International (ACEI)
http://www.acei.org

Association for Supervision and Curriculum Development (ASCD)
http://www.ascd.org

Birth Order and Intelligence
http://www.indiana.edu
Type in "birth order"

Building Family Strengths: Research to Application
http://www.clemson.edu
Click "search"; type in "family strengths"

Bureau of Indian Affairs
http://doi.gov/
Click "Bureau of Indian Affairs"

Bureau of Labor Statistics
http://www.bls.gov/

Center for Interventions, Treatment and Addiction Research
http://www.med.wright.edu/
Click "educational programs"; click "research"; click "substance abuse and treatment"; click "Center for Interventions, Treatment and Addiction Research"

Center for Substance Abuse Treatment
http://www.samhsa.gov/
Click "Center for Substance Abuse Treatment"

Center for the Child Care Workforce
http://ccw.cleverspin.org

Center on the Family
http://uhfamily.hawaii.edu/

Character Education Partnership
http://www.character.org

Child Care Aware
http://www.childcareaware.org

Child Welfare and Research on Families
http://www.childwelfare.com/
Type in "research"

Child Welfare League of America
http://www.cwla.org

Children Now
http://www.childrennow.org

Children's Defense Fund
http://www.childrensdefense.org

Children's Memorial Hospital (Chicago)—Neonatology
www.childrensmemorial.org
Click "departments and programs"; click "neonatology"

Children, Youth & Family Consortium
http://www.cyfc.umn.edu/

Coalition for Asian American Children and Families
http://www.cacf.org

Council for Exceptional Children
http://www.cec.sped.org/

Creating a Strong Family
http://www.ianr.unl.edu
Click "publications"; click "families"

Dads and Daughters
http://www.dadsanddaughters.org/

Department of Health and Human Services Administration on Children and Families
http://www.acf.dhhs.gov

Developmental Assets
www.search-institute.org/
Click "Developmental Assets"

Divorce Education and Mediation Program
http://www.hamiltontn.gov
Click "courts information"; click "circuit court clerk"; click "divorce education seminars"

Early Childhood Development
http://www.worldbank.org
Type in "early childhood"

Eastern Orthodox Church in America
http://www.oca.org

ERIC Clearinghouse on Disabilities and Gifted Education
http://ericec.org/

Clearinghouse on Early Education and Parenting
http://ceep.crc.uiuc.edu

Exceptional Parent Magazine
http://www.eparent.com/

Facing History and Ourselves
http://www.facinghistory.org/

Families and Work Institute
http://www.familiesandwork.org

Families in Crisis
http://www.Familiesincrisis.org

Family and Corrections Network
http://www.fcnetwork.org

Family Education Network
http://familyeducation.com/

Family Educational Rights and Privacy Act (FERPA)
http://www.ed.gov/
Click "policy"; type in "FERPA"

Family Focus
http://www.family-focus.org

Family Literacy
http://www.pabook.libraries.psu.edu
Click "family literacy activities"

Family Preservation and Child Welfare Network
http://www.familypreservation.com

Family Resilience
http://extension.missouri.edu
Type in "family resilience"

Family Support America
http://www.famillysupportamerica.org

Family Village
http://www.familyvillage.wisc.edu

Family Violence Prevention Fund
http://endabuse.org/

Federal Office of Child Support Enforcement
http://www.acf.dhhs.gov/
Select "Child Support Enforcement" on
  pull-down menu for ACF Programs

Federal Resource Center for Special Education
http://www.rrfcnetwork.org

Federal Resources for Educational Excellence (FREE)
http://www.ed.gov
Type in "free"

Federation for Children with Special Needs
http://www.fcsn.org

Forum on Child and Family Statistics
http://www.childstats.gov/

Foster Care
http://www.fostercare.net

Free Appropriate Public Education Site
http://www.wrightslaw.com Click "FAPE"

From Family Stress to Family Strengths
http://www.cdc.gov Type in "family stress"

Futures for Children
http://www.futuresforchildren.org

Health Coverage for Legal Immigrant Children
http://www.cbpp.org
Click "health policies"; click "2000"

Helping Children to Understand Divorce
http://www.muextension.missouri.edu
Type in "divorce"

Home Instruction Program for Preschool Youngsters (HIPPY)
http://www.hippyusa.org

Homeless Children's Network
http://www.hcnkids.org

Homes for the Homeless
http://www.homesforthehomeless.com/

Index of Native American Resources on the Internet
http://www.hanksville.org
Click "Index of Native American Resources
  on the Internet"

Individualizing Inclusion in Child Care
http://www.fpg.unc.edu/~inclusion/

Institute for Child and Family Policy
http://www.childpolicy.org/

Jewish Holidays
http://www.bnaibrith.org
Click "programs"; click "Jewish Holidays"

Kwanzaa
http://www.officialkwanzaawebsite.org

Latino Resources
http://www.latinoweb.com
http://latino.sscnet.ucla.edu/

Matthew Shepard Foundation
http://www.matthewsplace.org

Megaskills from the Home and School Institute
http://www.megaskillshsi.org

Migrant Education Program
http://www.ed.gov
Click "offices"; click "Office of Elementary and Secondary Education home page"; click "programs/initiatives"; click "office of migrant education"

Migrant Head Start
http://www.acf.dhhs.gov
Click "Head Start Bureau" on pull-down menu; click "programs/services"; click "migrant and seasonal program branch"

Multicultural Books Every Child Should Know
http://www.education.wisc.edu
Type in "multicultural"; click "Multicultural Literature Volume 2"

Multicultural Pavilion
http://curry.edschool.Virginia.edu
Click "A-Z index"; click "The Multicultural Pavilion"

Museum of Tolerance
http://www.wiesenthal.com
Select "Museum of Tolerance" from pull-down menu

National Association for Family Child Care
http://www.nafcc.org

National Association for Gifted Children
http://www.nagc.org

National Association for the Education of Homeless Children and Youth
http://www.naehcy.org

National Association for the Education of Young Children (NAEYC)
http://www.naeyc.org

National Association of Child Care Resource and Referral Agencies
http://www.naccrra.org

National Association of School Psychologists
http://www.naspcenter.org

National Black Child Development Institute
http://www.nbcdi.org

National Center for Children in Poverty
http://www.nccp.org

National Center for Education Statistics
http://nces.ed.gov/

National Center for Policy Analysis: Welfare
http://www.ncpa.org
Type in "welfare"

National Center on Addiction and Substance Abuse at Columbia University
http://www.casacolumbia.org/

National Child Care Information Center
http://nccic.org

National Clearinghouse for English Language Acquisition and Language Instruction Educational Programs
http://www.ncela.gwu.edu

National Clearinghouse on Child Abuse and Neglect Information
http://nccanch.acf.hhs.gov

National Coalition Against Domestic Violence
http://www.ncadv.org/

National Coalition for Parent Involvement in Education
http://www.ncpie.org/

National Council on Child Abuse and Family Violence
http://www.nccafv.org/

National Council on Family Relations
http://www.ncfr.org

National Dissemination Center for Children with Disabilities
http://www.nichcy.org

National Domestic Violence Hotline
http://www.ndvh.org/

National Head Start Association
http://www.nhsa.org/

National Network for Child Care
http://www.nncc.org/

National Parent Information Network
http://www.npin.org/

National Parent teacher Association (PTA)
http://www.pta.org/

Parent Teacher Organization (PTO)
http://www.ptotoday.com

Parents Action for Children
http://www.parentsaction.org

Parents Anonymous
http://www.parentsanonymous.org/

Parents as Teachers (PAT) National Center
http://www.parentsasteachers.org

Primary Project (School based prevention)
http://www.childrensinstitute.net
Click "programs for children"; click "primary project"

Project Resilience
www.projectresilience.com/

Research and Training Center on Family Support and Children's Mental Health
http://www.rtc.pdx.edu

Research Matters
http://www.researchmatters.harvard.edu

Sexual Orientation and Gender Identity
http://www.aclu.org
Click "lesbian and gay rights"

Special Child
http://www.specialchild.com

Stand for Children
http://www.stand.org

STARBRIGHT Foundation for Seriously Ill Children and Their Families
http://www.starbright.org

Teaching Strategies
http://www.TeachingStrategies.com

Teaching Tolerance
http://www.Tolerance.org

The Reading Connection
http://www.thereadingconnection.org/

Tufts University Child and Family Web Guide
http://www.cfw.tufts.edu

U.S. Census Bureau—Poverty
http://www.census.gov
Type in "poverty"

U.S. Government Publications for Parents
http://www.ed.gov
Click "publications"; click "A-Z index"; click "parents"

ZERO TO THREE
http://www.zerotothree.org/

The NAEYC Code of Ethical Conduct and Statement of Commitment*

Preamble

NAEYC recognizes that those who work with young children face many daily decisions that have moral and ethical implications. The NAEYC Code of Ethical Conduct offers guidelines for responsible behavior and sets forth a common basis for resolving the principal ethical dilemmas encountered in early childhood care and education. The Statement of Commitment is not part of the Code but is a personal acknowledgment of an individual's willingness to embrace the distinctive values and moral obligations of the field of early childhood care and education. The primary focus of the Code is on daily practice with children and their families in programs for children from birth through 8 years of age, such as infant/toddler programs, preschool and prekindergarten programs, child care centers, hospital and child life settings, family child care homes, kindergartens, and primary classrooms. When the issues involve young children, then these provisions also apply to specialists who do not work directly with children, including program administrators, parent educators, early childhood adult educators, and officials with responsibility for program monitoring and licensing. (Note: See also the "Code of Ethical Conduct: Supplement for Early Childhood Adult Educators," online at http://www.naeyc.org/about/positions/ethics04.asp.)

Core Values

Standards of ethical behavior in early childhood care and education are based on commitment to the following core values that are deeply rooted in the history of the field of early

*Code of Ethical Conduct and Statement of Commitment; A position statement of the National Association for the Education of Young Children; revised April 2005; endorsed by the Association for Childhood Education International.

childhood care and education. We have made a commitment to

- Appreciate childhood as a unique and valuable stage of the human life cycle

- Base our work on knowledge of how children develop and learn

- Appreciate and support the bond between the child and family

- Recognize that children are best understood and supported in the context of family, culture, community, and society

- Respect the dignity, worth, and uniqueness of each individual (child, family member, and colleague)

- Respect diversity in children, families, and colleagues

- Recognize that children and adults achieve their full potential in the context of relationships that are based on trust and respect

Conceptual Framework

The Code sets forth a framework of professional responsibilities in four sections. Each section addresses an area of professional relationships: (1) with children, (2) with families, (3) among colleagues, and (4) with the community and society. Each section includes an introduction to the primary responsibilities of the early childhood practitioner in that context. The introduction is followed by a set of ideals (I) that reflect exemplary professional practice and a set of principles (P) describing practices that are required, prohibited, or permitted.

The ideals reflect the aspirations of practitioners. The principles guide conduct and assist practitioners in resolving ethical dilemmas. Both ideals and principles are intended to direct practitioners to those questions which, when responsibly answered, can provide the basis

for conscientious decision making. While the Code provides specific direction for addressing some ethical dilemmas, many others will require the practitioner to combine the guidance of the Code with professional judgment.

The ideals and principles in this Code present a shared framework of professional responsibility that affirms our commitment to the core values of our field. The Code publicly acknowledges the responsibilities that we in the field have assumed and in so doing supports ethical behavior in our work. Practitioners who face situations with ethical dimensions are urged to seek guidance in the applicable parts of this Code and in the spirit that informs the whole.

Often, "the right answer"—the best ethical course of action to take—is not obvious. There may be no readily apparent, positive way to handle a situation. When one important value contradicts another, we face an ethical dilemma. When we face a dilemma, it is our professional responsibility to consult the Code and all relevant parties to find the most ethical resolution.

Section I
Ethical Responsibilities to Children

Childhood is a unique and valuable stage in the human life cycle. Our paramount responsibility is to provide care and education in settings that are safe, healthy, nurturing, and responsive for each child. We are committed to supporting children's development and learning; respecting individual differences; and helping children learn to live, play, and work cooperatively. We are also committed to promoting children's self-awareness, competence, self-worth, resiliency, and physical well-being.

Ideals

I-1.1   To be familiar with the knowledge base of early childhood care and education and to stay informed through continuing education and training.

I-1.2   To base program practices upon current knowledge and research in the field of early childhood education, child development, and related disciplines, as well as on particular knowledge of each child.

I-1.3   To recognize and respect the unique qualities, abilities, and potential of each child.

I-1.4   To appreciate the vulnerability of children and their dependence on adults.

I-1.5   To create and maintain safe and healthy settings that foster children's social, emotional, cognitive, and physical development and that respect their dignity and their contributions.

I-1.6   To use assessment instruments and strategies that are appropriate for the children to be assessed, that are used only for the purposes for which they were designed, and that have the potential to benefit children.

I-1.7   To use assessment information to understand and support children's development and learning, to support instruction, and to identify children who may need additional services.

I-1.8   To support the right of each child to play and learn in an inclusive environment that meets the needs of children with and without disabilities.

I-1.9   To advocate for and ensure that all children, including those with special needs, have access to the support services needed to be successful.

I-1.10   To ensure that each child's culture, language, ethnicity, and family structure are recognized and valued in the program.

I-1.11   To provide all children with experiences in a language that they know, as well as support children in maintaining the use of their home language and in learning English.

I-1.12   To work with families to provide a safe and smooth transition as children and families move from one program to the next.

Principles

P-1.1   Above all, we shall not harm children. We shall not participate in practices that are emotionally damaging, physically harmful, disrespectful, degrading, dangerous, exploitative, or intimidating to children. This principle has precedence over all others in this Code.

P-1.2   We shall care for and educate children in positive emotional and social environments that are cognitively stimulating and that support each child's culture, language, ethnicity, and family structure.

P-1.3   We shall not participate in practices that discriminate against children by denying benefits, giving special advantages, or excluding them from programs or activities on the basis of their sex, race, national origin, religious beliefs, medical condition, disability, or the marital status/family structure, sexual orientation, or religious beliefs or other affiliations of their families. (Aspects of this principle do not apply in programs that have a lawful mandate to provide services to a particular population of children.)

P-1.4   We shall involve all those with relevant knowledge (including families and staff) in decisions concerning a child, as appropriate, ensuring confidentiality of sensitive information.

P-1.5   We shall use appropriate assessment systems, which include multiple sources of information, to provide information on children's learning and development.

P-1.6   We shall strive to ensure that decisions such as those related to enrollment, retention, or assignment to special education services, will be based on multiple sources of information and will never be based on a single assessment, such as a test score or a single observation.

P-1.7   We shall strive to build individual relationships with each child; make individualized adaptations in teaching strategies, learning environments, and curricula; and consult with the family so that each child benefits from the program. If after such efforts have been exhausted, the current placement does not meet a child's needs, or the child is seriously jeopardizing the ability of other children to benefit from the program, we shall collaborate with the child's family and appropriate specialists to determine the additional services needed and/or the placement option(s) most likely to ensure the child's success. (Aspects of this principle may not apply in programs that have a lawful mandate to provide services to a particular population of children.)

P-1.8   We shall be familiar with the risk factors for and symptoms of child abuse and neglect, including physical, sexual, verbal, and emotional abuse and physical, emotional, educational, and medical neglect. We shall know and follow state laws and community procedures that protect children against abuse and neglect.

P-1.9   When we have reasonable cause to suspect child abuse or neglect, we shall report it to the appropriate community agency and follow up to ensure that appropriate action has been taken. When appropriate, parents or guardians will be informed that the referral will be or has been made.

P-1.10   When another person tells us of his or her suspicion that a child is being abused or neglected, we shall assist that person in taking appropriate action in order to protect the child.

P-1.11   When we become aware of a practice or situation that endangers the health, safety, or well-being of children, we have an ethical responsibility to protect children or inform parents and/or others who can.

Section II
Ethical Responsibilities to Families

Families are of primary importance in children's development. Because the family and the early childhood practitioner have a common interest in the child's well-being, we acknowledge a primary responsibility to bring about communication, cooperation, and collaboration between the home and early childhood program in ways that enhance the child's development.

Ideals

I-2.1   To be familiar with the knowledge base related to working effectively with families and to stay informed through continuing education and training.

I-2.2   To develop relationships of mutual trust and create partnerships with the families we serve.

I-2.3   To welcome all family members and encourage them to participate in the program.

I-2.4   To listen to families, acknowledge and build upon their strengths and competencies, and learn from families as we support them in their task of nurturing children.

I-2.5   To respect the dignity and preferences of each family and to make an effort to learn about its structure, culture, language, customs, and beliefs.

I-2.6   To acknowledge families' childrearing values and their right to make decisions for their children.

I-2.7   To share information about each child's education and development with families and to help them understand and appreciate the current knowledge base of the early childhood profession.

I-2.8   To help family members enhance their understanding of their children and support the continuing development of their skills as parents.

I-2.9   To participate in building support networks for families by providing them with opportunities to interact with program staff, other families, community resources, and professional services.

Principles

P-2.1 We shall not deny family members access to their child's classroom or program setting unless access is denied by court order or other legal restriction.

P-2.2 We shall inform families of program philosophy, policies, curriculum, assessment system, and personnel qualifications, and explain why we teach as we do—which should be in accordance with our ethical responsibilities to children (see Section I).

P-2.3 We shall inform families of and, when appropriate, involve them in policy decisions.

P-2.4 We shall involve the family in significant decisions affecting their child.

P-2.5 We shall make every effort to communicate effectively with all families in a language that they understand. We shall use community resources for translation and interpretation when we do not have sufficient resources in our own programs.

P-2.6 As families share information with us about their children and families, we shall consider this information to plan and implement the program.

P-2.7 We shall inform families about the nature and purpose of the program's child assessments and how data about their child will be used.

P-2.8 We shall treat child assessment information confidentially and share this information only when there is a legitimate need for it.

P-2.9 We shall inform the family of injuries and incidents involving their child, of risks such as exposures to communicable diseases that might result in infection, and of occurrences that might result in emotional stress.

P-2.10 Families shall be fully informed of any proposed research projects involving their children and shall have the opportunity to give or withhold consent without penalty. We shall not permit or participate in research that could in any way hinder the education, development, or well-being of children.

P-2.11 We shall not engage in or support exploitation of families. We shall not use our relationship with a family for private advantage or personal gain, or enter into relationships with family members that might impair our effectiveness working with their children.

P-2.12 We shall develop written policies for the protection of confidentiality and the disclosure of children's records. These policy documents shall be made available to all program personnel and families. Disclosure of children's records beyond family members, program personnel, and consultants having an obligation of confidentiality shall require familial consent (except in cases of abuse or neglect).

P-2.13 We shall maintain confidentiality and shall respect the family's right to privacy, refraining from disclosure of confidential information and intrusion into family life. However, when we have reason to believe that a child's welfare is at risk, it is permissible to share confidential information with agencies, as well as with individuals who have legal responsibility for intervening in the child's interest.

P-2.14 In cases where family members are in conflict with one another, we shall work openly, sharing our observations of the child, to help all parties involved make informed decisions. We shall refrain from becoming an advocate for one party.

P-2.15 We shall be familiar with and appropriately refer families to community resources and professional support services. After a referral has been made, we shall follow up to ensure that services have been appropriately provided.

Section III
Ethical Responsibilities to Colleagues

In a caring, cooperative workplace, human dignity is respected, professional satisfaction is promoted, and positive relationships are developed and sustained. Based upon our core values, our primary responsibility to colleagues is to establish and maintain settings and relationships that support productive work and meet professional needs. The same ideals that apply to children also apply as we interact with adults in the workplace.

A. Responsibilities to Coworkers

Ideals

I-3A.1   To establish and maintain relationships of respect, trust, confidentiality, collaboration, and cooperation with coworkers.

I-3A.2   To share resources with co-workers, collaborating to ensure that the best possible early childhood care and education program is provided.

I-3A.3   To support coworkers in meeting their professional needs and in their professional development.

I-3A.4   To accord coworkers due recognition of professional achievement.

Principles

P-3A.1   We shall recognize the contributions of colleagues to our program and not participate in practices that diminish their reputations or impair their effectiveness in working with children and families.

P-3A.2   When we have concerns about the professional behavior of a coworker, we shall first let that person know of our concern in a way that shows respect for personal dignity and for the diversity to be found among staff members, and then attempt to resolve the matter collegially and in a confidential manner.

P-3A.3   We shall exercise care in expressing views regarding the personal attributes or professional conduct of coworkers. Statements should be based on firsthand knowledge, not hearsay, and relevant to the interests of children and programs.

P-3A.4   We shall not participate in practices that discriminate against a coworker because of sex, race, national origin, religious beliefs or other affiliations, age, marital status/family structure, disability, or sexual orientation.

B. Responsibilities to Employers

Ideals

I-3B.1   To assist the program in providing the highest quality of service.

I-3B.2   To do nothing that diminishes the reputation of the program in which we work unless it is violating laws and regulations designed to protect children or is violating the provisions of this Code.

Principles

P-3B.1   We shall follow all program policies. When we do not agree with program policies, we shall attempt to effect change through constructive action within the organization.

P-3B.2   We shall speak or act on behalf of an organization only when authorized. We shall take care to acknowledge when we are speaking for the organization and when we are expressing a personal judgment.

P-3B.3   We shall not violate laws or regulations designed to protect children and shall take appropriate action consistent with this Code when aware of such violations.

P-3B.4 If we have concerns about a colleague's behavior, and children's well-being is not at risk, we may address the concern with that individual. If children are at risk or the situation does not improve after it has been brought to the colleague's attention, we shall report the colleague's unethical or incompetent behavior to an appropriate authority.

P-3B.5 When we have a concern about circumstances or conditions that impact the quality of care and education within the program, we shall inform the program's administration or, when necessary, other appropriate authorities.

C. Responsibilities to employees

Ideals

I-3C.1 To promote safe and healthy working conditions and policies that foster mutual respect, cooperation, collaboration, competence, well-being, confidentiality, and self-esteem in staff members.

I-3C.2 To create and maintain a climate of trust and candor that will enable staff to speak and act in the best interests of children, families, and the field of early childhood care and education.

I-3C.3 To strive to secure adequate and equitable compensation (salary and benefits) for those who work with or on behalf of young children.

I-3C.4 To encourage and support continual development of employees in becoming more skilled and knowledgeable practitioners.

Principles

P-3C.1 In decisions concerning children and programs, we shall draw upon the education, training, experience, and expertise of staff members.

P-3C.2 We shall provide staff members with safe and supportive working conditions that honor confidences and permit them to carry out their responsibilities through fair performance evaluation, written grievance procedures, constructive feedback, and opportunities for continuing professional development and advancement.

P-3C.3 We shall develop and maintain comprehensive written personnel policies that define program standards. These policies shall be given to new staff members and shall be available and easily accessible for review by all staff members.

P-3C.4 We shall inform employees whose performance does not meet program expectations of areas of concern and, when possible, assist in improving their performance.

P-3C.5 We shall conduct employee dismissals for just cause, in accordance with all applicable laws and regulations. We shall inform employees who are dismissed of the reasons for their termination. When a dismissal is for cause, justification must be based on evidence of inadequate or inappropriate behavior that is accurately documented, current, and available for the employee to review.

P-3C.6 In making evaluations and recommendations, we shall make judgments based on fact and relevant to the interests of children and programs.

P-3C.7 We shall make hiring, retention, termination, and promotion decisions based solely on a person's competence, record of accomplishment, ability to carry out the responsibilities of the position, and professional preparation specific to the developmental levels of children in his/her care.

P-3C.8 We shall not make hiring, retention, termination, and promotion decisions based on an individual's sex, race, national origin, religious beliefs or other affiliations, age, marital status/family structure, disability, or sexual orientation. We shall be familiar with and observe laws and regulations that pertain to employment discrimination. (Aspects of this principle do not apply to programs that have a lawful mandate to determine eligibility based on one or more of the criteria identified above.)

P-3C.9   We shall maintain confidentiality in dealing with issues related to an employee's job performance and shall respect an employee's right to privacy regarding personal issues.

Section IV
Ethical Responsibilities to Community and Society

Early childhood programs operate within the context of their immediate community made up of families and other institutions concerned with children's welfare. Our responsibilities to the community are to provide programs that meet the diverse needs of families, to cooperate with agencies and professions that share the responsibility for children, to assist families in gaining access to those agencies and allied professionals, and to assist in the development of community programs that are needed but not currently available.

As individuals, we acknowledge our responsibility to provide the best possible programs of care and education for children and to conduct ourselves with honesty and integrity. Because of our specialized expertise in early childhood development and education and because the larger society shares responsibility for the welfare and protection of young children, we acknowledge a collective obligation to advocate for the best interests of children within early childhood programs and in the larger community and to serve as a voice for young children everywhere.

The ideals and principles in this section are presented to distinguish between those that pertain to the work of the individual early childhood educator and those that more typically are engaged in collectively on behalf of the best interests of children—with the understanding that individual early childhood educators have a shared responsibility for addressing the ideals and principles that are identified as "collective."

Ideals (Individual)

I-4.1   To provide the community with high-quality early childhood care and education programs and services.

Ideals (Collective)

I-4.2   To promote cooperation among professionals and agencies and interdisciplinary collaboration among professions concerned with addressing issues in the health, education, and well-being of young children, their families, and their early childhood educators.

I-4.3   To work through education, research, and advocacy toward an environmentally safe world in which all children receive health care, food, and shelter; are nurtured; and live free from violence in their home and their communities.

I-4.4   To work through education, research, and advocacy toward a society in which all young children have access to high-quality early care and education programs.

I-4.5   To work to ensure that appropriate assessment systems, which include multiple sources of information, are used for purposes that benefit children.

I-4.6   To promote knowledge and understanding of young children and their needs. To work toward greater societal acknowledgment of children's rights and greater social acceptance of responsibility for the well-being of all children.

I-4.7   To support policies and laws that promote the well-being of children and families, and to work to change those that impair their well-being. To participate in developing policies and laws that are needed, and to cooperate with other individuals and groups in these efforts.

I-4.8 To further the professional development of the field of early childhood care and education and to strengthen its commitment to realizing its core values as reflected in this Code.

Principles (Individual)

P-4.1 We shall communicate openly and truthfully about the nature and extent of services that we provide.

P-4.2 We shall apply for, accept, and work in positions for which we are personally well-suited and professionally qualified. We shall not offer services that we do not have the competence, qualifications, or resources to provide.

P-4.3 We shall carefully check references and shall not hire or recommend for employment any person whose competence, qualifications, or character makes him or her unsuited for the position.

P-4.4 We shall be objective and accurate in reporting the knowledge upon which we base our program practices.

P-4.5 We shall be knowledgeable about the appropriate use of assessment strategies and instruments and interpret results accurately to families.

P-4.6 We shall be familiar with laws and regulations that serve to protect the children in our programs and be vigilant in ensuring that these laws and regulations are followed.

P-4.7 When we become aware of a practice or situation that endangers the health, safety, or well-being of children, we have an ethical responsibility to protect children or inform parents and/or others who can.

P-4.8 We shall not participate in practices that are in violation of laws and regulations that protect the children in our programs.

P-4.9 When we have evidence that an early childhood program is violating laws or regulations pro-tecting children, we shall report the violation to appropriate authorities who can be expected to remedy the situation.

P-4.10 When a program violates or requires its employees to violate this Code, it is permissible, after fair assessment of the evidence, to disclose the identity of that program.

Principles (Collective)

P-4.11 When policies are enacted for purposes that do not benefit children, we have a collective responsibility to work to change these practices.

P-4.12 When we have evidence that an agency that provides services intended to ensure children's well-being is failing to meet its obligations, we acknowledge a collective ethical responsibility to report the problem to appropriate authorities or to the public. We shall be vigilant in our follow-up until the situation is resolved.

P-4.13 When a child protection agency fails to provide adequate protection for abused or neglected children, we acknowledge a collective ethical responsibility to work toward the improvement of these services.

Glossary of Terms Related to Ethics

Code of Ethics defines the core values of the field and provides guidance for what professionals should do when they encounter conflicting obligations or responsibilities in their work.

Values, Qualities, or Principles that individuals believe to be desirable or worthwhile and that they prize for themselves, for others, and for the world in which they live.

Core Values Commitments held by a profession that are consciously and knowingly embraced by its practitioners because they make a contribution to society. There is a difference between personal values and the core values of a profession.

Morality   Peoples' views of what is good, right, and proper; their beliefs about their obligations; and their ideas about how they should behave.

Ethics   The study of right and wrong, or duty and obligation, that involves critical reflection on morality and the ability to make choices between values and the examination of the moral dimensions of relationships.

Professional Ethics   The moral commitments of a profession that involve moral reflection that extends and enhances the personal morality practitioners bring to their work, that concern actions of right and wrong in the workplace, and that help individuals resolve moral dilemmas they encounter in their work.

Ethical Responsibilities   Behaviors that one must or must not engage in. Ethical responsibilities are clear-cut and are spelled out in the Code of Ethical Conduct (for example, early childhood educators should never share confidential information about a child or family with a person who has no legitimate need for knowing).

Ethical Dilemma   A moral conflict that involves determining appropriate conduct when an individual faces conflicting professional values and responsibilities.

Sources for Glossary Terms and Definitions

Feeney, S., & N. Freeman. 1999. *Ethics and the early childhood educator: Using the NAEYC code.* Washington, DC: NAEYC.

Kidder, R.M. 1995. *How good people make tough choices: Resolving the dilemmas of ethical living.* New York: Fireside.

Kipnis, K. 1987. How to discuss professional ethics. *Young Children 42* (4): 26–30.

Work Group for the Revision of the Code of Ethical Conduct

Mary Ambery	Ruth Ann Ball	James Clay
Julie Olsen Edwards	Harriet Egertson	Anthony Fair
Stephanie Feeney	Jana Fleming	Nancy Freeman
Marla Israel	Allison McKinnon	Evelyn Wright Moore
Eva Moravcik	Christina Lopez Morgan	Sarah Mulligan
Nila Rinehart	Betty Holston Smith	Peter Pizzolongo, NAEYC Staff

The National Association for the Education of Young Children ("NAEYC") is a nonprofit corporation, tax exempt under Section 501(c)(3) of the Internal Revenue Code, dedicated to acting on behalf of the needs and interests of young children. The NAEYC Code of Ethical Conduct ("Code") has been developed in furtherance of NAEYC's nonprofit and tax exempt purposes. The information contained in the Code is intended to provide early childhood educators with guidelines for working with children from birth through age 8. Use, reference to, or review of the Code does not guarantee compliance with NAEYC Early Childhood Program Standards and Accreditation Performance Criteria and program accreditation procedures. It is recommended that the Code be used as guidance in connection with implementation of the NAEYC Program Standards, but such use is not a substitute for diligent review and application of the NAEYC Program Standards.

NAEYC has taken reasonable measures to develop the Code in a fair, reasonable, open, unbiased, and objective manner, based on currently available data. However, further research or developments may change the current state of knowledge. Neither NAEYC nor its officers, directors, members, employees, or agents will be liable for any loss, damage, or claim with respect to any liabilities, including direct, special, indirect, or consequential damages incurred in connection with the Code or reliance on the information presented.

Statement of Commitment

As an individual who works with young children, I commit myself to furthering the values of early childhood education as they are reflected in the ideals and principles of the NAEYC Code of Ethical Conduct. To the best of my ability I will

- Never harm children
- Ensure that programs for young children are based on current knowledge and research of child development and early childhood education.
- Respect and support families in their task of nurturing children.
- Respect colleagues in early childhood care and education and support them in maintaining the NAEYC Code of Ethical Conduct.
- Serve as an advocate for children, their families, and their teachers in community and society.
- Stay informed of and maintain high standards of professional conduct.
- Engage in an ongoing process of self-reflection, realizing that personal characteristics, biases, and beliefs have an impact on children and families.
- Be open to new ideas and be willing to learn from the suggestions of others.
- Continue to learn, grow, and contribute as a professional.
- Honor the ideals and principles of the NAEYC Code of Ethical Conduct

  1. Culture includes ethnicity, racial identity, economic level, family structure, language, and religious and political beliefs, which profoundly influence each child's development and relationship to the world.
  2. There is not necessarily a corresponding principle for each ideal.
  3. The term family may include those adults, besides parents, with the responsibility of being involved in educating, nurturing, and advocating for the child.
  4. This Statement of Commitment is not part of the Code but is a personal acknowledgement of the individual's willingness to embrace the distinctive values and moral obligations of the field of early childhood care and education. It is recognition of the moral obligations that lead to an individual becoming part of the profession.

This statement may be purchased as a brochure, and the Statement of Commitment is available as a poster suitable for framing. See our catalog for ordering information.

NAEYC Academy for Early Childhood Program Accreditation Standards and Topic Areas

Standard 1
NAEYC Accreditation Criteria for Relationships

Program Standard: The program promotes positive relationships among all children and adults to encourage each child's sense of individual worth and belonging as part of a community and to foster each child's ability to contribute as a responsible community member.

Topic Areas

1.A. Building Positive Relationships among Teachers and Families

1.B. Building Positive Relationships between Teachers and Children

1.C. Helping Children Make Friends

1.D. Creating a Predictable, Consistent, and Harmonious Classroom

1.E. Addressing Challenging Behaviors

1.F. Promoting Self-Regulation

Standard 2
NAEYC Accreditation Criteria for Curriculum

Program Standard: The program implements a curriculum that is consistent with its goals for children and promotes learning and development in each of the following areas: social, emotional, physical, language, and cognitive.

Topic Areas

2.A. Essential Characteristics

2.B. Areas of Development: Social-Emotional Development

2.C. Areas of Development: Physical Development

2.D. Areas of Development: Language Development

2.E. Curriculum Content Area for Cognitive Development: Early Literacy

2.F. Curriculum Content Area for Cognitive Development: Early Math

2.G. Curriculum Content Area for Cognitive Development: Science

2.H. Curriculum Content Area for Cognitive Development: Technology

To avoid confusion in the numbering system, there are no criteria labeled 2.I.

2.J. Curriculum Area for Cognitive Development: Creative Expression and Appreciation for the Arts

2.K. Curriculum Content Area for Cognitive Development: Health and Safety

2.L. Curriculum Content Area for Cognitive Development: Social Studies

Standard 3
NAEYC Accreditation Criteria for Teaching

Program Standard: The program uses developmentally, culturally, and linguistically appropriate and effective teaching approaches that enhance each child's learning and development in the context of the program's curriculum goals.

Topic Areas

3.A. Designing Enriched Learning Environments

3.B. Creating Caring Communities for Learning

3.C. Supervising Children

3.D. Using Time, Grouping, and Routines to Achieve Learning Goals

3.E. Responding to Children's Interests and Needs

3.F. Making Learning Meaningful for All Children

3.G. Using Instruction to Deepen Children's Understanding and Build Their Skills and Knowledge

Standard 4
NAEYC Accreditation Criteria for Assessment of Child Progress

Program Standard: The program is informed by ongoing systematic, formal, and informal assessment approaches to provide information on children's learning and development. These assessments occur within the context of reciprocal communications with families and with sensitivity to the cultural contexts in which children develop. Assessment results are used to benefit children by informing sound decisions about children, teaching, and program improvement.

Topic Areas

4.A. Creating an Assessment Plan

4.B. Using Appropriate Assessment Methods

4.C. Identifying Children's Interests and Needs and Describing Children's Progress

4.D. Adapting Curriculum, Individualizing Teaching, and Informing Program Development

4.E. Communicating with Families and Involving Families in the Assessment Process

Standard 5
NAEYC Accreditation Criteria for Health Standard

Program Standard: The program promotes the nutrition and health of children and protects children and staff from illness and injury.

Topic Areas

5.A. Promoting and Protecting Children's Health and Controlling Infectious Disease

5.B. Ensuring Children's Nutritional Well-being

5.C. Maintaining a Healthful Environment

Standard 6
NAEYC Accreditation Criteria for Teachers Standard

Program Standard: The program employs and supports a teaching staff that has the educational qualifications, knowledge, and professional commitment necessary to promote children's learning and development and to support families' diverse needs and interests.

Topic Areas

6.A. Preparation, Knowledge, and Skills of Teaching Staff

6.B. Teachers' Dispositions and Professional Commitment

Standard 7
NAEYC Accreditation Criteria for Families Standard

Program Standard: The program establishes and maintains collaborative relationships with each child's family to foster children's development in all settings. These relationships are sensitive to family composition, language, and culture.

Topic Areas

7.A. Knowing and Understanding the Program's Families

7.B. Sharing Information Between Staff and Families

7.C. Nurturing Families as Advocates for Their Children

Standard 8
NAEYC Accreditation Criteria for Community Relationships Standard

Program Standard: The program establishes relationships with and uses the resources of the children's communities to support the achievement of program goals.

Topic Areas

8.A. Linking with the Community

8.B. Accessing Community Resources

8.C. Acting as a Citizen in the Neighborhood and the Early Childhood Community

Standard 9
NAEYC Accreditation Criteria for Physical Environment Standard

Program Standard: The program has a safe and healthful environment that provides appropriate and well-maintained indoor and outdoor physical environments. The environment includes facilities, equipment, and materials to facilitate child and staff learning and development.

Topic Areas

9.A. Indoor and Outdoor Equipment, Materials, and Furnishings

9.B. Outdoor Environmental Design

9.C. Building and Physical Design

9.D Environmental Health

Standard 10
NAEYC Accreditation Criteria for Leadership and Management Standard

Program Standard: The program effectively implements policies, procedures, and systems that support stable staff and strong personnel, fiscal, and program management so all children, families, and staff have high-quality experiences.

Topic Areas

10.A. Leadership

10.B. Management Policies and Procedures

10.C. Fiscal Accountability Policies and Procedures

10.D. Health, Nutrition, and Safety Policies and Procedures

10.E. Personnel Policies

10.F. Program Evaluation, Accountability, and Continuous Improvement

Responding to Linguistic and Cultural Diversity Recommendations for Effective Early Childhood Education

A Position Statement of the National Association for the Education of Young Children (1995)

Linguistically and culturally diverse is an educational term used by the U.S. Department of Education to define children enrolled in educational programs who are either non-English-proficient (NEP) or limited-English-proficient (LEP). Educators use this phrase, linguistically and culturally diverse, to identify children from homes and communities where English is not the primary language of communication (Garciá, 1991). For the purposes of this statement, the phrase will be used in a similar manner. This document primarily describes linguistically and culturally diverse children who speak languages other than English. However, the recommendations of this position statement can also apply to children who, although they speak only English, are also linguistically and culturally diverse.

Introduction

The children and families served in early childhood programs reflect the ethnic, cultural, and linguistic diversity of the nation. The nation's children all deserve an early childhood education that is responsive to their families, communities, and racial, ethnic, and cultural backgrounds. For young children to develop and learn optimally, the early childhood professional must be prepared to meet their diverse developmental, cultural, linguistic, and educational needs. Early childhood educators face the challenge of how best to respond to these needs.

The acquisition of language is essential to children's cognitive and social development. Regardless of what language children speak, they still develop and learn. Educators recognize that linguistically and culturally diverse children come to early childhood programs with previously acquired knowledge and learning based upon the language used in their home. For young children, the language of the home is the language they have used since birth, the language they use to make and establish meaningful communicative relationships, and the language they use to begin to construct their knowledge and test their learning. The home language is tied to children's culture, and culture and language communicate traditions, values, and attitudes (Chang, 1993). Parents should be encouraged to use and develop children's home language; early childhood educators should respect children's linguistic and cultural backgrounds and their diverse learning styles. In so doing, adults will enhance children's learning and development.

Just as children learn and develop at different rates, individual differences exist in how children whose home language is not English acquire English. For example, some children may experience a silent period (of six or more months) while they acquire English; other children may practice their knowledge by mixing or combining languages (for example, "Mi mamá me put on mi coat"); still other children may seem to have acquired English-language skills (appropriate accent, use of vernacular, vocabulary, and grammatical rules) but are not truly proficient; yet some children will quickly acquire English-language proficiency. Each child's way of learning a new language should be viewed as acceptable, logical, and part of the ongoing development and learning of any new language.

Defining the Problem

At younger and younger ages, children are negotiating difficult transitions between their home and educational settings, requiring an adaptation to two or more diverse sets of rules, values, expectations, and behaviors. Educational programs and families must respect and reinforce each other as they work together to achieve the greatest benefit for all children. For some young children, entering any new environment—including early childhood programs—can be intimidating. The lives of many young children today are further complicated by having to communicate and learn in a language that may be unfamiliar. In the past, children entering U.S. schools from families whose home language is not English were expected to immerse themselves in the mainstream of schools, primarily through the use of English (Soto, 1991; Wong Fillmore, 1991). Sometimes the negative attitudes conveyed or expressed toward certain languages lead children to "give up" their home language. Early childhood professionals must recognize the feeling of loneliness, fear, and abandonment children may feel when they are thrust into settings that isolate them from their home community and language. The loss of children's home language may result **in the disruption of family communication patterns, which may lead to the loss of intergenerational wisdom; damage to individual and community esteem; and children's potential nonmastery of their home language or English.**

NAEYC's Position

NAEYC's goal is to build support for equal access to high-quality educational programs that recognize and promote all aspects of children's development and learning, enabling all children to become competent, successful, and socially responsible adults. Children's educational experiences should afford them the opportunity to learn and to become effective, functioning members of society. Language development is essential for learning, and the development of children's home language does not interfere with their ability to learn English. Because knowing more than one language is a cognitive asset (Hakuta & García, 1989), early education programs should encourage the development of children's home language while fostering the acquisition of English.

For the optimal development and learning of all children, educators must **accept** the legitimacy of children's home language, **respect** (hold in high regard) and **value** (esteem, appreciate) the home culture, and **promote** and **encourage** the active involvement and support of all families, including extended and nontraditional family units.

When early childhood educators acknowledge and respect children's home language and culture, ties between the family and programs are strengthened. This atmosphere provides increased opportunity for learning because young children feel supported, nurtured, and connected not only to their home communities and families but also to teachers and the educational setting.

The Challenges

The United States is a nation of great cultural diversity, and our diversity creates opportunities to learn and share both similar and different experiences. There are opportunities to learn about people from different backgrounds; the opportunity to foster a bilingual citizenry with skills necessary to succeed in a global economy; and opportunities to share one's own cherished heritage and traditions with others.

Historically, our nation has tended to regard differences, especially language differences, as cultural handicaps rather than cultural resources (Meier & Cazden, 1982). "Although most Americans are reluctant to say it publicly, many are anxious about the changing racial and ethnic composition of the country" (Sharry, 1994). As the early childhood profession transforms its thinking,

The challenge for early childhood educators is to become more knowledgeable about how to relate to children and families whose linguistic or cultural background is different from their own.

Between 1979 and 1989 the number of children in the United States from culturally and linguistically diverse backgrounds increased considerably (NCES, 1993), and, according to a report released by the Center for the Study of Social Policy (1992), that diversity is even more pronounced among children younger than age 6. Contrary to popular belief, many of these children are neither foreign born nor immigrants but were born in the United States (Waggoner, 1993). Approximately 9.9 million of the estimated 45 million school-age children, more than one in five, live in households in which languages other than English are spoken (Waggoner, 1994). In some communities, however, the number of children living in a family in which a language other than English is spoken is likely to be much larger. Head Start reports that the largest number of linguistically and culturally diverse children served through Head Start are Spanish speakers, with other language groups representing smaller but growing percentages (Head Start Bureau, 1995).

The challenge for teachers is to provide high-quality care and education for the increasing number of children who are likely to be linguistically and culturally diverse.

Families and communities are faced with increasingly complex responsibilities. Children used to be cared for by parents and family members who typically spoke the home language of their family, be it English or another language. With the increasing need of family members to work, even while children are very young, more and more children are placed in care and educational settings with adults who may not speak the child's home language or share their cultural background. Even so, children will spend an ever-increasing amount of their waking lives with these teachers. What happens in care will have a tremendous impact on the child's social, emotional, and cognitive development. These interactions will influence the child's values, view of the world, perspectives on family, and connections to community. This places a tremendous responsibility in the hands of the early childhood community.

Responding to linguistic and cultural diversity can be challenging. At times the challenges can be complicated further by the specific needs or issues of the child, the family, or the educational program. Solutions may not be evident. Individual circumstances can affect each situation differently. There are no easy answers, and often myths and misinformation may flourish. The challenges may even seem to be too numerous for any one teacher or provider to manage. Nonetheless, despite the complexity, it is the responsibility of all educators to assume the tasks and meet the challenges. Once a situation occurs, the early childhood educator should enter into a dialogue with colleagues, parents, and others in an effort to arrive at a negotiated agreement that will meet the best interest of the child. For example,

- A mother, father, and primary caregiver each have different cultural and linguistic backgrounds and do not speak English. Should the language of one of these persons be affirmed or respected above the others? How can the teacher affirm and respect the backgrounds of each of these individuals?

- The principal is concerned that all children learn English and, therefore, does not want any language other than English spoken in the early childhood setting. In the interest of the child, how should the educator respond?

- An educator questions whether a child will ever learn English if the home language is used as the primary language in the early childhood setting. How is this concern best addressed?

Solutions exist for each of these linguistic and cultural challenges, just as they do for the many other issues that early childhood educators confront within the early childhood setting. These challenges must be viewed as opportunities for the early childhood educator to reflect, question, and effectively respond to the needs of linguistically and culturally diverse children. Although appropriate responses to every linguistically and culturally diverse situation cannot be addressed through this document, early childhood educators should consider the following recommendations.

Recommendations for a Responsive Learning Environment

Early childhood educators should stop and reflect on the best ways to ensure appropriate educational and developmental experiences for all young children. The unique qualities and characteristics of each individual child must be acknowledged. Just as each child is different, methods and strategies to work with young children must vary.

The issue of home language and its importance to young children is also relevant for children who speak English but come from different cultural backgrounds, for example, speakers of English who have dialects, such as people from Appalachia or other regions having distinct patterns of speech, speakers of Black English, or second- and third-generation speakers of English who maintain the dominant accent of their heritage language. While this position statement basically responds to children who are from homes in which English is not the dominant language, the recommendations provided may be helpful when working with children who come from diverse cultural backgrounds, even when they only speak English. The overall goal for early childhood professionals, however, is to provide every child, including children who are linguistically and culturally diverse, with a responsive learning environment. The following recommendations help achieve this goal.

A. Recommendations for Working with Children

Recognize that all children are cognitively, linguistically, and emotionally connected to the language and culture of their home.

When program settings acknowledge and support children's home language and culture, ties between the family and school are strengthened. In a supportive atmosphere young children's home language is less likely to atrophy (Chang, 1993), a situation that could threaten the children's important ties to family and community.

Acknowledge that children can demonstrate their knowledge and capabilities in many ways.

In response to linguistic and cultural diversity, the goal for early childhood educators should be to make the most of children's potential, strengthening and building upon the skills they bring when they enter programs. Education, as Cummins states, implies "drawing out children's potential and making them more than they were" (1989, vii). Educational programs and practices must recognize the strengths that children possess. Whatever language children speak, they should be able to demonstrate their capabilities and also feel the success of being appreciated and valued. Teachers must build upon children's diversity of gifts and skills and provide young children opportunities to exhibit these skills in early childhood programs. The learning environment must focus on the learner and allow opportunities for children to express themselves across the curriculum, including art, music, dramatization, and even block building. By using a nondeficit approach (tapping and recognizing children's strengths rather than focusing the child's home environment on skills yet unlearned) in their teaching, teachers should take the time to observe and engage children in a variety of learning activities. Children's strengths should be celebrated, and they should be given numerous ways to express their interests and talents. In doing this, teachers will provide children an opportunity to display their intellect and knowledge that may far exceed the boundaries of language.

Understand that without comprehensible input, second-language learning can be difficult.

It takes time to become linguistically proficient and competent in any language. Linguistically and culturally diverse children may be able to master basic communication skills; however, mastery of the more cognitively complex language skills needed for academic learning (Cummins, 1989) is more dependent on the learning environment. Academic learning relies on significant amounts of information presented in decontextualized learning situations. Success in school becomes more and more difficult as children are required to learn, to be tested and evaluated based on ever-increasing amounts of information, consistently presented in a decontextualized manner. Children learn best when they are given a context in which to learn, and the knowledge that children acquire in "their first language can make second-language input much more comprehensible" (Krashen, 1992, 37). Young children can gain knowledge more easily when they obtain quality instruction through their first language. Children can acquire the necessary language and cognitive skills required to succeed in school when given an appropriate learning environment, one that is tailored to meet their needs (NAEYC & NAECS/SDE, 1991; Bredekamp & Rosegrant, 1992).

Although verbal proficiency in a second language can be accomplished within two to three years, the skills necessary to achieve the higher level educational skills of understanding academic content through reading and writing may require four or more years (Cummins, 1981; Collier, 1989). Young children may seem to be fluent and at ease with English but may not be capable of understanding or expressing themselves as competently as their English-speaking peers. Although children seem to be speaking a second language with ease, speaking a language does not equate to being proficient in that language. Full proficiency in the first language, including complex uses of the language, contributes to the development of the second language. Children who do not become proficient in their second language after two or three years of regular use probably are not proficient in their first language either.

Young children may seem to be fluent and at ease speaking a second language, but they may not be fully capable of understanding or expressing themselves in the more complex aspects of language and may demonstrate weaknesses in language-learning skills, including vocabulary skills, auditory memory and discrimination skills, simple problem-solving tasks, and the ability to follow sequenced directions. Language difficulties such as these often can result in the linguistically and culturally diverse child being over referred to special education, classified as learning disabled, or perceived as developmentally delayed.

B. Recommendations for Working with Families

Actively involve parents and families in the early learning program and setting.

Parents and families should be actively involved in the learning and development of their children. Teachers should actively seek parental involvement and pursue establishing a partnership with children's families. When possible, teachers should visit the child's community (for example, shops, churches, and playgrounds); read and learn about the community through the use of books, pictures, observations, and conversations with community members; and visit the home and meet with other family members.

Parents and families should be invited to share, participate, and engage in activities with their children. Parent involvement can be accomplished in a number of ways, including asking parents to share stories, songs, drawings, and experiences of their linguistic and cultural background and asking parents to serve as monitors or field trip organizers. Families and parents should be invited to share activities that are developmentally appropriate and meaningful within their culture. These opportunities demonstrate to the parent what their child is learning; increase the knowledge, information, and understanding of all children regarding people of different cultures and linguistic backgrounds; and establish a meaningful relationship with the parent. The early childhood educator should ensure that parents are informed and engaged with their child in meaningful activities that promote linkages between the home and the early care setting.

Encourage and assist all parents in becoming knowledgeable about the cognitive value for children of knowing more than one language, and provide them with strategies to support, maintain, and preserve home-language learning.

In an early childhood setting and atmosphere in which home language is preserved, acknowledged, and respected, all parents can learn the value of home-language development and the strength it provides children as they add to their existing knowledge and understanding. Parents and teachers can learn how to become advocates regarding the long-term benefits that result from bilingualism.

Parents and teachers recognize the acquisition of English as an intellectual accomplishment, an opportunity for economic growth and development, and a means for achieving academic success. There are even times when parents may wish for the ability, or have been mistakenly encouraged, to speak to their children only in English, a language of which the parents themselves may not have command. The educator should understand the effects that speaking only in English can have upon the child, the family, and the child's learning. The teacher must be able to explain that speaking to the child only in English can often result in communications being significantly hindered and verbal interactions being limited and unnatural between the parent and the child. In using limited English, parents may communicate to children using simple phrases and commands (for example, "Sit down" or "Stop"); modeling grammatically incorrect phrases (for example, "We no go store"); or demonstrating other incorrect usages of language that are common when persons acquire a second language. From these limited and incorrect verbal interactions, the amount of language the child is hearing is reduced, and the child's vocabulary growth is restricted, contributing to an overall decrease in verbal expression. When parents do not master the second language yet use the second language to communicate with their child, there is an increased likelihood that the child will not hear complex ideas or abstract thoughts—important skills needed for cognitive and language development. The teacher must explain that language is developed through natural language interactions. These natural interactions occur within the day-to-day setting, through radio and television, when using public transportation, and in play with children whose dominant language is English. The parent and the teacher must work collaboratively to achieve the goal of children's learning English.

Through the home language and culture, families transmit to their children a sense of identity, an understanding of how to relate to other people, and a sense of belonging. When parents and children cannot communicate with one another, family and community destabilization can occur. Children who are proficient in their home language are able to maintain a connectedness to their histories, their stories, and the day-to-day events shared by parents, grandparents, and other family members who may speak only the home language. Without the ability to communicate, parents are not able to socialize their children, share beliefs and value systems, and directly influence, coach, and model with their children.

Recognize that parents and families must rely on care-givers and educators to honor and support their children in the cultural values and norms of the home.

Parents depend on high-quality early childhood programs to assist them with their children's development and learning. Early childhood programs should make provisions to communicate with families in their home language and to provide parent–teacher encounters that both welcome and accommodate families. Partnerships between the home and the early childhood setting must be developed to ensure that practices of the home and expectations of the program are complementary. Linguistic and cultural continuity between the home and the early childhood program supports children's social and emotional development. By working together, parents and teachers have the opportunity to influence the understanding of language and culture and to encourage multicultural learning and acceptance in a positive way.

C. Recommendations for Professional Preparation

Provide early childhood educators with professional preparation and development in the areas of culture, language, and diversity.

Efforts to understand the languages and cultural backgrounds of young children are essential in helping children to learn. Uncertainty can exist when educators are unsure of how to relate to children and families of linguistic and cultural backgrounds different from their own. Early childhood educators need to understand and appreciate their own cultural and linguistic backgrounds. Adults' cultural background affects how they interact with and/or teach young children. The educator's background influences how children are taught, reinforced, and disciplined. The child's background influences how the child constructs knowledge, responds to discipline and praise, and interacts in the early childhood setting.

Preservice and inservice training opportunities in early childhood education programs assist educators in overcoming some of the linguistic and cultural challenges they may face in working with young children. Training institutions and programs can consider providing specific courses in the following topic areas or include these issues in current courses: language acquisition; second-language learning; use of translators; working with diverse families; sociolinguistics; cross-cultural communication; issues pertaining to the politics of race, language, and culture; and community involvement.

Recruit and support early childhood educators who are trained in languages other than English.

Within the field of early childhood education, there is a need for knowledgeable, trained, competent, and sensitive multilingual/multicultural early childhood educators. Early childhood educators who speak more than one language and are culturally knowledgeable are an invaluable resource in the early childhood setting. In some instances the educator may speak multiple languages or may be able to communicate using various linguistic regionalisms or dialects spoken by the child or the family. The educator may have an understanding of sociocultural and economic issues relevant within the local linguistically and culturally diverse community and can help support the family in the use and development of the child's home language and in the acquisition of English. The early childhood teacher who is trained in linguistic and cultural

diversity can be a much-needed resource for information about the community and can assist in the inservice cultural orientation and awareness training for the early childhood program. The bilingual educator also can be a strong advocate for family and community members.

Too often, however, bilingual early childhood professionals are called upon to provide numerous other services, some of which they may not be equipped to provide. For example, the bilingual professional, although a fluent speaker, may not have the vocabulary needed to effectively communicate with other adults or, in some instances, may be able to read and write only in English, not in the second language. In addition, bilingual teachers should not be expected to meet the needs of all linguistically and culturally diverse children and families in the program, especially those whose language they do not speak. Bilingual providers should not be asked to translate forms, particularly at a moment's notice, nor should they be required to stop their work in order to serve as interpreters. Bilingual teachers should not serve in roles, such as advising or counseling, in which they may lack professional training. These assignments may seem simple but often can be burdensome and must be viewed as added duties placed upon the bilingual teacher.

Preservice and inservice training programs are needed to support bilingual early childhood educators in furthering educators' knowledge and mastery of the language(s) other than English that they speak, and training should also credit content-based courses offered in languages other than English. Professional preparation instructors must urge all teachers to support multilingual/multicultural professionals in their role as advocates for linguistically and culturally diverse children. Early childhood professionals should be trained to work collaboratively with the bilingual early childhood teacher and should be informed of the vital role of the bilingual educator. Additionally, there is a need for continued research in the area of linguistic and cultural diversity of young children.

D. Recommendations for Programs and Practice

Recognize that children can and will acquire the use of English even when their home language is used and respected.

Children should build upon their current skills as they acquire new skills. While children maintain and build upon their home language skills and culture, children can organize and develop proficiency and knowledge in English. Bilingualism has been associated with higher levels of cognitive attainment (Hakuta & Garciá, 1989) and does not interfere with either language proficiency or cognitive development. Consistent learning opportunities to read, be read to, and see print messages should be given to linguistically and culturally diverse children. Literacy developed in the home language will transfer to the second language (Krashen, 1992). Bilingualism should be viewed as an asset and an educational achievement.

Support and preserve home language usage.

If the early childhood teacher *speaks* the child's home language, then the teacher can comfortably use this language around the child, thereby providing the child with opportunities to hear and use the home language within the early childhood setting. Use of the language should be clearly evident throughout the learning environment (e.g., in meeting charts, tape recordings, the library corner). Educators should develop a parent information board, using a language and reading level appropriate for the parents. Teachers should involve parents and community members in the early childhood program. Parents and community members can assist children in hearing the home language from many different adults, in addition to the teacher who speaks the home language. Parents and community members can assist other parents who may be unable to read, or they can assist the teacher in communicating with families whose home language may not have a written form.

If the early childhood educator *does not speak* the language, he or she should make efforts to provide visible signs of the home language throughout the learning environment through books and other relevant reading material in the child's language and with a parent bulletin board (get a bilingual colleague to help review for accuracy of written messages). The teacher can learn a few selected words in the child's language, thus demonstrating a willingness to take risks similar to the risks asked of children as they learn a second language. This effort by the teacher also helps to validate and affirm the child's language and culture, further demonstrating the teacher's esteem and respect for the child's linguistic and cultural background. The teacher should model appropriate use of English and provide the child with opportunities to use newly acquired vocabulary and language. The teacher also must actively involve the parent and the community in the program.

If the teacher is *faced with many different languages* in the program or classroom, the suggestions listed above are still relevant. Often teachers feel overwhelmed if more than one language is spoken in the program; however, they should remember that the goal is for children to learn, and that learning is made easier when children can build on knowledge in their home language. The teacher should consider grouping together at specific times during the day children who speak the same or similar languages so that the children can construct knowledge with others who speak their home language. The early childhood educator should ensure that these children do not become socially isolated as efforts are made to optimize their learning. Care should be taken to continually create an environment that provides for high learning expectations.

Develop and provide alternative and creative strategies for young children's learning.

Early childhood educators are encouraged to rely on their creative skills in working with children to infuse cultural and linguistic diversity in their programs. They should provide children with multiple opportunities to learn and ways for them to demonstrate their learning, participate in program activities, and work interactively with other children.

To learn more about working with linguistically and culturally diverse children, early childhood educators should collaborate with each other and with colleagues from other professions. To guide the implementation of a developmentally, linguistically, and culturally appropriate program, collaborative parent and teacher workgroups should be developed. These committees should discuss activities and strategies that would be effective for use with linguistically and culturally diverse children. Such committees promote good practices for children and shared learning between teachers and parents.

Summary

Early childhood educators can best help linguistic and culturally diverse children and their families by acknowledging and responding to the importance of the child's home language and culture. Administrative support for bilingualism as a goal is necessary within the educational setting. Educational practices should focus on educating children toward the "school culture" while preserving and respecting the diversity of the home language and culture that each child brings to the early learning setting. Early childhood professionals and families must work together to achieve high- quality care and education for all children.

References

Bredekamp, S., & T. Rosegrant, eds. 1992. *Reaching potentials: Appropriate curriculum and assessment for young children.* Vol. 1. Washington, DC: NAEYC.

Center for the Study of Social Policy. 1992. *The challenge of change: What the 1990 census tells us about children.* Washington, DC: Author.

Chang, H.N.-L. 1993. *Affirming children's roots: Cultural and linguistic diversity in early care and education.* San Francisco: California Tomorrow.

Collier, V. 1989. How long: A synthesis of research on academic achievement in second language. *TESOL Quarterly 23*: 509–531.

Cummins, J. 1981. The role of primary language development in promoting educational success for language minority students. In *Schooling and language minority students: A theoretical framework*, eds. M. Ortiz, D. Parker, & F. Tempes. Office of Bilingual Bicultural Education, California State Department of Education. Los Angeles: Evaluation, Dissemination, and Assessment Center, California State University.

Cummins, J. 1989. *Empowering minority students.* Sacramento: California Association for Bilingual Education.

Garciá, E. 1991. *The education of linguistically and culturally diverse students: Effective instructional practices.* Santa Cruz: National Center for Research on Cultural Diversity and Second Language Learning, University of California.

Hakuta, K., & E. Garciá. 1989. Bilingualism and education. *American Psychologist 44* (2): 374–379.

Head Start Bureau, Administration on Children, Youth, and Families, Department of Health and Human Services. 1995. Program information report. Washington, DC: Author.

Krashen, S. 1992. *Fundamentals of language education.* Torrance, CA: Laredo Publishing.

Meier, T.R., & C.B. Cazden. 1982. A focus on oral language and writing from a multicultural perspective. *Language Arts 59*: 504–512.

National Association for the Education of Young Children (NAEYC) and National Association of Early Childhood Specialists in State Departments of Education (NAECS/SDE). 1991. Guidelines for appropriate curriculum content and assessment in programs serving children ages 3 through 8. *Young Children 46* (3): 21–38.

National Center for Education Statistics (NCES). 1993. Language characteristics and schooling in the United States, a changing picture: 1979 and 1989. NCES 93-699. Washington, DC: U.S. Department of Education, Office of Educational Research and Improvement.

Sharry, F. 1994. *The rise of nativism in the United States and how to respond to it.* Washington, DC: National Education Forum.

Soto, L.D. 1991. Understanding bilingual/bicultural children. *Young Children 46* (2): 30–36.

Waggoner, D., ed. 1993. Numbers and needs: Ethnic and linguistic minorities in the United States 3 (6).

Waggoner, D. 1994. Language minority school age population now totals 9.9 million. *NABE News 18* (1): 1, 24–26.

Wong Fillmore, L. 1991. When learning a second language means losing the first. *Early Childhood Research Quarterly 6*: 323–346.

Resources

Banks, J. 1993. Multicultural education for young children: Racial and ethnic attitudes and their modification. In *Handbook of research on the education of young children,* ed. B. Spodek, 236–251. New York: Macmillan.

Collier, V. 1989. How long: A synthesis of research on academic achievement in second language. *TESOL Quarterly 23*: 509–531.

Collier, V., & C. Twyford. 1988. The effect of age on acquisition of a second language for school. *National Clearinghouse for Bilingual Education 2* (Winter): 1–12.

Derman-Sparks, L., & the A.B.C. Task Force. 1989. *Anti-bias curriculum: Tools for empowering young children.* Washington, DC: NAEYC.

McLaughlin, B. 1992. *Myths and misconceptions about second language learning: What every teacher needs to unlearn.* Santa Cruz: National Center for Research on Cultural Diversity and Second Language Learning, University of California.

Neugebauer, B., ed. 1992. *Alike and different: Exploring our humanity with young children.* Redmond, WA: Exchange Press, 1987. Reprint, Washington, DC: NAEYC.

Ogbu, J.U. 1978. *Minority education and caste: The American system in cross cultural perspective.* New York: Academic.

Phillips, C.B. 1988. Nurturing diversity for today's children and tomorrow's leaders. *Young Children 43* (2): 42–47.

Tharp, R.G. 1989. Psychocultural variables and constants: Effects on teaching and learning in schools. *American Psychologist 44*: 349–359.

APPENDIX E

Professional Preparation Excerpts from NAEYC Initial Licensing Standards for Early Childhood Teacher Certification

NAEYC Initial Licensure Standards

Introduction

Why have standards for early childhood professional preparation?

This document presents one part of NAEYC's standards for the preparation of early childhood professionals. The standards in this document are specifically intended for higher education programs that prepare practitioners at the "initial licensure" or certification level (usually a baccalaureate or master's degree). However, the standards, and the principles that these standards represent, are relevant to many other professional development settings. NAEYC recognizes and welcomes all those who teach young children—whatever their current education and experience—into the community of professional practice. NAEYC honors the commitment that draws so many talented people into this field, and we hope that these and other professional standards will help create a unified vision of excellence, with multiple, well-articulated professional pathways.

Standards and NAEYC's Mission

Why should NAEYC have standards for the preparation of early childhood professionals? NAEYC's mission is to improve the quality of services for children from birth through age 8. Over the years, NAEYC has supported that mission through its leadership in developing position statements, guidelines, and standards on behalf of the profession. Collaboratively developed standards can provide a solid, commonly held foundation from which diverse structures may arise, incorporating the wisdom of local communities, families, and practitioners. Connecting with others through standards By developing and revising standards for early childhood professional preparation, NAEYC connects its vision of excellence with that of many other groups that are concerned about teacher preparation and performance. The National Council for

Accreditation of Teacher Education (NCATE) has general, or "unit," standards that describe the kinds of knowledge, skills, and dispositions that all well-prepared education professionals should possess. NAEYC's "program" standards are closely aligned with those of NCATE but provide specific guidance about the preparation of early childhood professionals. Other NCATE-affiliated groups, including specialty professional associations like NAEYC but in elementary education, special education, reading, mathematics, science, and social studies, set their own expectations for high-quality professional preparation. NAEYC collaborates with those groups and works to coordinate its standards with theirs. **NAEYC works especially closely with the Division for Early Childhood (DEC) of the Council for Exceptional Children (CEC) to ensure that our standards complement and support one another, so that all early childhood teachers are well prepared to teach young children with and without developmental delays or disabilities.**

Finally, NAEYC's standards for professional preparation are part of a larger set of expectations, or standards, that together form an image of what is required if all young children are to receive the kind of early education they need and deserve.

The Context and Scope of the Early Childhood Field

Context As emphasized in NAEYC's last standards publication (NAEYC, 1996a) and elsewhere (e.g., NAEYC's 1997 position statement Licensing and Public Regulation of Early Childhood Programs), the field of early childhood education differs in significant ways from other domains of education, although it also shares common elements. As compared with elementary and secondary teachers, early childhood professionals work in many settings—not just public schools but also child care programs, private preschools and kindergartens, early intervention programs including Head Start and Early Head Start, family support and home-based programs, and so on. Similarly, the professional roles assumed by early childhood professionals are far more varied than those typical in elementary and secondary education—including roles as lead teachers, mentor teachers, education coordinators, early childhood trainers, inclusion specialists, resource and referral staff, technical assistance specialists, early childhood technology specialists, early interventionists, and home visitors. Even at institutions where the majority of graduates take teaching positions in public schools, high-quality early childhood professional preparation programs convey to candidates the range and complexity of those roles, most of which involve significant collaboration across professions, as well as collaboration with young children's families.

Scope NAEYC continues to define the "early childhood" period as spanning the years from birth through age 8. As in past editions of its standards, NAEYC recognizes that within that range, early childhood professionals—and the programs that prepare them—may choose to specialize within the early childhood spectrum (infants/toddlers, preschool, or kindergarten/primary). Teacher licensure complicates the picture, since states' definitions of the early childhood age span and its subdivisions vary greatly (McCarthy, Cruz, & Ratcliff, 1999). Specialization can be valuable, but NAEYC believes that all early childhood professionals At the center . . . positive outcomes for all young children . . . these standards now are organized into five core categories:

Promoting Child Development and Learning;
Building Family and Community Relationships;
Observing, Documenting, and Assessing to Support Young Children and Families;
Teaching and Learning; and
Becoming a Professional.

The five brief standards statements in this document offer a shared vision of early childhood professional preparation. But to make the vision real, the details must be constructed uniquely and personally, within particular communities of learners. Good early childhood settings may look very different from one another. In the same way, good professional preparation programs may find many pathways to help candidates meet high standards, so that they can effectively support young children and their families.

NAEYC Initial Licensure Standards

Standard 1. Promoting Child Development and Learning Candidates use their understanding of young children's characteristics and needs, and of multiple interacting influences on children's development and learning, to create environments that are healthy, respectful, supportive, and challenging for all children.

Standard 2. Building Family and Community Relationships Candidates know about, understand, and value the importance and complex characteristics of children's families and communities. They use this understanding to create respectful, reciprocal relationships that support and empower families, and to involve all families in their children's development and learning.

Standard 3. Observing, Documenting, and Assessing to Support Young Children and Families Candidates know about and understand the goals, benefits, and uses of assessment. They know about and use systematic observations, documentation, and other effective assessment strategies in a responsible way, in partnership with families and other professionals, to positively influence children's development and learning.

Standard 4. Teaching and Learning Candidates integrate their understanding of and relationships with children and families; their understanding of developmentally effective approaches to teaching and learning; and their knowledge of academic disciplines to design, implement, and evaluate experiences that promote positive development and learning for all children.

Sub-Standard 4a. Connecting with children and families Candidates know, understand, and use positive relationships and supportive interactions as the foundation for their work with young children.

Sub-Standard 4b. Using developmentally effective approaches Candidates know, understand, and use a wide array of effective approaches, strategies, and tools to positively influence children's development and learning.

Sub-Standard 4c. Understanding content knowledge in early education Candidates understand the importance of each content area in young children's learning. They know the essential concepts, inquiry tools, and structure of content areas including academic subjects and can identify resources to deepen their understanding.

Sub-Standard 4d. Building meaningful curriculum Candidates use their own knowledge and other resources to design, implement, and evaluate meaningful, challenging curriculum that promotes comprehensive develop-mental and learning outcomes for all young children.

Standard 5. Becoming a Professional Candidates identify and conduct themselves as members of the early childhood profession. They know and use ethical guidelines and other professional standards related to early childhood practice. They are continuous, collaborative learners who demonstrate knowledgeable, reflective, and critical perspectives on their work, making informed decisions that integrate knowledge from a variety of sources. They are informed advocates for sound educational practices and policies.

Standards Summary

Standard 1. Promoting Child Development and Learning

Candidates use their understanding of young children's characteristics and needs, and of multiple interacting influences on children's development and learning, to create environments that are healthy, respectful, supportive, and challenging for all children.

Supporting Explanation   The early childhood field has historically been grounded in a child development knowledge base, and early childhood programs have aimed to support a broad range of positive developmental outcomes for all young children. Although the scope and emphasis of that knowledge base have changed over the years, and although early childhood professionals recognize that other sources of knowledge are also important influences on curriculum and programs for young children, early childhood practice continues to be deeply linked with a "sympathetic understanding of the young child" (Elkind, 1994).

In basing their practice in child development, however, well-prepared early childhood professional candidates go beyond narrow or outdated developmental concepts. Their knowledge and understanding of young children's characteristics and needs encompasses multiple, interrelated areas of children's development and learning—including physical, cognitive, social, emotional, language, and aesthetic domains, play, activity, and learning processes, and motivation to learn—and is supported by coherent theoretical perspectives and by current research. Candidates also understand and apply their understanding of the many influences on young children's development and learning, and of how those influences may interact to affect development in both positive and negative ways. Candidates emphasize—both in their conceptual understanding and in their work with children—the multiple influences on development and learning. Those influences include the cultural and linguistic contexts for development, children's close relationships with adults and peers, economic conditions of children and families, health status and disabilities, children's individual developmental variations and learning styles, opportunities to play and learn, technology and the media, and family and community characteristics. Candidates also understand the potential influence of early childhood programs, including early intervention, on short- and long-term outcomes for children.

Candidates' competence is demonstrated in their ability to use developmental knowledge to create healthy, respectful, supportive, and challenging learning environments for all young children (including curriculum, interactions, teaching practices, and learning materials). Such environments reflect four critical features. First, the environments are healthy—that is, candidates possess the knowledge and skills needed to promote young children's physical and psychological health, safety, and sense of security. Second, the environments reflect respect—for each child as a feeling, thinking individual and then for each child's culture, home language, individual abilities or disabilities, family context, and community. In respectful environments, candidates model and affirm anti-bias perspectives on development and learning. Third, the learning environments created by early childhood teacher candidates are supportive—candidates demonstrate their belief in young children's ability to learn, and they show that they can use their understanding of children's development to help each child understand and make meaning from her or his experiences through play, spontaneous activity, and guided investigations. Finally, the learning environments that early childhood candidates create are appropriately challenging—in other words, candidates apply their knowledge of contemporary theory and research to construct learning environments that provide achievable and "stretching" experiences for all children—including children with special abilities and children with disabilities or developmental delays.

Key Elements of Standard 1

1a: Knowing and understanding young children's characteristics and needs

1b: Knowing and understanding the multiple influences on development and learning

1c: Using developmental knowledge to create healthy, respectful, supportive, and challenging learning environments

Rubrics for these key elements, outlining distinct levels of candidate performance and program evidence, are available online at http://www.naeyc.org.

Standard 2. Building Family and Community Relationships

Candidates know about, understand, and value the importance and complex characteristics of children's families and communities. They use this understanding to create respectful, reciprocal relationships that support and empower families, and to involve all families in their children's development and learning.

Supporting Explanation Because young children's lives are so embedded in their families and communities, and because research indicates that successful early childhood education depends upon partnerships with families and communities, early childhood professionals need to thoroughly understand and apply their knowledge in this area.

First, well-prepared candidates possess knowledge and understanding of family and community characteristics, and of the many influences on families and communities. Family theory and research provide a knowledge base. Socioeconomic conditions; family structures, relationships, stresses, and supports (including the impact of having a child with special needs); home language; cultural values; ethnicity; community resources, cohesiveness, and organization—knowledge of these and other factors creates a deeper understanding of young children's lives. The knowledge is critical to candidates' ability to help children learn and develop well.

Second, candidates possess the knowledge and skills needed to support and empower families through respectful, reciprocal relationships. Candidates understand how to build positive relationships, taking families' preferences and goals into account and incorporating knowledge of families' languages and cultures. Candidates demonstrate respect for variations across cultures in family strengths, expectations, values, and childrearing practices. Candidates consider family members to be resources for insight into their children, as well as resources for curriculum and program development. Candidates know about and demonstrate a variety of communication skills to foster such relationships, emphasizing informal conversations while also including such approaches as exchanging e-mails and posting information and children's work on the Web, with print copies sent home for families without Web access. In their work, early childhood teacher candidates support and empower diverse families, including those whose children have disabilities or special characteristics or learning needs; families who are facing multiple challenges in their lives; and families whose languages and cultures may differ from those of the early childhood professional. Candidates also understand that their relationships with families include assisting families in finding needed resources, such as mental health services, health care, adult education, English language instruction, and economic assistance, that may contribute directly or indirectly to their children's positive development and learning.

Well-prepared early childhood candidates are able to identify such resources and know how to connect families with services, including help with planning transitions from one educational or service system to another.

Finally, well-prepared candidates possess essential skills to involve families and communities in many aspects of children's development and learning. They understand and value the role of parents and other important family members as children's primary teachers. Candidates understand how to go beyond parent conferences to engage families in curriculum planning, assessing of children's learning, and planning for children's transitions to new programs. When their approaches to family involvement are not effective, candidates evaluate and modify those approaches rather than assuming that families "are just not interested."

Key Elements of Standard 2

2a: Knowing about and understanding family and community characteristics

2b: Supporting and empowering families and communities through respectful, reciprocal relationships

2c: Involving families and communities in their children's development and learning

Rubrics for these key elements, outlining distinct levels of candidate performance and program evidence, are available online at http://www.naeyc.org.

Standard 3. Observing, Documenting, and Assessing to Support Young Children and Families

Candidates know about and understand the goals, benefits, and uses of assessment. They know about and use systematic observations, documentation, and other effective assessment strategies in a responsible way, in partnership with families and other professionals, to positively influence children's development and learning.

Supporting Explanation Although definitions vary, in these standards the term "assessment" includes all methods through which early childhood professionals gain understanding of children's development and learning. Observation, documentation, and other forms of assessment are central to the practice of all early childhood professionals. Ongoing, systematic observations and other informal and formal assessments enable candidates to appreciate children's unique qualities, to develop appropriate goals, and to plan, implement, and evaluate effective curriculum. Although assessment may take many forms, early childhood candidates demonstrate its central role by embedding assessment-related activities in curriculum and in daily routines, so that assessment becomes a habitual part of professional life. Even as new professionals, they feel empowered by assessment rather than viewing assessment as a necessary evil imposed by others.

Well-prepared early childhood candidates recognize the central role that appropriate assessment plays in the design of effective programs and practices for young children. They can explain the central goals, benefits, and uses of assessment. In considering the goals of assessment, candidates articulate and apply the concept of "alignment"—good assessment is consistent with and connected to appropriate goals, curriculum, and teaching strategies for young children. At its best, assessment is a positive tool that supports children's development and learning, and that improves outcomes for young children and families. Positive assessment identifies the strengths of families and children; through appropriate screening and referral, assessment may also result in identifying children who may benefit from special services. Candidates are able to explain such positive uses of assessment and exemplify them in their own work, while also showing awareness of the potentially negative uses of assessment in early childhood programs and policies.

Early childhood assessment includes observation and documentation, plus other appropriate assessment strategies. Effective teaching of young children begins with thoughtful, appreciative, systematic observation and documentation of each child's unique qualities, strengths, and needs. Observing young children in classrooms, homes, and communities helps candidates develop a broad sense of who children are—as individuals, as group members, as family members, as members of cultural and linguistic communities. Observation gives insight into how young children develop and how they respond to opportunities and obstacles in their lives. Because spontaneous play is such a powerful window on all aspects of children's development, well-prepared candidates create opportunities to observe children in playful situations as well as in more formal learning contexts. All behavior has meaning, and well-prepared candidates demonstrate skill in reading young children's behavior cues; the skill is especially important for infants and toddlers and for children whose verbal abilities are limited. Candidates demonstrate skills in conducting systematic observations, interpreting those observations, and reflecting on their significance.

With observation and documentation as their foundation, well-prepared candidates know about a wide range of assessment tools and approaches. More than reciting a list of assessment strategies, early childhood candidates can explain the connections between specific assessment approaches and specific educational and developmental goals. They can also identify the characteristics, strengths, and limitations of specific assessment tools and strategies, including the use of technologies such as videotape and electronic record keeping. New practitioners are not assessment specialists; however, they do understand essential distinctions and definitions (e.g., screening, diagnostic assessment,

standardized testing, accountability assessment) and are familiar with essential concepts of reliability and validity and other psychometric concepts. Their understanding helps them in selecting appropriate formal assessment measures, critiquing the limitations of inappropriate measures, and discussing assessment issues as part of interdisciplinary teams. Within the classroom or program setting, candidates demonstrate skills in using varied assessments that are appropriate to their goals and children's characteristics, with emphasis on curriculum-embedded, performance assessments.

Many young children with disabilities are included in early childhood programs, and early identification of children with developmental delays or disabilities is very important. All beginning professionals, therefore, need essential knowledge about how to collect relevant information, including appropriate uses of screening tools and play-based assessments, not only for their own planning but also to share with families and with other professionals. Well-prepared candidates are able to choose valid tools that are developmentally, culturally, and linguistically appropriate; use the tools correctly; adapt tools as needed, using assistive technology as a resource; make appropriate referrals; and interpret assessment results, with the goal of obtaining valid, useful information to inform practice and decision making.

Although assessment can be a positive tool for early childhood professionals, it has also been used in inappropriate and harmful ways. Well-prepared candidates understand and practice responsible assessment. Candidates understand that responsible assessment is ethically grounded and guided by sound professional standards. It is collaborative and open. Responsible assessment supports children, rather than being used to exclude them or deny them services. Candidates demonstrate understanding of appropriate, responsible assessment practices for culturally and linguistically diverse children and for children with developmental delays, disabilities, or other special characteristics. Finally, candidates demonstrate knowledge of legal and ethical issues, current educational concerns and controversies, and appropriate practices in the assessment of diverse young children.

Many aspects of effective assessment require collaboration with families and with other professionals. Such assessment partnerships, when undertaken with sensitivity and sound knowledge, contribute positively to understanding children's development and learning. Both family members and, as appropriate, members of interprofessional teams may be involved in assessing children's development, strengths, and needs. As new practitioners, candidates may have had limited opportunities to experience such partnerships, but they demonstrate essential knowledge and core skills in team building and in communicating with families and colleagues from other disciplines.

Key Elements of Standard 3

3a: Understanding the goals, benefits, and uses of assessment

3b: Knowing about and using observation, documentation, and other appropriate assessment tools and approaches

3c: Understanding and practicing responsible assessment

3d: Knowing about assessment partnerships with families and other professionals

Rubrics for these key elements, outlining distinct levels of candidate performance and program evidence, are available online at http://www.naeyc.org.

Standard 4. Teaching and Learning Candidates integrate their understanding of and relationships with children and families; their understanding of developmentally effective approaches to teaching and learning; and their knowledge of academic disciplines to design, implement, and evaluate experiences that promote positive development and learning for all young children.

- Sub-Standard 4a. Connecting with children and families
- Sub-Standard 4b. Using developmentally effective approaches
- Sub-Standard 4c. Understanding content knowledge in early education
- Sub-Standard 4d. Building meaningful curriculum

Standard 4 is complex, with four Sub-Standards, because teaching and learning with young children is a complex enterprise, and its details vary depending on children's ages, characteristics, and the settings within which teaching and learning occur. Well-prepared early childhood professionals construct curriculum and program content from multiple sources. As described below, the early teaching and learning experiences that will support all children's success must be grounded in four interrelated elements:

(a) positive relationships and supportive interactions;

(b) a broad repertoire of appropriate, effective teaching/learning approaches;

(c) essential content knowledge and familiarity with significant resources in specific academic disciplines; and

(d) skills in developing, implementing, and evaluating curriculum that integrates those elements to promote positive outcomes.

Especially when planning curriculum and teaching strategies for young children with developmental delays or disabilities or are learning English, well-prepared candidates know about and have the skills to collaborate with professionals from other disciplines (e.g., special education, school psychology, speech and language). The following subsections describe each of the four substandards of the Teaching and Learning standard in detail.

Sub-Standard 4a. Connecting with Children and Families

Candidates know, understand, and use positive relationships and supportive interactions as the foundation for their work with young children.

Supporting Explanation Throughout the years that children spend in educational settings, their successful learning is dependent not just on "instruction" but also on personal connections with important adults who support and facilitate their learning. It is through those connections that children develop not only academic skills but also positive learning dispositions and confidence in themselves as learners.

Infants learn about the world through their relationships with their primary caregivers. Responsiveness in caregiving creates the conditions within which very young children can explore and learn about their world. Candidates who plan to work with children of any age must have skill in creating responsive relationships, although the nature of those relationships differs as children develop. The close attachments children develop with their teachers/caregivers, the expectations and beliefs that adults have about children's capacities, and the warmth and responsiveness of adult-child interactions are powerful influences on positive developmental and educational outcomes.

Early childhood candidates demonstrate that they understand the theories and research that support the importance of relationships and high-quality interactions in early education. In their practice, they display warm, nurturing interactions with individual children and their families, communicating genuine liking for and interest in young children's activities and characteristics.

Candidates demonstrate the essential dispositions and skills to develop positive, respectful relationships with children whose cultures and languages may differ from their own, as well as with children who may have developmental delays, disabilities, or other learning challenges. In making the transition from family to a group context, very young children need continuity between the caregiving practices of family members and those used by professionals in the early childhood setting. Their feelings of safety and confidence depend on that continuity. Candidates know the cultural practices and contexts of the young children they teach, and they adapt practices to be culturally sensitive. With older children, candidates continue to emphasize cultural sensitivity while also developing culturally relevant knowledge and skills in important academic domains.

Sub-Standard 4b. Using Developmentally Effective Approaches

Candidates know, understand, and use a wide array of effective approaches, strategies, and tools to positively influence young children's development and learning.

Supporting explanation Early childhood professionals need appropriate, effective approaches to help young children learn and develop well. Candidates must ground their curriculum in a set of core approaches to teaching that are supported by research and are closely linked to the processes of early development and learning. In a sense, those approaches are the curriculum for infants and toddlers, although academic content can certainly be embedded in each of them. With older children, the relative weight and explicitness of subject matter or academic content become more evident in the curriculum, and yet the core approaches or strategies remain as a consistent framework.

Although this subsection describes many of those approaches, they are not merely a list from which early childhood professionals may pick at random. Well-prepared candidates' professional decisions about approaches to early childhood teaching and learning are based on understanding of children as individuals and (in most cases) as part of a group, and on alignment with important educational and developmental goals. A flexible, research-based "continuum of teaching strategies" is the best support for children's developmental and educational needs. Well-prepared early childhood candidates understand and effectively use the following approaches, strategies, and tools to promote young children's development and learning:

Fostering oral language and communication Early childhood candidates embed every aspect of the curriculum within the context of rich oral language and other communication strategies, using technology as needed to augment communication for children with disabilities. Both verbal and nonverbal communication create links with children from infancy onward, not only supporting close relationships but also creating the foundations for literacy and cognitive development and later academic competence.

Drawing from a continuum of teaching strategies Well-prepared candidates display a broad range of interactive and instructional skills. They understand and use teaching approaches that span a continuum from child-initiated to adult-directed learning, and from free exploration to scaffolded support or teacher modeling. In selecting the approaches, candidates demonstrate that they are basing their selection on knowledge of individual children, on research evidence, and on understanding of appropriate, challenging teaching and learning goals.

Making the most of the environment and routines Especially for the youngest children, the curriculum is the physical and social environment and in particular the daily routines of feeding, bathing, napping, and playtime. Candidates know the power of the environment to foster security and to support exploration, and they create physical environments and routines that offer predictability as well as opportunities for oral language development, social interaction, and investigations. Candidates demonstrate understanding and skill in setting up all aspects of the indoor and outdoor environment to promote learning and development. Well-designed learning or activity centers can offer young children extensive opportunities to manipulate objects, build, paint, listen to stories or music, read, write, and challenge themselves. Candidates' work displays their skills in designing such centers and other features of the environment to support specific goals (including IEP and IFSP goals) and to expand children's learning. Well-prepared candidates also demonstrate skill in selecting and adapting bias-free, culturally relevant learning materials that support learning by all children, including those with developmental delays or disabilities. Daily, weekly, and longer-term schedules designed by candidates also provide evidence that candidates can apply their understanding of young children's need for balance, order, depth, variety, and challenge.

Capitalizing on incidental teaching Because so much of young children's learning takes place informally and spontaneously, early childhood practitioners must be skilled at "incidental teaching," identifying and taking advantage of informal opportunities to build children's language, concept development, and skills. For those candidates preparing specifically to work with infants and toddlers, this will be the primary approach to teaching, but all candidates require skills in this area if they are to be effective. Depending on children's ages and program settings, candidates use diapering, meals, clean-up times, outdoor play, dressing, and other routines and transitions to support children's learning. Engaging conversations, thought-provoking questions, provision of materials, and spontaneous activities are all evident in candidates' repertoire of teaching skills.

Focusing on children's characteristics, needs, and interests Another developmentally effective approach is to focus on children's individual characteristics, cultures, temperaments, and central developmental concerns, using families as important sources of insight. Again, such practices form the heart of teaching and learning for infants and toddlers, yet they are also effective approaches for children at the upper end of the early childhood period. And the focus on children's needs is also at the center of good practices for young children with disabilities, whose IEPs and IFSPs are based on individual and family goals. Well-prepared early childhood candidates keep the child as the center, while also paying close attention to important standards and learning outcomes, connecting new learning with children's prior knowledge and areas of individual fascination.

Linking children's language and culture to the early childhood program Before they come to school, all children learn and develop in their own unique and highly diverse linguistic, social, and cultural context. When previous learning and development are nurtured in early education programs, the overall benefits of early education are enhanced. Recognizing and using the child's and family's primary language ensures that early childhood education adds to and does not subtract from previous experiences at home and in the community. In implementing effective approaches to teaching and learning, candidates demonstrate that they use linguistic and cultural diversity as resources, rather than seeing diversity as a deficit or problem.

Teaching through social interactions Because so much of children's learning takes place in a social context, their peer group can be viewed as a teaching tool. When working with groups of children, candidates show competence in promoting positive social interactions and—depending on children's ages and social skills—engaging children in parallel or collaborative learning activities. Candidates understand that children who have limited social skills or who are rejected by others may have difficulty in other areas, and so candidates actively work to increase social competence in all children, treating this as an educational priority. Even as beginning teachers, they show a commitment to creating learning communities within early childhood classrooms, where children help and care for one another.

Creating support for play All early childhood professionals must demonstrate competence in using play as a foundation for young children's learning from infancy through the primary grades. Although most children play spontaneously, well-prepared candidates can create and support environments that enrich and extend children's play, knowing when to intervene with questions, suggestions, and challenges. Especially for children with disabilities and developmental delays, candidates explicitly model and facilitate appropriate play and social interactions. Candidates create and support play experiences that reflect gender equity, respect for cultural diversity, and principles of nonviolence. Candidates demonstrate understanding of the value of play in itself, as a way for children to make sense of their experiences and to develop a wide range of skills.

Addressing children's challenging behaviors "Classroom management" is the greatest difficulty reported by most novice practitioners. Well-prepared early childhood candidates demonstrate understanding of the multiple, underlying causes of children's challenging behaviors. Early childhood candidates demonstrate a varied repertoire of research-based guidance approaches to meet individual children's needs. Their work shows that they understand the importance of a supportive, interesting classroom environment and relationships as ways to prevent many challenging behaviors. In implementing guidance approaches, candidates aim to develop children's self-regulation and respect for others. Candidates also demonstrate knowledge and essential skills to meet the special needs of children whose behavioral difficulties are related to disabilities, family or community violence, or other stressful circumstances.

Supporting learning through technology Rather than being merely an enrichment or add-on to the curriculum, technology has taken a central place in early childhood programs. Candidates demonstrate sound knowledge and skills in using technology as a teaching and learning tool. Appropriate technology, including computer software, digital or Web content, cameras, and other peripherals, can support and expand young children's learning, including (through assistive technology) the learning of many children with disabilities. Candidates display awareness of the benefits and potential risks of technology, as well as issues of economic and gender equity in distribution of technology resources. Candidates demonstrate knowledge about how to combine appropriate software with other teaching tools to integrate and reinforce learning.

Using integrative approaches to curriculum Skills in developing integrated, thematic, or emergent curriculum are evident in the work of well-prepared early childhood candidates. Those skills go well beyond implementing prepackaged, superficial units of study about seasons and holidays. Depending on children's ages and developmental levels, an integrated "project approach" to teaching and learning frequently allows children to immerse themselves for extended periods in the study of a topic of high interest to an entire class or a small group. Candidates with strong subject-matter knowledge (as discussed in Sub-Standard 4c) can embed valuable content from mathematics, the arts, literacy, social studies, and other areas in such thematic studies.

Sub-Standard 4c. Understanding Content Knowledge in Early Education Candidates understand the importance of each content area in young children's learning. They know the essential concepts, inquiry tools, and structure of content areas including academic subjects and can identify resources to deepen their understanding.

Supporting explanation Good early childhood curriculum does not come out of a box or a teacher-proof manual. Early childhood professionals have an especially challenging task in developing effective curriculum. As suggested in Standard 1, well-prepared candidates ground their practice in a thorough, research-based understanding of young children's development and learning processes. In developing curriculum, they recognize that every child constructs knowledge in personally and culturally familiar ways. In addition, in order to make curriculum powerful and accessible to all, well-prepared candidates develop curriculum that is free of biases related to ethnicity, religion, gender, or ability status—and, in fact, the curriculum actively counters such biases.

Content areas for early childhood But these tasks are only part of the challenge. Guided by standards for early learning that are effective (NAEYC & NAECS/SDE, 2002), the teacher of children from birth through age 8 must also be well versed in the essentials of many academic disciplines and content areas. And because children are encountering those content areas for the first time, early childhood professionals set the foundations for later understanding and success. Well-prepared candidates choose their approaches to the task depending on the ages and developmental levels of the children they teach. With the youngest children, early childhood candidates emphasize the key experiences that will support later academic skills and understandings—with great reliance on the core approaches and strategies described in Sub-Standard 4b and with great emphasis on oral language and the development of children's background knowledge. Working with somewhat older or more skilled children, candidates also identify those aspects of each subject area that are critical to children's later academic competence. With all children, early childhood professionals support later success by modeling engagement in challenging subject matter and by building children's faith in themselves as young learners—as young mathematicians, scientists, artists, readers, writers, historians, economists, and geographers (although children may not think of themselves in such categories). Going beyond conveying isolated facts, then, well-prepared early childhood candidates possess the kind of content knowledge that focuses on the "big ideas," methods of investigation and expression, and organization of the major academic disciplines. Thus, the early childhood professional knows not only what is important in each content area but also why it is important—how it links with earlier and later understandings both within and across areas. The following sections outline some of this essential understanding in each major discipline.

However, early childhood educators cannot be experts in everything. Because of its central place in later academic competence, the domain of language and literacy requires in-depth research- based understanding and skill. Mathematics, too, is increasingly recognized as an essential foundation. Yet because early childhood professionals must be acquainted with such a breadth of content knowledge, additional resources are needed to supplement the basic knowledge of beginning practitioners. Items in the References and Resources section of this document, especially the professional associa-tion standards documents, offer greater depth and detail in all these content areas.

Common features in candidates' work across content areas Well-prepared candidates demonstrate certain competencies that cut across content areas or academic disciplines. Certain "basics" are common features in candidates' work, whether they are developing curriculum in language and literacy, the arts, mathematics, physical activity and physical education, science, or social studies. Well-prepared early childhood candidates understand the importance of each content area in children's development and learning. They demonstrate essential knowledge of the develop- mental foundations of children's interest in, and understanding of, each content area (i.e., how children's cognitive, language, physical, social, and emotional development influence their ability to understand and benefit from curriculum in each content area—as well as how that curriculum may support development in each domain). Candidates observe and describe the early roots of children's interest and capacities in each content area, and they know how early childhood programs can build on those interests. They demonstrate the essential knowledge and skills needed to provide appropriate environments that support learning in each content area for all children, beginning in infancy (through foundational developmental experiences) and extending through the primary grades—although the nature and depth of their knowledge and skills will vary depending on which sub-periods of early childhood their program emphasizes. Candidates demonstrate basic knowledge of the research base underlying each content area and they demonstrate basic knowledge of the core concepts and standards of professional organizations in each content area, relying on sound resources for that knowledge. Finally, candidates demonstrate that they can analyze and critique early childhood curriculum experiences in terms of the relationship of the experiences to the research base and to professional standards.

Language and literacy Early language and literacy form the basis for much later learning, and well-prepared candidates possess extensive, research-based knowledge and skill in the area, regardless of the age group or setting in which they intend to practice. Listening, speaking, reading, and writing are integrated elements. Verbal and nonverbal communication in its diverse forms, combined with competence as a reader and writer, are essential for children's later development. Even as infants and toddlers, children are building the foundations for literacy through early experiences.

Candidates—including those who are not currently teaching linguistically diverse young children—also demonstrate knowledge of second-language acquisition and of bilingualism. They know the home language environments of the children they teach and the possible effects on children when their classroom environment does not reflect the home language. Candidates know the sociopolitical contexts of major language groups and how those may affect children's motivation to learn English. Candidates understand the benefits of bilingualism and the special needs of young English language learners (ELLs), building on the home language systems that children already have developed and assisting them to add a second language to their repertoire. For young ELLs who are learning to read, candidates use, adapt, and assess research-based literacy activities and teaching methods that build on prior knowledge and support successful transitions for those learners.

Candidates are able to articulate priorities for high-quality, meaningful language and literacy experiences in early childhood, across a

developmental continuum. Across the years from infancy through third grade, those experiences should help children to, for example:

- Explore their environments and develop the conceptual, experiential, and language foundations for learning to read and write
- Develop their ability to converse at length and in depth on a topic in various settings (one-on-one with adults and peers, in small groups, etc.)
- Develop vocabulary that reflects their growing knowledge of the world around them
- Use language, reading, and writing to strengthen their own cultural identity, as well as to participate in the shared identity of the school environment
- Associate reading and writing with pleasure and enjoyment, as well as with skill development
- Use a range of strategies to derive meaning from stories and texts
- Use language, reading, and writing for various purposes
- Use a variety of print and non-print resources
- Develop basic concepts of print and understanding of sounds, letters, and letter-sound relationships

The arts: Music, creative movement, dance, drama, and art Even before children can speak, they move, gesture, and respond to color, sound, and rhythm. Their joy in the "hundred languages of children" shows the value of the arts in early childhood, both as important ends in themselves and as tools for success in other areas. Candidates are able to articulate priorities for high-quality, meaningful arts experiences in early childhood, across a developmental continuum. Depending on children's ages and other characteristics, those experiences should help children to, for example:

- Interact musically with others
- Express and interpret understandings of their world through structured and informal musical play
- Sing, play, and create music
- Respond to expressive characteristics of music—rhythm, melody, form—through speaking, singing, moving, and playing simple instruments
- Use music to express emotions, conflicts, and needs
- Move expressively to music of various tempos, meters, modes, genres, and cultures to express what they feel and hear
- Understand and apply artistic media, techniques, and processes
- Make connections between visual arts and other disciplines

Mathematics Strong mathematical foundations are associated with later academic competence, but international comparisons have found American mathematics education to be seriously deficient. Yet for curious young children, mathematics is a powerful, exciting tool to use in making sense of their world. Mathematics instruction should be guided by the principles and standards developed by the National Council of Teachers of Mathematics (NCTM) and by the joint position statement of NAEYC and NCTM (2002). Early childhood candidates apply the principles that guide all mathematics instruction, as well as the specific NCTM standards for preK–grade 2. The standards are based on the belief that "students learn important mathematical skills and processes with understanding" (NCTM, 2000, ix). According to NCTM, understanding develops through interaction with materials, peers, and supportive

adults in settings where students have opportunities to construct their own relationships when they first meet a new topic. As outlined by NCTM, well-prepared candidates understand and apply the following six principles, or "themes," of mathematics instruction:

- Equity: high expectations and strong support for all children
- Curriculum: more than a collection of activities: coherent, focused on important mathematics, and well integrated across grades and developmental levels
- Teaching: understanding what children already know and need to learn, and challenging and supporting them to learn it well
- Learning: children must learn with understanding, building new mathematical knowledge from experience and prior knowledge
- Assessment: should support the learning of important mathematics and give useful information to teachers and children
- Technology: is essential in teaching and learning mathematics; a tool to enhance learning

In addition to those principles, candidates understand which concepts and skills are developmentally appropriate for preK–grade 2 children in each of five content areas—operations, algebra, geometry, measurement, data analysis, and probability—as well as in the five process areas of problem solving, reasoning and proof, connections, communication, and representation. Early childhood candidates are able to link those two sets of standards together so that the process standards are used in teaching and learning mathematical content.

Physical activity and physical education For young children, moving and exploring what their bodies can do are essential elements of early learning. All children, with and without disabilities, set themselves physical challenges and investigate the frontiers of their physical capacities. Candidates are able to articulate priorities for high-quality, meaningful physical activity and physical education experiences in early childhood, across a developmental continuum. Depending on children's ages and other characteristics, those experiences should help children to, for example:

- Have varied, repeated experiences with functional movement and manipulation

- Demonstrate progress toward mature forms of selected physical skills

- Try new movement activities and skills

- Use feedback to improve performance

- Experience and express pleasure from participation in physical activity

- Apply rules, procedures, and safe practices

- Gain competence to provide increased enjoyment in movement

In promoting children's physical development, candidates are aware of cultural differences and gender expectations. They know when to respect children's and families' preferences regarding dress for physical activity and level of participation, and when to make adaptations to help children meet physical goals, yet support culturally sensitive practices.

Science Although their investigations may not be systematic and their ideas and questions may not be scientifically accurate, young children's intense curiosity and love of hands-on exploration give them much in common with more mature scientists. Early childhood offers unique opportunities to explore phenomena using skills of scientific inquiry, cultivate scientific dispositions, and build a foundation for understanding core scientific concepts.

Candidates are able to articulate priorities for high-quality, meaningful science experiences in early childhood, across a developmental continuum. Focused exploration of meaningful content (for example, the growth and development of a plant over time, or investigation of the properties of water at a water table) supports early scientific understanding. Depending on children's ages and other characteristics, those experiences should help children to, for example:

- Raise questions about objects and events around them

- Explore materials, objects, and events by acting upon them and noticing what happens

- Make careful observations of objects, organisms, and events using all their senses

- Describe, compare, sort, classify, and order in terms of observable characteristics and properties

- Use a variety of simple tools to extend their observations (e.g., hand lens, measuring tools, eye dropper)

- Engage in simple investigations including making predictions, gathering and interpreting data, recognizing simple patterns, and drawing conclusions

- Record observations, explanations, and ideas through multiple forms of representation

- Work collaboratively with others, share and discuss ideas, and listen to new perspectives

Social studies The social studies area presents special challenges to early childhood education. Because core concepts may be abstract or distant in time or space, providing many hands-on experiences is difficult yet essential for children's interest and understanding. Candidates are able to articulate priorities for high-quality, meaningful social studies experiences in early childhood, across a developmental continuum. Depending on children's ages and other characteristics, those experiences should help children to, for example:

Geography

- Make and use maps to locate themselves in space
- Observe the physical characteristics of the places in which they live and identify landforms, bodies of water, climate, soils, natural vegetation, and animal life of that place

History

- Use the methods of the historian, identifying questions, locating and analyzing information, and reaching conclusions
- Record and discuss the changes that occur in their lives, recalling their immediate past

Economics

- Develop awareness of the difference between wants and needs (the concept of scarcity)
- Develop interest in the economic system, understanding the contributions of those who produce goods and services

Social relations/Civics

- Become a participating member of the group, giving up some individuality for the greater good
- Recognizing similarities among people of many cultures
- Respecting others, including those who differ in gender, ethnicity, ability, or ideas
- Learn the principles of democracy, working cooperatively with others, sharing, and voting as they solve problems

Sub-Standard 4d: Building Meaningful Curriculum

Candidates use their own knowledge and other resources to design, implement, and evaluate meaningful, challenging curriculum that promotes comprehensive developmental and learning outcomes for all young children.

Supporting explanation In their work with young children, candidates demonstrate that they can draw upon all the preceding tools—relationships with young children and families; appropriate, effective approaches to early childhood teaching and learning; and meaningful content in the academic disciplines—to design, implement, and evaluate curriculum for young children. The complexity of the process requires candidates, as well as experienced teachers, to go beyond their own basic knowledge to identify and use high-quality resources, including books, standards documents, Web resources, and individuals who have specialized content expertise, in developing early childhood curriculum. Curriculum planning starts with clear, appropriate goals and desired outcomes for children. Although national or state standards or desired expectations may influence curriculum in positive ways, several larger goals are also important guides:

Security and self-regulation. Appropriate, effective curriculum creates a secure base from which young children can explore and tackle challenging problems. Well-implemented curriculum also helps children become better able to manage or regulate their expressions of emotion and, over time, to cope with frustration and manage impulses effectively, rather than creating high levels of frustration and anxiety.

Problem-solving and thinking skills. Candidates who have skills in developing and implementing meaningful, challenging curriculum will also support young children's ability—and motivation—to solve problems and think well.

Academic and social competence. Because good early childhood curriculum is aligned with young children's developmental and learning styles, it supports the growth of academic and social skills.

With these goals in mind, candidates develop curriculum to include both planned and spontaneous experiences that are developmentally appropriate, meaningful, and challenging for all young children, including those with developmental delays or disabilities; that address cultural and linguistic diversities; that lead to positive learning outcomes; and that—as children become older—develop positive dispositions toward learning within each content area.

Depending on children's ages and program settings, candidates demonstrate skill in building curriculum from relationships, daily interactions, and routines (the core elements of infant/toddler curriculum); in integrating academic disciplines with other content in an emergent, interdisciplinary, or thematic curriculum; and (especially for older children) in providing focused learning opportunities within a specific content area. Candidates demonstrate that they can implement plans in organized yet flexible ways, adapting the curriculum to meet the interests and needs of diverse children while proactively supporting their learning. They demonstrate essential skills in evaluating the curriculum in light of their own goals and of children's engagement in learning activities, and they modify curriculum in light of their own evaluation and feedback from supervisors.

Key elements of Standard 4

4a: Knowing, understanding, and using positive relationships and supportive interactions

4b: Knowing, understanding, and using effective approaches, strategies, and tools for early education

4c: Knowing and understanding the importance, central concepts, inquiry tools, and structures of content areas or academic disciplines

4d: Using own knowledge and other resources to design, implement, and evaluate meaningful, challenging curriculum to promote positive outcomes

Rubrics for these key elements, outlining distinct levels of candidate performance and program evidence, are available online at http://www.naeyc.org.

Standard 5. Becoming a Professional

Candidates identify and conduct themselves as members of the early childhood profession. They know and use ethical guidelines and other professional standards related to early childhood practice. They are continuous, collaborative learners who demonstrate knowledgeable, reflective, and critical perspectives on their work, making informed decisions that integrate knowledge from a variety of sources. They are informed advocates for sound educational practices and policies.

Supporting explanation   The early childhood field has a distinctive history, values, knowledge base, and mission. Early childhood professionals, including beginning teachers, have a strong identification and involvement with the early childhood field, to better serve young children and their families. Well-prepared candidates understand the nature of a profession. They know about the many connections between the early childhood field and other related disciplines and professions with which they may collaborate while serving diverse young children and families. Candidates are also aware of the broader contexts and challenges within which early childhood professionals work and might work in the future. Because young children are at such a critical point in their development and learning, and because they are vulnerable and cannot articulate their own rights and needs, early childhood professionals have compelling responsibilities to know about and uphold ethical guidelines and other professional standards.

The profession's code of ethical conduct guides the practice of responsible early childhood educators. Well-prepared candidates are very familiar with the NAEYC Code of Ethical

Conduct and are guided by its ideals and principles. This means honoring their responsibilities to uphold high standards of confidentiality, sensitivity, and respect for children, families, and colleagues. Candidates know how to use the Code to analyze and resolve professional ethical dilemmas and are able to give defensible justifications for their resolutions of those dilemmas. Well-prepared candidates also know and obey relevant laws such as those pertaining to child abuse, the rights of children with disabilities, and school attendance. Finally, candidates are familiar with relevant professional guidelines such as national, state, or local standards for content and child outcomes; position statements about, for example, early learning standards, linguistic and cultural diversity, early childhood mathematics, technology in early childhood, and prevention of child abuse; child care licensing requirements; and other professional standards affecting early childhood practice.

Continuous, collaborative learning to inform practice is a hallmark of a professional in any field. An attitude of inquiry is evident in well-prepared candidates' writing, discussion, and actions. Whether engaging in classroom-based research, investigating ways to improve their own practices, participating in conferences, or finding resources in libraries and Internet sites, candidates demonstrate self-motivated, purposeful learning that directly influences the quality of their work with young children. Candidates—and professional preparation programs—view graduation or licensure not as the final demonstration of competence but as one milestone among many, including for-credit and not-for-credit experiences.

At its most powerful, learning is socially constructed, in interaction with others. Even as beginning teachers, early childhood candidates demonstrate involvement in collaborative learning communities with other candidates, higher education faculty, and experienced early childhood practitioners. By working together on common challenges, with lively exchanges of ideas, members of such communities benefit from one another's perspectives. Candidates also demonstrate understanding of and essential skills in interdisciplinary collaboration. Because many children with disabilities and other special needs are included in early childhood programs, every practitioner needs to understand the role of the other professionals who may be involved in young children's care and education (e.g., special educators, reading specialists, speech and hearing specialists, physical and occupational therapists, school psychologists). Candidates demonstrate that they have the essential communication skills and knowledge base to engage in interdisciplinary team meetings as informed partners and to fulfill their roles as part of IEP/IFSP teams for children with developmental delays or disabilities.

As professionals prepared in four- and five-year higher education programs, early childhood candidates' decisions and advocacy efforts are grounded in multiple sources of knowledge and multiple perspectives. Even routine decisions about what materials to use for an activity, whether to intervene in a dispute between two children, how to organize nap time, what to say about curriculum in a newsletter, or what to tell families about new video games are informed by a professional context, research-based knowledge, and values.

Well-prepared candidates' practice is influenced by knowledgeable, reflective, and critical perspectives. In their work with young children, candidates show that they make and justify decisions on the basis of their knowledge of the central issues, professional values and standards, and research findings in their field. They also show evidence of reflective approaches to their work, analyzing their own practices in a broader context, and using reflections to modify and improve their work with young children.

Finally, well-prepared candidates display a critical stance, examining their own work, sources of professional knowledge, and the early childhood field with a questioning attitude. Their work demonstrates that they do not just accept a simplistic source of "truth"; instead, they recognize that while early childhood educators share the same core professional values, they do not agree on all of the field's central questions. Candidates demonstrate an understanding that through dialogue and attention to differences, early childhood professionals will continue to reach new levels of shared knowledge.

Finally, early childhood candidates demonstrate that they can engage in informed advocacy for children and the profession. They know about the central policy issues in the field, including professional compensation, financing of the early education system, and standards setting and assessment. They are aware of and engaged in examining ethical issues and societal concerns about program quality and provision of early childhood services and the implications of those issues for advocacy and policy change.

Candidates have a basic understanding of how public policies are developed, and they demonstrate essential advocacy skills, including verbal and written communication and collaboration with others around common issues.

Key elements of Standard 5

5a: Identifying and involving oneself with the early childhood field

5b: Knowing about and upholding ethical standards and other professional guidelines

5c: Engaging in continuous, collaborative learning to inform practice

5d: Integrating knowledgeable, reflective, and critical perspectives on early education

5e: Engaging in informed advocacy for children and the profession

Rubrics for these key elements, outlining distinct levels of candidate performance and program evidence, are available online at http://www.naeyc.org.

References and Resources

Publications

[Numbers in brackets denote items pertinent to one or more of the five standards; "G" denotes items of General usefulness.]

Adams, M.J. 1994. *Beginning to read: Thinking and learning about print.* Cambridge, MA: Bradford Books. [4]

August, D., & K. Hakuta, eds. 1998. *Educating language-minority children.* Washington, DC: National Academy Press. [1,4]

Barnett, W.S., & S.S. Boocock. 1998. *Early care and education for children in poverty: Promises, programs, and long-term results.* Albany, NY: State University of New York Press. [G]

Barnett, W.S., J.W. Young, & L.J. Schweinhart. 1998. How preschool education influences long-term cognitive development and school success. In *Early care and education for children in poverty,* eds. W.S. Barnett & S.S. Boocock, 167–84. Albany, NY: State University of New York Press. [G]

Barrera, I. 1996. Thoughts on the assessment of young children whose sociocultural background is unfamiliar to the assessor. In *New visions for the developmental assessment of infants and young children,* eds. S.J. Meisels & E. Fenichel, 69–84. Washington, DC: ZERO TO THREE/National Center for Infants, Toddlers, and Families. [3]

Beckman, P.J. 1996. *Strategies for working with families of young children with disabilities.* Baltimore, MD: Brookes. [2]

Bentzen, W.R. 1997. *Seeing young children: A guide to observing and recording behavior.* Albany, NY: Delmar. [1]

Bergen, D., R. Reid, & L. Torelli. 2001. *Educating and caring for very young children: The infant/toddler curriculum.* New York: Teachers College Press. [4]

Berk, L.E., & A. Winsler. 1995. *Scaffolding children's learning: Vygotsky and early childhood education.* Washington, DC: NAEYC. [1]

Bodrova, E., & D.J. Leong. 1996. *Tools of the mind: The Vygotskian approach to early childhood education.* Upper Saddle River, NJ: Prentice Hall. [4]

Bredekamp, S., & C. Copple, eds. 1997. *Developmentally appropriate practice in early childhood programs.* Rev. ed. Washington, DC: NAEYC. [G]

Bredekamp, S., & T. Rosegrant, series & vol. eds. 1992. *Reaching potentials. Vol.1: Appropriate curriculum and assessment for young children.* Washington, DC: NAEYC. [3,4]

Bredekamp, S., & T. Rosegrant, series & vol. eds. 1995. *Reaching potentials. Vol. 2: Transforming early childhood curriculum and assessment.* Washington, DC: NAEYC. [3,4]

Burns, M.S., P. Griffin, & C.E. Snow, eds. 1999. *Starting out right: A guide to promoting children's reading success.* Washington, DC: National Academy Press. [4]

Campbell, F.A., C.T. Ramey, E. Pungello, J. Sparling, & S. Miller-Johnson. 2002. Early childhood education: Young adult outcomes from the Abecedarian Project. *Applied Developmental Science 6* (1): 42–57.

Campbell, F.A., R. Harms, J.J. Sparling, & C.T. Ramey. 1998. Early childhood programs and success in school: The Abecedarian study. In *Early care and education for children in poverty*, eds. W.S. Barnett & S.S. Boocock, pp. 145–66. Albany, NY: State University of New York Press. [G]

Campbell, P.S., & C. Scott-Kassner, eds. 1995. *Music in childhood, from preschool through the early grades.* Belmont, CA: Wadsworth. [4]

Chafel, J., ed. 1997. Families and early childhood education. *Advances in Early Education and Day Care*, vol. 9. Stamford, CT: JAI Press. [2]

Chang, H.N., A. Muckelroy, & D. Pulido-Tobiassen. 1996. *Looking in, looking out: Redefining child care and early education in a diverse society.* San Francisco, CA: California Tomorrow. [G]

Chang, H.N., J.O. Edwards, C. Alvarado, D. Pulido-Tobiassen, & C.L. Morgan. 1999. *Transforming curriculum, empowering faculty: Deepening teachers' understanding of race, class, culture, and language.* San Francisco, CA: California Tomorrow. [G]

Child Mental Health Foundations and Agencies Network. 2000. *A good beginning: Sending America's children to school with the social and emotional competence they need to succeed.* Bethesda, MD: National Institute of Mental Health, Office of Communications and Public Liaison. [4]

Clements, D.H. 2001. Mathematics in the preschool. *Teaching Children Mathematics* 7: 270–75. [4]

Clements, D.H., & J. Sarama. 2000. Standards for preschoolers. *Teaching Children Mathematics* 7: 38–41. [4]

Clements, D.H., J. Sarama, & A.M. DiBiase, eds. In press. *Engaging young children in mathematics: Findings of the National 2000 Conference on Standards for Preschool and Kindergarten Mathematics Education.* Hillsdale, NJ: Erlbaum. [4]

Cohen, D.H., V. Stern, & N. Balaban. 1997. *Observing and recording the behavior of young children.* 4th ed. New York: Teachers College Press. [1]

Copley, J.V. 2000. *The young child and mathematics.* Washington, DC: NAEYC. [4]

Copley, J.V., ed. 1999. *Mathematics in the early years.* Reston, VA: National Council of Teachers of Mathematics; and Washington, DC: NAEYC. [4]

Darling-Hammond, L., J. Ancess, & B. Falk. 1993. *Authentic assessment in action: Studies of schools and students at work.* New York, NY: Teachers College Press. [3]

Darling-Hammond, L., L. Einbender, F. Frelow, & J. Ley-King. 1993. *Authentic assessment in practice: A collection of portfolios, performance tasks, exhibitions, and documentation.* New York: National Center for Restructuring Education, Schools, and Teaching (NCREST). [3]

Dunst, C.J., C.M. Trivette, & A.G. Deal. 1994. *Supporting and strengthening families: Methods, strategies, and practices.* Vol. 1. Cambridge, MA: Brookline Books. [2]

Edwards, P.A., H.M. Pleasants, & S.H. Franklin. 1999. *A path to follow: Learning to listen to parents.* Portsmouth, NH: Heinemann. [2]

Elkind, D. 1994. *A sympathetic understanding of the child: Birth to sixteen*, 3d ed. Boston: Allyn & Bacon.

Epstein, J.L., M.G. Sanders, & L.A. Clark. 1999. *Preparing educators for school-family-community partnerships: Results of a national survey of colleges and universities.* Baltimore, MD: Center for Research on the Education of Students Placed at Risk. [2]

Falk, B. 2000. *The heart of the matter: Using standards and assessment to learn.* Portsmouth, NH: Heinemann. [3]

Feeney, S., & N.K. Freeman. 1999. *Ethics and the early childhood educator: Using the NAEYC code.* Washington, DC: NAEYC. [5]

Feeney, S., N.K. Freeman, & E. Moravcik. 2000. *Teaching the NAEYC code of ethical conduct.* Washington, DC: NAEYC. [5]

Fillmore, L.W., & C.E. Snow. 2000. *What teachers need to know about language.* Washington, DC: Office of Educational Research and Improvement. [4]

Forman, G., & B. Fyfe. 1998. Negotiated learning through design, documentation, and discourse. In *The hundred languages of children: The Reggio Emilia approach—Advanced reflections,* 2d ed., eds. C. Edwards, L. Gandini, & G. Forman, 239–60. Greenwich, CT: Ablex. [4]

Gandini, L., & C.P. Edwards. 2001. *Bambini: The Italian approach to infant/toddler care.* New York: Teachers College Press. [4]

Gardner, H. 1993. *Frames of mind: The theory of multiple intelligences.* New York: Basic Books. [1]

Gregory, E., ed. 1997. *One child, many worlds: Early learning in multicultural communities.* New York: Teachers College Press. [2]

Guralnick, M.J., ed. 2001. *Early childhood inclusion: Focus on change.* Baltimore, MD: Brookes. [G]

Harbin, G.L., R.A. McWilliam, & J.J. Gallagher. 2000. Services for young children with disabilities and their families. In *Handbook of early childhood intervention,* 2nd ed., eds. J.P. Shonkoff & S.J. Meisels, 387–415. New York: Cambridge University Press. [G]

Hart, B., & T.R. Risley. 1995. *Meaningful differences in everyday experience of young American children.* Baltimore, MD: Brookes. [4]

Heath, S.B. 1983. *Ways with words: Language, life, and work in communities and classrooms.* New York: Cambridge University Press. [4]

Helm, J.H., S. Beneke, & K. Steinheimer. 1998. *Windows on learning: Documenting young children's work.* New York: Teachers College Press. [3]

Heubert, J.P., & R.M. Hauser. 1999. *High stakes: Testing for tracking, promotion, and graduation.* Washington, DC: National Academy Press. [3]

Hodgkinson, H.L. 1992. *A demographic look at tomorrow.* Washington, DC: Institute for Educational Leadership. [G]

Hodgkinson, H.L. 2003. *Leaving too many children behind: A demographer's view on the neglect of America's youngest children.* Washington, DC: Institute for Educational Leadership. [G]

Johnson, J., & J.B. McCracken, eds. 1994. *The early childhood career lattice: Perspectives on professional development.* Washington, DC: NAEYC. [5]

Johnson, L.J., M.J. LaMontagne, P.M. Elgas, & A.M. Bauer. 1998. *Early childhood education: Blending theory, blending practice.* Baltimore, MD: Brookes. [G]

Kaiser, B., & J.S. Rasminsky. 1999. *Meeting the challenge: Effective strategies for challenging behaviors in early childhood environments.* Ottawa, Canada: Canadian Child Care Federation. [4]

Katz, L.G., & S.C. Chard. 2000. *Engaging children's minds: The project approach.* 2d ed. Greenwich, CT: Ablex. [4]

Kohn, A. 1999. *The schools our children deserve: Moving beyond traditional classrooms and "tougher standards."* Boston, MA: Houghton Mifflin. [5]

Ladson-Billings, G. 2001. *Crossing over to Canaan: The journey of new teachers in diverse classrooms.* San Francisco: Jossey-Bass. [5]

Lally, J.R. 1995. *Caring for infants and toddlers in groups: Developmentally appropriate practice.* Arlington, VA: ZERO TO THREE/National Center for Clinical Infant Programs. [4]

Lamb, M., ed. 1999. *Parenting and child development in "nontraditional" families.* Mahwah, NJ: Erlbaum. [2]

Lee, E., D. Menkart, & M. Okazawa-Rey, eds. 1998. *Beyond heroes and holidays: A practical guide to K–12 anti-racist, multicultural education and staff development.* Washington, DC: Network of Educators on the Americas. [4]

Losardo, A., & A. Notari-Syverson. 2001. *Alternative approaches to assessing young children.* Baltimore, MD: Brookes. [3]

Lynch, E.W., & M.J. Hanson. 1998. *Developing cross-cultural competence: A guide for working with children and their families.* 2d ed. Baltimore, MD: Brookes. [1,2]

McCabe, A. 1995. *Chameleon readers: Teaching children to appreciate all kinds of good stories.* Columbus, OH: McGraw-Hill Higher Education. [4]

McCarthy, J., J. Cruz, & N. Ratcliff. 1999. *Early childhood teacher education licensure patterns and curriculum guidelines: A state by state analysis.* Washington, DC: Council for Professional Recognition. [G]

McWilliam, P.J., P.J. Winton, & E.R. Crais. 1996. *Practical strategies for family-centered intervention.* San Diego, CA: Singular Publishing Group. [2]

Mussen, P., ed. 1997. *Handbook of child psychology.* 5th ed. New York: Wiley. [1]

NAEYC. 1996a. *Guidelines for preparation of early childhood professionals.* Washington, DC: Author. [G]

NAEYC. 1996b. *Technology and young children: Ages 3 through 8.* Position Statement. Washington, DC: Author. [G]

NAEYC. 1997. *Code of ethical conduct and statement of commitment.* Position Statement. Washington, DC: Author. [G]

NAEYC. 1997. *Licensing and public regulation of early childhood programs.* Position Statement. Washington, DC: Author. [5]

NAEYC. 1998. *Accreditation criteria and procedures of the National Academy of Early Childhood Programs.* Position Statement. Washington, DC: Author. [G]

NAEYC & National Association of Early Childhood Specialists in State Departments of Education (NAECS/SDE). 2002. *Early learning standards: Creating the conditions for success.* Joint Position Statement. Washington, DC: NAEYC. [G]

NAEYC & National Council of Teachers of Mathematics (NCTM). 2002. *Early childhood mathematics: Promoting good beginnings.* Joint Position Statement. Washington, DC: NAEYC. [4]

National Commission on Teaching and America's Future. 1996. *What matters most: Teaching for America's future.* New York: Author. [G]

National Council of Teachers of Mathematics (NCTM). 2000. *Principles and standards for school mathematics.* Reston, VA: Author. [4]

National Institute of Child Health and Human Development. 2000. Report of the National Reading Panel. *Teaching children to read: An evidence-based assessment of the scientific research literature on reading and its implications for reading instruction.* NIH Publication No. 00-4769. Washington, DC: U.S. Government Printing Office. [4]

National Institute on Early Childhood Development and Education, U.S. Department of Education. 2000. *New teachers for a new century: The future of early childhood.*

National Research Council. 1998. *Preventing reading difficulties in young children,* eds. C.E. Snow, M.S. Burns, & P. Griffin. Committee on the Prevention of Reading Difficulties in Young Children, Commission on Behavioral and Social Sciences and Education. Washington, DC: National Academy Press. [4]

National Research Council. 1999. *How people learn: Brain, mind, experience, and school,* eds. J.D. Bransford, A.L. Brown, & R.R. Cocking. Committee on Developments in the Science of Learning, Commission on Behavioral and Social Sciences and Education. Washington, DC: National Academy Press. [G]

National Research Council. 2001a. *Adding it up: Helping children learn mathematics,* eds. J. Kilpatrick, J. Swafford, & B. Findell. Mathematics Learning Study Committee, Center for Education, Division of Behavioral and Social Sciences and Education. Washington, DC: National Academy Press. [4]

National Research Council. 2001b. *Eager to learn: Educating our preschoolers,* eds. B.T. Bowman, M.S. Donovan, & M.S. Burns. Committee on Early Childhood Pedagogy, Commission on Behavioral and Social Sciences and Education. Washington, DC: National Academy Press. [G]

National Research Council and Institute of Medicine. 2000. *From neurons to neighborhoods: The science of early childhood development,* eds. J.P. Shonkoff & D.A. Phillips. Board on Children, Youth, and Families, Commission on Behavioral and Social Sciences and Education. Washington, DC: National Academy Press. [G]

Neelly, L.P. 2001. Developmentally appropriate music practice: Children learn what they live. *Young Children 56* (3): 32–43. [4]

Neuman, S.B., & D.K. Dickinson. 2001. *Handbook of early literacy research.* New York: Guilford. [4]

Neuman, S.B., C. Copple, & S. Bredekamp. 1999. *Learning to read and write: Developmentally appropriate practices for young children.* Washington, DC: NAEYC. [4]

New Standards/Speaking and Listening Committee. 2001. *Speaking and listening for preschool through third grade.* Washington, DC: National Center on Education and the Economy. [4]

Peisner-Feinberg, E.S., M.R. Burchinal, R.M. Clifford, M.L. Culkin, C. Howes, S.L. Kagan, N. Yazejian, P. Byler, J. Rustici, & J. Zelazo. 1999. *The children of the Cost, Quality, and Outcomes Study go to school.* Chapel Hill: University of North Carolina at Chapel Hill, Frank Porter Graham Child Development Center. [G]

Reynolds, A.J., J.A. Temple, D.L. Robertson, & E.A. Mann. 2001. Long-term effects of an early childhood intervention on educational achievement and juvenile arrest: A 15-year follow-up of low-income children in public schools. *Journal of the American Medical Association 285* (18): 2339–46. [G]

Rosin, P., A.D. Whitehead, L.I. Tuchman, G.S. Jesien, A.L. Begun, & L. Irwin. 1996. *Partnerships in family-centered care: A guide to collaborative early intervention.* Baltimore, MD: Brookes. [2]

Sandall, S., M. McLean, & B. Smith. 2000. *DEC recommended practices in early intervention/early childhood special education.* Longmont, CO: Sopris West Educational Services. [G]

Seefeldt, C. 1995. Transforming curriculum in social studies. In *Reaching potentials. Vol. 2: Transforming early childhood curriculum and assessment,* eds. S. Bredekamp & T. Rosegrant, 145–66. Washington, DC: NAEYC. [4]

Seefeldt, C. 2001. *Social studies for the preschool/primary child.* 6th ed. Upper Saddle River, NJ: Prentice Hall/Merrill. [4]

Seefeldt, C., & A. Galper. 2000. *Active experiences for active children: Social studies.* Upper Saddle River, NJ: Prentice Hall/Merrill. [4]

Shartrand, A.M., H.B. Weiss, H.M. Kreider, & M.E. Lopez. 1997. *New skills for new schools.* Washington, DC: U.S. Department of Education. [2]

Shore, R. 1997. *Rethinking the brain: New insights into early development.* New York: Families and Work Institute. [G]

Sims, W.L. ed.; J. Cassidy, A. Freshwater, & C.D. Mack, assoc. eds. 1995. *Strategies for teaching: Prekindergarten music.* Reston, VA: National Association for Music Education (MENC). [4]

Snell, M.E., & R. Janney. 2000. *Teachers' guides to inclusive practices: Collaborative teaming.* Baltimore, MD: Brookes. [G]

Stauffer, S.L., & J. Davidson, eds. 1996. *Strategies for teaching: K-4 general music.* Reston, VA: National Association for Music Education (MENC). [4]

Tabors, P.O. 1997. *One child, two languages: A guide for preschool educators of children learning English as a second language.* Baltimore, MD: Brookes. [4]

Tabors, P.O. 1998. What early childhood educators need to know: Developing effective programs for linguistically and culturally diverse children and families. *Young Children* 53 (6): 20–26. [1,4]

Tabors, P.O., & C.E. Snow. 2001. Young bilingual children and early literacy development. In *Handbook of early literacy research,* eds. S.B. Neuman & D.K. Dickinson, 159–78. New York: Guilford. [4]

Teaching Children Mathematics. 2001. Focus issue: Mathematics and culture, 7 (6). [4]

Tertell, E.A., S.M. Klein, & J.L. Jewett, eds. 1998. *When teachers reflect: Journeys toward effective, inclusive practice.* Washington, DC: NAEYC. [5]

Turnbull, A.P., & H.R. Turnbull. 1997. *Families, professionals, and exceptionality: A special partnership.* 3d ed. Columbus, OH: Merrill. [2]

Van Scoter, J., E. Ellis, & J. Railsback. 2001. *Technology in early childhood education: Finding a balance.* Portland, OR: Northwest Regional Education Laboratory. [4]

Von Blackensee, L. 1999. *Technology tools for young learners.* Larchmont, NY: Eye on Education. [4]

Vygotsky, L.S. 1978. *Mind in society: The development of higher psychological processes.* Cambridge, MA: Harvard University Press. [1]

Whitebook, M., C. Howes, & D. Phillips. 1998. *Worthy work, unlivable wages: The National Child Care Staffing Study, 1988–97.* Washington, DC: National Center for the Early Childhood Work Force. [5].

Winton, P.J., J. McCollum, & C. Catlett, eds. 1997. *Reforming personnel preparation in early intervention: Issues, models, and practical strategies.* Baltimore, MD: Brookes. [G]

Wolery, M., & J.S. Wilbers, eds. 1994. *Including children with special needs in early childhood programs.* Washington, DC: NAEYC. [G]

Wozniak, R.H., & K.W. Fischer, eds. 1993. *Development in context: Acting and thinking in specific environments,* 3–44. Mahwah, NJ: Erlbaum. [1]

Yelland, N.J., ed. 2000. *Promoting meaningful learning: Innovations in educating early childhood professionals.* Washington, DC: NAEYC. [5] professional preparation. Jessup, MD: U.S. Department of Education, ED Publishing. [G]

Websites

American Associate Degree Early Childhood Educators, http://www.accessece.org

American Association of Colleges for Teacher Education, http://www.aacte.org

American Alliance for Health, Physical Education, Recreation, and Dance, http://www.aahperd.org

Center for the Improvement of Early Reading Achievement, http://www.ciera.org

CEO Forum on Education and Technology, Self-Assessment for Teacher Preparation, http://www.ceoforum.org

Children and Computers, http://www.childrenandcomputers.com

Council for Exceptional Children, http://www.cec.sped.org

Division for Early Childhood, http://www.dec-sped.org

ERIC Clearinghouse on Assessment and Evaluation, http://ericae.net

International Reading Association, http://www.reading.org

MENC: National Association for Music Education, http://www.menc.org

MuSICA: Music and Science Information Computer Archive, http://www.musica.uci.edu

National Association for Bilingual Education, http://www.nabe.org

National Association for Early Childhood Teacher Educators, http://www.naecte.org

National Association for the Education of Young Children, http://www.naeyc.org

National Center for Research on Evaluation, Standards, and Student Testing, http://cresst96.cse.ucla.edu

National Center on Education and the Economy, http://www.ncee.org

National Clearinghouse for English Language Acquisition and Language Instruction Educational Programs, http://www.ncela.gwu.edu

National Council of Teachers of Mathematics, http://www.nctm.org

National Early Childhood Technical Assistance Center, http://www.nectac.org

National Education Goals Panel, http://www.negp.gov

National Educational Technology Standards Projects, http://cnets.iste.org

National Geographic Society, National Standards for Geography, http://www.nationalgeographic.com/xpeditions/standards/

National Institute for Early Education Research, http://nieer.org/

Program for Infant/Toddler Caregivers, http://www.pitc.org

Technology & Young Children (NAEYC Technology & Young Children Interest Forum), http://techandyoungchildren.org/index.shtml

ZERO TO THREE, http://www.zerotothree.org

Initial Licensure Standards Work Group

NAEYC gratefully acknowledges the expertise and commitment of the members of the Initial Licensure Standards Work Group:

Linda Hassan-Anderson, National Black Child Development Institute (NBCDI)–Atlanta Affiliate

Nancy Barbour, Kent State University

Josué Cruz Jr., University of South Florida

John Johnston, University of Memphis

Ann Marie Leonard, James Madison University

NAEYC Staff

Marilou Hyson, Associate Executive Director for Professional Development

Parker Anderson, Assistant Director for Professional Development

Institutional affiliations reflect those held by the members at the time the Work Group

NAEYC Position Statement on the Prevention of Child Abuse in Early Childhood Programs and the Responsibilities of Early Childhood Professionals to Prevent Child Abuse*

Child abuse is any nonaccidental injury or pattern of injuries to a child for which there is no "reasonable" explanation (National Committee to Prevent Child Abuse, 1995). It includes physical, emotional, and sexual abuse. As the nation's largest organization of early childhood professionals and others dedicated to improving the quality of early childhood programs in centers, schools, and homes, the National Association for the Education of Young children (NAEYC) is committed to safeguarding the well-being of children. Child abuse violates children's health and safety and betrays their trust.

Most child abuse is perpetrated by family members; 1994 figures indicate that in 90% of reported cases of abuse, perpetrators were parents or other relatives (U.S. Department of Health and Human Services, 1996). Early childhood programs in centers, homes, and schools can help minimize the potential for this type of abuse by working to support families and providing referrals to appropriate helping services as needed. Although much less frequent than abuse by family members, child abuse also occurs in out-of-home settings such as schools, child care, foster care, and organized youth activities. Child abuse by those working with children violates the fundamental principle in NAEYC's *Code of Ethical Conduct* for working with young children: "Above all, we shall not harm children" (Feeney & Kipnis, 1992).

Estimates of the proportion of child abuse in out-of-home settings vary, ranging from 1% to 7% of reported rates of abuse (Wells et al., 1995). Fortunately, the majority of employees and volunteers working with young children are caring individuals committed to promoting children's safety, healthy development, and learning. However, because previous and potential abusers may seek opportunities with access to children, those organizing and operating any type of out-of-home setting for children and youth must take

*Adopted September 1996

proper precautions to minimize the potential for harm to children.

NAEYC deplores child abuse in any form in any setting and believes that all early childhood professionals, families, and communities must be vigilant in protecting children from all forms of abuse. NAEYC offers the following recommendations as strategies to prevent child abuse, including physical, emotional, and sexual abuse, in early childhood programs to the greatest extent possible. These recommendations outline specific roles for early childhood professionals, early childhood programs, family members, and public regulation. Particular attention is given to the role of early childhood programs, focusing on the importance of carefully planned and implemented policies with regard to practices with children, staff screening and recruitment, and partnerships with families. In addition, this statement outlines responsibilities of early childhood professionals to prevent child abuse in other settings. These recommendations focus on children from birth through age eight attending any type of group program, including child care centers and preschools, kindergarten and the primary grades, and family child care homes.

Role of Early Childhood Programs

NAEYC recommends that early childhood programs in centers, homes, and schools adopt policies consistent with the guidelines that follow. In some cases these policies will be set by a larger organizational structure, such as a school district, religious group, corporation, or community agency.

Program policies

1. Early childhood programs should employ an adequate number of qualified staff to work with children and to provide adequate supervision of program staff and volunteers.

Limiting the number of children for which each adult is responsible and the overall group size helps staff to better meet the individual needs of each child. Teachers are better able to provide supervision of all children and to recognize signs or changes in behavior that may indicate the possibility of abuse. NAEYC's accreditation criteria for centers (NAEYC, 1991) recommend group sizes of no more than 6 to 8 infants, 8 to 12 toddlers, 14 to 20 preschoolers, 16 to 20 kindergartners, and 20 to 24 primary grade children, always with at least 2 adults per group. Smaller numbers may be necessary for children with certain emotional or behavioral problems who require more intensive and direct supervision.

2. The program environment (including both indoor and outdoor areas) should be designed to reduce the possibility of private, hidden locations in which abuse may occur.

Young children need opportunities for solitude and quiet play in small groups throughout the day, but all early childhood program spaces should be regarded as public. Both indoor and outdoor areas can be designed and set up in ways that provide opportunities for solitude while also allowing for unobtrusive adult supervision. Likewise, the program environment should be designed to reduce the likelihood that staff members, volunteers, or others have opportunities for hidden interactions with children.

3. All program staff, substitutes, and volunteers should receive preservice orientation and refresher training at regular intervals that include but are not limited to (a) an understanding of what constitutes child abuse, (b) the program's discipline policy and appropriate guidance of children, (c) means of preventing potential abuse situations in group settings, (d) identification of signs of potential abuse, and (e) individual obligations and procedures for reporting suspected cases of abuse.

Individuals who work with young children and their families are obligated to report any suspicions of child abuse to the appropriate authorities. Ensuring that staff members and program volunteers understand and keep abreast of (a) strategies to reduce abuse, (b) ways to recognize potential signs of abuse, and (c) appropriate actions for reporting abuse helps reduce risks and meets legal obligations while minimizing the potential for false reports.

4. Centers, schools, and homes should have clear policies and procedures for maintaining a safe, secure environment.

Access to the facility should be controlled, for example, by requiring all visitors to sign in and sign out of the program area or to check in and check out with the administrative office. In the case of family child care homes, parents should be informed prior to the use of a substitute, and children should never be left in the care of an individual without their parents' knowledge.

5. Teachers and caregivers should be supervised by qualified personnel on an ongoing basis, and parents should be encouraged to spend time in the program.

In instances when a teacher or caregiver works primarily alone, periodic, drop-in visits by supervising personnel, parents, or others should be encouraged; such visits can reduce the isolation sometimes experienced by individual providers, thus minimizing the potential for abuse.

6. Programs should not institute "no-touch" policies to reduce the risk of abuse.

In the wake of well-publicized allegations of child abuse in out-of-home settings and increased concerns regarding liability, some programs have instituted such policies, either explicitly or implicitly. No-touch policies are misguided efforts that fail to recognize the importance of touch to children's healthy development. Touch is especially important for infants and toddlers. Warm, responsive touches convey regard and concern for children of any age. Adults should be sensitive to ensuring that their touches (such as pats on the back, hugs, or ruffling a child's hair) are welcomed by the children and appropriate to their individual characteristics and cultural experience. Careful, open communication between the program and families about the value of touch in children's development can help achieve consensus on acceptable ways for adults to show their respect and support for children in the program.

Staff Screening, Recruitment, and Retention Policies Programs should employ careful screening and recruitment practices to increase the likelihood of selecting appropriate candidates as staff, substitutes, or volunteers to work with children. NAEYC's recommendations reflect the screening decisionmaking model developed by the American Bar Association's Center for Children and the Law (Wells et al., 1995) that identifies a variety of potential screening mechanisms, including personal interviews, verification of personal and professional references and education qualifications, criminal record checks, and affidavits at-testing to history of conviction for abuse or other violent crimes. NAEYC recommends that all early childhood programs in centers, homes, and schools have a comprehensive screening policy in place and that this policy be publicized to existing and potential staff and volunteers, families and other interested policies.

NAEYC recommends the following guidelines be used in developing a screening policy.

1. At a minimum, basic screening should be conducted on all staff members, substitutes, volunteers, and other individuals who may have access to young children but do not have direct responsibility for their care and education.

For example, bus drivers, janitors, cooks, and administrative assistants should be screened in the cases of centers and schools, and all older children and adults present in a family child care provider's home (family members, friends, or employees) should be screened. The basic screening should include a signed, written application, careful review of employment record, checks of personal and professional references, and a personal interview. Additional screening, such as verification of educational status and checks of motor vehicle record, criminal record, and other registries may be appropriate depending upon the duration, frequency, and type of contact between the adult and children and the degree of supervision. In the case of self-employed family child care providers, public agencies should provide for screening and make the results of the screening available to parents on request.

2. All potential employees, substitutes, and volunteers should be required to attest to any previous convictions, in particular, whether they have ever been convicted of any crime against children or other violent crime.

Factors such as the relevance and recency of any conviction and demonstration of rehabilitation should be weighed in making hiring and placement decisions for individuals who admit to previous convictions. A volunteer's or employee's failure to fully disclose previous convictions should be viewed as automatic grounds for dismissal.

3. All potential employees and volunteers should be required to provide at least three personal references from previous employers, parents of children served, or educators.

Programs should check these references carefully.

4. All new employees and volunteers should be required to complete a mandatory probationary period.

Although new staff members or volunteers should have no unsupervised access to children during the probationary period, they should have supervised interactions with children so that their competencies in working with young children can be assessed.

5. In addition to screening policies designed to ensure that appropriate individuals are engaged in work in the program, early childhood programs should have policies designed to retain competent staff and remove others if necessary.

Programs that provide competitive salaries, good benefits and working conditions, and regular opportunities for advancement are more likely to recruit and retain competent staff who provide better quality care to children. In addition, the provision of employee assistance programs can provide support to staff facing stressful circumstances, thus minimizing the potential for abuse.

Policies also should provide for the removal of individuals whose performance on the job is deemed unacceptable or whose behavior outside the job could affect their performance (such as a bus driver being convicted for driving under the influence).

6. Clear procedures should be in place for responding to an accusation of abuse in the program.

These procedures should address steps to protect children and provide due process for the accused, and they should be publicized in advance to staff as well as parents.

Policies to Promote Close Partnerships with Families Ongoing program policies that strengthen partnerships with families also can help minimize the likelihood of abuse in the program. Examples of such policies follow.

1. Programs should strongly encourage and provide ample opportunity for family participation.

2. Family members should have access to any part of the center, school, or family child care home to which children have access while their children are in care.

3. Field trips should include parents when possible, be approved by the program administrator, be supervised by regular program personnel, and be conducted with written parental permission.

4. Programs should require that children be released only to parents or legal guardians or to those persons authorized in writing by their parents or guardians. Staff should check identification of authorized individuals who are unfamiliar to them.

5. Programs should inform parents about the characteristics of good quality programs and the signs of potential abuse. Parents should be informed also about the child protection practices implemented by the program through (a) written policies shared with parents and family members, (b) access to public records documenting regulatory compliance (when applicable), and (c) publicized mechanisms for registering complaints and the procedures to be followed in response to a complaint.

Close partnerships with families also can help reduce the potential for child abuse by family members. Early childhood programs can provide information to parents and families regarding child development and effective strategies for responding to children's behavior. Teachers and caregivers should be knowledge-able about and alert to signs of family stress and provide support to families. Early childhood professionals can collaborate with state agencies, such as protective services, to promote understanding of child development, support and empower families, and advocate for children. Working with families in this way may help break cycles of family violence and prevent children from becoming abusers themselves.

Role of Family Members

Parents and other family members can assist in the prevention of child abuse in early childhood programs by

- increasing their sensitivity to children's communications,
- participating in and observing their children's programs,
- talking regularly with other families who use the program, and
- understanding and using child abuse reporting procedures when appropriate.

Children have minimal responsibility in the prevention of child abuse. Indeed, many of the child-oriented abuse prevention materials and techniques that have been developed in the wake of highly publicized allegations of abuse do not reflect an understanding of children's development and learning. They can be confusing to children and promote anxiety and fear. Rather than placing the responsibility on children to prevent abuse, NAEYC believes it is the responsibility of parents, early childhood professionals, and other adults to ensure to the greatest degree possible that abuse does not occur by providing safe, well-planned, and well-supervised environments.

Role of Public Regulation

An effective regulation system is an essential component in public efforts to reduce the potential for abuse in early childhood programs. The nature of public regulatory systems governing early childhood programs varies by program auspice. States license or employ other means of regulation for the majority of programs in centers and schools. Nearly all states also have regulatory processes in place for family child care homes, although it is estimated that only a small fraction of family child care providers in the nation is indeed regulated (Willer et al., 1991).

Public regulatory processes help reduce the potential for abuse when

- all settings providing education and care to children of two or more families are subject to regulation;

- waivers that erode the intent of the regulatory standards are not allowed;

- funding is sufficient to provide adequate regulatory staff for inspection on at least an annual basis;

- regulatory personnel are knowledgeable about complaint and law enforcement procedures so that implementation of all regulatory requirements is ensured;

- regulatory standards require policies regarding parental access to programs, authorization of children's release, and parental notification and approval of children's participation on field trips; and

- parents and the public are provided information about what defines good quality care, regulatory standards and monitoring procedures, and complaint procedures.

Some child care settings, such as in-home care in which families employ someone to care for the child in their home or other private arrangements in which an individual provides care for only one family, are not subject to public regulation. Therefore, public mechanisms to prevent child abuse in out-of-home settings must extend beyond traditional licensing and regulatory processes.

Most states require individuals working in schools, centers, and family child care homes to successfully complete a criminal background check prior to full employment. NAEYC supports the use of such background checks but warns that they are only one of many necessary strategies to reduce risk. Even the most sophisticated system of criminal background checks is limited by the fact that many instances of abuse go unreported and therefore never result in a conviction. Also, no system for such checks can detect first-time or potential abusers. Because many problems exist with the current system of background checks, parents and the community should not be lulled into a false sense of complacency regarding children's safety when such a system is in place. Given this caveat, NAEYC offers these recommendations for the effective use of criminal record checks.

1. The costs of completing a criminal record background check should be kept as low as possible, and the check should be completed in a timely manner.

2. The scope of the check should be clear. State regulations vary as to which records are searched: local, state, and/or federal criminal convictions; child abuse registries; or sex of-fender registries. With regard to child abuse registries, states employ different standards as to the type of information recorded, resulting in serious shortcomings of these data. For example, some registries include unsubstantiated allegations, and some registries record instances of abuse by the name of the victim rather than the perpetrator, making it difficult to track abusers (Cohen, 1985).

3. If convictions are uncovered, clear procedures for action should be in place. Some states require individuals to undergo a background check before they can be hired to work with children but have no clear

procedures for action when substantiated convictions are found.

4. Results of background checks should be readily available to families, especially those families using in-home child care, family child care, or other settings exempt from public regulation. Some states have used technology to make information on background checks readily available to families and providers. Colorado has instituted a system that allows access to information at public libraries and child care resource-and-referral programs. California was the first state to institute a Child Care Trustline. This database includes current and potential child care providers who have successfully undergone a criminal record background check. Parents and programs can check potential employees against the database to ensure that their names appear (as opposed to a criminal background check in which being listed is a negative).

Role of Early Childhood Professionals

Monitoring by public agencies helps to ensure basic acceptable levels of quality in early childhood programs. However, it is the responsibility of early childhood professionals to

1. Promote standards of excellence toward which programs may strive. NAEYC encourages centers and eligible schools to pursue NAEYC accreditation. This process requires programs to undertake a rigorous self-study process and provides for an independent external assessment to determine whether high standards are met. Other accreditation systems are available for family child care homes and schools not eligible for NAEYC accreditation.

2. Assist in informing the public about the need for and the ingredients of high-quality early childhood programs.

3. Encourage the continued professional development of all early childhood professionals.

4. Advocate for well-designed, sufficiently funded, and effectively implemented public regulations and programs that reduce the incidence of abuse against children.

5. Understand their ethical obligations to recognize and report suspicions of abuse (see Feeney & Kipnis, 1992).

Early childhood professionals can also play an important role in helping to prevent the incidence of child abuse in other settings beyond early childhood programs. The vast majority of child abuse is committed by family members or others who are close to the family. By establishing supporting relationships with families, early childhood professionals may help reduce the likelihood of child abuse by family members. Programs should make readily available to families under stress appropriate information and referrals to community services and provide information and support for families regarding appropriate discipline and guidance of young children. In addition, early childhood professionals should advocate for effective community support services, including child protective services, social services, and mental health services that include sufficient numbers of qualified staff sensitive to meeting the individual needs of children and families.

Conclusion

The National Association for the Education of Young Children is strongly committed to promoting high quality in early childhood programs. Practices that lead to high-quality programs help reduce the likelihood of abuse of children in out-of-home settings, and high-quality programs can provide support to families to reduce instances of abuse in the home. Thus, the members of NAEYC pledge their commitment and expertise to work with other concerned individuals and groups to provide a safe and wholesome environment for all of America's children.

References

Cohen, A. 1985. Use of statewide central child abuse registries for purposes of screening child care workers: *False promises and troubling concerns.* San Francisco: Child Care Law Center.

Feeney, S., & Kipnis, K. 1992. *Code of ethical conduct & statement of professional commitment.* Washington, DC: NAEYC.

NAEYC. 1991. *Accreditation criteria and procedures of the National Academy of Early Childhood Programs* (rev. ed.). Washington, DC: Author.

National Committee to Prevent Child Abuse. 1995. *Annual survey of incidence of child abuse.* Chicago: Author.

U.S. Department of Health and Human Services. National Center on Child Abuse and Neglect. 1996. *Child maltreatment 1994: Reports from the states to the National Center on Child Abuse and Neglect.* Washington, DC: GPO.

Wells, S., Davis, N., Dennis, K., Chipman, R., Sandt, C., & Liss, M. 1995. *Effective screening of child care and youth service workers.* Washington, DC: American Bar Association Center on Children and the Law.

Willer, B., Hofferth, S. L., Ksiker, E. E., Divine-Hawkins, P., Farquhar, E., & Glantz, F. B.. 1991. *The demand and supply of child care in 1990.* Washington, DC: NAEYC.

Additional Resources

Code of Ethical Conduct and Statement of Commitment. 1992. S. Feeney & K. Kipnis. [Brochure available in English and Spanish editions.] NAEYC.

Healthy Young Children: A Manual for Programs. 1995 ed. A. S. Kendrick, R. Kaufmann, & K. P. Messenger, eds. Washington, DC: NAEYC.

NAEYC Position Statement on Violence in the Lives of Children. 1993. [Brochure.] Washington, DC: NAEYC.

National Committee to Prevent Child Abuse. 332 S. Michigan Ave., Chicago, IL 60604.

The Role of Educators in the Prevention and Treatment of Child Abuse and Neglect: The User Manual Series. 1992. C. C. Tower. U.S. Department of Health and Human Services, National Center on Child Abuse, and Neglect. DHHS publication No. (ACF) 92-30172.

accreditation: A voluntary process with a goal of increasing and maintaining high quality in early childhood programs

active listening: An interpersonal communication strategy that promotes clear and honest exchanges of information

adaptation: In family systems theory, a process that engages a family's recovery factors so that they bounce back after crises

adjustment: In family systems theory, a process that engages a family's protective factors to continue to function even with risks

adoption: A legal process of taking a child into one's family and raising that child as one's own

advocacy: Activities that support and call for support for children and families

anti-bias: An educational approach that fosters fairness, equity and inclusion in all areas, including culture, ethnicity, gender, language and more

at-risk children: Children at risk for developmental delays or disabilities due to family situations including poverty, psychopathology, loss of members, or inability to nurture

attachment: The psychological, and probably biological, process by which parents and children create emotional bonds with one another

authoritarian parenting: An approach to child-rearing that emphasizes adult control of children's behavior

authoritative parenting: An approach to child-rearing that includes stating expectations for children and communicating with them in respectful ways

balanced families: According to the circumplex model, families that demonstrate a balance in both cohesion and flexibility

bioecological theory: Theory proposed by Urie Bronfenbrenner that relates ecological systems to human development

birth order: The sequence in which children are born or adopted into families

blended families: Families in which one or both partners bring children from another relationship

buoyancy: In family systems theory, a family's ability to recover quickly from a challenge or transition

child abuse and neglect: Maltreatment of a child and the failure of parents or other responsible adults to provide necessary care and supervision

child care trilemma: The concern for quality, affordability, and accessibility of child care

chronosystem: According to bioecological theory, the sociohistorical context of an individual

circumplex model: A family systems model intended to demonstrate how all family members are interconnected

code of ethical conduct: A profession's expectations for appropriate, optimal behavior and practices for its members

codependency: When a person sacrifices his or her own needs to serve another person to an unhealthy extreme

cohesion: According to the circumplex model, family togetherness

community resources: Support available to children and families in a particular community

conflict resolution: Strategies for constructively processing differences between individuals or groups

congruence: The degree of similarity between home and school

contextualist theories: Approaches that demonstrate the importance of relationships among children, families, and communities that are crucial to effective family involvement in early childhood education

continuity: Efforts made to support children as they move from home to school or from one school setting to another

crises: In family systems theory, the possibility for a family's ongoing instability or dysfunction

culture: Socially transmitted behavior patterns typical of a population or of a community at a given time

developmental assets: Critical factors necessary for children's healthy development

developmental contextualism: A theoretical approach to understanding human development that considers both a strong biological foundation and family as the central social institution

developmentally appropriate practices (DAP): Those practices in early childhood education that are derived from deep knowledge of individual children and the context in which they develop and learn

disabilities: Physical, learning, or emotional factors that call for adaptations

diversity: The understanding that family structures, functions, characteristics, and interests are varied

donor insemination: The introduction of semen from a known or anonymous male into the female reproductive organs without sexual contact

downsizing: A phenomenon of corporations reducing number of employees

early childhood education: Any program of care and education for children from birth through eight years of age

early intervention: Comprehensive educational programs for young children who are at risk or who have been identified as having a disability

elasticity: In family systems theory, a family's capacity to maintain their ability to engage in established patterns of functioning after being challenged by risk factors

empathy: Understanding another's feelings, situation, values, and goals

empowering: The establishment of a model whereby all families can assert an active role in the education of their children

ethnicity: Identification with or belonging to a religious, racial, national, or cultural group

exosystem: According to bioecological theory, a system that has indirect effects on an individual

expressive role: Traditionally, the role that mothers have in providing the primary care and love for their children

extended family: Family members beyond parents and children, especially grandparents, aunts, uncles, and cousins

extended family relationships: The nature of the connection between an individual and extended family members

extreme families: According to the circumplex model, classification of families that are extreme in both cohesion and flexibility

family accord: Relates to a family's impression of competency in dealing with conflict

family coping: Strategies of families for dealing with stress

family-friendly work policies: Employer policies that consider the primacy of the family

family functions: Primary reasons for existence of the family unit

family life cycle: An approach to understanding families that considers how families typically change over time

family life education: A broad understanding of the influences in a child's life including quality of relationships with family members

family of orientation: The family into which one is born

family of procreation: The family that one creates by having children

family pride: Characteristics such as mutual respect, trust, loyalty, optimism, and shared values in a family

family protective factors: In family systems theory, a positive side of families' ability to cope when faced with stressors that lead to increases in a family's elasticity

family recovery factors: In family systems theory, a positive side of families' ability to cope when faced with stressors that lead to supporting a family's buoyancy

family size: The number of family members residing together

family strengths: An approach to understanding families that emphasizes characteristics of healthy family relationships

family structure: The unique ways that families organize

family support movement: A perspective that recognizes that families are responsible for their children's development and that no family can function alone

family systems theory: A framework that emphasizes the notion that everything that happens to any family member affects all other family members

family violence: Abuse or injury within families

FERPA: Family Education Rights and Privacy Act is a federal law designed to protect the privacy of students' academic records

flexibility: According to the circumplex model, a family's ability to deal with change

gender inequality: The phenomenon of males having greater power than females in society

gender role: Expected social behavior relating to being male or female

high-quality, affordable child care: Child care that local families can pay for and meets these criteria: child-centered curriculum, well-trained teachers, and planned family involvement

homeless: Having no home or refuge

horizontal stressors: According to family systems theory, stress-producing events that occur over time

home visiting: An educational practice whereby early childhood professionals meet with families in their homes

immigrant families: Families that leave one country to settle in another

incarcerated: Jailed or imprisoned; denied freedom

inclusion: An educational practice whereby programs enroll both typically developing children and children with identified disabilities

inclusiveness: An educational approach that is welcoming to all children and families

instrumental role: Traditionally, the role of fathers with their children that has a minimal role in caring for children

interdisciplinary collaboration: A consensus-building model that uses a variety of perspectives to determine a plan for family involvement in a child's education

interpersonal communication: Effective strategies of human interaction between or among people

irreducible needs of children: Those needs that are basic to children's survival and optimal development

linkages: The level, type, and frequency of communication between families and schools

literacy: The ability to use language, especially reading, writing, speaking, and listening in order to communicate

macrosystem: According to bioecological theory, the culture in which one lives

marital transition: Process involved in moving into or out of marriage

maternal employment: The number of hours mothers of young children are employed outside the home

mesosystem: According to bioecological theory, relationships between contexts in the microsystem

microsystem: According to bioecological theory, the setting in which one lives or the near environment

midrange families: According to the circumplex model, families that are extreme with either cohesion or flexibility and balanced with either cohesion or flexibility

migrant families: Families who travel from place to place in order to gain employment

nuclear family: Self-contained family unit consisting of parents and children

nurturance: Caring for and providing for children

overlapping spheres of influence: The understanding that families, schools, and communities are intermingled and not discrete

parent education: Providing a variety of sources of support for the parents' role in caring for their children

parental attachment: The strong emotional bond that exists between parents and their children

parental rights: An educational philosophy based on the understanding that parents have the primary role in their children's lives

parenting: Care, love, and guidance provided by parents to their children

permissive parenting: An approach to child-rearing that exercises little control over children and exerts few demands on children's behavior

permissive-indifferent parenting: A permissive approach to parenting that is disconnected in nature

permissive-indulgent parenting: A permissive approach to parenting that allows children to control their own behavior without much limit-setting

preschool inclusion: A preschool educational practice that provides planned programs for children with and without identified disabilities

primacy of parental rights: A view that upholds the strict limits of the U.S. Constitution to interfere with family life

professional associations: Groups with membership open to specific professions that often provide information about and guide current research, practice, and advocacy

professional standards and ethics: Guidelines used by early childhood educators for appropriate professional behavior and best educational practices

public policies: Federal, state, and local laws

quality indicators: Standards used by the National Parent Teacher Association to assess family involvement in schools

race: A group of people distinguished by more or less distinct genetically transmitted physical characteristics

referral: The process of seeking and acquiring additional or different educational or support services to meet needs of individual children

religiosity: The degree to which a family values or practices religious beliefs

resilience: In family systems theory, the property of the family system that enables it to be elastic and buoyant

resilient children: Children who exhibit good developmental outcomes despite high-risk family situations

right of family integrity: The legal basis for parents to bear and rear children according to their own beliefs

self-disclosure: Sharing information from one's own life situation

serious illness: Health conditions that are chronic or life-threatening

sibling relationships: Connections and interactions between or among children in the same family (sisters and brothers)

socialization: A parental responsibility to teach and support children in how to get along with others

sociocultural theory: Vygotsky's theory that emphasizes the relationship of the social environment, particularly cultural, to cognition and learning

spirituality: The quality of being concerned with the soul, God, and/or a religious institution

substance abuse: Illegal or overuse of drugs or alcohol

Temporary Assistance for Needy Families (TANF): Federal legislation that provides support to families in poverty

tolerance: Acts intended to promote equity, diversity, and inclusiveness, as well as to deter hate

transition to parenthood: Adjustment of an individual to new roles as a parent

two-way communication: Various educational practices that foster essential communication between home and school (as opposed to unilateral sharing of information in one direction only)

vertical stressors: According to family systems theory, stress-producing events that are embedded in particular families' patterns of relating

vulnerability: In family systems theory, a family's possibility of being faced with risk factors that may negatively affect functioning

zone of proximal development (ZPD): According to Vygotsky, the mechanism by which human development occurs

INDEX

Page numbers followed by f indicate figures

ZERO TO THREE National Center for Infants, Toddlers, and Families, 127, 128
1-2-3 Magic, summary and critique, 247f
One-way communication, 195–199, 208f
Two-way communication, 199–211
Two-year olds, 279–280
Six, Success By, 272–273

A

Abbott, C. F., 265
Abuse. *See* Child abuse and neglect
Academy for Early Childhood Program Accreditation, 19–22
Accreditation, 19–22, 76
  diversity guidelines, 53
  online resources, 21
Active listening, 206f, 207f, 211–212, 213f
Active Parenting, 241
  critique, 243f
  summary, 242f
Activities for Families with Young Children, 231
Adaptation and family resiliency, 134
Adjustment and family resiliency, 134
Adler, A., 241
Adolescent parents, 64, 116–117
Adoption, 111–113
Advocacy
  professionals, 183
  see also Big Ideas, evidence for child and family advocacy efforts
African American culture
  online resources, 30
  religiosity, 47
  variations in parenting and educational values, 35f
Aggression versus assertiveness, 217
Alcohol. *See* Substance abuse
Allen, C. T., 134
Allomothering, defined, 124
American Association for the Advancement of Science (AAAS), 224, 226–229, 228

American Association of Retired Persons (AARP), 115–116
American Indians. *See* Native American culture
American studies, 30
Announcements of child- and family-related activities, 199
Anti-bias activities, 232–233
Anti-Bias Curriculum, 177, 185–186
Appalachia, 49–50
Appell, L. J., Jr., 274
Archambault, C., 155
Artificial insemination, 110
Asian American culture
  online resources, 30
  variations in parenting and educational values, 35f
Assertive Discipline, summary and critique, 246f
Assertiveness versus aggression, 217
Assessment forms, 239f–240f
Assets, developmental, 4–5
At-risk children, 93
Attachment to caregiver, 118, 119
Authoritarian parenting, 120–122
Authoritative parenting, 120–122, 125, 128

B

Bailey, D. B., Jr., 267
Balanced families, 133–134
Banks, J. A., 34
Barnard, K. E., 123–124
Barriers to family involvement in education, 168
Barriers to multiculturalism, 185
Baumrind, D., 120–121
Bender, S. M., 264
Besaw, A., 91–92
Best practices, school policies based on, 178f
Big Ideas, evidence for child and family advocacy efforts, 274–281
  biological and ecological factors influencing development, 276
  differences in children, understanding of, 277–278
  discrimination for or against children, 278

experiences, effect on development, 277
families as teachers, 276–277
individual differences in children, understanding of, 277–278
infancy, rapid growth and development, 279
prenatal health, 275
preschool children, developmentally effective education, 280
"terrible twos" or "terrific toddlers," 279–280
Bilchik, S., 156, 157, 158
Bilingualism, 9–10
  case study: English language learners, 303–304
  National Association for Education of Young Children (NAEYC) position statement on linguistically and culturally diversity, 321–335
Binding-in, defined, 123
Bioecological theory, 7–8, 9f
  and barriers to family involvement in children's education, 168
  concentric circle model of bioecological theory, 9f
  developmental issues in families, 59–60
  early childhood education, 261–262
  extended families, 88
  family strengths, functions, and structure, 88
  nature vs. nurture, 7–8
  nuclear family, 88
  nurturance and child care, 118
  online resources, 7
  parent education, 237–238
  social environment, 29
  support for learning at home, 223
  theoretical perspectives, 107–108
Biological factors influencing development, 276
Birth (biological) parents, 109–115
Birth order, 101–102
Black culture. *See* African American culture
Blended families, 100, 111
Boards of trustees and advisory boards, 263

Bodrova, E., 225
Boethel, M., 51–52
Boot Camp for New Dads, 63–64
Boss, P., 134
Boulos, S., 109
Boundaries and expectations, 4
Boutte. G., 185
Bowman, B., 103, 176
Boyce, P., 63
Brain development, 256, 272f
Brazelton, T. B., 4–6, 75, 143, 278
Bredekamp, S., 16–17, 52, 278
   see also Developmentally Appropriate
      Practices (DAP)
Brody, G. H., 67
Brodzinsky, D. M., 112–113
Bronfenbrenner, U., 7–8, 29, 59–60,
      88, 108, 118, 223, 237–238
   family and school continuity,
      172–173
   online resources, 7
   see also Bioecological theory
Brooks, R., 93–94
Brooks-Gunn, J., 116–117
Brothers and sisters. *See* Sibling
      relationships
Buoyancy, 134
Business community, 274

C

Cable, S., 155, 156, 157f
Caldwell, B., 103
Careers and parenting, 70–77
Caregiver attachment, 118, 119
Carter, B., 13–14, 60, 88–90
Caspar, L. M., 143, 144
Castellino, D. R., 109
Celebrating diversity, 50
Certified Family Life Educators
      (CFLEs), 248–250
Character education, 120
Chavkin, N. F., 153, 154
Cheal, D., 36–37
Child abuse and neglect, 137–141
   Child Abuse Prevention and
      Treatment Act of 1974, 137
   effects of abuse, 139f
   implications for schools, 142f
   indicators of abuse and neglect,
      140f–141f
   National Association for Education
      of Young Children (NAEYC)
      position statement, 361–368
   online resources, 136, 141

Child care, 74–77
   case study, supporting families in
      infant care programs,
      287, 288
   Child Care and Development Block
      Grant (CCDBG), 76–77
   online resources, 76
   "trilemma," defined, 75–76
Child Development Block Grant
      (CCDBG), 280
Child welfare programs and recipients,
      35–39
Childhood obesity, 257
Children of incarcerated parents,
      156–159
Children's Defense Fund (CDF),
      34–35, 35–36, 47–48, 76,
      117–118
   online resources, 37
Children's Health Insurance Program
      (CHIP), 118
Chrisman, C., 178
Chrisman, K., 228
Christensen, D., 184, 187
Christian, L. G., 168
Chronosystem, 7–8, 108
Church. *See* Religiosity
Churchill, S., 177
Churchill, Winston, 279
Cicchetti, D., 139, 142f
Circumplex family system model,
      12–13
Clarke, Dr., 171
Cochrane, M., 181
Code of Ethical Conduct, 275
Codependency, 205f
Cohabiting families, 100
Cohesion in families, 12–13
Coleman, J., 181
Coleman, M., 155, 156, 157f, 177
Colker, L. J., 229
Collaboration among agencies and
      programs, 183, 273
Coltrane, S., 126
Comer Schools, 265, 266–267
Commitment to learning, 4
Communication, 211–220
   within families, 12
   between staff and parents
      assertiveness versus
         aggression, 217
      criticism, giving and receiving,
         216–217
      effective, 211–216

      ineffective, 214–215, 219
      one-way, 195–199
      two-way, 199–211
      written, 194–199
Communities, 263–264
   caring communities, 263–264
   community involvement standard,
      21, 21f–22f
   community-school-family
      partnership, 180f
   importance of, 3–25
   involvement in early childhood
      education, 262–263
Competencies, social, 4
Concentric circle model, 7–8, 9f, 59
Condon, J. T., 63
Confidentiality, 182–183
Conflict resolution, 207f, 217–220
Congregations to Leave No Child
      Behind, 47–48
Congruence, 171
*Connecting Head Start Parents to the
      Public School Setting,* 173
Constructive use of time, 4
Contextualist theories, 5–16
   Bronfenbrenner's bioecological
      theory, 7–8, 9f
   and family differences, 29–50
      application to early childhood
         education programs
         celebrating diversity, 50
         inclusiveness, 50–52
      ethical considerations, 52–55
         family support principles,
            54–55, 81
         NAEYC accreditation
            guidelines, 53
         Professional Code of Ethical
            Conduct, 54, 81–82
         relating diversity to
            developmentally appropriate
            practice, 52
         relating diversity to programs
            for children with special
            needs, 53
      ways in which families are
         different, 31–50
         economic differences in
            families, 34–39
         ethnicity, race, and culture,
            31–34
         families and religiosity,
            46–48
         geographic region, 48–50

family systems theory, 11–16
Vygotsky's sociocultural theory, 8–11
Continuity and transitions at school, 170–176
Cook, M., 229
Copley, J., 230
Copple, C., 16–17, 52, 278
see also Developmentally appropriate practices (DAP)
Corkindale, C. J., 63
Cornell Empowerment Group, 96
Cost of raising a child, 117–118
Council on Exceptional Children (CEC) Division for Early Childhood (DEC), 23–24, 24, 53
online resources, 24
Crises, 134
Criticism, giving and receiving, 206f, 216–217
Crowley, K., 226, 227–228
Culture, 9–10, 33–34
communication about culture, 211
cultural diversity, 29–34
multiculturalism. *See* Multiculturalism
online resources, 10, 30, 33, 50
Curtis, D., 97

D
Daily information sheets, 199
Day care. *See* Child care
Dean, C., 181
DeFrain, J., 238
Department of Education, United States (U.S.), 194
Depression, 62–64
Derman-Sparks, L., 177, 185–186, 232–233
Developmental Approaches to Science, Health and Technology (DASH), 228
Developmental assets, 4–5
Developmental contextualism, 11–12, 108–109
Developmental issues in families with young children, 59–83
bioecological theory, 59–60
Code of Ethical Conduct, 81–82
extended family relationships, 77–81
family support principles, 81
family systems theory, 60–61
sibling relationships, 64–69

stressors, 134
transition to parenthood, 61–64
work and family, 70–77
Developmental stressors, 134
Developmentally appropriate practices (DAP), 16–18, 252
case study: helping family members and staff understand developmentally appropriate practice, 292–295
diversity, 52
online resources, 18
Dickinson, D. K., 226
Differences in children, understanding of, 277–278
Dinkmeyer, D., 241
see also Systematic Training for Effective Parenting (STEP)
Disabilities, 147–150
case study: early child inclusive practices, 299–301
conditions of grieving, 148f
online resources, 148
see also Exceptional children
Discipline, 122
Assertive Discipline, summary and critique, 246f
Discrimination
gender, 137
for or against children, 278
Diversity, 29–50, 184–188
anti-bias curriculum, 185–186
application to early childhood education programs
celebrating diversity, 50
inclusiveness, 50–52
barriers to multiculturalism, 185
ethical considerations, 52–55
Code of Ethical Conduct, 54
family support principles, 54–55
NAEYC accreditation guidelines, 53
relating diversity to developmentally appropriate practices, 52
relating diversity to programs for children with special needs, 53
immigrants. *See* Immigrant families
online resources, 10, 30, 50
ways in which families are different, 31–50
economic differences in families, 34–39
ethnicity, race, and culture, 31–34

gender role identity, 39–46
geographic region, 48–50
religiosity, 46–48
see also Family differences; Multiculturalism
Division for Early Childhood (DEC) of the Council on Exceptional Children (CEC)
diversity, 53
online resources, 24
recommended practices in family-based practices, 23–24
Divorce and separation, 143–145
online resources, 145
stepfamilies, 100, 101
see also Single-parent families
Domestic violence. *See* Family violence
Donor insemination, 110
Doucette-Dudman, D., 114–116
Downsizing, 71
Dreikurs, D., 241
Drew, C. Ray, 43
Drugs. *See* Substance abuse
Drummet, A. R., 155, 156, 157f
Dunn, C., 181
Dunn, L., 145, 147
Dunst, C., 23, 149

E
Early childhood education, family-based philosophy, 167–176
barriers, 168
continuity and transitions, 170–176
families in democracy, 170
Head Start, 168–170
Early childhood educators, 160
topics for parent education
childhood obesity, 257
developmentally appropriate practice, 252
early brain development, 256
family literacy, 256
financial responsibility, 257
homework, 255
play for young children, value of, 251
positive guidance, 253
sexuality development, 255
television limitations, 253
Early childhood programs, 16–25
accreditation, 19–22, 53, 76
diversity in, 50–52
early childhood program standards, 19f

Early childhood programs (*Continued*)
  exceptional children, 23–24
  family support, 24–25, 103
  family-staff relationship, 193–220
  guidelines for Developmentally
      Appropriate Practice, 16–18
  inclusion, 18–19
  interactions with parents, 127–128
  online resources, 76
  special needs, 53
Early intervention, 267–270
Early Years Science blog, 229
Ecological factors influencing
      development, 276
Economic factors
  economic diversity, 34–39
  responsibilities of parents, 117–118
  single-parent families, 102–103
Edelman, M.W., 35–36, 47, 282
"Educare," 103
Education for All Handicapped
      Children Act of 1975, 149f
Effective communication. *See*
      Communication
Egg donation, 109–110
Elasticity, 134
Electronic mail, 210
Elkind, D., 39
E-mail, 210
Emery, R. E., 144
Empathy, 194, 206f
Employment and parenting, 70–77
Empowering parents, 177, 181
Empowerment, 4
Environmental systems, 7–8
Epstein, J., 171, 189–180, 223,
      224, 228
Epstein's Framework for School,
      Family and Community
      Partnerships, 189–180
Ethics. *See* Professional ethics
Ethnicity, 31–32
  online resources, 50
  see also Diversity; Multiculturalism
Exceptional children, 23–24
  diversity in programs for, 53
  see also Disabilities
Exosystem, 7, 108
Expectant nurturing, 123–124
Expectations, boundaries and, 4
Experiences, effect on
      development, 277
Expressive parental role, 122–123
Extended families, 77–81, 98
  bioecological theory, 88

building and maintaining
      relationships, 119–120
"It takes a village to raise a child,"
      3–5
variations in family structure, 100
  see also Grandparents
External assets, 4–5
Extreme families, 133
Eye contact, 215–216

F
Faber, A., 65, 69, 241
Facial expressions, 215–216
Faith. *See* Religiosity
Falbo, T., 66–67
Fallon, M. A., 155
Families
  barriers to family involvement in
      education, 168
  case studies: challenges of increasing
      family involvement, 289–291
  cohesion, 12–13
  communication, 12
  coping, 134
  in democracy, 170
  developmental issues, 59–83
  differences in. *See* Family differences
  extended families. *See* Extended
      families
  extended family relationships, 77–81
  families standard, 19–21
  family accord, 87
  family functions, 87–90
    causes of change in family
        functions, 96–97
    family law, 97–98
    historical and contemporary
        purposes of families, 94–96
    online resources, 95
  family structure. *See* Family structure
  family systems theory. *See* Family
      systems theory
  family-friendly work policies, 70,
      72, 74
  flexibility, 12–13
  functions of, 87–90, 94–98
  at home learning. *See* Learning at
      home
  illnesses. *See* Illnesses in family
  immigrants. *See* Immigrant families
  importance of, in children's lives,
      3–25
  importance of families in children's
      lives, 3–25
  integrity, 97

involvement, 189f
  barriers to family involvement in
      education, 168
  Parent Teacher Association
      (PTA), 181–182
  Partnership for Family
      Involvement in
      Education, 178
life cycle, 13–16
migrants. *See* Migrant families
military. *See* Military families
online resources, 45, 66, 70, 78, 92,
      93, 95, 98, 102, 125
pride, 87, 91, 97f
resilience, 93–94, 134
roles, 170f
school friendliness, 180f
and school responsibilities, 176–177
size, 66–67
size of, 66–67
status changes, 88–90
strengths, 87–94
  online resources, 92, 93
  resilient children, 93–94
stresses on. *See* Stresses on families
structure. *See* Family structure
structure of, 87–90, 98–102
support, 24–25
  developmental issues in families,
      81–82
  diversity and inclusion, 54–55
  empowering parents, 177
  family and school responsibilities,
      176–177
  family strengths, functions, and
      structure, 102–103
as teachers, 276–277
violence. *See* Family violence
  see also Parenting
Families and Work Institute, 73–74
  online resources, 70
Family differences, 29–50
  application to early childhood
      education programs
    celebrating diversity, 50
    inclusiveness, 50–52
  ethical considerations, 52–55
    Code of Ethical Conduct, 54
    family support principles, 54–55
    NAEYC accreditation
        guidelines, 53
    relating diversity to
        developmentally appropriate
        practice, 52
    relating diversity to programs for

children with special
needs, 53
online resources, 10, 30
ways in which families are different,
31–50
economic differences in
families, 34–39
ethnicity, race, and culture, 31–34
families and religiosity, 46–48
gender role identity, 39–46
geographic region, 48–50
structure, 87–90, 98–102
Family Education Rights and Privacy
Act (FERPA), 183
online resources, 183
Family law, 97–98
online resources, 98
Family life education, 248–250
Grigg's criteria for evaluating family
life education materials, 249f
Family literacy, 256
Family of orientation, 98
Family of procreation, 98
Family protective factors (FPF), 134
Family recovery factors (FRF), 134
Family structure, 87–90
the meaning of birth order, 101–102
variations in family form, 98–101
Family systems theory, 11–16, 133–135
communication, 193
developmental issues in families,
60–61
family status changes, 88–90
horizontal stressors, 134–135
role of culture, 30
Family violence, 135–137
online resources, 136
see also Child abuse and neglect
Family-based philosophy in early
childhood education,
167–176
barriers, 168
continuity and transitions, 170–176
families in democracy, 170
Head Start, 168–170
Family-based practices, 23–24
Family-centered interprofessional
collaboration, 273–274
Family-Friendly Communication for Early
Childhood Programs, 197
Family-friendly work policies, 70, 72, 74
Family-school-community partnership,
180f
Family-staff relationship
building relationships, 193–195

communication
assertiveness versus
aggression, 217
effective interpersonal
communication, 211–216
one-way communication, 195–199
two-way communication, 199–211
conflict resolution, 217–220
helpful attitudes for effective
interpersonal
communication, 219–220
some ineffective and
inappropriate practices to
avoid in interpersonal
communication, 219
Fathers, 124–127
online resources, 45, 125
role of, 44–46
transition to parenthood, 61–64
Feeney, S., 184, 187
Fertility issues, 109–111
Fields, J., 143, 144
Financial responsibility, teaching, 257
Flexibility, family, 12–13
Focus on Our Future, United
Way's, 271–272
Foster parenting, 113–114
FPF (family protective factors), 134
Frameworks for partnerships
additional frameworks, 181–182
Epstein's framework, 179–180
online resources, 181
FRF (family recovery factors), 134
Functional families, 91
Furman, E., 44

G
Galco, J., 226–228, 227
Galen, H., 188
Galinsky, E., 73–74
Gay and lesbian parents, 30–31,
39–46, 100
online resources, 40
Gender inequality, 137
Gender roles and identity, 30–31,
39–46
online resources, 40
transition to parenthood, 61–64
see also Fathers; Mothers
Geographic diversity, 48–50
Gerber, M., 103
Gestures, 215–216
Ghandi, 278
GIC Voice, The, 115–116
Ginott, H., 241

Gold, S., 265
Goldstein, S., 93–94
Golombok, S., 109–110
Gordon, T., 213
Grandparents, 77–81
online resources, 78
parenting their grandchildren, 100,
114–116
see also Extended families
Grassroots Success!, 262
Greenspan, S., 4–6, 75, 278
Group Parent Meeting, sample
assessments,
239f, 240f
Guggenheim, M., 97
Guidelines for developmentally
appropriate practice.
See Developmentally
appropriate practices (DAP)

H
Hale, J., 47
Hall, J., 215–216
Hamner, T. J., 120, 145, 147
Han, S., 134
Hanna, S. L., 194, 212, 219
Head Start, 168–170, 173, 174f, 265,
266, 270, 276–277
Head Start Handbook of the Parent
Involvement Vision and
Strategies (1996), 169
Health. See Illnesses in family
Hennessy, K., 139, 142f
Henninger, M., 225
Hensen, R., 225
Hernandez, D. J., 66, 67
Hetherington, E. M., 69
Higginbotham, J., 113
Hispanic/Latino culture
online resources, 30
variations in parenting and
educational values, 35f
HIV/AIDS, 152f
online resources, 151
Holidays, 48f, 50, 52, 55
Home Instruction Program for
Preschool Youngsters
(HIPPY), 245–248
claimed benefits, 246–247
evaluation research, 247–248
seven steps to start, 246
Home visits, 174–176, 210–211
Homeless families, 145–147
Homeless Assistance Act of 1987, 147
online resources, 146, 147

Homework, 255
Homosexuality. *See* Gay and lesbian parents
Horizontal stressors, 14, 134–135
How to be a Perfect Stranger: A Guide to Etiquette in Other People's Religious Ceremonies, 47
How to Talk So Kids Will Listen and Listen So Kids Will Talk, 241
  critique, 244f
  highlights, 243f
Howe, L. K., 32
Huang, G., 154

I

Identity
  ethnic, racial, and cultural, 31–34
  gender roles, 39–46
  positive, 4
IEP (Individual Education Plan), 149–150
IFSP (Individualized Family Service Plan), 150
Illnesses in family, 151, 153f
  online resources, 151
I-messages, 213–214
Immigrant families, 51–52, 151–153
  online resources, 152
In vitro fertilization (IVF), 109–110
Inappropriate communication, 219
Incarcerated parents, 156–159
  online resources, 158
  rights and advocacy for children, 159f
Inclusion and inclusiveness, 18–19, 50–52
  case study: early child inclusive practices, 299–301
  family support principles, 54–55
Indians. *See* Native American culture
Individual differences in children, understanding of, 277–278
Individual Education Plan (IEP), 149–150
Individual with Disabilities Education Act (IDEA), 149, 220
Individualized Family Service Plan (IFSP), 150
Individuals with Disabilities Education Act (PL 105-17 IDEA), 270, 280
Indulgent parenting, 121
Ineffective communication, 214–215, 219

Infancy
  case study, supporting families in infant care programs, 287, 288
  Infants and Toddlers with Disabilities Act (ITDA), 149f
  rapid growth and development, 279
Infertility, 109–111
Institute for Child and Family Policy, 70
Institute for Responsive Education, 24
Instructional Support Teams (IST), 271
Instrumental parental role, 123
Interdisciplinary collaboration, 183, 273
Interfaith Child Advocacy Network, 47–48
Internal assets, 4–5
International Reading Association (IRA), 224, 227
Interpersonal communication
  effective, 211–220
  ineffective, 214–215, 219
Involvement, parent, 174f, 188f, 189f
Irreducible needs of children, 4–6
"It takes a village to raise a child," 3–5
Iverson, T. J., 138

J

Jails. *See* Incarcerated parents
Jefferson-Smith, C. J., 157, 158
Jewish culture, 48f
  online resources, 52
Joint-custody families, 100
Journaling, 210

K

Kagan, S. L., 6, 16, 92
Kalt, J., 91–92
Kendell, K., 43
Kentucky Educational Reform Act (KERA), 265
Kling, N., 145, 147
Knapp, M. L., 215–216
Kohlberg, 242
Koralek, D., 229, 231
Kornhaber, A., 77–80
Kostelnik, M. J., 177
Krech, B., 197
Kreider, H. M., 168, 182
Kreisher, K., 156, 157, 158
Kwanzaa, 50

L

LaCure, J. R., 114–116
Lamb, M., 125
Language
  body language, 203–204, 215–216
  case study: English language learners, 303–304
  diversity, 9–10
Latino culture
  online resources, 30
  variations in parenting and educational values, 35f
Layoffs, 71
Learning
  commitment to, 4
Learning at home
  online resources, 224, 227, 229
  overview, 223–224
  subjects
    literacy, 225–227
    mathematics, 230–232
    science, 226–229
    social studies, 232–233
  theoretical foundations, 223
Leave No Child Behind, 282
  NCLB (No Child Left Behind Act), 220
Lee, A., 91–92
LeMasters, E., 238
Leong, D., 225
Lerner, R. M., 11, 109
  see also Developmental contextualism
Lesbian and gay parents, 30–31, 39–46
  online resources, 40
Lewis, C., 120
Licensing
  National Association for Education of Young Children (NAEYC) Initial Licensure Standards, 336–360
Lickona, T., 120, 241
Lieberman, A. F., 151, 152
Life cycle, family, 13–16
Linguistic diversity, 9–10
  case study: English language learners, 303–304
  National Association for Education of Young Children (NAEYC) position statement on linguistically and culturally diversity, 321–335
Linkages, 171
Listening, 206f, 207f, 211–212
Literacy, 225–227
  online resources, 224, 227

Local school boards, 262–263
Lopez, G. R., 153, 154
Lopez, M. E., 168, 182
Lott, J., 231
Lowe, A. D., 97
Lynn, L., 181

M

Macrosystem, 8, 108
Mahitivanichcha, K., 153, 154
Mancini, D. L., 155
Marital transitions, 143–145
   online resources, 145
Married nuclear families, 100
Maternal employment, 70–73
Mathematics, 230–232
   online resources, 224
Mazlish, E., 65, 69, 241
McCubbin, H. I., 134
McCubbin, M. A., 134
McGoldrick, M., 13–14, 40, 88–90
McKay, G., 241
   see also Systematic Training for
      Effective Parenting (STEP)
McKinney Homeless Assistance
      Act of 1987, 147
McLean, M. E., 23
McWilliam, P. J., 267
Mead, Margaret, 4
Menaghan, E. G., 72–73
Menchaca, V. D., 154
Menninger, K., 61
Mesosystem, 7, 223
Microsystem, 7, 29, 108
Midrange families, 133
Migrant families, 153–155
   online resources, 155
Military families, 155–156, 157f
   specific areas for family life
      educators to focus on,
      248–250
Mistral, G., 6, 278
Money, teaching financial
      responsibility, 257
Moore, E., 16
Moore, M. R., 116–117
Moral development, 120
Moravcik, E., 184, 187
Moses, K., 147
Mothers, 123–124
   transition to parenthood, 61–64
   working mothers, 70–73
Mother's Day Guest Commentary, 43
Multiculturalism, 33
   barriers to, 185

communication about culture, 211
National Association for Education
   of Young Children (NAEYC)
   position statement on
   linguistically and culturally
   diversity, 321–335
online resources, 30, 50
   see also Diversity
Murphy, Justice F. T., 141

N

National Association for Education of
      Young Children (NAEYC),
      10, 230, 275
   Academy for Early Childhood
      Programs, 19–22
      Accreditation Standards and
         Topic Areas, 321–324
   accreditation, 76
      diversity guidelines, 54–55
      performance criteria, 19–22
   child abuse and neglect, position
      statement, 361–368
   Code of Ethical Conduct, 54, 81–82
   code of ethical conduct, 183,
      310–321
   community involvement standard,
      21, 21f–22f
   developmental issues in families,
      81–82
   families standard, 19–21
   licensure standards, 336–360
   position statement on accreditation
      criteria, 21
National Coalition for Parent
      Involvement in Education,
      220
National Commission on Children, 103
National Council for the Social Studies
      (NCSS), 224
National Council of Family Relations
      (NCFR), 250
National Council of Teachers of
      Mathematics (NCTM), 224,
      230, 231, 232
National Education Goals Panel, 264
National Network of Partnership
      Schools (NNPS), 181, 223,
      224, 228
   online resources, 181
National Parent Teacher Association
      (PTA), 180–182
   online resources, 181
   understanding family involvement,
      181–182

National Program Accreditation
      Guidelines, 19–22
National Science Foundation (NSF),
      228
National Science Teachers Association
      (NSTA), 229
Native American culture
   family strengthening initiatives,
      91–92
   online resources, 30
   variations in parenting and
      educational
      values, 35f
Nature vs. nurture, 7–8
NCLB (No Child Left Behind
      Act), 220
Needs assessments, 239f
Neglect. See Child abuse and neglect
Neglect and abuse, child. See Child
      abuse and neglect
Neugebauer, B., 52
New Fathers Network, 63
Newsletters, 195–198
No Child Left Behind
   federal legislation, 220
   movement, 282
Nonverbal communication, 203–204,
      215–216
Northwest Regional Educational
      Laboratory, 220
Notes to parents, 198–200
NSF. See National Science Foundation
Nuclear family, 98, 100
   bioecological theory, 88
Nurturance
   and child care, 118–119
   by fathers, 126
   by mothers, 123–124
   nature vs. nurture, 7–8

O

Oakley, J., 145, 147
Obesity, 257
Olson, D. H., 12–13, 133
One-two-three Magic. See 1-2-3 Magic
One-way communication, 195–199,
      208f
Overlapping spheres of influence, 179
Overweight children, 257
Overworked parents, 70–71
Owocki, G., 225

P

Pacific Islander American culture, 35f
Parcel, T. L., 72–73

Parent education
    Active Parenting. *See* Active
        Parenting
    assessing needs and effects, 238–240
    format of programs, 240–241
    HIPPY. *See* Home Instruction
        Program for Preschool
        Youngsters (HIPPY)
    parent education books, 241–242
    parent education packages, 241
    PAT. *See* Parents as Teachers (PAT)
    philosophy of programs, 238–241
    STEP. *See* Systematic Training for
        Effective Parenting (STEP)
Parent education methods, 241–248
Parent empowerment, 177, 181
Parent interview form, 196f
Parent involvement, 174f, 188f, 189f
    barriers to family involvement in
        education, 168
    case studies: challenges of increasing
        family involvement, 289–291
    Parent Teacher Association (PTA),
        181–182
    Partnership for Family Involvement
        in Education, 178
Parent Meeting, sample assessments,
    239f, 240f
Parental rights, 97, 170
Parenting
    difficult parents, 218f
    gay and lesbian parents, 30–31,
        39–46
        online resources, 40
    motherhood and fatherhood
        fathering, 44–46, 124–127
        mothering, 123–124
            working mothers, 70–73
    online resources, 122, 125
    parental rights, 97
    parenting styles and beliefs, 120–122
        child development and the role of
            children in families, 127
        interactions with early childhood
            educators, 127–128
        trends in beliefs about discipline
            strategies, 122
    responsibilities of parents
        attachment and socialization, 119
        building and maintaining
            relationships, 119–120
        character education and
            spirituality, 120
        collaborating with social
            institutions, 120

economic, 117–118
    nurturance and child care,
        118–119
single-parent families, 40
theoretical perspectives
    bioecological theory, 107–108
    developmental contextualism,
        108–109
transition to, 61–64
ways to parenthood
    adoption, 111–113
    biological and fertility alternatives,
        109–111
    blended families, 111
    foster parents, 113–114
    grandparents as parents, 114–116
    teen parents, 116–117
    working parents, 70–77
Parents, reticent, reaching out, 187f
Parents and teachers, linking
    parents as consumers, 177
    supporting school policy and
        families, 177–179
Parents as consumers, 177
Parents as Teachers (PAT), 243–245
    The Born to Learn Curriculum, 245
    evaluation research, 244
    four components, 244
    two premises, 243
Parents' Jobs and Children's Lives, 72–73
Parent-teacher conferences, 175f,
    200–209
Parke, R., 44–46
Parr, M., 62–63
Partnership among families, schools,
    and communities, 3–25
Partnership for Family Involvement
    in Education, 178
Partnership for Science Literacy,
    228–229
Part-time employment, 71–73
Pearl, P. T., 116
Permissive parenting, 120–121
Personal space, 215
Phillips, C., 33–34
Phone calls to parents, 209–210
Pinderhuges, E., 112–113
Play, the value for young children, 251
Popkin, M., 241
    see also Active Parenting
Positive guidance, 253
Positive identity, 4
Positive values, 4
Postpartum depression, 62–63
Poverty, 34–39

online resources, 37
    see also Economic factors; Homeless
        families
Powell, D., 170, 171, 172, 240–241
Pregnancy, 123
    transition to parenthood, 63
Prenatal health, 275
Preschool children
    developmentally effective
        education, 280
    HIPPY. *See* Home Instruction
        Program for Preschool
        Youngsters (HIPPY)
    preschool inclusion, 270–271
Primacy of parental rights, 97
Primary education, design of, 280–281
Prisons. *See* Incarcerated parents
Process-person-context-time
    model, 7–8
Professional associations, 224
Professional development websites,
    305–309
Professional ethics, 52–55, 54, 81–82,
    275, 281–282
    Code of Ethical Conduct, 52–55,
        81–82
    developmental issues in families,
        81–82
    developmentally appropriate
        practices (DAP), 52
    diversity, 52–55
    family support principles, 54–55
    NAEYC accreditation guidelines, 53
    special needs, 53
Professional standards, 281–282
    National Association for Education
        of Young Children (NAEYC)
        Initial Licensure Standards,
        336–360
Professionalism in early childhood
    education, 182–184, 274–282
    advocacy, 183
    collaboration, 183
    confidentiality, 182–183
    continuing professional
        development, 281–282
    knowledge base, 274–281
    Leave No Child Behind, 282
    record-keeping, 184
    roles and boundaries, 183–184
    see also Big Ideas, evidence for child
        and family advocacy efforts
Program accreditation, 19–22
Program models, 266–273
    Comer Schools, 265, 266–267

early intervention, 267–270
Head Start, 265, 266, 270, 276–277
Instructional Support Teams, 271
Project Even Start, 273
United Way Success By 6, 272–273
United Way's Focus on Our Future, 271–272
Project Even Start, 273
PTA (National Parent Teacher Association), 180–182
online resources, 181
understanding family involvement, 181–182
Public law 99-457, 267
Public law 105-17 (1997 amendments to the Individuals with Disabilities Act), 267

Q

Quality indicators, 180f, 181

R

Race, 33
online resources, 50
Raising Good Children from Birth through the Teenage Years, 241
summary and critique, 245f
Raising Our Children's Children, 115
Ramey, C. T., 270
Ramey, S. L., 270
Rank, M. R., 38–39, 41
Reading, 225–227
online resources, 224, 227
Ready Schools, 264
Recommended practices in family-based practices, 23–24
Record-keeping, 184
Referring children for services, 264–266
Reflecting, Discussing, Exploring: Questions and Follow-Up Activities, 229
Reflective dialogue, 212–213
Regional differences, 48–50
Religiosity, 46–48
family strengths, 88
online resources, 47, 52
responsibilities of parents, 120
Report of the National Task Force on School Readiness, 1991, 263, 264
Reproductive technology, 109–111
Resilience and resilient children, 93–94, 134, 135f

Reticent parents, reaching out, 187f
Ribbens, J., 41–42, 44
Rights of families, 97
Riley, R., 120
Rogers, M. F., 152
Roles and boundaries, 183–184
role of early childhood educators, 160
Rosenberg, E., 111, 112
Rothbaum, F., 109
Rothenberg, D., 116
Ruiz-Escalante, J. A., 154
Russell, C. S., 133
Russo, T. J., 155
Ryan-Wenger, N. A., 155, 156

S

Same-sex families, 30–31, 39–46, 100
online resources, 40
Sandall, S., 23
Schaps, E., 120
School policies
based on best practices, 178f
and families, 177–179, 180f
family friendliness, 180f
School-family-community partnership, 180f
Science, 226–229
online resources, 224, 229
Scribner, J. D., 153, 154
Search Institute, 4, 264
Segal, M., 138
Self-disclosure, 194, 205f
Separation and divorce, 143–145
online resources, 145
Serious illness, 151, 153f
online resources, 151
Sex discrimination, 137
Sexual orientation, 30–31, 39–46
online resources, 40
Sexuality development, healthy, 255
Seymour, C., 156, 157, 158
Shartrand, A. M., 168, 181, 182
Shotland, J., 154
Sibling relationships, 64–69
birth order, 101–102
during family transitions, 101
online resources, 66
Siblings Without Rivalry, 65
Sickness. *See* Illnesses in family
Simonds, R. J., 152
Simons, R., 147–150

Single-parent families, 40, 100, 143–145
economic stressors, 102–103
Sisters and brothers. *See* Sibling relationships
Six, Success By, 272–273
Smith, B. J., 23
Smith, J., 91–92
Smith, S. S., 231
Social capital, 181
Social competencies, 4
Social Services Block Grant (SSBG), 77
Social studies, 232–233
online resources, 224
Socialization, 119
Societal institutions, 120
Sociocultural theory, 8–11
cultural diversity, 29–30
online resources, 10
Soderman, A. K., 177
Solchany, J. E., 123–124
Soltz, V., 241
Space Coast Early Intervention Center (SCEIC), 268–269f
Special needs, 53
online resources, 66
Spirituality and spiritual needs, 120
see also Religiosity
Sprenkle, D. H., 133
Standardized assessment: case study, 302
Standards. *See* Professional standards
Starting Small, 177, 232
Status changes, family, 88–90
Stein, L. C., 177
STEP. *See* Systematic Training for Effective Parenting
Stepfamilies, 100, 101
Stewart B. McKinney Homeless Assistance Act of 1987, 147
Stoneman, Z., 68
Straus, M. A., 135
Strengthening and Supporting Families, 103
Stresses on families
definition, 133
horizontal stressors, 134–135
unpredictable stressors, 135–159
child abuse, 137–141
children of incarcerated parents, 156–159
disabilities, 147–150
family violence, 135–137
homeless families, 145–147
immigrant families, 151–153

Stresses on families (*Continued*)
    marital transitions and single
        parenting, 143–145
    migrant families, 153–155
    military families, 155–156
    serious illnesses, 151
    substance abuse, 141–143
Stressors, horizontal and vertical, 14
Substance abuse, 141–143
    online resources, 143
Success By 6, United Way, 272–273
Swick, K., 185, 216, 280
Systematic Training for Effective
        Parenting (STEP), 241
    critique, 243f
    summary, 242f

T

Tabors, P. O., 226
Teachers, families as, 276–277
Teachers and parents, linking
    parents as consumers, 177
    supporting school policy and
        families, 177–179
Teale, W., 225
Teen parents, 64, 116–117
Telephone calls to parents, 209–210
Television, limiting, 254
Temporary Assistance for Needy
        Families (TANF), 35–36,
        77, 280
"Terrible twos," 279–280
"Terrific toddlers," 279–280
Testing
    standardized assessment: case
        study, 302
Test-tube babies, 110
Thompson, A. I., 134
Time
    constructive use of, 4
    see also Chronosystem
Toddlers
    Infants and Toddlers with
        Disabilities Act (ITDA), 149f
    "Terrific toddlers," 279–280

Togetherness, family, 12–13
Tolerance
    anti-bias activities, 232–233
    online resources, 50
    see also Diversity
Toth, S. L., 139, 142f
Transition to parenthood, 61–64
Transitions and continuity at school,
        170–176
"Transitions to School: A Planning
        Guide for Parents,"
        174, 175f
Trawick-Smith, J., 34, 184
"Trilemma," defined, 75–76
Trivette, C., 23, 149
Turner, P. H., 120, 145, 147
Two-way communication,
        199–211
Two-year olds, 279–280

U

U.S. Department of Education,
        194
Unemployment, 71
Uninvolved parenting, 121, 125
United Way
    United Way Success By 6,
        272–273
    United Way's Focus on Our Future,
        271–272
Unpredictable stressors
    child abuse, 137–141
    children of incarcerated parents,
        156–159
    disabilities, 147–150
    family violence, 135–137
    homeless families, 145–147
    immigrant families, 151–153
    marital transitions and single
        parenting, 143–145
    migrant families, 153–155
    military families, 155–156
    serious illnesses, 151
    substance abuse, 141–143

V

Values, positive, 4
Van Egeren, L., 61–62
Van Scoy, I., 185
Vertical stressors, 14
"Village, it takes a," 3–25
Violence. *See* Family violence
Vulnerability, 134
Vygotsky, L., 8–11
    on cultural diversity, 29
    online resources, 10

W

Wages and Quality, 77
Weiss, H. B., 168, 182
Weissbourd, B., 92
Welfare programs and recipients,
        35–37, 35–39
    Temporary Assistance for Needy
        Families (TANF), 35–36,
        77, 280
    Women, Infants & Children
        (WIC), 275
We-messages, 213–214
Werner, E. E., 93
Whiren, A. P., 177
White, L. J., 282
Wilson, J. B., 91–92
Women, Infants & Children
        (WIC), 275
Woodward, K. L., 77–78, 80
Woollett, A., 62–63
Working parents, 70–77
Written communication, 194–199

Y

Yarde, E., 115
Young, D. S., 157, 158

Z

Zemler, M., 91–92
Zone of proximal development
        (ZPD), 10–11
Zuckerman, B., 143